Gregg College Typing

Series Six

Complete Course

Scot Ober, Ph.D.

Professor, Department of
Administrative Services
Central Michigan University
Mount Pleasant, Michigan

Robert P. Poland, Ph.D.

Professor, Business and
Distributive Education
Michigan State University
East Lansing, Michigan

Robert N. Hanson, Ed.D.

Professor, Department of
Office Administration and
Business Education
Northern Michigan University
Marquette, Michigan

Albert D. Rossetti, Ed.D.

Professor, Department of
Business Education and Office
Systems Administration
Montclair State College
Montclair, New Jersey

Alan C. Lloyd, Ph.D.

Former Director,
Employment Testing
The Olsten Corporation
Westbury, New York

Fred E. Winger, Ed.D.

Former Professor, Office
Administration and
Business Education
Oregon State University
Corvallis, Oregon

Gregg Division
McGRAW-HILL PUBLISHING COMPANY

New York Atlanta Dallas St. Louis San Francisco
Auckland Bogotá Caracas Hamburg Lisbon
London Madrid Mexico Milan Montreal New Delhi
Paris San Juan São Paulo Singapore
Sydney Tokyo Toronto

Sponsoring Editor ■ Audrey S. Rubin
Editing Supervisor ■ Nicola von Schreiber
Design and Art Supervisor/Cover and Interior Design ■ Caryl Valerie Spinka
Production Supervisor ■ Mirabel Flores

Cover Photography ■ Nick Koudis
Interior Photography ■ James D'Addio, Nick Koudis, Bonnie West
Technical Studio ■ Burmar Technical Corporation

Library of Congress Cataloging-in-Publication Data
Gregg college typing, series six.

   Includes index.
   I. Typewriting.   I. Ober, Scot.
II. McGraw-Hill Book Company. Gregg Division.
Z49.G813   1989   652.3   88-27211
ISBN 0-07-038396-0

Gregg College Typing, Series Six
Complete Course

Lessons 1–60 of this publication are published simultaneously as part of the work
entitled *Gregg College Typing, Basic;* Lessons 61–120, as part of the work entitled
Gregg College Typing, Intermediate; and Lessons 121–180, as part of the work
entitled *Gregg College Typing, Advanced.*

1 2 3 4 5 6 7 8 9 0   DOWDOW   8 9 6 5 4 3 2 1 0 9

ISBN 0-07-038396-0

Contents

Index

TIMED WRITINGS

12-Second Sprints	1-Minute	
Page	Page	Words
24	5	10
40	6	12
46	8	13
56	9	14
289	11	15
	12	16
	14	17
	15	18
	17	19

2-Minute		3-Minute	
Page	Words	Page	Words
18	38	40	84
20	40	44	87
21	42	47	90
23	44	52	93
25	46	56	96
27	48	61	99
28	50	65	102
30	52	69	105
31	54	73	105
33	56	77	108
		84	108
		93	108
		98	114
		102	114
		106	117
		110	117
		114	120
		118	120
		122	120
		130	120

5-Minute			
Page	Words	Page	Words
133	200	243	250
137	205	247	250
141	205	251	250
145	205	257	250
149	210	261	250
153	210	265	250
157	215	269	255
161	215	273	255
165	215	277	260
167	216	281	260
172	220	285	260
176	220	289	265
180	225	303	270
184	225	313	275
188	225	323	280
192	230	333	285
196	230	347	290
200	235	357	295
204	235	367	300
208	235	375	300
215	240	379	300
225	245	383	300
235	250		

Preface

Gregg College Typing, Series Six is a multicomponent instructional system designed to give the student and the instructor a high degree of flexibility and a high degree of success in meeting their respective goals. To facilitate the choice and use of materials, the core components of this teaching-learning system are available in either a kit format or a book format. The *Keyboarding, Second Edition* text is also available for the development of touch inputting skills for use on computer keyboards.

THE KIT FORMAT

Gregg College Typing, Series Six gives the student and the instructor the opportunity to obtain a complete kit of materials for each of the three semesters in the typing curriculum generally offered by colleges. Each of the kits, which are briefly described below, contains a softcover textbook, a pad of workbook materials, and a cardboard easel for use as a copyholder.

The text in each kit contains instructional materials for 60 lessons, each 45–50 minutes long. Each workbook—called a *Workguide*—provides a technique evaluation form; learning guides, letterheads and other stationery for use in completing the production jobs, placement guides, and materials for improving students' language-arts skills.

Kit 1: Basic. This kit provides the text and Workguide materials for Lessons 1 through 60. Since this kit is designed for the beginning student, its major objectives are to develop touch control of the keyboard and proper typing techniques, build basic speed and accuracy skills, and provide practice in applying those basic skills to the production of letters, reports, tables, memos, forms, and other kinds of personal, personal-business, and business communications.

Kit 2: Intermediate. This kit includes the text and Workguide materials for Lessons 61 through 120. This second-semester course continues the development of basic typing skills and emphasizes the production

of various kinds of business correspondence, reports, tabulations, and forms from unarranged and rough-draft copy sources.

Kit 3: Advanced. This kit, which covers Lessons 121 through 180, is designed for the third semester. After a brief review of basic production techniques, each unit in this kit places the student in a different office situation where the emphasis is on such important modern office skills as editing, decision making, abstracting information, setting priorities, work flow, following directions, and working under pressure and with interruptions.

Format Guides. A pad of self-check keys is available for each of the three kits to enable students to check the correct format of all typed material.

THE BOOK FORMAT

For the convenience of those who wish to obtain the core instructional materials in separate volumes, the **Gregg College Typing, Series Six** system offers the following hardcover textbooks, workbooks, and self-check keys. In each instance, the content of the *Gregg College Typing* components is identical with that of the corresponding part or parts in the kit format.

Textbooks. *Gregg College Typing, Intensive Course* contains Lessons 1 through 120. The content and objectives of this two-semester hardcover text exactly match the content and objectives of the softcover textbooks in the *Basic* and *Intermediate* kits.

Gregg College Typing, Complete Course contains the text materials for Lessons 1 through 180. Thus it combines in one hardcover volume all the lessons contained in the three softcover textbooks included in the three kits.

Workbooks. The *Workguide* for each semester's work is available separately for use with the *Intensive* and *Complete* hardcover texts. These three workbooks are identical in content and purpose with those in the kits.

Format Guides. These self-check keys are also available for use with the *Intensive* and *Complete* hardcover texts.

SUPPORTING MATERIALS

The **Gregg College Typing, Series Six** system includes the following additional components for use with either the kits or the hardcover texts.

Progress Folders. These folders provide a lesson-by-lesson guide to the text activities, performance goals, and related instructional recordings and software for each of the three semesters.

Instructor's Materials. The special materials provided for the instructor can be used with either the **Gregg College Typing, Series Six** kits or the hardcover texts. These materials include special Instructor's Editions of each of the three semesters. Also available are keys to the drills and production exercises for each semester and a manual of teaching suggestions.

Computer Software. Two microcomputer software programs are correlated directly with *Gregg College Typing* for those classes using computers rather than typewriters:

1. The Keyboarding software (Lessons 1–25) provides instruction and practice on the alphabet, number, symbol, and 10-key number pad keys, as well as the basics of word processing including centering, underscoring, insert and delete functions, formatting, and so on.

2. The Skill Measurement Timings software (Lessons 1–180) provides unlimited opportunity for practice; administers and scores all Skill Measurement and test timings; scores the timings and highlights errors; reports speed and accuracy scores; and maintains complete records.

ACKNOWLEDGMENTS

We wish to express our appreciation to all the instructors and students who have used the previous editions and who have contributed much to this Sixth Edition.

The Authors

STANDARD FORMAT FOR LETTERS

Line length: 6-inch (60 pica/70 elite)
Style: modified-block
Paper: letterhead (business); plain (personal-business)
Paragraphs: blocked
Spacing: single
Date: line 15

ZIP Code: 1 space after state abbreviation
Punctuation: colon after salutation; comma after complimentary closing
Enumerations: numbers at left margin; turnover lines indented 4 spaces
Personal-business letter: no reference initials; return address in closing lines

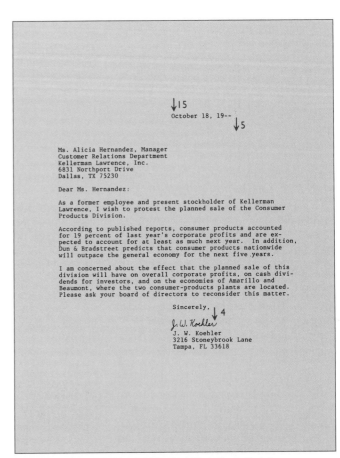

Employment Assistance Corporation
5133 Glentree Drive / San Jose, CA 95129

↓15
October 18, 19-- ↓5

Mr. James J. Novotny
Director of Human Resources
The Mitchell Company
7042 East Wesley Avenue
Denver, CO 80224-2536

Dear Mr. Novotny:

We would be happy to explore with you the possibility of our developing and validating an employment test for applicants for the position of assembler at your two plants. As shown in the enclosed brochure, we have developed many such tests for other companies during the ten years that our firm has been involved in employee testing.

On the basis of our preliminary discussions, the two main legal constraints we must be concerned with are as follows:

1. The test must accurately and reliably predict success on
4→the job if it is to be used to make hiring decisions.

2. The test must not exclude a greater number of minority members than nonminority members.

I am asking Jeffrey Munter, one of our testing specialists, to call to set up an appointment with your personnel staff to explore this matter further. We look forward to serving you.

Sincerely, ↓4

Eleanor Wainwright
Eleanor Wainwright
Marketing Manager ↓2

dco
Enclosure
c: Jeffrey Munter

BUSINESS LETTER (Modified-Block Style)

↓15
October 18, 19-- ↓5

Ms. Alicia Hernandez, Manager
Customer Relations Department
Kellerman Lawrence, Inc.
6831 Northport Drive
Dallas, TX 75230

Dear Ms. Hernandez:

As a former employee and present stockholder of Kellerman Lawrence, I wish to protest the planned sale of the Consumer Products Division.

According to published reports, consumer products accounted for 19 percent of last year's corporate profits and are expected to account for at least as much next year. In addition, Dun & Bradstreet predicts that consumer products nationwide will outpace the general economy for the next five years.

I am concerned about the effect that the planned sale of this division will have on overall corporate profits, on cash dividends for investors, and on the economies of Amarillo and Beaumont, where the two consumer-products plants are located. Please ask your board of directors to reconsider this matter.

Sincerely, ↓4

J. W. Koehler
J. W. Koehler
3216 Stoneybrook Lane
Tampa, FL 33618

PERSONAL-BUSINESS LETTER (Modified-Block Style)

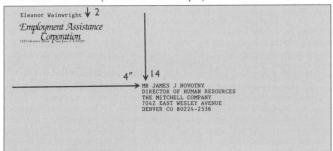

Eleanor Wainwright ↓2
Employment Assistance Corporation
5133 Glentree Drive / San Jose, CA 95129

4"   ↓14
MR JAMES J NOVOTNY
DIRECTOR OF HUMAN RESOURCES
THE MITCHELL COMPANY
7042 EAST WESLEY AVENUE
DENVER CO 80224-2536

LARGE BUSINESS ENVELOPE (No. 10)

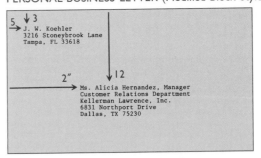

5 ↓3
J. W. Koehler
3216 Stoneybrook Lane
Tampa, FL 33618

2"   ↓12
Ms. Alicia Hernandez, Manager
Customer Relations Department
Kellerman Lawrence, Inc.
6831 Northport Drive
Dallas, TX 75230

SMALL PLAIN ENVELOPE (No. 6¾)

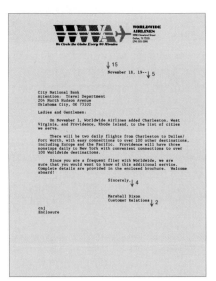

MODIFIED-BLOCK WITH INDENTED PARAGRAPHS (Standard Punctuation)

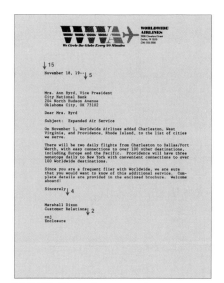

BLOCK (Open Punctuation)

SIMPLIFIED

BLOCK (Formatted for Window Envelope)

BLOCK STYLE ON MONARCH STATIONERY

BLOCK STYLE ON BARONIAL STATIONERY

STANDARD FORMAT FOR MONARCH STATIONERY

Size: 7¼ by 10½ inches
Line length: 5-inch (50 pica/60 elite)
Spacing: single
Date: line 14
Inside address: Begins on 5th line below date

STANDARD FORMAT FOR BARONIAL STATIONERY

Size: 5½ by 8½ inches
Line length: 4-inch (40 pica/50 elite)
Spacing: single
Date: line 12
Inside address: Begins on 4th line below date

```
                              February 18, 19--



          Consolidated Football League
          Attention:  General Counsel
          2430 Pennsylvania Avenue, NW
          Washington, DC 20037

          Ladies and Gentlemen:↓ 2

          Subject:  Contract Renegotiation↓ 2

          I am happy to report to you on the latest progress regarding
          the renegotiation for the contracts of the members of the na-
```

```
          to meeting with you and giving you a tour of our new high-tech
          center and research park.

                              Sincerely yours,↓ 2

                              CYRANO ELECTRONICS, INC.↓ 4



                              R. J. Foley, President ↓ 2

          lem
          Enclosure
          Express Mail
          c:  Marianne Lester ↓ 2

          PS: If Mrs. Pevey is available, we would enjoy having her ac-
          company you on your visit to our company.
```

SPECIAL LETTER PARTS

Attention Line. An attention line is sometimes used when a letter is addressed to a company rather than to an individual. The company name is typed as the first line of the inside address, and the attention line is typed on the second line. An appropriate salutation for a letter containing an attention line is *Ladies and Gentlemen:, Gentlemen:,* or *Ladies:.*

Subject Line. A subject line is sometimes used to indicate the topic of the letter. The term *Subject:, Re:,* or *In re:* may be used. The subject line is typed below the salutation, with 1 blank line above and below it.

Company Name in Closing Lines. If the company name is included in the closing lines, it should be typed in all-capital letters below the complimentary closing, with 1 blank line above and 3 blank lines below it.

Enclosure Notation. Whenever an item is to be enclosed

with the letter, an enclosure notation should be used. It is typed a single space below the reference initials. For more than one item, type *2 Enclosures, 3 Enclosures,* and so on.

Mailing Notation. If a mailing notation is included, it is typed on the line below the enclosure notation (if used) or on the line below the reference initials. A mailing notation comes before any copy notation.

Copy Notation. If someone other than the addressee is to receive a copy of the letter, a copy *(c)* notation is typed on the line below the mailing notation, the enclosure notation, or the reference initials, whichever comes last.

Postscript Notation. If a postscript is added to the letter, it is typed as the last item in the letter, preceded by 1 blank line. If the paragraphs in the letter are indented, the first line of the postscript should be indented as well.

Enumeration. An enumeration in the body of the letter is begun at the left margin, and turnover lines are indented 4 spaces. Leave 2 spaces after the number and period. The items within an enumeration are single-spaced, with double spacing between the items.

```
          are therefore happy to offer you the following accommodations
          for your convention:↓ 2

          1.  Between 180-200 double-occupancy rooms ↓ 2

          2.  Eight meeting rooms.  Each room will seat 50 people audi-
              torium style or 32 people at tables.  The rooms will be
              available to you throughout the convention.↓ 2

          3.  One complimentary two-bedroom suite for three nights↓ 2

          I hope these arrangements are satisfactory with you and your
          committee.  Please indicate your agreement by signing and re-
```

```
          ↓ 7
          Mr. Arthur O. Peters
          Page 2
          April 23, 19-- ↓ 3

          If you agree with these two suggestions, I'm ready to endorse
          your appraisal form and to seek the president's approval to
```

```
          ↓ 7
          Mr. Arthur O. Peters       Page 2          April 23, 19-- ↓ 3

          If you agree with these two suggestions, I'm ready to endorse
          your appraisal form and to seek the president's approval to
```

Two-Page Letters. The first page of a two-page letter is typed on letterhead stationery, and the second page is typed on plain paper. Leave at least a 1-inch bottom margin on the first page. On the second page, type the addressee's name, the page number, and the date beginning on line 7, either blocked at the left margin or displayed in one line across the page.

STANDARD FORMAT FOR MEMOS

Line length: 6-inch (60 pica/70 elite)
Paragraphs: blocked
Spacing: single
Paper: printed form, plain paper, or letterhead
Top margin: 2 inches (full sheet);
        1 inch (half sheet)
Writer's initials: optional; typed a double space below
        the body beginning at the center point

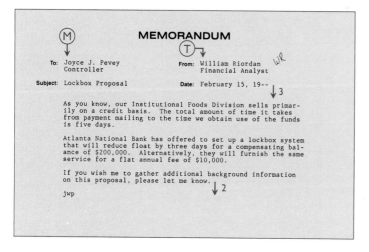

INTEROFFICE MEMORANDUM (Printed Form—Half Sheet)

STANDARD FORMAT FOR REPORTS

Line length: 6-inch (60 pica/70 elite)
Bound: Move both margins and all tab stops
        3 spaces to the right.
Paragraphs: indented 5 spaces
Spacing: double
Top margin: 2 inches (page 1);
        1 inch (other pages)
Bottom margin: at least 1 inch

↓13

MEMO TO: Joyce J. Pevey, Controller ↓2

FROM: William Riordan, Financial Analyst WR

DATE: February 15, 19-- ↓2

SUBJECT: Lockbox Proposal ↓3

As you know, our Institutional Foods Division sells primarily on a credit basis, with collections from this division averaging $10,000 a day. The total amount of time it takes from payment mailing to the time we obtain use of the funds is five days. Our opportunity costs on short-term funds are considered to be 8 percent.

Atlanta National Bank has offered to set up a lockbox system that will reduce float by three days for a compensating balance of $200,000. Alternatively, they will furnish the same service for a flat annual fee of $10,000.

Further details of the ANB proposal are contained in Garrison Boyd's letter of January 27, which is attached. Note especially Item 8, stating that this offer must be accepted by April 1 and will run for an 18-month period.

If you wish me to gather additional background information so that our Finance Committee can consider this proposal further, please let me know. ↓2

jwp
Attachment

INTEROFFICE MEMORANDUM (Plain Paper)

↓13

TYPING FORMAL REPORTS ↓2

Formatting Guidelines for Typists ↓2

By Stuart Lessin ↓3

Typing formal reports is not a difficult task if you just take the time to study the technical aspects involved. This report discusses report headings, page numbers, margins, reference citations, and the bibliography. ↓3

HEADINGS ↓2

The major heading in a report is the title. It should be centered in all-capital letters on line 13. A subtitle or byline, if used, is typed in initial capitals a double space below the title. The body of the report begins on the third line below the title or byline.

Side Headings. A side heading (such as the one shown above) is typed at the left margin in all-capital letters. Leave 2 blank lines before and 1 blank line after it.

Paragraph Headings. A paragraph heading is indented and typed a double space below the preceding paragraph. The words of the heading are capitalized, underscored, and followed by a period. The text begins on the same line. ↓3

PAGE NUMBERING ↓2

The first page of the body of the report is counted as page 1 but is not numbered. All the other pages are numbered

UNBOUND REPORT (Page 1)

UNBOUND REPORT WITH FOOTNOTES (Page 2)

↓7
2
↓3

at the top right on line 7, with the first line of text beginning on the third line below the page number. The page number
is typed without the word Page. The page number of the first
page of a special section, such as the bibliography, is centered on line 7 from the bottom of the page.
↓3

MARGINS

The following margins should be used for a report:
↓2
1. A 6-inch line (60 pica spaces and 70 elite spaces). If
4→the report is to be bound at the left, move both margins
    and all tab stops 3 spaces to the right.

2. A 2-inch top margin on the first page and a 1-inch top
    margin on all other pages of the body of the report.

3. A 1-inch bottom margin on all pages.
↓3

REFERENCE CITATIONS

Reference citations supply the reader with specific references to sources used in preparing the report. According to
Turabian, "Short . . . quotations should be incorporated into
the text of the paper and enclosed in double quotation marks."[1]
For longer quotations, Daly stipulates:
↓2
5→A quotation that contains four or more typewritten ←5
    lines should be set off from the text in single
    spacing and indented 5 spaces from both margins,
    with no quotation marks at the beginning or end.
    Double-space before and after the quotation.[2]
                                                    ↓1
――――――――――― ↓2
[1]Kate L. Turabian, A Manual for Writers of Term Papers,
Theses, and Dissertations, 4th ed., The University of Chicago
Press, Chicago, 1973, p. 64. ↓2
[2]Ferdinand J. Daly, "Formatting for Electronic Applications," Journal of Academic Research, Vol. 24, No. 3, September
1988, p. 49.

UNBOUND REPORT WITH FOOTNOTES (Page 2)

UNBOUND REPORT WITH FOOTNOTES (Partial Page)

↓7
3   ↓3

Footnotes. Footnote citations are typed at the bottom
of the page on which the references occur and are separated
from the text by a line of underscores 2 inches long. Single-
space before and double-space after the divider line. Each
footnote is indented and single-spaced, with double spacing
used between footnotes. On a partial page, the divider line
and the footnotes go at the bottom of the page.[3]

Endnotes. Endnotes perform the same function as footnotes except that they are numbered consecutively throughout
the report and are typed on a separate NOTES page at the end
of the report.[4] The notes are single-spaced, with double
spacing between them. The identifying number is typed on the
line (not as a superior figure), followed by a period and 2
spaces.

――――――――――― ↓2
[3]William A. Sabin, The Gregg Reference Manual, 6th ed.,
McGraw-Hill, New York, 1985, p. 335.

[4]Ibid., p. 337.
↑7

UNBOUND REPORT WITH FOOTNOTES (Partial Page)

BOUND REPORT WITH ENDNOTE REFERENCES

↓7
2
↓3

at the top right on line 7, with the first line of text beginning on the third line below the page number. The page number
is typed without the word Page. The page number of the first
page of a special section, such as the bibliography, is centered on line 7 from the bottom of the page.
↓3

MARGINS

The following margins should be used for a report:
↓2
1. A 6-inch line (60 pica spaces and 70 elite spaces). If
4→the report is to be bound at the left, move both margins
    and all tab stops 3 spaces to the right.

2. A 2-inch top margin on the first page and a 1-inch top
    margin on all other pages of the body of the report.

3. A 1-inch bottom margin on all pages.
↓3

REFERENCE CITATIONS ↓2

Reference citations supply the reader with specific references to sources used in preparing the report. According to
Turabian, "Short . . . quotations should be incorporated into
the text of the paper and enclosed in double quotation marks."[1]
For longer quotations, Daly stipulates:

5→A quotation that contains four or more typewritten ←5
    lines should be set off from the text in single
    spacing and indented 5 spaces from both margins,
    with no quotation marks at the beginning or end.
    Double-space before and after the quotation.[2]
                                                    ↓2
Footnotes. Footnote citations are typed at the bottom
of the page on which the references occur and are separated
from the text by a line of underscores 2 inches long. Single-
space before and double-space after the divider line. Each

BOUND REPORT WITH ENDNOTE REFERENCES

ENDNOTES FOR BOUND REPORT

↓13
NOTES
↓3

1. Kate L. Turabian, A Manual for Writers of Term
Papers, Theses, and Dissertations, 4th ed., The University
of Chicago Press, Chicago, 1973, p. 64. ↓2

2. Ferdinand J. Daly, "Formatting for Electronic Applications," Journal of Academic Research, Vol. 24, No. 3,
September 1988, p. 49.

3. William A. Sabin, The Gregg Reference Manual, 6th
ed., McGraw-Hill, New York, 1985, p. 335.

4. Ibid., p. 337.

5. Angela L. Boxer, A Manual of Style for Graduate
School, 3d ed., Consortium of Graduate Schools of Education,
Los Angeles, 1987, pp. 34-35.

6. Daly, p. 50.

7. H. L. Matthews, "New Research Reporting Standards,"
The New York Examiner, September 18, 1988, p. A2.

9
↑7

ENDNOTES FOR BOUND REPORT

REFERENCE SECTION

BOUND REPORT WITH AUTHOR/YEAR CITATIONS

COMPUTERIZED TRAVEL RESERVATIONS

By Miriam Caruso

Business people can now use their personal computers to make travel reservations. They can search data bases of hundreds of thousands of flights in seconds to customize their own travel schedule and save time and money. In addition, hotel reservations can be made on line (Rex, 1987).

ON-LINE AIRLINE RESERVATIONS

Using an electronic information service such as The Source or CompuServe, managers can identify flights and fares through a special service operated by the airline industry. The service will then display available flights from its records of more than 3 million flights (Barnes, 1987, p. 183).

All the information the on-line program needs is requested from the user in question-and-answer format. Users must enter the name of their departure and arrival cities, the travel dates, and the preferred times of departure. The on-line program then displays all relevant flights, including flight numbers, arrival and departure times, and fares.

Some of the computerized reservation services actually allow users to book their flights, paying for them by credit card. An added bonus of such services is that the passenger is automatically enrolled in the airline's frequent-flier

TITLE PAGE

↓13
TYPING FORMAL REPORTS

Formatting Guidelines for Typists

Line 33 → A Report Prepared for

ADS 301: Business Research

Professor Norman Pendergraft

Prepared by

Hiroshi Yoshimoto

November 18, 19--
↑13

TABLE OF CONTENTS

Ⓜ
↓13
CONTENTS ↓3

BIBLIOGRAPHY

↓13
BIBLIOGRAPHY ↓3

Boxer, Angela L., _A Manual of Style for Graduate School_,
5 → 3d ed., Consortium of Graduate Schools of Education, Los Angeles, 1987.

Daly, Ferdinand J., "Formatting for Electronic Applications," _Journal of Academic Research_, Vol. 24, No. 3, September 1988, pp. 46-50.

Matthews, H. L., "New Research Reporting Standards," _The New York Examiner_, September 18, 1988.

Sabin, William A., _The Gregg Reference Manual_, 6th ed., McGraw-Hill, New York, 1985.

Salerno, Nicholas, et al., "How to Communicate With Your Typist," _Journal of Modern Communication_, Vol. 14, No. 8, December 1988, pp. 25-27.

"You Can Type Your Research Report Yourself," _Current Business Careers_, June 19, 1987, pp. 39-42.

12
↑7

STANDARD FORMAT FOR TABLES

TITLE. Centered in all-capital letters and single-spaced.

SUBTITLE. Centered a double space below the title.

BODY. Centered horizontally, with 6 blank spaces between columns; single-spaced or double-spaced.

COLUMNS. Word columns align at the left; number columns align at the right.

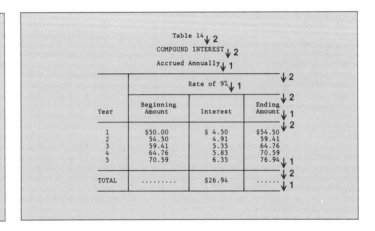

TRI-STATE PROFESSIONALS
FRINGE-BENEFIT ANALYSIS ↓2

January 1, 19-- ↓3

Component	Costs	Average Increase
Paid Time Off	$ 5,080	7%
Retirement	3,105	5%
Taxes	2,750	3%
Medical Plan	2,495	107%
Miscellaneous	2,650	14%
TOTALS	$16,080	16%

COLUMN HEADINGS. Centered over the column and underscored.

The $ signs appear only before the first number and the total and align vertically.

The % sign is repeated after each number if the column heading does *not* clearly indicate that the figures under it are percentages.

SALARY INCREASES* ↓2
Marketing Division ↓1

Name	Old Salary	New Salary	Increase ↓2↓1↓2
Arndt, Daniel R.	$38,480	$48,000	24.74%
Lavine, Rhonda	16,210	19,700	21.53%
Weber, Kathy M.	14,890	16,500	10.81%
Rogers, Kristin	31,567	34,500	9.29%
King, Jon J.	29,420	31,000	5.37% ↓1
AVERAGE	$26,113	$29,940	14.66% ↓1

*Effective March 1, 19--

Table 14 ↓2
COMPOUND INTEREST ↓2
Accrued Annually ↓1

Rate of 9% ↓1

Year	Beginning Amount	Interest	Ending Amount
1	$50.00	$ 4.50	$54.50
2	54.50	4.91	59.41
3	59.41	5.35	64.76
4	64.76	5.83	70.59
5	70.59	6.35	76.94
TOTAL	....	$26.94	....

STANDARD FORMAT FOR FORMS

NUMBER COLUMNS. Aligned at the right and centered visually within each ruled area.

WORD COLUMNS (or combination word and number columns). Aligned at the left, 2 or 3 spaces after the vertical rule.

LEFT MARGIN AND TABS. Left margin set for the first column and tabs set for each additional column.

DOLLAR SIGN. Omitted from amount columns.

TURNOVER LINES. Indented 2 or 3 spaces.

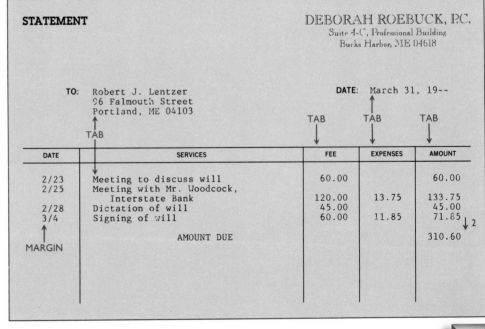

STATEMENT

DEBORAH ROEBUCK, P.C.
Suite 4-C, Professional Building
Bucks Harbor, ME 04618

TO: Robert J. Lentzer
96 Falmouth Street
Portland, ME 04103
↑ TAB

DATE: March 31, 19--

TAB   TAB   TAB

DATE	SERVICES	FEE	EXPENSES	AMOUNT
2/23	Meeting to discuss will	60.00		60.00
2/25	Meeting with Mr. Woodcock, Interstate Bank	120.00	13.75	133.75
2/28	Dictation of will	45.00		45.00
3/4	Signing of will	60.00	11.85	71.85 ↓2
	AMOUNT DUE			310.60

↑ MARGIN

WORD-DIVISION RULES

1. Do not divide words pronounced as one syllable (*thoughts, planned*), contractions (*shouldn't, haven't*), or abbreviations (*UNICEF, assoc.*).

2. Divide words only between syllables. Whenever you are unsure of where a syllable ends, consult a dictionary.

3. Leave at least three characters (the last will be a hyphen) on the upper line, and carry at least three characters (the last may be a punctuation mark) to the next line. Thus *de- lay* and *af- ter,* but not *a- maze* or *trick- y.*

4. Divide compound words either at the hyphen (*self-confidence*) or where the two words join to make a solid compound. Thus *master- piece,* not *mas- terpiece.*

PROOFREADERS' MARKS

Proofreaders' Mark	Draft	Final Copy	Proofreaders' Mark	Draft	Final Copy
ss Single-space	ss ⌈first line / second line	first line / second line	*new* ~~old~~ Change word	and ~~if~~ *when* you	and when you
ds Double-space	ds ⌈first line / second line	first line / second line	Delete	a ~~true~~ fact	a fact
¶ Make new paragraph	¶ If he is	If he is	⋯ Don't delete	a ~~true~~ story	a true story
∽ Transpose	(it / is) so	is it so	Delete and close up	co-operation	cooperation
∧ Insert word	and ∧it is	and so it is	≡ Capitalize	Fifth avenue	Fifth Avenue
V or ∧ Insert punctuation	if he's not∧	if he's not,	/ Use lowercase letter	our President	our president
# ∧ Insert space	all∧ready to	all ready to	◯ Spell out	the only ①	the only one
◡ Omit space	court⁀room	courtroom	⊙ Make it a period	one way⊙	one other way.
			Move as shown	no (other) way	no way

PUNCTUATION AND SPACING POINTERS

AMPERSAND. One space before and after.

CLOSING QUOTATION MARK. (*a*) Typed *after* a period or comma and *before* a colon or semicolon. *Always.* (*b*) Typed *after* a question mark or exclamation point if the quoted material is a question or an exclamation; otherwise, it is typed *before* the question mark or exclamation point.

COLON. Two spaces after.

COMMA. One space after.

EQUALS SIGN. One space before and after.

EXCLAMATION POINT. Two spaces after.

PERIOD. (*a*) Two spaces after a period at the end of a sentence; (*b*) one space after the period following someone's initials or the abbreviation of a single word (e.g., *Mrs.* Jones); (*c*) no space after each internal period in an abbreviation (e.g., *a.m.*).

QUESTION MARK. Two spaces after.

SEMICOLON. One space after.

TABLE COLUMNS. Six spaces between.

UNDERSCORE. (*a*) To type a magazine or book title, underscore the entire title, including internal spaces and punctuation. (*b*) To stress individual words, underscore them separately; do not underscore the punctuation or the spaces between the words.

ZIP CODE. One space before.

PUNCTUATION

COMMAS

1. Use a comma after an introductory expression (that is, a word, phrase, or clause that comes before the subject and verb of the independent clause).

First, she must place the diskette in Drive A.
When you finish the letters, type the report.
But: Type the report when you finish the letters.

2. Use commas to separate names used in direct address.

Thank you, Mrs. Liu, for your contribution.
Thank you for typing the monthly report, Mike.

3. Use commas to separate three or more items in a series when the last item is preceded by *and, or,* or *nor.*

Patsy, Kris, or Bill will be elected.
He saved the document, exited the word processing program, and then shut off the machine.

4. Use a comma to separate the two independent clauses in a compound sentence when they are joined by *and, but, or,* or *nor.*

I want to attend the concert, but Diana has tickets for the game.
Ellen left her job in May, and she and her sister went to Paris.
But: Ellen left her job in May and went to Paris with her sister.

5. Use commas to set off a nonessential expression (that is, a word, phrase, or clause that may be omitted without changing the basic meaning or the completeness of the sentence).

Our present projections, you must admit, are inadequate.
But: You must admit that the projections are inadequate.
It was mailed on Tuesday, the day your order was received.
But: Your item was mailed the day your order was received.

6. Separate the year with commas for a complete date.

The reunion will be held on May 2, 1990, in Minneapolis.
But: The reunion will be held on May 2 in Minneapolis.
But: In March 1988 the firm was incorporated.

7. When two adjectives modify the same noun, use a comma to separate the adjectives if they are not joined by *and.* (**Note:** If the first adjective modifies the combined idea of the second adjective plus the noun, do not separate the adjectives with a comma.)

Rob is an intelligent, understanding counselor.
But: Rob is an intelligent and understanding counselor.
The chair was a compassionate, generous person.
But: The director bought eight new computers.

8. Use commas to set off an expression in apposition (that is, a word, phrase, or clause that identifies or explains other terms).

The projectionist, Debbie Burke, will show the film at 8 p.m.
They shall fly to Denver on Thursday, August 21.

9. Use commas to set off a transitional expression (such as *therefore*) or an independent comment (such as *of course*).

Teresa told him, however, that the new printers would arrive within the next two weeks.
In the first place, the committee members have not yet come to an agreement on the selection.

10. Use commas to separate the name of a state or country following a city name.

The wide receiver moved to Cleveland, Ohio, in June.
But: The wide receiver moved to Cleveland in June.

SEMICOLONS

11. Use a semicolon to separate two independent clauses that are not joined by *and, but,* or *nor.*

Leslie worked on Labor Day; Jean did not.
But: Leslie worked on Labor Day, but Jean did not.

12. Use a semicolon to separate items in a series if any of the items already contain commas.

Staff meetings were held on Monday, March 5; Monday, March 12; and Wednesday, March 21.

COLONS

13. When a clause contains an expression such as *the following, as follows,* or *these* and is followed by a series of explanatory words, use a colon between the clause and the series.

The two most important criteria are these: an appropriate degree and relevant work experience.
But: The two most important criteria are an appropriate degree and relevant work experience.

HYPHENS

14. Hyphenate a compound adjective (two or more words that function as a unit to describe a noun) that comes *before* a noun. **Exception:** If the first word is an adverb ending in *ly,* do not hyphenate such adjectives.

The determination of production goals for each of the plants is a high-level decision.
But: Decisions about production goals are made at a high level.
All new employees will receive an on-the-job orientation.
But: New employees will receive an orientation on the job.

UNDERSCORES AND QUOTATION MARKS

15. Underscore titles of complete published works, and use quotation marks around titles that represent only a part of a complete published work.

The chapter entitled "IRAs and Personal Financial Planning" will be discussed in class tomorrow.
The sales director reported that excellent results had been obtained from advertisements in the Chicago Tribune.

PERIODS

16. Use a period to end a sentence that is a polite request, suggestion, or command if you expect the reader to respond by *acting* rather than by giving a yes-or-no answer.

Will you please send the report by overnight express.

May I have a copy of the income statement before the meeting.

But: Will you be able to arrange your schedule so that you can go?

APOSTROPHES

17. To make a singular noun possessive, place the apostrophe before the *s*.

a customer's request   the company's profits

18. To make a possessive from a singular noun that ends in an *s* sound, be guided by the way the word is pronounced. If a new syllable is formed by making the noun possessive, add an apostrophe and an *s* (*my boss's office, the witness's testimony*). If the addition of the extra syllable would make a word that is hard to pronounce, add only the apostrophe (*Mr. Phillips' career, Mrs. Hodges' friend*).

19. To make a plural noun not ending in *s* possessive, place the apostrophe before the *s*.

the women's offices   the children's school

20. To make a possessive from a plural noun ending in *s*, place the apostrophe after the *s*.

the secretaries' computers   the Halls' reception

21. Do not use an apostrophe with possessive pronouns.

The new house is ours.   The team won its first three debates.

But: It's time for their mid-semester exams.

NUMBER EXPRESSION

GENERAL RULES

1. Spell out numbers 1 through 10, and use figures for numbers above 10.

She invited seven managers to the meeting.
There were 20 people at the seminar.

2. If two or more *related* numbers both below and above 10 are used in the same sentence, use figures for all numbers.

We have 11 desks, 6 chairs, and 5 tables.

3. To express even millions or billions, use the following style:

20 million (**Not:** 20,000,000)   15.5 billion (**Not:** 15,500,000,000)

4. When two numbers come together in a sentence and one is part of a compound adjective, spell out the first number unless the second number would make a much shorter word.

three 9-room suites   175 six-page reports

5. Spell out fractions that stand alone, and use figures for mixed numbers.

four-fifths of the market   7⅜ yards   14½ inches

6. Spell out a number at the beginning of a sentence.

Fifty-five clerks approved the motion.
Two and one-half inches of snow fell today.

7. Use commas to separate thousands, millions, and billions.

8,567   213,489,000   10,476,890,000

ADDRESSES

8. Use figures for house numbers.

308 Summit Street   10 DuPont Circle

9. Spell out numbered streets 1 through 10, and use figures for numbered streets above 10. Omit *st, d,* or *th* if a word such as *West* precedes the street number.

550 Third Avenue   550 33d Street   550 East 33 Street

AMOUNTS OF MONEY

10. Do not use a decimal with even amounts of money.

$550 (**Not:** $550.00)

11. Use the word *cents* for amounts under $1.

75 cents (**Not:** $.75 or 75¢)

12. To express even millions or billions of dollars, use the following style:

$17 million (**Not:** $17,000,000)
$19.4 billion (**Not:** $19,400,000,000)

DATES

13. Use *st, d,* or *th* only if the day precedes the month.

Start work on the 3d of June. **But:** Start work on June 3.

TIME

14. Use figures to express time, whether with *o'clock* or with *a.m.* and *p.m.* (The abbreviations *a.m.* and *p.m.* should be typed in small letters without spaces.)

9 o'clock (**Not:** nine o'clock)
I left at 8:30 a.m. and returned at 5 p.m.

PERCENTAGES

15. Express percentages in figures, and spell out the word *percent.* **Note:** The percent sign (%) may be used in tables.

7 percent   15.6 percent

AGES AND ANNIVERSARIES

16. When ages are used as significant statistics, express them in figures. Otherwise, spell them out.

You may drive at the age of 16.
He can run for office when he is 21.
My father is seventy-five years old.

17. Spell out ordinals (*first, second,* and so on) in birthdays and anniversaries. However, if more than two words would be needed, use figures.

his third anniversary   our 155th anniversary

CAPITALIZATION

1. Capitalize every proper noun and every adjective derived from a proper noun. A proper noun is the official name of a particular person, place, or thing. In general, do not capitalize prepositions of fewer than four letters (such as *of*). The articles *a* and *an* are not capitalized; the article *the* is capitalized only under special circumstances.

the Empire State   Penn State University
Kansas City   Tuesday, January 13
Thanksgiving Day   The Wall Street Journal

2. Capitalize common organizational terms such as *advertising department* and *finance committee* when they are the actual names of units within the writer's own organization and are modified by the word *the*.

the Board of Trustees of our college meets on Tuesday.
The advertising department of A & G will reorganize.
Our Board of Trustees acted on all personnel decisions.

3. Capitalize all official titles when they precede personal names. Do *not* capitalize an official title when the personal name that follows is in apposition and is set off by commas, when the title follows a personal name, or when the title is used in place of a personal name.

President Susan H. Melrose   Susan H. Melrose, president
our president, Susan H. Melrose   The president of the company

4. Capitalize *north, south, east,* and *west* only when they designate definite regions or are an integral part of a proper name.

She lives in the Southwest.
They went to ski in western Massachusetts.
Go north on route 23 and then west on 202.

5. Capitalize a noun followed by a number or letter that indicates sequence. **Exception:** Do not capitalize the nouns *page, paragraph, size,* or *line.*

Invoice D120   page 17   Platform 3
Lesson 1   Table 12   size 12

6. In titles of published works and in headings, capitalize *(a)* the first and last words, *(b)* the first word following a colon or dash, and *(c)* all other words *except* articles (*the, a, an*), short conjunctions (*and, but, or*), and prepositions that contain three or fewer letters (*in, for, to*).

"Success in the World of Work"
Management Theories: A Constant Challenge

7. Capitalize names of important historical or commemorative events; of periods; of specific treaties, bills, acts, and laws; and of names of awards and medals.

the Declaration of Independence   the Bicentennial
Vocational Education Act   Pulitzer Prize winners

8. Capitalize names of holidays, both legal and religious, as well as names of months and days of the week.

Memorial Day   Tuesday, August 18   Passover

9. Capitalize the first word of a quoted sentence.

According to Rinaldi, "Employment rates in office jobs should rise considerably."
But: Crane, however, believes that office jobs will "show a slight drop."

10. Capitalize the first word of each item displayed in an enumerated list.

The following items should be taken for registration:
1. Proof of full-time status
2. Previous transcript
3. Student identification

11. Do not capitalize *(a)* the first word of an indirect quotation, *(b)* the names of school courses that are not proper nouns, or *(c)* the names of seasons.

Charles said that he would vote in the fall.
She is taking Spanish and office procedures this quarter.
We will hold our sales meeting in the spring this year.

GRAMMAR

SUBJECTS AND VERBS

1. When two or more subjects are joined by *or, either . . . or, neither . . . nor,* or *not only . . . but also:*
a. If both subjects are singular, use a singular verb.
b. If both subjects are plural, use a plural verb.
c. If one subject is singular and one is plural, it is best to place the plural subject immediately before the verb and use a plural verb.

Neither the owner nor the sales manager was in the store.
Neither the owners nor the sales managers were in the store.
Neither the owner nor the sales managers were in the store.

2. The following pronouns are always singular and take singular verbs: *each, either, neither, much,* and pronouns ending in *body, thing,* and *one.*

Neither of the clerks is using the microcomputer.
Each has his or her ticket to the concert.
Everyone is expected to produce mailable copy.

3. When establishing agreement between subject and verb, disregard intervening phrases and clauses.

Only one of the doctors is working on that floor.
The doctor, not the interns, is working on that floor.
The doctor, as well as the interns, is working on that floor.

4. Verbs in the subjunctive mood (those that talk of conditions which are improbable, doubtful, or contrary to fact) require the plural form.

I wish that I were on the Alaskan fishing trip.
If I were she, I would use a different format.

PRONOUNS

5. Use a singular pronoun with a singular antecedent (the word for which the pronoun stands) and a plural pronoun with a plural antecedent.

Neither Karla nor Marie must change her coat.
Everyone must have his or her text today.
Neither Mr. Brown nor his aides finished their work.

6. Use nominative pronouns (*I, he, she, we, they,* and so on) as subjects of a sentence or clause and after forms of the verb *to be.*

The receptionist and he are reviewing the data sheet.
It is she who likes this microcomputer program.

7. Use objective pronouns (*me, him, her, us, them,* and so on) as objects in a sentence or clause.

Louis thanked John for me.   The folders are for Susan and him.
The attendant asked Mike and them for the tickets.

ADJECTIVES AND ADVERBS

8. Use comparative adjectives and adverbs (*er, more,* and *less*) in referring to two persons, places, or things; use superlative adjectives and adverbs (*est, most,* and *least*) in referring to more than two.

He is the quicker of the two basketball players.
He is the quickest of the three basketball players.
This unit is the more capable of the two printers.
This unit is the most capable of the three printers.

ABBREVIATIONS

CAPITALIZATION AND HYPHENATION

1. Abbreviations usually follow the capitalization and hyphenation of the full words for which they stand.

Wed.	Wednesday	p.m.	post meridiem
ft-lb	foot-pound	N.C.	North Carolina

PUNCTUATION AND SPACING WITH ABBREVIATIONS

2. In lowercase abbreviations made up of single initials, use a period after each initial but no space after each internal period.

p.m.   i.e.   f.o.b.   e.o.m.

3. In all-capital abbreviations made up of single initials, do not use periods or internal spaces.

AICPA   IRS   UN   UAW

Exception: Retain the periods in abbreviations of geographical names, academic degrees, and a few miscellaneous expressions.

U.S.S.R.   M.S.   B.C.   R.S.V.P.

4. Leave one space following an abbreviation within a sentence unless another mark of punctuation follows immediately.

She arrived at 9 a.m. and left at 2 p.m. for Atlanta.
Steve works in New York, N.Y., but his home is in Connecticut.

PERSONAL NAMES, INITIALS, AND TITLES

5. Use a period and one space following each initial of a person's name; however, when personal initials stand alone, type them without periods or spaces.

Patricia A. Rocconi   A. D. Virtue   LBJ

6a. Always use the following abbreviated titles when they are used with personal names.

Mr.	Messrs. (plural or Mr.) Ms. Mses. or Mss. (plural of Ms.)
Mrs.	Mmes. (plural of Mrs.) Dr. Drs. (plural of Dr.)

6b. In general, spell out all other titles used with personal names.

Professor Primiano   President Cooper   Sister O'Hagen

6c. Always abbreviate *Jr., Sr.,* and *Esq.* when they follow personal names.

Mr. H. A. Smith, Jr.   George L. Barr, Esq.

COMPASS POINTS

7. Spell out compass points used as ordinary nouns and adjectives or when included in street names.

He purchased a lot on the southwest corner.
143 North Maple Avenue   12 East Franklin Street

8. Abbreviate compass points without periods when they are used *following* a street name.

18 East 30 Street, NW   84 Dupont Circle, SW

MEASUREMENTS

9a. In nontechnical writing, spell out units of measure.

a 5-quart bottle   12 yards of material
3½ by 5 inches   a 110-acre development

9b. Abbreviate units of measure when they occur frequently, as in technical or scientific work, forms, and tables. Do not use periods.

14 oz   6 qts   5 ft 10 in   55 mph

MAJOR PARTS OF AN ELECTRONIC TYPEWRITER

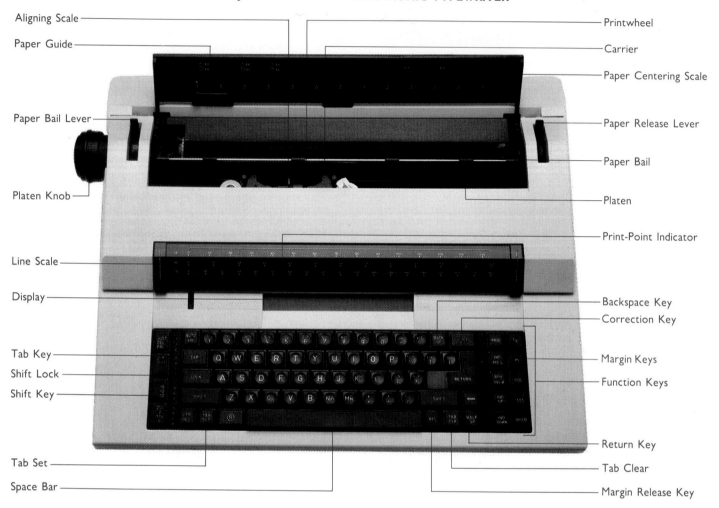

ALIGNING SCALE. Aids in positioning the carrier on a line of text for inserting or deleting characters.

BACKSPACE KEY. Moves the carrier to the left 1 space at a time.

CARRIER. Moves from left to right, carrying the printwheel across the paper.

CORRECTION KEY. Engages correction tape and lifts off an error.

DISPLAY. Allows the typist to view the text as it is typed into memory and before it is printed on the paper.

FUNCTION KEYS. Perform special functions, such as automatic centering and moving to the beginning or end of the document.

LINE SCALE. Indicates horizontal spaces across the length of the platen, carrier position, and margin stops.

MARGIN KEYS. Used to set left and right margins.

MARGIN RELEASE KEY. Temporarily unlocks the left or right margin.

PAPER BAIL. Holds the paper against the platen.

PAPER-BAIL LEVER. Controls the paper bail.

PAPER CENTERING SCALE. Used to center any size of paper in the machine.

PAPER GUIDE. Guides and aligns the paper as it is inserted into the machine.

PAPER RELEASE LEVER. Loosens the paper for straightening or removing.

PLATEN. Large cylinder around which the paper is rolled.

PLATEN KNOB. Used to turn the platen by hand. The *variable platen* in the left platen knob can be pushed in to turn the platen freely for slight vertical adjustments.

PRINT-POINT INDICATOR. Shows the exact point on the line at which the next character will be printed.

PRINTWHEEL. A printing element that has each character engraved at the end of a spoke. When a key is struck, the printwheel spins and prints the corresponding character.

RETURN KEY. Returns the carrier to the start of a new line.

SHIFT KEY. Positions the carrier so that a capital letter can be typed.

SHIFT LOCK. Locks the shift key so that the machine prints in all capitals.

SPACE BAR. Moves the carrier to the right 1 space at a time.

TAB CLEAR. Removes tabs.

TAB KEY. Moves the carrier to a point where a tab has been set.

TAB SET. Sets tabs at desired points.

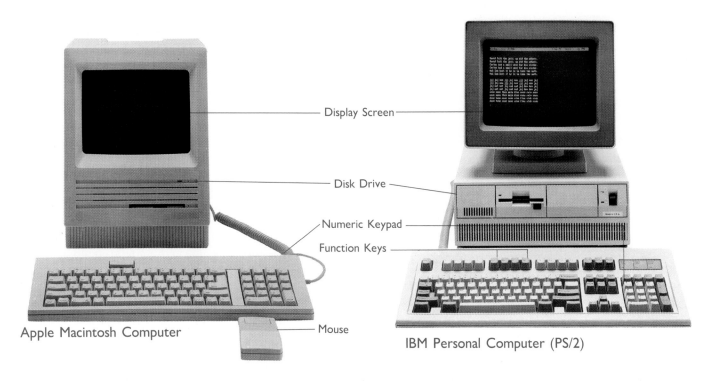

Display Screen

Disk Drive

Numeric Keypad

Function Keys

Apple Macintosh Computer

Mouse

IBM Personal Computer (PS/2)

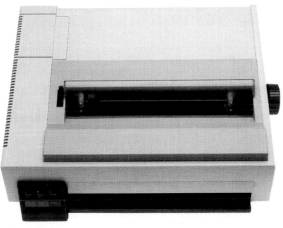

Printer

DISK DRIVE. The component into which a diskette is inserted so that data can be read from or written onto the diskette.

DISPLAY SCREEN. A device similar to a television screen used to display text and graphics. Also called a monitor.

FUNCTION KEYS. Keys that perform special functions, such as saving a document, centering a line, or moving the cursor to the beginning or end of a document.

MOUSE. A hand-operated electronic device used to move the cursor around on the display screen.

NUMERIC KEYPAD. The ten number keys arranged in calculator style to allow one-handed touch-typing of numeric data.

PRINTER. The component that prints the copy on paper.

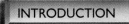

COUNTING THE SPACES

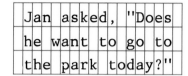

Jan	asked,	"Does
he	want	to	go	to
the	park	today?"

When a key or the space bar is tapped, the carrier advances 1 space. On most typewriters each space is the same size because most machines space uniformly, as though they were printing on graph paper.

These spaces can be counted by using the line scale. This scale shows a number every fifth or tenth space so that you can find any particular space across the width of the paper.

Each machine also has a special marker (called the carrier position indicator or the print-point indicator) that points to the space at which the machine is ready to print. For example, if the marker points to 58, the machine is ready to print at 58.

TYPE SIZE

```
1234567890    Pica
123456789012  Elite
```

Most typewriters use either *pica* or *elite* type. *Pica* type (also called 10 pitch) is larger than elite and prints 10 characters to an inch. *Elite* type (also called 12 pitch) prints 12 characters to an inch.

Thus a full line of typing on a standard sheet of paper ($8\frac{1}{2}$ inches wide) will contain 85 pica characters ($8\frac{1}{2} \times 10$) or 102 elite characters ($8\frac{1}{2} \times 12$).

Many electronic typewriters and computer printers also have other type sizes. For example, some machines print 15 characters to an inch, while others have proportional spacing, which means that small letters (such as *i*) require less space than large letters (such as *m* or *w*).

Although distinctions between pica and elite size type do not matter in forms, tables, or drills, these distinctions are important in letters and reports, because line lengths are commonly expressed in inches.

Find out which size type your machine has by typing the numbers 1 through 0 and comparing your typed copy with the illustration above.

PLANNING MARGINS AND SETTING MARGIN STOPS

Margin stops are used to center typed material across the paper. To plan the left and right margin settings:

Left Margin.   Subtract half the desired line length from the center point. For example, for a 60-space line, subtract 30 from the centering point you are using.

Right Margin.   Add half the desired line length to the center point plus 5 extra spaces to allow for line-ending decisions. See the table below.

MARGIN SETTINGS

Type Size	Line Length Spaces	Inches	Margin Settings Left	Right
Pica	40	4"	22	67
	50	5"	17	72
	60	6"	12	77
	70	7"	7	82
Elite	40	3⅓"	30	75
	50*	4"	25	80
	60	5"	20	85
	70*	6"	15	90

*Rounded off.

Margin Stops.   Margin stops for electronic typewriters are typically set by moving the carrier to the correct point on the margin scale and then depressing either the left or the right margin key.

Margin stops for electric typewriters can be set by pushing in the left and right margin stops and sliding them to the correct settings on the line scale.

On a computer, the word processing software generally has a default (preset) margin setting. To change the margin settings, consult the operating instructions provided by the manufacturer or ask your instructor for assistance.

SETTING TABS

Tab settings enable you to indent paragraphs consistently and to format columns of data efficiently. To set tabs:

1. Clear all tabs already set. On electronic typewriters, depress the tab clear key wherever a tab has been set. On electric typewriters, move the carrier to the right margin, and then hold down the tab clear key as you return the carrier. Software commands control the tab settings in word processing.

2. Set a new tab. Depress the space bar the number of spaces you wish to indent (usually 5 for a paragraph indention), and press the tab set key.

3. Test the new tab setting. Return the carrier to the left margin, and then firmly depress the tab key. The carrier should move directly to the point where you set the tab.

Note: You will not have to set any tabs until Lesson 10.

SETTING LINE SPACING

The amount of space between lines of typing is controlled by a line space selector (electric typewriters), by a line space key (electronic typewriters), or by a software command (word processing software).

On a typewriter, set the controls at 1 for single spacing (no blank space between lines) and at 2 for double spacing (1 blank line between typed lines). Some machines also have 1½ spacing (½ blank line between typed lines) and triple spacing (2 blank lines between typed lines).

LINE SPACING

Set at 1	Set at 1½	Set at 2	Set at 3
single	one and a half	double	triple
single			
single	one and a half	double	
single	one and a half		triple

INSERTING PAPER

To insert paper into the machine:

1. Confirm the paper guide setting.
2. Pull the paper bail forward.
3. With your left hand, place the paper behind the platen and against the paper guide. Use your right hand to turn the right platen knob clockwise to draw in the paper. Advance the paper until about a third of the sheet is visible.

Note: Electronic typewriters automatically feed the paper into the machine.

4. Check that the paper is straight by aligning the left edges of the front and back against the paper guide.

If the edges of the paper do not align, pull the paper release lever forward, straighten the paper, and then push the paper release lever back.

5. Place the paper bail back against the paper. Adjust the small rollers on the paper bail so that they are spaced evenly across the paper.

6. To prepare to type, turn the paper back until about ¼ inch shows above the paper bail.

REMOVING PAPER

To remove paper from the machine:

1. Pull the paper bail forward.
2. Pull the paper release lever toward you with your right hand as you silently draw out the paper with your left hand.
3. Return the paper release lever and paper bail to their normal positions.

DAILY ROUTINE

Perform these steps at the start of each class:

1. Arrange your work area: typewriter even with the front edge of the desk; typing paper on one side of the machine and textbook on the other, tilted for ease of reading.

2. Open the textbook to the correct lesson, and note the directions in the heading.

3. Make the necessary machine adjustments—set margins, tabs, and line spacing.

4. Insert a sheet of paper; straighten it if necessary.

5. Assume the correct typing posture, and begin typing the Warmup drill for the lesson.

STARTING A LESSON

¹**Line:** 60 spaces
²**Tab:** 5, center
³**Spacing:** single
⁴**Drills:** 2 times
⁵**Workguide:** 207–209

⁶**Goals:** To type 46 wam/5'/5e; to format billing forms.

Each lesson heading includes a display to tell what machine adjustments are needed at the start of the lesson and what supplementary materials will be needed somewhere in the lesson. The example in the left margin tells you to (1) use a 60-space line, (2) set a tab stop for a 5-space paragraph indention and another at the center point, (3) use single spacing, (4) type each drill line two times, and (5) use the forms on Workguide pages 207–209 to type the production jobs in the lesson.

The goals for the lesson (6) are (a) to type 46 words a minute on a 5-minute timed writing with no more than 5 errors and (b) to format billing forms.

BUILDING SKILL

Speed	Accuracy
aw awaken awhile	aw awaken awhile
aw awaken awhile	se severe seized
	rd ordeal burden
se severe seized	aw awaken awhile
se severe seized	se severe seized
	rd ordeal burden
rd ordeal burden	
rd ordeal burden	

WARMUPS. Line 1 of each lesson's Warmup builds speed, line 2 builds accuracy, and line 3 builds skill in number typing. The three lines of the Warmup provide practice on all the number and alphabet keys.

DRILLS. For speed development, repeat each *individual* drill line the designated number of times. For accuracy improvement, repeat each *group* of drill lines (as though they were a paragraph) the designated number of times.

TIMED WRITINGS

¹⁷ The procedures for han
²⁰
careful manner. Of course,
²²
outgoing and the incoming m
²⁵
in either case, it is vital
²⁷
carefully followed. Recent

All timed writings in this text are the exact length needed to reach the speed goal that is set for each lesson. Thus if you finish the timed writing, you know you have reached your speed goal.

The syllabic intensity (the average number of syllables per word) of all timed writings in this text is between 1.40 and 1.50, which means that the copy is of average difficulty.

Your speed on a timed writing is the number of words you typed divided by the number of minutes you typed. Round off a fraction to the nearest whole number.

All timed writings in this book contain small numbers, called speed markers, above the copy. When you take a 5-minute timed writing, the highest number that you reach is your *wam* (words-a-minute) speed.

BUILDING PRODUCTION SKILL

MARGINAL NOTES AND ARROWS. Marginal notes and arrows are sometimes used to remind you of line length, spacing, and so on. These aids are gradually reduced as you gain experience in typing each kind of job.

Some jobs have special explanations with them, positioned as close to the point of use as possible. Always look for and read marginal notes before you begin to type.

Horizontal arrows ($\rightarrow$) indicate the point at which to begin typing. For example, $\rightarrow$20 means begin typing 20 spaces from the left edge. Down arrows ($\downarrow$) indicate how many lines down the next line should be typed. For example, $\downarrow^{12}$ means begin typing on line 12.

$\downarrow^{12}$

$\rightarrow$20 Mr. Edward Whitman
Smith & Whitman Inc.

LEAVE I SPACE
BETWEEN STATE
AND ZIP CODE

1047 Fifth Avenue
New York, NY 10028

TYPING POSTURE

Typing speed and accuracy are both affected by your posture.

COMPUTER SOFTWARE

The miniature disk pictured above appears throughout the book as a reminder to use the correlated software—if you are learning to type on a computer rather than a typewriter.

WORD PROCESSING

The symbol above is designed to call your attention to information about word processing concepts or applications that you will encounter throughout this text. These special notations are provided to help you understand how to use the word processing features of an electronic typewriter or a computer with word processing software. As you learn how to format different types of documents on a typewriter, you will also be told how similar operations would be performed in a word processing environment.

Body centered opposite the J key, leaning forward.

Head erect, turned to face the book.

Feet apart and firmly braced.

Wrists straight and fingers curved. Position your fingertips on the home keys: left hand on A, S, D, and F; right hand on J, K, L, and ; (semicolon).

Note: Do not rest your hands or wrists on the equipment or on the desk.

PART I
THE TYPEWRITER ■
THE ALPHABET
AND NUMBER KEYS

OBJECTIVES

KEYBOARDING SKILL

To operate the letter and number keys by touch.

To make all machine adjustments needed to set margins, tabs, and line spacing; to remove paper efficiently.

To type 28 words a minute on a 2-minute timed writing with no more than 5 errors.

PROOFREADING SKILL

To proofread typewritten copy, mark and count errors, and compute typing speed.

TECHNICAL SKILL

To answer correctly at least 90 percent of the questions on an objective test.

FORMATTING SKILL

To center typed material both horizontally and vertically.

■ To understand how word processing hardware and software would function if used to format various production assignments.

TEST 9-D
TABLE 72
BOXED TABLE WITH BRACED
HEADINGS

Spacing: double
Paper: Workguide 499

Enrollment by Membership and Location
for Personnel Management Programs

19 - -

City	Employee Discipline		Employee Recordkeeping	
	Member	Nonmember	Member	Nonmember
Costa Mesa	30	6	27	3
Denver	22	4	19	5
East Lansing	41	2	33	6
Indianapolis	18	1	15	4
TOTAL	111	13	94	18

TEST 9-E
FORM 57
STATEMENT OF ACCOUNT

Paper: Workguide 499

PIXIE MARKETS

2168 Wildwood Lane   Jackson, MI 49203

Statement of Account
WITH: Apex Cafe
1330 Sandhurst Drive
Lansing, MI 48910

DATE: July 1, 19--

Amount Enclosed
$_____

Please return this stub with your check.

DATE	REFERENCE	CHARGES	CREDITS	BALANCE
June 1	Brought forward			565.80
2	Payment on account		450.00	
10	Invoice No. 2132	220.25		
25	Invoice No. 3168	16.80		
28	Payment on account		165.80	
29	Credit memo No. 345		10.50	
30	Payment on account		150.00	

Figure balance
for each transaction
and format form

Pay the last amount
in this column.

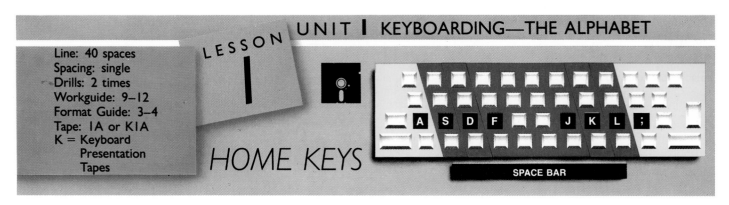

LESSON 1

Line: 40 spaces
Spacing: single
Drills: 2 times
Workguide: 9–12
Format Guide: 3–4
Tape: 1A or K1A
K = Keyboard
Presentation
Tapes

HOME KEYS

Goal: To control the home keys (A S D F J K L ;) and space bar.

I-A. PRACTICE THE SPACE BAR

With all fingers held motionless in home position, poise your right thumb about ¼ inch above the space bar. Tap the space bar in its center, and bounce your thumb off.

Space once (*tap the space bar once*) . . . twice (*tap the space bar twice*) . . . once . . . once . . . twice . . . once . . . twice . . . once . . . twice . . . twice . . . once . . . once . . . Repeat.

I-B. PRACTICE THE RETURN/ENTER KEY

On many computers, the return key is called *the enter key*.

In a quick, stabbing motion (1) extend the fourth finger of your right hand to the return key; (2) lightly tap the return key, causing the carrier to return automatically; and (3) "zip" the finger back to its home-key position.

Practice using the return key until you can do so with confidence and without raising your eyes from the book.

Space once . . . twice . . . once . . . twice . . . Return! Home! (*fingers on home keys*) . . . Repeat.

I-C. PRACTICE THE FOREFINGER KEYS

I-C. Using your right thumb and both forefingers (with other fingers in home position), type these three lines. Tap the keys lightly. Do not space after the last letter in the line before the return.

Left forefinger on F key
Right thumb on space bar

fff fff ff ff f f ff ff f f

Right forefinger on J key
Right thumb on space bar

jjj jjj jj jj j j jj jj j j

Left forefinger on F key
Right forefinger on J key
Right thumb on space bar

fff jjj ff jj f j ff jj f j

ITINREARY for CONSTANCE LAWLOR   6

June 3 - 5, 19--   9

Monday, June 3   12

    9:45 a.m.   Depart Detroit, ^Detroit Metropolitan Airport, NW 579.   24

   11:30 a.m.   Arrive ^Seattle, Seattle/Tacoma International Airport.   37
                     Reservations at Olympic Hotel.   43

    7:15 p.m.   Dinner with Mr. Alex Montgomery (Areo Space   53
                     Industries).   56

Tuesday, June 4   59

    8:00 a.m.   Breakfast with Ms. Barbara Lombardini (Areo   69
                     Space Industries)   73

   12:00 noon   Lunch with Areo space Industries Enginners.   83

    3:45 p.m.   Depart Seattle, ^Seattle/Tacoma International Airport, UA 2306.   98

    4:24 p.m.   Arrive Portland, ^Portland International Airport.   109
                     Reservations at Benson Hotel.   115

    6:30 p.m.   Reception--National Association of Electronic   126
                     Engineers--Rose City ballroom.   132

Wednesday, June 5   135

    8:00 a.m.   Opening session of conference--Mt. Hood Room   146

   10:30 a.m.   Presentation--Rose City Ballroom.   155

   12:00 noon   Luncheon--Columbia River Ballroom. ~~Mt. Hood Room.~~   163

    3:30 p.m.   Depart, ^Portland Portland International Airport,   175
                     NW 471.   176

   11:15 p.m.   Arrive Detroit, ^Detroit Metropolitan Airport.   187

LEFT HAND

Forefinger	F
Second finger	D
Third finger	S
Fourth finger	A

RIGHT HAND

J	Forefinger
K	Second finger
L	Third finger
;	Fourth finger
Space bar	Thumb

SPACE BAR

Leave 1 blank line (return twice) before starting a new drill.

1-D. PRACTICE THE F AND J KEYS

Use the forefingers on F and J keys. Tap the space bar with your right thumb.

1 fff fff jjj jjj fff jjj ff jj ff jj f j
   fff fff jjj jjj fff jjj ff jj ff jj f j

1-E. PRACTICE THE D AND K KEYS

Use the second fingers.

2 ddd ddd kkk kkk ddd kkk dd kk dd kk d k
   ddd ddd kkk kkk ddd kkk dd kk dd kk d k

1-F. PRACTICE THE S AND L KEYS

Use the third fingers.

3 sss sss lll lll sss lll ss ll ss ll s l
   sss sss lll lll sss lll ss ll ss ll s l

1-G. PRACTICE THE A AND ; KEYS

Use the fourth fingers.

4 aaa aaa ;;; ;;; aaa ;;; aa ;; aa ;; a ;
   aaa aaa ;;; ;;; aaa ;;; aa ;; aa ;; a ;

1-H. WORD BUILDING: SHORT WORDS

Type lines 5–11 two times each. Leave a blank line after each pair. Note word patterns.

5 lll aaa ddd lad lad fff aaa ddd fad fad

6 ddd aaa ddd dad dad aaa sss kkk ask ask

7 aaa sss ;;; as; as; aaa ddd ;;; ad; ad;

1-I. WORD BUILDING: LONGER WORDS

Space once after a semicolon.

8 a ad add adds; l la lad lads; a ad ads;

9 f fa fad fads; a as ask asks; d da dad;

10 l la las lass; f fa fal fall; s sa sad;

1-J. SKILL MEASUREMENT

Compare your Lesson 1 typing with that shown on Workguide pages 9–10, and then complete Workguide pages 11 and 12.

11 a dad; a fall; ask a lass; add a salad;

(Current date)   4

Ms. Frances Kelly   7
134 Robert S. Kerr Avenue, NW   13
Oklahoma City, OK 73102   18

Dear Ms. Kelly: 21

Subject: Dividend Reinvestment Program   29

Thank you for your interest in Oklahoma Bank's   38
Dividend Reinvestment Program. We are pleased to   48
be able to provide this service for our shareholders. 59
With our automated system, we are able to carry   69
forward funds and add them to the next   76
dividend. The status of your account is as follows: 87

1. The amount carried forward from the previous   97
   quarter is $242.   100

2. The cash dividend for the current quarter is   110
   $.24 a share. Your cash dividend for the   118
   quarter is $111.60.   122

3. The market price for Oklahoma Bank's stock   131
   on the day of purchase was $17.50. The   139
   number of shares purchased for you under   147
   the program was six, for a total of $105.   156

4. The amount to be carried forward is $9.02.   165

If you have any questions about your dividend   174
reinvestment account, please call Darla   182
Radbaugh or Ann Hammer at (405)555-8361.   190

Sincerely yours,   193

Charles T. Longworth   197
Shareholder Relations Department   204

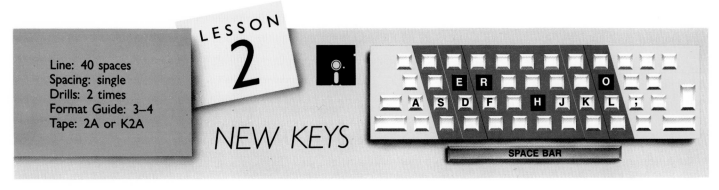

NEW KEYS

Line: 40 spaces
Spacing: single
Drills: 2 times
Format Guide: 3–4
Tape: 2A or K2A

Goal: To control the H, E, O, and R keys.

From now on, your fingers are named for the home keys on which they rest. For example, the D finger is the second finger on the left hand.

Use the J finger.

Note: Leave 1 space after a semicolon.

Use the D finger.

Use the L finger.

Use the F finger.

2-A. WARMUP

1 fff jjj ddd kkk sss lll aaa ;;; fff jjj
2 ask a lass; a fad; alas a lad; a salad;

2-B. PRACTICE THE H KEY

3 jjj jhj jhj hjh jjj jhj jhj hjh jjj jhj
4 has has had had aha aha ash ash hah hah
5 shah shad hall dash lash sash half hash
6 add a dash; a lass has half; as dad had

2-C. PRACTICE THE E KEY

7 ddd ded ded ede ddd ded ded ede ddd ded
8 led fee lee sea fed ade she he; see lea
9 feed held lead ease seal head fake keel
10 she sees a shed; he led a lass; a lease

2-D. PRACTICE THE O KEY

11 lll lol lol olo lll lol lol olo lll lol
12 sod old ode odd oak oh; hod foe off doe
13 oleo solo does odes joke kook look shoe
14 she held a lease; a lad solos; old oak;

2-E. PRACTICE THE R KEY

15 fff frf frf rfr fff frf frf rfr fff frf
16 red are her oar rod era rah err ore ark
17 door rare role read fare dear soar oars
18 she offered a rare jar; a dark red oar;

PROGRESS TEST ON PART 9

Ask your instructor for the General Information Test on Part 9.

TEST 9-A
5-MINUTE TIMED WRITING

Line: 60 spaces
Tab: 5
Spacing: double
Paper: Workguide 493

You have just completed a course in which you acquired   12
some of the most valuable skills needed for seeking employ-   24
ment in the business world today. They are required in all   36
facets of business to process information. Whether you are   48
an office worker or a manager, the skills will help you ad-   60
vance on the job. You have strived hard to acquire greater   72
proficiency in language arts, abstracting, decision making,   84
editing, formatting, following directions, human relations,   96
setting priorities, and working under pressure and with in-   108
terruptions. Each of these skills was developed or refined   120
as you perfected a high degree of competence in keyboarding   132
and typewriting. A good typist must maintain these skills.   144
It is amazing the changes that have taken place in the   156
office. No one would have expected the standard typewriter   168
to have given way to the electric, magnetic, and electronic   180
typewriters a few years ago. These machines are now giving   192
way to personal computers in most offices. A personal com-   204
puter permits words to be added or deleted, margins changed   216
at will, paragraphs moved, or the spelling checked by soft-   228
ware programs--and this is all completed in front of you on   240
a screen before a job is printed out. Although such equip-   252
ment is available and in use, all of today's businesspeople   264
must possess basic skills to process information accurately   276
and quickly. A software program is only as good as the op-   288
erator using it. A mind is still necessary to communicate.   300

| 1 | 2 | 3 | 4 | 5 | 6 | 7 | 8 | 9 | 10 | 11 | 12

2-F. BUILD SKILL ON WORD FAMILIES

Do not pause at the vertical lines that mark off the word families.

19 sold fold hold old; |hale sale kale dale
20 sash dash lash ash; |seed heed deed feed
21 rear sear dear ear; |rake sake fake lake

2-G. Take three 1-minute timings. Try to complete both lines each time.

2-G. SKILL MEASUREMENT: 1-MINUTE TIMED WRITING

22 she heard dad ask for a roll; she asked
23 for a jar;

LESSON
3

Line: 40 spaces
Spacing: single
Drills: 2 times
Format Guide: 3–4
Tape: 3A or K3A

NEW KEYS

SPACE BAR

Goal: To control the M, T, I, and C keys.

3-A. WARMUP

1 aa ;; ss ll dd kk ff jj hh ee oo rr aa;
2 he fed a doe; she sold a dark red shoe;

3-B. PRACTICE THE M KEY

Use the J finger.

3 jjj jmj jmj mjm jjj jmj jmj mjm jjj jmj
4 mar ham ma; ram dam me; jam am; mom mad
5 same lame room fame make roam loam arms
6 she made more room for more of her jam;

3-C. PRACTICE THE T KEY

Use the F finger.

7 fff ftf ftf tft fff ftf ftf tft fff ftf
8 tar ate sat lot mat tam rat eat jot hot
9 tool fate mart date late told take mate
10 she took the tools from store to store;

REPORT 100
BOUND-REPORT PAGE WITH
SIDE HEADINGS AND
FOOTNOTE

Paper: plain, full sheet

This is page 7 of a bound report.

Editing

Editng is the ~~method~~ *process* of revising a ~~paper~~ *document* to change the

spelling of a word, add or deleted a words or words, change

s/entnces *ences* or paragraphs to ~~help~~ *improve* the flow of words, and make

other essential corrections for producing a mainable *document* ~~paper~~.

The editingprocess ~~varys~~ *varies* from one type of equipment to

another.

On ~~a~~ *the* typewriter, the typist or originata *or* records

corrections on draft copy and them re types the entire *document* ~~paper~~.

When use *ing* a micocomputer and a word processing ~~software~~ *program* are

used, editing is *done* through a series of commands that differe

according to the ~~method~~ *procedure* and the software program being

~~implemented~~ *used*. Correct potrions of the text reamin untouched,

so it is not necessary to retype *the entire document.*

Proofreaders' Marks

Sabin⁹ states that proof reading is the ~~method~~ *process* by which

~~one~~ *you* confirms that the copy ~~one is~~ *you are* looking at faithfully re-

produces the orighal material in the ~~correct~~ *intended* form. He futher

~~states~~ *indicates* that if the copy devaites in anyway from the original

you have to make it ~~at once for~~ *mark* correction, and once the

corrections are made; you have to proof read the altered

material to ~~make sure~~ *ensure* that everything is ~~know~~ *now* as it should be.

Triple space

---

⁹William Sabin, The Gregg Reference Manual, Sixth Edition,
Gregg Division, McGraw-Hill Book Company, New York, 1985,
p. 240.

3-D. PRACTICE THE I KEY

Use the K finger.

11 kkk kik kik iki kkk kik kik iki kkk kik
12 air lid did sit kit rim him sir dim fir
13 iris tide site item fire idea tile tire
14 this time he left his tie at the store;

3-E. PRACTICE THE C KEY

Use the D finger.

15 ddd dcd dcd cdc ddd dcd dcd cdc ddd dcd
16 cot ace ice arc cat coo car act cod sac
17 deck coat itch aces face chat tack rich
18 he lets his old cat catch lots of mice;

3-F. BUILD SKILL ON WORD FAMILIES

19 mace face lace ace; | sail tail rail fail
20 mire tire fire ire; | dots tots jots lots
21 jade fade made ade; | seed deed feed heed
22 fads cads lads ads; | hale tale sale dale

3-G. BUILD SKILL ON SHORT SENTENCES

23 he told his joke; she is tired of them;
24 she took the feed seed to the old farm;
25 her date is late; she said he is ideal;
26 she met him at the dock; he liked that;

3-H. Take three 1-minute timings. Try to complete both lines each time.

3-H. SKILL MEASUREMENT: 1-MINUTE TIMED WRITING

27 the local store had a fire sale to sell
28 off some old clocks;

SKILLBUILDING AND REPORT REVIEW

Line: 60 spaces
Tab: 5
Spacing: single
Drills: 2 times
Format Guide: 185

Goals: To type 60 wam/5'/5e; to review formatting a report with side headings and a footnote.

180-B. Spacing: double. Record your score.

180-A.   WARMUP

S 1 Did Jake and Cy take the bus to Sidney, or how did they go?
A 2 Pam Fawaz's quick tally showed that just six drivers began.
N 3 Will he need Nos. 157, 394, and 806 for the sale on June 2?

SKILLBUILDING

180-B.   SKILL MEASUREMENT: 5-MINUTE TIMED WRITING

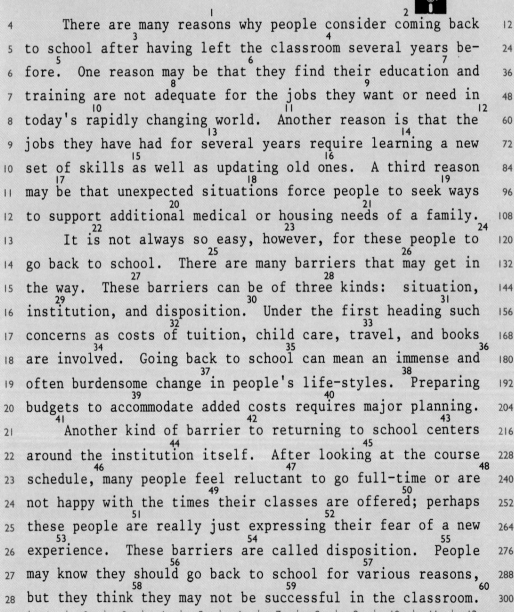

4   There are many reasons why people consider coming back   12
5   to school after having left the classroom several years be-   24
6   fore. One reason may be that they find their education and   36
7   training are not adequate for the jobs they want or need in   48
8   today's rapidly changing world. Another reason is that the   60
9   jobs they have had for several years require learning a new   72
10 set of skills as well as updating old ones. A third reason   84
11 may be that unexpected situations force people to seek ways   96
12 to support additional medical or housing needs of a family. 108
13   It is not always so easy, however, for these people to 120
14 go back to school. There are many barriers that may get in 132
15 the way. These barriers can be of three kinds: situation, 144
16 institution, and disposition. Under the first heading such 156
17 concerns as costs of tuition, child care, travel, and books 168
18 are involved. Going back to school can mean an immense and 180
19 often burdensome change in people's life-styles. Preparing 192
20 budgets to accommodate added costs requires major planning. 204
21   Another kind of barrier to returning to school centers 216
22 around the institution itself. After looking at the course 228
23 schedule, many people feel reluctant to go full-time or are 240
24 not happy with the times their classes are offered; perhaps 252
25 these people are really just expressing their fear of a new 264
26 experience. These barriers are called disposition. People 276
27 may know they should go back to school for various reasons, 288
28 but they think they may not be successful in the classroom. 300

| 1 | 2 | 3 | 4 | 5 | 6 | 7 | 8 | 9 | 10 | 11 | 12 |

Line: 40 spaces
Spacing: single
Drills: 2 times
Workguide: 13
Format Guide: 3–4
Tape: 4A or K4A

NEW KEYS

Goals: To control the right shift, V, and period keys; to count errors.

4-A. WARMUP

1 the jets had left as she came too late;
2 the farmer hired him to feed the mares;

To capitalize any letter that is on the left half of the keyboard:
1. With the J finger home, press and hold down the right shift key with the Sem finger.
2. Strike the letter key.
3. Release the shift key, and return fingers to home position.

4-B. PRACTICE THE RIGHT SHIFT KEY

3 ;;; ;A; ;A; ;;; ;S; ;S; ;;; ;D; ;D; ;;;
4 Ada Sam Rae Ted Dee Sam Tom Sal Alf Art
5 Dick Sara Todd Amos Carl Elsa Edie Chet
6 Amos Dale Ford married Emma Dee Carter;

4-C. PRACTICE THE V KEY

Use the F finger.

7 fff fvf fvf vfv fff fvf fvf vfv fff fvf
8 vie Ava vet Viv vis vim via Eva eve Val
9 vote move Vera vast ever Vida have live
10 Victor Vida moved to Vassar to see Eve;

4-D. PRACTICE THE . KEY

Use the L finger.

Space once after a period following an abbreviation but none after a period within an abbreviation. Space twice after a period at the end of a sentence.

11 lll l.l l.l .l. lll l.l l.l .l. lll l.l
12 sr. sr. dr. dr. ea. ea. Dr. Dr. Sr. Sr.
13 a.m. i.e. loc. cit. A.D. jr. D.C. misc.
14 She left. Sam cried. Sarah came home.

4-E. BUILD SKILL ON SHORT SENTENCES

Maintain a smooth and steady pace. Speed up on the second copy of each sentence.

15 Dr. Drake called Sam; he asked for Ted.
16 Vera told a tale to her old classmates.
17 Todd asked Cal to stack five old rails.
18 Del asked if he had read the last tale.

179-H. TABLE AND FORMS REVIEW

TABLE 70
RULED TABLE WITH
FOOTNOTE

Paper: full sheet

Special: double-space the column entries.

Selected Vehicle Trade-Ins — 5

Vehicle Number	Year Purchased	Trade-In Year*	Current Mileage	
				10
				16
15	1985	1989	15,321	19
21	1986	1990	12,113	22
24	1987	1991	10,131	25
25	1987	1991	6,432	28
26	1988	1992	4,351	31

*Estimated trade-in year. — 36

TABLE 71
BOXED TABLE WITH BRACED
HEADING

Paper: full sheet

Special: double-space the column entries.

CURRENT WORKERS BY YEARS OF EMPLOYMENT — 8

	Number				
Years	Male	Female	Total	Percent	14
0-5	10	8	18	22.5	17
6-10	15	12	27	33.8	20
11-15	8	8	16	20.0	22
16-20	6	6	12	15.0	25
21-Up	4	3	7	8.7	27
total	43	37	80	100.0	30

FORM 55
PURCHASE ORDER

Paper: Workguide 491

PURCHASE ORDER 4378. On November 15, 19—, the Purchasing Department processes Purchase Requisition 3265 and orders the following items from Winkler Supplies, 2400 Market Street, Harrisburg, PA 17103: 2 Ace videowriters (Catalog No. 828) @ $799.95 = $1,599.90; 3 oak lateral files (No. 842) @ $229.95 = $689.85; 1 litigation bag (No. 662) @ $249.25; and 1 seafarer's clock (No. 639) @ $59.90; TOTAL = $2,598.90.

FORM 56
INVOICE

Paper: Workguide 491

INVOICE 6340. On November 27, 19—, Winkler Supplies invoices Wade Stores, 1001 State Street, Erie, PA 16501, for its Purchase Order 4378 for the following items: 2 Ace videowriters, #828, @ $799.95 = $1,599.90; 3 oak lateral files, #842, @ $229.95 = $689.85; 1 litigation bag, #662, @ $249.25; and 1 seafarer's clock, #639, @ $59.90; for a total of $2,598.90; less 8% trade discount of $207.91; plus tax of $87.16; total amount due = $2,478.15.

4-F. COUNTING ERRORS

Compare with lines 19–21 below.

(Davod) ordered steaks; Sal liked steaks_②.
[1]   [2]
[3]
David ordered steaks⑤ Sal (likedsteaks).
Viola sold (m st) of the (itemS) at a loss.
[4]   [5]
Viola sold most the items at (at) a loss.
[6]   [7]
[9]   [8]
Al (him asked) for three jars of red jam.
Al asked him for three jars of red (jaj .)
[10]

After studying 4-F, complete Workguide page 13.

As indicated in the examples above, count it an error when:

1. Any stroke is incorrect.
2. Any punctuation after a word is incorrect or omitted.
3. The spacing after a word or after its punctuation is incorrect.
4. Any stroke is so light that it does not show clearly.
5. One stroke is made over another.
6. A word is omitted.
7. A word is repeated.
8. Words are transposed.
9. A direction about spacing, indenting, and so on, is violated.
10. Only one error is charged to any one word, no matter how many errors it may contain.

4-G. BUILD SKILL ON SHORT SENTENCES

4-G. After typing each line 2 times, circle and count your errors.

19 David ordered steaks; Sal liked steaks.

20 Viola sold most of the items at a loss.

21 Al asked him for three jars of red jam.

4-H. SKILL MEASUREMENT: 1-MINUTE TIMED WRITING

4-H. Take three 1-minute timings. Try to complete both lines each time.

22 Ed asked them to tell the major to come

23 after Vic left for home.

LESSON 5

REVIEW

Line: 40 spaces
Spacing: single
Drills: 2 times
Workguide: 14
Format Guide: 3–4
Tape: 5A or K5A

Goals: To strengthen all controls; to learn how to measure speed.

5-A. WARMUP

1 The jet took Ed to Asia after the race.

2 Vera liked the meal; Art loved the jam.

Line: 60 spaces
Tab: 5, center
Spacing: single
Drills: 2 times
Workguide: 491
Format Guide: 183

LESSON
179

SKILLBUILDING AND TABLE AND FORMS REVIEW

Goals: To improve speed and accuracy; to review formatting ruled tables with footnotes and braced headings; to review formatting business forms.

179-A. WARMUP

S 1 Did they handle the profit right for their auditor in Kent?
A 2 Mary, Jenny, and I will quietly pack five dozen huge boxes.
N 3 Do they plan to ship Order Nos. 5106 and 3789 on August 24?

SKILLBUILDING

179-B. PACED PRACTICE

Turn to the Paced Practice routine at the back of the book. Take several 2-minute timings, starting at the point where you left off the last time. Record your progress on Workguide page 290.

179-C. Take several 1-minute timings. Slow down while typing the symbols, but keep your eyes on the copy.

179-C. SYMBOL TYPING

4   The clerk* said $469 was too much for Desk #87. Desks   12
5 at Able & Jones cost 1/10 less. They (Able & Jones) didn't   24
6 have add-on taxes--just the sales price. The "Journal" ads   36
7 listed pens at $2.35. What a deal! Did you see these ads?   48
8 They also listed the following: tablets, tapes, and paper.   60
    | 1 | 2 | 3 | 4 | 5 | 6 | 7 | 8 | 9 | 10 | 11 | 12

PRETEST. Take a 1-minute timing; compute your speed and count errors.

179-D. PRETEST: ALTERNATE- AND ONE-HAND WORDS

9   A few men in Cascade and Reserve are eager to join the   12
10 antique-car race in Ohio. It is the only authentic race in   24
11 the world for an antique car. It is their goal to go there   36
12 in July. The fare to Mantau is better than average by air.   48
13 The men are free to go when their usual extra work is done.   60
    | 1 | 2 | 3 | 4 | 5 | 6 | 7 | 8 | 9 | 10 | 11 | 12

PRACTICE.
  Speed Emphasis: If you made no errors on the Pretest, type each line twice.
  Accuracy Emphasis: If you made 1 or more errors on the Pretest, type each group of lines (as though it were a paragraph) twice.

179-E. PRACTICE: ALTERNATE-HAND WORDS

14 also angle field profit problem formal signs throw and form
15 goal usual signs eighty element social chair blend big make
16 town amend world emblem visible visual their blame cut fish
17 firm eight lapel enrich auditor island snaps laugh aid lake

179-F. PRACTICE: ONE-HAND WORDS

18 hook craft nippy eraser average adverb draws pupil pull joy
19 seed draft onion afraid catered breeze hilly junky deed red
20 milk exact plump limply million regret fewer based moon mop
21 gave crave knoll extras acreage better defer award upon far

POSTTEST. Repeat the Pretest and compare performance.

179-G. POSTTEST: ALTERNATE- AND ONE-HAND WORDS

5-B. BUILD SKILL ON SHORT SENTENCES

3 Vickie loved the fame she had achieved.
4 Save the three rolls of dimes for Chad.
5 Todd had sold a set of tires to Victor.
6 The old farmer deeded the farm to Eric.

5-C. BUILD SKILL ON WORD FAMILIES

7 fame tame lame same|lace face mace race
8 fold cold mold told|mail tail sail rail
9 feed seed deed heed|mate late date fate

5-D. After studying 5-D, complete Workguide page 14.

If you are using the keyboarding software, your speed will be computed automatically.

5-D. MEASURING SPEED

Type for an exact number of minutes while someone times you.

Find out how many "average" words you have typed. Every 5 strokes count as 1 average word as marked off by the horizontal scales and, in paragraph copy, as cumulatively totaled after each line. The first example below contains (8 + 8 + 2) 18 words.

The second example contains (24 + 4) 28 words.

3. Divide the words typed by the number of minutes typed. If you type 28 words in 2 minutes, for example, you type (28 ÷ 2) 14 wam (words a minute); in 1 minute, (28 ÷ 1) 28 wam; or in ½ minute, (28 ÷ ½) 56 wam.

Compare with line 12.

Emma races small cars at a short track.
Emma races small cars at a short track.
Emma races
| | | 2 | 3 | 4 | 5 | 6 | 7 | 8

Compare with lines 13–15.

Dale took Tom home to see David. David
cooked a dish of fresh catfish for him.
Dale served Tom his homemade ice cream.
Dale took Tom home
| | | 2 | 3 | 4 | 5 | 6 | 7 | 8

5-E. If you can be timed, take a 1-minute timing on each line instead of typing it twice. Compute your speed; circle and count errors.

5-E. BUILD SKILL ON SHORT SENTENCES

10 Sara had five half liters of cold milk.
11 Rich visited Alaska after he left home.
12 Emma races small cars at a short track.
| | | 2 | 3 | 4 | 5 | 6 | 7 | 8 = 5-stroke words

5-F. If you can be timed, take two 1-minute timings instead of typing the paragraph twice. Compute your speed and count errors.

5-F. BUILD SKILL ON A SHORT PARAGRAPH

CUMULATIVE WORDS

13 Dale took Tom home to see David. David   8
14 cooked a dish of fresh catfish for him.   16
15 Dale served Tom his homemade ice cream.   24
| | | 2 | 3 | 4 | 5 | 6 | 7 | 8

5-G. Take three 1-minute timings. Try to complete both lines each time. Compute your speed and count errors.

5-G. SKILL MEASUREMENT: 1-MINUTE TIMED WRITING

16 Carla asked Vi Filmore if she liked her   8
17 red jacket. Vi said she did.   14
| | | 2 | 3 | 4 | 5 | 6 | 7 | 8

MEMO 36

Paper: Workguide 489

178-C.   MEMORANDUM REVIEW

(TO:) All Employees / (FROM:) Wilma Bates / Employee Relations / 9
(DATE:) (*Current date*) / (SUBJECT:) Jury Duty 15

The company recognizes the civic responsibility of employees to 27
serve on a jury and makes provision for them to perform such duty 41
without loss of pay. 45

The company will compensate employees called to jury duty for the 58
difference between the pay received from the court and the normal 71
take-home pay. The employee's fringe benefits will continue. The em- 85
ployee must notify his or her department head of the call to jury duty as 100
soon as it is received and must give proof of the jury duty pay to the 114
Payroll Department. The employee is expected to report for regular 127
work when temporarily excused from attendance at court. 138

Full cooperation is expected between the employee, the supervisor, 152
and the department head involved to ensure minimal disruption in the 166
production and service responsibilities of the unit. 176

MEMO 37
MEMO WITH OPEN TABLE

Paper: plain

MEMO TO: All Supervisors / FROM: Clinton Bates / Personnel Director / 12
DATE: (*Current date*) / SUBJECT: Employee Services and Opportunities 26

Listed below are some of the services and opportunities that are 39
widely used by employees. Please make sure that all employees are in- 53
formed of these activities. 58

Service/Opportunity	Office	Telephone	
Emergencies	Safety	555-1200	70
Credit Union	Credit Union	555-1238	76
Education	Employee Benefits	555-6500	83
Health Care	Clinic	555-5000	88
Lost and Found	Main Office	555-6300	95
Minority Programs	Human Relations	555-6510	103
Payroll	Payroll Office	555-6506	108
Public Relations	Public Relations	555-6570	116
Transportation	Auto Services	555-1250	123

LESSON
6

NEW KEYS

Line: 40 spaces
Spacing: single
Drills: 2 times
Workguide: 15–16
Format Guide: 3–4
Tape: 6A or K6A

Goals: To control the N, W, comma, and G keys; to type 15 wam/1'/3e.

"15 wam/1'/3e" means to type at the rate of 15 words a minute for 1 minute with no more than 3 errors.

6-A.   WARMUP

1 A market sold major food items at cost.
2 David sat at his desk for a short time.

6-B.   PRACTICE THE N KEY

Use the J finger.

3 jjj jnj jnj njn jjj jnj jnj njn jjj jnj
4 not and tan tin kin den sin ran fan man
5 none then seen find cent even rain sane
6 Ann cannot enter the old main entrance.

6-C.   PRACTICE THE W KEY

Use the S finger.

7 sss sws sws wsw sss sws sws wsw sss sws
8 saw few law who row wow how tow two now
9 wave saws wait warm wine when will want
10 Wanda will want to walk with Walt Shaw.

6-D.   TECHNIQUE TYPING: SPACE BAR

11 Sam let Art do it. Fred drove to work.
12 Al is not in. Ed is in. Ed can do it.

6-E.   PRACTICE THE , KEY

Use the K finger.

Space once after a comma.

13 kkk k,k k,k ,k, kkk k,k k,k ,k, kkk k,k
14 do, so, is, if, no, it, oh, to, of, or,
15 too, it is it, as soon as, if so, what,
16 Amos, Fred, Clark, and Daniel left too.

SKILLBUILDING AND MEMORANDUM REVIEW

Line: 60 spaces
Tab: 5
Spacing: single
Drills: 2 times
Workguide: 489
Format Guide: 183

Goals: To type 60 wam/5'/5e; to review formatting memorandums.

178-A. WARMUP

S 1 They may fish with us if it is all right for them to do so.
A 2 James and Glenn quickly explored the varying sizes of bows.
N 3 There were 26,789 votes for Lee and 34,510 votes for Jones.

SKILLBUILDING

178-B. Spacing: double. Record your score.

178-B. SKILL MEASUREMENT: 5-MINUTE TIMED WRITING

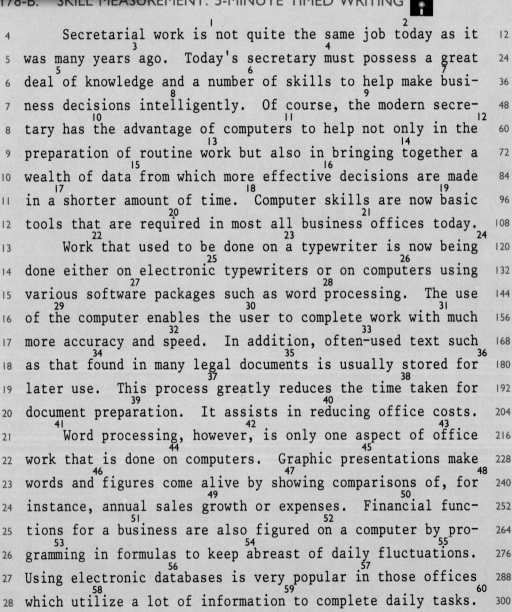

```
 4        Secretarial work is not quite the same job today as it    12
 5   was many years ago.  Today's secretary must possess a great    24
 6   deal of knowledge and a number of skills to help make busi-    36
 7   ness decisions intelligently.  Of course, the modern secre-    48
 8   tary has the advantage of computers to help not only in the    60
 9   preparation of routine work but also in bringing together a    72
10   wealth of data from which more effective decisions are made    84
11   in a shorter amount of time.  Computer skills are now basic    96
12   tools that are required in most all business offices today.   108
13        Work that used to be done on a typewriter is now being   120
14   done either on electronic typewriters or on computers using   132
15   various software packages such as word processing.  The use   144
16   of the computer enables the user to complete work with much   156
17   more accuracy and speed.  In addition, often-used text such   168
18   as that found in many legal documents is usually stored for   180
19   later use.  This process greatly reduces the time taken for   192
20   document preparation.  It assists in reducing office costs.   204
21        Word processing, however, is only one aspect of office   216
22   work that is done on computers.  Graphic presentations make   228
23   words and figures come alive by showing comparisons of, for   240
24   instance, annual sales growth or expenses.  Financial func-   252
25   tions for a business are also figured on a computer by pro-   264
26   gramming in formulas to keep abreast of daily fluctuations.   276
27   Using electronic databases is very popular in those offices   288
28   which utilize a lot of information to complete daily tasks.   300

     |  1  |  2  |  3  |  4  |  5  |  6  |  7  |  8  |  9  | 10  | 11  | 12
```

6-F. PRACTICE THE **G** KEY

Use the F finger.

17 fff fgf fgf gfg fff fgf fgf gfg fff fgf
18 got leg get sag tag nag age egg rag log
19 gain wage gown grew wing rage grow sage
20 The old green gown sagged in the front.

6-G. SKILL MEASUREMENT: 1-MINUTE TIMED WRITING

6-G. Take two 1-minute timings; compute your speed and circle errors.
(**Note:** Beginning with Lesson 7, you will not be reminded to circle errors.)

WORDS

21 Wilma joined the team for the last five   8
22 games. The coach liked her skills.   15

| | | | 2 | 3 | 4 | 5 | 6 | 7 | 8

LESSON 7

Line: 40 spaces
Spacing: single
Drills: 2 times
Workguide: 17–18
Format Guide: 5–6
Tape: 7A or K7A

NEW KEYS

Goals: To control the left shift, U, B, and colon keys; to type 16 wam/1'/3e.

7-A. WARMUP

1 Cora and Ed liked cats, dogs, and fish.
2 Evie jogged more than a mile with Walt.

To capitalize any letter that is on the right half of the keyboard:
1. With the F finger home, press and hold down the left shift key with the A finger.
2. Strike the letter key.
3. Release the shift key, and return fingers to home position.

7-B. PRACTICE THE LEFT **SHIFT** KEY

3 aaa Jaa Jaa aaa Kaa Kaa aaa Laa Laa aaa
4 Jed Ken Mel Kit Ned Hal Ira Kim Joe Lee
5 Jose Hans Mark Nita Iris Kate Hank John
6 Olga Hall went with Mike Lee to Kenton.

7-C. PRACTICE THE **U** KEY

Use the J finger.

7 jjj juj juj uju jjj juj juj uju jjj juj
8 urn sun lug sue jug due run rut cue dug
9 just hulk junk must hums sulk dunk nuns
10 Joe Uhl urged Hugh to ask Manuel Sturm.

177-H. LETTER REVIEW

LETTER 105
SIMPLIFIED STYLE WITH
ENCLOSURE NOTATION

Paper: Workguide 487–488

(*Current date*) / Ms. Carla Craven / 3520 | 8
Mountain View Drive / Anchorage, AK 99508 / | 16
Equipment Leasing | 19

Welcome to the multibillion-dollar business | 28
of equipment leasing. Equipment leasing has | 37
become a major factor in the financial strategy | 47
of contemporary business, with approximately | 56
$240 billion worth of equipment on lease, and | 65
is one of the fastest-growing forms of capital | 74
investment today. | 78

We are happy to have you as a limited part- | 86
ner in our fund. Through your investment in | 95
Mars, you will pool your resources with thou- | 104
sands of other similar investors and gain access | 114
to the high-yielding opportunities of this so- | 123
phisticated industry that are not normally | 131
within the reach of the typical private investor. | 141

Enclosed are a recent article about equip- | 149
ment leasing income funds from *National In-* | 158
vestor magazine and a reply card for request- | 166
ing additional information about our current | 175
offerings. | 177

Thank you for your confidence in Mars | 185
Leasing's expertise and staying power to ac- | 194
complish your partnership objectives. Please | 203
feel free to contact us if we can be of service to | 213
you. | 214

Lorenzo White / President / Enclosures | 221

LETTER 106
PERSONAL-BUSINESS LETTER IN
MODIFIED-BLOCK STYLE WITH
ENUMERATION

Paper: plain

(*Current date*) / Mr. Lorenzo White / President / | 9
Mars Leasing / 405 Olive Way / Seattle, WA | 17
98101 / Dear Mr. White: | 21

Thank you for your recent letter informing | 29
me about my limited partnership in Mars Leas- | 38
ing. | 39

I am happy to learn of the volume of dollars | 48
spent on equipment leasing by today's busi- | 56

ness firms. The article from *National Investor* | 66
was very informative. | 70

My broker indicated that you would be | 78
sending me the following materials: | 85
1. A confirmation of my investment. | 92
2. Quarterly and annual reports, with status | 101
updates. | 103
3. Quarterly distribution checks (if applica- | 112
ble). | 113
4. Schedule K-1 tax information. | 119

When should I expect to receive a confirma- | 128
tion of my investment and Schedule K-1 tax | 136
information? I am particularly concerned | 145
about these materials, as I am to meet with my | 154
accountant within the next three weeks. | 162

Sincerely yours, / Carla Craven / 3520 Moun- | 169
tain View Drive / Anchorage, AK 99508 | 176

LETTER 107
PERSONAL-BUSINESS LETTER IN
MODIFIED-BLOCK STYLE WITH
INDENTED PARAGRAPHS AND
FOREIGN ADDRESS

Paper: plain

(*Current date*) / Mr. Hans Schmidt / Graf-Adolf | 9
Strasse 100 / Dusseldorf 4000 / GERMANY / | 16
Dear Mr. Schmidt: | 19

I would like to take this opportunity on be- | 28
half of the International Marketing Association | 38
to invite you to be the keynote speaker at its | 47
annual convention in New York City on April | 56
6, 19—. | 57

As you are an internationally recognized | 66
consultant for the automobile industry, we | 74
would like to have you share with us your | 83
viewpoints regarding the industry during the | 92
next decade. We are particularly interested in | 101
your predictions concerning the impact of | 110
protectionist trade laws, the demand for auto- | 119
mobiles in the Third World, and the American | 128
share of the automobile market. We are aware | 137
of your research and publications in these | 145
three areas. | 148

The association will reimburse you for all | 156
expenses incurred in delivering your address. | 166
We hope that you will be able to accept our | 175
invitation. | 177

Sincerely yours, / Addison Fales / 160 Bea- | 184
con Street / Boston, MA 02116 | 189

7-D. PRACTICE EACH ROW

Top Row 11 We were told to take a train to Westin.

12 There were two tired men waiting there.

13 Write to their hometown to inform them.

Home Row 14 Jake asked his dad for small red flags.

15 Sara added a dash of salt to the salad.

16 Dale said she had a fall sale in Elson.

Bottom Row 17 He can come at five for nine old canes.

18 Melvin came to vote with vim and vigor.

19 Val had nerve to come via a moving van.

7-E. PRACTICE THE **B** KEY

Use the F finger.

20 fff fbf fbf bfb fff fbf fbf bfb fff fbf

21 big job bag bin bit bid bow bun cab orb

22 back bend blew bunt bent bulb bask bush

23 Robb burned the big bag of bad berries.

7-F. PRACTICE THE **:** KEY

The colon is the shift of the semicolon.

Use the Sem finger.

Space twice after a colon; once after a period following an abbreviation.

24 ;;; ;:; ;:; :;: ;;; ;:; ;:; :;: ;;; ;:;

25 Ms. See: Dr. Roe: Mrs. Low: Mr. Uhl:

26 Dear Mrs. Jones: Dear Jack: Dear Nan:

27 Date: To: From: Subject: as listed:

7-G. Take two 1-minute timings; compute your speed and count errors.

7-G. SKILL MEASUREMENT: 1-MINUTE TIMED WRITING

WORDS

28 Dear Fred: Bev would like to take Beth   8

29 to a Jets game. She can come tomorrow.   16

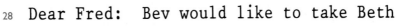

Line: 60 spaces
Tab: 5, center
Spacing: single
Drills: 2 times
Workguide: 487–488
Format Guide: 181

LESSON
177

SKILLBUILDING AND LETTER REVIEW

Goals: To improve speed and accuracy; to review formatting personal-business letters and simplified-style letters.

177-A. WARMUP

S 1 They did the work for that auditor with some help from Mel.
A 2 Jerry loves pizzas and got quite a few when Alex came back.
N 3 Our Invoice 4389 listed 20 desks, 17 chairs, and 56 tables.

SKILLBUILDING

177-B. Compare this paragraph with the second paragraph of Letter 102 on page 376. Type a list of the words that contain errors, correcting the errors as you type.

177-B. PRODUCTION PRACTICE: PROOFREADING

4 The house has eight rooms. Their are five rooms and
5 half beth on the first flour. the second floor has a main
6 bedroom and bath as welll as three bedrooms and one bath,
7 The family room with halve bath and a utility room is in the
8 basement. The inside of the house was painted within
9 the last six weeks. The exterior is in good condition, and
10 you need to repaint it.

PRETEST. Take a 1-minute timing; compute your speed and count errors.

177-C. PRETEST: CLOSE REACHES

11 Many employers often have policies that employees feel   12
12 do not treat everyone the same. Employers try to avoid any   24
13 notion of partiality. It is a myth to say that policies do   36
14 not work, for they do; policies help lift morale in offices   48
15 when an employee understands their usage and their results.   60
   | 1 | 2 | 3 | 4 | 5 | 6 | 7 | 8 | 9 | 10 | 11 | 12

PRACTICE.
Speed Emphasis: If you made no errors on the Pretest, type each line twice.
Accuracy Emphasis: If you made 1 or more errors on the Pretest, type each group of lines (as though it were a paragraph) twice.

177-D. PRACTICE: ADJACENT KEYS

16 tr true treat straw stray strap tracer betray metric citric
17 po pool polar spoil epoch spoon policy podium spoken spoils
18 sa said sales salad essay usage salute salary sesame disarm
19 oi oils oiler toils hoist avoid voiced boiled poison rejoin

177-E. PRACTICE: CONSECUTIVE FINGERS

20 my army pygmy seamy foamy grimy myself mystic stormy shimmy
21 ft lift often after lefty nifty rafter sifted gifted deftly
22 ny many nymph phony loony peony canyon mutiny grainy botany
23 lo look locus color igloo aglow looses hollow ballot employ

POSTTEST. Repeat the Pretest and compare performance.

177-F. POSTTEST: CLOSE REACHES

177-G. PROGRESSIVE PRACTICE: NUMBERS

Turn to the Progressive Practice: Numbers routine at the back of the book. Take several 30-second timings, starting at the point where you left off the last time. Record your progress on Workguide page 289.

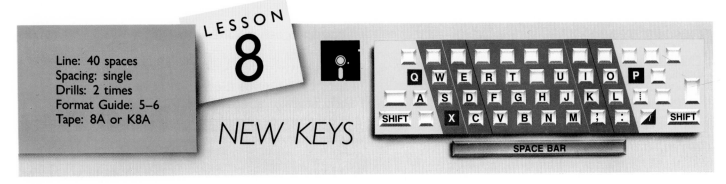

Line: 40 spaces
Spacing: single
Drills: 2 times
Format Guide: 5–6
Tape: 8A or K8A

Goals: To control the P, Q, diagonal, and X keys; to type 17 wam/1'/3e.

8-A. WARMUP

1 Wade bought Vi a jade ring at the mall.
2 Fred asked Merlin if Cora was at fault.

8-B. PRACTICE THE P KEY

Use the Sem finger.

3 ;;; ;p; ;p; p;p ;;; ;p; ;p; p;p ;;; ;p;
4 pan rip pat dip lip sip pen pad rap sap
5 page pale stop trip park palm peep pace
6 His pace kept him in step with Pauline.

8-C. PRACTICE THE Q KEY

Use the A finger.

7 aaa aqa aqa qaq aaa aqa aqa qaq aaa aqa
8 quip aqua quite quack equip quiet quick
9 quell quark quests quills quarts quotas
10 The quiet quints quilted an aqua quilt.

8-D. TECHNIQUE TYPING: SHIFT KEY

11 Elgin, Ohio; Sitka, Alaska; Ola, Idaho;
12 Mr. Ben Roth; Ms. Sue King; Ames, Iowa;
13 Mr. Vail; Miss Rubin; Mr. and Mrs. Mee;

8-E. PRACTICE THE / KEY

Use the Sem finger.

Leave no space before or after a diagonal.

14 ;;; ;/; ;/; /;/ ;;; ;/; ;/; /;/ ;;; ;/;
15 his/her him/her he/she either/or ad/add
16 do/due/dew hale/hail fir/fur heard/herd
17 Ask him/her if he/she and/or Al can go.

176-C.   LETTER REVIEW

LETTER 102
MODIFIED-BLOCK STYLE WITH
STANDARD PUNCTUATION,
ATTENTION LINE, POSTSCRIPT

Paper: Workguide 481–482

(*Current date*) / The Elite Decorators, Inc. / 9
Attention: Mr. James F. Black / 331 East Brook- 18
line / Boston, MA 02118 / Ladies and Gentle- 25
men: 26

Your letter asking about our new Apollo 34
Floor Carpets came on the same day we mailed 43
you and all other decorators a complete bro- 52
chure. Let me answer the questions you asked 61
in your letter. 64

First, as a well-known office decorator, you 73
will have the first opportunity to recommend 82
this carpet to your clients. 88

Second, you will be able to come in at your 96
convenience and select samples that you wish 105
to use in designing your current and future of- 115
fice layouts. 117

Third, you can assure your clients that our 126
carpets are guaranteed, under normal wear, for 135
six years. 137

The Apollo Floor Carpets are ready for im- 146
mediate sale. If you have further questions, 155
please call me. 158

Sincerely yours, / Nathan J. Green / Sales 165
Manager / PS: I know that you, of all people, 175
will like this new carpet. 180

LETTER 103
BLOCK STYLE WITH OPEN PUNCTUATION,
SUBJECT LINE, ENUMERATION, COPY NOTATION

Paper: Workguide 483–484

(*Current date*) / Ms. Louise Lopez / President / 9
Top Notch Products, Inc. / 3770 Frew Road / 17
Charlotte, NC 28206 / Dear Ms. Lopez / Sub- 24
ject: The Executive Suite 29

Thank you for your inquiry about our new 38
line of office furniture—The Executive Suite. 47

We believe that we have designed the ulti- 55
mate line of furniture for the successful execu- 64
tive. You will be able to create an atmosphere 74
of warmth and luxury at an unbelievably low 83
price. 84

The Executive Suite consists of the follow- 92
ing: 93
1.   Executive desks, 60 by 30 inches (29 101
inches high), with file and box drawers and a 111
handy storage shelf under the desk. 118
2.   Executive armchairs with thick, form- 126
fitted, pillowlike fabric and upholstered arm 135
rests. 136
3.   Executive credenzas, 72 by 20 inches. 144

Our sales representative, Ms. Ada Thomas, 153
will call to make an appointment for you to see 162
this quality-crafted wood furniture. 169

Sincerely yours / Lance Seymour / Sales Man- 177
ager / c: Ada Thomas 181

LETTER 104
MODIFIED-BLOCK STYLE WITH INDENTED
PARAGRAPHS, OPEN PUNCTUATION, COMPANY
NAME, ENCLOSURE NOTATION

Paper: Workguide 485–486

(*Current date*) / Mr. Adam Gray / 625 South 9
Phillips Avenue / Sioux Falls, SD 57104 / Dear 17
Mr. Gray 18

We have found the Richmond home you 26
wanted. I am enclosing five photographs and a 35
floor plan. 37

The house has nine rooms. There are five 46
rooms and a half bath on the first floor. The 55
second floor has a master bedroom and a bath 64
as well as three other bedrooms and one bath. 73
A family room with a half bath and a utility 82
room are in the basement. The outside of the 92
house was painted within the last six months. 101
The interior is in excellent condition, and you 111
will not need to repaint it. 116

The asking price is $185,000, but I believe 125
that we can get the house for about $182,500. 134
The current owner's mortgage can be renego- 143
tiated at 11 percent and the remainder fi- 151
nanced at 15 percent. 155

The house appears close to the details you 164
defined in your letter last week. There have 173
been a number of inquiries from other real es- 182
tate agents about this fine property. Please let 192
me know if you are interested in the home and 201
if I should make an offer for you. 208

Sincerely yours / A-ONE REALTORS, INC. / 215
Malcolm Schultz / Agent / Enclosures 222

8-F. PRACTICE THE X KEY

Use the S finger.

18 sss sxs sxs xsx sss sxs sxs xsx sss sxs
19 vex box fox hex lax lux wax mix nix tax
20 next taxi apex flex flax text flux axle
21 Max coaxed six men to fix a sixth taxi.

8-G. Take two 1-minute timings; compute your speed and
count errors.

8-G. SKILL MEASUREMENT: 1-MINUTE TIMED WRITING

WORDS

22 Jan packed her box with five quilts and   8
23 rugs. She had more but no plan to sell   16
24 them.   17

    | | | 2 | 3 | 4 | 5 | 6 | 7 | 8

LESSON 9

NEW KEYS

Line: 40 spaces
Spacing: single
Drills: 2 times
Format Guide: 5–6
Tape: 9A or K9A

Goals: To control the
hyphen, Z, Y, and ? keys; to
type 18 wam/1'/3e.

9-A. WARMUP

1 Susan packed two boxes of green grapes.
2 I have quit the marketing job in Idaho.

9-B. PRACTICE THE — KEY

Use the Sem finger.

A hyphen is typed without a
space before or after it.

Keep the J finger in home position to help guide your hand back
after reaching to the hyphen.

3 ;;; ;p; ;-; -;- ;;; ;p; ;-; -;- ;;; ;-;
4 self-made one-third one-fifth one-sixth
5 ice-cold has-been show-off ha-ha tie-in
6 Ms. Ward-Smith was a well-to-do matron.

9-C. PRACTICE THE Z KEY

Use the A finger.

7 aaa aza aza zaz aaa aza aza zaz aaa aza
8 zoo zap zig zip fez fizz jazz buzz daze
9 zest doze zing zinc zone zoom quiz gaze
10 The size of the prized pizza amazed us.

LESSON
176

SKILLBUILDING AND LETTER REVIEW

Line: 60 spaces
Tab: 5, center
Spacing: single
Drills: 2 times
Workguide: 481–486
Format Guide: 179

Goals: To type 60 wam/5'/5e; to review formatting block and modified-block letters.

176-A. WARMUP

S 1 The eight girls did work with vigor to pay for their visit.
A 2 Judge Fryxell was very much puzzled by Bo's quick thinking.
N 3 Who has any of these winning stubs: 48, 32, 19, 65, or 70?

SKILLBUILDING

176-B. Spacing: double.
Record your score.

176-B. SKILL MEASUREMENT: 5-MINUTE TIMED WRITING

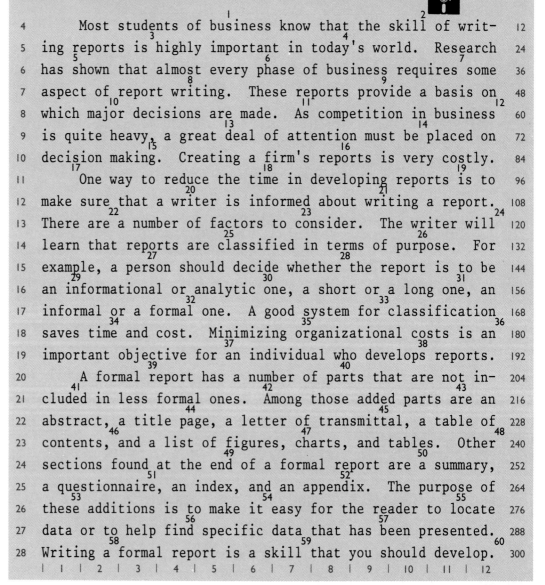

4   Most students of business know that the skill of writ-   12
5   ing reports is highly important in today's world. Research   24
6   has shown that almost every phase of business requires some   36
7   aspect of report writing. These reports provide a basis on   48
8   which major decisions are made. As competition in business   60
9   is quite heavy, a great deal of attention must be placed on   72
10   decision making. Creating a firm's reports is very costly.   84
11   One way to reduce the time in developing reports is to   96
12   make sure that a writer is informed about writing a report.   108
13   There are a number of factors to consider. The writer will   120
14   learn that reports are classified in terms of purpose. For   132
15   example, a person should decide whether the report is to be   144
16   an informational or analytic one, a short or a long one, an   156
17   informal or a formal one. A good system for classification   168
18   saves time and cost. Minimizing organizational costs is an   180
19   important objective for an individual who develops reports.   192
20   A formal report has a number of parts that are not in-   204
21   cluded in less formal ones. Among those added parts are an   216
22   abstract, a title page, a letter of transmittal, a table of   228
23   contents, and a list of figures, charts, and tables. Other   240
24   sections found at the end of a formal report are a summary,   252
25   a questionnaire, an index, and an appendix. The purpose of   264
26   these additions is to make it easy for the reader to locate   276
27   data or to help find specific data that has been presented.   288
28   Writing a formal report is a skill that you should develop.   300
    | 1 | 2 | 3 | 4 | 5 | 6 | 7 | 8 | 9 | 10 | 11 | 12

Elbow Control. Keep your elbows in close, hanging loosely by your sides. They should not swing out. Keep your shoulders relaxed and your fingers curved.

9-D. PRACTICE THE Y KEY

Use the J finger.

11 jjj jyj jyj yjy jjj jyj jyj yjy jjj jyj
12 eye yes yet yam joy you may way say ray
13 yarn year yawn yard holy fray eyed duty
14 Lazy Andy stayed in Troy to buy a ruby.

9-E. PRACTICE THE ? KEY

The question mark is the shift of the diagonal.

Use the Sem finger.

Space twice after a question mark at the end of a sentence.

15 ;;; ;/? ;/? ?;? ;;; ;/? ;/? ?;? ;;; ;?;
16 Can Ken go? If not him, who? Can Joe?
17 Is that you? Can it be? Who will see?
18 Did she ask? Can you go? Why not him?

9-F. TECHNIQUE TYPING: HYPHEN KEY

Hyphens are used:
1. To show that a word is divided (line 19).
2. To make a dash, with two hyphens (lines 20 and 23).
3. To join words in a compound (lines 21, 22, and 24).

19 Can Jerry go to the next tennis tourna-
20 ment? I am positive he--like you--will
21 find it a first-class sports event. If
22 he can go, I will get first-rate seats.
23 Zane--like Alice--liked to write texts.
24 Jill took Mary to a drive-in for lunch.

9-G. SKILL MEASUREMENT: 1-MINUTE TIMED WRITING

9-G. Take two 1-minute timings; compute your speed and count errors.

WORDS

25 Eliza landed a new job. She packed six   8
26 bags, quit her job, and moved away from   16
27 Michigan.   18

| | 1 | | 2 | 3 | 4 | 5 | 6 | 7 | 8

Mr. William Joyce, regional manager of the Phoenix Major Medical Company, has visited with Dr. Miller concerning the areas in which the company will cover medical expenses for some of his patients. Dr. Miller **drafted the following letter to be sent to Mrs. Holly Adams, 8317 East Thomas Road, Scottsdale, AZ 85251. Please send a blind copy to Mr. Joyce.**

SUBJECT: MEDical Expenses Covered by YOUR INSURANCE   10

Your major medical insurance carrier, Phoenix Major Medical   22
Company, has informed us that they cover a broad scope of medical   36
expenses whether incured in the hospital or not. We thought we   48
should review these with you. They include, but are not limited to,   62
the following expenses that either are not covered by your base   75
plan or are in excess of the coverage provided in your base plan.   88

1. Physicians' charges for diagnosis, treatment, or surgery   100
   (in hospital, office, clinic, or home).   108
2. Drugs requiring a writen prescription.   116
3. Hospital (inpatient at the hospital's semiprivate-room rate   129
   and outpatient).   132
4. Alergy shorts.   136
5. Private duty nrusing by rns, lpns, visiting nurses, and   149
   nurse's aides for nursing duties only.   157
6. Periodontal survery.   161
7. Physical and speech therapy.   168
8. Artificial limbs and certain other prosthetic devices.   179
9. Extended care facility for up to 200 days of continuous   191
   confinement.   194
10. Emotional disorders--hospital inpatient (outpatient cov-   206
    erage is limited to the employee out of work for 30 days   217
    and prior to return to work).   223
11. Cost of administration of anesthetics by a physician or   235
    professional anesthetist.   240
12. Local ambulance service.   246
13. Blood or blood plasma.   251

The Phoenix major Medical Company provides for continuation of   264
coverage during retirement for employees insured under this plan   277
immediately prior to retirement who retire in accordance with   289
your employers' formal retirement plan.   297

If you have questions concerning your coverage, please contact   310
the Phoenix Major Medical company or your employee benefits   322
office.   323

single-space each item

align item numbers

Line: 40 spaces
Spacing: single
Drills: 2 times
Format Guide: 5–6
Tape: 10A or K10A

Goals: To strengthen all controls; to format paragraph copy; to type 19 wam/1'/3e.

10-A. WARMUP

1 Gwen Dunne expects too much from a job.
2 Keith had a very quiet, lazy afternoon.

10-B. INDICATING A NEW PARAGRAPH

See "Setting Tabs" in the Introduction, page xviii.

The word counts in this book credit you with 1 word (5 strokes) for each paragraph indention in a timing. Press the tab key after the timing starts.

When a paragraph is double-spaced, indent the first word 5 spaces. Use the tab key for this indention. Study the steps for setting tabs on page xviii.

When a paragraph is single-spaced, precede it with 1 blank line. The first word may be either indented 5 spaces or blocked at the left margin. (See illustrations below.)

```
Dear George:
     I would like to visit you
next month.  What plans do you
have during June?
     We could go to Avon for a
trip down the river.  We had a
good time last year.
```
Double-spaced, indented.

```
Dear George:
     I would like to visit you
next month.  What plans do you
have during June?
     We could go to Avon for a
trip down the river.  We had a
good time last year.
     Can you let me know how a
trip like this sounds?  A raft
is a lot of fun, as you know.
```
Single-spaced, indented.

```
Dear George:
I would like to visit you next
month.  What plans do you have
during June?

We could go to Avon for a trip
down the river.  We had a good
time last year.

Can you let me know how a trip
like this sounds?  A raft is a
lot of fun, as you know.
```
Single-spaced, blocked.

SKILLBUILDING

10-C. Spacing—single; tab—5. Take a 1-minute timing on each paragraph, or type one complete copy. Compute your speed and count errors. Use the tab key to indent.

10-C. BUILD SKILL ON SHORT PARAGRAPHS

	WORDS
3 Jenny asked if Alex had taken Vera	8
4 to work. She had planned to ask her to	16
5 ride to work.	19
6 Her car was in the M-Z Garage. It	8
7 needed to have one quart of fluid added	16
8 for the brakes.	19

| 1 | 2 | 3 | 4 | 5 | 6 | 7 | 8 |

REPORT 95 (Continued)

The cystic artery and cystic duct were to- 301
gether. The cystic artery was just overlying the 311
cystic duct. This last structure was relatively 321
small in caliber but had quite a few adhesions 331
and was a little bit longer. It measured close to 341
2 cm in length. The artery was dissected, dou- 350
bly clipped, and cut, and then the cystic duct 359
was clamped between right angle clamps and 368
transected. The gallbladder was then removed 377
from the gallbladder bed with the electrosurgi- 386
cal unit cauterizing the bleeders on the gall- 395
bladder fossa. A Morris spec was then placed 405
against the gallbladder fossa and held in that 414
position. A cholangiogram was then obtained 423
by making an opening through the cystic duct, 432
inserting a #5 feeding tube, and injecting 50 441
percent 15 cc's of Hypaque. 447

One set of X rays was obtained and showed a 456
good picture of the common bile duct and 464
common hepatic ducts on the left. The right 473
did not visualize very well. There was no evi- 482
dence of obstruction or any dilatation of the 491
duct. The feeding tube was then removed, and 500
the cystic duct was ligated and clipped close to 510
the junction of the common hepatic duct. The 519
suprahepatic area was then irrigated with nor- 528
mal saline and aspirated. An attempt was then 538
made to localize and remove the appendix; 546
however, the cecum was down in the pelvis, 555
and the appendix was not removed. 561

The packs were then removed, the count 569
was correct, and the wound was closed in lay- 578
ers, with #1-Dexon used for the peritoneum 587
and posterior rectus sheath as well as the infe- 596
rior rectus sheath. Superficial fascia was closed 606
with 2-0 Dexon in a running stitch with 3-0 to 616
the skin edges and 1″ Steristrips. No drains 625
were used. The dressing was applied. 632

The patient tolerated the procedure well 640
and returned to the RR in good condition. 649

LETTER 100
LETTER WITH TABLE   Paper: Workguide 477–478

**Please type the following letter to Tucson Medical Sup-
plies, Inc., 245 East Broadway, Tucson, AZ 85701, Attention: Mr. Hector Lopez. In the closing type *Sincerely
yours* and my name, Grace Horvath, R.N. I wrote this
letter in a hurry, so please check for any spelling, grammatical, or punctuation errors I might have made.**

Ladies and Gentlemen,   4

Have you received are latest order 11
dated May 28, 19--. We are 17
in ergent need of the supplys. 23
They were: 25

Items	Cost	
2 Stethoscopes	$ 88.00	31
2 Cuffs	23.60	34
1 Tuning fork	11.10	37
2 Percussion hammers	20.00	42
10 Boxes of gloves	40.80	47
	$183.70	48

If you have not received our order 55
of May 28, please let me know 61
immediatly. We always no 67
that we can count on Tuscon 73
Medical Supplies, Inc., for the 79
finest in medical equip. 85

REPORT 98
HUMAN RELATIONS   Paper: plain

A patient calls from home and insists that she must speak to
Dr. Miller immediately. She is known to call for either doctor
on "emergencies" that turn out to be minor. Dr. Miller is visiting a terminally ill patient and will not be in for the rest of the
day. How would you handle this situation? Prepare a brief
report for Dr. Miller.

REPORT 99
HUMAN RELATIONS   Paper: plain

Right after a patient has complained to you that he has been
waiting more than 30 minutes past his appointment time, a
lady you know to be long-winded comes in and asks you to
slip her in to see the doctor "for just a few minutes." Describe
how you would handle this situation.

10-D. ALPHABET REVIEW

Type each line twice.

9 Alma Adams asked Alda to fly to Alaska.
10 Both Bill and Barbara liked basketball.
11 Can Cass accept a classic car in Clare?
12 David did dine in the diner in Drayton.
13 Earl says Elmer edited the entire text.
14 Four fables focused on the five friars.
15 Gina gave a bag of green grapes to Gil.
16 Hal hoped Seth had helped haughty Hugh.
17 Irene liked to pickle pickles in brine.
18 Jody Judd joined a junior jogging team.
19 Keith kept a kayak for a trip to Koyuk.
20 Lance played a razzle-dazzle ball game.
21 Martha made more money on many markups.
22 Nan knew ten men in a main dining room.
23 Opal Olah opened four boxes of oranges.
24 Pat paid to park the plane on the ramp.
25 Quincy quickly quit his quarterly quiz.
26 Robin read rare books in their library.
27 Sal signed, sealed, and sent the lease.
28 Todd caught trout in the little stream.
29 Uncle Marty urged Julie to go to Utica.
30 Viva Vista vetoed the five voice votes.
31 Walt waited while Wilma went to Weston.
32 Xu mixed extra extract exactly as told.
33 Yes, your young sister played a cymbal.
34 Zesty zebras zigzagged in the Ohio zoo.

10-E. Take two 1-minute timings; compute your speed and count errors.

10-E. SKILL MEASUREMENT: 1-MINUTE TIMED WRITING

WORDS

35   Buzz expected a quiet evening with   8
36 his family. His sister, Kim, was to be   16
37 home from Java.   19

| 1 | 2 | 3 | 4 | 5 | 6 | 7 | 8 |

REPORT 96 Paper: plain

As you are transcribing your report, Dr. Hernandez brings you page 7 of her paper. She asks that you retype the page and make the necessary corrections now, as she wants to mail it today. After you have retyped the page, you *plan* to continue transcribing the Brower report.

Page 7

Under the ~~asupiees~~ *direction* of several national health organiza- 12
tions, a drive is ~~going forwarde~~ *underway* to convince millions of peo- 23
ple ~~they should~~ *to* get their blood cholesterol levels checked. 34
New limits of risk have been set so that cholesterol levels 46
that were ~~previously~~ *once* considered normal are now judged to be too 57
high. A new emphasis is being placed on effective treatment 70
for ~~people~~ *those* who are found to be at risk. 77
~~Is it possible~~ *Could* we ~~are~~ *be* over playing the importance of 86
cholesterol? I am not suggesting that high blood cholesterol 98
levels are not important. Certainly, we ~~all know~~ *would be* better off 110
if we kept ours below the new recommended levels. For many, *otherwise* 124
healthy individuals, this ~~becomes a problem~~ *is not an easy task to do.* For senior citi- 138
zens, those over 60, the evidence is not ~~that positive~~ *convincing* that 149
the benefits of lower cholesterol call for ~~any~~ *either* drastic dietary 163
modification or treatment with drugs. If you are 40 or older, 175
moderate risk now begins ~~earlier~~ with a blood cholesterol 185
level of 240, and anything over 260 is ~~dangerously high.~~ *considered to be high risk.* 198
   At this point I would like to point out that I ~~am totally~~ *have no* 209
~~in agreement~~ *argument* with the goals of preventative medicine ~~and~~ *or* the 221
a value of a sound and prudent diet. In fact, I ~~endorse~~ *believe in* the 233
"risk factor" theory of heart disease. A large body of data 245
strongly suggests that high blood pressure, cigarette smoking, 258
and high blood cholesterol are ~~three of the~~ *the most* important con- 268
trollable contributors to heart attacks and ~~responsible for~~ *the early* 279
~~the~~ onset of cardiovascular disease. 286

REPORT 97
HUMAN RELATIONS Paper: plain

Just as you finish page 7 of Dr. Hernandez's paper, a patient comes to your desk to pay his bill. He asks you what he owes and wants to pay by check, but that very morning the bank advised you that his previous check bounced. Prepare a brief report of your conversation with the patient. After you have dealt with the patient, you continue transcribing the Brower report.

LESSON **11**

HORIZONTAL CENTERING

Line: 50 spaces
Tab: 5, center
Spacing: single
Drills: 2 times
Workguide: 19
Format Guide: 5–6
Tape: 11A or K11A

Goals: To type 19 wam/2′/5e; to center horizontally.

S = Speed

A = Accuracy

11-A. WARMUP

S 1 Jack went with Pam to the ball game last evening.
A 2 Fay quickly jumped over the two dozen huge boxes.

SKILLBUILDING

PRETEST. Take a 1-minute timing; compute your speed and count errors.

11-B. PRETEST: VERTICAL REACHES

WORDS

3   He knew about the rival races away from home 10
4 and ordered Gilbert to skip the seventh race.   19

| | 1 | | 2 | 3 | 4 | 5 | 6 | 7 | 8 | 9 | 10

PRACTICE.
   Speed Emphasis: If you made 2 or fewer errors on the Pretest, type each line twice.
   Accuracy Emphasis: If you made 3 or more errors, type each group of lines (e.g., lines 5–8) as though it were a paragraph, twice.

11-C. PRACTICE: UP REACHES

5 aw aware flaws drawn crawl hawks sawed awful flaw
6 se seven reset seams sedan loses eases serve used
7 ki skids kings kinks skill kitty kites kilts kits
8 rd board horde wards sword award beard third cord

11-D. PRACTICE: DOWN REACHES

9 ac races pacer backs ached acute laced facts each
10 kn knave knack knife knows knoll knots knelt knew
11 ab about abide label above abide sable abbey drab
12 va evade avail value vapor divan rival naval vain

POSTTEST. Repeat the Pretest and compare performance.

11-E. POSTTEST: VERTICAL REACHES

11-F. Take two 2-minute timings; or type two copies. Compute your speed and count errors. Record your score on Workguide page 3.

11-F. SKILL MEASUREMENT: 2-MINUTE TIMED WRITING

WORDS

13   Zeke applied for the job some time last week 10
14 and was told to report to work this Tuesday.   19
15   Max would like you to help us locate a quiet   29
16 room with a sweeping view of the big harbor.   38

| | 1 | | 2 | 3 | 4 | 5 | 6 | 7 | 8 | 9 | 10

LETTER 99
LETTER WITH SUBJECT LINE
AND POSTSCRIPT

Paper: Workguide 473–474

Please type the following letter to Dr. Thomas Holden, president, Arizona Medical Association, 2201 North Central Avenue, Phoenix, AZ 85004. Use the subject line *Cholesterol Paper.* Dr. Hernandez wrote this letter in a hurry, so please check any spelling, grammatical, and punctuation errors she might have made. Dr. Hernandez is revising one page of the paper to be enclosed with this letter and will have it to you shortly.

As you know, I agreed to present a paper on new questions about cholesterole. Enclosed is one of the pages on which I am having the most difficulty.

Do you agree that we could overplay the importance of cholesterol to public. Should I stress the importance of people of all ages monitering their chlorestal level?

I really want to get across to all members of the Ariz. Med. Asso. the importance of cholesterol levels and how they relate to pateint health.

L. Hernandez

PS: Please call me as soon as you can so I can proceed with my paper.

REPORT 95
OPERATIVE REPORT

Paper: Workguide 475 and plain paper

Dr. Miller referred one of his patients to Dr. Fitzgerald for surgery, and Dr. Miller would like to have an operative report typed from the cassette the surgeon has sent to the office. Use the operative report form for the first page; type subsequent pages on plain paper with name of patient, hospital number, and date of operation as headings. The whole report should be single-spaced.

This is Dr. Herman Fitzgerald. I will be dictating an operative report for Eldon Brower.

Hospital Number: 317-67, Room Number: 546, Preoperative Diagnosis: Chronic Cholecystitis with Cholelithiasis, Postoperative Diagnosis: Same, Operation/Procedure: Cholecystectomy with Cholangiogram, Anesthesia: General, Procedure Date: May 23, 19—, Discharge Date: May 30, 19—. Procedure: Under adequate general anesthesia with endotracheal intubation administered by Dr. Able and staff, the upper abdomen was shaved and then prepped with Betadine scrub followed with Betadine paint and then draped in a sterile manner.

A right subcostal incision was made, roughly 10 to 12 cm long, starting just to the left of the midline and extending to the mid-axillary line on the right side and roughly 2 cm below the right costal margin. The right rectus muscles as well as the sheaths, anterior and posterior, were transected with the electrosurgical unit. After the abdominal cavity was entered, exploration was carried out. With palpation of the lesion in the small bowel, the loop was then brought out of the abdominal cavity, and the blood supply and the mesentery to this lesion were clamped in two stages, cut, and ligated with 2-0 Dexon. After this was done, additional palpations of the rest of the small bowel failed to reveal other tumors. The duodenum was then packed inferiorly, and the adhesions that involved the gallbladder, which were moderately extensive, were dissected out and the gallbladder freed. A Balfour self-retaining type of retractor was then applied with the large blade inferiorly. Porta hepatis exposed, Hartmann's pouch of the gallbladder was then grasped with a Kelly clamp.

11-G. Complete Workguide page 19 before doing 11-G.

11-G. HORIZONTAL CENTERING

To center words across the page:
1. Set the carrier at the center point of the paper (50 elite/42 pica).
2. Locate the backspace key in the upper right corner of the keyboard. This key is controlled by the Sem finger.
3. Say the strokes (including spaces) to yourself in pairs, pressing and releasing the backspace key one time for each pair of strokes. For example:

Practice 1. Center each of these names:

Toledo
Florence
Woodhaven
Osco
South Otter Creek

Check: The letter *O* aligns vertically.

Br|uc|e |E.| E|dw|ar|ds

Caution: If you have a letter left over after calling out the pairs, *do not* backspace for this letter. For example:

Al|la|n |Le|ro|y |Fr|os |t

4. Type the words. They should appear centered on the line.

Practice 2. Center each of these names:

Bruce E. Edwards
Martha Lee Donaldson
Allan Leroy Frost
Christopher Lakowski
Elizabeth Anne Webster

Check: The letter *S* aligns vertically.

LESSON 12

TYPING IN ALL CAPITALS

Line: 50 spaces
Tab: 5, center
Spacing: single
Drills: 2 times
Format Guide: 5–6
Tape: 12A or K12A

Goals: To type 20 wam/2'/5e; to type in all capitals.

12-A. WARMUP

S 1 Dad is going to bake two pies for you and me now.
A 2 Joe quietly picked six razors from the woven bag.

SKILLBUILDING

12-B. BUILD SKILL ON PHRASES

3 to do|you can|for us|at a time|do not|you will be
4 will have been|has been able|to be able|he is not
5 of this|in a|for me|you were|due to|for it|can be
6 will go|on the|with us|should have been|she and I

12-C. BUILD SKILL ON WORD FAMILIES

7 are fare mare tare bare care hare pare dare glare
8 end bend send mend tend vend lend fend rend blend
9 old told sold mold bold fold gold cold hold scold
10 ill till hill sill mill pill dill kill will still

This is a physical examination report for Leonard Pat- copy on the appropriate form.
terson prepared by Dr. Miller. Please type this longhand

Drugs :
No allergy
Th--Naprosyn 250 mg b.i.d.
Hydrochlorothiazide 50 mg daily for BP

Past History :
Arthritis started in the knee with swelling about 5 weeks ago.
Cleft palate -- successful operation
Hemorrhoidectomy -- 1975
Tobacco -- one pack a day
Recent tests -- Venogram
                Xray of leg at Valley General Hospital

Family History :
Mother died of cancer at 55
Father is fine at 72
Brother had cancer of trachea
Sister had mastectomy
No diabetes in family

Physical :
Has had chest pain substernally off and on
No coughing
Postnasal drip
No indigestion or vomiting
BM is OK
No weight change

ENT, neck, chest, heart -- OK
Good carotid pulses
Chest is clear to P and A
Heart is rhythmic; no murmur
134/80
Pulse 75/minute regular
Abdomen -- no mass felt
Genitalia -- OK
Rectal -- normal digital examination
EKG -- normal

Plan -- LP-I fasting
       Chest Xray
       Stool for blood

12-D. Make two copies. Copy 1: Type each sentence on a separate line. Copy 2: Type each sentence on a separate line, but tab-indent it 5 spaces.

12-D. TECHNIQUE TYPING: RETURN/ENTER AND TAB KEYS

11 It is now ours. He is. Ask her. Call me later.
12 Open the door. You can go. Let me see. He may.
13 Go for it. Right now. You can do it. Watch me.
14 You will. Giorgio left. He should. Write Mary.

12-E. PUNCTUATION PRACTICE

Space once after a semicolon and comma; twice after a period and question mark at the end of a sentence; twice after a colon.

15 Paul writes; Sam sings. Is it warm? It is cold.
16 Pat, May, and Jo like to read. Can Mike go? No.
17 I can go also. How is Kate? I will stay; hurry.
18 Did Jill go too? I hope so. Can William decide?

12-F. Take two 2-minute timings; compute your speed and count errors. Record your score on Workguide page 3.

12-F. SKILL MEASUREMENT: 2-MINUTE TIMED WRITING

WORDS

19   You briskly jogged exactly five miles taking 10
20 you past the gray dwelling that marks the zenith. 20
21   Jessie quipped that you cut five minutes off 30
22 your time due to the barking dog who lives there. 40

| | | 1 | | | 2 | | 3 | | 4 | | 5 | | 6 | | 7 | | 8 | | 9 | | 10

12-G. TYPING IN ALL CAPITALS

To type in all capitals:
1. Depress the shift lock on a typewriter or the caps lock on a computer.

2. Type the word or words.
3. Release the shift lock by touching the right shift key.

Practice. Center each of these five lines horizontally. The letter *W* lines up.

MINNESOTA TYPEWRITING CONTEST
Held on Wednesday
FIVE BIG AWARDS GIVEN
Call John Wilbur Hall
WHITEWATER

Line: 50 spaces
Tab: 5, center
Spacing: single
Drills: 2 times
Workguide: 20
Format Guide: 7–8
Tape: 13A or K1B

LESSON 13

VERTICAL CENTERING

Goals: To type 21 wam/2'/5e; to center material vertically.

13-A. WARMUP

s 1 Joan can go to the show with Max if she wants to.
A 2 Mack Jacoby had a powerful zest for quiet living.

TABLES 68–69
Paper: plain
OPEN TABLES WITH SUBTITLES

Using the appointment book for today (*Workguide page 468*), prepare an appointment reference sheet for each doctor. Don't forget to make a copy for me. I'll need it when I pull the files.

FORM 54
Paper: Workguide 468
APPOINTMENT BOOK ENTRY

The telephone rings. After identifying the office with "Better Health Associates" and your name, you find that Mr. William Morris would like an appointment with Dr. Miller on Thursday morning, June 7. You check your appointment book (Workguide page 468) for that date and continue your discussion with Mr. Morris. You are able to determine a mutually agreeable time and make the appropriate entries in the appointment book. His telephone number is 555-6939. He has never seen either Dr. Miller or Dr. Hernandez before and has been having frequent backaches for the past two weeks.

REPORT 91
Paper: Workguide 469
REPORT OF CONSULTATION

Dr. Hernandez would like to have a report of consultation typed from the cassette she prepared last evening.

This is Dr. Hernandez. I will be dictating a report of consultation for Nathan Arnold. 3

Room Number: 456, Hospital Number: 31, 4 Attending Physician: Dr. Louise Hernandez, 8 Consulting Physician: Dr. James Issac, Reason 11 for Consultation: Episodes of Chest Pain. History: This is a 49-year-old gentleman with a 23 history of bronchospastic lung disease and 31 hypertension who is undergoing evaluation for 41 episodes of chest pain. Physical Examination: 50 The resting blood pressure is 160/84, the heart 59 rate 72 and regular, and the respirations 18. 69 The lungs have scattered rhonchi. The cardiac 78 exam shows that the S1 and S2 are normal. No 87 S3, S4, or murmur. The resting ECG shows 96 sinus rhythm with PR interval of .16, QRS interval .10, QT interval .38, axis + 60 degrees; 114 it is within normal limits. 120

The patient was exercised according to 127 Bruce Protocol. Exercise was terminated after 137 7 minutes of exercise, which corresponds to 146 Stage III of the Bruce Protocol and an exertion 155 level of approximately 9 METS. The exercise 164 was terminated because of dyspnea. There 173 were no symptoms of chest pain during the 181 test. At peak exercise, the heart rate was 141 191 beats per minute, which represents 87 percent 200 of maximum predicted heart rate when 100 208 percent of maximum heart rate is considered 217 as 161 beats per minute. The blood pressure 226 and heart rate response to exercise were normal. There were rare isolated PVCs observed 244 during the test. At peak heart rate, there was 253 less than 1 mm of upsloping ST segment depression in any lead of the 12-lead ECG. 269

Final Diagnosis: Exercise treadmill test was 279 negative for angina pectoris or ECG evidence 288 of myocardial ischemia. 292

REPORT 92
Paper: plain
HUMAN RELATIONS

A patient, Mrs. Alice Moore, leaves Dr. Hernandez's office and comes to your desk to pay her bill. You know Mrs. Moore to be a friendly but inquisitive person. While writing her check, she casually inquires about her friend Erma Johnson, asking how she made out on her visit to the doctor a few days earlier. Type a report on how you would handle this situation.

REPORT 93
Paper: plain
ABSTRACT OF A REPORT

Sometimes our patients need to be reminded about our office hours and payment policies. In addition, I'm not sure that they really know what information we need when they call for an appointment. I'd like you to compose, from the information in the Procedures Manual, a one-page information sheet explaining these three things. Give the information sheet the title "Better Health Associates," and use three questions as side headings. Type it double-spaced on one page. We'll duplicate your information sheet and hand it out to both new patients and people who request this information.

13-B. PRETEST: DISCRIMINATION PRACTICE

3   Opal alerted an astute older man to wear the 10
4 proper colored suit to the opera. His godson did 20
5 too. 21
   | | | 2 | 3 | 4 | 5 | 6 | 7 | 8 | 9 | 10

PRETEST. Take a 1-minute timing; compute your speed and count errors.

13-C. PRACTICE: LEFT HAND

6 rtr sport train alert courts assert tragic truest
7 asa usage cased cease astute dashed masked castle
8 sds winds bands seeds godson woodsy shreds wields
9 rer overt rerun older before entire surest better

PRACTICE.
   Speed Emphasis: If you made 2 or fewer errors on the Pretest, type each line twice.
   Accuracy Emphasis: If you made 3 or more errors, type each group of lines (as though it were a paragraph) twice.

13-D. PRACTICE: RIGHT HAND

10 mnm hymns unmet manly mental namely manner number
11 pop opera pools opens polite proper police oppose
12 olo solos color lower locker oldest lowest frolic
13 iui fruit suits built medium guided helium podium

13-E. POSTTEST: DISCRIMINATION PRACTICE

POSTTEST. Repeat the Pretest and compare performance.

13-F. TECHNIQUE TYPING: TAB KEY

13-F. Set a tab every 10 spaces from the left margin. Then type lines 14–17, pressing the tab key after typing each word. Type each line twice.

14 dear TAB→ loan TAB→ care TAB→ idea TAB→ hike
15 your   quip   unit   name   four
16 item   zone   very   able   uses
17 same   lamb   etch   peel   year

13-G. ALPHABET REVIEW

18 aria bulb chic dead edge fife gage hash iris jive
19 kite lilt memo nine oleo plop quip rare skis tilt
20 undo veto waxy axes yoga zoom area bomb coca died
21 Jack Powell was quite vexed by such lazy farming.

13-H. SKILL MEASUREMENT: 2-MINUTE TIMED WRITING

13-H. Take two 2-minute timings; compute your speed and count errors. Record your score on Workguide page 3.

WORDS
22   Have you ever read the want-ad sections of a 10
23 paper? It is often possible to read of good bar- 20
24 gains. 21
25   In just a few lines of print you can read of 31
26 quality clothing, cars, prized gems, and pets for 41
27 sale. 42
   | | | 2 | 3 | 4 | 5 | 6 | 7 | 8 | 9 | 10

Situation: Today is Monday, June 4, 19—. You are a medical secretary for Better Health Associates, 1810 North Arrowhead Drive, Chandler, AZ 85224. You are working for John F. Miller, M.D., and Louise Hernandez, M.D., two of the ten doctors in the firm. You report directly to the office manager, Grace Horvath, R.N.

Your work includes making, changing, and canceling appointments; preparing medical documents; composing and transcribing medical reports, letters, and memorandums; and dealing with patients in person in the reception area or by telephone.

Ms. Horvath has explained that no matter how carefully the day is planned, interruptions and emergencies will alter your schedule. If they do, she has advised you to rearrange your work and move ahead. She has given you the first page of the Better Health Associates Procedures Manual and asked you to study it carefully before the first patients arrive at 10 a.m.

BETTER HEALTH ASSOCIATES PROCEDURES MANUAL

The goal of Better Health Associates is to maintain good health for the entire family—from the very young to the aged. We realize that an illness can affect not only the patient but family members as well. We want to become acquainted with and treat every member of the family. This will help us to deal more effectively with both the patient and the family when a health problem occurs.

The office is open from 9 a.m. to 5 p.m. Monday through Thursday and from 9 a.m. to noon on Fridays. An answering service takes all incoming calls when the office is closed and contacts the doctors in emergency situations. Patients are seen by appointment only, and patients requiring immediate care are seen only if the doctors' schedules can be adjusted without causing a prolonged wait for other patients. Patients needing emergency care are referred to Emergency Admissions at Valley General Hospital.

When a patient calls for an appointment, the following information must be obtained: (1) name of family member to be seen, (2) age, (3) doctor to be seen, and (4) reason for visit. If a patient does not specify a doctor, an appointment should be made with the doctor who has the most convenient appointment time available or is the appropriate specialist.

It is important during the phone call to inform or remind the patient about our policy of collecting payment for services immediately upon completion of the appointment. The patient is given a receipt that also serves as a completed insurance form; the patient is responsible for dealing with the insurance company.

Appointments are to be made by penciling in the patients' names in the appointment book. The hours when no appointments are to be made should be crossed out to ensure that a patient is not scheduled during those hours. The name, phone number, and reason for the appointment should be noted in the book under the name of the appropriate doctor. New patients and physical examinations require one-hour appointments; others are to be scheduled for 30 minutes.

The hours during which each physician is available for appointments are listed in the next column.

Dr. Miller		Dr. Hernandez	
Mon.:	10–12, 1–5	Mon.:	10–12, 1–5
Tues.:	10–12, 1–5	Tues.:	10–12, 1–5
Wed.:	10–12, off	Wed.:	off, 1–5
Thurs.:	10–12, 1–5	Thurs.:	10–12, 1–5
Fri.:	10–12	Fri.:	10–12

Each day the medical secretary's first task is to prepare an appointment reference sheet for each doctor with a carbon copy. The original is kept on the doctors' desks. The carbon is given to Ms. Horvath so that she can pull the necessary patient files. The appointment sheet is formatted on plain paper and includes the appointment time, the patient's name, and the reason for the visit. As appointments are changed, pen corrections have to be made on the doctors' appointment sheets. Ms. Horvath will update her copy of the sheet. The following appointment sheet is provided as a sample:

APPOINTMENTS FOR DR. MILLER

Monday, March 15

10:00 a.m.	Alex Brown	fever
10:30 a.m.	Mary Forman	asthma
11:00 a.m.	William Joyce	physical
1:00 p.m.	Lois Purcell	eye infection
1:30 p.m.	Sherry Davis	stitches out
2:00 p.m.	James Mosenthal	sore back
3:30 p.m.	David Yen	cold
4:00 p.m.	Behzad Yamini	consultation report
4:30 p.m.	Helen Pinnavaia	postoperative report

Unless otherwise specified, letters are to be formatted in the block style with standard punctuation. The closing lines are as follows:

Sincerely yours,   Sincerely yours,

John F. Miller, M.D.   Louise Hernandez, M.D.

13-I. Complete Workguide page 20 before doing 13-I.

WP If you are using a computer with word processing software, you may use a *menu* to indicate the depth of the top margin. The vertical centering is then done either automatically or manually.

Also note that the copy in the practice exercises may not be centered exactly as described. It will depend on the word processing software you are using.

13-I. VERTICAL CENTERING

For material to look centered, the top and bottom margins must appear to be the same.

To center a group of lines and to provide for an equal top and bottom margin:
1. Count the lines (including blank ones) that the material will occupy when typed.
2. Subtract that number from the number of lines available on your paper. Most typewriters space 6 lines to an inch. Standard typing paper is 11 inches long.

Therefore, 11 × 6 = 66 lines on a full page or 33 lines on a half page.
3. Divide the remainder by 2 (drop any fraction) to find the number of the line, counting from the top, on which to begin typing.

Example: To center 5 double-spaced lines on a half sheet, you need 9 lines (5 typed, 4 blank); 33 − 9 = 24 ÷ 2 = 12. Begin typing on line 12.

Practice 1. Center the material below on a half sheet. Double-space. Center each line horizontally. The letter *T* aligns vertically.

```
CITIES
Portland
Waters
Eastlake
Montrose
```

Practice 2. Center the material below on a half sheet. Double-space. Center each line horizontally. The letter *I* aligns.

```
APPRAISERS
Dunnings
Levine
Main
Pattison
```

LESSON 14
BLOCK CENTERING

Line: 50 spaces
Tab: 5, center
Spacing: single
Drills: 2 times
Format Guide: 7–8
Tape: 14A or K2B

Goals: To type 22 wam/2'/5e; to block-center material.

14-A. WARMUP

S 1 Joe has to stay at home today to take care of me.
A 2 Gaze at views of my jonquil or red phlox in back.

SKILLBUILDING

14-B. TECHNIQUE TYPING: SHIFT/CAPS LOCK

3 Her FOR RENT sign was run down by ROLLS TRUCKING.
4 Carpets ON SALE for this week ONLY--FREE PADDING.
5 Come see the TALKING BEAR. Certain to AMAZE YOU.
6 Add ZIP to your ad with OUR HELP. CALL ADS-RITE.

14-C. PUNCTUATION PRACTICE

Space once after a comma; twice after a colon.

7 The ties were brown, gray, and tan. I like them.
8 The list was as follows: milk, eggs, and cereal.
9 Jake wanted these items: books, pens, and paper.
10 We sit, read, and eat. They run, swim, and talk.

L. PACED PRACTICE

Turn to the Paced Practice routine at the back of the book. Take several 2-minute timings, starting at the point where you left off the last time. Record your progress on Workguide page 290.

M. Spacing: double.
Record your score.

M. SKILL MEASUREMENT: 5-MINUTE TIMED WRITING

```
37        You have just been hired in one of the fastest-growing    12
38  occupational areas in our country--the health-related occu-     24
39  pations.  The health-related professions are providing many     36
40  exciting opportunities for young men and women such as you.     48
41  There are many excellent careers in this professional area.     60
42        Health-related jobs are found in medical supply firms,    72
43  clinics, nursing homes, public health departments, research     84
44  agencies, industrial firms, and doctors' offices.  You have     96
45  selected employment in a medical center working with one of    108
46  the best groups of professional specialists in the country.    120
47        The doctors you will work with have been in practice a    132
48  number of years and attend a variety of patients both young    144
49  and old.  You were hired not only because of your excellent    156
50  secretarial skills but also because of your superior knowl-    168
51  edge of the terminology and procedures demanded on the job.    180
52        You will be expected to carry out your duties with the    192
53  highest ethical standards found in any profession.  Some of    204
54  your duties will be helping patients who are ill and desire    216
55  to see one of the doctors for the first time, who are being    228
56  referred to a specialist, or who are making a return visit.    240
57        One of the most important skills required of a medical    252
58  secretary is that of human relations.  You will face a num-    264
59  ber of amazing problems every day as you work with patients    276
60  who want to see a doctor right now, who ask for medical in-    288
61  formation you cannot give, or who are behind with payments.    300
     |  1  |  2  |  3  |  4  |  5  |  6  |  7  |  8  |  9  |  10  |  11  |  12
```

N. INTEGRATED OFFICE PROJECT: BETTER HEALTH ASSOCIATES

Complete each of the medical office jobs in the order in which they are presented.

14-D.   CONCENTRATION PRACTICE

11 The provocative statement caused an insurrection.
12 A congregation in Connecticut intervened quickly.
13 A lackadaisical traveler crisscrossed continents.
14 All resignations were interpreted as irrevocable.

14-E.   BUILD SKILL ON SHORT SENTENCES

Maintain an even pace.

15 It runs. Stand up. She works. Use it. He may.
16 Read the books. Come by. Drop it. Lay it down.
17 Pick him. Walk the dog. Watch the time. Go up.
18 Calm down. He likes it. You may not. They can.

14-F.   SKILL MEASUREMENT: 2-MINUTE TIMED WRITING

14-F. Take two 2-minute timings; compute your speed and count errors. Record your score on Workguide page 3.

		WORDS
19	The new girl on the block wants to study law	10
20	when she is out of school and to work for a large	20
21	law firm.	22
22	If she is a success, in seven years she will	32
23	expect to be a judge and quote from great lawyers	42
24	with zeal.	44

| 1 | 2 | 3 | 4 | 5 | 6 | 7 | 8 | 9 | 10

14-G.   BLOCK CENTERING

To block-center a paragraph, center the longest line of the paragraph.

When several lines are to be listed, center them as a group, or a block:
1. Backspace-center and type the title.
2. Select the longest item.

3. Backspace to center that item, and set the left margin stop at the point to which you have backspaced.
4. Type the list, beginning each item at the left margin.

Practice 1. Block-center the display below on a half sheet of paper. Single-space. Leave 2 blank lines below the title.

Practice 2. Block-center the 2-minute timing, 14-F, on a half sheet. Include the title *LAW CAREERS*. Use double spacing. Leave 2 blank lines between the title and first paragraph.

Practice 3. Block-center the display below on a half sheet of paper. Double-space. Leave 2 blank lines below the title.

PARTS OF A LETTER ↓3

Date
Inside Address
Salutation
Subject
Body
Complimentary Closing
Signature
Writer's Identification
Reference Initials
Enclosure Notation
Postscript

RIVERS ↓3

Colorado
Hudson
Maumee
Mississippi
Missouri
Ohio

F. These words are among the 225 most frequently misspelled words in business correspondence.

F.   PRODUCTION PRACTICE: SPELLING

16 audit general present through property important activities
17 other service support balance personal reference supervisor
18 based follows officer similar location directors provisions
19 which receive subject section academic secretary especially
20 there faculty whether absence judgment procedure provisions

G. Type the paragraph twice, or take two 1-minute timings.

G.   SYMBOL TYPING

21   The clerk* read that Jones & Smith would pay $950 as a   12
22 fee to the lawyer (Hill) for help with the following cases: 24
23 #16, #32, and #47. Dick and/or Sue thought the "extras" to   36
24 be appropriate in all cases. They thought an 8% add-on tax   48
25 demanded by that city was out of line; Hill thought so too!   60
  | | | 2 | 3 | 4 | 5 | 6 | 7 | 8 | 9 | 10 | 11 | 12

H.   PROGRESSIVE PRACTICE: NUMBERS

Turn to the Progressive Practice: Numbers routine at the back of the book. Take several 30-second timings, starting at the point where you left off the last time. Record your progress on Workguide page 289.

I. Compare this paragraph with the first paragraph of the timing on page 367. Type a list of the words that contain errors, correcting the errors as you type.

I.   PRODUCTION PRACTICE: PROOFREADING

26   You have just hired been in one of the fastest-gorwing
27 occupational areas in are country--the health related occu-
28 pations. The health-related professsions are providing many
29 excitiing opportunities for youngmen and women such as you.
30 There are meny excellent carrers in this professional area.

J. Type this paragraph once, incorporating the indicated revisions. Then take several 1-minute timings, trying to increase your speed each time.

J.   CONCENTRATION PRACTICE

31 When you have finished all eight of the integrated projects   12
32 of this work, you will have had the opportunity to completed   24
33 a variety of office jobs. Some of the tasks could be simi-   36
34 lar in format but different in nature. formatting requires   48
35 a high degree of decision-making abilities on the part of all 60
36 workers. The ability will aid you get ahead on the job.   72
  | | | 2 | 3 | 4 | 5 | 6 | 7 | 8 | 9 | 10 | 11 | 12

K.   PROGRESSIVE PRACTICE: ALPHABET

Turn to the Progressive Practice: Alphabet routine at the back of the book. Take several 30-second timings, starting at the point where you left off the last time. Record your progress on Workguide page 289.

Line: 50 spaces
Tab: 5, center
Spacing: single
Drills: 2 times
Workguide: 21–22
Format Guide: 7–8
Tape: 15A or K3B

SPREAD CENTERING

Goals: To type 23 wam/2'/5e; to spread-center material.

15-A. WARMUP

s 1 If you will call me, I will give you the new key.
A 2 The big quick lynx from the zoo just waved a paw.

SKILLBUILDING

15-B. BUILD SKILL ON PHRASES

3 which was|made up|came from|with them|about their
4 for a few|it can|speak up|all of you|in regard to
5 there are|as many as|it may be|if you can|into it

15-C. TECHNIQUE TYPING: SHIFT KEY

6 Joe Tao Sal Ann Yuk Sue Pat Jae Tab Fay Vera Rosa
7 Dick Fern Juan Mike Andre Fidel Pedro Chong Alice
8 Karen Ojars Marta Scott Carlos Maria Julie Ceasar

15-D. Take three 12-second timings on each line or type each line twice. The scale gives your wam score for each 12-second timing.

15-D. 12-SECOND SPRINTS

9 Jim cited the law to prove his case against Paul.
10 The unusual sights affected the men tremendously.
11 I accepted all conditions except this second one.
12 All the seniors played in the last football game.

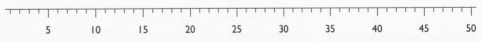

5   10   15   20   25   30   35   40   45   50

15-E. PUNCTUATION PRACTICE

When you make the reach to the hyphen, keep the other fingers and the elbow relatively still.

13 Jan Brooks-Smith was a go-between for the author.
14 The off-the-record comment led to a free-for-all.
15 Louis was a jack-of-all-trades as a clerk-typist.
16 Ask Juliet--she's with Central Data--to find out.
17 Joanne is too old-fashioned to be that outspoken.

INTEGRATED OFFICE PROJECT: MEDICAL

Line: 60 spaces
Tab: 5, center
Spacing: single
Drills: 2 times
Workguide: 467–480
Format Guide: 173

GOALS FOR UNIT 35

1. To type 60 wam for 5 minutes with no more than 5 errors.
2. To improve alphabet, number, and symbol skills.
3. To type tables, reports, and letters, applying rules of capitalization and punctuation.
4. To make decisions based on office policies under simulated conditions.
5. To proofread and retype draft report copy.
6. To make decisions and formulate responses in situations dealing with interpersonal relations.

A. WARMUP

S 1 Pamela is to go to town with Cyrus if it is her time to go.
A 2 Rex says Jack played a very quiet game of bridge with Inez.
N 3 I bought tickets 10, 29, 38, 47, and 56 for the five of us.

SKILLBUILDING

PRETEST. Take a 1-minute timing; compute your speed and count errors.

B. PRETEST: COMMON LETTER COMBINATIONS

4   The condo committee was hoping the motion would not be   12
5 forced upon it, realizing that viable solutions ought to be   24
6 developed. It was forceful in seeking a period of time for   36
7 tensions to cool. All concerned wanted the problem solved.   48
       | 1 | 2 | 3 | 4 | 5 | 6 | 7 | 8 | 9 | 10 | 11 | 12

PRACTICE.
   Speed Emphasis: If you made no errors on the Pretest, type each line twice.
   Accuracy Emphasis: If you made 1 or more errors on the Pretest, type each group of lines (as though it were a paragraph) twice.

C. PRACTICE: WORD BEGINNINGS

8 for forum forge forced forgot formal forest foreign forerun
9 con conks conic consul confer convey convex contact concern
10 per perks peril person period perish permit percale percent
11 com combs comet combat comedy comics common compete complex

D. PRACTICE: WORD ENDINGS

12 ing tying hiking liking edging bowing hoping having nursing
13 ble fable pebble treble tumble viable dabble fumble fusible
14 ion union legion nation region motion potion option bastion
15 ful awful cupful fitful joyful lawful earful artful tearful

POSTTEST. Repeat the Pretest and compare performance.

E. POSTTEST: COMMON LETTER COMBINATIONS

15-F. CONCENTRATION PRACTICE

18 The headmaster reprimanded an old procrastinator.
19 His mathematicians matriculated in Massachusetts.
20 An optimistic orchestra director was remunerated.
21 The ingenuous announcer was infatuated with news.

15-G. Take two 2-minute timings; compute your speed and count errors. Record your score on Workguide page 3.

15-G. SKILL MEASUREMENT: 2-MINUTE TIMED WRITING

		WORDS
22	Franz left out a vital model when he shipped	10
23	six big crates of new machines to the retailer in	20
24	a nearby town.	23
25	He was quick to see his error and made out a	33
26	new job order to send the extra model right away.	43
27	They were sold.	46

| 1 | 2 | 3 | 4 | 5 | 6 | 7 | 8 | 9 | 10

15-H. SPREAD CENTERING

To spread-center a line of type for greater emphasis, leave 1 space between letters and 3 spaces between words. To do this: back-space from center (a) once for each letter (except the last one) and (b) once for each space between words.

Practice. Spread-center these lines. Single-space. Leave 2 blank lines below the title.

C L A S S   R O S T E R   ↓3

C H E S S E M A N N
E S T I L L
H A S S B U R G
P A S T U R A N
S I P E

The letter *S* should align vertically.

15-I. This drill reviews the skills you have learned in centering display copy:
Vertical centering
Horizontal centering
Spread centering
Block (list) centering

If you are using a word processor or a computer, you will want to take advantage of its automatic centering feature where appropriate.

15-I. CENTERING REVIEW

Practice 1. Center the display below on a full sheet of paper. Center each line separately. Double-space. Leave 2 blank lines below the title.

Practice 2. Block-center the display below on a half sheet of paper. Single-space. Spread-center the title. Leave 2 blank lines below the title.

ACCOUNTING TERMINOLOGY   ↓3

Account
Asset
Capital
Credit
Data and Information
Debit
Income
Liability
Value

E D I T I N G   ↓3

Capitalization
Grammar
Number Usage
Omissions
Punctuation
Repetitions
Spelling
Typographical Errors
Word Division

FORM 52
DOCKET SHEET

Paper: Workguide 463

Mr. Cline maintains a handwritten record of the time he devotes and the expenses he incurs for each client. This data is recorded on a docket sheet. At the end of the month or when a particular legal task has been completed, he wants you to prepare a typewritten copy of the docket. When a line is drawn below the last entry on a docket page, it indicates that the legal action on that matter has been completed. The following information should be included on the docket sheet that you type for Susan B. Johnson.

Single-space each entry; double-space between entries.

DOCKET

CLIENT Susan B. Johnson   3

TYPE OF MATTER Preparation of Last Will and Testament   11

FEE $75 an hour plus disbursements   17

Date	Explanation	Hours	Disbursements	
3/8/--	Meeting with Mrs. Susan B. Johnson to discuss will	1 ½		24 / 29
3/9/--	Meeting with Mr. Tom Burns, trust officer at Lubbock Trust Company	1		37 / 44
3/9/--	Travel to Lubbock to meet with Mr. Burns		$13.50	51 / 54
3/10/--	Research to prepare will	1		60
3/11/--	Preparation of will	1 ½		67
3/14/--	Coordinate signing of will	1		73

FORM 53
STATEMENT

Paper: Workguide 465

The information from the docket sheet is used to submit a bill for services rendered by Mr. Cline. A sample statement form is illustrated at the right. Prepare a similar statement form to be sent to Susan B. Johnson at 155 Fairbanks Street, Plainview, TX 79072, for the work Mr. Cline did in preparing her last will and testament. In the Services column of the statement, you'll have to summarize briefly the explanations from the docket sheet. The fee for each entry, as well as a Total figure at the bottom, must be computed.

STATEMENT

Mr. James Baldwin
15 Pepperhill Street
Tulia, TX 79088

Date February 16, 19--

To: STEPHEN L. CLINE • ATTORNEY AT LAW
Sheffield Building   72 Bentley Place   Plainview TX 79072

Date	Services	Fee or Retainer	Disbursements	Total
2/10	Meeting to discuss will	$ 75.00		
2/11	Meeting at Tulia Savings	112.50		
2/11	Mileage to Tulia		$14.00	
2/13	Research for will	75.00		
2/13	Mileage to Lubbock		13.50	
2/14	Signing of will	75.00		$365.00

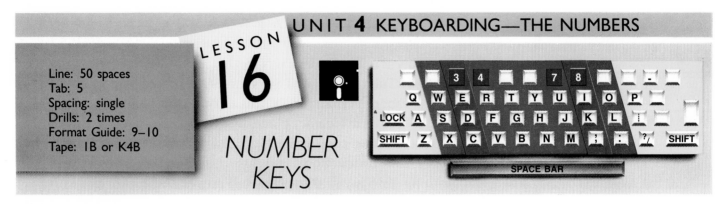

LESSON
16

NUMBER
KEYS

Line: 50 spaces
Tab: 5
Spacing: single
Drills: 2 times
Format Guide: 9–10
Tape: 1B or K4B

Goals: To control the 4, 7, 3, and 8 keys; to type 24 wam/2'/5e.

16-A. WARMUP

s 1 The small girl had a problem with the giant fish.
A 2 Packing jam for the dozen boxes was quite lively.

16-B. PRACTICE THE **4** KEY

Use the F finger.

3 fr4f fr4f f44f f44f f4f4 f4f4 4 44 444 4,444 4:44
4 44 flakes 44 fans 44 figs 44 feet 44 fish 44 fins
5 The 44 pupils went to 4 different movies at 4:44.
6 The 44 adults were in charge of the 444 children.

16-C. PRACTICE THE **7** KEY

Use the J finger.

7 ju7j ju7j j77j j77j j7j7 j7j7 7 77 777 7,777 7:77
8 77 jewels 77 jars 77 jets 77 jugs 77 jobs 77 jigs
9 Bus No. 7 made 7 stops and handled 77 passengers.
10 Joseph had 47 books, 74 magazines, and 77 videos.

16-D. REVIEW THE 4 AND 7 KEYS

11 The 44 tickets were for the April 4 show at 7:44.
12 Anne was to read pages 44, 47, 74, and 77 to him.
13 When Jack turned 47, they had a party for 74 men.
14 Kate planted 44 tulips, 47 mums, and 74 petunias.

16-E. PRACTICE THE **3** KEY

Use the D finger.

15 de3d de3d d33d d33d d3d3 d3d3 3 33 333 3,333 3:33
16 33 drains 33 dogs 33 days 33 dine 33 died 33 doze
17 The 33 boys had 33 books with 33 stamps in total.
18 If Charles adds 43, 44, and 347, he will get 434.

16-F. PRACTICE THE **8** KEY

Use the K finger.

19 ki8k ki8k k88k k88k k8k8 k8k8 8 88 888 8,888 8:88
20 88 knives 88 kids 88 kits 88 keys 88 inns 88 inks
21 Flight 88 left at 7:38 and got to Boston at 8:38.
22 Please call Sue at 347-8833 or 847-3883 at 8 a.m.

REPORT 90
POWER OF ATTORNEY

Spacing: double
Paper: Workguide: 461
Start: line 13

Always triple-space before a signature line.

POWER OF ATTORNEY

KNOW ALL MEN BY THESE PRESENTS that I, ANTHONY FERNAN- | 17
DEZ, of the City of Tulia, County of Swisher, State of Texas, do hereby | 32
appoint my son, Robert Fernandez, of this City, County, and State my | 45
attorney-in-fact to act in my name, place, and stead as my agent in the | 60
management of real estate transactions, chattel and goods transactions, | 74
banking and securities transactions, and business operating transactions, | 89
giving and granting unto my said attorney full power and authority to do | 104
and perform all and every act and thing whatsoever requisite and neces- | 118
sary to be done in the said management as fully, to all intents and pur- | 132
poses, as I might or could do if personally present, with full power of | 146
revocation, hereby ratifying and confirming all that my said attorney | 160
shall lawfully do or shall cause to be done by virtue hereof: | 172

IN WITNESS WHEREOF, I have hereunto set my hand and seal this | 185
thirteenth day of April, 19—. | 191

_____(L.S.) | 192

SIGNED and affirmed in the presence of | 200

_____ and _____ | 201

TABLE 67
BOXED TABLE WITH BRACED HEADING

Spacing: double
Paper: plain, full sheet

Calculate the percent change for the last column of the table. Use one decimal place.

In the Percent Change column, show minus percent change with a hyphen; plus will be assumed.

HALE COUNTY CLIENTS FOR LEGAL SERVICES

City/Town	NUMBER OF CLIENTS		Percent Change
	Last Year	This Year	
Abernathy	11	13	
Hale Center	8	10	?
Happy	3	2	
Petersburg	9	13	
Plainview	62	70	
Seth Ward	5	4	
TOTAL	98	112	?

16-G.   REVIEW THE 3 AND 8 KEYS

23 Jack took the 8:38 train from Track 33 to Boston.
24 There were 838 men and 383 women at the 33 games.
25 On March 8 the 38 boys walked 8 miles to see him.
26 She added 3, 8, 33, 38, 83, and 88 to their bill.

SKILLBUILDING

16-H.   SUSTAINED TYPING: SYLLABIC INTENSITY

16-H. Take a 1-minute timing on the first paragraph to establish your base speed. Then take successive 1-minute timings on the other paragraphs. As soon as you equal or exceed your base speed on one paragraph, advance to the next one.

27   There is no question that we have entered an   10
28 age of information. Many new processes and smart   20
29 equipment can now provide more data in less time.   30

30   The entire telecommunications industry has a   10
31 very bright future. With the use of the computer   20
32 and the phone, many data bases will be available.   30

33   The ease with which financial records can be   10
34 updated and revised is truly phenomenal. Visit a   20
35 nearby financial institution for a demonstration.   30

36   Inventory control has become simpler with an   10
37 emphasis on technology. Optical scanning devices   20
38 can help businesses with their inventory records.   30

  | | | 2 | 3 | 4 | 5 | 6 | 7 | 8 | 9 | 10

16-I.   SKILL MEASUREMENT: 2-MINUTE TIMED WRITING

16-I. Spacing: double. Record your score on Workguide page 3.

39   The personal computer has affected the lives   10
40 of many people in the past decade. With software   20
41 programs appearing on a regular basis, people are   30
42 finding that the personal computer does help them   40
43 to do many long tasks in much less time.   48

  | | | 2 | 3 | 4 | 5 | 6 | 7 | 8 | 9 | 10

LESSON 17

REVIEW

Line: 50 spaces
Tab: 5
Spacing: single
Drills: 2 times
Format Guide: 9–10
Tape: 2B or K5B

Goals: To strengthen the manipulation of various machine parts; to type 25 wam/2'/5e.

S = Speed

A = Accuracy

N = Numbers

17-A.   WARMUP

S 1 She hopes that they will have a good time in May.
A 2 Lazy brown dogs do not jump over the quick foxes.
N 3 Adding 43, 47, 73, 84, and 87 would give you 334.

REPORT 89 (Continued)

For the remainder of this document, Mr. Cline has used the will that he drew up for Susan B. Johnson several years ago. Make appropriate changes as indicated.

Note: On legal documents, wording that is valid in one state may not be valid in other states.

Be sure that all the signature lines are on the same page—that of the testatrix and those of the witnesses. In order to accomplish this, it may be necessary to have the next-to-last page be just a partially typed page. In that case type the page number just 3 lines below the last line typed.

IN WITNESS WHEREOF, I subscribe my name this ~~10th~~ *14th* | 1055

March 1989
day of ~~June, 1977~~, at Plainview, Texas. | 1063

↓3

Susan B. Johnson
SUSAN B. JOHNSON ↓3 | 1066

The foregoing instrument, consisting of this and | 1076
Please check
(three (3)) preceding typewritten pages, was signed, published, | 1088

and declared by SUSAN B. JOHNSON, the Testatrix, to be her | 1100

Last Will and Testament, in the presence of each of us, pres- | 1112

ent at the same time, and we, at her request and in her pres- | 1124

ence, and in the presence of each other, have hereunto sub- | 1135

14th   *March 1989*
scribed our names as witnesses this ~~10th~~ day of ~~June, 1977~~, at | 1148

Plainview, Texas. | 1152

↓3

77 Dowling Street
~~Richard F. Cornish~~   of ~~81 Harrison Avenue~~ | 1156
~~Richard F. Cornish~~ | 1159
Leroy A. Kennedy   Plainview, TX 79072 | 1163
                              ↓3

Sandra B. Lanzi   of 165 Witkowski Way | 1167
Sandra B. Lanzi | 1170
                              Plainview, TX 79072 | 1173
                              ↓3
                              181 Buckingham Road
~~Rita B. Saunders~~   of ~~57 Bennett Street~~ | 1178
~~Rita B. Saunders~~ | 1181
Mary B. Kehayes   Plainview, TX 79072 | 1185

(PAGE THREE OF THREE) | 1188

Please check

17-B.   ALPHABET REVIEW

4 Jo quietly picked sixty sizes from the woven bag.
5 John quickly drew six zippers from the level bag.
6 Becky was amazed that Joe could quit giving help.
7 Pamela quickly fixed the valve for Jim and Buzzy.

17-C.   NUMBER TYPING

8 Jeff was to read pages 37, 48, 74, and 83 to him.
9 The 7:38 bus did not come to our stop until 8:44.
10 Invoice 8 had ticket sales of 78, 44, 83, and 37.
11 We invited 43 boys, 48 girls, 7 men, and 8 women.

17-D.   TECHNIQUE TYPING: RETURN/ENTER KEY

17-D. Type each sentence on a separate line.

12 Al won. Sheila lost. The team won. She forgot.
13 Will you go? Can he win? Who won? Where is he?
14 What speed did you reach? How accurate were you?
15 Tom will jog. Sue will bowl. Katie is swimming.

17-E.   TECHNIQUE TYPING: TAB KEY

17-E. Set tabs every 10 spaces. Use the tab key to go from column to column.

16 You	should	be	able	to
17 use	the	tab	key	with
18 speed	and	control	without	looking
19 at	what	you	are	typing.

17-F.   TECHNIQUE TYPING: SHIFT/CAPS LOCK

Use the shift lock when a word or series of words is typed in all capitals.

20 Review PAST DUE ACCOUNTS RECEIVABLE by AUGUST 10.
21 We will buy either a TOY POODLE or a FOX TERRIER.
22 Please R.S.V.P. to SUE KANE about the SHORE TRIP.

17-G.   TECHNIQUE TYPING: SPACE BAR

23 a b c d e f g h i j k l m n o p q r s t u v w x y
24 is to go an it we if by in so at of or me and the
25 He is to be here as soon as he can buy a new bat.
26 You can buy a new boat with credit if you desire.

17-H.   SKILL MEASUREMENT: 2-MINUTE TIMED WRITING

17-H. Spacing: double. Record your score.

27   Personal computers are creating a big impact 10
28 on all of our lives. We see them in the home and 20
29 on the job. Expect sizes and prices to change in 30
30 the future. Quite a change will also be noted in 40
31 the kinds of software programs that will be used. 50

| 1 | 2 | 3 | 4 | 5 | 6 | 7 | 8 | 9 | 10 |

This is a continuation of the last will and testament of Susan B. Johnson. Follow the format that was begun on the first page as you continue keyboarding this will.

(B) Twenty-five percent (25%) to my beloved son, THOMAS A. JOHNSON, or his surviving issue, per stirpes; 265 273 278

(C) Twenty-five percent (25%) to my beloved daughter, LYNN A. JOHNSON, or her surviving issue, per stirpes; 286 294 300

(D) Twenty-five percent (25%) to my beloved daughter, DIANE L. JOHNSON, or her surviving issue, per stirpes; 307 316 321

(E) In the event any of my beloved children predecease me leaving no issue surviving, I hereby give, devise, and bequeath said share of my estate to my surviving children, or their surviving issue, per stirpes. 330 339 348 357 363

FOURTH: If any minor becomes entitled, during his or her minority, to a share of my estate, I direct that my Trustee shall not deliver said share to such minor until such minor shall attain the age of eighteen (18) years; and I direct that such share shall be held by my Trustee for the following uses and purposes: to use and apply for the education, health, and support of such minor, so much of the principal and income of such share as said Trustee, in her absolute and uncontrolled discretion, may deem proper. Said Trustee may make payment of any income or principal so applied to the use of the minor by making such payment to the guardian of such minor or by applying same for the benefit of such minor, and the receipt of such guardian of evidence of the expenditure of such money for the benefit of such minor shall be a full and sufficient discharge to the Trustee for any such payment, whether or not there be any legal guardian for such minor at the time of any such payment or application, and regardless of such minor's other sources of income; or, in case such minor shall die before distribution of all the property held in trust for his or her benefit, to the executor or administrator of the estate of such minor, the receipt of the person or persons to whom any such payment or distribution is so made being a sufficient discharge 371 380 390 400 409 417 427 436 445 455 464 473 482 490 499 508 516 525 534 543 553 562 571 579 588 598 608 617 625 634

thereof, even though my Executor or Trustee may be such persons. 643 647

FIFTH: I give to my Executor, hereinafter named, full power: 655 659

(A) To retain, in kind, any investment, security, or property which I may own at the time of my death, or, in his discretion, to change such investment and to invest in securities whether or not they are legal investments for trust funds under the laws of the State of Texas; 668 677 686 695 704 714

(B) To sell, lease, mortgage, exchange, assign, transfer, release, convey, or in any other way dispose of any part or all of my estate, real, personal, or mixed, on such conditions and on such terms as may seem to him advisable, without the approval of any court therefore obtained, to make, execute, and deliver all proper instruments and papers necessary in connection therewith. 722 732 742 751 760 768 777 786 790

SIXTH: I hereby nominate, constitute, and appoint my beloved daughter, CHARLOTTE J. FITZPATRICK, as Trustee of the trust provisions created under my Last Will and Testament. I direct that my Trustee shall not be required to furnish a bond or other character of security for the faithful execution of her duties in any jurisdiction, or, if a bond be required, no sureties shall be required to be furnished thereon. 799 807 815 824 833 843 853 863 871 873

SEVENTH: I hereby nominate, constitute, and appoint my beloved husband, RALPH V. JOHNSON, as sole Executor of this, my Last Will and Testament. In the event my beloved husband, RALPH V. JOHNSON, should predecease me, fail to qualify, or for any cause whatsoever fail or cease to act as Executor under this, my Last Will and Testament, then, and in any of those events, I do nominate, constitute, and appoint my beloved daughter, CHARLOTTE J. FITZPATRICK, as Executrix of this, my Last Will and Testament, in place and stead of my beloved husband, RALPH V. JOHNSON. I direct that none of the parties named in this Will as Executor or Executrix shall be required to furnish a bond or other character of security for the faithful execution of their duties in any jurisdiction, or, if a bond be required, no sureties shall be required to be furnished thereon. 881 889 898 907 914 924 932 942 951 959 968 977 985 995 1004 1014 1023 1032 1042 1045

(Continued on page 362.)

17-I. Center a double-spaced copy on a half sheet. Center each line horizontally.

17-I. CENTERING PRACTICE

FALL FOLIAGE TRIP
↓3
Kittatinny Mountain Range
Saturday, October 8
Bus Leaves Parking Lot at 7 a.m.

Line: 50 spaces
Tab: 5
Spacing: single
Drills: 2 times
Format Guide: 9–10
Tape: 3B or K6B

LESSON 18

NUMBER KEYS

Goals: To control the 2, 9, 1, and 0 keys; to type 26 wam/2'/5e.

18-A. WARMUP

S 1 Is he to visit the client in Chicago or New York?
A 2 Quietly pack more new boxes with five dozen jugs.
N 3 Flight 374 will be departing Gate 37 at 8:48 p.m.

18-B. PRACTICE THE 2 KEY

Use the S finger.

4 sw2s sw2s s22s s22s s2s2 s2s2 2 22 222 2,222 2:22
5 22 sports 22 sets 22 sons 22 seas 22 suns 22 subs
6 The 22 students in Room 222 sold all 222 tickets.
7 We will be there May 23 and 24 or June 27 and 28.

18-C. PRACTICE THE 9 KEY

Use the L finger.

8 lo9l lo9l 1991 1991 1919 1919 9 99 999 9,999 9:99
9 99 lights 99 logs 99 lips 99 legs 99 labs 99 lads
10 The 9 boys and 9 girls in Room 9 sold 999 towels.
11 He got 38 pens, 29 pads, 74 pencils, and 9 clips.

18-D. REVIEW THE 2 AND 9 KEYS

12 On 9/2 the group ate 292 hot dogs and 99 burgers.
13 You get 479 when you add 22, 29, 92, 99, and 237.
14 She had test scores of 92, 94, and 97 in English.
15 On 2/28 Michelle typed 29 wam with only 2 errors.

18-E. PRACTICE THE 1 KEY

Use the A finger.

16 aq1a aq1a a11a a11a a1a1 a1a1 1 11 111 1,111 1:11
17 11 arenas 11 aces 11 axes 11 aims 11 arts 11 adds
18 Sam got 1,111 votes; Sue had 1,181; Vi had 1,119.
19 By 1991 he will have 17 new clients in 11 cities.

LAST WILL AND TESTAMENT

Paper: Workguide 451–459

Legal style: Indent paragraphs 10 spaces.

Legal documents are often typed on ruled stationery, which is 8½ by 11 inches. Margin stops are set a space or two inside the double rule.

WP Some word processing software will allow the storage of the constant text of a legal form with stop codes where the variable text should be inserted. This saves keyboarding and proofreading time, allowing the secretary to be more productive.

Subheadings of a given paragraph may be indented 20 spaces.

The next few pages represent a rough draft of the last will and testament of Susan B. Johnson. Please type a final copy.

LAST WILL AND TESTAMENT   5

OF   5

SUSAN B. JOHNSON   8

I, Susan B. Johnson, of Plainview, County of Hale,   18
Texas, being of disposing and sound mind, memory, and under-   30
standing, do make, publish and declare this to be my last   42
Will and Testament, and here by revoke any and all Wills and   54
Codicils heretofore made by me.   60

FIRST: I direct that all my just debts and funeral ex-   71
penses be paid as soon after my decease as may be practicable.   83

Second: I give, devise, and bequeath all the rest,   94
residue, and remainder of my property, real, personal, or   105
mixed, of whatsoever kind of nature and whereso ever situated,   118
including property over which I have any power of appointment   130
at my death, to my beloved husband, Ralph V. Johnson, to his   142
own use, absolutely and forever.   149

Third: If my beloved husband, RALPH V. JOHNSON,   159
should predecease me, I direct that the provisions of PARA-   170
GRAPH SECOND of this will shall be void, and in lieu there of,   183
I give, devise and bequeath the rest, residue and remainder of   196
my property, real, personal or mixed, of whatso ever kind or   208
nature and wheresoever situated, including property over which   220
I hold a power of appointment at my death, as follows: 231

(A) Twenty-five (25%) percent to my be-   239
loved daughter, CHARLOTTE J. FITZPATRICK, or her surviving   251
issue, per stirpes;   254

PAGE ONE OF FIVE   258

(Continued on page 361.)

18-F. PRACTICE THE **0** KEY

Use the Sem finger.

20 ;p0; ;p0; ;00; ;00; ;0;0 ;0;0 0 00 000 0,000 0:00
21 100 parks 10 pens 10 pins 10 pits 10 pegs 10 pads
22 You will get 220 when you add 30, 40, 70, and 80.
23 The 20 employees should go to personnel at 10:10.

18-G. REVIEW THE I AND 0 KEYS

24 Mary read the 10 scripts and 11 texts in 10 days.
25 Please call her at 291-0011 or at 290-1001 today.
26 The 101 employees left at 10:11 instead of 11:01.
27 Raymond added 1, 10, 100, and 1,000 to get 1,111.

18-H. Spacing: double. Record your score.

18-H. SKILL MEASUREMENT: 2-MINUTE TIMED WRITING

28   We can expect quite a few changes in our job   10
29 market in the next few decades. People will have   20
30 jobs that will require new skills due to the many   30
31 uses of the computer. We will have a gain in the   40
32 size of the labor force, with more people working   50
33 in offices.   52

| | | | 2 | 3 | 4 | 5 | 6 | 7 | 8 | 9 | 10

LESSON 19 REVIEW

Line: 50 spaces
Tab: 5
Spacing: single
Drills: 2 times
Format Guide: 9–11
Tape: 4B or K7B

Goals: To improve speed and accuracy; to improve control of number keys; to type 27 wam/2'/5e.

19-A. WARMUP

S 1 The new worker had a small problem with the bank.
A 2 Jan quickly moved the six dozen big pink flowers.
N 3 Jeff got tickets 10, 29, 38, and 47 for the show.

SKILLBUILDING

19-B. PACED PRACTICE

Turn to the Paced Practice routine at the back of the book. Take several 2-minute timings, starting at the point where you left off the last time. Record your progress on Workguide page 6.

Tab: 10
Spacing: double
Paper: plain, ruled*

*The double lines should be 1½ inches from the left; the single line, ½ inch from the right.

Spread-center the title.

Standard manuscript procedures are used for vertical placement of copy in legal documents. One-page documents are vertically centered on the page. The first page of a multiple-page document has a top margin of 2 inches; subsequent pages have a 1-inch top margin. The bottom margins of all pages are from 1 to 1½ inches in depth.

It is common to have a 10-space indention for each paragraph in a legal document.

EMPLOYMENT CONTRACT   7

   This agreement, made and concluded this *ninth* ~~eighth~~ day   17
of April, 19--, between Baker Temporary Services of 174 Foley   30
Street, Tulia, Texas, party of the first part, and Charlotte   42
McMullen, 17 Fritz Avenue, Plainview, Texas, *party of the second part*. 56
   Article 1. Services. The said party of the second   66
part covenants and agrees to and with the party of the (1st)   79
part ~~as;~~ to furnish her services to the said party of the   90
first part as Computer ~~Specialists~~ *Applications* Training Consultant two (2) 102
days a week for three (3) calendar months, beginning January   115
1, 19--, and ending ~~April 30~~ *March 31*, 19--; and the said party of the 127
second part covenants and agrees to conduct training sessions   139
in the use of commonly used soft ware applications programs in   152
word processing, database, spreadsheets, and graphics. In   163
addition, the party of the second part agrees to conduct fea-   175
sibility studies for selected ~~businesses~~ *firms* to determine the 186
needed hardware purchases that ~~might~~ *should* be made to improve the 198
management of information systems. It is agreed that the   210
number of businesses to be serviced will not exceed six (6) ~~a~~   222
~~month.~~ *during the term of this contract.*   228
   Article 2. Wages. The said party of the first part   239
covenants and agrees to pay the said party of the second part,   252
for the same, the sum of seven thousand two hundred dollars   264
($7,200), as follows: the sum of two thousand four hundred   276
dollars ($2,400), the last day of each month beginning on (Jan.)   289
31, 19--.   291
   In witness whereof, the parties to the employment   301
contract have here unto set their hands the day and year first   313
above written. ↓3   316

_____   _____
Charlotte McMullen   Eleanor Baker, President   324
                                         Baker Temporary Services ↓3   329

_____   _____
Witness to Signature   Witness to Signature   337

19-C. NUMBER TYPING

4 The 44 students bought tickets for the 4:44 show.
5 With 77 packets of thread, she made 777 sweaters.
6 Ticket No. 333 was entitled to 3,333 jelly beans.
7 She took Train No. 888 through 8 different towns.
8 Matt lived at 222 Lincoln with 2 dogs and 2 cats.

9 I threw only 99 pitches in the 9 innings pitched.
10 Gloria ran the 11 miles in 1 hour and 11 minutes.
11 When you add 10, 20, 30, 80, and 90, you get 230.
12 Order No. 2839 had 27 fewer crates than I wanted.
13 Call Robert at 724-3890 or 812-4410 for the data.

PRETEST. Take a 1-minute timing; compute your speed and count errors.

19-D. PRETEST: HORIZONTAL REACHES

14 The legal facts gave our lawyer a sense that 10
15 we had the upper hand. All written testimony had 20
16 impacted negatively on the young farmhand who was 30
17 being charged with several pyrotechnic incidents. 40

| | 1 | 2 | 3 | 4 | 5 | 6 | 7 | 8 | 9 | 10 |

PRACTICE.
   Speed Emphasis: If you made 2 or fewer errors on the Pretest, type each line twice.
   Accuracy Emphasis: If you made 3 or more errors, type each group of lines (as though it were a paragraph) twice.

19-E. PRACTICE: IN REACHES

18 wr wrap writ wren wreak wrist wrote wrong wreaths
19 ou pout ours outs ounce cough fouls dough coupons
20 ad adds dead wade adult ready blade adopt adheres
21 py pyre copy pyro pygmy pylon happy weepy pyramid

19-F. PRACTICE: OUT REACHES

22 yo yolk yoga your youth yodel yowls yokel younger
23 fa fact afar farm faith sofas fakes fades defames
24 up upon soup cups upset group upper super upsurge
25 ga gate saga gave cigar gains legal gasps garbage

POSTTEST. Repeat the Pretest and compare performance.

19-G. POSTTEST: HORIZONTAL REACHES

19-H. Spacing: double.

19-H. SKILL MEASUREMENT: 2-MINUTE TIMED WRITING

26 Technology is making it possible for workers 10
27 at different sites to share more and more data in 20
28 less time. Experts tell us that by combining our 30
29 phones and computers we can have information that 40
30 will quickly zoom from one location to another to 50
31 help all jobholders. 54

| | 1 | 2 | 3 | 4 | 5 | 6 | 7 | 8 | 9 | 10 |

N. INTEGRATED OFFICE PROJECT: STEPHEN L. CLINE, ATTORNEY-AT-LAW

Situation: Today is Monday, April 12. You are secretary to Mr. Stephen L. Cline, attorney-at-law. His office is in the Sheffield Building at 72 Bentley Place, Plainview, TX 79072.

You handle all the administrative duties of the office as well as prepare all the correspondence and legal documents that Mr. Cline must have typed. He prefers to use the block letter style and open punctuation. Closing lines are as follows:

```
Sincerely yours


Stephen L. Cline
Attorney-at-Law
```

LETTER 98
TWO-PAGE LETTER   Paper: Workguide 447–448

Mr. Cline has dictated the following letter for you to type. The table within the letter should be arranged as a two-column open table.

Send this letter to mr . . . thomas applebaum   4
. . . president . . . financial investors . . . 77   11
gateway towers . . . plainview . . . tx . . .   16
79072 . . . dear mr . . . applebaum . . .   21

i enjoyed meeting you this afternoon and   29
discussing the approach to take in handling the   39
large number of clients that you have with past   48
. . . due accounts . . . as we concluded . . . this   56
is creating a serious cash flow problem for   64
your business and must be corrected as   72
quickly as possible . . .   76

mr . . . lorenzini of your accounting depart-   84
ment has provided me with the following in-   92
formation indicating the number of clients   101
who have past . . . due accounts (*arrange the*   106
following information in two columns) . . .

overdue more than 30 days . . . 38 . . . over-   113
due more than 60 days . . . 21 . . . overdue   119
more than 90 days . . . 20 . . . overdue more   125
than 120 days . . . 16 . . . overdue more than   132
180 days . . . 10 . . . overdue more than a year   139

. . . 8 . . .   139

mr . . . lorenzini has given me the names and   147
addresses of each of the clients in each of the   157
above categories . . . after i prepare an appro-   165
priate letter to be sent to these people . . . i   174
will meet with you to get your approval on its   183
contents . . .   185

as i indicated in our discussion . . . i will use   194
a low . . . key approach in all the communica-   202
tions . . . past experience has shown that this is   211
the best approach to take when making this   220
first attempt to collect on past . . . due ac-   228
counts . . . if that approach does not get results   237
. . . i will then take a stronger stand to ensure   246
collection . . .   248

again . . . thank you for meeting with me . . .   256
i will look forward to working with you as we   265
attempt to collect on your past . . . due ac-   273
counts . . . i will call your office next week to   282
set up an appointment for our next meeting   291
. . .

FORMS 50–51
VOUCHER CHECKS   Paper: Workguide 449

Mr. Cline asks you to type two voucher checks.

The first check is for payment of the utility bill for the past month. Make the check payable to Lone Star Electric & Gas, 57 Bradley Street, Lubbock, TX 79403, for $347.63.

The second check, for $865.50, is payable to Ellis Office Equipment for the new electronic typewriter that was just delivered. The check is in payment of Invoice 4632. The Ellis office is located at 67 Harris Drive, Amarillo, TX 79103.

REPORT 88
EMPLOYMENT CONTRACT

Mr. Cline would like to have a typed copy of the employment contract found on page 359. This was typed as a rough draft last week.

19-1. Center a double-spaced copy on a half sheet. Center each line horizontally.

19-1. CENTERING PRACTICE

SEMINAR ON DATA COMMUNICATIONS ↓3
Featuring Dr. Albert B. Coleman
Professor of Business, Highlands University
Wednesday, October 18, 7:30 p.m.
Mountainview Resort
Highlands, Vermont

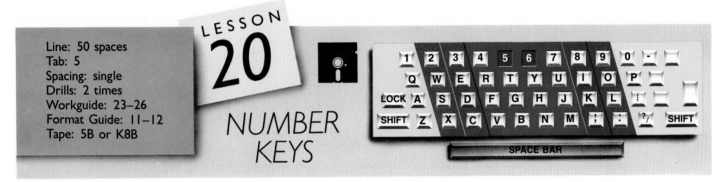

Line: 50 spaces
Tab: 5
Spacing: single
Drills: 2 times
Workguide: 23–26
Format Guide: 11–12
Tape: 5B or K8B

LESSON 20
NUMBER KEYS

Goals: To control the 5 and 6 keys; to type 28 wam/2'/5e.

20-A. WARMUP

S 1 They had problems with their profits from August.
A 2 Quickly pack the box with five dozen jars of gum.
N 3 Sue went from 380 29th Street to 471 27th Street.

20-B. PRACTICE THE 5 KEY

Use the F finger.

4 fr5f fr5f f55f f55f f5f5 f5f5 5 55 555 5,555 5:55
5 55 favors 55 furs 55 fads 55 fibs 55 foes 55 fury
6 The 55 students read the 555 pages in 55 minutes.
7 She found items 5, 10, and 29; I found 47 and 38.

20-C. PRACTICE THE 6 KEY

Use the J finger.

8 jy6j jy6j j66j j66j j6j6 j6j6 6 66 666 6,666 6:66
9 66 jewels 66 join 66 jabs 66 jump 66 jams 66 jots
10 At the age of 66, Tom moved from 66 Lincoln Road.
11 There are 53,640 people in Lodi; 28,179 in Alpha.

20-D. REVIEW THE 5 AND 6 KEYS

After doing 20-D, complete Workguide pages 23 and 24, the Punctuation Learning Guide.

12 The 65 adults went to 5566 Wooster Avenue on 6/5.
13 On 5/6 at the age of 6, Andrew weighed 65 pounds.
14 If Gail takes 10 percent of 650, she will get 65.
15 Call Jeffrey at 555-8407 or 555-5143 by 8:30 p.m.

K. Type each line twice. Concentrate on the infrequently used letters of the alphabet.

K. ALPHABET REVIEW: INFREQUENTLY USED KEYS

J 49 Jack enjoyed joining Joe and John for a June trip to Japan.
Q 50 A quick, quiet, and unique banquet might look quite quaint.
X 51 Maxine expects sixty extra boxes of index cards next month.
Z 52 Prizes dazzled the amazed citizens and puzzled Zola and Oz.

L. PACED PRACTICE

Turn to the Paced Practice routine at the back of the book. Take several 2-minute timings, starting at the point where you left off the last time. Record your progress on Workguide page 290.

M. Spacing: double.
Record your score.

M. SKILL MEASUREMENT: 5-MINUTE TIMED WRITING

53   The need for advice and help on legal matters is known   12
54 to be on the increase. Due to this rise, there is a demand   24
55 for more office workers who understand the many legal forms   36
56 that can be found in law offices today. Experts in the law   48
57 field want workers who understand these various forms.   59
58   One of the most common forms used by many lawyers is a   71
59 simple contract. This involves an agreement between two or   83
60 more parties to meet certain requirements. A contract will   95
61 provide all details about who will do what and when it will   107
62 be done. This basic legal form has existed many years.   118
63   Another form which has had a long history in the legal   130
64 field is the last will and testament. Most adults now know   142
65 that it is quite important to have such a document. When a   154
66 person dies intestate, the time and process for settling an   166
67 estate might become quite complex and more cumbersome.   177
68   Two other legal forms often used on the job in a legal   189
69 office should be understood. A power of attorney is issued   201
70 when one person wishes another to act in his behalf for any   213
71 reason. A statement adopted by a group or organization for   225
72 an individual or cause is referred to as a resolution.   236
73   At the present time, job openings for persons desiring   248
74 to work in the legal field are good. The special forms and   260
75 documents used in the law office should be understood. The   272
76 expectation for high production means that those people who   284
77 work in law offices can expect higher salary benefits.   295
    | | 2 | 3 | 4 | 5 | 6 | 7 | 8 | 9 | 10 | 11 | 12

20-E. NUMBER TYPING

20-E. Take two 1-minute tim- ings. Note that the last two digits of each number are a cumulative word count.

16 1101 1102 1103 1104 1105 1106 1107 1108 1109 1110
17 2211 2212 2213 2214 2215 2216 2217 2218 2219 2220
18 3321 3322 3323 3324 3325 3326 3327 3328 3329 3330
19 4431 4432 4433 4434 4435 4436 4437 4438 4439 4440

20-E. Take two 1-minute tim- ings. Note that the last two digits of each number are a cumulative word count.

20-F. SUSTAINED TYPING: NUMBERS

20-F. Take a 1-minute timing on the first paragraph to estab- lish your base speed. Then take successive 1-minute timings on the other paragraphs. As soon as you equal or exceed your base speed on one paragraph, advance to the next one.

20   In the past quarter, we have added the names   10
21 of 78 clients to our data base. This gives us an   20
22 exciting total of 249 clients in this first year.   30
23   Of the 249 clients, 91 were being handled by   10
24 Charles Thompson; 85 were controlled by Charlotte   20
25 Baines; and 73 were being serviced by Gail Banks.   30
26   We got 24 clients in July from 107 contacts;   10
27 August brought us 29 clients from 168 contacts; a   20
28 record of 35 clients was gained during September.   30
29   We were able to get 249 clients in our first   10
30 year; our aim is 350, 425, and 500 clients in the   20
31 next three years--or 1,524 clients in four years.   30

| | | 2 | 3 | 4 | 5 | 6 | 7 | 8 | 9 | 10

20-G. SKILL MEASUREMENT: 2-MINUTE TIMED WRITING

20-G. Spacing: double. Record your score.

32   The purpose for all the new technology is to   10
33 make workers more productive. If this happens, a   20
34 decrease in the number of hours on the job may be   30
35 noticed. This could mean that workers would have   40
36 extra time off. This could be quite a benefit to   50
37 a sizable number of employees.   56

| | | 2 | 3 | 4 | 5 | 6 | 7 | 8 | 9 | 10

20-H. CENTERING PRACTICE

20-H. Center a double-spaced copy on a half sheet. Spread- center the heading. Center each line.

ANNUAL FIREWORKS
Wednesday, July 4   ↓3
Valley Road Park
Manchester, New Hampshire
Sponsored by Chamber of Commerce
Music starting at 7:30 p.m.
Fireworks beginning at 9 p.m.

F. These words are recognized as "spelling demons."

F. PRODUCTION PRACTICE: SPELLING

16 acquaint calendar cigarette criticism particular government
17 accuracy schedule interpret technique appreciate discipline
18 favorite strength knowledge privilege facilitate ingredient
19 quantity surprise recognize prejudice accumulate tremendous

G. Keep your eyes on the copy, and try not to slow down for the capital letters.

G. TECHNIQUE TYPING: SHIFT KEY

20 Mr. Olsen became president of RMS Company in Utah on May 5.
21 Sue, Pete, and Jerry saw the Statue of Liberty in New York.
22 Mr. and Mrs. James Mancini left for St. Thomas on April 11.
23 Prints in the Tampa Museum of Art came from Rome and Paris.

H. Compare this paragraph with the last paragraph of the timing on page 357. Type a list of the words that contain errors, correcting the errors as you type.

H. PRODUCTION PRACTICE: PROOFREADING

24   At the present time, job openings for persons desireing
25 to work in the legel field are good. The special farms and
26 documents used in the law office shuld be understood. The
27 expectation for high production means that the people who
28 work in law offices can expect higher salary benfits.

I. As you type this paragraph, untangle the transpositions. This means that you must read ahead for understanding.

I. CONCENTRATION PRACTICE

29   Employee benefits, also known as benefits fringe, must
30 be carefully evaluated when select you a job. The benefits
31 received from a job be can equal to one-third of salary the
32 received. Thus the of importance benefits be must obvious.

J. Take a 1-minute timing on the first paragraph to establish your base speed. Then take several 1-minute timings on the other paragraphs. As soon as you equal or exceed your base speed on one paragraph, advance to the next one.

J. SUSTAINED TYPING: NUMBERS

33   Our real estate sales agency office at 15 Hemlock Road   12
34 recently achieved a new record. Sale of existing homes for   24
35 the month of February was 12. Sale of completely new homes   36
36 for the month totaled 6. These are exciting sales figures.   48

37   The 12 branch offices of Hemlock Sales have a total of   12
38 89 sales associates. There are 53 men and 36 women. There   24
39 has been a total increase of 14 associates since we had our   36
40 last corporate gathering in Amarillo a number of years ago.   48

41   One of the Hemlock agents sold one house for $237,500;   12
42 she sold another one for $178,650 seven days later. She is   24
43 already at her sales quota for the month. Since that first   36
44 sale fifteen years ago, she has sold a total of 182 houses.   48

45   The median price of homes sold by Hemlock was $102,500   12
46 last year. The year before that it was $93,600, and in the   24
47 prior year it was $84,200. The increases of 11 percent and   36
48 9.5 percent have made real estate an attractive investment.   48

| 1 | 2 | 3 | 4 | 5 | 6 | 7 | 8 | 9 | 10 | 11 | 12

Ask your instructor for the General Information Test on Part 1.

PROGRESS TEST ON PART 1

TEST 1-A
2-MINUTE TIMED WRITING ON ALPHABETIC COPY

Line: 50 spaces
Tab: 5
Spacing: double
Paper: Workguide 27
Start: 6 lines from top

Let it snow. If those three words make your   10
pulse race, you probably like winter sports. You   20
may like to ski, skate, or sled in Vail.   28

The three words cause you to gaze quietly in   38
the distance as you don and adjust the right gear   48
for your expected trip to winter sports.   56

| | | 2 | 3 | 4 | 5 | 6 | 7 | 8 | 9 | 10

TEST 1-B
2-MINUTE TIMED WRITING ON COPY WITH NUMBERS

Line: 50 spaces
Tab: 5
Spacing: double
Paper: Workguide 27
Start: 6 lines from top

San Francisco has a public library system of   10
26 branches. The budget was over 13.2 million in   20
1986 for this 26-branch library system.   28

There are over 1,950,684 volumes in the sys-   38
tem and a circulation of over 2,695,510. Many of   48
the 712,753 citizens use the libraries.   56

| | | 2 | 3 | 4 | 5 | 6 | 7 | 8 | 9 | 10

TEST 1-C
HORIZONTAL AND VERTICAL CENTERING

Title displayed:
  Spread-centered
  2 blank lines
Line: center longest line; block-center listing
Tab: center only
Spacing: as shown
Paper: Workguide 29
Start: to center on half sheet

C R U I S E S

The Hill-Rowe Travel Company is pleased to announce its annual winter cruises to the Caribbean. The cruises include stops at:

Antigua
Barbados
Grenada
Guadeloupe
Martinique
St. Lucia
St. Maarten

Line: 60 spaces
Tab: 5, center
Spacing: single
Drills: 2 times
Workguide: 447–465
Format Guide: 169

LESSONS 166–170

INTEGRATED OFFICE PROJECT: LEGAL

GOALS FOR UNIT 34

1. To type 59 wam for 5 minutes with no more than 5 errors.
2. To improve number-typing skills.
3. To format a two-page letter in block style, applying rules of punctuation and capitalization.
4. To format legal documents—employment contract, last will and testament, and power of attorney.
5. To format forms and voucher checks.
6. To format a boxed table with a braced heading.
7. To perform calculations.

A.   WARMUP

S 1 When Jan visits the island, she will plan to see the autos.
A 2 Because he was very lazy, Jack paid for six games and quit.
N 3 Model 1342 sold for $2,190.70; model 2109 sold for $326.85.

SKILLBUILDING

PRETEST. Take a 1-minute timing; compute your speed and
count errors.

B.   PRETEST: HORIZONTAL REACHES

4   Some employees were engaged in a market survey to rate   12
5   the data gathered from the campus. Some of the data within   24
6   the study eluded the employees because they were puzzled by   36
7   the range of ages of students and by the high dropout rate.   48
    | | | 2 | 3 | 4 | 5 | 6 | 7 | 8 | 9 | 10 | 11 | 12

PRACTICE.
   Speed Emphasis: If you made
no errors on the Pretest, type
each line twice.
   Accuracy Emphasis: If you
made 1 or more errors on the
Pretest, type each group of lines
(as though it were a paragraph)
twice.

C.   PRACTICE: IN REACHES

8   oy ploy toys boys voyage joyous decoys employ oyster busboy
9   ar arch yard fear argued market soared embark dollar artist
10 pu punt spun spur puzzle spunky deputy campus pushed repute
11 lu luck club plus luxury eluded salute unplug fluffy lugged

D.   PRACTICE: OUT REACHES

12 ge germ ages wage genius urgent agents merged engage gentle
13 da data soda daze danger update payday agenda pedals daring
14 hi high thin chip hinder shield hiking behind hiring within
15 ra rate brag rare ratify traced ranged afraid ramble betray

POSTTEST. Repeat the Pretest
and compare performance.

E.   POSTTEST: HORIZONTAL REACHES

TEST 1-D
BLOCK CENTERING

Title displayed:
  Centered
  2 blank lines
Line: to center longest item
Tab: center
Spacing: single
Paper: Workguide 29
Start: to center on half sheet

MODERN U.S. SUSPENSION BRIDGES

      Bronx-Whitestone
      Delaware Memorial
      Gas Pipe Line
      George Washington
      Golden Gate
      Mackinac Straits
      Seaway Skyway
      Tacoma Narrows
      Transbay
      Verrazano-Narrows

TEST 1-E
LINE CENTERING

Title displayed:
  Centered
  2 blank lines
Line: center each line
      horizontally
Tab: center
Spacing: double
Paper: Workguide 31
Start: to center on half sheet

FOREIGN EXCHANGE

British Pound

Canadian Dollar

French Franc

German Mark

Japanese Yen

Mexican Peso

Swiss Franc

TEST 1-F
BLOCK CENTERING

Title displayed:
  Spread-centered
  2 blank lines
Line: to center longest item
Tab: center
Spacing: single
Paper: Workguide 31
Start: to center on half sheet

TEN LARGEST U.S. CITIES

New York
Los Angeles
Chicago
Houston
Philadelphia
Detroit
Dallas
San Antonio
Phoenix
San Francisco

Mr. Schober will be taking a business trip to San Francisco during the week of March 24 in order to attend the NERDA convention and to visit with prospective customers. Type a final copy of this edited itinerary.

Begin on line → Itinerary for Mr. Frank Schober   ALL CAPS
7

March ~~22-25~~, 19--
24-27

Sunday, March ~~22~~ 4

  6:30 p.m.   Depart Lambert-St. Louis International #
          Airport, TWA Flight 233.

  7:40 p.m.   Arrive San Francisco International Airport;
          (Ron) Schmidt, California (rep), will meet
          you.
+1 SPACE
  8:30 p.m.   Dinner with Messrs. Tate and Mancini of
     ↓3   Redwood ~~Systems.~~
          Electronics.

Monday, March ~~2~~ 5

  7:30 a.m.   Breakfast--Mr. Jack Morris, *Belmont Systems.*

  9:00 a.m.   ~~Attend~~ opening general session of NERDA
          convention.

+1 SPACE
 10:30 a.m.   Work at booth in exhibitors' room.
 12:00 noon   NERDA ^ Luncheon--Golden Gate Ballroom.

  2:00 p.m.   Attend ~~meeting~~ "Security System ~~Electronics~~."
            seminar   Trends

  7:00 p.m.   ↓3 Attend ^ banquet--Golden Gate Ballroom.

Tuesday, March 2~~4~~ 6   NERDA

  7:30 a.m.   Breakfast--Todd Dilts, Marie King, and ~~Jack~~ Rob
          Ross of Empire Electronics in San Carlos.

  9:00 a.m.   Spend day at Empire Electronics--tour
  (indent 1 more char.) facilities, ~~have~~ lunch with officers,
          and ^ sales presentation.
          make

  6:00 p.m. ↓3 Dinner with son and daughter-in-law.

Wednesday, March 2~~5~~ 7

 12:00 noon   NERDA ^ Luncheon--Golden Gate Ballroom.

  3:30 p.m.   Leave San Francisco International Airport,
          TWA Flight 222.
+1 SPACE
  9:35 p.m.   Arrive Lambert-St. Louis International
          Airport.

PART 2

SKILLBUILDING■
LETTERS, REPORTS,
AND TABLES

OBJECTIVES

KEYBOARDING SKILL
To operate the entire keyboard by touch.

To type 36 words a minute on a 3-minute timed writing with no more than 5 errors.

PROOFREADING SKILL
To proofread typewritten material, mark and count errors, correct errors, and compute typing speed.

TECHNICAL SKILL
To answer correctly at least 90 percent of the questions on an objective test.

FORMATTING SKILL
To make correct word divisions and line-ending decisions.

To format business letters and personal-business letters.

To format one-page reports, enumerations, and bibliographies.

To format tables with column headings.

■ To understand how word processing equipment and software would function if used to format various production assignments.

TABLE 66
RULED TABLE

Paper: plain

Spacing: Group the items in sets of five. Single-space, with double spacing between sets.

Strategic Security Systems needs a complete directory of all new customers that they have handled this year. Prepare a table with the name of the company, the city and state, the phone number, and the contact person. Mr. Schober will be able to share this information with the sales representatives in the different territories for follow-up calls.

STRATEGIC SECURITY SYSTEMS
New Clients in Past Year

Company	City, State	Phone	Contact	
ABD ~~Company~~ Controls	Rogers, AR	(501) 555-90(24) 515	Donald Guidi	26
Chester Products	Boone, IA	(~~913~~) 555-1565	Thomas Perez	36
Crane Electronics	Newport, AR	(501) 555-1420	~~Ruth~~ Rita Clarke	46
Datatronics, Inc.	Austin, ~~MI~~ MN	(507) 555-3148	Vera Crispen	57
Electro Group	~~Lebanon~~ Monett, MO	(~~507~~) 417 555-2731	Richard Cruse	67
Electronic Barn	Fulton, MO	(314) 555-8730	Fred ~~Jackson~~ Johnson	77
Harlan Electronics	Harlan, IA	(712) 555-4487	Sam Hutchins	88
Integrity Systems	Auburn, NE	(402) 555-1890	Robert Freman	99
Jaspen Associates	Murray, KY	(502) 555-~~4132~~ 3142	James Bennett	110
~~JCA~~ Jenco Controls	Fairbury, NE	(402) 555-9032	Susan Belmont	120
L & M Associates	Pana, IL	(217) 555-8437	Jack Thompson	130
National Sterling	Iowa City, IA	(319) 555-2280	Albert Eng	141
PCT Systems	Canton, IL	(309) 555-7818	Nick DeMassi	151
PAM, Inc.	Mayfield, KY	(502) 555-8837	Steve Ricci	160
Radco Electronics	Mexico, MO	(314) 555-8122	Charles Motti	171
Searcy Electronics	Searcy, A~~K~~R	(501) 555-~~4877~~ 3766	Estelle Macey	182
Sentinel Security	Parsons, KS	(316) 555-8400	Donna Cline	192
Tencor Products	Trenton, MO	(816) 555-1579	Ste~~phen~~ve ~~Krey~~ Klein	202
Tomco Electronics	St. Paul, ~~MI~~ MN	(612) 555-3440	Harry Bentley	214
TRC Distributors	Hibbing, ~~MI~~ MN	(218) 555-6832	David Prugh	224
Wayne Electronics	Wayne, NE	(402) 555-7132	Anita Jansko	234
Western Electronics	Bolivar, MO	(417) 555-8407	Thomas Catan	245
Bell Security	Olathe, KS	(913) 555-1565	Jason Velez	255
Herrin Electronics	Herrin, IL	(618) 555-5684	Joan Tracey	266
Thomas Electronics	Columbia, MO	(314) 555-6907	Roger Allgor	277

Alphabetize in table!

LESSON
21

SYMBOLS AND WORD DIVISION

Line: 60 spaces
Tab: 5
Spacing: single
Drills: 2 times
Format Guide: 11–12
Tape: 6B or K9B

Goals: To control the **#**, **(**, and **)** keys; to improve speed and accuracy; to make correct word-division decisions.

21-A. WARMUP

S 1 The man took the keys that he had in his hand to the truck.
A 2 The four women in the jury box quickly spotted Dave dozing.
N 3 Seats 10, 29, 38, 47, and 56 are still unsold for tomorrow.

21-B. PRACTICE THE # KEY

NUMBER (if before a figure) or POUNDS (if after a figure) is the shift of 3. Use the D finger.

4 ded de3d d3d d3#d d3#d d##d d##d #3 #33 #38 #383 #3,383 d#d
5 I want 33# of #200, 37# of #300, and 38# of #400 by Friday.
6 Package #47 weighs 65#; #51 weighs 84#; and #83 weighs 42#.
7 My favorite tours for this year are #29, #38, #47, and #56.

21-C. PRACTICE THE (AND) KEYS

PARENTHESES are the shifts of 9 and 0. Use the L and Sem fingers.

8 1091 191 19(1 1(1 1(1 ;p0; ;0; ;0); ;); ;); (2) (4) (6) (8)
9 Please ask (1) Tom, (2) Pat, (3) Anne, (4) Sue, and (5) Ed.
10 David brought some (1) skis, (2) sleds, and (3) ice skates.
11 The typist is (1) speedy, (2) accurate, and (3) productive.

12 Three of our workers (Parks, Lemay, and Eng) were rewarded.
13 The manager (Ms. Holden) went to Albany on Friday (June 5).
14 The man from Illinois (Mr. Roberts) will vote yes (not no).
15 My bingo is (1) B5, (2) I21, (3) N36, (4) G54, and (5) O73.

SKILLBUILDING

21-D. NUMBER TYPING

16 On the cruise ship Sunup, Cabins 20 and 19 were very small.
17 I know a man who is 21; his aunt is also 21; his dad is 60.
18 The tour had 874 people, 387 from Hope and 487 from Bangor.
19 We ordered 90 cartons and 43 boxes when we called 555-5536.

21-E. Compare these two paragraphs with the first two paragraphs of the timed writing in 22-J on page 40. Type a list of the words that contain errors, correcting the errors as you type.

21-E. PRODUCTION PRACTICE: PROOFREADING

20 Jobs in busness require good comunication skills for
21 sucess. Confirmation of this fact can be found in various
22 magzines and books.
23   It is expected that a new worker on business will have
24 the ability to speak and write clearly and properly. These
25 are critcal skills.

LETTERS 96–97
MODIFIED-BLOCK STYLE

Paper: Workguide 439–442

Mr. Schober has dictated the following two letters for you to transcribe when you have time. He has identified the paragraphs, but you will have to supply the correct punctuation and capitalization.

Send this letter to mr . . . harvey domino . . . 3
town electronics . . . 181 wright street . . . 10
jonesboro . . . ar . . . 72401 . . . dear mr . . . 16
domino . . . 17

thank you for your recent inquiry about our 26
security systems . . . we have carried a line of 35
residential and industrial security systems for 44
the past fifty years . . . 49

we have just recently begun to service ac- 57
counts in the jonesboro area . . . mr . . . ken- 64
neth kardux is our new sales representative 73
handling accounts in that area . . . i will for- 82
ward your letter to him and request that he 91
contact you within the next few weeks to an- 99
swer any questions you might have about our 108
products and service . . . 112

i plan to attend the trade show sponsored by 121
the national electronics research and develop- 130
ment association in san francisco . . . where 138
we will exhibit some of our new products . . . 147
if you plan to be there . . . please stop by our 156
exhibit booth and introduce yourself . . . sin- 164
cerely yours . . . 166

Send this second letter to mr . . . paul baines 3
. . . chamber of commerce . . . 157 village 9
square . . . kirkwood . . . mo . . . 63122 . . . 14
dear mr . . . baines . . . 17

i enjoyed attending the recent luncheon 25
held by the kirkwood chamber of commerce at 34
the village inn . . . i especially enjoyed having a 44
chance to speak with many of our business 52
leaders from kirkwood . . . 56

it was very enlightening to hear of the many 65
plans that the chamber has made for the next 74
twelve months . . . the plans for the day fair to 84
be held on saturday . . . april 20 . . . sound 91

very exciting . . . this can be a real boost for all 101
our business establishments in kirkwood . . . 109

if the plans to prepare a program booklet for 118
that day materialize . . . i want to be sure to be 127
included as a supporter . . . please contact me 136
about purchasing a booster page . . . sincerely 144
yours . . . 146

MEMO 35

Paper: Workguide 443

Mr. Schober would like Ronald Schmidt, our sales agent in California, to know of his upcoming plans to be in San Francisco. Please type the following memo to Mr. Schmidt.

TO: Ronald Schmidt, California Agent   6
FROM: Frank Schober, Marketing Manager   13
RE: San Francisco Trip   16
DATE: March 15, 19—   19

As I indicated in our last telephone conver- 28
sation, I plan to fly to San Francisco on March 37
24 to attend the NERDA convention and visit 46
with a few prospective customers. 53

I will arrive on Sunday, March 24, at 7:40 61
p.m. on TWA Flight 233. I would very much 70
appreciate it if you could meet me at the air- 79
port and then join me for dinner with Messrs. 88
Tate and Mancini of Redwood Electronics. 96

I will spend all day Monday at the NERDA 104
convention. On Tuesday I will be with officials 114
of Empire Electronics in San Carlos. I'd like 124
you to spend that day with me also. 131

If you have any questions, please give me a 139
call. 140

FORMS 48–49
INVOICES

Paper: Workguide 445

Mrs. Cull has asked you to type the following two invoices. Get the price information for the items from the price schedule you typed (page 348). Be sure that your calculations for unit price, total price, and total cost are accurate. Include the catalog number along with the item name in the Description column.

The first invoice (#1130) goes to R & S Systems at 156 Oaktree Road, Sikeston, MO 63801. We have shipped them 2 Entry Delay Warning Devices, 2 Automatic Alarm Shutoffs, and 1 Panic Alarm.

The second invoice (#1131) goes to Bentley & Sons, 11 Westfield Place, Clarinda, IA 51632. We have shipped them 2 Combustion Detectors, 2 Delay Disable Switches, and 1 Security Phone Dialer.

21-F. SUSTAINED TYPING: SYLLABIC INTENSITY

21-F. Take a 1-minute timing on the first paragraph to establish your base speed. Then take successive 1-minute timings on the other paragraphs. As soon as you equal or exceed your base speed on one paragraph, advance to the next one.

26	One should always attempt to maintain good health. As	12
27	the first step in keeping good health, one should avoid the	24
28	habit of smoking. Volumes have been written on this topic.	36
29	A second habit that will help maintain your health for	12
30	decades is consuming an appropriate amount of water, day in	24
31	and day out; most physicians recommend eight glasses a day.	36
32	Making exercise a habit is another important trait for	12
33	staying in good health. Most experts agree that spending a	24
34	few minutes a day in regular, vigorous exercise is helpful.	36
35	A final habit of importance is maintaining appropriate	12
36	body weight. The key to maintaining weight is developing a	24
37	positive eating pattern. Calculating calories will assist.	36

| 1 | 2 | 3 | 4 | 5 | 6 | 7 | 8 | 9 | 10 | 11 | 12 |

21-G. WORD DIVISION

21-G. It is preferable not to divide a word at the end of a line. If it is necessary, however, follow the rules given here.

WP

Many word processors have an automatic hyphenation feature that will (a) automatically divide words too long to fit on one line or (b) highlight those words so that you can insert a hyphen at the appropriate point.

1. Do not divide (a) words pronounced as one syllable *(thoughts, planned)*, (b) contractions *(shouldn't, haven't)*, or (c) abbreviations *(UNICEF, assoc.)*.
2. Divide words only between syllables. Whenever you are unsure of where a syllable ends, consult a dictionary.
3. Leave at least three characters (the last will be a hyphen) on the upper line, and carry at least three characters (the last may be a punctuation mark) to the next line. Thus *de- lay* and *but- ter*, but not *a- maze* or *trick- y*.
4. Divide compound words either at the hyphen *(self- confidence)* or where the two words join to make a solid compound. Thus *master- piece*, not *mas- terpiece*.

21-H. PRODUCTION PRACTICE: WORD DIVISION

21-H. Select the words in each line that can be divided, and type them with a hyphen to show where the division should be (example: *con- sult*).

38	rhythm	aren't	going
39	safety	figment	ILGWU
40	grandfather	straight	planned
41	excess	because	couldn't
42	nation	mailbox	stressed
43	children	AMVETS	leading

21-I. CENTERING PRACTICE

21-I. Center a double-spaced copy on a half sheet of paper. Spread-center the heading, and block-center the body.

```
          S P R I N G   V A C A T I O N
          Daytona Beach, Florida
          March 24-31
          Leave from STUDENT CENTER
          Reasonable Cost for Food, Lodging, and Travel
          Call DEBBIE at 555-3244
```

REPORT 86
ANNOUNCEMENT

Paper: plain

Mrs. Cull has received this handwritten notice that Mr. Schober wants to have as an announcement of the new security system. Arrange it as an attractive one-page flier so that it can be distributed at the trade show in San Francisco. Type the notice as soon as possible so that Mr. Schober can consider any possible revisions before sending it to the printer. Arrange the material attractively on the page.

(ALL CAPS & CENTER) STRATEGIC SECURITY SYSTEMS — 10

(Spread-center) ANNOUNCES — 14

(CAPS & center) The OBSERVER -- MODEL 1023 — 24

(center) (A Complete, Inexpensive Home Security System) — 33

ss ← Strategic Security Systems is pleased to announce — 43
the introduction of its newest home security system-- — 54
the OBSERVER, MODEL 1023! — 59

Standard Features Include: — 64

5 → * State-of-the-art infrared motion detection system. — 74
* Built-in microprocessor to eliminate false alarms. — 85
* Eight door and window sensors for maximum security. — 95
ds * Combination 100-decibel siren and 300-watt strobe. — 106
* Battery power -- works through power failure! — 115
* Integral smoke/fire alarm. — 120
* Easy-to-use control panel. — 126
* Easy installation. — 130

ss ← Strategic Security is pleased to offer a two-year — 140
warranty with this new system. The cost — 148
of the system to dealers is $450. Suggested — 157
retail price is $625. Discounts available — 166
for large orders. — 169

ss ← For any technical questions about — 176
this new product, contact our engineers — 184
at 1-800-555-3473. For any sales infor- — 192
mation, contact our marketing personnel — 200
at 1-800-555-3797. — 203

SYMBOLS AND WORD DIVISION

Line: 60 spaces
Tab: 5
Spacing: single
Drills: 2 times
Format Guide: 13–14
Tape: 7B or K10B

Goals: To control the %, ', and '' keys; to type 28 wam/3'/5e.

22-A. WARMUP

S 1 Todd might fish in the big lake when he visits that island.
A 2 Jack quietly moved up front and seized the big ball of wax.
N 3 He went to Rome on May 30, 1975, and left on July 24, 1986.

22-B. PRACTICE THE % KEY

PERCENT is the shift of 5. Use the F finger.

4 ftf ft5f f5f f5%f f5%f f%%f f%%f 5% 55% 78% 52.5% 67.5% f%f
5 Saul was quoted rates of 8%, 9%, 11%, and 13% on the loans.
6 Ramos scored 93% on the test, Sue had 88%, and Al made 84%.

22-C. PRACTICE THE ' KEY

APOSTROPHE is to the right of the semicolon. Use the Sem finger.

7 ;'; ''' ;'; ''' Can't we go on Sue's boat and Chad's plane?
8 Pat's hat, Paul's gloves, and Steve's scarf were all taken.
9 It's Lynn's job to cover Maria's telephone when she's gone.

22-D. PRACTICE THE " KEY

QUOTATION is the shift of the apostrophe. Use the Sem finger.

10 ;'; '"' ;"; '"' "Super," she said.   "That was a super job."
11 The theme of next week's meeting is "Stress in the Office."
12 I watched "Meet the Mets" and "Yankee Power" on the screen.

22-E. Study these rules before typing lines 13–17.

22-E. PLACEMENT OF QUOTATION MARKS

Remember these rules about the placement of quotation marks:
1. The closing quotation mark is always typed *after* a period or comma but *before* a colon or semicolon.
2. The closing quotation mark is typed *after* a question mark or exclamation point if the quoted material is a question or an exclamation; otherwise, the quotation mark is typed *before* the question mark or exclamation point.

13 "Hello," she said.   "My name is Stephanie; I'm from Miami."
14 Sara read the article from the text, "Can She Succeed Now?"
15 You said, "I'll mail the check"; however, you didn't do it.
16 Did Jane end the meeting by saying, "We may hit our quota"?
17 Please mark the following items "Important":   G361 and F75.

SKILLBUILDING

22-F. NUMBER TYPING

18 She called us at 555-5873 with the 6 orders on September 7.
19 Read Chapters 7, 8, 9, and 10 on pages 60, 75, 85, and 100.
20 On May 28 we will expect to hear from 47 boys and 68 girls.
21 There were 395 votes for Tom, 649 for Sue, and 758 for Pat.

LETTER 95
COMPOSED LETTER

Paper: Workguide 433–434

Mr. Schober has just received this purchase order from Gull Electronics. Compose a letter to the firm indicating that the last two items will be shipped immediately; however, Model 1020 is no longer available. It has been replaced by Model 1023, which will be announced at the trade show in San Francisco. Explain that our sales agent in their area, Mr. Jack Osur, will contact them to explain the features of Model 1023 and that we will be delighted to ship it to them when Mr. Osur confirms the order. Enclose a copy of the promotional flier (page 351). Send a copy of the letter to Jack Osur.

GULL ELECTRONICS
57 Livingston Parkway
Moberly, MO 65270

Purchase Order No. 1574

To: Strategic Security Systems
11 Wilson Avenue
Kirkwood, MO 63122

Date: March 2, 19--

PLEASE SHIP AND BILL US FOR THE GOODS LISTED BELOW.
IF FOR ANY REASON YOU CANNOT DELIVER WITHIN 30 DAYS,
LET US KNOW AT ONCE. PLEASE REFER TO OUR PURCHASE
ORDER NUMBER (ABOVE) IN ALL COMMUNICATIONS.

QUANTITY	CAT. NO.	DESCRIPTION	UNIT PRICE	AMOUNT
2	SS-721	Alarm Processing System--Model 1020	399.75	799.50
4	SS-412	Automatic Alarm Shutoff	22.50	90.00
2	SS-232	Combustion Detector	61.50	123.00
		TOTAL		1,012.50

NOTE: YOUR BILL TO US SHOULD INDICATE ALL YOUR USUAL DIS-
COUNTS. PAYMENT WILL BE MADE UPON RECEIPT OF BILL WITH GOODS.

Sandra Walmach _____ Purchasing Agent

MEMO 33
COMPOSED MEMORANDUM

Paper: Workguide 435

Prepare a memo to Jack Osur, sales agent, informing him of the letter that was sent to Gull Electronics. Include a copy of the letter you wrote to Gull Electronics along with their purchase order. Ask Jack to contact them as soon as possible to finalize the order for Model 1023.

MEMO 34
COMPOSED MEMORANDUM

Paper: Workguide 437

Prepare a memo to Thomas Butler, Shipping Department, asking him to ship the automatic alarm shutoffs and the combustion detectors to Gull Electronics. Provide him with a copy of the purchase order, and give the reason for the partial shipment as you explained it in the letter to Gull Electronics.

22-G. CONCENTRATION PRACTICE

22-G. Spell out all numbers as you type lines 22–25. All lines will end evenly.

22 There were 4 girls and 7 boys at the birthday party.
23 We saw 2 movies, 4 concerts, and 5 plays last week.
24 She wants 2 more workers, 9 altogether, here at 7.
25 The 2 girls won 1st and 3rd place in the 6th event.

22-H. 12-SECOND SPRINTS

22-H. Take three 12-second timings on each line. The scale gives your wam speed for each 12-second timing. (If you cannot be timed, type each line twice.)

26 Plan to join our team at the mall when you finish your job.
27 When it is time to work, be sure that you do the very best.
28 Find a quiet place when it is time to do all your homework.
29 The trip being planned for this weekend should be pleasant.

```
        5    10    15    20    25    30    35    40    45    50    55    60
```

22-I. PACED PRACTICE

Turn to the Paced Practice routine at the back of the book. Take several 2-minute timings, starting at the point where you left off the last time. Record your progress on Workguide page 6.

22-J. SKILL MEASUREMENT: 3-MINUTE TIMED WRITING

22-J. Spacing: double. Record your score.

30 Jobs in business require good communication skills for 12
31 success. Confirmation of this fact can be found in various 24
32 magazines and books. 28
33 It is expected that a new worker in business will have 40
34 the ability to speak and write clearly and properly. These 52
35 are critical skills. 56
36 While there are many attributes needed for success, it 68
37 should be obvious that having good communication skills can 80
38 be a gigantic asset. 84

```
 |   |   2   |   3   |   4   |   5   |   6   |   7   |   8   |   9   |  10  |  11  |  12
```

22-K. PRODUCTION PRACTICE: WORD DIVISION

22-K. Select the words that can be divided, and type them with a hyphen to show where the division should be (example: *under- stand*).

39 understand	USSR	maintain
40 along	thoughts	wasn't
41 abundant	staged	varsity
42 person	self-evident	planned
43 isn't	mailable	awake
44 NABTE	section	design
45 weighed	transmit	o'clock
46 withhold	breach	service
47 through	shouldn't	senator-elect

11 Wilson Avenue **STRATEGIC SECURITY SYSTEMS** Kirkwood, MO 63122

(314) 555-3400

March 5, 19--   3

Ms. Phyllis Berkowitz   7
15 Park East (Rd.)   10
Aurora, CO 80010   13

Dear Ms. Berkowitz: 17

I am pleased to learn that our add in the latest issue of the   29
magazine Electronics Developments has prompted you to seek more   42
information. Thank you for returning the inquiry card that   54
was part of that add.   58

Strategic Security is a comprehensive supplier of all types of security   73
systems that can be purchased for the home and/or business   84
establishment. Our newest security system, Model 1023, is   96
designed to alert you of a forced entry into a protected area   111
or signal an alarm if a fire alarm conditions exists. This   123
system becomes your Alarm Processing Center.   132

in the event
The burglar alarm section provides for ~~two~~ three zones of operation.   145
This enables the installation to be ~~broken down~~ separated into three   156
areas of protection. The fire alarm part of the system oper-   168
ates on a 24-hour basis. ~~and operates on~~ a one-zone concept.   179
                          It uses

Enclosed is a brochure that describes this system in detail.   191
Please review this information, and I will plan to have our few   203
marketing representative ~~agent~~ in your area contact you within the next ~~three~~   217
weeks to answer any questions you may have.   226

                                    Sincerely yours,   229
                               ds   Strategic Security Systems   234

                                    Frank Schober   237
                                    Marketing Manager   240

urs   241
Enclosures   243

SYMBOLS AND LINE-ENDING DECISIONS

Line: 60 spaces
Tab: 5
Spacing: single
Drills: 2 times
Workguide: 33–34
Format Guide: 13–14
Tape: 8B or K11B

Goals: To control the &, $, and _ keys; to make correct line-ending decisions; to improve speed and accuracy.

23-A. WARMUP

S 1 If the work is done correctly, the group may make a profit.
A 2 Working quietly, Max alphabetized the census of vital jobs.
N 3 Our store will be open from 7:30 to 9:45 on December 18-26.

&
7
AMPERSAND (sign for *and*) is the shift of 7. Use the J finger.

23-B. PRACTICE THE & KEY

4 juj ju7j j7j j7&j j&&j j&&j Max & Di & Sue & Tom & Vi & Kay
5 The case of Ball & Trup vs. Crane & Vens will start May 10.
6 Rudd & Sons bought their ten tickets from Cross & Thompson.

$
4
DOLLAR is the shift of 4. Use the F finger.

23-C. PRACTICE THE $ KEY

7 frf fr4f f4f f4$f f$$f f$$f $44, $444, $4,444, $44.40, $440
8 She received quotes of $48, $52, and $76 for the old radio.
9 Our insurance paid $625 for the accident; I paid only $150.

UNDERSCORE is the shift of the hyphen. Use the Sem finger.
Note: Underscore individual words separately; for a book title, underscore the entire title, including the spaces.

23-D. PRACTICE THE ⎯ KEY

10 ;p; ;p-; ;-; ;-_; ;__; ;__; wouldn't or couldn't; me or we;
11 Rebecca should use The American Heritage School Dictionary.
12 Be sure that you used the words to, too, and two correctly.

WP
Some word processing software has an automatic underscore feature that can underscore as you type. However, some programs require typing the copy first and then using a function key to underscore.

23-F. Select and insert *you, your,* or *you're* in place of each dash.

23-E. TECHNIQUE TYPING: SHIFT/CAPS LOCK

13 MR. ANGELO P. ANGELOZZI of 241 Fifth Avenue was the winner.
14 Will they be going to SAN DIEGO or to PITTSBURGH next week?
15 The important GAME pits EAST CHESTNUT HIGH vs. BATTON HIGH.
16 Our BETA SIGMA chapter will attend the meeting in PORTLAND.

23-F. CONCENTRATION PRACTICE

17 -- should buy -- three tickets to the show by next week.
18 -- quite correct when -- note that -- bill is wrong.
19 -- correct in noting that -- thoughts make -- happy.
20 -- should balance -- checkbook with -- bank statement.

N. INTEGRATED OFFICE PROJECT: STRATEGIC SECURITY SYSTEMS

Situation: Today is Monday, March 4. You are a secretary for Strategic Security Systems in Kirkwood, Missouri. You work for Mrs. Louise Cull, administrative assistant to Mr. Frank Schober, the marketing manager at Strategic. Working for Mrs. Cull, you perform a variety of tasks, including typing letters, memorandums, forms, tables, and reports. All letters from Strategic Security Systems are typed in the modified-block style with standard punctuation. The closing lines of all external communications include the name of the firm.

Sincerely yours,

STRATEGIC SECURITY SYSTEMS

(Name)
(Title)

FORM 47   Paper: Workguide 425
JOB PRIORITY LIST

Before you begin your work, review the items in the project. Then, on Workguide page 425, assign a 1, 2, or 3 priority to each item.

TABLE 65   Paper: Workguide 427
PRICE SCHEDULE

Mr. Schober has dictated the following material. Please transcribe it.

This is Mr. Schober. I would like to have a price list of selected products that are optional for our security systems. Put the information in a table format, with the title Price Schedule for Security Systems Optional Items. *As a subtitle for the table, use* Prices Effective April 1, 19—. *Type it double-spaced on our letterhead; I don't need this until next week.*

Column headings are item . . . catalog number . . . dealer cost . . . *and* suggested resale price . . .

the first entry is entry delay warning device . . . *the catalog number is* SS-105 . . . *the dealer cost is*

$59.95 . . . *the suggested resale price is* $79.90 . . . *the second entry is* combustion detector . . . SS-232 . . . $64.50 . . . $90.30 . . . *the third item is* delay disable switch . . . SS-351 . . . $19.95 . . . $25.60 . . . *the next item is* automatic alarm shutoff . . . SS-412 . . . $24.00 . . . $33.60 . . . *the next item is* panic alarm . . . SS-514 . . . $39.95 . . . $54.00 . . . *the final item is* security phone dialer . . . SS-601 . . . $14.95 . . . $19.90.

LETTERS 93–94   Paper: Workguide 429–432

Mrs. Cull has attached this note to the letter on the next page. Please follow the instructions.

Mr. Schober would like these two letters to be sent out as soon as possible. Please type the first letter to Ms. Berkowitz. Then make changes as needed and type the same letter to Roger A. Allgor, 1151 Tall Oaks Drive, Ft. Dodge, Iowa. Look up the ZIP Code for Mr. Allgor's address.

23-G. NUMBER TYPING

23-G. Take two 1-minute timings. Note that the last two digits of each number provide a cumulative word count to help you determine your speed.

21	4701	3802	2903	1004	5605	7406	8307	9208	6509	4710	3811	2912
22	1013	5614	7415	8316	9217	6518	4719	3820	2921	1022	5623	7424
23	8325	9226	6527	4728	3829	2930	1031	5632	7433	8334	9235	6536
24	4737	3838	2939	1040	5641	7442	8343	9244	6545	4746	3847	2948

23-H. MAKING LINE-ENDING DECISIONS

23-H. Not all typewriters are alike, so check yours to see how many spaces are left after the warning bell rings and before the keys lock at the right margin.

WP
Computers and word processors have an automatic carrier return called *word wrap* that advances to the next line as each line becomes full. The automatic word wrap eliminates the need for a manual return at the end of a line.

When you cannot type material line for line, you must decide where each line should end. To help you end lines *without looking up*, a bell rings when the carrier is 8 to 10 spaces from the right margin. For example, if you wish lines to end at 75 and have therefore set the margin at 80, the bell may ring when the carrier reaches 70—signaling that you have 10 spaces left before the keys lock at the margin, and only 5 spaces left before you reach the *desired* ending point of 75. When the bell rings, end the line as near to the *desired* line ending as possible (preferably without dividing a word).

For example, if your typewriter gives an 8-space warning, here are some typical line-ending decisions you might encounter:

DESIRED ENDING		RETURN AFTER TYPING
BELL	LOCK	
Winter isn't pleasant		isn't
With pleasant hopes		pleasant
The calamity struck		calamity
Members maintained		main-

23-I. PRODUCTION PRACTICE: LINE-ENDING DECISIONS

The timed writing in 22-J on page 40 is shown on a 60-space line. Set your margins for a 50-space line and type it again. Decide where to end each line. Listen for the bell and *do not look up*. If time permits, repeat the exercise using a 70-space line.

23-J. CENTERING PRACTICE

23-J. Center the exercise on a half sheet of paper. Spread-center the title, and block-center the notice.

N O T I C E ↓3

The Affirmative Action Committee will be meeting on Thursday, October 18, in Room C-310. The meeting will be chaired by Connie Walters, director. The following items will be discussed: ↓2

1. Current Profile of Support Personnel
2. Current Profile of Professional Staff
3. Revision of Reporting Forms
4. Change in Interviewing Form
5. Goal for Hiring of Support Personnel
6. Goal for Hiring of Professional Staff

K. Type this paragraph once, concentrating on each letter typed. Then take a few 1-minute timings, trying to increase your speed each time.

K. CONCENTRATION PRACTICE

45   El uso de la bicicleta es muy popular en Barranquilla.   12
46 Cuando el tiempo es bueno a toda la gente joven le gusta ir   24
47 a pasear en bicicletas. Me gusta ir a montar en bicicleta.   36

| 1 | 2 | 3 | 4 | 5 | 6 | 7 | 8 | 9 | 10 | 11 | 12 |

L. PACED PRACTICE

Turn to the Paced Practice routine at the back of the book. Take several 2-minute timings, starting at the point where you left off the last time. Record your progress on Workguide page 290.

M. Spacing: double. Record your score.

M. SKILL MEASUREMENT: 5-MINUTE TIMED WRITING

48   In the past two decades, we have noted an explosion in   12
49 the growth and development of electronic equipment. It has   24
50 been quite evident in all phases of our society. It can be   36
51 seen in the home, in schools, and in the workplace. It can   48
52 easily be noted in how we handle personal business.   58
53   It is becoming very common to find a home that has all   70
54 the new conveniences of the electronic world. Some of this   82
55 technology can be seen in elaborate stereo systems, compact   94
56 discs, videocassette recorders, and microwave ovens. Home-   106
57 owners are also buying many new telephone services.   116
58   When it comes to school, we are finding that using the   128
59 personal computer is having a big impact. Many schools are   140
60 making plans to be sure that all students are becoming more   152
61 proficient at operating and using the personal computer. A   164
62 student must be computer-literate for future living.   174
63   When it comes to the world of work, it is very evident   186
64 that electronics has been quite significant. Factories and   198
65 offices throughout the land have been making use of the new   210
66 technologies in order to improve the speed and quality with   222
67 which all different types of work can be completed.   232
68   In conducting personal business, it is possible to see   244
69 more and more use of new technology. Judging by the growth   256
70 of automated teller windows and the growing use of shopping   268
71 and banking at home, it is easy to recognize that the newer   280
72 technologies can help simplify our personal affairs.   290

| 1 | 2 | 3 | 4 | 5 | 6 | 7 | 8 | 9 | 10 | 11 | 12 |

Line: 60 spaces
Tab: 5
Spacing: single
Drills: 2 times
Format Guide: 13–14
Tape: 9B or K12B

LESSON
24

SYMBOLS AND ERROR CORRECTION

Goals: To control the @ and * keys; to learn different error-correction processes; to type 29 wam/3'/5e.

24-A. WARMUP

S 1 The downtown firms that produce maps of islands have moved.
A 2 The day her film took a prize box, Jacqueline was vigorous.
N 3 With 37,548 fans screaming, we won the game 10-9 on May 26.

24-B. PRACTICE THE @ KEY

@
2 AT is the shift of 2. Use the S finger.

4 sws sw2s s2s s2@s s2@s s@@s s@@s Buy 15 @ $44 and 18 @ $55.
5 We will sell him 14 units @ $9, 8 units @ $15, and 5 @ $21.
6 Order 12 items @ $114, 9 @ $99, and another 18 items @ $87.

24-C. PRACTICE THE * KEY

*
8 ASTERISK is the shift of 8. Use the K finger.

7 kik ki8k k8k k8*k k8*k k**k k**k *** Tom's article* is new.
8 The * sign, the asterisk, is used for reference purposes.**
9 The asterisk symbol, ***, is ideal for typing a border. ***

SKILLBUILDING

PRETEST. Take a 1-minute timing; compute your speed and count errors.

24-D. PRETEST: COMMON LETTER COMBINATIONS

10   The manager tried to react with total control. He was   12
11 indeed annoyed and devoted all his efforts to being fair to   24
12 the entire staff. His daily schedule was rampant with ways   36
13 in which to confront the situation and to apply good sense.   48
    | 1 | 2 | 3 | 4 | 5 | 6 | 7 | 8 | 9 | 10 | 11 | 12

PRACTICE.
    Speed Emphasis: If you made 2 or fewer errors on the Pretest, type each line twice.
    Accuracy Emphasis: If you made 3 or more errors, type each group of lines (e.g., 14–17) as though it were a paragraph, twice.

24-E. PRACTICE: WORD BEGINNINGS

14 re relay react reply reuse reason record return results red
15 in index inept incur inset inning indeed insure interns ink
16 be beast berry being beeps berate belong became beavers bet
17 de dealt death decay devil detest devote derive depicts den

24-F. PRACTICE: WORD ENDINGS

18 ly dimly daily apply lowly barely deeply unruly finally sly
19 ed cured moved tamed tried amused billed busted creamed fed
20 nt mount blunt front stunt absent rodent splint rampant ant
21 al canal total local equal plural rental verbal logical pal

POSTTEST. Repeat the Pretest and compare performance.

24-G. POSTTEST: COMMON LETTER COMBINATIONS

24-H. ERROR CORRECTION

An error should be corrected as soon as it is made. Since you may not know when you make an error, however, always be sure to proofread your work carefully and

F. Take two 1-minute timings. Note that the last two digits of each number are a cumulative word count and give your wam speed.

F. NUMBER TYPING

16   3301 5502 6603 8804 2205 4406 9907 7708 1109 2110 3111 4112
17   5613 6714 2015 3816 9117 9018 3719 5220 1921 7922 5923 2024
18   8225 5026 4127 8728 4229 7930 2131 6432 5833 2834 3035 9736
19   1437 3638 1239 8240 5441 9142 3443 7844 6845 4046 9547 8248

G. This drill gives practice in typing words that end in *ant* or *ent*.

G. PRODUCTION PRACTICE: SPELLING

20   abundant applicant defendant important dominant significant
21   arrogant resistant attendant observant ignorant extravagant
22   apparent competent expedient insurgent accident independent
23   frequent impatient excellent different obedient magnificent

H. Tab: every 12 spaces.

H. TECHNIQUE TYPING: TAB KEY

24   Thomas   Brenda   Wesley   Carolyn   Michael
25   Virginia   Valentino   Gina   Ludevina   Dino
26   Venice   Munich   London   Moscow   Tokyo
27   Italy   Germany   England   Russia   Japan

I. Compare this paragraph with the last paragraph of the timing on page 347. Type a list of the words that contain errors, correcting the errors as you type.

I. PRODUCTION PRACTICE: PROOFREADING

28   In conducting personal busness, it is possible to see
29   more and more use of new technolgy. Judging by the growth
30   of autamated teller windows and the growing use of shoping
31   and banking at home, it is easy to recognise that the newer
32   technologies can help simplify our personel affairs.

J. Take a 1-minute timing on the first paragraph to establish your base speed. Then take several 1-minute timings on the other paragraphs. As soon as you equal or exceed your base speed on one paragraph, advance to the next one.

J. SUSTAINED TYPING: ROUGH DRAFT

33   When you begin a new job, a few things can help ensure   12
34   success. The first deals with getting along with others in   24
35   the workplace. Maintaining a good rapport with supervisors   36
36   and coworkers should always be a prime goal of new workers.   48

37   Listen~ing~ carefully to instructions and endeavoring to   12
38   ~~finish~~ complete assigned tasks accurately are quite important. It   24
39   is ~~necessary~~ essential that a new worker understand what must be done   36
40   and then finish th~at~e task in an efficient, accurate manner.   48

41   Another useful tip is being a ~~cooperative~~ dependable worker. When   12
42   a new worker maintains a ~~fine~~ good attendance pattern, its just   24
43   like a good credit rating. Do not be late for work, and be   36
44   very certain that your absences from work are at a minimum.   48

     | 1 | 2 | 3 | 4 | 5 | 6 | 7 | 8 | 9 | 10 | 11 | 12

correct any errors that you find *before* removing the paper from the typewriter or before storing a document on a word processor. Correcting errors while the paper is still in the machine is much easier than having to reinsert the paper and align the type. Also, correcting an error on a computer before a document is stored saves the time of recalling the document and making the correction.

Use one of the following techniques to correct errors:

Correction Ribbon. Typewriters with correction capabilities contain a correction ribbon as well as a special backspace key that engages the correction ribbon. (1) Use the special backspace key to backspace to the error. (2) Retype the error so that the coating on the correction ribbon lifts the error off the typing page. (3) Type the correction.

Backspace/Strikeover. To correct an error on electronic typewriters, word processors, or computers: (1) Depress the backspace key or correction key to erase the incorrect characters. (2) Type the correct characters. The correct characters replace the incorrect ones. This method may vary according to the equipment used.

Correction Paper. Slips of paper that contain a light coating of chalk can also be used to correct an error. (1) Backspace to the error and place the correction paper between the typing paper and the typewriter ribbon (coated side toward the typing paper). (2) Retype the error. (The chalk from the correction paper will conceal the error.) (3) Remove the correction paper, backspace, and type the correction.

Correction Fluid. Correction fluid works similarly to correction paper in that it covers the error. (1) Turn the paper forward or backward. (2) Brush the fluid sparingly over the error. (3) Let the fluid dry. (4) Type the correction.

Typing Eraser. (1) Lift the paper bail and turn the platen to move the error into position for easy access. (2) To keep eraser crumbs from falling into the mechanism, move the carrier to the extreme left or right—away from the error. (3) Use a stiff ink eraser and a *light* up-and-down motion to erase the error. (4) Return to the typing line and type the correction.

24-I. Type lines 22–25; then make the following corrections:
Lines 22 and 23: Change *Kim* to *Jim.*
Lines 24 and 25: Change *four* to *five.*

24-I. PRODUCTION PRACTICE: ERROR CORRECTION

22 Kim's brother showed Kim how to fix the damaged automobile.
23 When Kim went to Sue's house, Kim found the old photograph.
24 The four students took twelve trips in the past four years.
25 Four errors are usually allowed in timings of four minutes.

| SKILLBUILDING |

24-J. Spacing: double.
Record your score.

24-J. SKILL MEASUREMENT: 3-MINUTE TIMED WRITING

26 Airports can be interesting places to visit. Being in   12
27 a crowded airport lobby will make one realize just how much   24
28 our society is on the move.   29
29   The number of people who fly on any given day is quite   41
30 high. Experts say the number of passengers will get higher   53
31 in the next several years.   58
32   As the number of flights increases at many airports, a   70
33 good number of flights are delayed in departing. Officials   82
34 hope to solve the problem.   87

| | | 2 | 3 | 4 | 5 | 6 | 7 | 8 | 9 | 10 | 11 | 12

INTEGRATED OFFICE
PROJECT: ELECTRONICS

Line: 60 spaces
Tab: 5, center
Spacing: single
Drills: 2 times
Workguide: 425–445
Format Guide: 163

GOALS FOR UNIT 33

1. To type 58 wam for 5 minutes with no more than 5 errors.
2. To format letters, invoices, reports, tables, and memorandums.
3. To apply rules for punctuation and capitalization in formatting.
4. To compose a business letter and memorandums.
5. To perform calculations.
6. To set priorities.
7. To use reference works.

A. WARMUP

S 1 When we went home, he took the pair of socks from the auto.
A 2 Jack requested that Liz buy six new games to have for Paul.
N 3 Model 4380 sold for $5,647.90 less 10 percent on August 21.

SKILLBUILDING

PRETEST. Take a 1-minute timing; compute your speed and count errors.

B. PRETEST: DISCRIMINATION PRACTICE

4   Losing income can make one very uneasy. Debts quickly   12
5   mount. A merry attitude gets flung aside, and the weeks in   24
6   which there is no income make one behave differently. This   36
7   is a time to look at all options and consider viable moves.   48

  | 1 | 2 | 3 | 4 | 5 | 6 | 7 | 8 | 9 | 10 | 11 | 12

PRACTICE.
  Speed Emphasis: If you made no errors on the Pretest, type each line twice.
  Accuracy Emphasis: If you made 1 or more errors on the Pretest, type each group of lines (as though it were a paragraph) twice.

C. PRACTICE: LEFT HAND

8   vbv bevy vibe above brave bevel beaver viable adverb behave
9   wew were week twine jewel where glowed twelve review brewer
10 ded dead bead added tweed edits graded doomed impede decide
11 fgf figs golf defog gaffe flung finger gifted flight forgot

D. PRACTICE: RIGHT HAND

12 klk milk like bulky klutz locks kettle linked buckle tackle
13 uyu your buys youth unify bushy uneasy yogurt runway hourly
14 oio boil oily ivory optic comic income orient losing choice
15 jhj jump head juror heavy eject hasten jovial reject wishes

POSTTEST. Repeat the Pretest and compare performance.

E. POSTTEST: DISCRIMINATION PRACTICE

Line: 60 spaces
Tab: 5
Spacing: single
Drills: 2 times
Format Guide: 13–16
Tape: 10B or K12B

SYMBOLS

Goals: To control optional symbols; to construct special symbols; to improve speed and accuracy.

25-A. WARMUP

S 1 Half of the corn in that big field may be cut by six hands.
A 2 Jack quietly gave some of his prize boxes to the dog owner.
N 3 The 29 teachers and 754 students arrived at 8:30 on May 16.

25-B. Take 1-minute timings on each paragraph. Then take a 2-minute timing on both paragraphs together. Stress technique and accuracy rather than speed.

25-B. SYMBOL TYPING

4   Sam said, "Order 33# of the #100 crates." You can try
5 to order them from Smith & Clay (call V & J if needed). If
6 the old price of 1 pound @ $3 holds, the total will be $99.
7   Since our 25% discount was not shown on Invoice #3434,
8 Mr. DeVries will not want to send the check for $543 unless
9 B & W sends a debit memo (or letter) to correct the record.

¢
6

CENT is the shift of 6 on some keyboards. Use the J finger.

!
1

EXCLAMATION is the shift of the 1 on most keyboards. Use the A finger.

+
=

EQUAL is to the right of the hyphen on most keyboards. Use the sem finger.

+
=

PLUS is the shift of EQUAL. Use the Sem finger.

25-C. PRACTICE THE ¢, !, =, AND + KEYS

10 jyj jy6j j6j j6¢j j6¢j j¢¢j j¢¢j Alan paid 6¢ and 56¢ each.
11 They spent 10¢, 29¢, 38¢, 47¢, and 56¢ for the new pencils.
12 aqa aq1a a1a a1!a a1!a a!!a a!!a Where! What! Why! When!
13 The blast-off is nearing: Five! Four! Three! Two! One!
14 ;=; ;=; ;==; ;==; ;==; Let A = 50; Let B = 75; Let C = 100!
15 If B = 10, then 60; if B = 20, then 70; if B = 30, then 80.
16 ;=; ;=+; ;=+; ;++; ;++; 8 + 8 = 16; 7 + 7 = 14; 6 + 6 = 12.
17 When you add 30 + 40 + 50 + 60 + 70 + 80 + 90, you get 420.

25-D. CONSTRUCTING SPECIAL SYMBOLS

times	18 What is 9 x 6?	Small letter x.
minus	19 129 - 73 = 56.	Hyphen.
divided by	20 121 ÷ 11 = 11.	Colon, backspace, hyphen.
feet and inches	21 Rose is 5' 7".	Apostrophe (feet), quotation marks (inches).
fractions	22 8/10 = 80/100.	Numerator, diagonal, denominator.
minutes and seconds	23 10' 45" to go.	Apostrophe (minutes), quotation mark (seconds).
exclamation	24 I will not go!	Period, backspace, apostrophe.
brackets	25 They /‾Indians‾/	Diagonals, with underscores facing inside.

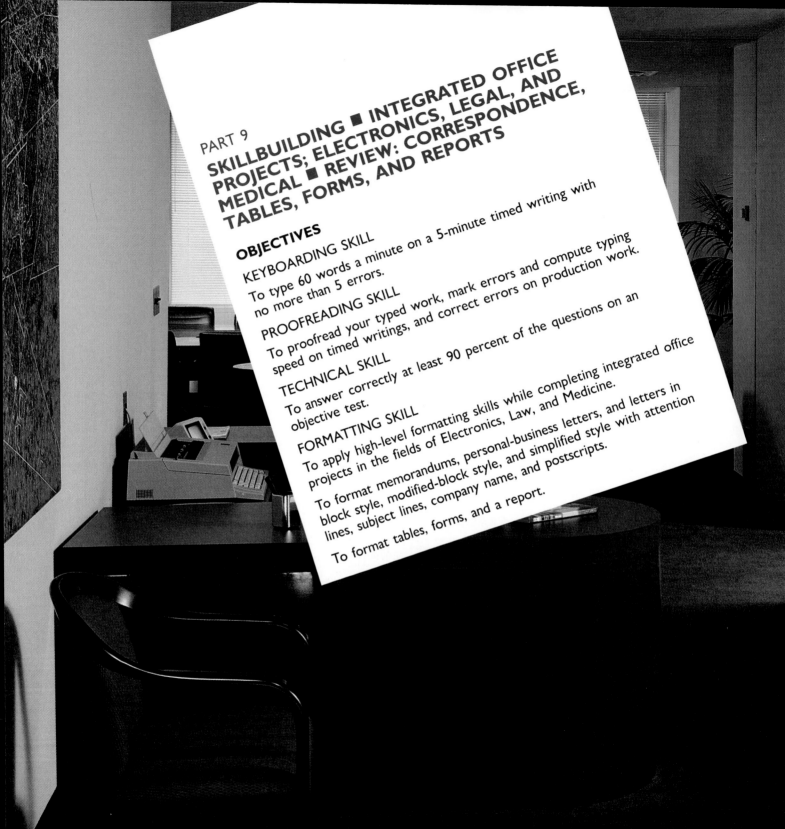

PART 9

SKILLBUILDING ■ INTEGRATED OFFICE PROJECTS; ELECTRONICS, LEGAL, AND MEDICAL ■ REVIEW: CORRESPONDENCE, TABLES, FORMS, AND REPORTS

OBJECTIVES

KEYBOARDING SKILL

To type 60 words a minute on a 5-minute timed writing with no more than 5 errors.

PROOFREADING SKILL

To proofread your typed work, mark errors and compute typing speed on timed writings, and correct errors on production work.

TECHNICAL SKILL

To answer correctly at least 90 percent of the questions on an objective test.

FORMATTING SKILL

To apply high-level formatting skills while completing integrated office projects in the fields of Electronics, Law, and Medicine.

To format memorandums, personal-business letters, and letters in block style, modified-block style, and simplified style with attention lines, subject lines, company name, and postscripts.

To format tables, forms, and a report.

25-E. TECHNIQUE TYPING: TAB KEY

25-E. Set tabs every 15 spaces. Use the tab key to go from column to column.

26	Being	productive	at	information
27	processing	will	be	enhanced
28	by	having	individuals	who
29	know	how	to	keyboard.

25-F. TECHNIQUE TYPING: RETURN/ENTER KEY

25-F. Type each sentence on a separate line.

30 Where are they going? Who is going? When will you return?
31 The hat was red. The scarf was pink. The gloves were tan.
32 Joe sang. Stu read. Ro walked. Vin cried. Pat screamed.
33 What score did you get on the test? Was it an improvement?

25-G. PRODUCTION PRACTICE: LINE-ENDING DECISIONS

The skill measurement timed writing in 24-J on page 44 is shown on a 60-space line. Set your margins for a 70-space line, and type the three paragraphs. Decide for yourself where to end each line. Listen for the bell and *do not look up*. If time permits, repeat this exercise using a 50-space line.

25-H. SUSTAINED TYPING: NUMBERS AND SYMBOLS

25-H. Take a 1-minute timing on the first paragraph to establish your base speed. Then take successive 1-minute timings on the other paragraphs. As soon as you equal or exceed your base speed on one paragraph, advance to the next one.

34   Our sales to Johnson & Clark showed an increase of 30%   12
35 over the same month last year. Last year we sold them $650   24
36 worth of merchandise in May; sales for this year were $845.   36
37   Shipment of items on Invoice #478 (radios, tape decks,   12
38 & stereos) was to be postponed to June 12. The delay would   24
39 mean that our cash flow for May would be reduced by $3,605.   36
40   Errors were found on these invoices: (#336, #391, and   12
41 #402). The errors resulted in a shortfall of revenue. For   24
42 the year, errors have gone up 22%. This must be corrected!   36
     | | | 2 | 3 | 4 | 5 | 6 | 7 | 8 | 9 | 10 | 11 | 12

25-I. 12-SECOND SPRINTS

25-I. Take three 12-second timings on each line. The scale gives your wam speed for each 12-second timing.

X 43 Max took the sixty extra index cards from the box for Alex.
J 44 Jack, John, and Jacob just enjoyed the juice from Al's jug.
Q 45 That unique equation on the quiz made Quentin quit quickly.
Z 46 Zeke was amazed at the prize that Lizzy won at that bazaar.

     5   10   15   20   25   30   35   40   45   50   55   60

25-J. CENTERING PRACTICE

25-J. Center a double-spaced copy on a half sheet of paper. Spread-center the title, and block-center the body.

P B L   W I N N E R S
Transcription: Eileen Murray
Public Speaking: Susan Angelozzi
Future Teacher: Stanley Barusiwicz
Typewriting: Stephen White
Shorthand: Mary Rubino
Business Math: Elaine Gallo

TEST 8-D
TABLE 64
RULED TABLE

Spacing: double
Paper: Workguide 421

SAVINGS RATES 3

Effective January 1, 19-- 8

Type	Rate	Minimum Amount	Annual Yield	
				10
				14
Passbook	5.50%	none	5.58%	18
Christmas Club	5.75%	none	5.83%	24
Check Plus	1.00%	none	1.00%	29
NOW Account	5.50%	$500.00	5.65%	34
Super NOW Account	5.50%	$1,000.00	5.65%	42
IRA Accounts:				44
Variable	7.00%	none	7.25%	49
Fixed	7.00%	none	7.25%	52
Money Market	7.00%	none	7.25%	58

TEST 8-E
MEMO 32
MEMO REPORT

Paper: Workguide 423

Please prepare a memo report addressed to All Employees from me, Joanne 4
Sloan-Riley, Manager. Use today's date and FCS (Favored Customer Service) as 18
the subject.

An exciting new dimension has been added to the PRIME frequent-flyer 32
program offered by National Airlines. All the usual benefits of PRIME will 47
continue as in the past. In addition, the FCS (Favored Customer Service) 62
system has been established. (*Now type a side heading labeled "Fea-* 68
tures.") Through the FCS system, we can now establish a special com- 81
puter file (for either an individual or a group) that automatically "re- 95
members" every travel request, from special menus to billing 107
procedures, and fulfills it with speed and accuracy. The profile can be 122
developed to reflect preferences in such items as flight times, aircraft, 136
seating, special services, car rentals, and hotels. (*Now type a second side* 147
heading labeled "Advantages.") One obvious advantage of FCS is the 156
saving of valuable time for both the traveler and the travel agent. It 170
assures the traveler of custom service every step of the way, with each 185
detail reliably confirmed. This type of personalized service will help 199
retain our clients so that we can continue to serve their travel needs. 213
(*Paragraph*) Copies of the brochure, *FCS Traveler Benefits,* will be dis- 225
tributed as soon as they are received. 232

LESSON 26

LETTER TYPING

Line: 60 spaces
Tab: 5
Spacing: single
Drills: 2 times
Workguide: 35–41
Format Guide: 15–16
Tape: 11B

Goals: To type 30 wam/3'/5e; to format a business letter.

26-A. WARMUP

S 1 They paid the four men to handle the forty bushels of corn.
A 2 Jay gave an expert a quick breakdown of all the sizes made.
N 3 Call 555-3190 and clarify our $826.47 charge for equipment.

SKILLBUILDING

26-B. Type lines 4–7 twice each. In these We-23 drills, each number uses the same reaches as the preceding word.

26-B. NUMBER TYPING

4 we 23 et 35 ore 943 tie 483 rot 495 toy 596 the 563 you 697
5 up 70 re 43 pie 083 ire 843 top 590 yet 635 owe 923 owl 929
6 it 85 or 94 yet 635 pup 070 wit 285 pit 085 out 975 rip 480
7 to 59 ie 83 pet 035 yet 635 two 529 tip 580 wet 235 put 075

26-C. Type line 8. Then type lines 9–11 reading the words from right to left.

26-C. CONCENTRATION PRACTICE

8 When keyboarding, always strive for complete concentration.
9 concentration. complete for strive always keyboarding, When
10 left. to right from sentence the typing by up looking Avoid
11 words. over skips often copy the from up looks who typist A

26-D. Compare this paragraph with the second paragraph of the letter on page 49. Type a list of the words that contain errors, correcting the errors as you type.

26-D. PRODUCTION PRACTICE: PROOFREADING

12 We would like to invite you to a special sesion, desined to
13 provide more detailed formation about our service, which we
14 are sponsering for people from the Dallas area. The session
15 will be held on Tuesday, March 6, in Raybern Hall of the
16 Dallas Convention center. It will begin at 9 a.m.

26-E. Spacing: double. Record your score.

26-E. SKILL MEASUREMENT: 3-MINUTE TIMED WRITING

17 Time is precious. Whether you are at work or at home, 12
18 you only have a set number of hours at your disposal. Plan 24
19 to use all your time wisely. 30
20 Employers like to see workers who zip along at a quick 42
21 pace. Of course, it is just as important that the work you 54
22 complete be free of mistakes. 60
23 Be sure that you take time for yourself at home. If a 72
24 few extra minutes or hours become available, consider doing 84
25 a special treat for yourself. 90

I am honored to be asked to present a paper at the Air Safety Collo- 94
quium that you have scheduled in connection with the opening of the 108
new aviation exhibit. I accept your invitation and will make plans to 122
attend the colloquium on August 21. 129

There are two topics that I might discuss. Please let me know which 143
one you prefer. 146
  1. The air safety records of domestic and foreign manufacturers. 159
  2. The air safety records of domestic and foreign airlines. 171
I shall look forward to both the opening of the aviation exhibit and the 185
colloquium. 188

TEST 8-C
FORM 46
EXPENSE REPORT

ALICE K. SLADE / Deputy Director   193

Paper: Workguide 419

EXPENSE REPORT

FROM __6/12/--__   NAME __Alice K. Slade__
TO __6/14/--__   LOCATION __Washington, DC - Chicago, IL__
DATE AUTHORIZED __6/4/--__   AUTHORIZED BY _____   PURPOSE OF TRIP __Meeting with Midway Airport Manager__

DATE	CITY	BREAKFAST	LUNCH	DINNER	HOTEL	Pub. Trans.	Car Rental	TOLLS	PHONE	1 ENTERTAINMENT	2 AUTO	3 MISC.	TOTAL
6/12	Chicago		11.25	24.00	100.58	188.00			6.85		6.40		337.08
6/13	Chicago	9.40			100.58				24.30	87.40		7.30	228.98
6/14	Chicago	8.70	12.20			188.00					6.40	48.00	263.30
TOTALS (Including Tips)		18.10	23.45	24.00	201.16	376.00			31.15	87.40	12.80	55.30	829.36

1 ENTER ALL REIMBURSABLE ENTERTAINMENT EXPENSES. LIST EACH OCCASION SEPARATELY. GIVE THE COMPLETE DETAILS OF WHO, WHERE, AND WHY. ENTER DAILY AMOUNTS UNDER #1 ABOVE.

ENTERTAINMENT

DATE	EXPLANATION	AMOUNT
6/13	Dinner with Jason E. Walker, Manager of Midway Airport; Michigan Shores Restaurant and Lounge, Chicago; Topic: Quarterly Air Safety Report	87.40

XXXXXXXXXXXXXXXXXXXXXXXXXXXXXXXXXXXXXXXXXXXXXXX   TOTAL   87.40

REQUEST FOR ADVANCE

CATEGORY	ESTIMATED EXPENSE	ACTUAL EXPENSE
FOOD/LODGING		
TRANSPORTATION		
ENTERTAINMENT		
MISC. (Tolls & Phone)		
TOTAL		
ADVANCE AMOUNT REQUESTED		

I DO HEREBY AGREE TO REPAY ANY AMOUNT NOT ACCOUNTED FOR WITH BUSINESS RECEIPTS WITHIN 30 DAYS OF FILING A COMPLETED EXPENSE REPORT.

Name _____ Date _____
APPROVED BY
_____ Date _____
ADVANCE RECEIVED BY
_____ Date _____

2 ALL AUTOMOBILE EXPENSES SHOULD BE ENTERED BELOW BY DATE INCURRED. SHOW MILEAGE FOR GAS. ENTER TOTAL UNDER #2 ABOVE.

AUTOMOBILE

DATE	EXPLANATION	AMOUNT
6/12	To airport from home (32 miles)	6.40
6/14	To home from airport (32 miles)	6.40

XXXXXXXXXXXXXXXX   TOTAL   12.80

3 ANY ADDITIONAL EXPENSE SHOULD BE ENTERED HERE WITH APPROPRIATE RECEIPTS BY DATE. ENTER TOTAL UNDER #3 ABOVE.

MISC.

DATE	EXPLANATION	AMOUNT
6/13	Supplies	7.30
6/14	Typing and Duplicating	36.00
	Airport Parking	12.00

XXXXXXXXXXXXXXXX   TOTAL   55.30

EXPENSE REPORT SUMMARY

TOTAL EXPENSES	829.36
LESS CHARGES	0.00
LESS CASH ADVANCE	0.00
AMT DUE	829.36
COMPLETED BY AND DATE	
AUDITED BY AND DATE	
APPROVED FOR PAYMENT BY AND DATE	

ATTACH RECEIPTS FOR ANY EXPENSES OVER $10.00. FILE EXPENSE REPORT WITHIN 2 WEEKS OF BUSINESS TRIP.

26-F. BASIC PARTS OF A BUSINESS LETTER

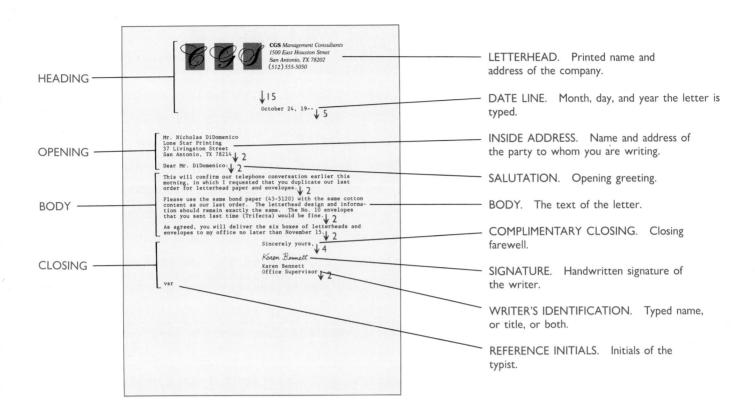

HEADING

OPENING

BODY

CLOSING

LETTERHEAD. Printed name and address of the company.

DATE LINE. Month, day, and year the letter is typed.

INSIDE ADDRESS. Name and address of the party to whom you are writing.

SALUTATION. Opening greeting.

BODY. The text of the letter.

COMPLIMENTARY CLOSING. Closing farewell.

SIGNATURE. Handwritten signature of the writer.

WRITER'S IDENTIFICATION. Typed name, or title, or both.

REFERENCE INITIALS. Initials of the typist.

26-G. FORMATTING A BUSINESS LETTER

Method 1: Using the Visual Guide. Detach Workguide page 37, the visual guide for letter placement. Read and follow the directions on the guide to correctly format business letters and to develop the judgment you need to estimate placement.

Method 2: Using a Placement Formula

1. For all letters use a 6-inch line (60 pica/70 elite). Set a tab stop at the center point.
2. Type the date on line 15 from the top of the paper, beginning at center.
3. Space down 5 lines, and type the inside address at the left margin on line 20.
4. Double-space before and after the salutation.

5. Single-space the body of the letter, but double-space between paragraphs.
6. Begin the complimentary closing at center, a double space below the body.
7. Begin the writer's identification at center, 4 lines below the complimentary closing.

Note: In order to make the letter appear centered on the page, you may adjust the number of blank lines—as few as 2 blank lines for a long letter to as many as 6 blank lines for a very short letter.

8. Type your initials at the left margin a double space below the last line of the writer's identification. Use lowercase letters without periods.

26-H. BUSINESS LETTERS

Complete Workguide pages 35–36 before typing the letters in this unit. Then, using the visual guide for letter placement on Workguide page 37 and the letterheads on Workguide pages 39 and 41, type the letters on the next page.

Ask your instructor for the General Information Test on Part 8.

PROGRESS TEST ON PART 8

```
             1                              2
As you move along in your career, you likely will find      12
     3                               4
that you spend significantly more time at various meetings.  24
   5                       6                      7
You will soon realize that superior decisions are made when  36
                         8                    9
persons share different points of view and thus become more  48
          10                  11                       12
informed about an issue.  As your career moves forward, you  60
                        13                    14
will want to acquire the very best group discussion skills.  72
          15                      16
Those who hope to influence other members of the group       84
     17                     18                      19
must be willing to do their homework.  This means that both  96
                 20                    21
sides of an issue must be explored in advance so that sound 108
         22                    23                       24
judgments can be made.  Even the unsophisticated members of 120
                       25                      26
a group will quickly detect that a speaker is not informed. 132
           27                        28
In addition to being knowledgeable about a topic under      144
      29                    30                       31
discussion, you will want to demonstrate a type of attitude 156
                 32                    33
that will attract others to your position.  A calm voice, a 168
        34                      35                      36
nondefensive manner, and a willingness to listen to persons 180
                        37                    38
with opposite views will be more fruitful than a squabbling 192
         39                    40
style.  People who retain their composure when those around 204
      41                    42                       43
them are falling apart earn the respect of their coworkers. 216
                 44                    45
You will be able to learn the art of compromise if you      228
        46                    47                       48
have an open mind.  Some people think that to compromise is 240
                        49                    50
to renounce one's integrity.  Nothing could be further from 252
              51                    52
the truth.  People who become good at making decisions know 264
    53                    54                       55
that positions may need to be modified.  There will even be 276
                      56                    57
times when opinions will be totally reversed.               285
| 1 | 2 | 3 | 4 | 5 | 6 | 7 | 8 | 9 | 10 | 11 | 12
```

Ask your instructor for the General Information Test on Part 8.

TEST 8-A
5-MINUTE TIMED WRITING

Line: 60 spaces
Tab: 5
Paper: Workguide 415

TEST 8-B
LETTER 92
INFORMAL GOVERNMENT LETTER

Line: 6½ inches (1-inch side margins)
Tab: 5
Paper: Workguide 417

June 12, 19— / Reply to attention of TPAS / Subject: Air Safety Collo-   7
quium on August 21, 19— / Mr. William R. Buchholz, Curator / Smith-   19
sonian Institution / 1000 Jefferson Drive, SW / Washington, DC 20560   31

Thank you for providing the update on your aviation history project   45
and the opening of your new aviation exhibit in August. Interested per-   59
sons throughout the world look forward to both the publication of the   73
history and the opening of the exhibit.   *(Continued on page 342.)*   81

LETTER 1
MODIFIED-BLOCK STYLE

Line: 6 inches (60 pica/70 elite)
Tab: center
Date: current
Paper: Workguide 39, 41

Leave 1 space between the state
and the ZIP Code.

Standard punctuation: Colon
after the salutation and comma
after the complimentary closing.

CGS *Management Consultants*
1500 East Houston Street
San Antonio, TX 78202
(512) 555-5050

(Current Date)   4

LETTER 2
MODIFIED-BLOCK STYLE

Using the same date, body, and
closing, retype Letter 1, addressing it to Mr. Charles LoPresti,
Personnel Manager, Sunbelt Financial Services, 1335 Johnson
Boulevard, Dallas, TX 75208.

Ms. Suzanne Dodds, President   10
Texas Business Forms, Inc.   15
15 South Walnut Street   19
Dallas, TX 75201   22

Dear Ms. Dodds: 25

Thank you for visiting our exhibit booth at the recent meeting   38
that was sponsored by the Texas Association for Training and   50
Development. We were extremely pleased with the number of   62
people who expressed an interest in our services.   72

We would like to invite you to a special session, designed to   84
provide more detailed information about our services, which we   97
are sponsoring for people from the Dallas area. The session   109
will be held on Tuesday, March 7, in Rayburn Hall of the   120
Dallas Convention Center. It will begin at 9 a.m.   130

If you would like to attend, please call my office for a   142
reservation. We would like you to be our guest at a luncheon   154
that will follow the morning session.   162

                    Sincerely yours,   165

                    Clifford G. Smiley   168
                    President   170

Type your own initials for the
reference initials.   vsr   171

Business letter in modified-block style with (*a*) date and closing lines beginning at center, (*b*) all other
lines beginning at left margin, and (*c*) single spacing.

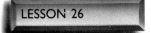

REPORT 84

Paper: plain

FORMAL REPORT IN OFFICE-STYLE DICTATION

Please transcribe this dictation of a formal report I've drafted. You'll need to "listen to" (*read through*) the entire dictation before starting to type, since I've made a few changes later in the dictation that affect the earlier parts of the report. Also, I would like you to look up some information in reference works to fill in various parts of the report.

The title of this report is Alamo Exploration Strategies, *with a byline* By Courtland J. Brantley, Jr. *Here is the body of the report.*   4 9 11

Ever since the Arab Oil Embargo of . . .   20

(*Would you please look up the year that the Arab Oil Embargo started and insert the correct year here.*)

. . ., the United States has enacted many measures to try to become more energy self-sufficient. As a result, today Americans are using energy more efficiently than ever before, and total oil consumption has declined since 1973.   27 36 46 55 64

At the same time that this country was trying to encourage greater exploration of its own energy resources, Congress was adopting such legislation as the Clean Water Act, which was passed in 75 84 93 103 106

(*Please look up the year that this act was passed and insert it here.*)

Thus oil exploration and refinery companies were, in fact, receiving mixed signals from the government: On the one hand, produce more; on the other hand, pay more attention to environmental concerns.   115 124 133 142 146

As Alamo and other oil companies develop their long-range plans, it is likely that such planning will continue to encompass both expanded production and expanded concern for the environment.   154 164 172 180 184

The U.S. government is now in the process of developing a request for proposals for commercial oil companies to explore off-shore sites under government jurisdiction. The site that Alamo is most interested in is off the coast of Maine, an area measuring about . . .   194 203 212 221 231 239

(*I know the area measures 200 square miles, but I don't know how many square kilometers that is. Would you please find out how to convert square miles to square kilometers and then insert the correct figure here.*)

. . . square kilometers.   243

It is likely that other companies will also be interested in this site. Specifically, Atlantic Richfield Company . . .   252 262 275

(*Please look up the address of this company's headquarters in Los Angeles and type it in parentheses here.*)

. . . will probably submit a bid. Mobil and Prairie Oil are also likely to be interested in this venture.   284 294 295

(*This report is getting so long that I will have to divide it into sections. Please insert a side heading labeled "The Dilemma" after the first paragraph and one labeled "The Stakes" after the third paragraph. Then, right here, insert the third side heading, labeled "The Recommendation."*)

Alamo should try to interest another, larger company in forming a limited partnership specifically to explore this new site. Dr. Armand Hammer, . . .   308 317 326 339

(*I'm not sure what Dr. Hammer's exact title is. Would you please look it up and put it here—for example, president of XYZ Company.*)

. . ., would be a key person to act as a go-between for us. He has wide industry and government contacts that would help us form a partnership in a timely and efficient manner.   347 356 364 373

REPORT 85

Paper: plain

COMPOSED ABSTRACT OF FORMAL REPORT

The report that you just transcribed is about 300 words long, and President Gaffga will want a shorter version to study. Would you please compose a summary (or abstract) of this report of 50 to 75 words. Use the same title and byline, but add the word *Abstract* as the subtitle. Since the abstract will be only one or two paragraphs long, you will not need side headings.

Line: 60 spaces
Tab: 5
Spacing: single
Drills: 2 times
Workguide: 43–47
Format Guide: 15–18
Tape: 12B

LESSON 27

BUSINESS LETTERS

Goals: To improve speed and accuracy; to format business letters.

27-A. WARMUP

S 1 The eight men plan to go to the lake so that they can fish.
A 2 Because he was very lazy, Jack paid for six games and quit.
N 3 Order No. 3874 for $165.20 did not arrive until October 19.

SKILLBUILDING

PRETEST. Take a 1-minute timing; compute your speed and count errors.

27-B. PRETEST: CLOSE REACHES

4   We were hoping to agree on the need to check the value   12
5 of our assets. No one should be opposed to finding answers   24
6 that would give us our worth. Old records and ledgers will   36
7 be sorted, and we will unite in our effort to get the data.   48
   | 1 | 2 | 3 | 4 | 5 | 6 | 7 | 8 | 9 | 10 | 11 | 12

PRACTICE.
   Speed Emphasis: If you made 2 or fewer errors on the Pretest, type each line twice.
   Accuracy Emphasis: If you made 3 or more errors, type each group of lines (as though it were a paragraph) twice.

27-C. PRACTICE: ADJACENT KEYS

8 as ashes cases class asset astute passes chased creases ask
9 op optic ropes grope snoop oppose copied proper trooper top
10 we weave tweed towed weigh wealth twenty fewest answers wet
11 rt worth alert party smart artist sorted charts turtles art

27-D. PRACTICE: CONSECUTIVE FINGERS

12 sw sweet swarm swing swift switch answer swampy swims swirl
13 un undue bunch stung begun united punish outrun untie funny
14 gr grand agree angry grade growth egress hungry group graph
15 ol older solid tools spool volume evolve uphold olive scold

POSTTEST. Repeat the Pretest and compare performance.
27-F. The opening lines of a letter require the quick operation of the return key. Type these six opening lines 3 times as quickly as possible.

27-E. POSTTEST: CLOSE REACHES

27-F. PRODUCTION PRACTICE: LETTER PARTS

                    (Current Date) ↓5

Ms. Naomi Rodriquez
Rex Travel Agency
18 South Liberty Place
Ogden, UT 84401 ↓2

Dear Ms. Rodriquez:

27-G. BUSINESS LETTERS

Use the visual guide for letter placement on Workguide page 37 and the letterheads on Workguide pages 43–47 to type Letters 3–5 on page 51. Use a 6-inch line (60 pica/70 elite spaces) and the modified-block style illustrated on page 49.

Please prepare two purchase orders for equipment we'll need for our new engineering wing here at headquarters. Please calculate the totals for the Amount column.

Since both companies we're purchasing from pay the shipping costs if the order is accompanied by payment, please prepare two voucher checks for the total amount due for each purchase order. In the Memo blank on the checks, type "Purchase Order (*number*)." On the voucher, type "Check (*number*), dated August 14, 19—, in payment of Purchase Order (*number*)." Then type the payee's name and address in the blank on the voucher.

FORMS 42–43
PURCHASE ORDERS
Paper: Workguide 411

FORMS 44–45
VOUCHER CHECKS
Paper: Workguide 413

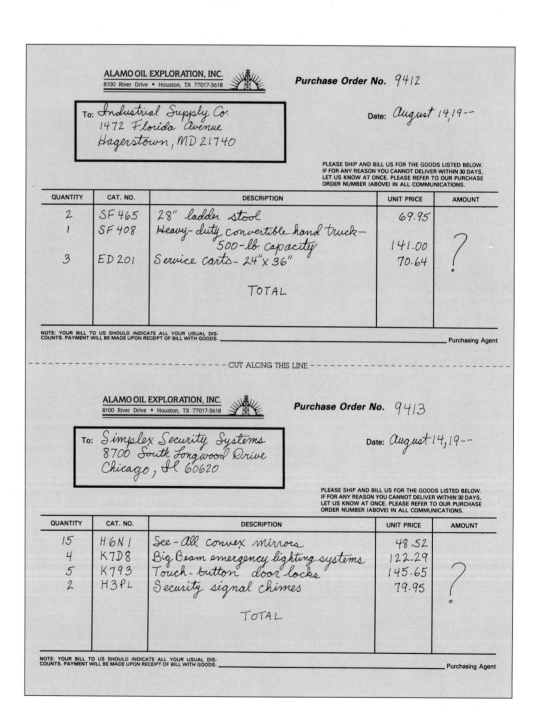

TITLES IN BUSINESS CORRESPONDENCE

Courtesy titles always precede an individual's name in the inside address of a letter; for example, *Mr., Mrs., Ms.,* or *Dr.* In the closing lines, however, a courtesy title does not precede a man's name; a woman may include a courtesy title in either her handwritten name or her typed name.

A job title may be typed on the same line as the person's name, on a line by itself, or on the same line as the company name, depending on which arrangement gives the best visual balance.

INSIDE ADDRESS:	CLOSING LINES:
Mr. Joel Chiang, President Fairweather Travel, Inc.	Sincerely yours, *(Ms) Pilar Figueroa*
Dr. Maryellen B. Gorman Resident Physician Westfield Medical Center	Pilar Figueroa Loan Officer Cordially yours,
Ms. Charlotte Townfield Manager, Grove Finances	*Kathy Troy* Miss Kathy Troy, Manager Personnel Department

LETTER 3
MODIFIED-BLOCK STYLE

Line: 6 inches (60 pica/70 elite)
Tab: center
Date: line 15
Paper: Workguide 43

(Current Date) / Mr. Raymond Bentley / Personnel Director / Adam	12
Metal Products / P.O. Box 408 / Stillwater, OK 74074 / Dear Mr. Bentley:	25
Thank you for responding to our advertisement regarding the special	39
seminars we sponsor for supervisory and middle management personnel.	52
We are in a position to provide a series of classes and/or seminars for	67
the supervisors at your plant, or if you prefer, we can invite you to enroll	82
selected supervisors at workshops that will be held in your area for	96
individuals from various firms.	102
I will call you next week to set up an appointment so that I can explain	117
our programs and answer any questions you may have.	127
Sincerely yours, / Clifford G. Smiley / President / *(Your Initials)*	136

LETTER 4
MODIFIED-BLOCK STYLE

Paper: Workguide 45

(Current Date) / Ms. Dorothy Garcia, Manager / Kearfott Defense Sys-	13
tems / 1130 Lee Highway / San Angelo, TX 76903 / Dear Ms. Garcia:	25
Thank you for your complimentary letter concerning the seminars we	38
sponsored for your supervisors last week.	46
I plan to share your letter with our instructor, Mr. Edward Min. I know	61
he will be delighted with the rating he received and with the comments	75
that were included by some of the participants.	85
I think that your suggestion for a follow-up seminar with Mr. Min is an	99
excellent idea. I will call you early next month to discuss possible dates.	114
Yours truly, / (Ms.) Luanne A. Chekarsky / Training Director / *(Your*	126
Initials)	

LETTER 5
MODIFIED-BLOCK STYLE

Paper: Workguide 47

(Current Date) / Mr. Charles McGinnis, President / Schiffenhaus, Inc. /	14
61A Binghamton Place / Roswell, NM 88201 / Dear Mr. McGinnis:	25
Use the same body and closing lines as in Letter 3.	136

Please type an itinerary for my upcoming California trip. Arrange the material attractively on the page.

ITINERARY FOR C. J. BRANTLEY
September 8-10, 19--

Monday, September 8

1 p.m.   Leave for airport; United Flight 834
                         to Los Angeles leaves at 2:45 p.m.

4:05 p.m.   Arrive LAX; met by Adam Broderick, chief
                         engineer, Natural Gas Division. Single-
                         room reservation guaranteed for late
                         arrival at Airport Hilton.

7 p.m.   Dinner at Hollywood & Vine Restaurant;
                         party of four: C. J. Brantley (host),
                         Adam Broderick, Ethel Agnew (Wastewater
                         Management, Inc.), and Roger L. Schutte
                         (Bureau of Land Management).

Tuesday, September 9

9 a.m. - 1 p.m.   Tour of wastewater treatment plants in
                         southern California.

Afternoon & Evening   Free; stay overnight at Airport Hilton.

Wednesday, September 10

8:45 a.m.   Leave for LAX airport; American Flight
                         206 to Sacramento leaves at 10 a.m.;
                         arrives at 11:15 a.m. Take taxi to
                         state capitol.

12 noon   Lunch with Assemblyman O. J. Wolfe at
                         J. C. Crawford's. Topic: Senate Bill
                         1045-68 (Clean Rivers Amendment).

Afternoon   Call on various legislators as avail-
                         able. Accompanied by Assemblyman Wolfe.

5:30 p.m.   Leave for airport; United Flight 307
                         to Houston leaves at 7 p.m.; arrives
                         in Houston at 11:15 p.m.

Line: 60 spaces
Tab: 5
Spacing: single
Drills: 2 times
Workguide: 49–51
Format Guide: 17–18
Tape: 12B

LESSON 28

BUSINESS LETTERS

Goals: To type 31 wam/3'/5e; to format business letters.

28-A. WARMUP

S 1 They may wish to help me fight the problem to the very end.
A 2 David quickly put the frozen jars away in small gray boxes.
N 3 Al's sales for the last month went from $35,786 to $41,290.

SKILLBUILDING

28-B. PROGRESSIVE PRACTICE: ALPHABET

Turn to the Progressive Practice: Alphabet routine at the back of the book. Take several 30-second timings, starting at the point where you left off the last time. Record your progress on Workguide page 5.

28-C. Take two 1-minute timings. The last two digits of each number provide a cumulative word count to help you determine your wam speed.

28-C. NUMBER TYPING

4 3801 4702 1803 9304 6305 8006 2807 3308 5909 6110 9011 1212
5 4813 1914 7915 5316 8117 2418 7619 3720 9421 5922 7023 2324
6 8825 4126 6827 3128 9629 7530 5831 2632 1733 8834 6235 4036
7 2737 8538 5539 1140 3941 4642 9943 6744 7345 8146 3947 5248

28-D. Type lines 8–11 twice each. Then take two 1-minute timings on lines 12–15.

28-D. SYMBOL TYPING

8 sws sw2s s2s s@s s2s@s s2@s frf fr4f f4f f$f f4f$f f4$f $44
9 lol lo9l 191 1(1 191(1 19(1 ded de3d d3d d#d d3d#d d3#d #33
10 ju7 ju7j j7j j&j j7j&j j7&j frf fr5f f5f f%f f5f%f f5%f 55%
11 ;p; ;p0; ;0; ;); ;0;); ;0); kik ki8k k8k k*k k8k*k k8*k ***
12 Invoice #3212 to Klekburg & Baines requested the following:
13 (1) 9 disks @ $2.60 each, (2) 7 tapes @ $2 each, (3) 8 pens
14 @ $1.10 each, and 18 records @ $6 each. The total for this
15 bill is $154.20, with a 7% sales tax adding another $10.79.

28-E. Spacing: double. Record your score.

28-E. SKILL MEASUREMENT: 3-MINUTE TIMED WRITING

16   Have you ever heard it said that attitude can help you   12
17 achieve a higher altitude than your aptitude? Just think a   24
18 minute about what this is implying.   31
19   It is still essential that you acquire many skills and   43
20 that you learn all the important concepts and principles of   55
21 the career that you might pursue.   62
22   Keep in mind, though, that experts say that it is your   74
23 attitude that helps you get to the top. How do you size up   86
24 when one evaluates your attitude?   93
   | 1 | 2 | 3 | 4 | 5 | 6 | 7 | 8 | 9 | 10 | 11 | 12

MEMO 31
MEMO REPORT

Paper: plain

Yesterday (August 12), President Gaffga asked me to draft a memo for him. Please prepare a memo addressed to All Employees, Midland Refinery, from John F. Gaffga, President. The subject is Closing of Midland Refinery.

The purpose of this memorandum is to discuss 9
with you the Board of Directors' decision yes- 18
terday to close the refinery in Midland on De- 27
cember 31, 19—. (*Now type a side heading* 30
labeled "Reasons for Closing.") The stringent 37
legislation recently passed by the U.S. Con- 45
gress has made this action necessary. It would 55
cost more than $8 million to install new equip- 64
ment and to make extensive modifications in 73
our present plant that would enable us to con- 82
form to the new regulations. This amount can- 91
not be justified in light of the estimated de- 100
creased productivity of the refinery. 107
(*Paragraph*) Although recent installations 113
have reduced the amount of pollution dis- 121
charged into the atmosphere, our diligent ef- 130
forts to diminish pollution still do not enable 140
us to meet the new standards. Thus, in order to 150
comply with the law, we have made the painful 159
decision to close the refinery. (*The second side* 165
heading is labeled "Effect on Midland Work- 169
ers.") We appreciate fully the gravity of this 178
decision to our 460 valued Midland employ- 186
ees. Ms. Katherine Sandhusen, director of per- 195
sonnel, has been instructed to canvass the 204
nearby area to seek new positions for each of 213
you. Her staff will interview each of you to sug- 223
gest possible transfer to one of our other refin- 233
eries or to other companies. Possible early re- 242
tirement without penalty for employees over 251
age 55 will also be discussed. (*Paragraph*) 257
Please be assured that we will work with you 266
in every way possible to ensure financial secu- 275
rity for you and your families. More informa- 284
tion will be forthcoming shortly. 291

LETTER 91
BLOCK STYLE ON BARONIAL STATIONERY

Paper: Workguide 409–410

I drafted this letter in a hurry on my portable computer. Please clean it up and type it in block style on baronial stationery. Correct any errors you find.

Mr. Steven Small, Engineer 5
City of Edmond 8
2105 Stepping Stone Trail 13
Edmond, OK 73034 16

Dear Steve: 18

Thank you again for the priviledge of examining 28
your municipal wastewater installation. Largely 38
because of my visit, our subsidiary the salem pa- 47
per company has resolved to build a wastewater 57
treatment plant as soon as possible. 64

Could you suggest reference sources that our Engineers 75
should study before we commit ourselfs to a con- 85
tract for this custom-built plant? 92

Again Steve I appreciate you guidance on this 101
project. Please let me know when I can return the 112
favor. 113

Sincerly, 115

Courtland J. Brantley, Jr. 120
Manager, Enviromnental Control 126

LETTER 6
MODIFIED-BLOCK STYLE

Paper: Workguide 49

28-F. BUSINESS LETTERS

Use the date April 15 to type this letter from Luanne A. Chekarsky / Training Director. Send the letter to Ms. Charlotte Luna / Personnel Manager / Wilmont Financial Securities / 1575 Longhorn Boulevard / Corpus Christi, TX 78402 / (Supply a salutation and closing lines.)

In reviewing my records, I note that we submitted	10
a proposal to you on March 15 to conduct two seminars	21
for your administrative support personnel during the	31
week of June 24.	35
If you are still interested in having these workshops,	46
please let me know within the next two weeks so	55
that I can schedule the speaker and prepare the	65
necessary materials.	69
If I do not hear from you by May 1, I will	77
assume that you no longer wish to sponsor the	87
seminar at this time. If you have any questions or	97
need further information, please don't hesitate to call me.	109

LETTER 7
MODIFIED-BLOCK STYLE

Paper: Workguide 51

Use the date April 15 to type this letter from Clifford G. Smiley / President. Send the letter to Mr. Wayne Johnson / Johnson Travel Agency / 1107 Cedarcrest Avenue / San Antonio, TX 78204 / Dear Wayne: / (Supply an appropriate closing.)

I am delighted that you will be able to make	9
arrangements for our company-sponsored trip to Hawaii	20
during the second week of July. As I indicated to	30
you on the phone, this trip is an incentive bonus for	41
employees who demonstrated consistently superior performance	53
during the last 12 months.	58
Enclosed are the names and addresses of the individuals	69
who have won this recognition. The group will leave together	82
from the local airport. I understand that there will be	93
one stop in Los Angeles on the way to Honolulu. Is that	105
correct?	106
When you have all the information regarding time of	117
departure and hotel reservations, please call me so that	128
I can stop by to discuss the arrangements with you.	138

Note: To indicate that an item is enclosed with a letter, type the word *Enclosure* a single space below the reference initials of a business letter. Example:

```
urs
Enclosure
```

Insert an enclosure notation in the closing lines.

Please type these minutes in final format. Type the title & side headings in all capitals & triple-space between sections.

CJB

Refinery Consultants' Conference
Minutes of the Meeting
August 1, 19--

Attendance	Alamo Operations Committee; Evan Rudolph, Editor, Petroleum Weekly; Sharon J. Sink, General Manager, Midland Refinery; George L. Weaver, Professor of Petroleum Economics, Texas A & M University; Thomas Weirich, Senior Partner, Woodridge and Weirich.	26 36 46 55 64 65
Introduction	C. J. Brantley, Manager of Environmental Control, called the conference to order at 8:30 a.m. He discussed the major purpose of the conference: to provide information to help the Operations Committee determine whether to close Midland Refinery.	78 88 98 108 117
Midland Financial Conditions	Sharon Sink discussed financial conditions at Midland and the effect new federal legislation will have on profitability.	129 141 146
Industry Update	George Weaver discussed current economic trends in the energy industry in general and the petroleum industry in particular.	158 169 174
Washington Outlook	Evan Rudolph discussed current and proposed federal legislation that affects the oil industry, especially the pending antitrust legislation regarding Consolidated Oil.	186 198 207 210
Environmental Concerns	Tom Weirich discussed the political and social trends regarding environmental concerns. He also summarized the recent public opinion poll Alamo commissioned regarding public attitudes about the environment.	222 233 242 250 256
Adjournment	The meeting was adjourned at 3 p.m.	265

PERSONAL-BUSINESS LETTERS

Line: 60 spaces
Tab: 5
Spacing: single
Drills: 2 times
Format Guide: 17–20
Tape: 13B

Goals: To improve speed and accuracy; to format personal-business letters.

29-A. WARMUP

S 1 Go to the mall and see what might be the problem with Todd.
A 2 Two sax players in the jazz band gave a quick demo for Tom.
N 3 Seats 30, 31, 47, 48, 56, and 57 in Section 29 were unsold.

SKILLBUILDING

29-B. PROGRESSIVE PRACTICE: NUMBERS

Turn to the Progressive Practice: Numbers routine at the back of the book. Take several 30-second timings, starting at the point where you left off the last time. Record your progress on Workguide page 5.

29-C. Take a 1-minute timing on the first paragraph to establish your base speed. Then take successive 1-minute timings on the other paragraphs. As soon as you equal or exceed your base speed on one paragraph, advance to the next one.

29-C. SUSTAINED TYPING: SYLLABIC INTENSITY

4   There are many types of buyers to be found in society.   12
5 One common type is known as the bargain hound. This person   24
6 goes all out to find items marked below the sticker prices.   36
7   Another type of consumer is called an emotional buyer.   12
8 Buying decisions are made with the heart, not the head. It   24
9 seems this buyer is trying to buy a feeling, not an object.   36
10   A third type of consumer that can be identified is the   12
11 compulsive shopper. This buyer doesn't really need what is   24
12 purchased but continually desires to go on shopping binges.   36
13   The sensible shopper has the advantage over the others   12
14 described. This shopper establishes a dollar limit for the   24
15 needed purchases and then compares store prices for values.   36
    | 1 | 2 | 3 | 4 | 5 | 6 | 7 | 8 | 9 | 10 | 11 | 12

29-D. The closing lines of a letter require the quick operation of the return and tab keys. Type these closing lines 3 times as quickly as possible.

Tab: center

29-D. PRODUCTION PRACTICE: LETTER PARTS

TAB→   Sincerely yours, ↓4

TAB→   Thomas C. Butler
TAB→   Personnel Manager ↓2

urs
Enclosure

REPORT 81
MEETING AGENDA

Paper: plain

Please type a final copy of this meeting agenda. Use standard report margins, and triple-space between each item. (*See rough-draft agenda below.*)

POSTCARDS 6–8

Paper: Workguide 407–408

Please send a postcard to Dr. Weaver (Petroleum Economics Department, Texas A & M University, College Station, TX 77843). Use block style for the postcard and my complete name and title (Manager, Environmental Control) in the closing lines. Here's the message:

Just a short note to remind you that you are scheduled to speak on the topic "Industry Update" at our Refinery Consultants' Conference on August 1 in the Board of Directors' Room at our headquarters. Your presentation is scheduled from 10 a.m. until 11 a.m.

Please send the same postcard to Mr. Rudolph (Petroleum Weekly, P.O. Box 1076, Washington, DC 20013) and Mr. Weirich (Woodridge and Weirich, 4500 Spellman Road, Houston, TX 77035. Use the appropriate topic and times for each speaker.

	REFINERY CONSULTANT'S CONFERENCE	6
	Meeting Agenda	9
	August 1, 19--	12
8:30- 9:00	Introduction .... C. J. Brantley	19
9:00-10:00	Financial condition of Midland .... Sharon J. Sink	30
	(Ms. Sink is the general manager of Midland	39
	Refinery.)	41
10:00-11:00	Industry update .... Dr. George L. Weaver	49
	(Dr. Weaver is a professor of Petroleum Eco-	58
	nomics at Texas A & M University.)	65
11:00-12:00	The Washington outlook .... Evan Rudolph	74
	(Mr. Rudolph is the editor of Petroleum	82
	Weekly.)	83
12:00- 1:30	Luncheon .... Top of the Tens Restaurant	92
	(1021 Main Street, Houston)	98
1:30- 2:30	Environmental concerns .... Thomas Weirich	107
	(Mr. Weirich is the senior partner at Woodridge	116
	and Weirich, Environmental Consultants, Hous-	126
	ton.)	
2:30- 3:00	Conference Wrap-Up .... C. J. Brantley	135
3:00	Adjournment	138

29-E. FORMATTING PERSONAL-BUSINESS LETTERS

Personal-business letters are written to conduct one's own personal-business affairs. Since they are typed on plain paper, the writer's return address must be included as part of the letter. In the illustration below, the return address is typed below the name in the closing lines. This style, although not the traditional one, is becoming increasingly popular. In the more conventional style, the writer's address is typed above the date on lines 13 and 14. Reference initials are not used with either format.

LETTER 8
PERSONAL-BUSINESS LETTER IN MODIFIED-BLOCK STYLE

Line: 6 inches (60 pica/70 elite)
Tab: center
Date: line 15
Paper: plain

If a letter is addressed to a company rather than to an individual, the appropriate salutation is *Ladies and Gentlemen* or *Gentlemen*.

↓15

(Current Date)   4
↓5

Gonzales Investment Services   10
15 Plainfield Avenue   14
Ft. Lauderdale, FL 33302   18

Ladies and Gentlemen: 23

Your advertisement in today's newspaper is of great interest   35
to me. I have a certificate of deposit that will be maturing   47
in another six weeks, and I am considering the various   58
investment options that are open to me.   66

The ad states that you have a service available whereby a   78
representative from your firm will do a complete financial   89
analysis free of charge. I am interested in having such an   101
analysis done. Since I have a full-time job, it would be   113
necessary to have an evening appointment.   121

Please have someone call me at 555-8407 to arrange a time that   134
would be convenient. I am usually home from work by 6 p.m.   146
every day.   148
↓2

Sincerely yours,   151
↓4

(Miss) Karen S. Rinaldi   156
156 Pleasantview Drive   160
Dania, FL 33004   163

Reference initials are not needed in letters you type for yourself.

LETTER 9
PERSONAL-BUSINESS LETTER IN MODIFIED-BLOCK STYLE

Paper: plain

Using the same return address, date, body, and closing lines, retype Letter 8, addressing it to Mr. Roger Allgor / Empire Financial Services / 75 Canfield Avenue / Hollywood, FL 33003 / Dear Mr. Allgor:

O. INTEGRATED OFFICE PROJECT: ALAMO OIL EXPLORATION, INC.

Situation: Today is July 17, 19—, and you are secretary to Mr. Courtland J. Brantley, Jr., manager of Environmental Control at Alamo Oil Exploration, Inc., in Houston, Texas. In addition to its oil exploration and refining divisions, Alamo owns several subsidiary companies.

TABLE 63
ABSTRACTED TABLE
IN BOXED FORMAT

Paper: plain, full sheet

We are considering building a hydroelectric plant in the West in cooperation with the Western Utility Consortium. Please prepare a table showing the present hydroelectric plants in the states of California, Oregon, and Washington. Arrange the plants in descending order of capacity by state, with the states in alphabetic order. Single-space the items within each state, but double-space between states. We do not need the owners listed. Show the source of the data, and arrange the table in boxed format as shown below.

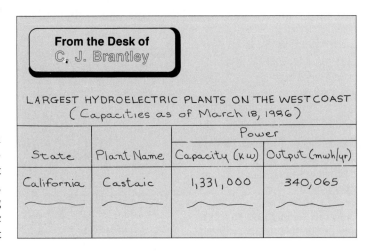

From the Desk of C. J. Brantley

LARGEST HYDROELECTRIC PLANTS ON THE WEST COAST
(Capacities as of March 18, 1986)

State	Plant Name	Power	
		Capacity (kw)	Output (mwh/yr)
California	Castaic	1,331,000	340,065

Largest Hydroelectric Plants in U.S.
(Capacities as of March 18, 1986)

Plant name	State	Owner	Installed capacity (kw)	Annual generation (mwh)
Coulee Dam	Washington	USBR-Pacific NW Region	6,494,000	19,124,443
John Day	Oregon	USCE-North Pacific Div.	2,160,000	10,429,203
Chief Joseph	Washington	USCE-North Pacific Div.	2,069,000	10,732,096
LD Pump Station	Michigan	Consumers Power Co.	1,978,800	−873,961
Moses Niagara	New York	Power Authy of St of N.Y.	1,950,000	17,316,318
Dalles Dam	Oregon	USCE-North Pacific Div.	1,806,800	8,169,938
Raccoon Mountain	Tennessee	Tennessee Valley Auth.	1,530,000	−408,424
Castaic	California	Los Angeles (City of)	1,331,000	340,065
Rocky Reach	Washington	Chelan Pub. Util. Dist. #1	1,213,950	6,521,378
Glen Canyon	Arizona	USBR-Upper Colorado Reg.	1,206,240	7,663,582
Helms	California	Pacific Gas & Electric	1,125,000	79,971
Bonneville	Oregon	USCE-North Pacific Div.	1,076,000	5,472,508
Bath County	Virginia	Virginia Elec. & Power Co.	1,050,000	−30,705
Blenheim G	New York	Power Authy of St of N.Y.	1,000,000	−982,674
McNary	Oregon	USCE-North Pacific Div.	980,000	6,843,037
Moses Dam	New York	Power Authy of St of N.Y.	912,000	7,282,683
Northfield Mountain	Massachusetts	W. Massachusetts Elec. Co.	846,000	−359,219
Boundary	Washington	Seattle (City of)	834,100	3,634,623
Wanapum	Washington	Grant Pub. Util. Dist. #2	831,250	4,879,769
Little Goose	Washington	USCE-North Pacific Div.	810,000	2,849,363
Monumental	Washington	USCE-North Pacific Div.	810,000	2,751,730
Lower Granite	Washington	USCE-North Pacific Div.	810,000	2,865,150
Muddy Run	Pennsylvania	Philadelphia Elec. Co.	800,000	−519,065
Priest Rapids	Washington	Grant Pub. Util. Dist. #2	788,500	4,991,728
Wells	Washington	Douglas Pub. Util. Dist. #1	774,300	3,973,404
Hoover Dam	Nevada	USBR-Lower Colorado Reg	672,500	4,308,659
Hoover Dam	Arizona	USBR-Lower Colorado Reg	667,500	3,844,416
Edward Hyatt	California	California (State of)	644,250	1,473,461
Wilson Dam	Alabama	Tennessee Valley Auth.	629,840	1,738,490
Rock Island	Washington	Chelan Pub. Util. Dist. #1	622,500	2,815,011
Jocassee	South Carolina	Duke Power Co.	610,000	−290,728
Ice Harbor	Washington	USCE-North Pacific Div.	603,000	2,664,426
Bear Swamp	Massachusetts	New England Elec. System	600,000	−151,062
Oahe	South Dakota	USCE-Omaha District	595,000	2,621,014
Brownlee	Idaho	Idaho Power Co.	585,400	2,983,072
Smith Mountain	Virginia	Appalachian Power Co.	547,250	6,570
Shasta Dam	California	USBR-Mid. Pacific Region	535,000	1,558,344

Source: *The World Almanac and Book of Facts, 1987,* Pharos Books, New York, 1986.

Line: 60 spaces
Tab: 5, center
Spacing: single
Drills: 2 times
Workguide: 53–55
Format Guide: 19–20
Tape: 13B

LESSON 30

LETTER REVIEW

Goals: To type 32 wam/3'/5e; to format personal-business and business letters.

30-A. WARMUP

S 1 The bills from last week came in the mail at the same time.
A 2 Zeb gave Holly six dozen pears to make two quarts of juice.
N 3 Our sales for May increased $13,470, to a total of $98,652.

SKILLBUILDING

30-B. Take three 12-second timings on each line. The scale gives your wam speed for each 12-second timing.

30-B. 12-SECOND SPRINTS

J 4 John just enjoyed a jitney ride with Jerry, Joan, and Jeff.
Q 5 Quincy was not quite equal to quoting the quip from Quebec.
Z 6 Zeblin was dazzled by the size of the prize for the puzzle.

| 5   10   15   20   25   30   35   40   45   50   55   60 |

30-C. Use the shift lock when a word or series of words is typed in all caps.

30-C. TECHNIQUE TYPING: SHIFT/CAPS LOCK

7 Send the package to CRANE TRAVEL AGENCY in SPRINGFIELD, IL.
8 The SAILING CARRIER leaves MIAMI every Saturday in OCTOBER.
9 They REQUEST that the DEBIT MEMO be sent by MARCH 15, 1992.
10 ANN PAIGE got the leading part of ISABELLE in MY HOME TOWN.

30-D. PRODUCTION PRACTICE: LINE-ENDING DECISIONS

The skill measurement timed writing in 28-E on page 52 is shown on a 60-space line. Set your margins for a 40-space line, and type the three paragraphs, deciding for yourself where to end each line. Listen for the bell; *do not look up.* After typing the paragraphs on a 40-space line, change your margins for a 50-space line and repeat the exercise.

30-E. Spacing: double. Record your score.

30-E. SKILL MEASUREMENT: 3-MINUTE TIMED WRITING

11   When you start a new office job, strive to learn about   12
12 the flow of work as quickly as possible. Explore how forms   24
13 and letters are processed and handled.   32
14   One way to learn about the flow of work is to consider   44
15 the roles that are played by each office worker. Strive to   56
16 learn about the work done by each one.   64
17   Think through how work is done in your office. If you   76
18 take time to analyze who does what and in what order, it is   88
19 likely that you will be a good worker.   96

| 1 | 1 | 1 | 2 | 1 | 3 | 1 | 4 | 1 | 5 | 1 | 6 | 1 | 7 | 1 | 8 | 1 | 9 | 1 | 10 | 1 | 11 | 1 | 12 |

L. Compare this paragraph with Section B on page 331. Type a list of the words that contain errors, correcting the errors as you type.

L. PRODUCTION PRACTICE: PROOFREADING

47   Janice and her escort were late for the dance at a re-
48 sort. The drumers in the band had just started playing as
49 they come in. It seems janice injured the back of her head
50 on the bank of the river, during a curise late that morning.

M. PROGRESSIVE PRACTICE: ALPHABET

Turn to the Progressive Practice: Alphabet routine at the back of the book. Take several 30-second timings, starting at the point where you left off the last time. Record your progress on Workguide page 289.

N. Spacing: double. Record your score.

N. SKILL MEASUREMENT: 5-MINUTE TIMED WRITING

51   In the early eighteen hundreds, Americans were writing   12
52 with goose-quill pens that were dipped in ink made of poke-   24
53 berry juices. The only pencils available were manufactured   36
54 in Europe and cost one quarter. During that period a quar-   48
55 ter would buy one week's worth of groceries.   57
56   American sailing ships returning from the Orient would   69
57 have the holds filled with graphite for ballast. This min-   81
58 eral was selected because it was heavy, easy to handle, and   93
59 cheap. Upon landing, the sailors dumped that graphite into   105
60 the shallow waters of the bay, abandoning it.   114
61   An enterprising young American pulverized the graphite   126
62 and mixed it with clay. Then he added just enough water to   138
63 make a stiff dough. Rolling this into the form of a cylin-   150
64 der, he baked the pencil lead in a brick oven. The problem   162
65 was how to insert the lead inside the pencil.   171
66   He cut two pieces of round cedar wood, making a groove   183
67 down the center of the flat, inside surface. He placed the   195
68 hardened lead in the groove of one of the pieces, glued the   207
69 two separate sections together, and then sharpened the end.   219
70 This became the first pencil made in America.   228
71   It was not a perfect instrument, but a beginning. The   240
72 pencil business, however, didn't make any headway until the   252
73 Civil War; soldiers wanted to write letters home, but quill   264
74 pens and pokeberry ink couldn't be carried in backpacks. A   276
75 portable writing instrument was the solution.   285

    | 1 | 2 | 3 | 4 | 5 | 6 | 7 | 8 | 9 | 10 | 11 | 12

30-F. LETTER REVIEW

Assignment	Style	Special Instructions	Words
Letter 10 Plain Paper	Personal-Business	Arrange as shown below, with return address after the writer's identification.	184
Letter 11 Workguide: 53	Modified-Block	Omit return address; add your reference initials.	174
Letter 12 Workguide: 55	Modified-Block	Same as Letter 11, except add this final sentence to paragraph 3: "As a token of my appreciation for the work already done, please accept the enclosed centennial certificate." Add your reference initials and an enclosure notation.	197

LETTER 10
PERSONAL-BUSINESS LETTER IN
MODIFIED-BLOCK STYLE

WP

If you had typed Letter 10 on a word processor, the only part that you would have to type for Letter 11 would be the reference initials (you would also need to delete the return address). The body and closing lines would not need to be retyped.

(Current Date)   4

Ms. ~~Judith~~ *Jolene* Durish, President   10
Flair Entertainment Company   15
15 South Montrose ~~Street~~   20
Pasadena, CA 91103   23

Dear Ms. Durish: 27

The information you ~~provided~~ *forwarded to* me concerning the possibility of   40
providing "The Leading Edge" for a concert at our upcoming   52
celebration is *very* much appreciated.   59

After consulting with members of ~~the~~ *our* planning committee and   71
checking our financial status for this event, we have decided   83
that we would like to explore this with you further. Could   95
you ~~arrange~~ *plan* to meet with a group of our committee members? We   107
meet every Thursday evening from 7 to 10 p.m. Please let me   119
know what would be convenient ~~Friday~~ *Thursday* night for you.   130

We ~~will~~ look forward to meeting with you and to possibly   140
making final arrangements for booking "The Leading Edge" as   152
the main attraction at the celebration of our town's   163
centennial.   165

Sincerely yours,   168

Peter Lazzaro, Chairperson   173
Pomona Centennial
15 Greenmont Terrace   182
Pomona, CA 91702   185

G. TECHNIQUE TYPING: SHIFT KEY

G. All 26 capital letters are included in these sentences. Keep your eyes on the copy, and try not to slow down for the capital letters.

16 Ella X. Lee visited her Aunt Beth in Gary, Indiana, in May.
17 Quinn was at a New Year's Day sale in Santa Fe, New Mexico.
18 I heard Judge Paul O'Connell's speech "What You Must Know."
19 Did Z. U. Thomas run for Attorney General in West Virginia?
20 Radio City Music Hall is in Rockefeller Center in New York.

H. PRODUCTION PRACTICE: SPELLING

H. These words are among the 400 most frequently misspelled words in business correspondence.

21 these foreign products administrative calendar cannot weeks
22 shown carried policies transportation industry fiscal value
23 hours closing specific specifications students family labor
24 total develop programs responsibility continue access phase
25 union summary capacity administration internal budget sewer

I. SUSTAINED TYPING: SYLLABIC INTENSITY

I. Take a 1-minute timing on the first paragraph to establish your base speed. Then take several 1-minute timings on the other paragraphs. As soon as you equal or exceed your base speed on one paragraph, advance to the next one.

26   One of the most basic forms of energy is the yo-yo; it   12
27 is just a flywheel on a string. It is made up of two disks   24
28 that are joined by a peg or axle and comes with a cord that   36
29 is wrapped around it. Kids may spin them for hours on end.   48

30   The player loops the free end of the string around one   12
31 finger and then releases the yo-yo. It spins in and out of   24
32 the hand as the string unwinds and rewinds. Although there   36
33 are no rules to the game, there are many complex maneuvers.   48

34   The cardinal principle at work in the yo-yo is the law   12
35 of conservation of energy. A yo-yo at rest in the hand has   24
36 potential energy. When the yo-yo is released, this energy,   36
37 plus the force of the toss, is made available to the yo-yo.   48

38   As the yo-yo goes down, its energy is channeled in two   12
39 directions--the translational energy of its movement toward   24
40 the ground and the rotational energy of its spinning around   36
41 and around during the process of unwinding from the string.   48

   | 1 | 2 | 3 | 4 | 5 | 6 | 7 | 8 | 9 | 10 | 11 | 12

J. TECHNIQUE TYPING: SPACE BAR

J. These sentences are made up of very short words, requiring the frequent use of the space bar. Type them twice. Do not pause before or after the space bar.

42 We can do it if you or he can go on a jet to see a big dog.
43 All of the air in the old bag is OK, but it may be too dry.
44 It was sad to see the son of Al who was at an old, dim pub.
45 If she is so bad, why did she win the bet a day or two ago?
46 Her dog dug up an old bag and a jar of jam at the oak tree.

K. PROGRESSIVE PRACTICE: NUMBERS

Turn to the Progressive Practice: Numbers routine at the back of the book. Take several 30-second timings, starting at the point where you left off the last time. Record your progress on Workguide page 289.

LESSON
31
ONE-PAGE REPORTS

Line: 60 spaces
Tab: 5
Spacing: single
Drills: 2 times
Workguide: 57–60
Format Guide: 21–22
Tape: 14B

Goals: To improve speed and accuracy; to use proofreaders' marks; to format a one-page report.

31-A. WARMUP

S 1 Jaime said that the rich man may fix the pens if they leak.
A 2 Godfrey monopolized conversations with six quite bad jokes.
N 3 Exactly 604 were bought and 523 sold at that store in 1987.

SKILLBUILDING

PRETEST. Take a 1-minute timing; compute your speed and count errors.

31-B. PRETEST: ALTERNATE- AND ONE-HAND WORDS

4   The chairman of the committee will handle the downtown   12
5 tax problem. If they reverse their earlier opinion, social   24
6 pressures might affect the way future problems are handled.   36
    | | | 2 | 3 | 4 | 5 | 6 | 7 | 8 | 9 | 10 | 11 | 12

PRACTICE.
   Speed Emphasis: If you made 2 or fewer errors on the Pretest, type each line twice.
   Accuracy Emphasis: If you made 3 or more errors, type each group of lines (as though it were a paragraph) 2 times.

31-C. PRACTICE: ALTERNATE HANDS

7 of the with girl right blame handle island antique chairman
8 is for wish town their panel formal social problem downtown
9 if sit work make tight amend profit eighty element neighbor
10 it pan busy they flair signs thrown theory signals problems

31-D. PRACTICE: ONE HAND

11 gas lip fact yolk taxes yummy affect poplin reverse pumpkin
12 far you cast kill draws jumpy grease uphill wagered opinion
13 tea pin cage lump beard hilly served limply bravest minimum
14 fat hip tree only great bully garage unhook reserve million

POSTTEST: Repeat the Pretest and compare performance.

31-E. POSTTEST: ALTERNATE- AND ONE-HAND WORDS

31-F. Set tabs every 12 spaces. Use the tab key to go from column to column. Type only once.

31-F. TECHNIQUE TYPING: TAB KEY

15 assets	awning	basket	blinds	boiler
16 breeze	bucket	canary	center	cinder
17 clocks	convoy	custom	debate	desert
18 detail	docket	effort	embryo	fiance
19 gopher	houses	icicle	jewels	knight
20 ladder	master	notion	optics	pantry
21 piracy	pencil	quarry	rating	riddle
22 saddle	senior	tennis	ticket	upward
23 violin	weaver	xylene	yeoman	zither

UNIT 32

Line: 60 spaces
Tab: 5, center
Spacing: single
Drills: 2 times
Workguide: 407–413
Format Guide: 157

INTEGRATED OFFICE PROJECT: ENERGY

GOALS FOR UNIT 32

1. To type 57 wam for 5 minutes with no more than 5 errors.
2. To format complex letters, memos, reports, tables, and forms.
3. To edit documents while typing, correcting spelling errors and applying rules of grammar, punctuation, and typing style.
4. To collect business information, using reference works.
5. To compose an abstract of a longer document.
6. To follow directions.

A.   WARMUP

S 1   Do they own those downtown firms which make maps of cities?
A 2   Ben may give quite a few extra prizes for their old jacket.
N 3   We won the March 29 game by 106-98 in front of 34,725 fans.

SKILLBUILDING

PRETEST. Take a 1-minute timing; compute your speed and count errors.

B.   PRETEST: VERTICAL REACHES

4   Janice and her escort were late for a dance at the re-   12
5   sort. The drummers in the band had just started to play as   24
6   they came in. It seems Janice injured the back of her knee   36
7   on the bank of the river during a cruise late that morning.   48
   | 1 | 2 | 3 | 4 | 5 | 6 | 7 | 8 | 9 | 10 | 11 | 12

PRACTICE.
   Speed Emphasis: If you made no errors on the Pretest, type each line twice.
   Accuracy Emphasis: If you made 1 or more errors on the Pretest, type each group of lines (as though it were a paragraph) twice.

C.   PRACTICE: UP REACHES

8   at late flatly rebate atomic rather repeat attest atom what
9   dr draw drowsy sundry driver adrift drying tundra drum drug
10 ju jump junior justly jumble adjust injure jurist jury junk
11 es ages thesis access esteem resort smiles escape desk nest

D.   PRACTICE: DOWN REACHES

12 ca scat scales cattle casual scarce recall fiscal cash call
13 nk rank blanks anklet unkind donkey tinker chunky wink bank
14 ba tuba ballot cabana bakery abates global basket balk band
15 sc disc script ascend scheme escort fiasco scolds scar scab

POSTTEST. Repeat the Pretest and compare performance.

E.   POSTTEST: VERTICAL REACHES

F.   PACED PRACTICE

Turn to the Paced Practice routine at the back of the book. Take several 2-minute timings, starting at the point where you left off the last time. Record your progress on Workguide page 290.

31-G. BASIC PARTS OF A REPORT

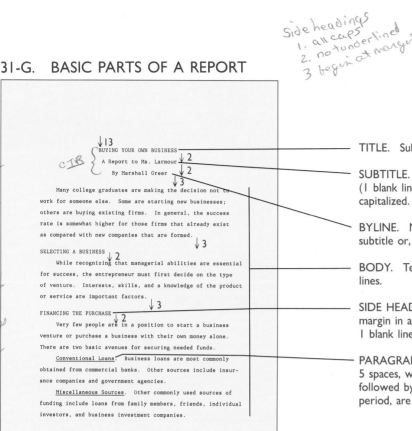

Handwritten notes (top):
Side headings
1. all caps
2. no t underlined
3. begin at margin

¶ heading
1. Keywords Cap.
2. do underscore
3. begin indented
4. Period at end of ¶ heading

Handwritten notes (left margin):
*Tab at Center
DIS
¶line + body Triple Space
¶Tab at 5 space in.

TITLE. Subject of the report; centered and typed in all-capital letters.

SUBTITLE. Secondary or explanatory title; centered a double space (1 blank line) below the title, with first and principal words capitalized.

BYLINE. Name of the writer; centered a double space below the subtitle or, if no subtitle is used, a double space below the title.

BODY. Text of the report; separated from the heading by 2 blank lines.

SIDE HEADING. Major subdivision of the report; typed at the left margin in all-capital letters; preceded by 2 blank lines and followed by 1 blank line.

PARAGRAPH HEADING. Minor subdivision of the report; indented 5 spaces, with first and principal words capitalized; underscored and followed by a period. (The spaces between the words, but not the period, are also underscored.)

31-H. FORMATTING A ONE-PAGE REPORT

Line Length. 6 inches (60 pica/70 elite).
Tab Stops. Always set two—one for indenting paragraphs and one for centering titles and subtitles.
Top Margin. 2 inches; center the title on line 13.
Spacing. Double-space the title block (title, subtitle, and byline) and the body of the report. Leave 2 blank lines (a triple space) between the title block and the body.
Bottom Reminder. Before inserting the paper, pencil in two very light lines (to be erased later): one line about an inch from the bottom to indicate where the last line of typing should go, and a second line about an inch higher to serve as a warning.

Note: The easiest way to format a report is to use a *visual guide*—a sheet on which the margins are marked off in heavy lines. When this sheet is placed behind the paper on which you will type, the ruled lines show through to indicate the correct placement of margins and copy. Workguide pages 59 and 60 are visual guides for use in formatting reports.

Before typing Report 1, complete Workguide pages 57–58.

31-I. PROOFREADERS' MARKS

The proofreaders' marks shown below are used by writers and typists to indicate the changes to be made in typed copy when it is being revised for final typing. These marks are used in the report on the next page.

Proofreaders' Mark		Draft	Final Copy	Proofreaders' Mark		Draft	Final Copy
⌒	Omit space	blue bird	bluebird	∧	Insert word	she may go (*not*)	she may not go
∾	Transpose	which will you	which you will	ℓ	Delete	a ~~rough~~ draft	a draft
¶	Paragraph	¶ Most of the	Most of the	≡	Capitalize	Norwood street	Norwood Street

REPORT 80
ILLUSTRATION

Paper: Workguide 403

Please type the title and labels on this illustration, which will be used in an accident report. You will need to use the paper release lever of your typewriter and adjust your paper so that each label aligns correctly.

FORM 41
EXPENSE REPORT

Paper: Workguide 405

Finally, please type an expense report for an accident inspection tour that Ms. Slade took in Newark, New Jersey. Proofread the figures carefully.

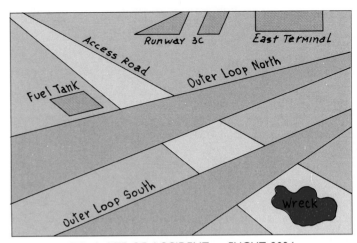

FIG. I SITE OF ACCIDENT — FLIGHT 2034

EXPENSE REPORT

FROM _4/3/--_   NAME _Alice K. Slade_
TO _4/5/--_   LOCATION _Washington, DC - Newark, NJ_
DATE AUTHORIZED _4/2/--_   AUTHORIZED BY _JWL_   PURPOSE OF TRIP _Accident Inspection Tour_

DATE	CITY	BREAKFAST	LUNCH	DINNER	HOTEL	Pub. Trans.	Car Rental	TOLLS	PHONE	1 ENTERTAINMENT	2 AUTO	3 MISC.	TOTAL
4/3	Newark				106.50	98.00				74.50	8.40		287.40
4/4	Newark	9.25	12.00		106.50		52.30	4.25		103.00		18.50	305.80
4/5	Newark	10.30	14.25			98.00			13.50		8.40	13.25	157.70
TOTALS (Including Tips)		19.55	26.25		213.00	196.00	52.30	4.25	13.50	177.50	16.80	31.75	750.90

1 ENTERTAINMENT — ENTER ALL REIMBURSABLE ENTERTAINMENT EXPENSES. LIST EACH OCCASION SEPARATELY. GIVE THE COMPLETE DETAILS OF WHO, WHERE, AND WHY. ENTER DAILY AMOUNTS UNDER #1 ABOVE.

DATE	EXPLANATION	AMOUNT
4/3	Dinner with Don Wagner, Asst. Operations Officer, Newark Int'l Airport; LaBelle Restaurant, Newark; Topic: Flight 2034 accident	74.50
4/4	Dinner with Patricia Edmunds and Tom Hendley, Cabin Attendants; Club 001, West Caldwell; Topic: Flight 2034 accident	103.00
XXXXXXXXXXXXXXXXXXXXXXXXXXXXXXXXXXXXXXXXX TOTAL		177.50

REQUEST FOR ADVANCE

CATEGORY	ESTIMATED EXPENSE	ACTUAL EXPENSE
FOOD/LODGING		
TRANSPORTATION		
ENTERTAINMENT		
MISC. (Tolls & Phone)		
TOTAL		
ADVANCE AMOUNT REQUESTED		

I DO HEREBY AGREE TO REPAY ANY AMOUNT NOT ACCOUNTED FOR WITH BUSINESS RECEIPTS WITHIN 30 DAYS OF FILING A COMPLETED EXPENSE REPORT.

Name _____ Date _____
APPROVED BY
_____ Date _____
ADVANCE RECEIVED BY
_____ Date _____

2 AUTOMOBILE — ALL AUTOMOBILE EXPENSES SHOULD BE ENTERED BELOW BY DATE INCURRED. SHOW MILEAGE FOR GAS. ENTER TOTAL UNDER #2 ABOVE.

DATE	EXPLANATION	AMOUNT
4/3	To Airport (42 mi)	8.40
4/5	From Airport (42 mi)	8.40
XXXXXXXXXXXXXXXX TOTAL		16.80

3 MISC. — ANY ADDITIONAL EXPENSE SHOULD BE ENTERED HERE WITH APPROPRIATE RECEIPTS BY DATE. ENTER TOTAL UNDER #3 ABOVE.

DATE	EXPLANATION	AMOUNT
4/4	Photocopy Logs	18.50
4/5	Supplies	4.25
4/5	Airport Parking	9.00
XXXXXXXXXXXXXX TOTAL		31.75

EXPENSE REPORT SUMMARY

TOTAL EXPENSES	750.90
LESS CHARGES	0.00
LESS CASH ADVANCE	0.00
AMT DUE	750.90
COMPLETED BY AND DATE	
AUDITED BY AND DATE	
APPROVED FOR PAYMENT BY AND DATE	

ATTACH RECEIPTS FOR ANY EXPENSES OVER $10.00. FILE EXPENSE REPORT WITHIN 2 WEEKS OF BUSINESS TRIP.

31-J. ONE-PAGE REPORT

Type Report 1, using double spacing and making the corrections indicated by the proofreaders' marks. Use the visual guide on Workguide page 59.

REPORT I

Line: 6 inches (60 pica/70 elite)
Tab: 5, center
Spacing: double
Paper: plain
Workguide: 59

WP
Word processing programs allow a block of text (a character, word, sentence, or paragraph) to be automatically inserted (∧) into or deleted (ℐ) from the existing text.

↓13	
FORMS OF BUSINESS ORGANIZATION	6
A Report for Introduction to Business ↓2	13
By Patti Zhuang ↓2	16
↓3	

Nearly every business organization in the United States 28

is owned by an individual or by a group of ∧private citizens. Sole 41

proprietorships, partnerships, and corporations are ~~by far~~ 51

the most common ∧forms of business ∧organization ~~types.~~ 61
↓3

SOLE PROPRIETORSHIPS 65

A sole proprietorship is a business that is owned by one 76

person. this individual receives all of the profits earned 89

by that business but is also (responsible/personally) for all 100

of the liabilities incurred. ~~This is~~ Sole proprietorships are ∧ the most prevalent type 116

of owner ship in the country. 122

PARTNERSHIPS 124

ℐ Partnerships are businesses owned and managed by two or more 136

persons. In this type of organization, the profits and re- 148

sponsibilities are shared by all members of the partner ship. 160

Each partner's role is usually described in writing. 171

CORPORATIONS 173

A corporation is the most common form of ownership for 184

∧larger business firms. In this form of ownership, a ∧group ~~bunch~~ of people 198

create a legal entity that assumes all risks and functions 210

independently of the owners. 215

REPORT 79
SCHEDULE PROPOSAL

Line: 6 inches (60 pica/70 elite)
Tab: 15, center
Paper: plain

A frequent job in many government offices is preparing schedule proposals for management. These proposals are often speaker requests, like the one below. Use standard report margins.

WP
Many word processors have a columnar text feature that enables text to be set up in two columns like this automatically.

SCHEDULE PROPOSAL FOR THE DEPUTY DIRECTOR   8
↓3

SPEECH: "Aviation Safety--The Legislative Scene"   18
↓3

MEETING: Annual Convention, Aviation Writers Association   29
                 of North America   32

WHEN/WHERE: November 13, 19--, 2:15-2:50 p.m.
                 October 11, 19--, 8:15-9:15 a.m., Jack Tar   43
                 Hotel, 701 Van Ness Avenue, San Francisco,   52
                 California. ^94102   55

PARTICIPANTS: 350 aviation writers: 300 newspaper journal-   66
                 ists (most from big-city newspapers), and 30   75
                 magazine journalists, and 20 book authors.   83

BACKGROUND: AWANA has frequently given the administration   94
                 negative press coverage during this term,   103
                 partly because of a preception that the Presi-   112
                 dent has not given aviation safety a high pri-   121
                 ority. Some hostile questions can be expected   130
                 at the end of the speech. The purpose of the   139
                 speech would be to highlight the Administra-   148
                 tion's efforts to increase public aviation   157
                 safety and to lobby for passage of HB 1045- 32.   166

MEDIA   The participants typically file stories with   176
COVERAGE: their home newspapers. In addition, ② or ③   188
                 local San Francisco television stations would   197
                 probably cover the session.   202

STAFF   Wilbur J. Oliver, your staff assistant, would   214
COORDINATORS: prepare the briefing material; Jan Donnovan, ice   226
                 public information officer (Ext. 073), would   235
                 draft the speech and handle meeting arrange-   243
                 ments.   245
                 (Ext. 324)

PROPOSED BY: Janice Donnovan, Public Information Office   256

ONE-PAGE REPORTS

Line: 60 spaces
Tab: 5, center
Spacing: single
Drills: 2 times
Workguide: 57–60
Format Guide: 21–22
Tape: 14B

Goals: To type 33 wam/3'/5e; to format one-page reports.

32-A. WARMUP

S 1 Six men met them when the bus jerked to a stop at the gate.
A 2 Jacki Baxter cleverly equipped a dozen white magnetometers.
N 3 Lynn moved from 369 South 42 Street to 508 North 17 Street.

SKILLBUILDING

32-B. SUSTAINED TYPING: SYLLABIC INTENSITY

32-B. Take a 1-minute timing on the first paragraph to establish your base speed. Then take several 1-minute timings on the remaining paragraphs. As soon as you equal or exceed your base speed on one paragraph, advance to the next one.

4   Some young people do not know that the number one goal   12
5 for business is to earn money for the owners. Persons will   24
6 not invest their money if there is little chance of profit.   36

7   When they invest the money, they also provide new jobs   12
8 for workers. These workers can then support themselves and   24
9 their families and not depend on public funds for a living.   36

10   More money quietly flows into the local economy as the   12
11 paychecks of these workers are expended. This enables some   24
12 more people to work, and the work force size keeps growing.   36

13   When people are aware that the profit motive is a most   12
14 important objective for business investors, they are a good   24
15 deal more appreciative of the functions of a business firm.   36

| | | 2 | 3 | 4 | 5 | 6 | 7 | 8 | 9 | 10 | 11 | 12

32-C. DIAGNOSTIC TYPING: ALPHABET

Turn to the Diagnostic Typing: Alphabet routine on pages SB-1–SB-3. Take the Pretest, and record your performance on Workguide page 5. Then practice the drill lines for those reaches on which you made errors.

32-D. SKILL MEASUREMENT: 3-MINUTE TIMED WRITING

32-D. Spacing: double. Record your score.

16   It is natural for a new college graduate to think that   12
17 the perfect job is waiting. Some of my friends have found,   24
18 though, that it might not turn out this way.   33
19   What experience have you had? This is often the first   45
20 question that is asked. And, of course, the young graduate   57
21 is amazed that the degree alone won't do it.   66
22   And if you can't get a job, how do you get experience?   78
23 Some succeed by securing part-time work; others are able to   90
24 get free-lance assignments in related areas.   99

| | | 2 | 3 | 4 | 5 | 6 | 7 | 8 | 9 | 10 | 11 | 12

Ms. Slade would like some transparencies for the speech you typed earlier. We'll have the transparencies made from the masters you type. Please center the material attractively on the special forms we have available. Spread-center the title of each transparency, and leave plenty of space between the lines.

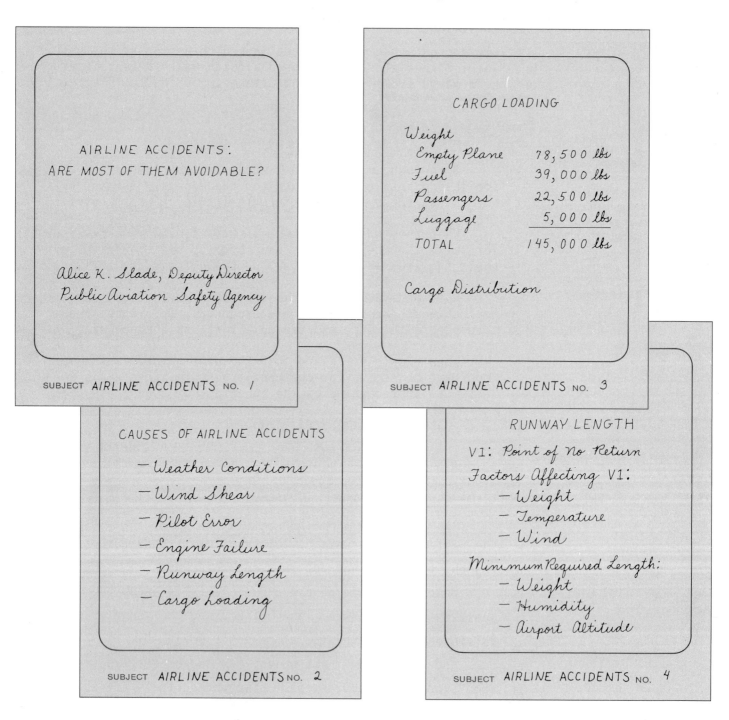

AIRLINE ACCIDENTS:
ARE MOST OF THEM AVOIDABLE?

Alice K. Slade, Deputy Director
Public Aviation Safety Agency

SUBJECT AIRLINE ACCIDENTS NO. 1

CARGO LOADING

Weight
Empty Plane   78,500 lbs
Fuel   39,000 lbs
Passengers   22,500 lbs
Luggage   5,000 lbs
TOTAL   145,000 lbs

Cargo Distribution

SUBJECT AIRLINE ACCIDENTS NO. 3

CAUSES OF AIRLINE ACCIDENTS

— Weather Conditions
— Wind Shear
— Pilot Error
— Engine Failure
— Runway Length
— Cargo Loading

SUBJECT AIRLINE ACCIDENTS NO. 2

RUNWAY LENGTH

V1: Point of No Return
Factors Affecting V1:
    — Weight
    — Temperature
    — Wind
Minimum Required Length:
    — Weight
    — Humidity
    — Airport Altitude

SUBJECT AIRLINE ACCIDENTS NO. 4

32-E. ONE-PAGE REPORTS

Type Reports 2 and 3, using double spacing and making the corrections indicated by the proofreaders' marks. Use the visual guide found on Workguide page 59.

REPORT 2
ONE-PAGE REPORT

Line: 6 inches (60 pica/70 elite)
Tab: 5, center
Spacing: double
Paper: plain
Workguide: 59

You must listen for the bell to end your lines, as some words have been changed.

WP

Input is information that is sent to word processors for processing. Examples of input are longhand, shorthand, and dictation. After the input is typed, changes (called *revisions*) are often made in a document. Only the changed material must be retyped, as the original document is stored on a disk in the word processor.

REPORT 3

Retype Report 2 with these changes:
1. Add the subtitle *A Report for Beginning Typing.*
2. Delete the two paragraph headings.

PARTS OF A REPORT   3

By Susan L. Dixon   7

A class report may contain several special parts in addition to   20

the body of the report. Some of these special additional parts come   31

before the body, and some come after it.   39

INTRODUCTORY PARTS   43

The title page and the table of contents are parts of a   54

report that come before the main body.   61

   Title Page. The title page is the cover page for a long   72

report. It identifies the author, title, and date of the   84

report. The number and name of the course for which the re-   95

port is being prepared should also be shown.   104

   Table of contents. The table of contents lists the main sec-   116

tions and the pages on which each of these sections begins.   128

It is not required for a report of only a few pages.   139

Bibliography   141

   The bibliography comes at the end of the report. It   152

lists all the journals, books, and other sources that the   163

writer used to prepare the report. With this listing, the   175

reader is able to refer to the same study publications for additional   188

information. Therefore, there should be enough information   197

should be provided so that the reader can locate a particular source in   211

the library.   214

LETTER 90
TWO-PAGE FORMAL GOVERNMENT LETTER

Paper: Workguide 393–394

Since the Sandhusen letter is going to a private individual (instead of to another government office), please transcribe it as a formal government letter, using the models at the right as a guide.

Line: 6½ inches (1-inch side margins)
Date: line 7
Subject: line 11
Punctuation: standard
Inside Address: line 14
Paragraphs: blocked
Second Page: addressee and page number on line 7; text follows on second line below
Writer's Name: in all capitals

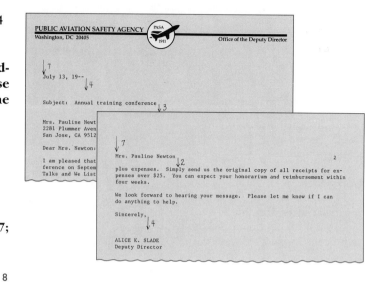

May 13, 19— / Subject: Airline passenger   8
safety tips / Mr. William J. Sandhusen / Carriage   17
House, Apt. 1086 / 1463 Springfield Avenue /   25
New Providence, NJ 07974 / Dear Mr.   31
Sandhusen: 33

Although the safety of commercial aviation   42
in this country is unsurpassed in the world,   51
your travel club is wise to explore ways of   60
improving your chances of surviving a plane   68
crash. The information below comes from our   77
extensive study of airline safety involving   86
many thousands of flights yearly. You may in-   95
clude any of this information you wish in your   105
monthly newsletter.   108

If the plane's engines are under its wings,   117
you should pick a seat in the tail area. How-   126
ever, if the engines are mounted near the tail,   136
you should sit near an exit over the wing. The   145
best seats are by the window or along the aisle.   155
Either location offers a clearer path to an exit.   165

Unlike car accidents in which passengers are   174
jolted at high force as the car rapidly stops, an   184
airplane sliding along the ground slows gradu-   193
ally and is somewhat cushioned as cargo areas   202
underneath the passenger area absorb the   211
force of impact. The tail area often is least dam-   221
aged, and common sense says that is the best   230
place to sit. But if the plane's engines are   239
mounted near its tail, beware of the rear. Heat   249
from the engine fire could cause injury or   257
damage the emergency exits.   263

Knowledge of the plane itself can also help   271
you to survive an accident. Experts recom-   280
mend the following tactics: 285

1. As you take your seat, look for the nearest   295
door and window exits. If possible, look to see   305
how to open the exits. Check for strips of   313
lights on the aisle floors, leading to exits.   322

2. Listen to the cabin attendant's briefing,   332
and read the passenger information card—no   340
matter how often you fly. Different planes have   350
different emergency procedures.   356

3. If you'll be over water, check under your   366
seat for a life preserver. If you don't find one,   376
notify an attendant.   380

4. Fasten your seat belt snugly over your   388
hips, not over your stomach.   394

Finally, if a plane does crash, you should wait   404
until it comes to a complete rest and then try   413
to get out quickly without jeopardizing other   422
passengers' safety. Don't try to take anything   432
with you; and if cabin attendants are giving in-   441
structions, follow them. An emergency slide   450
will inflate as the emergency door opens.   459
Don't try to sit down and slide; just jump onto   468
the slide to make the fastest exit possible.   477

I am pleased to provide this information for   486
your travel club. I would also like to reassure   496
your group of the safety of commercial avia-   504
tion in this country. For example, there were   514
5.6 million commercial plane departures in   522
this country in 1985 and only four fatal plane   532
accidents. This is a record of which the Public   542
Aviation Safety Agency is extremely proud.   550

Sincerely, / ALICE K. SLADE / Deputy Director   558

Line: 60 spaces
Tab: 5, center
Spacing: single
Drills: 2 times
Format Guide: 21–24
Tape: 15B

ENUMERATIONS

Goals: To improve speed and accuracy; to improve proofreading skills; to format enumerations.

33-A.   WARMUP

S 1 Both girls wore yellow formal gowns to the prom last night.
A 2 Max quickly amazed Joan Bishop with five magic card tricks.
N 3 New inventory counts were 370 as compared with 425 in 1986.

SKILLBUILDING

33-B. Type the exercise and correct all errors.

33-B.   PRODUCTION PRACTICE: PROOFREADING

4   Do you enjoy expensive paintings but can not afford
5 the huge sums of money required for thier purchase. Just
6 as one might rent a cadillac for a special trip, it is
7 possible to have an expensive painting in your home.
8 While policies do vary, 60-day rentals commonly are priced
9 at approximatley ten per cent of the retail price.
10   Art museums throughout the country have adopted
11 this marketing strategy. if the renter decides to buy
12 the painting, the rental price is commonly applied to
13 the purchase price. As you would expect, your credit
14 histry and your character must be verified in advanse.

33-C.   Center each line: Tab to center, backspace once for every 2 strokes, and then type the entry. Use double spacing.
   Check: The letter *o* aligns vertically.

33-C.   HORIZONTAL-CENTERING PRACTICE

15 Roy S. Foreman
16 Edward A. Rodenberger
17 Fern Stoddard
18 Kim M. Roberts
19 Kevin L. Kronschnabel
20 B. J. Cloutier
21 Carolyn Soderman
22 David Olsen

33-D.   PACED PRACTICE

Turn to the Paced Practice routine at the back of the book. Take several 2-minute timings, starting at the point where you left off the last time. Record your progress on Workguide page 6.

REPORT 74 (Continued)

DISPLAY TRANSPARENCY 3: CARGO LOAD-ING. 432 433

LET'S CONSIDER CARGO LOADING FOR A TYPICAL COMMERCIAL PLANE. THE MD80 IS A WORKHORSE OF THE AVIATION INDUSTRY AND IS FLOWN BY FOUR MAJOR AIRLINES. THE MD80 IS RATED BY ITS MANUFACTURER FOR A MAXIMUM TAKEOFF WEIGHT OF 147,000 POUNDS. IT WEIGHS 78,500 POUNDS WITHOUT FUEL, AND ITS FUEL WEIGHS ABOUT 39,000 POUNDS. 440 448 454 461 468 475 482 489 496

THE AVERAGE NUMBER OF PASSENGERS PER FLIGHT FOR ALL MD80'S FLYING COMMERCIAL ROUTES LAST YEAR WAS 155. THE AVERAGE SUMMER WEIGHT PER PASSENGER IS 145 POUNDS. (OBVIOUSLY, THE WEIGHT IN WINTER IS HIGHER BECAUSE OF HEAVIER CLOTHING AND TYPICALLY MORE CARRY-ON LUGGAGE.) THUS THE PEOPLE ON BOARD TYPICALLY WEIGH ABOUT 22,500 POUNDS. 502 509 517 524 532 540 547 553 560 562

THROW IN AN AVERAGE OF 5,000 POUNDS OF LUGGAGE PER FLIGHT, AND YOU CAN SEE THAT THE WEIGHT OF A TYPI- 568 574 582

CAL LOADED MD80 IS 145,000 POUNDS— JUST 2,000 POUNDS LESS THAN ITS MAXIMUM CAPACITY. 589 596 599

STILL, IT IS NOT THE WEIGHT OF THE LOADED AIRCRAFT THAT IS SO CRUCIAL— IT'S HOW THE CARGO HAS BEEN LOADED. IF THE LOAD IS IMPROPERLY DISTRIBUTED, IT CREATES PROBLEMS BY SHIFTING THE PLANE'S CENTER OF GRAVITY TOO FAR FORWARD OR AFT. 606 613 620 628 635 642 645

FORTUNATELY, MOST COMMERCIAL JETS ARE NOT TOO SENSITIVE, AND A COUPLE THOUSAND POUNDS OF BAGGAGE DOESN'T BOTHER THEM. DURING THE PAST FOUR YEARS, IN NOT ONE OF THE PLANE ACCIDENTS THAT WE'VE REVIEWED HAS CARGO LOADING BEEN RULED AS THE PRIMARY CAUSE. 652 659 666 673 680 687 694 695

MORE SERIOUS, CONSIDERING TODAY'S LARGE JETS AND MORE CROWDED AIRPORTS, IS THE MATTER OF RUNWAY LENGTH. 702 708 714 716

DISPLAY TRANSPARENCY 4: RUNWAY LENGTH. 722 724

TABLE 62
RULED TABLE

Spacing: single
Paper: plain, full sheet

Ms. Slade has asked for a list of the busiest airports in the United States. Please prepare a ruled table, taking the data from the table below. Use the same title and subtitle. Type the table in two columns, and list the airports in order from busiest to least busy. After the last entry, insert a line labeled *AVERAGE* (with a ruled line above and below); then calculate the mean number of takeoffs and landings (add the numbers in the *Total* column and divide the sum by 20), and type the result in the *Total* column.

WP Many software programs would sort this information in descending (or ascending) order.

THE TWENTY BUSIEST U.S. AIRPORTS 6

Total Takeoffs and Landings 12

Airport	Total	Airport	Total	
Atlanta International	749,909	Newark	400,204	22
Boston Logan	402,695	Oakland International	370,619	32
Chicago O'Hare International	768,079	Phoenix Sky Harbor International	394,306	47
Dallas/Ft. Worth International	547,901	Pittsburgh Greater International	360,859	62
Denver Stapleton International	502,897	San Francisco	396,161	73
Detroit Metropolitan	366,261	San Jose Municipal	364,846	84
La Guardia (New York City)	367,256	Santa Ana	521,630	93
Long Beach	398,559	Seattle Boeing	383,478	101
Los Angeles International	545,973	St. Louis International	411,288	113
Minneapolis/St. Paul International	361,961	Van Nuys	503,488	125

Source: Federal Aviation Administration.

33-E. FORMATTING ENUMERATIONS

Read the information in Report 4 before you type the assignments in this section. Study the format so that you get a mental picture of the layout before you begin typing.

↓13

ENUMERATIONS   2

↓3

REPORT 4
ENUMERATION

Line: 6 inches (60 pica/70 elite)
Tab: 4
Spacing: single
Paper: plain

WP Many software programs have a tab indent feature or temporary left margin that allows the operator to use word wrap on enumerations.

1. An enumeration may be any series of numbered items. How-   14
   ever, to most people the word means a displayed listing   26
   like this one, with the numbers standing out at the left.   37
   ↓2

2. The numbers are typed at the left margin and are followed   49
   by a period and 2 spaces. To align the turnover lines of   61
   copy, a tab stop is set 4 spaces in from the left margin.   72

3. Items are single-spaced without any blank lines between   84
   them if most items take one line or less. However, if   95
   most items require more than one line (as in this   105
   enumeration), they are single-spaced with 1 blank line   116
   between items.   119

4. The periods following the numbers should be vertically   131
   aligned. If the enumeration runs to ten or more items,   142
   the left margin must be reset 1 space to the left.   152

↓13

CITY OF ST. CLOUD   3

↓3

REPORT 5
OUTLINE

Line: block center horizontally
Tab: 4, 8
Spacing: single
Paper: plain

WP Some software programs contain an outlining feature that automatically formats different levels of headings and allows the operator to rearrange headings easily.

Use the margin release lever to backspace for roman numerals II and III. The periods will then align vertically.

   I. ADMINISTRATIVE OFFICES   9
   ↓2
      A. City Manager   12
      B. Finance and Accounting   17
      C. City Clerk   20
      ↓3
  II. SERVICE DEPARTMENTS   25

      A. Fire Department   28
      B. Parks and Recreation Department   35
         1. Indoor sports facilities   41
         2. Outdoor sports facilities   47
         3. Parks and marinas   51
      C. Police Department   55

III. UTILITIES OFFICES   60

      A. Board of Light and Power   65
      B. Sewage Disposal Plant   70
      C. Water and Street Department 77

REPORT 74
SPEECH

Line: 50 spaces
Paper: plain

Would you please transcribe the first several pages of a speech that Ms. Slade will be presenting in the fall. She likes her speeches typed on a 50-space line, with the body of the speech double-spaced and typed in all capitals.

Quadruple-space between paragraphs, and do not break a paragraph between two pages. Use standard top and bottom margins, and number each page as you normally do in reports. Please underline each reference to a transparency. Here's a previous speech to use as a guide in formatting.

```
              ↓13
        AIRLINE SAFETY:  WHOSE RESPONSIBILITY?
                                          ↓2
   Speech Presented at April 2, 19-- PASA Conference
         By Alice K. Slade, Deputy Director,
            Public Aviation Safety Agency
                                   ↓4

        THANK YOU, MS. AMES, FOR THAT NICE INTRODUCTION.

   IT IS MY PLEASURE TO DISCUSS WITH YOU TODAY THE TOPIC

   OF AIRLINE SAFETY.
                      ↓4

        DISPLAY TRANSPARENCY 1:  AIRLINE SAFETY:  WHOSE

   RESPONSIBILITY?
                  ↓4
```

AIRLINE ACCIDENTS: ARE MOST OF THEM AVOIDABLE? 7 9

Speech Presented on September 3, 19—, in Milwaukee, Wisconsin, at the Annual Recognition Dinner of the American Airline Association by Alice K. Slade, Deputy Director, Public Aviation Safety Agency 18 26 35 45 49

THANK YOU, MR. BEASLEY, FOR THAT NICE INTRODUCTION. ON BEHALF OF DIRECTOR LOGAN AND THE OTHER MEMBERS OF THE PUBLIC AVIATION SAFETY AGENCY, I AM PLEASED TO BRING YOU GREETINGS TONIGHT AND TO SPEND A FEW MOMENTS TALKING TO YOU ON THE TOPIC OF THE CAUSES OF AIRLINE ACCIDENTS. 56 63 70 77 84 91 98 104

DISPLAY TRANSPARENCY 1: AIRLINE ACCIDENTS: ARE MOST OF THEM AVOIDABLE? 111 118

OBVIOUSLY, IN A PERFECT WORLD THERE WOULD BE NO NEED FOR MY SPEECH TONIGHT. WE AT PASA WORK VERY HARD TO ENSURE THAT AIRLINE ACCIDENTS DON'T HAPPEN. AND WE'RE EXTREMELY PROUD OF THE AIRLINE SAFETY RECORD THAT HAS ACCUMULATED DURING THIS ADMINISTRATION. 126 132 140 147 154 161 168 169

LAST YEAR THIS COUNTRY EXPERIENCED FEWER COMMERCIAL AIRLINE ACCIDENTS THAN ANY OTHER DEVELOPED COUNTRY IN THE FREE WORLD—DESPITE THE FACT THAT OUR SKIES AND OUR AIRPORTS ARE THE BUSIEST IN TERMS OF AVIATION TRAFFIC. 176 183 190 197 204 212 212

BUT—THIS IS NOT A PERFECT WORLD, AND ACCIDENTS DO HAPPEN OCCASIONALLY. WHEN THEY DO, IT IS OUR JOB TO 219 226 233

STUDY THE DATA DEVELOPED BY THE NATIONAL TRANSPORTATION SAFETY BOARD IN ORDER TO INSTITUTE NEW TRAINING PROGRAMS, NEW PROCEDURES, NEW LEGISLATION, OR WHATEVER IT TAKES TO ENSURE THAT SUCH ACCIDENTS DO NOT RECUR. 240 247 254 261 268 274 275

IN THE COURSE OF STUDYING AIRLINE ACCIDENTS, WE'VE ACCUMULATED DATA REGARDING THEIR CAUSES THAT TENDS TO DISCREDIT IN MANY WAYS THE TRADITIONAL WISDOM REGARDING AIRLINE SAFETY; AND I'D LIKE TO SHARE SOME OF THAT DATA WITH YOU THIS EVENING. 282 289 296 303 309 317 323

SPECIFICALLY, I'LL BE DISCUSSING SOME RECENT DATA REGARDING SIX COMMON CAUSES OF COMMERCIAL AIRLINE ACCIDENTS: 331 337 344 345

DISPLAY TRANSPARENCY 2: CAUSES OF AIRLINE ACCIDENTS. 352 356

THE SIX MOST COMMON CAUSES OF COMMERCIAL AIRLINE ACCIDENTS IN THIS COUNTRY SINCE PASA BEGAN KEEPING RECORDS IN 1911 ARE AS FOLLOWS: 362 369 376 382

—WEATHER CONDITIONS 386
—WIND SHEAR 388
—PILOT ERROR 391
—ENGINE FAILURE 394
—RUNWAY LENGTH 397
—CARGO LOADING 400

I'D LIKE TO DISCUSS THESE IN INCREASING ORDER OF IMPORTANCE, WITH CARGO LOADING BEING THE LEAST FREQUENT SOURCE OF PROBLEMS. 407 415 421 425

(Continued on page 326.)

Line: 60 spaces
Tab: 5, center
Spacing: single
Drills: 2 times
Format Guide: 23–24
Tape: 16A

ONE-PAGE REPORTS

Goals: To type 34 wam/3'/5e; to format reports from rough-draft copy.

34-A. WARMUP

S 1 They said they will not take a jet when they take the trip.
A 2 Jess quit before two lazy men excavated gravel in the park.
N 3 Prices on lots 398 and 621 were raised from 47 to 50 cents.

SKILLBUILDING

34-B. Make two copies. Copy 1: Type each sentence on a separate line. Copy 2: Type each sentence on a separate line, but tab-indent it 5 spaces.

34-B. TECHNIQUE TYPING: RETURN/ENTER KEY

4 Where is the new office? It is located on the fifth floor.
5 Is there sufficient space? Yes, it is a very large office.
6 Will I have my own office? No, room dividers will be used.

7 Three telephone lines are needed. A recorder will be used.
8 New furniture has been ordered. We will install carpeting.
9 Office supplies have been ordered. Storage room is scarce.

10 We will move on December 1. Will a moving company be used?
11 One new person will be employed. What will that person do?
12 We will be in a new building. Are there parking lots near?

34-C. DIAGNOSTIC TYPING: NUMBERS

Turn to the Diagnostic Typing: Numbers routine on pages SB-4–SB-5. Take the Pretest, and record your performance on Workguide page 5. Then practice the drill lines for those reaches on which you made errors.

34-D. Spacing: double. Record your score.

34-D. SKILL MEASUREMENT: 3-MINUTE TIMED WRITING

13   Nonverbal communication gives extra meaning to what we   12
14 say. Posture, hand gestures, and facial expressions convey   24
15 our inner thoughts more accurately than words do.   34
16   One can stress a point with just a nod of the head and   46
17 by a change of expression. Eye contact may signal a person   58
18 that you are listening or you couldn't care less.   68
19   The use of such extras in a formal speech adds zest to   80
20 what may be quite boring. And at times, unknown to the one   92
21 speaking, their power may carry the true message.   102

| 1 | 2 | 3 | 4 | 5 | 6 | 7 | 8 | 9 | 10 | 11 | 12 |

L.   INTEGRATED OFFICE PROJECT: PUBLIC AVIATION SAFETY AGENCY

Situation. Today is Monday, May 13, your first day as a typist in the office of Alice K. Slade, Deputy Director of the Public Aviation Safety Agency, a government agency in Washington, D.C. Your supervisor is Randy Blanchard, Ms. Slade's administrative assistant.

Because government offices format many types of documents differently than industry, you must pay special attention to the formatting details that are provided with each job. In addition, you should correct any spelling or grammar errors you find and submit all jobs in mailable form.

The informal letter is the most common style used by government. It is similar to an office memorandum.

Capitalize only the first word and proper nouns in the subject line.

The address is positioned to show through a window envelope.

Informal government letters do not contain a salutation or complimentary closing.

Indent the first line of a subparagraph 5 spaces; begin turnover lines at the left margin.

Type the writer's name in all capitals.

On the file copy (but not on the original letter), the typist inserts a reference line (which identifies the office symbol, writer, typist, and date) on the second line below the last closing line. Example:

Enclosure

TPAS:AKSlade:urs 5-13---

LETTER 89
INFORMAL GOVERNMENT
LETTER

Line: 6½ inches (1-inch side margins)
Tab: 5
Paper: Workguide 391–392

Please retype the Buchholz letter that our temporary worker prepared yesterday. Although it's in the correct format, it contains several grammar and spelling errors that must be corrected. Since this is your first day on the job, I've marked the letter with formatting guidelines.

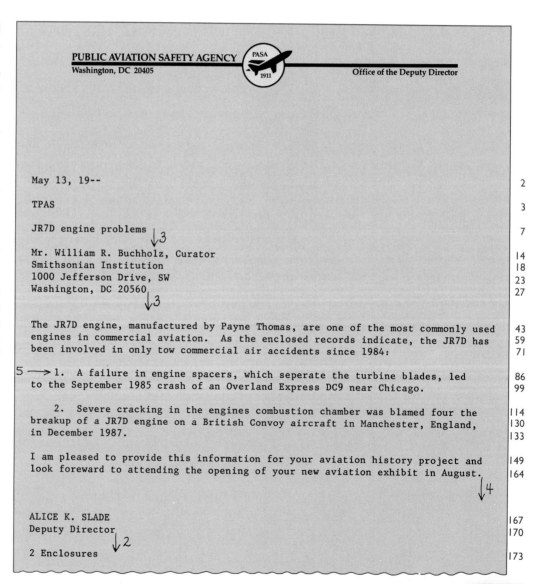

PUBLIC AVIATION SAFETY AGENCY
Washington, DC 20405
PASA
1911
Office of the Deputy Director

May 13, 19--   2

TPAS   3

JR7D engine problems ↓3   7

Mr. William R. Buchholz, Curator   14
Smithsonian Institution   18
1000 Jefferson Drive, SW   23
Washington, DC 20560 ↓3   27

The JR7D engine, manufactured by Payne Thomas, are one of the most commonly used   43
engines in commercial aviation. As the enclosed records indicate, the JR7D has   59
been involved in only tow commercial air accidents since 1984:   71

5 → 1. A failure in engine spacers, which seperate the turbine blades, led   86
to the September 1985 crash of an Overland Express DC9 near Chicago.   99

  2. Severe cracking in the engines combustion chamber was blamed four the   114
breakup of a JR7D engine on a British Convoy aircraft in Manchester, England,   130
in December 1987.   133

I am pleased to provide this information for your aviation history project and   149
look foreward to attending the opening of your new aviation exhibit in August. ↓4   164

ALICE K. SLADE   167
Deputy Director   170

2 Enclosures ↓2   173

34-E. ONE-PAGE REPORTS

Type Reports 6 and 7. Use double spacing, and make the corrections indicated by the proofreaders' marks. Use Workguide page 59 as a visual guide, and preview the revisions before you begin typing.

REPORT 6
ONE-PAGE REPORT

Line: 6 inches
Spacing: double
Paper: plain
Workguide: 59

Using proofreaders' marks to edit and revise a document prior to producing the final copy is called *editing*.

REPORT 7

Retype Report 6, but add the subtitle *A Report for Introduction to Business* and two paragraph headings: *Home Insurance* before the third paragraph and *Auto Insurance* before the fourth paragraph.

TYPES OF INSURANCE	4
By Patti Zhuang	7

All of us are exposed to a variety of risks every day. 18
Insurance is designed to provide protection against ordinary 30
risks. Among the many kinds of available insurance, the fol- 42
lowing are types of policies held by most people. 52

PROPERTY INSURANCE 55

Property insurance is designed to cover financial losses in- 67
curred by damage or destruction of property. home and auto 79
auto insurance are two examples of this type of coverage. 89

Home insurance covers losses from damage to a home and/or 100
its contents. This could include such things as fire, 111
vandalism, or even lightning. 117

Automobile insurance protects against losses from damage 129
to or by an automobile. Accidents, fire, theft, and 139
liability lawsuits are usual coverages. 147

HEALTH INSURANCE 150

Health insurance coverage is commonly purchased by business firms for 164
their employees as well as by individuals. possible coverages 177
include hospitalization, dental, optical, and disability 188
insurance. Few people can afford the high cost of medical 200
services today without health insurance protection. 210

J. Compare these lines with Sections C and D on page 321. Type a list of the words that contain errors, correcting the errors as you type.

J. PRODUCTION PRACTICE: PROOFREADING

40 maps visual suspect amendment turndown visible height sings
41 from profit penalty shamrocks brandish problem thrown chair
42 snap emblem dormant authentic clemency figment island usual
43 half signal auditer endowment ornament element handle amend

44 serve uphill exceess killjoy carefree homonym terarce onion
45 trade poplon greater pumpkin eastward plumply barrage holly
46 difer unhook reserve minimum abstract million scatter slump
47 exact kimono created minikin casettes opinion seaweed union

K. Spacing: double
Record your score.

K. SKILL MEASUREMENT: 5-MINUTE TIMED WRITING

48   Dress shirts are designed to be worn on occasions that   12
49 require ties and jackets. They come in two main varieties: 24
50 basic and fancy. Basic shirts are either white, bluish, or   36
51 light beige. Fancy shirts come in such colors as yellow or   48
52 pink and have bold stripes or patterns.   56

53   The most common type of shirt is fashioned from broad-   68
54 cloth or oxford cloth. Oxford cloth is a soft cotton cloth   80
55 or a blended cloth with a basket weave, and broadcloth is a   92
56 closely woven fabric with a plain weave. Cotton fibers are 104
57 not quite as popular as blended fibers.   112

58   All-cotton shirts are cooler than combinations of cot-   124
59 ton and some other fabric. They are more difficult to iron 136
60 but look better than the blend shirts when ironed properly. 148
61 Blends are easy to maintain, needing only touch-up ironing. 160
62 In addition, blends are less expensive.   168

63   To distinguish a good-quality shirt from one of lesser   180
64 quality, first examine the yarns. The better the yarn from 192
65 which the fabric is woven, the better the shirt is going to 204
66 wear. Twisted yarns are the best, and single-needle sewing 216
67 is utilized for its superior strength.   224

68   If you wear a dress shirt no more frequently than once   236
69 weekly and care for it properly, it will last several years 248
70 or longer. Heavy bleaching shortens the shirt's life span. 260
71 Authorities indicate that the average man probably outgrows 272
72 shirts more often than wearing them out.   280

| 1 | 2 | 3 | 4 | 5 | 6 | 7 | 8 | 9 | 10 | 11 | 12 |

Line: 60 spaces
Tab: 5, center
Spacing: single
Drills: 2 times
Format Guide: 23–26
Tape: 16A

Goals: To improve speed and accuracy; to improve word-division skills; to improve the skill of formatting from rough-draft copy; to format a report with an enumeration and a bibliography.

35-A. WARMUP

S 1 Pam lost an ax at the first lake when she went there today.
A 2 He picked two extra biology quizzes for Marv, Jan, and Hal.
N 3 The population of the city had grown by 237,645 since 1980.

SKILLBUILDING

35-B. Select the words that can be divided, and type them with a hyphen to show where the division should be (example: *fore-front*).

35-B. PRODUCTION PRACTICE: WORD DIVISION

4	brought	account	business
5	divide	haven't	borderline
6	weekly	USMC	thrilled
7	isn't	knowledge	TWA
8	tabletop	ahead	self-assured

35-C. Take a 1-minute timing on the first paragraph to establish your base speed. Then take several 1-minute timings on the remaining paragraphs. As soon as you equal or exceed your base speed on one paragraph, advance to the next one. All lines should end evenly at the right margin.

35-C. SUSTAINED TYPING: ROUGH DRAFT

9 Several of our subscribers have reported that they get   12
10 a lot of junk mail these days that publicizes the many get-   24
11 rich schemes awaiting them. A word for the wise: Be wary.   36
12 ¶It is true that fortunes are made by entrepreneurs who   12
13 capitalize on an idea and make millions. the excitement of   24
14 such challenges can help fulfill the lives of many persons.   36
15 But it is quite true that there have been thousands of   12
16 aspiring millionaires who have lost sizeable investments. a   24
17 proposal to make others rich should be looked at carefully.   36
18 modern investors are seeking increasingly the services   12
19 of financial consultants. They have special regular qualifications   24
20 in family financial planning and weighing investment risks.   36

| 1 | 2 | 3 | 4 | 5 | 6 | 7 | 8 | 9 | 10 | 11 | 12 |

F. PROGRESSIVE PRACTICE: NUMBERS

Turn to the Progressive Practice: Numbers routine at the back of the book. Take several 30-second timings, starting at the point where you left off the last time. Record your progress on Workguide page 289.

G. SUSTAINED TYPING: ALTERNATE-HAND WORDS

G. Take a 1-minute timing on the first paragraph to establish your base speed. Then take several 1-minute timings on the other paragraphs. As soon as you equal or exceed your base speed on one paragraph, advance to the next one.

```
16        A downturn in world fuel prices signals a lower profit   12
17   for the giant oil firms.  In fact, most downtown firms will    24
18   see the usual sign of tight credit and other problems.  The    36
19   city must get down to business and make plans for the fall.    48

20        The hungry turkeys ate eight bushels of corn that were    12
21   thrown to them by our neighbors next door.  They also drank    24
22   the five bowls of water that were left in the yard.  All in    36
23   all, the birds caused quite a bit of chaos in the barnyard.   48

24        A debate on what to do about that extra acreage in the    12
25   desert dragged on for eight hours.  One problem is what the    24
26   effect may be of moving the ancient Indian ruins to a safer    36
27   place.  City council has a duty to protect our environment.   48

28        Molly Babbage was dressed in a bright pink gown at the    12
29   spring dance held on the deserted island near Traverse City   24
30   last week.  Her date, Philip Carter, was dressed in a black   36
31   three-piece suit, with a green shamrock in his right lapel.   48
     |   |   | 2 | 3 | 4 | 5 | 6 | 7 | 8 | 9 | 10 | 11 | 12
```

H. DIAGNOSTIC TYPING: ALPHABET

Turn to the Diagnostic Typing: Alphabet routine at the back of the book. Take the Pretest, and record your performance on Workguide page 289. Then practice the drill lines for those reaches on which you made errors.

I. SYMBOL TYPING

I. Type line 32 twice. Then take several 1-minute timings on lines 33–39. Maintain a smooth, even rhythm, and try to keep your eyes on the copy.

```
32   d3#d 19(1 ;0); f5%f ;''; ;'"; j7&j f4$f s2@s k8*k ;-_; ;/?;

33        At 3:40 p.m. on July 8, 1987, Melon & Day (our first--   12
34   but not our last--counsel) met John's partner and asked him   24
35   to pay the $3,200 plus 8% interest for the 10,000# of scrap   36
36   he purchased for a "steal" @ $.32.  Is Hostel* now required   48
37   to pay that amount and/or explain why not?  I would hope he   60
38   paid the 8.70% tax--amounting to $278.40--that was due last   72
39   Friday, July 1.  Isn't Melon & Day looking into that angle?   84
     |   |   | 2 | 3 | 4 | 5 | 6 | 7 | 8 | 9 | 10 | 11 | 12
```

35-D. FORMATTING A REPORT WITH AN ENUMERATION AND A BIBLIOGRAPHY

Read Report 8 for the information it contains. Then carefully follow the instructions at the left, noting that the tab must be reset for the single-spaced numbered items.

REPORT 8
REPORT WITH ENUMERATION

Tab: 5, center
Spacing: double

The lines for each numbered item are single-spaced. However, double spacing is used between items.

Turnover lines are indented 4 spaces.

PREPARING A BIBLIOGRAPHY   5

By Heidi Keltjen   8

¶ A bibliography is, *an alphabetic* a listing of sources and is placed at the   22
end of the report, following these guide lines.   32
1. Use the *report* length/line: 60 pica or 70 elite spaces.   44
2. Center the title in all-capital letters on line 13.   55
    Two ~~three~~ blank lines precede the body.   62
3. Arrange book information in in this order: *author,* title,   74
    publisher, place of publication, and date.   82
4. Arrange information for journals *articles* in this order: 94
    author, title of article (in quotation marks), title of   105
    journal (underscored), series number, volume number,   116
    issue number, date, and page number or numbers.   125

REPORT 9
BIBLIOGRAPHY

Tab: 5
Spacing: single

BIBLIOGRAPHY ↓3   2

Organization as author

Distributive Education Clubs of America, <u>Preparing for the</u>   14
    <u>Job Interview</u>, Educational Association Clearinghouse,   25
    San Francisco, 1981. ↓2   29

Book by one author

Faux, Marian, <u>The Executive Interview</u>, St. Martin's Press,   41
    New York, 1985.   44

Article—no author

"How They Sell to You Is How They'll Sell for You," <u>Sales &</u>   56
    <u>Marketing Management</u>, Vol. CXXXIII, No. 3, August 13,   67
    1984, pp. 77-78.   70

Book by two authors

Meyer, Mary Coeli, and Inge M. Berchtold, <u>Getting the Job:</u>   82
    <u>How to Interview Successfully</u>, Petrocelli Books,   92
    Princeton, N.J., 1982.   96

Article by three or more authors
(*et al.* means "and others")

Scott, Richard A., et al., "On-Campus Recruiting: The Students Speak Up," <u>Journal of Accountancy</u>, Vol. CLIX,   108
    No. 1, January 1985, pp. 60-62.   118
    124

Article by one author

Solomon, Robert J., "Using the Interview in Small Business,"   136
    <u>Journal of Small Business Management</u>, Vol. XXII,   146
    No. 4, October 1984, pp. 17-23.   152

Line: 60 spaces
Tab: 5, center
Spacing: single
Drills: 2 times
Workguide: 391–405
Format Guide: 151

LESSONS 151–155

INTEGRATED OFFICE PROJECT: GOVERNMENT

GOALS FOR UNIT 31

1. To type 56 wam for 5 minutes with no more than 5 errors.
2. To format formal and informal correspondence according to U.S. government guidelines.
3. To format complex reports, tables, and forms.
4. To extract data from one document and format new copy.
5. To follow directions.
6. To edit documents while typing, correcting spelling errors and applying rules of grammar, punctuation, and typing style.
7. To perform simple mathematical calculations.

A. WARMUP

S 1 Bob owns a pair of ancient bicycles and a giant ivory bowl.
A 2 The five major exams were quickly graded in pencil by Buzz.
N 3 I now live at 6318 First Street, Apt. 597, Macon, GA 31201.

SKILLBUILDING

PRETEST. Take a 1-minute timing; compute your speed and count errors.

B. PRETEST: ALTERNATE- AND ONE-HAND WORDS

4   In their opinion, the ornamental bicycle from Honolulu   12
5 may be regarded as an authentic antique. It deserves to be   24
6 treated well because it will attract many new visitors from   36
7 Texas and Ohio to most downtown streets in July and August.   48
    | 1 | 2 | 3 | 4 | 5 | 6 | 7 | 8 | 9 | 10 | 11 | 12

PRACTICE.
   Speed Emphasis: If you made no errors on the Pretest, type each line twice.
   Accuracy Emphasis: If you made 1 or more errors on the Pretest, type each group of lines (as though it were a paragraph) twice.

C. PRACTICE: ALTERNATE-HAND WORDS

8 maps visual suspend amendment turndown visible height signs
9 form profit penalty shamrocks blandish problem thrown chair
10 snap emblem dormant authentic clemency figment island usual
11 half signal auditor endowment ornament element handle amend

D. PRACTICE: ONE-HAND WORDS

12 serve uphill exceeds killjoy carefree homonym terrace onion
13 trade poplin greater pumpkin eastward plumply barrage holly
14 defer unhook reserve minimum attracts million scatter plump
15 exact kimono created minikin cassette opinion seaweed union

POSTTEST. Repeat the Pretest and compare performance.

E. POSTTEST: ALTERNATE- AND ONE-HAND WORDS

LESSON 36

TABLES

Line: 60 spaces
Tab: 5
Spacing: single
Drills: 2 times
Workguide: 63
Format Guide: 25
Tape: 17A

Goals: To type 35 wam/3'/5e; to format 2- and 3-column tables.

36-A. WARMUP

S 1 Fritz saw many old jets at the air show held in the spring.
A 2 Jim kept Gil away because four dozen taxi drivers had quit.
N 3 Tickets were incorrectly numbered from 49801 through 53762.

SKILLBUILDING

36-B. PACED PRACTICE

Turn to the Paced Practice routine at the back of the book. Take several 2-minute timings, starting at the point where you left off the last time. Record your progress on Workguide page 6.

36-C. Spacing: double. Record your score.

36-C. SKILL MEASUREMENT: 3-MINUTE TIMED WRITING

4   You have to realize that your phone work can be a real   12
5 plus for your firm's image. Don't jabber like some do when   24
6 on the phone, as some customer might react negatively.   35
7   It is important to answer the telephone graciously, as   47
8 this conveys a positive image for your company. The caller   59
9 must be aware that the correct party has been reached.   70
10   A friendly greeting will help to put a caller at ease.   82
11 Next, you should state the name of the company and your own   94
12 name. Have references handy for those hard questions.   105

| 1 | 2 | 3 | 4 | 5 | 6 | 7 | 8 | 9 | 10 | 11 | 12

36-D. BASIC PARTS OF A TABLE

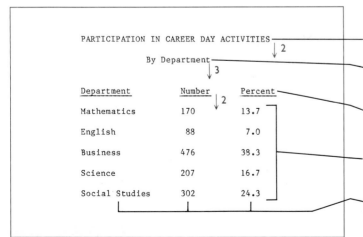

TITLE. Identifies contents of table. Center and type in all-capital letters.

SUBTITLE. Sometimes used to give more information about the table. Center a double space below the title, with the first and all principal words capitalized.

COLUMN HEADINGS. Tell what is in each column. Either begin at left of column or center over the column. Underscore, and leave 2 blank lines before and 1 blank line after.

BODY. Consists of the columns in the table. Center horizontally, usually with 6 spaces between columns; may be either single-spaced or double-spaced.

COLUMN. Is a listing of information. Word columns align at the left. Columns of whole numbers align at the right; columns of decimal amounts align on the decimal point.

I'll also need the comparative bookings/sales data for each of the three branches. Make an individual table for each branch, and use the location of the branch as part of the heading. When you extract the names of the salespeople according to branch, please list them on the basis of highest to lowest bookings for this year. For example, in the Muncie table Madeline D. Huls will be first, and James A. Quinnell will be last. Don't put the names in groups of four, as there will be only five or six names in each table. Give totals for this year and last year and the total percent change for each branch. You can calculate the total percent change by dividing the difference between the two total bookings amounts by the total bookings for last year. Type the tables across the length of the paper.

This is a cover letter for a questionnaire that I'll want you to type. Type the date, inside address, and salutation lines as you normally do for a letter in which the merge feature will be used to personalize the letter. (*See Letters 81–83 on page 307.*)

as one who has used the services of our office	10
. . . you can help us by taking a few minutes to	18
complete the enclosed questionnaire and returning it to us at your earliest convenience	27
	36
. . .	
worldwide travel places top priority on the	45
needs of people like you who use our services	54
. . . by providing us with responses to the	62
questions . . . you will help us to provide services designed specifically for you . . .	70
	77

This questionnaire should help us to do a better job of meeting the needs of our travelers. Please retype it, and then we'll decide which method of duplication we'll use to make the number of copies we need.

```
WORLD WIDE TRAVEL                    Traveler Questionnaire    8

   1.  How many times you have been served by Worldwide Travel?   20
          _____ 1              _____ 6-10                     21
          _____ 2-5 usually   _____ 11 or more               23
   2.  Which Worldwide branch serves your travel needs?           35
       _____ Terre Haute _____ Indianapolis _____ Muncie   41
   3.  How would you rate our service?                            48
          _____ Excellent    _____ Fair                      51
          _____ Good         _____ Poor                      52
       Comments:_____  54
       _____

   4.  Is most of your travelling done for business or pleasure? 66
          _____ Business     _____ Pleasure                  69
   5.  What do you consider to be the most important ser-         80
       vices of a Travel Agency?                                  85
       _____

       _____

   6.  What new services would you like to see offered by World- 97
       wide Travel?                                              99
       _____

       _____
```

36-E. FORMATTING A TABLE

Before you begin, clear all tabs and move the margins to the extreme left and right.

1. Select the Key Line. The key line consists of the longest item in each column, plus 6.blank spaces for each open area between columns.

2. Set the Left Margin. From the center, backspace once for every 2 characters or spaces in the key line, and set the left margin at the point to which you have backspaced.

Example: se/nt/en/ce/12/34/56/th/ou/gh/12/34/56/ta/bl/es

Note: Do not backspace for an extra stroke at the end of the line.

3. Set Tabs. Space across the paper once for *each* letter and *each* space in the longest entry of the first column plus the 6 blank spaces, and set a tab for the second column. Do the same for the longest entry in the second column plus the 6 blank spaces, and set a tab for the third column.

4. Compute the Top Margin. To center the table vertically, subtract the number of lines (including blank lines) in the table from either 66 (a full sheet of paper) or 33 (a half sheet) and divide by 2. If a fraction is left, drop it.

Example: 33 − 12 = 21; 21 ÷ 2 = 10½; begin typing on line 10.

5. Type the Table. Backspace-center the title in all-capital letters. Then leave 2 blank lines and type the body.

Note: Use the tab key to move across from column to column.

Practice. Center this double-spaced table on a half sheet.

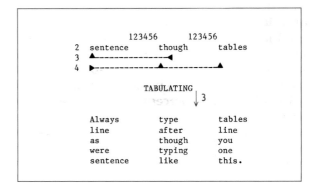

Before typing Tables 1 and 2, complete Workguide page 63.

36-F. TABLES

Type Tables 1 and 2 on half sheets of paper, double-spacing the body of each table. Leave the machine on single spacing until you are ready to begin typing the column entries.

Remember to clear all tab stops and to move the margins to the extreme left and right before formatting each table.

TABLE 1
3-COLUMN TABLE

Spacing: double
Paper: plain, half sheet

Number columns with decimals align on the decimal point.

FIRST-QUARTER SALES ↓2			4
As a Percentage of Target Goal ↓3			10
Connecticut	Malcolm W. Tarsun	106.5	16
New Jersey	Ingrid S. Torgeson	112.2	23
New York	Elise R. Estivant	98.3	29
Pennsylvania	J. D. Greenberg	104.7	35

Key Line: Pennsylvania 123456 Ingrid S. Torgeson 123456 106.5

TABLE 2
2-COLUMN TABLE

Spacing: double
Paper: plain, half sheet

ANNIVERSARY PLANNING COMMITTEE		6
M. Choy	Human Resources	10
J. Ortega	Quality Control	15
D. Pierce	Mail Services	20
T. West	Accounts Receivable	25

TABLE 58
RULED TABLE

Paper: plain, full sheet

Please type this table showing comparative sales for the last two years. The table goes with the memo (*page 318*). As the table is quite wide, type it across the length of the paper.

Compute the total amount for this year and the percentage of increase for this year as compared with last year. Compute the percentage by dividing the total amount of increase by the total amount for last year. Please leave the names in sets of four for ease of reading. Prepare an extra copy of the table for use in the preparation of Tables 59–61 (*page 320*).

WORLDWIDE TRAVEL AGENCY
COMPARATIVE BOOKINGS/SALES OF CURRENT YEAR AND LAST YEAR

Salesperson	Branch	Bookings Last Year	Bookings This Year	Percent Change
Andersen, Jeffrey S.	Terre Haute	$ 375,682	$ 392,643	4.5
Behling, Shannon L.	Muncie	326,783	336,488	3.0
Bradley, Brian	Terre Haute	174,924	187,466	7.2
Carlson, Bobbi Jo	Indianapolis	293,491	314,832	7.3
Frazier, R. G.	Indianapolis	360,420	379,141	5.2
Huls, Madeline D.	Muncie	420,734	431,724	2.6
King-Sager, Karen	Terre Haute	307,859	311,567	1.2
Kokaviska, David J.	Terre Haute	294,786	255,006	-13.5
Mancini, Gregory R.	Indianapolis	293,745	305,709	4.1
McDowell, Mark L.	Indianapolis	257,056	261,115	1.6
Quinnell, James A.	Muncie	182,482	184,002	0.8
Schuenemann, Kelly A.	Muncie	190,581	205,904	8.0
Scott, Charlene A.	Terre Haute	337,691	316,724	-6.2
Sequera, Pedro	Muncie	268,990	274,823	2.2
Vezzetti, Joy M.	Terre Haute	394,008	407,890	3.5
Young, Mildred F.	Indianapolis	265,559	298,791	12.5
TOTALS		$4,744,791	$4,863,825	

TABLES WITH BLOCKED COLUMN HEADINGS

Line: 60 spaces
Tab: 5
Spacing: single
Drills: 2 times
Format Guide: 25–27
Tape: 18A

Goals: To improve speed and accuracy; to format tables with blocked column headings.

37-A. WARMUP

S 1 They caught the last boat back to the mainland at the dock.
A 2 Fay's wipers quit just when Marv locked the zoo's gate box.
N 3 The left-hand keys are 12345, and the right ones are 67890.

SKILLBUILDING

PRETEST. Take a 1-minute timing; compute your speed and count errors.

37-B. PRETEST: VERTICAL REACHES

4   Some lawmakers in Washington attribute our basic bank-   12
5 ing success to judicious or scientific cash reserve manage-   24
6 ment. A bank just cannot be drawn into dropping its guard.   36
   | 1 | 2 | 3 | 4 | 5 | 6 | 7 | 8 | 9 | 10 | 11 | 12

PRACTICE.
Speed Emphasis: If you made 2 or fewer errors on the Pretest, type each line twice.
Accuracy Emphasis: If you made 3 or more errors on the Pretest, type lines 7–14 once; then repeat.

37-C. PRACTICE: UP REACHES

7 at atlas plate water later batch fatal match late gate atom
8 dr draft drift drums drawn drain drama dress drab drag drop
9 ju jumpy juror junky jumbo juice julep judge just judo jump
10 es essay press bless crest quest fresh rises less best pest

37-D. PRACTICE: DOWN REACHES

11 ca cable cabin cadet camel cameo candy carve cash case cane
12 nk trunk drink rinks prank brink drank crank sink monk bank
13 ba batch badge bagel baked banjo barge basis bank back bass
14 sc scale scald scrub scalp scare scout scarf scan scar scat

POSTTEST. Repeat the Pretest and compare performance.

37-E. POSTTEST: VERTICAL REACHES

37-F. FORMATTING TABLES WITH BLOCKED COLUMN HEADINGS

Underscored column headings are used to identify the information in the columns. Blocked headings (as shown at the right) are becoming increasingly popular because they are quick and easy to format. The first column heading begins at the left margin. The second column heading begins at the tab setting for the second column, and so on.

When items are selected for the key line, the column heading is considered as one of the column entries; that is, it is selected for the key line if it is the longest entry in the column.

Follow the steps for formatting a table outlined on page 70.

SILICON VALLEY LODGING, INC.

November 1, 19--
↓3

Name of Motel	City	Rooms
Rainbow Motel	Cupertino	114
Red Horse Ranch	Los Gatos	53
Airport Motel	San Jose	78
Friendship Inn	Santa Clara	96
Kamdahl's Motel	Sunnyvale	102

Key Line: Red Horse Ranch₁₂₃₄₅₆Santa Clara₁₂₃₄₅₆Rooms

REPORT 72
JUSTIFIED DISPLAY

Line: 31 spaces
Spacing: double
Paper: plain, full sheet

It is possible to have all lines end evenly at the right margin by leaving extra spaces at selected places on the typed lines. The result is referred to as a *justified dis-*

play. As we will use this procedure for our company newsletter, which we are starting next week, practice the preparation of such a display as described in this copy from our procedures manual. First read the copy, and then prepare a copy exactly as shown, remembering to include the # symbol in the first display.

This copy shows the justified copy with extra spaces inserted between the words.

You would not use this method when typing regular correspondence, but it is an excellent technique for a special typing display.

WP

A word processor can print out justified copy upon receiving one command from the operator, eliminating the step of typing a draft copy.

12.1 JUSTIFYING LINES   4

Justifying typing (making all   10
the lines of typing end evenly)   17
is done as follows: 20
1. Begin by typing a draft,#   26
ending all lines as close as###   32
possible to the point where you   39
want them to end. Except for##   45
lines which are at the end of##   51
paragraphs, fill in short lines   57
with # signs to show how many##   64
extra spaces will be needed.   69
2. You are now ready to type   75
the good copy. Be sure that###   81
extra spaces are inserted. The   88
copy will look better if the###   94
spaces are scattered so that### 100
they do not come together.   105

Justifying typing (making all
the lines of typing end evenly)
is done as follows:
1. Begin by typing a draft,
ending all lines as close as
possible to the point where you
want them to end. Except for
lines which are at the end of
paragraphs, fill in short lines
with # signs to show how many
extra spaces will be needed.
2. You are now ready to type
the good copy. Be sure that
extra spaces are inserted. The
copy will look better if the
spaces are scattered so that
they do not come together.

MEMOS 29–30
COVER MEMORANDUMS

Paper: plain, full sheets

Tuesday Aug 15
From: Ms. Joanne Sloan Riley

Along with two memorandums, you'll also have to prepare the four tables to which I refer. Type this memorandum twice, once to Loretta Kendall, manager of the Muncie branch, and once to Mike Britton, manager of

the Indianapolis branch. The subject of the memos is Bookings/Sales for Worldwide Travel Agency. When you prepare the tables, remember to make the extra copies that are needed. As I wrote the draft in a hurry, please correct any errors you find. Fill in the missing numbers after you have computed them from the summary table for all three branches on page 319.

You probably have been looking   6
forward to recieving the bookings/sales   14
report for the Worldwide travel   21
agency. Enclosed are four tables   28
that contain information for each   34
of the three offices. In addition, a   42
summery report is enclosed for   48
all three branches. Besides sales for   56
both last year and this year for   63
each sales person the percentage   69
of change is shown.   73

¶ Compare the total Worldwide   79
amount of $ for last year   86
with $ for this year. This   93
     per cent increase reflects the 100
good job that our three branches   106
are doing.   108
¶ We can understand that you   114
and those on your staff are   119
eager to see the latest sales   125
figures. Congratulations and best   132
wishes for next year.   137

TABLE 3
3-COLUMN TABLE

Spacing: double
Paper: plain, full sheet

STOCK MARKET GROUPS WITH LARGEST GAINS ↓2 8

For Quarter Ending March 31, 19-- ↓3 14

No.	Leading Industries	Leading Company ↓2	21
1	Retail—Discount	Marco, Inc.	27
2	Retail—Clothing	Fairview Stores	33
3	Personal Services	Liv-Rite Dynamics	40
4	Drug Manufacturers	Cleveland International	48
5	Shoe Manufacturers	Kise Leather Company	56
6	Retail—Gift Specialty	Dahlstrom Brothers	64

TABLE 4
3-COLUMN TABLE

Spacing: double
Paper: plain, full sheet

SUPERIOR INVESTMENTS ↓2 4

Five-Year Share Price Comparisons ↓3 11

Mutual Fund	1984	1989 ↓2	14
Superior Growth	11.08	32.84	19
Superior High Yield	23.87	42.38	25
Superior Income	53.61	96.35	30
Superior International	48.32	54.72	37
Superior Tax-Free Bond	35.78	69.06	43
Superior Technology	13.81	18.56	49
Superior Utilities	49.02	55.79	54

TABLE 5
3-COLUMN TABLE

Spacing: double
Paper: plain, full sheet

SUGGESTED READING LIST 4

Title	Author	Publisher	
The Great Depression	Willard P. McCarty	Econ Press	18
The Postwar Boom	Bonnie F. Meinert	Ashton Publishing	28
War and the Economy	Wanda M. Dellies	Dobsons, Inc.	38
The Mid-80s Bear	Laura L. Ohman	Cierra Books	46
Recession in the 1970s	Robert J. Sachs	Scanlon Publishers	57
Inflation Theories	James D. Wilson Jr.	Cordero & Sons	67
The New Economists	K. V. Fung	Collegiate Books	76

LETTER 87
FORM LETTER

Paper: plain, full sheet

honeymoon trips, so we are going to do a large mailing to stimulate additional business. This form letter has been edited and is ready for final typing. Please check the spelling of those words which I've circled.

We know that our agency has to do more to promote

(Date)

(Name)
(Street)
(City, State Zip)

(Salutation)

If your typewriter does not have an exclamation mark, use a period and an apostrophe.

Congratulations on your engagement! This is such an exciting | 12
time for you! You will soon begin planing for your wedding, | 25
and you probably have already started thinking about where you | 37
will go for your honeymoon. Locations that are particularly | 49
popular in the colder months are the Carribbean Islands, the | 61
Bahamas, Mexico, California, and Florida. Some summer sites | 73
for those who enjoy the outdoors are New England, Minnesota, | 86
Glacier National Park, and the Upper Peninsula of Mich. The | 99
resorts of the Pocono Mountains provide packages for skiing, | 111
skating, and snowmobiling in the winter and for golf, tennis, | 123
and water skiing in the summer. Always popular honeymoon | 135
trips, of course, are a visit to Niagara Falls and an ocean | 147
cruise. | 148

Come in, and one of our agents will be happy to make your | 160
reservations. By doing so early, you will get the best prices | 172
and accomodations. | 176

We extend our wishes for happiness to both of you and look for | 188
ward to serving you. | 192

Sincerely yours, | 196

Joanne Sloan-Riley | 199
Manager | 201

Use your own reference initials, of course.

urs | 202

P.S. We can also arrange flights and room | 210
reservations for your wedding guests. | 217

Line: 60 spaces
Tab: 5
Spacing: single
Drills: 2 times
Format Guide: 27
Tape: 19A

LESSON
38

TABLES WITH SHORT CENTERED COLUMN HEADINGS

Goals: To type 35 wam/3'/5e; to format tables with short centered column headings.

38-A.   WARMUP

S 1 They will take their rowboat when they go back to the lake.
A 2 Mac Wiker did prize the five or six big quarterly journals.
N 3 Nina said that 27 of the 30 clients had read pages 491-568.

SKILLBUILDING

38-B. Take a 1-minute timing on the first paragraph to establish your base speed. Then take several 1-minute timings on the remaining paragraphs. As soon as you equal or exceed your base speed on one paragraph, advance to the next one.

38-B.   SUSTAINED TYPING: NUMBERS

4   Michael learned through firsthand experience last week   12
5 that the cost of a week on the water can vary a great deal.   24
6 He says that a rowboat would be about right for his wallet.   36

7   His Uncle Bob told him that when he was his age he had   12
8 rented a small cabin for the huge sum of $105 for one week.   24
9 For $23 more, he rented a small boat and an outboard motor.   36

10   Then Uncle Bob went on to say that when he rented that   12
11 same cabin last year the cost had gone up to either $395 or   24
12 $410. The boat and motor rentals now cost from $62 to $87.   36

13   Aunt Kate said that she and her husband will be paying   12
14 either $1,946 or $2,073 for one week's sailing on a 53-foot   24
15 yacht. The boat has a 4-person crew and was built in 1982.   36
   | | | 2 | 3 | 4 | 5 | 6 | 7 | 8 | 9 | 10 | 11 | 12

38-C.   PROGRESSIVE PRACTICE: ALPHABET

Turn to the Progressive Practice: Alphabet routine at the back of the book. Take several 30-second timings, starting at the point where you left off the last time. Record your progress on Workguide page 6.

38-D. Spacing: double. Record your score.

38-D.   SKILL MEASUREMENT: 3-MINUTE TIMED WRITING

16   Each office has its own plan which is used for storing   12
17 and retrieving written information. This process is called   24
18 filing. All of us realize that things do differ because of   36
19 differences in offices, but the basic approach is the same.   48
20   A good filing system can help to make your office more   60
21 efficient. If you know where your documents are located, a   72
22 great deal of time can be saved. This time can be used for   84
23 the myriad of extra office jobs. Quick and easy access are   96
24 things to look for in a good records system.   105
   | | | 2 | 3 | 4 | 5 | 6 | 7 | 8 | 9 | 10 | 11 | 12

LETTER 86　　　　　Paper: Workguide 387–388
COVER LETTER

Here's the cover letter to go along with the Norway tour report. Date the letter with today's date, and use Norway Tour as the subject line. Since this is a duplicated form letter, there won't be a need for an inside address; just type the salutation where it would usually go. Please attach this letter to the report you typed for the Norway tour.

dear norway travelers . . . i have finalized the　　9
plans for our tour of norway . . . and i wanted　　17
to bring you up to date on our plans . . .　　25

　　i have attached a report that spells out our　　34

flight schedule and other details concerning　　43
our flight out of the united states . . . once we　　52
reach oslo . . . i will give each of you a copy of　　61
the final itinerary for our ten days in norway　　71
. . . a detailed schedule for our return to the　　79
united states will also be provided at that time　　89
. . .

　　thank you for joining us on our tour . . . i am　　98
sure you will enjoy the trip . . . if you have any　　107
questions or concerns . . . please contact me　　116
. . . our staff joins me in extending best wishes　　125
for a wonderful vacation trip . . .　　131

MEMO 28　　　　　Paper: plain, full sheet

As you know, airline policies are still undergoing a great deal of change. The NAA and major airlines have been working for some time to structure the following guidelines for children traveling alone. All employees of Worldwide must share the responsibility for bringing these policies to the attention of our clients. Please type a copy of this memorandum, correcting any errors you may find.

```
MEMO TO:  All Employees                                        5

FROM:     Joanne Sloan-Riley                                  11
          Manager

DATE:                                                         15

SUBJECT:  Guidelines for Children Who Travel Alone            25
      + 1#                 new policies
The airlines have issued rules for children who travel alone.  39
Please keep these guide lines posted so that you can refer to  51
them frequently.                                              54

1.  No children under 5 years of age will be accepted without  67
    an adult.                                                  69

2.  Children aged 5, 6, or 7 will be accepted on nonstop       80
    flights.  They must be met by an adult however.            90

3.  Children aged 8 through 11 will be accepted on nonstop     101
    connecting flights.  They must be met by an adult.  The    113
    airline will assist children in making connections.        123

4.  Children unaccompanied will be charged an adult fare.      134

5.  Children aged 12 through 15 may recieve help in making a   146
    connecting flight if help is requested.                    154

6.  The adults meeting a child must show proper identification 166
    and sign a document before they take the child.            175

    Remember, there are no exceptions to these policies.       186
```

38-E. FORMATTING TABLES WITH SHORT CENTERED COLUMN HEADINGS

Tables with short centered column headings are formatted almost like those with blocked column headings, as described on page 71: (1) Select the key line. (2) Backspace-center to set the left margin. (3) Space across to set the column tabs.

To compute the number of spaces that each column heading should be indented from the start of its column:

1. Subtract the number of spaces in the column heading from the number of spaces in the longest item of the column.
2. Divide the answer by 2 (drop any fraction), and indent the column heading that number of spaces.

The computations shown here are for the two column headings illustrated at the right:

Column 1: $18 - 4 = 14$; $14 \div 2 = 7$; indent the heading 7 spaces.

Column 2: $12 - 5 = 7$; $7 \div 2 = 3\frac{1}{2}$; indent the heading 3 spaces.

You may want to pencil in each indention reminder on the copy as shown so that you will not forget to indent.

```
              COMPANY PRESIDENTS
                                 ↓3

     7⌋Name              3⌋Years
                                 ↓2
     John A. Price          1946-1953
     William P. Hocking     1954-1968
     Roberto S. Ojeda       1969-1984
     Carol E. Herndon       1985-Present
```

Short centered column headings are capitalized, underscored, preceded by 2 blank lines, and followed by 1 blank line.

TABLE 6
3-COLUMN TABLE WITH
SHORT COLUMN HEADINGS

Spacing: double
Paper: plain, half sheet

The $ sign is not repeated in a column of figures.

WP Most word processing software has a decimal tab feature that aligns the decimal points in a column of figures.

TOP UNITED WAY CONTRIBUTORS   5

Department	Leader	Amount	10
Purchasing	Kellee A. Dillon	$3,073.00	17
Operations and Maintenance	Gregory J. Hulbert	2,979.25	27
Research and Development	Mary L. Nardi	2,482.50	36
Shipping	Robert C. Higgins	2,146.00	43
Accounting	John P. Touchinski	1,850.60	50
Publications	Clarence L. Roth	1,752.60	57
Sales	Paulette L. Skehen	1,467.00	63

TABLE 7
3-COLUMN TABLE WITH
SHORT COLUMN HEADINGS

Spacing: double
Paper: plain, half sheet

WP Some word processors have a column-layout feature that automatically aligns column headings with the column entries.

ASHTON PUBLISHING   3
Print Titles for December 19—   9

Title	Author	Editor	13
Emerging Mutual Funds	Bernadette M. Chow	Maria A. Sartorelli	24
The Glitter of Gold	Lester A. Frazier	Paul J. Spalding	35
Guide to Buying Stocks	Alfred E. Hughes	Joan G. Valentine	46
A Model Portfolio	Kimberly Ferns Ewing	Pablo J. Menendez	57
Selecting a Home Mortgage	Mike D. Reynolds	Sharon B. Dohrman	68
Starting Your Own Business	Elise M. Harrington	Philip L. Knox	80

Please retype the information for the Norway tour. When you finish typing the corrected copy, I'll dictate a cover letter for it.

NORWAY TOUR   2

While business reports ordinarily are typed with double spacing, single spacing may be used.

The official date of departure for the trip to Norway is   14
September 7. The following information is provided so that you   26
will be kept up to date on final arrangements. The flight   38
return will leave Oslo on September 18.   46

Airline	Flight No.	Terminal Airport	Time	
				47
				52
United	513	Lv. Indianapolis	5:12 p.m.	59
		Arr. N.Y. Kennedy	6:33 p.m.	64
Northwest	102	Lv. N.Y. Kennedy	9:05 p.m.	72
		Arr. Oslo	12:00 noon	75
Northwest	104	Lv. Oslo	2:05 p.m.	81
		Arr. N.Y. Kennedy	3:50 p.m.	86
United	1631	Lv. N.Y. Kennedy	6:15 p.m.	93
		Arr. Indianapolis	7:35 p.m.	99

Use abbreviations in tables when there are space limitations.

Please be at Gate 16 at Indianapolis international airport one   110
hour in advance of our departure flights tickets will be at   122
the gate, and all travelers will be issued individual boarding   134
passes.   136

Side headings usually are typed in all-capital letters without underscores. It is acceptable, however, to capitalize only important words; when doing so, underscore the side headings.

Luggage   137

According to International flight regulations, each per-   148
son may check one piece of luggage weighing up to 44 pounds.   161
All luggage will be checked through to Oslo. You may also   172
carry one small bag to be stored under your seat on the plane.   185
Other personal items, such as coats and cameras, may be stored   198
in the over head compartments.   204

Passports   205

Upon boarding Northwest in New York, you will need to   216
present your passport. Please keep it handy, and be careful   228
not to misplace or loose it.   234

Line: 60 spaces
Tab: 5
Spacing: single
Drills: 2 times
Workguide: 64
Format Guide: 27–29
Tape: 20A

TABLES WITH LONG CENTERED COLUMN HEADINGS

Goals: To improve speed and accuracy; to improve proofreading skills; to format long centered column headings.

39-A. WARMUP

S 1 Dick said that the next sign might be the one for the show.
A 2 Big Chuck Jarvey quoted amounts for extra prizes last week.
N 3 My balcony seats are those numbered 10, 29, 38, 47, and 56.

SKILLBUILDING

39-B. Type the paragraph and correct the errors.

39-B. PRODUCTION PRACTICE: PROOFREADING

4 All members of hte Toledoe Data Prosessors Association will
5 be asked ot vote next weak. Desisions will be made about a
6 merjer with the Toledoe PC Club. Speakers will present the
7 arguments for bot sides ofthe issue befor the members vote.

39-C. PROGRESSIVE PRACTICE: NUMBERS

Turn to the Progressive Practice: Numbers routine at the back of the book. Take several 30-second timings, starting at the point where you left off the last time. Record your progress on Workguide page 6.

39-D. FORMATTING TABLES WITH LONG CENTERED COLUMN HEADINGS

The table below illustrates three types of centered headings: short, long, and two-line.

LAKEVIEW MANOR APARTMENTS ↓2		
January 1, 19--, Rate Schedule ↓3		
Type of Unit	Number of Units	Monthly Rental Cost per Unit
Three bedrooms, three baths	24	$1,240.50
Two bedrooms, two baths	12	960.00
Two bedrooms, one bath	36	787.50
One bedroom, one bath	24	595.50
Studio, one bath	24	390.00

Short Centered Column Headings. The first one—the short centered column heading—is centered above the column as described in Lesson 38 on page 74 ($27 - 12 = 15$ and $15 \div 2 = 7\frac{1}{2}$; indent 7 spaces).

Long Centered Column Headings. The second column heading is longer than any of the column entries and is, therefore, part of the key line. To determine the horizontal placement of the column:

1. Subtract the number of spaces in the longest item in the column from the number of spaces in the column heading.
2. Divide the answer by 2 (drop any fraction), and indent the column that number of spaces. In the illustration, $15 - 2 = 13$ and $13 \div 2 = 6\frac{1}{2}$. Indent the column 6 spaces.

Two-Line Column Headings. The third column heading is so long that it requires two lines. Both lines are underscored, and the second one aligns horizontally with the other column headings. The shorter line is centered under the longer one ($19 - 8 = 11$ and $11 \div 2 = 5\frac{1}{2}$). Indent the second line of the heading 5 spaces.

Before typing Tables 8–10, complete Workguide page 64.

N. INTEGRATED OFFICE PROJECT: WORLDWIDE TRAVEL AGENCY

Before you begin your assignment at the Worldwide Travel Agency, sharpen your language arts skills by completing Workguide pages 297–298. The Worldwide project provides realistic office experiences that relate to the travel industry. Begin your work by establishing priorities for the different jobs in the project.

Situation: Today is Tuesday, August 15, 19—. You are working as a secretary at the Worldwide Travel Agency, located in Terre Haute, Indiana. Your supervisor is Ms. Joanne Sloan-Riley, manager of the Terre Haute branch office of Worldwide located in the Gateway Mall.

Ms. Sloan-Riley has a number of jobs ready for you to complete. You will want to read through the materials first so that you can ask for any clarification right away. Ms. Sloan-Riley has a very hectic schedule, heavily involved with supervision and in meeting deadlines. Therefore, she likes a secretary who can work well without direct supervision.

Use the modified-block letter style with standard punctuation for all outgoing correspondence, and include this closing:

```
           Sincerely yours,



           Joanne Sloan-Riley
           Manager
```

Once you have looked over your work assignments and have cleared up any questions, you will need to prioritize the jobs. Determine the priority levels (1, 2, and 3) of the jobs according to these guidelines:

1. Those items which have been identified by Ms. Sloan-Riley as having high priority or which, in your judgment, should be in this category.
2. Those items which are timely but, on the basis of their content, do not warrant a high-priority label.
3. Those items which may be delayed until after you have completed the jobs in levels 1 and 2.

FORM 40   Paper: Workguide 383
JOB PRIORITY LIST

Review the jobs in this project on the basis of the guidelines for prioritizing listed above. Then assign a 1, 2, or 3 priority to each job. List the jobs by level on Workguide page 383, and complete them accordingly.

LETTER 85   Paper: Workguide 385–386

An unusual inquiry arrived in today's mail. Mrs. Myrtle A. Cook of 347 Cummins Drive, Muncie, IN 47304, has inquired about scenic automobile routes from Muncie through New England and the Boston area. I was in a hurry when I dashed off this reply. I'd appreciate your correcting any errors. Please get this letter out this afternoon. I will be in Indianapolis for a meeting—so sign my name, and remember to add your initials.

A trip from Muncie thru	5
New England and the Boston area	12
is a good choice for late September.	19
I am sorry to inform you however	26
that our office does not provide	33
detailed plans for automobile travel.	40
Perhaps your insurance agent,	46
or your automobile club can	52
provide this service. In addition,	59
you can obtain useful informasion	66
from state tourist bureaus as	72
well as the chamber of commerce	78
in each area you plan to visit.	84
I am enclosing an informative	90
broshure about Boston that includes	98
a discriptive list of hotels and	104
motels. I hope you will find	110
it helpful.	112
When ever you plan to use	117
commercial transportation for	123
your travels, we shall be	129
happy to help plan your trip.	134

TABLE 8
4-COLUMN TABLE

Spacing: single
Paper: plain, half sheet

TRI-CITIES BUSINESS SCHOOL
Home Backgrounds of Students, October 19-- | 14

Location	Men	Women	Total	
Farm	86	104	190	20
Small Town	83	59	142	24
Small City	175	166	341	27
Medium-Size City	384	372	756	32
Large City	92	134	226	36

(18 — Location header line)

TABLE 9
3-COLUMN TABLE

Spacing: double
Paper: plain, full sheet

AVERAGE GRAIN YIELDS | 4

Chippewa County, 19— | 8

(handwritten: 8-4= 4÷2=[2]   16-4=12÷2=[6]   13-9=4÷2=2)

(handwritten: 24 42 ; 2)48 -24 ; ∠m = 18)

Crop	Bushels Per Acre	Compared With Last Year	
Barley	55.0	106.8%	20
Corn	84.6	103.3%	23
Oats	71.9	98.6%	25
Soybeans	42.7	92.2%	29
Wheat	45.3	107.6%	32

(11, 17 — Compared With Last Year header)

keyline: Soybeans 123456 Bushels Per Acre 123456 Compared With

TABLE 10
4-COLUMN TABLE

Spacing: double
Paper: plain, full sheet

Center and single-space each line of a two-line title. If possible, the first line should be longer than the second.

WORK STATUS OF STUDENTS AT | 5
APEX BUSINESS SCHOOL | 9

Enrollment and Work Status	1987	1988	1989	
Full-time student/no job	16%	12%	14%	23
Full-time student/part-time job	41%	46%	47%	31
Full-time student/full-time job	3%	4%	3%	39
Part-time student/no job	7%	4%	5%	45
Part-time student/part-time job	14%	16%	13%	53
Part-time student/full-time job	19%	18%	18%	61

(17 — Enrollment and Work Status header)

K. PACED PRACTICE

Turn to the Paced Practice routine at the back of the book. Take several 2-minute timings, starting at the point where you left off the last time. Record your progress on Workguide page 290.

L. Take several 1-minute timings on each line.

L. TECHNIQUE TYPING: SHIFT KEY

39 Pat and Joannie took Brandon to the Guthrie Theater in May.   12
40 Aunt Beth gave Kara and Tom a set of Classic Grafton china.   12
41 Our Midwest trip took us to Duluth, Green Bay, and Chicago.   12
   | 1 | 2 | 3 | 4 | 5 | 6 | 7 | 8 | 9 | 10 | 11 | 12

M. Spacing: double. Record your score.

M. SKILL MEASUREMENT: 5-MINUTE TIMED WRITING

42   Airline travel for both personal and business purposes   12
43 is fairly routine today. However, there continue to be the   24
44 dreaded delays, overbooked flights, missed connections, and   36
45 cancellations. There are a few things that you might do to   48
46 help your next junket go smoothly.   55
47   First, make sure that those reservations are in order.   67
48 Even then, you will want to be among the early birds at the   79
49 gate because of overbookings. Also, your seat choices will   91
50 be much better. You have a right to sit in that nonsmoking   103
51 section; stand up for your rights.   110
52   Second, you should realize that many airline decisions   122
53 affecting delays and cancellations are made for the purpose   134
54 of saving your life. Some factors affecting such decisions   146
55 are weather, a plane's mechanical condition, and the volume   158
56 of air traffic. Try to be patient.   165
57   Third, acquaint yourself with the schedules of all the   177
58 airlines that serve your community. Expect any delays that   189
59 might be encountered and plan accordingly. Avoid flying at   201
60 peak periods, such as Friday afternoons or Sunday evenings,   213
61 and at the start or end of holidays.   220
62   Fourth, remember that time means money in the business   232
63 world, and the delay or cancellation of a flight could mean   244
64 problems. Contingency plans are required for meetings that   256
65 are particularly crucial. My friend Jerry always flies one   268
66 day early for meetings of this type.   275
   | 1 | 2 | 3 | 4 | 5 | 6 | 7 | 8 | 9 | 10 | 11 | 12

TABLE, REPORT, AND LETTER REVIEW

Line: 60 spaces
Tab: 5, center
Spacing: single
Drills: 2 times
Workguide: 65
Format Guide: 29–30

Goals: To type 36 wam/3'/5e; to format a table, a report, and a letter.

40-A.   WARMUP

S 1 He had a right to the profits from the two bushels of corn.
A 2 Fritz Krebs may join pushy crowds at quaint Texas villages.
N 3 She transferred from Flight 238 to Flight 749 at 10:56 p.m.

SKILLBUILDING

40-B. Take a 1-minute timing on the first paragraph to establish your base speed. Then take several 1-minute timings on the remaining paragraphs. As soon as you equal or exceed your base speed on one paragraph, advance to the next one.

40-B.   SUSTAINED TYPING: SYMBOLS

4   It was quite normal that Patty was somewhat nervous as   12
5   she entered the college building. After four years of work   24
6   as a clerk, she was here to take the college entrance exam.   36

7   Just as you have likely done, Patty took her #2 pencil   12
8   and began to fill in the score sheet. A test administrator   24
9   (Mr. Gillam) had said that a grade of 75% would be passing.   36

10   Patty had come to Room #68 (a large lecture hall) from   12
11   the Ballou & Ingerham accounting firm. It's a "mighty long   24
12   hike," and almost 100% of the examinees were already there.   36

13   For a $25 fee, everyone in Room #68 (the large lecture   12
14   hall) answered the "carefully chosen" true-false questions.   24
15   About 40% had prepared by using Carr & Teugh's Study Guide.   36

| | | 2 | 3 | 4 | 5 | 6 | 7 | 8 | 9 | 10 | 11 | 12 |

40-C.   DIAGNOSTIC TYPING: ALPHABET

Turn to the Diagnostic Typing: Alphabet routine at the back of the book. Take the Pretest, and record your performance on Workguide page 6. Then practice the drill lines for those reaches on which you made errors.

40-D. Spacing: double. Record your score.

40-D.   SKILL MEASUREMENT: 3-MINUTE TIMED WRITING

16   Some of us can recall when a computer was a rare thing   12
17   in an office. Early models were huge and had quite limited   24
18   storage. It is hard to believe that things change so fast.   36
19   If we examine the uses of the early computers, we very   48
20   quickly realize that the processing of numbers was the only   60
21   activity. Use of computer jargon was in its early infancy.   72
22   The use of word processing is now one of the most com- 84
23   mon ways in which these giant tools are used. What a great   96
24   thing to have this pure magic at the tips of one's fingers. 108

| | | 2 | 3 | 4 | 5 | 6 | 7 | 8 | 9 | 10 | 11 | 12 |

F. DIAGNOSTIC TYPING: ALPHABET

Turn to the Diagnostic Typing: Alphabet routine at the back of the book. Take the Pretest, and record your performance on Workguide page 289. Then practice the drill lines for those reaches on which you made errors.

G. Take a 1-minute timing on each line; compute your speed and count errors.

G. TECHNIQUE PRACTICE: INFREQUENT LETTERS

16 Jeff jogs, jumps rope, and does judo just in June and July. 12
17 Kent kept the keys to the truck and took Kim's kitten home. 12
18 He requested many quality quilts to fill his quota quickly. 12
19 Max boxed six bouts in the Texas exhibition for extra cash. 12
20 Yes, you may go play in the park and buy some sticky candy. 12
21 Dozens of crazy zookeepers zipped past the zebras and zebu. 12

| | 1 | | 2 | 3 | 4 | 5 | 6 | 7 | 8 | 9 | 10 | 11 | 12

H. Compare these lines with Sections C and D on page 311. Type a list of the words that contain errors, correcting the errors as you type.

H. PRODUCTION PRACTICE: PROOFREADING

22 as mast last post easy vase beast waste taost reason castle
23 op hope flip open mops rope oprea droop scope copier trophy
24 we went owed went weld weed weigh weary wedge wealth plowed
25 rt hurt sort cart dirt font court party start hearty parted

26 sw swat swim swam swig swap swift sweat sword switch swirly
27 un tune spun unit punt dune under prune sunny hunter uneasy
28 gr grow grin grab grub grew great grave gripe grease grassy
29 ol role oleo pool sold hole troll jolly polka stoled oldest

I. Take a 1-minute timing on the first paragraph to establish your base speed. Then take several 1-minute timings on the other paragraphs. As soon as you equal or exceed your base speed on one paragraph, advance to the next one.

I. SUSTAINED TYPING: NUMBERS

30   Jill told me that there were only 18 second graders in 12
31 her classroom in School District 409. That is roughly half 24
32 the number enrolled in her first-grade classroom last year. 36

33   When the 71 elementary teachers in School District 409 12
34 were asked about class size, 68 indicated that they thought 24
35 class size shouldn't exceed 25; the other 3 didn't respond. 36

36   Kindergarten and grade 1 classes in the district aver- 12
37 age 18 students per class; grades 2 and 3, 27; and grades 4 24
38 and 5, 31. School District 409 needs 6 more good teachers. 36

| | 1 | | 2 | 3 | 4 | 5 | 6 | 7 | 8 | 9 | 10 | 11 | 12

J. DIAGNOSTIC TYPING: NUMBERS

Turn to the Diagnostic Typing: Numbers routine at the back of the book. Take the Pretest, and record your performance on Workguide page 289. Then practice the drill lines for those reaches on which you made errors.

40-E. FORMATTING REVIEW

Before typing these jobs, review table typing (pages 69, 70, and 74), report typing (page 59), and letter typing (page 48) if necessary.

TABLE 11
4-COLUMN TABLE

Spacing: single
Paper: plain, half sheet

QUARTERLY USED-CAR SALES				5
Lincoln Park Location				9
Type	July	August	September	14
Compact	43	34	50	16
Midsize	27	23	25	19
Luxury Sedan	17	21	14	22
Sports	9	7	16	24
Station Wagon	8	8	17	28

REPORT 10

Spacing: double
Paper: plain, full sheet

LINCOLN PARK SALES REPORT 5

Third Quarter, 19— 9

Sales at the Lincoln Park used-car lot for the third quarter of 19— 23
were up 17.4 percent from the previous year. The total monthly auto 36
sales were as follows: July, 104; August, 93; and September, 122. There 51
appear to be two reasons for our success. 59

BUILDING AND LOT IMPROVEMENTS 65
After Saxton Auto Sales, Inc. purchased Lincoln Park in March, several 80
landscaping and building renovation projects were implemented at our 93
lot. The result has been an attractive location that promotes an atmos- 108
phere of quality and confidence. 114

INCREASE IN ADVERTISING 119
We think that the 43 percent increase in advertising expenditures 132
since March has also paid dividends. This increase has been in the news- 146
paper, radio, and television media. 153
We look forward to even better sales during the fourth quarter. 166

LETTER 13
MODIFIED-BLOCK STYLE

Paper: Workguide 65

When a letter has more than one enclosure, use the correct numeral and the word *Enclosures*. Example: *2 Enclosures*.

(Current date) / Mr. J. L. Payton, President / Saxton Auto Sales, Inc. / 14
3280 Ridge Street / Chicago Heights, IL 60411 / Dear Mr. Payton: 26
As members of the Saxton team, we at Lincoln Park are indeed proud 39
to send you our sales report for the third quarter. The staff and I are 54
pleased to be a part of your organization. 62
In addition to a copy of our sales report for the third quarter, a listing 77
of sales by type of car for each of the months of July, August, and Septem- 92
ber is also enclosed. 96
Sincerely, / Tom J. Giesen / Sales Manager / *(Your initials)* / 2 Enclo- 105
sures 106

INTEGRATED OFFICE PROJECT: TRAVEL

Line: 60 spaces
Tab: 5, center
Spacing: single
Drills: 2 times
Workguide: 383–390
Format Guide: 147

GOALS FOR UNIT 30

1. To improve speed and accuracy on alphabetic and numeric copy.
2. To type 55 wam for 5 minutes with no more than 5 errors.
3. To improve skills in formatting from handwritten and rough-draft copy.
4. To improve arithmetic skills.
5. To improve formatting skills.
6. To set priorities.
7. To correct common language arts errors.
8. To use reference works.

A. WARMUP

S 1 He had to pay big bucks for a chair and a bed for his flat.
A 2 A black fox was roving among the puny jonquils and azaleas.
N 3 Ed counted 278 cars, 150 trucks, 69 tractors, and 34 buses.

SKILLBUILDING

PRETEST. Take a 1-minute timing; compute your speed and count errors.

B. PRETEST: CLOSE REACHES

4   Casey hoped that we were not wasting good grub. After   12
5   the sun went down, he swiftly put the oleo and plums in the   24
6   cart. Bart opened a copy of an old book, Grant had a swim,   36
7   and Curtis unearthed a sword in a hole in that grassy dune.   48
    | 1 | 2 | 3 | 4 | 5 | 6 | 7 | 8 | 9 | 10 | 11 | 12

PRACTICE.
  Speed Emphasis: If you made no errors on the Pretest, type each line twice.
  Accuracy Emphasis: If you made 1 or more errors on the Pretest, type each group of lines (as though it were a paragraph) twice.

C. PRACTICE: ADJACENT KEYS

8   as mask last past easy vase beast waste toast reason castle
9   op hope flop open mops rope opera droop scope copier trophy
10 we west owed went weld weep weigh weary wedge wealth plowed
11 rt hurt port cart dirt fort court party start hearty parted

D. PRACTICE: CONSECUTIVE FINGERS

12 sw swat swim swan swig swap swift sweet sword switch swirly
13 un tune spun unit dune punt under prune sunny hunter uneasy
14 gr grow grim grab grub grew great graze gripe grease grassy
15 ol role oleo pool sold hole troll folly polka stolen oldest

POSTTEST. Repeat the Pretest and compare performance.

E. POSTTEST: CLOSE REACHES

Ask your instructor for the General Information Test on Part 2.

T E S T 2

PROGRESS TEST ON PART 2

TEST 2-A
3-MINUTE TIMED WRITING

Line: 60 spaces
Tab: 5
Spacing: double
Paper: Workguide 67
Start: 6 lines from top

```
               1          2           3          4
Now that you have completed the first forty lessons of      12
        5           6          7          8
this text, let us hope that you are quite pleased with your   24
      9         10           11            12
level of progress thus far.  Learning to type the different  36
        13          14           15             16
keys by touch was followed by attempts to improve the speed  48
         17          18          19           20
and accuracy of your stroking.  You have now completed your  60
        21         22           23            24
first cycle of typing letters, reports, and tables.  If you  72
        25          26           27             28
analyze the next part of the text, you will see a continued  84
          29         30            31           32
push to increase your stroking skill.  There will also be a  96
       33          34          35            36
great deal of emphasis put on increasing production skills.  108
|  1  |  2  |  3  |  4  |  5  |  6  |  7  |  8  |  9  | 10  | 11  | 12
```

TEST 2-B
LETTER 14
MODIFIED-BLOCK STYLE

Paper: Workguide 69

(Current date) / Ms. Gail Hentz / Vice President for Administration /   13
Oliver Temporary Services / 65 McPherson Street / Danville, KY 40422 /   26
Dear Ms. Hentz: 29

Are you having difficulty finding individuals who possess the skills and   43
training that employers look for in their temporary employees? Could   57
you benefit from having prospective employees who have additional   71
appropriate skills?   74

Take a few minutes to read through the enclosed brochure. It de-   87
scribes a training program that we have developed to help you train your   102
temporary workers in those skills which are in high demand by potential   116
employers.   118

If you wish, we will send you this instructional package on a free,   132
ten-day trial basis. Just use the order slip in the brochure to get your   147
copy. We are confident that once you use this exciting new program,   160
you will be able to increase your rate of placement of temporary   173
workers.   174

Sincerely yours, / Donald C. Williams / Account Executive / *(Your*   184
initials) / Enclosure   187

Paper: plain, full sheet

I would like you to retype the memorandum report I have prepared concerning the microcomputer work-shops that are going to be offered to our staff. This memo is going out to all full- and part-time employees. The subject is Microcomputer Workshops. Date the memorandum November 16. Use the standard memo report format with double spacing.

MEMO TO: 9

FROM: 17

DATE: 21

SUBJECT: 28

All full-and part-time employees are being encouraged to participate 42
in the microcomputer workshops that have been scheduled for 54
the months of Dec. and Jan. Jim Stakeman, director of per- 67
sonnel has issued the following statement regarding released 81
time: 82

policy

All employees who are interested in attending a 91
microcomputer workshop are eligible for released 101
time from their regular duties. In order to 110
maintain adequate departmental coverage during 120
workshop periods, it is necessary to coordinate 129
this released time with the employees immediate 139
supervisor. 141

Work Coverage 144

All employees who see a need for microcomputer skills are 155
encouraged to attend these valuable sessions. Because the 167
workshops are limited in size, it is important that interested 180
employees discuss their wishes with their immediate supervisor 192
within the next week so that an acceptable schedule can be 204
developed. Each supervisor is responsible for maintaining 216
appropriate coverage within the department. 226

work

A variety of policies regarding released time exist within our 238
organization This announcement is intended to standardize 250
those policies so that employees can take advantage of future 263
work shops without penalty. 268

Tentative Topics 271

workshop

While a complete list of Topics has not been finalized, there 285
will likely be a basic orientation to word processing, spread- 297
sheet, graphics and database software programs. 307

WP Many word processing software packages have a feature that will indent display paragraphs 5 spaces from both margins.

WP With a word processor, it is possible to move blocks of copy anywhere within the document.

REPRODATA EQUIPMENT, INC.

Copier Sales for October

Model	Number	Percent
Paramount D2000	347	35.1
Zenith C4000	210	21.2
Embassy 21XL50	148	14.9
Zenith C3051	121	12.2
Paramount D1200	89	9.0
Embassy 40XX20	57	5.8
Paramount D4000	18	1.8

NEW PHONE SERVICES

By Gail Okun

Telephone service has become quiet [quite] sophisticated in the past few years. Call forwarding, call waiting, and speed call service are already available to some [many] customers. Two new services will soon be available to many [some] private and business clients: return call and call screening.

RETURN CALL

This service will enable [allow] a customer to return the most recent incoming call, even if it was not answered. This feature will help to call back that person who might call you at an inopportune time when you can't answer the telephone.

Call Screening

Screening calls can be extremely beneficial to any customer. Two services are call block and call trace.

Call Block. This feature will give the client [customer] the ability to stop all calls originating from specific telephone numbers. The caller hears a ring, but the client [customer] does not. This means that one can chose not to talk to selected individuals.

Call Trace. This service will allow [enable] a customer to initiate an automatic trace of the last call recieved. This can assist one who is receiving anonymous calls of any type.

REPORT 70
ENUMERATION

Paper: plain, full sheet

Use **IN-SERVICE WORKSHOP EVALUATION** as the main title for this report and Miscellaneous Comments as the subtitle. Six participants wrote comments for item 7 of the questionnaire. I've taped their comments together. Please type them as an enumerated list. Although we do not want to change the respondents' thoughts, I would like you to correct errors in grammar, punctuation, capitalization, and spelling as you type the enumeration.

1. 7. Additional comments: As I can't afford to go to college at night this Winter; I really appreciate the bank helping me.   6 / 14 / 21

2. 7. Additional comments: I can practice at home because one of my friend's said she would borrow her computer to me.   26 / 33 / 39

3. 7. Additional comments: It would help me if I could attend a more advanced session dealing with our data base program.   44 / 52 / 58

4. 7. Additional comments: You gave us to much in one day. My head was spinning and I dont remember much.   63 / 70 / 76

5. 7. Additional comments: Some people had to work during the workshop, and I think there should be another one for them.   81 / 89 / 95

6. 7. Additional comments: This was the best of the two workshops I have attended. Keep up the good work!   102 / 110 / 112

PART 3

SKILLBUILDING■ CORRESPONDENCE, REPORTS, AND FORMS

OBJECTIVES

KEYBOARDING SKILL

To operate the entire keyboard by touch.

To type 40 words a minute on a 3-minute timed writing with no more than 5 errors.

PROOFREADING SKILL

To proofread your typed work, mark and count errors, correct errors, and compute typing speed.

TECHNICAL SKILL

To answer correctly at least 90 percent of the questions on an objective test.

FORMATTING SKILL

To format memorandums on plain paper, letterhead stationery, and printed forms.

To format postcards and envelopes.

To format two-page bound reports with footnotes, endnotes, and supplementary pages.

To prepare job-application papers, including a personal data sheet, a job-application form, and a letter of application.

■ To understand how word processing equipment and software would function if used to format various assignments.

FORM 38
CHANGE OF ADDRESS

Paper: Workguide 379

Mr. Ronald B. Ruecker, whose old address is 2207 Fairfax Drive, Charlotte, NC 28209, telephones to inform you that he has moved to 314 Marcus Court, Charlotte, NC 28213, but wants to continue his accounts. His new telephone number is (704) 555-6342. After the call, you reach for a pen and a change-of-address form and go to the files to obtain additional information. His social security number is 462-52-6378, and his checking account number is 125-639-2. He has an IRA account (number 936427), a safe-deposit box, and an installment loan for the purchase of an automobile.

Mr. Ruecker has been told that he will receive a change-of-address form in the mail and that he must sign it and return it to the bank. You type the information on a second form, proofread it carefully, and send it to Mr. Ruecker.

FORM 39
STOP PAYMENT

Paper: Workguide 381

This is your day for phone calls. At 3:20 p.m., Miss Shirley A. Morris of 6431 Chandworth Road, Charlotte, NC 28210, calls to inform you that her check #1063 dated October 15 has been lost in the mail. You write the information on a stop-payment form and ask some questions. The check was made payable to Jerome D. Johnson in the amount of $137.80 on account number 121-543-2. Miss Morris's phone number is (704) 555-4763.

You type the information on a second form, sign your name as the person putting the form on file, and forward it to the bookkeeping department.

REPORT 68
QUESTIONNAIRE WITH FILL-INS

Paper: 2 copies of evaluation form from Report 67 on page 306

It looks as though we've received all the replies to the in-service workshop survey that we're going to get. The returns are pretty good: Out of the 35 employees surveyed, 28 responded.

If you would get two copies of the questionnaire you filed (*Report 67, page 306*), I'll read out the results to you. You can write in the results on one copy and type them right on the second copy. Verify that the numbers for each question total 28, the number of respondents. Label the typed copy WORKSHOP EVALUATION RESULTS at the top. Ready for question 1?

1. 11 excellent; 14 good; 3 fair; 0 poor
2. 8 excellent; 14 good; 5 fair; 1 poor
5. 6 too long; 10 too short; 12 just right
6. 12 complete/informative; 4 complete/uninformative; 11 incomplete/informative; 1 incomplete/uninformative

REPORT 69
BAR CHART

Paper: plain, full sheet

I think that question 1, which asks for a general reaction to the workshop, will be of particular interest to the president and the members of the board of directors. Would you please prepare a bar chart showing the results for this question. Use the instructions and sample from our procedures manual to make the bar chart. First, you'll have to compute the percentages by dividing the number of respondents who checked each choice by the total number of respondents—28. Round off all percentages to the nearest whole number, check that they total 100, and show the percentages in increments of 20. Use GENERAL REACTIONS TO WORKSHOP as the title for the bar chart.

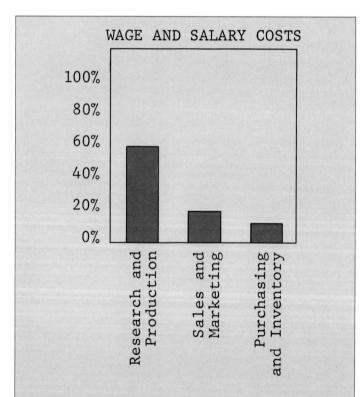

Bar charts are used to show graphically the relationship between different sets of data. The widths of the bars should be the same; the height of a bar shows the percentage value. Center the chart by eye judgment on the page, and draw the lines using either the underscore key or black ink. You may type the bar labels at the bottom horizontally (if you have room), or you may turn the paper sideways to type them, making sure that all lines end at the same point.

LESSON
41

Line: 60 spaces
Tab: 5
Spacing: single
Drills: 2 times
Workguide: 75
Format Guide: 31–32
Tape: 21A

MEMORANDUMS

Goals: To improve speed and accuracy; to format interoffice memorandums.

41-A. WARMUP

S 1 She may make eight right angles when she works on the maps.
A 2 Sixty-five amazed children kept quiet with our big justice.
N 3 They won the three games by 46 to 20, 35 to 9, and 17 to 8.

SKILLBUILDING

PRETEST. Take a 1-minute timing; compute your speed and count errors.

41-B. PRETEST: DISCRIMINATION PRACTICE

4   Few of you were as lucky as Bev was when she joined us   12
5 for golf. She just dreaded the looks of the work crew when   24
6 she goofed. But she neatly swung a club and aced the hole.   36
   | 1 | 2 | 3 | 4 | 5 | 6 | 7 | 8 | 9 | 10 | 11 | 12

PRACTICE.
   Speed Emphasis: If you made 2 or fewer errors on the Pretest, type each line twice.
   Accuracy Emphasis: If you made 3 or more errors, type each group of lines as though it were a paragraph, twice.

41-C. PRACTICE: LEFT HAND

7 vbv verb bevy vibes bevel brave above verbal bovine behaves
8 wew west weep threw wedge weave fewer weight sewing dewdrop
9 ded deed seed bride guide dealt cried secede parted precede
10 fgf gulf gift fight fudge fugue flags flight golfer feigned

41-D. PRACTICE: RIGHT HAND

11 klk kiln lake knoll lanky locks liken kettle kindle knuckle
12 uyu buys your usury unity youth buoys unruly untidy younger
13 oio coin lion oiled foils foist prior oilcan iodine iodized
14 jhj jury huge enjoy three judge habit adjust slight jasmine

POSTTEST. Repeat the Pretest and compare performance.

41-E. POSTTEST: DISCRIMINATION PRACTICE

41-F. DIAGNOSTIC TYPING: NUMBERS

Turn to the Diagnostic Typing: Numbers routine at the back of the book. Take the Pretest, and record your performance on Workguide page 5. Then practice the drill lines for those reaches on which you made errors.

41-G. FORMATTING AN INTEROFFICE MEMORANDUM

An interoffice memorandum is a message from one person to another in the same organization. It may be typed on plain paper, on a special memorandum form, or on letterhead stationery, using either a half sheet or a full sheet of paper. Follow these steps in typing a memorandum on either plain paper or letterhead stationery:

1. Use a 6-inch line (60 pica/70 elite).
2. Begin typing the heading on line 7 on half sheets of paper and on line 13 on full sheets of paper.
3. Set a 10-space tab to align the heading information.
4. Leave 2 blank lines before the body of the memorandum.
5. Include your reference initials. (The writer's initials are optional.)

LETTERS 81–83 Paper: Workguide 371–376
FORM LETTERS

Three loan accounts are overdue, and reminder letters must be sent. Form Letter 5 has been drafted and proofread carefully and is ready to be typed. The Loan Department has provided the following information. Type the letters to the three people, inserting the appropriate information in each letter.

Mr. Ronald E. McKeen	Mr. M. L. Grove	Ms. Olivia Karnes
450 Marshall Avenue	212 Rockview Court	318 Culloden Court
Charlotte, NC 28208	Charlotte, NC 28211	Charlotte, NC 28214
$285	$725	$335

WP

By storing text and merge commands in a "primary file" and variable information with merge codes in a "secondary merge file," it is possible to merge the two files together to produce form letters that are personalized with specific information for each individual.

(Date)   3

+ 2#

(Name)   7
(Street)   11
(City, State Zip)   15

(Salutation):   18

This is a busy time of the year for all of us, so I decided to   31
send you a ~~brief~~ reminder concerning your loan payment.   42
Please use the self-addressed envelope provided to forward   54
(amount) by return mail.   58

Is there some ~~cause~~ reason why we haven't recieved your payment? If 70
so, please contact me immediately about your account. If you   83
have already sent your payment, please disregard this re-   94
minder. We do appreciate your excellent record with our bank.   106

                                    Sincerely,   108

                                    Thomas P. Ryan   111
                                    Vice President   114
                                    and Cashier   116

LETTER 84 Paper: Workguide 377–378

I would like you to type a letter concerning the sale of a mortgaged vehicle. The letter should be sent to Mr. Adam Larsch, 313 Travis Avenue, Charlotte 28204.

dear mr. larsch . . . we would like to inform   8
you that we have sold the 1986 pontiac sun-   16
bird . . . which was the security on your loan   25
number 007835 . . . the vehicle was sold for   33
the sum of five thousand four hundred dollars   37
. . . and we applied the proceeds from the sale   45
to your loan balance . . . however . . . there is 53
still an outstanding balance of seven hundred   60
thirty-three dollars that is your responsibility   66
. . .

please contact me as soon as you receive   75
this letter to arrange for payment of this   83
amount . . .   85

Let's add a postscript:

we will consider monthly payments of sixty-   93
eight dollars and forty-two cents for a year . . . 97

MEMO 1

Line: 6 inches (60 pica/70 elite)
Tab: 10
Paper: plain, half sheet

↓7
Tab

MEMO TO: Shirley DeWitt, Accounting Department   9
↓2

FROM: Michael Andresen, Manager   16
↓2

DATE: November 10, 19--   22
↓2

SUBJECT: Meeting on Computer Networking   30
↓3

This will confirm this morning's telephone conversation in   42
which I indicated that I would like to meet with all depart-   53
ment heads in our Finance Division concerning the implementa-   65
tion of computer networking.   71
↓2

The meeting will begin at 9 a.m. on November 21 and will be   83
held in the conference room on the sixth floor. Peter Frank,   94
vice president for information services, will address the   106
group and will be available for questions.   115
↓2

kae   116

MEMO 2

Line: 6 inches (60 pica/70 elite)
Tab: 10
Paper: Workguide 75

WP
Some word pro-
cessors enable the user to
program margins and tab
stops that will then be saved
for future use. Others store
the heading lines so that
only variable text has to be
keyed in.

↓13
Tab

MEMO TO: Earl L. Schlee, Senior Vice President   7
↓2

FROM: Michael Andresen, Manager   12
↓2

DATE: November 22, 19—   16
↓2

SUBJECT: Computer Networking in Finance Division   24
↓3

Computer networking in the Finance Division was discussed at a meet-   37
ing on November 21, and the staff was very receptive to the ideas pre-   51
sented.   52
↓2

Peter Frank, vice president for information services, addressed the   66
group on the advantages and disadvantages of networking. He also out-   80
lined a five-phase plan to integrate networking into our present system.   94
Following the presentation, a number of questions and ideas were dis-   108
cussed.   109
↓2

Specific departmental applications will be addressed at our next meeting   124
early in December.   128
↓2

kae   129

REPORT 67 (Cont.)
EVALUATION FORM

Shown in pica.

Two additional copies of this form will be needed for later use on page 308.

State Bank of Charlotte

5

Workshop evaluation form

9

1. The entire program was: 2# (check one)

17

_____ Excellent   _____ Fair

20

_____ Good   _____ Poor

22

Comments: _____

23

_____

2. In general, the new (info) provided was: (check one)

36

_____ Excellent   _____ Fair

38

_____ Good   _____ Poor

40

Comments: _____

42

_____

3. I enjoyed especially these topics and/or ~~people~~ speakers:

53

a. _____

53

b. _____

53

4. I was disappointed in# these topics and/or ~~people~~ speakers:

64

a. _____

65

b. _____

65

5. The work shop was: (check one)

72

_____ Too long

74

_____ Too short

75

_____ _____ just right

77

6. The ~~procedures~~ manual is: (check one)

86

_____ Complete/informative

90

_____ Complete/uninformative

94

_____ Incomplete/informative

99

_____ Incomplete/uninformative

103

7. Additional Comments: _____

108

_____

_____

MEMORANDUMS

Line: 60 spaces
Tab: 5
Spacing: single
Drills: 2 times
Format Guide: 31–32
Tape: 22A

Goals: To type 36 wam/3'/5e; to improve skills in typing punctuation marks; to format interoffice memorandums.

42-A. WARMUP

S 1 Henry got six tickets to the game for half the usual price.
A 2 Dave and Peggy quickly mixed the frozen berries with juice.
N 3 The three doctors delivered 305 girls and 264 boys in 1987.

SKILLBUILDING

42-B. Take a 1-minute timing on the first paragraph to establish your base speed. Then take several 1-minute timings on the remaining paragraphs. As soon as you equal or exceed your base speed on one paragraph, advance to the next one.

42-B. SUSTAINED TYPING: PUNCTUATION

4   Changes in federal tax laws in recent years have had a   12
5 real effect on the paychecks of office workers. The social   24
6 security tax rate went up while income tax rates went down.   36
7   However, the result has been modest increases in take-   12
8 home pay for most people. Some workers are now looking for   24
9 places to invest; they want their savings to work for them.   36
10   Safety must be the <u>small</u> investor's main concern; rate   12
11 of return and availability are secondary. Will those sure-   24
12 fire, unbeatable schemes lead you to think any differently?   36
13   Those investments (savings) won't make one rich, but a   12
14 regular investment plan <u>will help</u> to "ease one into retire-   24
15 ment." A first-rate rule is: Watch for a tempter's snare.   36
     | | | 2 | 3 | 4 | 5 | 6 | 7 | 8 | 9 | 10 | 11 | 12

42-C. PACED PRACTICE

Turn to the Paced Practice routine at the back of the book. Take several 2-minute timings, starting at the speed at which you left off the last time. Record your progress on Workguide page 6.

42-D. Spacing: double. Record your score.

42-D. SKILL MEASUREMENT: 3-MINUTE TIMED WRITING

16   We must not make the mistake of thinking that computer   12
17 technology is limited to the office. A stop at a fast-food   24
18 place recently forced me to think about this for some time.   36
19   My friend and I quickly gave our orders to a young man   48
20 at the counter. The young man keyed in codes for each item   60
21 and then turned to the next one in line. We could see five   72
22 cooks through an opening that I would judge to be four feet   84
23 by six feet in size. One of the cooks read our orders on a   96
24 kitchen monitor; our bill was being automatically computed.   108
     | | | 2 | 3 | 4 | 5 | 6 | 7 | 8 | 9 | 10 | 11 | 12

TABLE 57
RULED TABLE

Paper: plain, full sheet

Please type this table showing the new savings rates for our various accounts. Center the table vertically and horizontally on a sheet of plain paper. Double-space the column entries, including the different kinds of IRA accounts, so that the table will be easier to read. Indent the three types of IRA accounts 3 spaces.

Type	Rate	Minimum Amount	Annual Yield	
SAVINGS RATES				3
Effective November 1, 19--				8
		Minimum	Annual	10
Type	Rate	Amount	Yield	14
Passbook	5.00%	None	5.06%	19
Christmas Club	5.25%	None	5.32%	24
Check Plus	1.00%	None	1.00%	29
NOW Account	5.00%	$500	5.12%	34
Super NOW Account	5.00%	$1,000	5.12%	41
IRA Accounts				43
Variable	6.50%	None	6.72%	47
Fixed	6.50%	None	6.72%	51
Money Market	6.50%	None	6.72%	56

REPORT 67
EVALUATION FORM

Paper: plain, full sheet

I would like some feedback concerning the in-service workshop to determine if it was worthwhile, so I have prepared an evaluation form to be completed by the participants. Please type the form (*see page 306*) using the standard report format.

MEMO 26
COVER MEMO

Paper: Workguide 367

We will need a cover memo to accompany the evaluation form. Please address the memo to Workshop Partic- ipants and use In-Service Evaluation for the subject line. Date the memo November 11.

now that our in-service employee workshop is 9
over . . . i would like you to share your com- 17
ments concerning the workshop with me . . . 25
in order to evaluate the effectiveness of the 34
workshop . . . i need some feedback from you 43
. . . please complete the attached evaluation 51
form and return it to me by november 15 . . . 59
    the information gained from this survey will 68
enable us to develop a training program specif- 77
ically geared to your needs . . . please be spe- 85
cific in your answers and comments . . . all re- 94
sponses will be kept confidential . . . thank you 103
for your cooperation . . . 107

POSTCARD 5
FOLLOW-UP REMINDER

Paper: Workguide 369

Let's type a follow-up reminder right away for those employees who do not return their evaluation forms by November 15. Please prepare a postcard for duplication and date it November 16. Here is my handwritten draft.

To Workshop Participants: 5

November 15 has come and gone, 11
but we did not receive your 17
Workshop Evaluation Form. If 23
you haven't already done so, 29
please complete the questionnaire 35
and return it to us. It is our 42
hope that the survey results will 49
help us to design a beneficial 55
training program. 58

Tom Ryan 60
Vice President and Cashier 65

42-E. MEMORANDUMS

Type the memorandums below, using the same formatting procedures that were used for the memorandums on page 83. Work to improve your speed as you quickly move through the *MEMO TO, FROM, DATE,* and *SUBJECT* lines.

MEMO 3

Paper: plain, half sheet

MEMO TO: Elmer Foster, General Manager / FROM: Elizabeth Blom- 13
quist, Computer Operations / DATE: November 18, 19— / SUBJECT: 25
Implementation of Word Processing Center 33

   I have compiled the data you requested regarding the need for a word 47
processing center for our central offices. There are many advantages to 62
the implementation of such a system. During the past month, informa- 75
tion has been gathered from various departments regarding their antici- 89
pated use of the center. 94

   As we agreed in our telephone conversation earlier this morning, I will 108
send you a comprehensive report of my findings in the next few days. 122
We will then meet to discuss the report on November 26. / *(Your* 133
initials) 134

MEMO 4

Paper: plain, full sheet

WP Many word processors have a rapid form-fill-in feature that automatically prints each line of the heading for a memo, pausing to allow the operator to key in the variable information on each line.

An attachment notation is used if the material mentioned is to be physically attached to the memorandum. An enclosure notation is used if the material is enclosed in the same envelope with the memorandum. Type either notation at the left margin, a single space below the reference initials.

```
MEMO TO:    Elmer Foster                                        4
            General Manager                                     7
FROM:       Elizabeth Bloomquist                               13
            Computer Operations                                17
DATE:       November 22, 19--                                  22
SUBJECT:    Implementation of Word Processing Center           32


                         18
In my memo of November 17, I said that I would forward my      44
recommendations for the implementation of a word processing    56
                                  detailed
center at our central offices.  A report is attached.          68

Our current level of secretarial support appears to be inade-  80
quate.  There are often delays of from four to seven days.     92

There micro computers with word processing software will be    104
made available to the computer center.  We think that delays   116
can be held to two days by retraining present employees.  I    128
                             m
will expand on these recomendations at our meeting on november 140
26.                                                            141
pck                                                            142
Attachment                                                     144
```

N. INTEGRATED OFFICE PROJECT: STATE BANK OF CHARLOTTE

Situation: Today is Tuesday, October 25. You are secretary to Mr. Thomas P. Ryan, vice president and cashier at the State Bank of Charlotte in Charlotte, North Carolina. You are expected to format documents properly and to capitalize correctly, insert punctuation as needed, and edit where necessary. Mr. Ryan prefers the modified-block letter style with standard punctuation and these closing lines:

Sincerely,

Thomas P. Ryan
Vice President
and Cashier

TABLE 56
WORKSHOP AGENDA

Paper: plain, full sheet

Please type this agenda, which will be attached to a cover for distribution. Double-space the body, leave 6 spaces between the two columns, and pivot the items in the second column from the right margin.

IN-SERVICE EMPLOYEE WORKSHOP		6
Workshop Agenda		9
November 10, 19--		12
Opening Remarks	Tom Ryan	17
Mortgage Loans	Louise Abb	21
Installment Loans	J. William Hakes	28
Checking/Savings	Ralph Peters	34
Buffet Luncheon	11:45 a.m.-1:15 p.m.	41
Certificates of Deposit	Lorraine Li	47
Club Memberships	Hank Heers	53
Series EE Bonds	Richard De May	58
NOW Accounts	Joni Cli	62

MEMO 25
COVER MEMO

Paper: Workguide 363

Please type this cover memo for the workshop agenda. The memo should be addressed to Workshop Participants, from me (Tom Ryan). Use today's date. The subject is In-Service Employee Workshop.

please look over the attached agenda for the	9
in-service workshop scheduled for november	18
10 . . . each speaker has been asked to prepare	26
a 15 minute presentation . . . a question and	35
answer session will be held after each speech	44
. . .	
this workshop has been scheduled for the	52
purpose of bringing employees up to date on	61
policies and procedures . . . copies of the new	70
procedures manual will be distributed . . .	77
a continental breakfast will be available at	86
8:15 am . . . and a luncheon will be provided at	96
noon . . .	97
i look forward to seeing you on november	105
10 . . .	106

LETTER 80
COMPOSED LETTER

Paper: Workguide 365–366

Please compose a letter to be sent to J. William Hakes at the Carolina School of Banking, 2406 East Market Street, Greensboro, North Carolina. The ZIP Code is 27401.

Use "Dear Bill" for the salutation, and remind him that our employee workshop will begin with a continental breakfast at 8:15 a.m. on November 10.

Tell him that a copy of the workshop agenda is enclosed with the letter. Though I have discussed this with him on the phone, be sure to confirm that in addition to speaking on installment loans, he will be serving as our external consultant throughout the day.

Close the letter by saying that we are looking forward to having him with us and that he should call if he has any questions about the workshop.

POSTCARDS

Line: 60 spaces
Spacing: single
Drills: 2 times
Workguide: 77–80
Format Guide: 33–34
Tape: 23A

Goals: To improve speed and accuracy; to improve proof-reading skills; to format postcards.

43-A. WARMUP

S 1 Mel and Pam may take a bus to visit their aunt in late May.
A 2 Geoffrey Braxmont quickly drove past the wild jazz concert.
N 3 There were 1,602 students compared with 534 in August 1987.

SKILLBUILDING

43-B. Retype this announce-ment, correcting errors as you type.

43-B. PRODUCTION PRACTICE: PROOFREADING

4 A new service weill be provided for all employes of Dobson,
5 Inc beginnning on january 1, 19--. The new Human Resources
6 Department will initiate a series of worksshops onthe topic
7 of "Personal Financial planning". After covering the topic
8 of budjets, we well give attention to such things as these:
9 how to save, bying, a house, taxes, investments, retirement
10 planing, wills, estate planing, and subjects of interest...

43-C. FORMATTING A POSTCARD

Study the illustration and notations below and in the left margin; then, using the post-card forms on Workguide pages 77–80, type Postcards 1–4.

POSTCARD 1

Line: 45 pica/55 elite spaces
Tab: 2 inches, center
Spacing: single
Paper: Workguide 77–78

RETURN ADDRESS. Blocked on line 3, ½ inch from left edge. The personal title *Mr.* should not be used, but other titles such as *Dr.* or *Mrs.* may be used.
ADDRESS. Blocked on line 12, 2 inches from left edge.

Note: Single-space all ad-dresses. Type the city, state, and ZIP Code on one line; leave 1 space between the state abbrevi-ation and the ZIP Code.

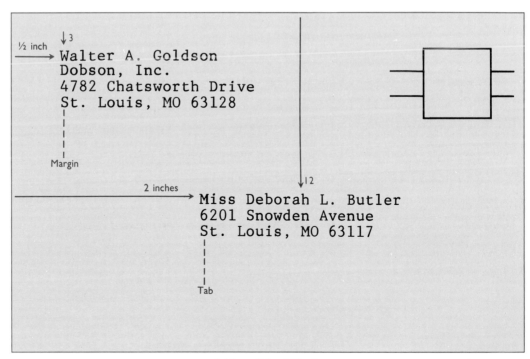

½ inch ↓3
Walter A. Goldson
Dobson, Inc.
4782 Chatsworth Drive
St. Louis, MO 63128

Margin

2 inches ↓12
Miss Deborah L. Butler
6201 Snowden Avenue
St. Louis, MO 63117

Tab

Address Side of Card

K. Select the words in each line that can be divided, and type them with a hyphen to show where the division should be (example: *manage- ment*).

K. PRODUCTION PRACTICE: WORD DIVISION

41	unique	issue	hadn't
42	part-time	types	sized
43	schedule	ready	NCAA
44	knockout	parsnip	cloudy
45	juggle	furthermore	apron
46	prayer	mirror	futile

L. PACED PRACTICE

Turn to the Paced Practice routine at the back of the book. Take several 2-minute timings, starting at the point where you left off the last time. Record your progress on Workguide page 290.

M. Spacing: double. Record your score.

M. SKILL MEASUREMENT: 5-MINUTE TIMED WRITING

47	Few office managers have been formally prepared in the	12
48	field of education. It is also true that most will confirm	24
49	that they devote a lot of time to teaching. There are many	36
50	traits in the management of employees that are very similar	48
51	to those in teaching students.	54
52	Of these, the trait that is probably the most critical	66
53	is patience. When orienting an employee to new procedures,	78
54	the manager must let the individual learn at his or her own	90
55	pace. Managers, like teachers, must not require perfection	102
56	without adequate learning time.	108
57	Sensible managers know the importance of communicating	120
58	effectively with their workers, just as expert teachers use	132
59	these skills in working with students. An important aspect	144
60	of communication that is often overlooked is listening; the	156
61	effective communicator listens.	162
62	While at the same time acting as supervisor, an office	174
63	manager must provide guidance for many workers. Along with	186
64	teaching new techniques and procedures to workers, there is	198
65	a need to guide them in completing their work correctly and	210
66	in completing it on schedule.	216
67	If your goal is to become a manager, remember that you	228
68	will need the skills of a teacher. You will be expected to	240
69	demonstrate that you are patient with the employees and can	252
70	communicate well with them. You will also provide guidance	264
71	so that work is done properly.	270

| 1 | 2 | 3 | 4 | 5 | 6 | 7 | 8 | 9 | 10 | 11 | 12 |

MARGINS. ½ inch on each side. Start the date on line 3 at center.
CLOSING. At center. Leave room for a signature if required; otherwise, leave 1 blank line. The complimentary closing is generally omitted.
REFERENCE INITIALS. Your own.
CARD SIZE. Postcards are 5½ by 3½ inches.

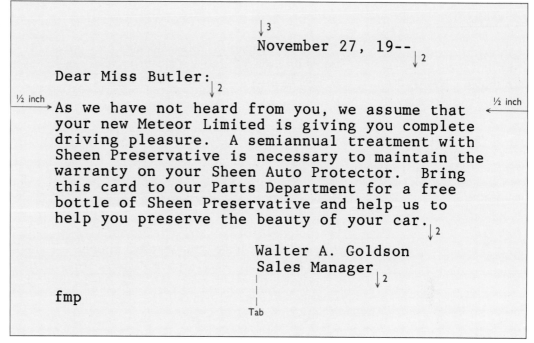

↓3
November 27, 19--
↓2

Dear Miss Butler: ↓2

½ inch →As we have not heard from you, we assume that   ½ inch ←
your new Meteor Limited is giving you complete
driving pleasure. A semiannual treatment with
Sheen Preservative is necessary to maintain the
warranty on your Sheen Auto Protector. Bring
this card to our Parts Department for a free
bottle of Sheen Preservative and help us to
help you preserve the beauty of your car. ↓2

                    Walter A. Goldson
                    Sales Manager ↓2

fmp

Tab

Message Side of Card

POSTCARD 2
Paper: Workguide 77–78

Send the message in Postcard 1 above from Mr. Goldson to Mr. Robert F. Keeley / 38 Overview Court / St. Louis, MO 63128. Use the current date and an appropriate salutation.

POSTCARD 3
Paper: Workguide 79–80

Type a postcard with the following message from Mr. Goldson to Mrs. Joylynn Weston / 3416 Millett Street / East St. Louis, IL 62201.

It was a pleasure for me to meet you when you stopped at our showroom   21
last evening. When I told Jim Burns that you had stopped in, he was truly   36
disappointed that he was not here to see you. I told him that you were   51
considering the purchase of a new car, so he may have called you by the   64
time this card arrives. As our inventory is at an all-time high, Jim will be 79
able to help you find just the car you want.   96

POSTCARD 4
Paper: Workguide 79–80

The last postcard contains the following message from Mr. Goldson to Mr. William J. Arthur / 8725 Bremerton Road / St. Louis, MO 63144.

Dear Bill: We at Dobson are as pleased as you are that the convertible   18
you bought last year has not given you any problems. You should be   32
aware, however, that the original one-year warranty expires on the first   46
of next month. Consequently, we recommend that you consider pur-   59
chasing an extended coverage policy for continued protection. I shall   73
look forward to your call at 555-3864; or if convenient, please stop in for   88
a cup of coffee.   98

F. DIAGNOSTIC TYPING: ALPHABET

Turn to the Diagnostic Typing: Alphabet routine at the back of the book. Take the Pretest, and record your performance on Workguide page 289. Then practice the drill lines for those reaches on which you made errors.

G. TECHNIQUE TYPING: RETURN/ENTER AND TAB KEYS

G. Make two copies. Copy 1: Type each sentence on a separate line. Copy 2: Type each sentence on a separate line, but tab-indent it 5 spaces.

16   Where do you work? I work for a firm in Chicago, Illinois.
17   What department are you in? I work in the finance section.
18   Do you enjoy your job? Yes, it is quite fun and rewarding.
19   Do you work long hours? I work the normal forty-hour week.
20   Do you put in any overtime? Yes, I do when it's very busy.
21   How long have you worked there? I have worked three years.
22   Are you up for a promotion? Yes, I may move up the ladder.
23   What job will you get? I could become the department head.

H. PRODUCTION PRACTICE: PROOFREADING

H. Compare these lines with Sections C and D on page 301. Type a list of the words that contain errors, correcting the errors as you type.

24   re redo retack reform remake revamp return rewrite reactive
25   in into imcome invent insole intact intone invalid indebted
26   be bema belong become before bemuse betray betruth befuddle
27   de defy decide defend design detain device depress deformed

28   ly duly likly calmly gamely hardly kindly clearly direcetly
29   ed aged handed fanned melted played traded reached sheilded
30   nt dent repent patant invent recant cement figment poignant
31   al dial rental cereal bridal fungal normal literal unformal

I. SUSTAINED TYPING: SYLLABIC INTENSITY

I. Take a 1-minute timing on the first paragraph to establish your base speed. Then take several 1-minute timings on the other paragraphs. As soon as you equal or exceed your base speed on one paragraph, advance to the next one.

32   Many routine factory jobs and tasks are often not done   12
33   by people. Machines now perform some work that was done by   24
34   members of the labor force. What happens to these persons?   36

35   Perhaps you think that this brings about a shortage of   12
36   jobs for those who are laid off. This does not necessarily   24
37   happen because jobs are increasing in many technical areas.   36

38   In order to take advantage of these new emerging jobs,   12
39   young people must continue their education after completing   24
40   high school. People who have special skills are in demand.   36
     | | 2 | 3 | 4 | 5 | 6 | 7 | 8 | 9 | 10 | 11 | 12

J. DIAGNOSTIC TYPING: NUMBERS

Turn to the Diagnostic Typing: Numbers routine at the back of the book. Take the Pretest, and record your performance on Workguide page 289. Then practice the drill lines for those reaches on which you made errors.

Line: 60 spaces
Tab: 5
Spacing: single
Drills: 2 times
Workguide: 81–86
Format Guide: 33–36
Tape: 23A

LESSON
44

FORMATTING ENVELOPES AND FOLDING LETTERS

Goals: To improve symbol-typing skills; to type 37 wam/ 3'/5e; to format large and small envelopes; to fold letters for large and small envelopes.

44-A. WARMUP

S 1 A right turn may take them down the road by the clear lake.
A 2 Max questioned Peg Clay as to which five frozen jars broke.
N 3 He saw 26 goats, 57 pigs, 38 cows, 19 horses, and 40 ducks.

SKILLBUILDING

44-B. DIAGNOSTIC TYPING: ALPHABET

Turn to the Diagnostic Typing: Alphabet routine at the back of the book. Take the Pretest, and record your performance on Workguide page 5. Then practice the drill lines for those reaches on which you made errors.

44-C. SYMBOL TYPING

4   The Study Guide* sold @ $9 <u>less</u> a 10% "cash discount."
5 It's likely that Patty and/or her next-door neighbor (Jaime
6 Egan) will do well and get jobs at Kuhn & Mohr at #738 Elm.

7   Gaines & Maxton* sold 7 sets @ $450, a 33 1/3% markup.
8 Janis Roberts (their <u>top</u> salesperson) hasn't sold any #268s
9 yet, but she is "gunning" for the year-end trip to Florida.

44-D. Spacing: double.
Record your score.

44-D. SKILL MEASUREMENT: 3-MINUTE TIMED WRITING

10   To be loyal does have different meanings. We might be   12
11 thinking of the trait as it is applied to family members or   24
12 friends. We would all agree that it is used as a patriotic   36
13 word.   37
14   A third use is one with which beginning workers should   49
15 become acquainted. Loyalty to your job and the company for   61
16 which you work is extremely important. You should show you   73
17 care.   74
18   Some of those with whom you work may like to criticize   86
19 the boss or the company in the lounge at every opportunity.   98
20 You, however, can avoid gossip and work for the good of the   110
21 firm.   111

| 1 | | 2 | 3 | 4 | 5 | 6 | 7 | 8 | 9 | 10 | 11 | 12

Line: 60 spaces
Tab: 5, center
Spacing: single
Drills: 2 times
Workguide: 363–381
Format Guide: 139

LESSONS 141–145

INTEGRATED OFFICE PROJECT: BANKING

GOALS FOR UNIT 29

1. To improve speed and accuracy on alphabetic and numeric copy.
2. To type 54 wam for 5 minutes with no more than 5 errors.
3. To improve composition skills.
4. To improve proofreading skills.
5. To improve word-division skills.
6. To improve arithmetic skills.
7. To develop skills needed for formatting letters, memorandums, postcards, tables, agendas, forms, and reports used in bank offices.

A. WARMUP

S 1 I had a big hot dog and a soda when I got to that ballpark.
A 2 He quickly boxed up the five new jazz records this morning.
N 3 The March 4, 1987, meeting started at 2:05 p.m. in Room 36.

SKILLBUILDING

PRETEST. Take a 1-minute timing; compute your speed and count errors.

B. PRETEST: COMMON LETTER COMBINATIONS

4   Della Kily will return to Detroit because she believes 12
5 her income will increase. She will share an apartment with 24
6 Joanne to save on rent. Their rental was lowered, however, 36
7 because of the intense complaints of the outraged dwellers. 48
   | 1 | 2 | 3 | 4 | 5 | 6 | 7 | 8 | 9 | 10 | 11 | 12

PRACTICE.
  Speed Emphasis: If you made no errors on the Pretest, type each line twice.
  Accuracy Emphasis: If you made 1 or more errors on the Pretest, type each group of lines (as though it were a paragraph) twice.

C. PRACTICE: WORD BEGINNINGS

8 re redo retake reform remake revamp return rewrite reactive
9 in into income indent insole intact intone invalid indebted
10 be beam belong become before bemuse betray betroth befuddle
11 de deny decide defend design detain devise depress deformed

D. PRACTICE: WORD ENDINGS

12 ly duly likely calmly gamely hardly kindly clearly directly
13 ed aged handed farmed melted played traded reached shielded
14 nt dent relent patent invent recant cement figment poignant
15 al dial mental cereal bridal fungal normal literal informal

POSTTEST. Repeat the Pretest and compare performance.

E. POSTTEST: COMMON LETTER COMBINATIONS

44-E. FORMATTING ENVELOPES

Note: The format used for addressing this large envelope is recommended by the U.S. Postal Service for bulk mail that will be sorted by an electronic scanning device. The address is typed in all-capital letters with no punctuation, and it also incorporates the nine-digit ZIP Code. Either format illustrated is acceptable for first-class mail.

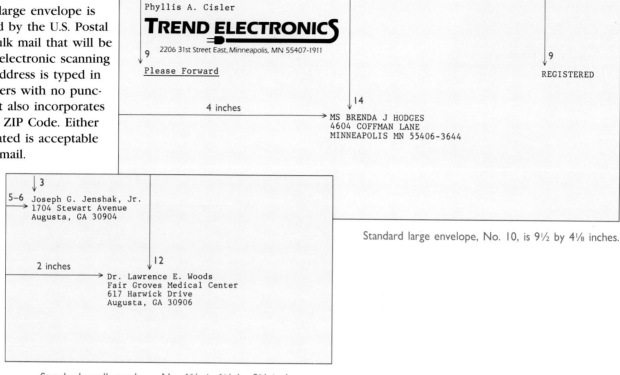

Phyllis A. Cisler

TREND ELECTRONICS

9   2206 31st Street East, Minneapolis, MN 55407-1911

Please Forward

4 inches

14

MS BRENDA J HODGES
4604 COFFMAN LANE
MINNEAPOLIS MN 55406-3644

9

REGISTERED

Standard large envelope, No. 10, is 9½ by 4⅛ inches.

3

5-6   Joseph G. Jenshak, Jr.
1704 Stewart Avenue
Augusta, GA 30904

2 inches

12

Dr. Lawrence E. Woods
Fair Groves Medical Center
617 Harwick Drive
Augusta, GA 30906

Standard small envelope, No. 6¾, is 6½ by 3⅝ inches.

I. RETURN ADDRESS. Business envelopes have a return address printed on the envelope. The writer's name may be typed above the address. On the envelope for a personal letter, the return address begins ½ inch (about 5 or 6 spaces) from the left edge on line 3. Lines are single-spaced and blocked at the left. The personal title *Mr.* should not be used, but other titles may be.

2. ON-ARRIVAL DIRECTIONS. Any on-arrival directions, such as *Personal, Confidential, Please Forward,* or *Hold for Arrival,* should be typed on line 9 and aligned on the left with the return address. These words are typed in capital and lowercase letters and underscored.

3. ADDRESS. Begin the name and address for a small envelope on line 12, 2 inches (about 20 pica/25 elite spaces) from the left edge; and for a large envelope on line 14, 4 inches (about 40 pica/50 elite spaces) from the left edge. Single-space and block all lines, with the city, state, and ZIP Code on the same line. Type the two-letter abbreviation of the state name, with 1 space before the ZIP Code.

When typing foreign addresses, type the name of the country on a separate final line, in all capitals.

4. SPECIAL MAIL SERVICE. Directions for such mail services as *special delivery, airmail* (overseas only), or *registered* are typed in all-capital letters on line 9. The notation should end ½ inch (about 5 spaces) from the right edge.

ENVELOPE I NO. 10 Workguide: 81	From Phyllis A. Cisler. SPECIAL DELIVERY to MR CHARLES R HARRISON / RELIABLE SOFTWARE INC / 5613 BRUNSWICK AVENUE NORTH / MINNEAPOLIS MN 55429-2714	10 19 25
ENVELOPE 2 NO. 6¾ Workguide: 83	Confidential from Dr. Carlos P. Decker / 2407 Reed Avenue / Norman, OK 73071. To Ms. Wanda B. Russell / 702 Allenhurst Street / Norman, OK 73071.	11 23 24
ENVELOPE 3 NO. 6¾ Workguide: 83	From J. L. Rogers / Leola Court Apartments, #23 / 3426 Bayou Road / LeBeau, LA 71345. To Mrs. Ellen L. Moreau / 2936 Pineacre Avenue / Davenport, IA 52803.	11 22 26

PART 8
SKILLBUILDING ■ INTEGRATED OFFICE PROJECTS; BANKING, TRAVEL, GOVERNMENT, AND ENERGY

OBJECTIVES

KEYBOARDING SKILL
To type 57 words a minute on a 5-minute timed writing with no more than 5 errors.

PROOFREADING SKILL
To proofread your typed work, mark errors and compute typing speed on timed writings, and correct errors on production work.

TECHNICAL SKILL
To answer correctly at least 90 percent of the questions on an objective test.

FORMATTING SKILL
To apply high-level formatting skills while completing integrated office projects in the fields of Banking, Travel, Government, and Energy.

44-F. FOLDING LETTERS

To fold a letter for a large (No. 10) envelope:
1. Fold up the bottom third of the letter.
2. Fold the top third down to ½ inch from the first crease.
3. Insert the last crease into the envelope first, with the flap facing up.

To fold a letter for a small (No. 6¾) envelope:
1. Fold up the bottom half to ½ inch from the top.
2. Fold the right third over to the left.
3. Fold the left third over to ½ inch from the right crease.
4. Insert the last crease into the envelope first, with the flap facing up.

LETTER 15
MODIFIED-BLOCK STYLE

Paper: Workguide 85

Use the current date and your own reference initials.

Mr. Alvin S. Gumbel	4
Assistant Manager	7
Diplomat Hotel	10
823 North Michigan Avenue	15
Chicago, IL 60611	18
Dear Mr. Gumbel:	22
We are pleased that you will be able to handle the	32
arrangements for our annual convention to be held at	42
your hotel from March 16 through 19.	50
From our perspective, the preliminary meeting with you	61
last week went very well. Our tentative convention	71
program will be ready in about two weeks.	79
With the professional assistance of you and your staff,	90
we look forward to the best convention ever.	99
Sincerely,	101
Harold R. Ottoson	105
President - Elect	108

ENVELOPE 4

Paper: Workguide 86

Type a No. 10 envelope for Letter 15.

will be used to determine eligibility for company benefits   12

that require a service waiting period.   19

DENTAL PLAN   22

Eligibility. All ~~workers~~ employees working 50 75 per cent time or   34

more and th~~ere~~eir eligible dependents are covered by a the dental   46

plan. This coverage is also provided for retirees and their   58

eligble dependents or survivors.   65

Coverage. The plan covers ~~fifty~~ 50 percent of the usual,   75

cutsomary, and reasonable costs of preventative, diagnostic,   88

rsetorative, pros~~thontic~~thodontic, and orthodontic services. The plan provides an   103

~~individual employee~~ maximum of $7~~00~~50 per calendar year for charges covered   116

and includes limitations regarding the number of services pay   128

able per year (~~e.g.,~~ i.e., routine examinations); orthodontic cover-   140

age is limited to those under 19 years of age and is subject to   153

an individual maximum lifetime of $750.   161

Cost. The plan is fully paid by the company for full-   172

time employees; part-time employees receive an one-half or   183

three-quarters contribution on the basis of the~~re~~ir per cent age of   196

employment.   198

LONG-TERM disability   202

Eligibility, Coverage ~~of~~ under the long-term Disability Plan   214

is available to ~~workers~~ employees who are employed full-time for ~~ten~~ nine   227

months. Employees may receive benefits after ~~seven~~ six months of   239

continuous disability.   243

LESSON 45

LETTERS WITH COPIES

Goals: To improve speed and accuracy; to prepare letters with carbon copies; to correct errors on carbon copies.

45-A. WARMUP

S 1 Eight of their girls may take the big van when they can go.
A 2 Liz fixed Vivian's car; it goes quickly with jumper cables.
N 3 Panian had 1,209 votes, Smythe had 734, and Nelson had 658.

SKILLBUILDING

45-B. PACED PRACTICE

Turn to the Paced Practice routine at the back of the book. Take several 2-minute timings, starting at the speed at which you left off the last time. Record your progress on Workguide page 6.

45-C. CARBON COPIES

It is good business practice to keep a copy of all typed materials, either in the form of a *hard copy* (paper copy) in the files or in the form of *soft copy* that is stored in the computer or on a disk. A copy may also be sent to one or more individuals other than the addressed party. Copies can be made by typing with carbon paper, by printing out a second original copy on the printer, or by using a photocopy machine. Whatever method is used, indicate on the original document that copies have been sent to others. Follow the steps below for making carbon copies.

WP

On a word processor, additional copies can be made by (1) inserting a carbon pack into the printer (the piece of equipment that actually types out what has been entered on the word processor) or (2) having the system print out as many copies of the document as needed.

1. Assemble the carbon pack: *(a)* the sheet of paper on which you will type, *(b)* the carbon paper (shiny side down), and *(c)* the onionskin or other thin sheet of paper on which you wish to make the copy.
2. Insert the carbon pack into the typewriter: *(a)* Straighten the sides and top. *(b)* Insert the pack into the machine with the carbon side (and the copy paper) facing you. *(c)* Hold the pack with one hand, and use the automatic paper feed with the other. *(d)* Before you start to type, check to be sure that the letterhead or top sheet, as well as the dull side of the carbon paper, is facing you. Note: When using an electric typewriter, hold the paper pack in the left hand and turn the platen knob with the right.
3. To make corrections on carbon copies: *(a)* Use a soft (pencil) eraser to erase errors on the copy paper. *(b)* Place a stiff card under the sheet on which you erase to keep smudges from appearing on the copies beneath. (If you find an error after removing your paper, erase and correct on each sheet separately.)

A copy (c) notation is added to a letter if someone is to get a copy of it. Type a small letter c on the line below the reference initials (or below the enclosure notation if there is one).

```
                              Sincerely yours,


                              Pat Dorf, Director

          slk
          c:  Barbara J. Reeder
```

Send this letter to Allied Dental Plan, to the attention of Mr. Paul Gross, at 3720 Wash- 15
ington Avenue, St. Louis, MO 63108. Send a copy of the letter to John J. Melnick. Supply 21
an appropriate salutation and complimentary closing. 25

As you requested in your letter last week, 34
we are enclosing a copy of a description of the 43
new employee dental plan that was renegoti- 52
ated with your firm. 56

You will see that we have indicated that all 65
employees who are working 75 percent of the 74
time or more are covered by the plan, as are 83
their eligible dependents. 88

The plan covers 50 percent of the usual, cus- 97
tomary, and reasonable costs of preventative, 106
diagnostic, restorative, prosthodontic, and or- 115
thodontic services. Do you think we should 124

describe these services further, or will the bro- 133
chure you are sending to each employee suf- 142
fice? 143

Under the terms of the new contract, we 151
point out to part-time employees that they will 160
receive a one-half or three-quarters contribu- 169
tion on the basis of their percentage of em- 178
ployment. 180

Please let me know what changes, if any, you 189
would suggest to clarify this new plan. 197

Allison McGregor / Employee Relations 213

A FIVE-YEAR COMPARISON OF ELECTRONIC 7
Typewriter Sales 10

Store	Total Sales		Percent of Increase/Decrease
	1985	1990	
Atlanta	1,305	2,360	80.8	25
Chicago	1,960	4,350	76.8	29
Nashville	730	1,460	100.0	33
Detroit	1,530	1,530	−16.8	38
New York	2,400	4,600	38.3	42
Philadelphia	1,890	1,450	−26.4	48

13
15
21

LETTER 16
MODIFIED-BLOCK STYLE

Date: current
Carbons: 1
Spacing: single
Workguide: 87

Enumerations within a letter are arranged with the numbers at the left margin and turnover lines indented 4 spaces.

ENVELOPES 5 AND 6

Workguide: 88–90

Type a No. 10 envelope for Letter 16 and a No. 6¾ envelope for Letter 17.

Mr. Jeffrey B. Baldwin 8
Baldwin's Department store 14
1732 Euclid Avenue East 18
Des Moines, IA 50313 22

Dear Mr. Baldwin: 26

I am happy to report ~~that many~~ *on several* developments *that* have occured since 40
you wrote *to* inquiring about our newest sportswear line: 50

1. ~~Several~~ fabric sample ~~pieces, as well as~~ *and* copies of our 58
   new catalogs were sent last friday. 65

2. Application forms for a 30-day open charge account have *also* 78
   been mailed to you. As soon as these forms ~~have been~~ *are returned to us and* pro- 92
   cessed, we can begin ~~begin~~ sending you the latest in mens 102
   and women's sports wear. 107

3. *I have just learned that* I will be visiting your area during the next two weeks *If you are available, I would like* to 132
   show you some of our latest styles. 139

As soon as my travel plans are finalized, I will call you to 151
set up an appointment *with you*. I look forward to meeting you. 164

Sincerely yours,
Frazier T. Moen 170
Sales Representative 174

evy 174
c: Ms. Gloria S. Berg 179

LETTER 17
MODIFIED-BLOCK STYLE

Carbons: 1
Workguide: 89

ENUMERATION. Treat each numbered item as a separate paragraph with numbers at the left margin and turnover lines indented 4 spaces.

(Current date) / Mr. Timothy J. Dickinson / Commercial Loan Depart- 13
ment / Union National Bank / 7232 Hokulani Street / Honolulu, HI 96825/ 25
Dear Mr. Dickinson: 29

The following information is provided as a follow-up to my earlier loan 44
application form on behalf of Mid-Way Fabricators: 1. Mid-Way was 57
founded by Mr. Alvin R. Chong in 1965. 2. Detailed itemizations of cur- 71
rent assets and liabilities are provided on the enclosed balance sheet 85
dated June 30, 19—, the end of our last fiscal period. 3. An income 99
statement is provided for the same fiscal period. 109

I look forward to seeing you on *(one week from today)*. 119

Sincerely yours, / Eileen F. Blanchard / Treasurer / *(Your initials)* / 128
Enclosures 2 / c: Donald B. Taylor 135

Ask your instructor
for the General
Information Test on
Part 7.

PROGRESS TEST ON PART 7

TEST 7-A
5-MINUTE TIMED WRITING

Line: 60 spaces
Tab: 5
Spacing: double
Paper: Workguide 355

Perhaps the topic of time management is an old one, an   12

overworked subject studied many times throughout our school   24

years. But the ability to use one's time wisely is a valu-   36

able skill in office work. To waste time is to waste money   48

or even worse. The employee who wishes to excel on the job   60

must master the skill of good time management. This talent   72

is quite easy to acquire, but it requires lots of planning.   84

Employees should try to list all of those things which   96

they think could interfere with job performance. Often the   108

use of the telephone is a major time waster. A call should   120

be made only after determining all points that are relevant   132

to the subject. Small talk must be curtailed, but one need   144

not be rude on the other hand. This same policy applies to   156

office visitors. Conversations, while polite, should avoid   168

unnecessary discussion regarding the firm or its employees.   180

Keeping a time log is one of the best ways to begin an   192

in-depth study of how one's time is being spent. It should   204

indicate whether one's time is being used efficiently or if   216

too much time is squandered on many unnecessary activities.   228

Analyzing this time log will reveal the areas of a person's   240

workday that were wasted. Every activity that proves to be   252

inefficient must be thrown out or revised for better use of   264

time.   265

| | 1 | 2 | 3 | 4 | 5 | 6 | 7 | 8 | 9 | 10 | 11 | 12

LESSON
46

BOUND REPORTS

Line: 60 spaces
Tab: 5, center
Spacing: single
Drills: 2 times
Workguide: 91–92
Format Guide: 37–38
Tape: 16B

Goals: To use additional proofreaders' marks; to type 37 wam/3'/5e; to format a two-page bound report.

46-B. Spacing: double. Record your score.

46-A.   WARMUP

S 1   Do not blame the eight girls who own the six pairs of keys.
A 2   A crazy dog was seen jumping quickly over a badly hurt fox.
N 3   Prices for new parts increased from 49% to 65% on 12/30/87.

46-B.   SKILL MEASUREMENT: 3-MINUTE TIMED WRITING

```
                 1              2              3              4
 4      Most office workers find that some phase of their jobs    12
          5          6              7                    8
 5   relates to records control, no matter what their job title.  24
            9           10             11                12
 6   Quite often, such duties take up as much as a fourth of the  36
          13              14                  15            16
 7   time for secretaries, clerk-typists, and accounting clerks.  48
              17            18            19              20
 8      Regardless of the size of a firm or the type of record    60
           21            22                23              24
 9   system that it uses, the job description of a records clerk   72
             25               26              27            28
10   will, of course, include the task of sorting and filing all  84
            29            30              31              32
11   kinds of letters, memos, or forms.  Records clerks may also  96
               33              34              35          36
12   set up coding systems and construct indexes or other cross-  108
            37
13   reference aids.                                              111

     |  |  2  |  3  |  4  |  5  |  6  |  7  |  8  |  9  |  10  |  11  |  12
```

46-C.   PROOFREADERS' MARKS

The six most frequently used proofreaders' marks were introduced in Lesson 31. These six marks, plus 11 additional proofreaders' marks, are presented below. Study all the marks carefully and complete Workguide pages 91–92 before typing Report 12.

Proofreaders' Mark		Draft	Final Copy	Proofreaders' Mark		Draft	Final Copy
ss	Single-space	*ss* [first line / second line	first line second line	*new* old̶	Change word	and i̶f̶ you	and when you
ds	Double-space	*ds* [first line / second line	first line / second line	ℐ	Delete	a t̶r̶u̶e̶ fact	a fact
⁋	Make new paragraph	⁋ If he is	If he is	...	Don't delete	a t̶r̶u̶e̶ story	a true story
∪	Transpose	(it / is) so	is it so	ℐ	Delete and close up	co‿operation	cooperation
∧	Insert word	and∧ it is	and so it is	≡	Capitalize	Fifth avenue	Fifth Avenue
∨ or ∧	Insert punctuation	if he's not∧	if he's not,	/	Use lowercase letter	our P̸resident	our president
⌗∧	Insert space	all⌗ready to	all ready to	◯	Spell out	the only ①	the only one
⌒	Omit space	court⌒room	courtroom	⊙	Make it a period	one way⊙	one other way.
				♂	Move as shown	no (other) way	no way

Ms. McIntosh plans to conduct a review of the performance of each sales representative. Since she will be on the road to work with these people during the third week of August, she wants an itinerary to give her supervisor when she meets with him tomorrow.

ITINERARY FOR JOYCE McINTOSH ← Begin on line 7   6

Third Week of August   10

      Center

Monday, August 16   13

    9 a.m.   Spend morning with (Maureen DeVries.)   21

    1 p.m.   Spend afternoon with (Mario Principi.)   30
                                  ↓3

Tuesday, August 17   33
                            Robert
    9 a.m.   Meet with ~~Bob~~ Brady of Delray Prininting   43
              to review final proofs for advertising   51
              brochure on new deferred compensation   58
              plan.   59

    12 noon   Attend the luncheon and meeting of the   68
              Lawrence Civic Association at Bray Inn.76

    2 p.m.   Spend afternoon with Ernest Thompson.   85
                                    ↓3

Wednesday, August 18   89

    9 a.m.   Spend morning with Richard Cornish.   97

    1 p.m.   Spend afternoon with Victoria Sek.   105
                                  ↓3

Thursday, August 19   109

    9 a.m.   Spend morning with Matilda Ruiz.   116

    1 p.m.   Spend afternoon in office getting ready   126
              for the sales meeting to be held ~~on~~   132
              ~~Friday, 8/20.~~   134
              tomorrow.   ↓3

Friday, August 20   137
                              in office
    9 a.m.   Sales meeting ^with six sales represen-   148
              tatives.   150
              Pick up   at
    11:30 a.m.   ~~Get~~ advertising brochures ~~from~~ Delray   160
              Printing.   161

    1 p.m.   Spend afternoon in office reviewing all   171
              correspondence received during the week   179
              and preparing written evaluations of the   187
              visits with the sales representatives   194
              during the week.   198

46-D. FORMATTING A TWO-PAGE BOUND REPORT

If you do not have the visual guide for bound reports, make a light pencil mark in the margin an inch or so from the bottom of your paper to guide you in ending your first page at an appropriate point. Erase the mark later.

A bound report requires a wider left margin for binding. To format a bound report: (1) use the visual guide on Workguide page 60; (2) move both margins and all tab stops 3 spaces to the right. The first page of a two-page report is formatted in the same manner as a one-page report.

To format the second page: (1) Type the page number (without the word *page*) on line 7 at the right margin. (Do not type a page number on the first page.) (2) Begin the text of the report on line 10, a triple space below the page number.

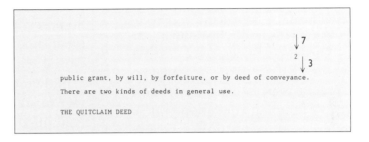

public grant, by will, by forfeiture, or by deed of conveyance.
There are two kinds of deeds in general use.

THE QUITCLAIM DEED

REPORT 12
TWO-PAGE BOUND REPORT

Line: 6 inches (60 pica/70 elite)
Paper: plain
Visual guide: Workguide 60

Determine where to end your first page in order to leave a 1-inch bottom margin.

REPORT 13
UNBOUND REPORT

Paper: plain
Visual guide: Workguide 59

Retype Report 12, this time in unbound format. Use your own name in the byline.

COMPUTERIZED TRAVEL RESERVATIONS] ds	6
By Miriam Caruso	10

Businesspeople can now use their personal computers to make travel reservations. They can search databases of hundreds of thousands of flights in seconds to customize their own travel schedule and save time and money. In addition, hotel reservations can be made on line.

ON-LINE AIRLINE RESERVATIONS

Using an electronic information service such as the source or CompuServe, managers can identify flights and fares through a special service operated by the air line industry; the service will then display flights from it's records of more than 3 million records of available flights.

All of the information the on-line program needs is requested from the user in question-and-answer format. Users must enter the name of thier departure and arrival cities, the travel dates, and the preferred times of departure. The on-line program then displays all relevant flights, including flight numbers, arrival and departure times, and fares. ¶Some of the computerized reservation services allow users to actually book their flights, paying for them by credit card. An added bonus of such services is

21
33
45
57
64

70
80
94
106
121
124

134
146
157
168
179
190
202
214
225

LETTERS 76–78
Paper: Workguide 347–352
BLOCK STYLE, OPEN PUNCTUATION

Mr. Arnold Speert, the claims supervisor, has dictated the following three letters for you to transcribe. He has indicated the correct paragraphs, but you will have to be sure to punctuate and capitalize correctly. Be careful to use the apostrophe for contractions or to indicate possession.

Send this first letter to mr . . . john kane . . . executive director . . . kansas insurance institute . . . 15 capital street . . . topeka . . . ks . . . 66603 . . . dear mr . . . kane . . . 6 / 15 / 22 / 23

in the most recent issue of your newsletter . . . i read of the continuing education course that will be offered at the institutes facility beginning on thursday . . . september 15 . . . im pleased to note that the course will deal with appraising property damage from fire . . . 32 / 41 / 51 / 58 / 67 / 76

since we have a claims adjuster who recently joined our staff . . . i would like more information on that course so that i might enroll him . . . please send me complete details on class meeting times . . . the cost of enrollment . . . an application for admission . . . and the complete course description . . . in addition . . . please provide me with the name of the individual who will be teaching the course and the name of the textbook that will be used . . . 83 / 92 / 101 / 110 / 118 / 126 / 134 / 142 / 152 / 160 / 161

every time we have arranged for one of our employees to attend one of your continuing education courses . . . we have been extremely pleased with the growth we have noted when the individual returns to the job . . . sincerely yours . . . 170 / 178 / 185 / 193 / 202 / 212

Send this second letter to ms . . . patricia cummings . . . 15 bedford street . . . lawrence . . . ks . . . 66044 . . . dear ms . . . cummings . . . 6 / 13 / 17

i am pleased to notify you that your claim for damage suffered to the aluminum siding on your home from the storm of august 11 has been resolved . . . of course . . . we are sorry for any inconvenience you were caused . . . 27 / 35 / 44 / 52 / 59

the claims adjuster who visited with you on august 22 completed all the work necessary to verify that you were entitled to have that damage repaired under the coverage you have with homeowners policy #189-3471 . . . which you have had with midwest insurance for the past seven years . . . the damage suffered was estimated to be $3,870 . . . allowing for your 80 percent coinsurance clause . . . your settlement amount is $3,096 . . . the check is enclosed with this letter . . . 68 / 77 / 86 / 96 / 103 / 112 / 120 / 129 / 137 / 145 / 150

midwest insurance is pleased to be of service to you at this time . . . we appreciate your continued support of our insurance program and will be happy to answer any questions you may have concerning this settlement . . . sincerely yours . . . 158 / 167 / 176 / 185 / 193 / 204

Send this third letter to mr . . . bernard . . . c . . . thompson . . . 148 sullivan drive . . . baldwin city . . . ks . . . 66006 . . . dear mr . . . thompson . . . 6 / 14 / 19

i am delighted to send you this check for $4,050 to cover the cost of repairing the damage to your automobile that resulted from the collision you had on route 59 in ottawa on thursday . . . july 20 . . . 27 / 36 / 45 / 54 / 58

a customers claim for any damage suffered is a priority item here at midwest . . . we try to process each claim as quickly as possible . . . since we realize that the customer is depending on us at this critical time . . . we hope that youre pleased with the speed with which we processed your claim . . . we also wish you good luck with your repaired automobile . . . 67 / 76 / 84 / 93 / 102 / 111 / 119 / 127

if you have any questions regarding this settlement . . . please get in touch with me . . . i will be happy to answer any of your questions . . . sincerely yours . . . 136 / 144 / 153 / 165

FORMS 36–37
Paper: Workguide 353
VOUCHER CHECKS

Mr. Speert will need two voucher checks to be enclosed with two of the letters that he dictated above. Please type a voucher check for $3,096 payable to Patricia Cummings and one payable to Bernard C. Thompson for $4,050. Use checks 1305 and 1306.

Provide an appropriate page 2 heading.

WP   Software is now being developed that can be "taught" to read handwriting (which is written on a special digital tablet) and then display the text directly on the computer screen for editing.

that the passenger is automatically enrolled in the air- 236
lines' frequent-flier program and is able to receive free 248
travel as he or she accumulates mileage on the airline. 259
There is no charge to join any of the frequent-flier pro- 271
grams. 272

Other services require that the computer user contact a 283
Travel Agent or airline to purchase the ticket. However, 295
the user can still be assured of getting the most convenient 307
or most economical flight by previewing the available 318
flights via a computer. 322

ON-LINE HOTEL RESERVATIONS 327

The Hotel Directory is another useful 335
on-line service available to computer 343
users. It provides up-to-date and com- 350
prehensive listings of more than 20,000 358
hotels worldwide. 362

Information Provided. For each of the 369
hotels listed, the program provides the 377
street address, the location (such as down- 386
town, airport, or ocean-front), the local 394
and any toll-free telephone numbers, the 402
number and types of rooms available, 410
room rates, credit cards accepted, and any 418
special facilities (such as health clubs, 427
heated pools, secretarial services, and the 436
like). 437

Access Procedures. Computer users 444
can search for a hotel by specifying a city, 453
the hotel name or chain, a range of room 461
rates, or the type of special facility de- 469
sired. If, for example, a city is selected, 478
all available hotels and motels in that 486
area will be listed. 490

REPORT 64
TWO-PAGE REPORT

Paper: plain

Ms. McIntosh wants to have this report for distribution at the sales meeting on August 20.

Use the standard report format to prepare this report.

There are eight misspelled words in this report. Please correct them as you format the report.

Due to the increased interest in reducing taxes that many individual clients have expressed, Midwest Insurance has entered into an agreement with Bradley National Pension Company. This new investment plan will enable us to market a deferred compensation plan whereby individuals from selected business organazations may agree to set aside a portion of their income before it is federally taxed. The following paragraphs discuss three questions that you should be able to answer for any prospective clients.

WHY SHOULD ONE JOIN?

A very strong reason for joining is the fact that the client pays less in current federal income taxes, since current taxible income is reduced. In adition, the deferred salary is invested, and it will accummulate earnings that are also free from federal income tax. Finally, the deferred salary is received at retirement time, when income will most likely be lower; thus the income tax rate will also be lower.

HOW IS MONEY INVESTED?

The individual investor decides how the deferred compensation will be invested. There are three choices available for the investment funds. The first choice involves a Fixed Income Fund, which invests moneys in high-quality corporate and goverment bonds. It should be understood that bond values may fluctuate according to bond market conditions. The second choice is an Equity Fund, which invests in a deversified common stock portfolio, selected for long-term capital appreciation. It should be understood that this can be risky, but it may offer the greatest possibility for increases in value. The final choice is a Money Market Fund, which invests in short-term debt obligations. The goal is to try to maximize current income while preserving capital through investments such as short-term United States government securities, bank certificates of deposit, and commercial paper.

HOW DOES IT WORK?

A client interested in joining this plan must complete an application through one of our sales representatives. The application will request information on the amount of income to be deferred, information on benificiaries, and the choice of where the funds will be invested. The amount of the deferral may be increased, decreased, or suspended at any time.

This is an exciting new marketing venture that Midwest will be able to provide for its clients. Informational brochures will be availible for all sales representatives to distribute to prospective clients. These have complete information on this new plan.

Use standard bound-report format.

Underline the italicized paragraph headings.

WP
Many word processors have an automatic page-break feature that provides the correct top and bottom margins on a multipage report.

Note: Never type a heading as the last line on a page. Also, if you must divide a paragraph between two pages, leave at least two lines of the paragraph at the bottom of one page and carry forward at least two lines to the next page.

RETAILING ORGANIZATIONS   5
The Last Stage of the Distribution Channel   13
By Kimberly J. Buckley   17

Retailers represent the last stage of the distribution channel that   31
goods follow on their journey from producer to consumer. Retailers   45
sell goods to the ultimate consumer for personal use. They merchandise   59
the goods using either in-store or out-of-store operations.   71

IN-STORE RETAILERS   74

In-store retailers use conventional store facilities, such as super-   88
markets or department stores, to provide goods for their customers.   102
They represent by far the largest category of retailers.   113

Independent Stores. An independent store is an individual retail store,   127
usually a small family-owned business. Most independents sell a rela-   141
tively narrow line of products, such as auto parts or records and tapes.   156

Chain Stores. A chain store is one of a group of similar stores owned   170
by the same company. The parent company normally buys products   183
directly from the manufacturer and distributes them to the individual   197
stores for sale to the final consumer.   204

OUT-OF-STORE RETAILERS   209

Out-of-store retailers do not use conventional retail facilities to sell   223
their goods. Instead, they rely on a variety of other promotional and   237
marketing techniques. Although both house-to-house sales and vending-   251
machine sales account for considerable volume, most out-of-store sales   266
are generated by either telephone or mail.   274

Telephone Retailing. In telephone retailing, salespeople call prospects   289
or follow up on the customer's response to promotional campaigns. In-   302
creases in printing and mailing costs, combined with new features pro-   316
vided by the telephone companies, have increased the use of this tech-   330
nique.   331

Mail-Order Retailing. Mail-order retailers ask buyers to order prod-   345
ucts from catalogs or from brochures sent directly to their homes or by   359
using order blanks placed in newspapers and magazines. Some compa-   372
nies distribute all their products through mail sales; others use catalogs   387
to supplement in-store retailing operations.   396

Line: 6 inches (60 pica/70 elite)
Tab: 5, center
Spacing: double
Paper: plain, full sheet

From the left margin, spread *NEWS RELEASE*. Leave 1 space between letters and 3 spaces between words. Begin *From Joyce McIntosh* at center.

Ms. McIntosh wants this news release to be typed and submitted to the *Lawrence Star* as soon as possible.

If you are using a word processor, you may want to justify the right margin to meet the needs of the newspaper.

Any material (such as a news release) that is to be published is double-spaced to allow for editing.

N E W S   R E L E A S E   From Joyce McIntosh   8
                                 Midwest Insurance Company   13
                                 125 Ridgefield Avenue   18
                                 Lawrence, KS 66044   21
                                        ↓2

                                 Release August 6, 19--   26
                                        ↓3

                     MIDWEST HONORS MATILDA RUIZ   31
                                ↓3

      Lawrence, Kans., August 3--Ms. Charlotte Kirsh, president   43
of Midwest Insurance, presented ~~Mattie~~ *Matilda* Ruiz with an award for   55
being the top sales representative of Midwest for the second   67
consecutive year. The award was presented to Ms. Ruiz on   79
Saturday, July 16, at the Camelot Inn. ~~About~~ *Over 100* ~~90~~ employees   91
attended the banquet. In recognition of her ~~accomplishments,~~ *achievement,*   102
Ms. Ruiz was presented with a cash award and a desk set. ~~that~~   114
~~was appropriately inscribed.~~

      Ms. Kirsh outlined the contributions made by Ms. Ruiz ~~in~~   124
~~the past several years~~ since becoming a sales associate with   132
Midwest. In addition, Ms. Ruiz was responsible for generating   145
sales of *over* $325,000 during the last four months. Policies were   158
sold by ~~Ms. Ruiz~~ *her* for homeowner's, (automobile,) and life insur-   169
ance coverage. Ms. Ruiz is responsible for clients in Doug-   181
las, Jefferson, and Johnson counties.   188

      Excerpts from letters that have been written by satisfied   200
clients concerning the service provided by Ms. Ruiz ~~was~~ *were* read   212
by Ms. Kirsh. Ms. Ruiz has been a sales associate with Mid-   224
west for the past four years. She received her B.S. degree in   237
marketing from East Kansas University. ~~and~~ *Ms. Ruiz* lives in De Soto   250
with her husband and two children.   257

FOOTNOTES

Line: 60 spaces
Tab: 5, center
Spacing: single
Drills: 2 times
Format Guide: 39–40
Tape: 18B

Goals: To type 38 wam/3'/5e; to format a report with footnotes.

48-A. WARMUP

S 1 Your major problem with the ivory handle is that it sticks.
A 2 Jack said Inez played a very quiet game of bridge with Rex.
N 3 Log on to Data File 89762 at 3:20 and log off before 12:45.

SKILLBUILDING

48-B. CONCENTRATION PRACTICE

48-B. Take several 30-second timings on each line. Try to maintain the same speed on all these lines.

4 It is up to you and me to do it if it is to be done at all.
5 Much of what they have said means that your plan will lose.
6 Conscientious secretaries transcribed their correspondence.
| | | 2 | 3 | 4 | 5 | 6 | 7 | 8 | 9 | 10 | 11 | 12

48-C. SKILL MEASUREMENT: 3-MINUTE TIMED WRITING

48-C. Spacing: double. Record your score.

7 Both at home and in the office, color affects the mood 12
8 and physical comfort of people. The decreased use of over- 24
9 head light fixtures in the modern office requires new color 36
10 patterns. 38
11 Red creates feelings of warmth but too much red causes 50
12 stress. Yellow is seen as cheerful, white will emphasize a 62
13 feeling of lightness, and blue or green look quite cool and 74
14 relaxing. 76
15 Just two or three colors should be combined in the of- 88
16 fice. Too many colors tend to look choppy. The colors you 100
17 choose for the office must reflect the type of work that is 112
18 performed. 114
| | | 2 | 3 | 4 | 5 | 6 | 7 | 8 | 9 | 10 | 11 | 12

48-D. FORMATTING REPORTS WITH FOOTNOTES

Footnote references indicate the sources of facts or ideas in a report. A superscript (raised) number is typed after the fact or idea in the body of the report, and the footnote reference is typed at the bottom of the same page. To format footnotes:

1. Single-space after the last line of text, and type a 2-inch underscore to separate the text from the footnotes.
2. Double-space, indent 5 spaces, and type the superscript footnote number and the reference. Single-space the lines of a footnote, but double-space between footnotes.

Note: When the last page of a multipage report contains a

it does not make any difference."[1] Most newspapers formerly paid $25 per page for typesetting, but with the desktop publishing software, the cost has dropped to $8 per page.[2]
—————————
[1]Louise Plachta and Leonard E. Flannery, The Desktop Publishing Revolution, 2d ed., Computer Publications, Inc., Los Angeles, 1987, pp. 558-559.

[2]Terry Denton, "Newspaper Cuts Costs, Increases Quality," The Monthly Press, October 1986, p. 135.

footnote, the divider line and footnotes are typed at the bottom of the page—not immediately below the last line of text.

Ms. McIntosh has completed some research on the total population found in some of the eastern counties of Kansas and has collected data on the number of policies in effect in each county. She wants to use this as a discussion topic at the upcoming meeting for sales representatives. Arrange this table in boxed format.

POPULATION AND POLICIES IN EASTERN KANSAS COUNTIES

County	Population	Number of Policies		
		Homeowner's	Auto	Life
Atchison	18,397	183	354	1,754
Doniphan	9,268	91	180	987
Douglas	67,640	705	1,521	7,110
Franklin	21,813	224	420	2,175
Jackson	11,644	98	210	1,076
Jefferson	15,207	164	320	1,619
Johnson	270,269	2,841	4,740	26,239
Leavenworth	54,809	576	1,110	5,509
Miami	21,618	240	475	2,008
Nemaha	11,211	114	222	1,084
Osage	15,319	187	375	1,527
Pottawatomie	14,782	138	269	1,444
Shawnee	154,916	1,642	3,469	16,328
Wabaunsee	6,687	70	152	583
Wyandotte	172,335	1,840	3,864	17,340
TOTAL	865,915	9,113	17,681	86,783

TABLE 54
RULED TABLE

Spacing: double
Paper: plain, full sheet

For the same sales meeting, Ms. McIntosh will need information on the number of policies written during the last quarter by the six sales representatives in eastern Kansas. Title of table: MIDWEST FOURTH-QUARTER SALES.

Sales Representative	Homeowner's	Auto	Life
Cornish, Richard	17	24	32
DeVries, Maureen	15	20	24
Principi, Mario	14	18	21
Ruiz, Matilda	25	32	38
Sek, Victoria	18	30	28
Thompson, Ernest	21	22	26

Paper: plain
Visual guide: Workguide 59

WP Many word processors have a special feature that enables you to position footnotes quickly and automatically, without having to determine where the divider line should go.

Note: As you type each superscript in the body of a report, estimate the number of lines needed for the corresponding footnote. Then place a light pencil mark in the left margin at the point where you should stop typing the text in order to leave enough room at the bottom of the page for the footnote.

Footnotes may also be typed with regular numbers followed by a period—for example:

1. "Software Leaves . . .

USING MICROCOMPUTERS IN ELECTIONS *(TO WIN)*   7

Politicians throughout the country are *increasingly* turning to micro-   21
computers to help them run a more effective campaign. Comput-   33
ers have long been used for mass mailings and to help manage   45
campaign finances. Now they are *also* being used to help campaign   59
managers plan *more effective strategies* winning campaigns.   67

For example, it is estimated that at least (10) different   74
software programs are available that contain maps with census   86
information.[1] The campaign manager can have a map with the   96
most recent voting patterns for each precinct appear on his or *the*   99
her computer screen. Each precinct can be highlighted to show   122
the number of eligible voters, the number who actually voted   134
in the last election, and the distribution of voters *among* between   146
the political parties. ¶ Some software programs even allow   157
users to combine census and political data. Angela South Pick,   170
a Political Consultant who has used such a program, said, "For   182
example, you can ask to see all the areas in a district that   195
have at least voted 75 per cent republican over the past (4)   207
years and that have a *median* medium family income of between $40,000   219
and $60,000."[2]   221

    225
_____

[1]"Software Leaves the Business Office," Information World   237
Weekly, Februrary 18, 1986, pp. 43-48.   244
[2]Jon N. Nicholas and Suzanne Rydahl-Fleming, Winning   255
Strategies for the Electronic Age, National Policy Center   267
for Voter Education, Washington, D.C., *1986,* p. 179.   277

N. INTEGRATED OFFICE PROJECT: MIDWEST INSURANCE COMPANY

Situation: Today is Monday, August 2. You are employed in the office of Midwest Insurance Company at 125 Ridgefield Avenue in Lawrence, Kansas. Midwest handles automobile, homeowner's, and life insurance. You work for both Mr. Arnold Speert, claims supervisor, and Ms. Joyce McIntosh, sales manager. The company expects all correspondence to be typed in block style with open punctuation. Be sure to make any corrections for incorrect spelling, grammar, or punctuation in the tasks that must be completed in the following jobs.

FORM 35
OPERATOR'S LOG   Paper: Workguide 337

As a step toward measuring productivity in office work, Midwest Insurance requires its office staff to keep a record in an operator's log of all work performed during the day. The instructions for completing this log are given on the log form itself. The turnaround time on your log sheet is the total time the job was in your hands. Complete this log with information about each job that you complete in this unit.

REPORT 62
BOILERPLATE PARAGRAPHS   Paper: plain

Mr. Speert has decided to prepare some standard paragraphs that can be used when clients inquire about an insurance matter with Midwest. Prepare a one-page report entitled "Boilerplate Paragraphs." Use a 6-inch line, with a 1-inch top margin and single spacing. Indent the first line of each paragraph.

Para. 1. Your inquiry about processing a claim through your automobile insurance policy with Midwest has been received. I was sorry to hear of your accident, but I can assure you that your claim will be handled efficiently as soon as we collect all the necessary information. — 8, 17, 26, 35, 45, 54, 55

Para. 2. Your inquiry about processing a claim through your automobile insurance policy with Midwest has been received. I was sorry to hear that your auto was stolen, but I can assure you that your claim will be handled very quickly as soon as we receive the proper forms. — 64, 72, 81, 90, 100, 109, 110

Para. 3. Your inquiry about processing a claim through your homeowner's insurance — 119, 127

policy with Midwest has been received. I am extremely sorry to hear about the burglary that took place at your home. We will handle your claim as quickly as possible as soon as the necessary paperwork has been completed. — 136, 144, 154, 163, 171

Para. 4. Please submit the police report of the accident, along with the estimate that you received for repairing the damage to your auto. I will then have our claims adjuster schedule a visit with you so that final processing can begin. — 180, 190, 198, 207, 216, 219

Para. 5. Please send us a copy of the police form that was completed when your car was stolen. In addition, submit a copy of the leasing agreement that you signed with the car agency for the rental of a replacement vehicle. — 228, 237, 247, 256, 264

Para. 6. Please submit the record filed by your local police department in investigating the burglary. In addition, submit an itemized list of the items that were taken during the burglary, with the market value assigned to each item. — 273, 282, 291, 300, 309, 311

Para. 7. This entire process should take no more than one month prior to settlement taking place. If you have any questions, please get in touch with me. — 319, 325, 333, 339, 342

Para. 8. As soon as we receive all the necessary paperwork, we will expedite payment for your stolen car under the comprehensive coverage plan that you have with us. — 349, 356, 363, 370, 375

Para. 9. I will assign one of our adjusters to visit your home as soon as our office receives the forms outlined above. — 382, 389, 395, 399

Line: 60 spaces
Tab: 5, center
Spacing: single
Drills: 2 times
Format Guide: 39–42
Tape: 18B

Goals: To increase speed and accuracy; to type a report with endnotes.

49-A. WARMUP

S 1 The big man did not burn the ivory handle of the oak chair.
A 2 Because he was very lazy, Jack paid for six games and quit.
N 3 I got 98 of 147 items correct on the ENG 605 test at 12:30.

SKILLBUILDING

49-B. Take a 1-minute timing on the first paragraph to establish your base speed. Then take several 1-minute timings on the remaining paragraphs. As soon as you equal or exceed your base speed on one paragraph, advance to the next one.

49-B. SUSTAINED TYPING: ROUGH DRAFT

4   Buying office chairs is not as simple as it may sound. 12
5 Computer operators must now stay seated for long periods of 24
6 time and assume certain positions unique to their function. 36

7   The needs of these operators can not be met by the tra- 12
8 ditional office chairs. So Furniture makers now produce new 24
9 chairs designed to enhance the comfort of office ~~personal~~ personnel. 36

10   For a chairs to be comfortable, ~~they~~ it must have an adjust- 12
11 able seat. It must have the same contour of a typical human 24
12 body, and it must move in the same way that the body moves. 36

13   Seat hieght should ~~must~~ be adjustable so that there is ~~very~~ quite 12
14 little pressure on the legs when the feet are ~~resting~~ on the floor. 24
15 Chairs should also allow operators to shift in their seats. 36

| | 1 | | 2 | | 3 | | 4 | | 5 | | 6 | | 7 | | 8 | | 9 | | 10 | | 11 | | 12

49-C. ENDNOTES

Like footnotes, endnote references indicate the sources for statements cited. However, instead of placing the references at the bottom of the page, you type them on a separate page at the end of the report. To format endnotes:

1. Center the heading *NOTES* in all capitals on line 13.
2. Triple-space (leave 2 blank lines), indent 5 spaces, and type the reference number (not a superscript), followed by a period, 2 spaces, and the reference. Single-space the lines of an endnote, but double-space between endnotes.
3. Center the page number 1 inch from the bottom of the page.

↓13
NOTES
↓3

    1. "Software Leaves the Business Office," <u>Information World Weekly</u>, February 18, 1986, pp. 43-48.

    2. Jon N. Nicholas and Suzanne Rydahl-Fleming, <u>Winning Strategies for the Electronic Age</u>, National Policy Center for Voter Education, Washington, D.C., 1986, p. 179.

    3. Louise Plachta and Leonard E. Flannery, <u>The Desktop Publishing Revolution</u>, 2d ed., Computer Publications, Inc., Los Angeles, 1987, pp. 558-559.

    4. Terry Denton, "Newspaper Cuts Costs, Increases Quality," <u>The Monthly Press</u>, October 1986, p. 135.

L.   12-SECOND SPRINTS

42 Judge Jones justly joined Judge Jettig on a major judgment.
43 Kathy had a quick snack with baked cookies, cake, and milk.
44 Quentin quietly and quickly quoted that eloquent quotation.
45 Alex took extra time to execute the exercise on a tax exam.
46 Buzz was amazed at the size of the dozen zebras at the zoo.

|||||||||||||
5   10   15   20   25   30   35   40   45   50   55   60

M. Spacing: double. Record your score.

M.   SKILL MEASUREMENT: 5-MINUTE TIMED WRITING

47   Protection against an economic loss has always been an   12
48 important concept. This is precisely what is meant when we   24
49 talk about insurance. This is accomplished by sharing risk   36
50 with a large number of other persons. There are many types   48
51 of insurance to deal with.   53
52   It is quite important to have auto insurance. This is   65
53 to cover the cost of injury to other people or to cover the   77
54 cost of damage to property caused by an auto. Some factors   89
55 that determine the cost of insurance include your age, sex, 101
56 and past driving record.   106
57   Life insurance is extremely important. To protect for 118
58 major economic losses due to death, many people secure some 130
59 type of life insurance that will enable their dependents to 142
60 continue meeting their living expenses. Age of the insured 154
61 is one major cost factor.   159
62   Home and property insurance is also quite critical. A 171
63 person should have insurance to cover the cost to fix or to 183
64 rebuild a home after a fire or some other type of disaster. 195
65 Coverage might also include losses for stolen property that 207
66 occur due to a burglary.   212
67   There are many other types of insurance which might be 224
68 purchased. It is important to analyze what losses might be 236
69 met or what economic risks might occur. When this is done, 248
70 it will be possible to determine whether some other type of 260
71 insurance might be needed.   265

| 1 | 2 | 3 | 4 | 5 | 6 | 7 | 8 | 9 | 10 | 11 | 12 |

THE INFORMATION PROCESSING MANAGER   7

By *(Your name)*   11

The information processing manager is responsible for providing sup-   25
port for those departments which are involved in planning, installing,   39
operating, and maintaining integrated information processing systems.   53
These systems include word processing, electronic mail, and decision-   67
support systems.   70

PLANNING AND COORDINATION   75

A recent survey indicated that most IP managers spend about 15 per-   88
cent of their time in planning and coordinating information processing   103
systems.[1] They first obtain user input and gather other information on   117
the requirements of data communication, including the kinds of applica-   131
tions needed as well as the storage requirements for data.   143

They must also research such areas as available software, networking   156
capabilities, and license agreements. Prior to making any purchase deci-   171
sions, the IP manager should also complete a facility impact study to   185
determine power requirements, environmental factors, and other build-   198
ing considerations.[2]   202

ESTABLISHING POLICIES AND PROCEDURES   210

As much as a fourth of the IP manager's time is devoted to establishing   224
systemwide policies and procedures for the overall information process-   238
ing function.[3] Policies and procedures must be established for data stor-   253
age, equipment maintenance, and user priority. Also included in this   267
function is the training program that must be an ongoing part of any   280
effective information processing operation.   289

Reynolds best summarized the IP manager's responsibility when he   302
said, "Any manager who devotes all his or her energies to purchase deci-   316
sions and who neglects the thousand other, less glamorous, details, will   331
surely live to regret that decision later."[4]   340

If you must divide a paragraph between two pages, always leave at least two lines of the paragraph at the bottom of one page and bring forward at least two lines to the second page. Do not have a side heading as the last line of a page. Do not divide the last word on a page.

Endnotes go on a separate page.

NOTES   341

1. Neal Morningstar, "The IP Manager: Who's Minding the Store?" *MIS*   355
Journal, January 1988, p. 153.   361
2. I-Ming Aron and Robert Aron, *Information Processing,* Bird's Eye   374
Publications, Inc., Boston, 1987, pp. 385–386.   384
3. Morningstar, p. 155.   388
4. LeRoy Reynolds, *Administration and Supervision: Theory and*   401
Practice, 3d ed., The University of York Press, York, Mich., 1988, p. 389.   416

F. PRODUCTION PRACTICE: SPELLING

16 abundance entrance assistance attendance annoyance distance
17 clearance reliance remittance observance fragrance elegance
18 influence audience conference occurrence inference presence
19 reference violence abstinence competence innocence sentence

G. TECHNIQUE TYPING: SHIFT KEY

20 Aaron Albert Betty Bess Carl Calvin Dolly Denise Earl Eddie
21 Fanny Felice Gomez Gabe Hedy Hester Jerry Joseph Kiki Karen
22 Lenny Lionel Mindy Mary Nick Norman Olive Odette Paul Peter
23 Robin Ramona Sammy Stew Tara Tricia Upton Urbino Vera Vicki

H. PRODUCTION PRACTICE: PROOFREADING

24   There are other types of insurance which might be
25 purchased. It is important to analyse what losses might be
26 met or what economic rizks might occur. When this is done,
27 it will be possable to determine whether some other type of
28 insurance hight be needed.

I. CONCENTRATION PRACTICE

29 Jan met mr. and mrs. rocconi when they flew to los angeles.
30 Continental flight 38 to st. thomas made a stop in atlanta.
31 Vicki and frank left for virginia on saturday, november 13.
32 Fenway park is two miles south of the bunker hill monument.

J. PROGRESSIVE PRACTICE: ALPHABET

Turn to the Progressive Practice: Alphabet routine at the back of the book. Take several 30-second timings, starting at the point where you left off the last time. Record your progress on Workguide page 289.

K. SUSTAINED TYPING: NUMBERS

33   The magazine subscription service prepared an ad to be   12
34 aired on cable television on September 29 and 30. For this   24
35 ad to be a success, calls from 300 customers were required.   36

36   After the ad was aired on September 29, 182 calls were   12
37 received. The service received 246 calls for September 30.   24
38 A grand total of 428 calls were processed from that one ad.   36

39   With each subscription averaging $30, gross sales from   12
40 that ad were $12,840. Sales for August were $9,870; the ad   24
41 on September 29 and 30 helped increase the sales by $2,970.   36

  | 1 | 2 | 3 | 4 | 5 | 6 | 7 | 8 | 9 | 10 | 11 | 12

SPECIAL REPORT PAGES

Line: 60 spaces
Tab: 5, center
Spacing: single
Drills: 2 times
Format Guide: 42–52
Tape: 19B

Goals: To type 38 wam/3'/5e; to format a report title page and a table of contents.

50-A. WARMUP

S 1 I wish to work with the busy chap who owns the eight autos.
A 2 Ken bought Mary five or six dozen pieces of quaint jewelry.
N 3 The 23 percent raise brought her 1987 salary up to $45,026.

SKILLBUILDING

50-B. Compare this paragraph with the first paragraph of Report 16 on page 101. Then type a copy, correcting the errors as you type.

50-B. PRODUCTION PRACTICE: PROOFREADING

4   The information processing manger is responsable
5 for providing support for the departments which are in-
6 involved in planning, installing, opperating, and main-
7 taining intergrated information-processing systems. These
8 systems may include word processing, electronic mail and
9 decicion-suppport systems.

50-C. Spacing: double. Record your score.

50-C. SKILL MEASUREMENT: 3-MINUTE TIMED WRITING

10   Some firms experience high turnover in their mailrooms   12
11 since jobs there are frequently low-paying. Thus, it is no   24
12 surprise that some firms have switched to machines to lower   36
13 costs. One new way to deliver mail inside of a firm is the   48
14 mobile mail unit. The unit is a self-propelled cart; it is   60
15 guided by an invisible path painted on the floor or carpet.   72
16 An electronic tracking system keeps the cart on track as it   84
17 zips up and down the halls. The cart makes regular rounds,   96
18 stopping at set spots to allow workers to remove their mail   108
19 and to insert mail for others.   114

| 1 | 2 | 3 | 4 | 5 | 6 | 7 | 8 | 9 | 10 | 11 | 12 |

50-D. FORMATTING A TITLE PAGE AND A TABLE OF CONTENTS

Reports prepared for college or business often include a title page and a table of contents. The title page should appear centered horizontally and vertically. The information it contains may vary, but it always includes at least the report title, the writer's name, and the date.

The table of contents for a report should be on a separate page, with the heading typed in all-capital letters on line 13.

Line: 60 spaces
Tab: 5, center
Spacing: single
Drills: 2 times
Workguide: 337–353
Format Guide: 133

INTEGRATED OFFICE PROJECT: INSURANCE

GOALS FOR UNIT 28

1. To type 53 wam for 5 minutes with no more than 5 errors.
2. To format letters in block style with open punctuation.
3. To format a memorandum and tables.
4. To format a standard report.
5. To format specialized reports—a news release and an itinerary.
6. To format voucher checks.
7. To apply rules of punctuation and capitalization when formatting selected documents.

A.   WARMUP

S 1   You will want to do some fishing when you visit the island.
A 2   Max quietly gave Jack a zinger about his pesky new friends.
N 3   Call 859-0672 when you begin processing check #34 for $176.

PRETEST. Take a 1-minute timing; compute your speed and count errors.

B.   PRETEST: HORIZONTAL REACHES

4   Our advisers were to discuss your affairs at the legal   12
5   meeting. Upon returning to the office, they should write a   24
6   short brief to advise you of the wrongs they have gathered.   36
7   We will be happy to give you a copy as soon as it is ready.   48
       | 1 | 2 | 3 | 4 | 5 | 6 | 7 | 8 | 9 | 10 | 11 | 12

PRACTICE.
    Speed Emphasis: If you made no errors on the Pretest, type each line twice.
    Accuracy Emphasis: If you made 1 or more errors on the Pretest, type each group of lines (as though it were a paragraph) twice.

C.   PRACTICE: IN REACHES

8   wr writes dowry wrong unwrap wrench awry writhe wren wreath
9   ou output rough ounce source double ouch detour ours ouster
10 ad advise ready adore leader steady adds spread fade admits
11 py pylons happy pygmy spying floppy pyre snappy copy python

D.   PRACTICE: OUT REACHES

12 yo yonder mayor yodel myopic joyous your crayon yowl yogurt
13 fa factor offal fades affair unfair fast prefab sofa faulty
14 up uplift erupt upset supply coupon upon markup cups upturn
15 ga gazing legal gavel negate slogan gave frugal toga gather

POSTTEST. Repeat the Pretest and compare performance.

E.   POSTTEST: HORIZONTAL REACHES

REPORT 17
TITLE PAGE

Paper: plain
Tab: center
Style as shown

If a report title or subtitle must be divided between two lines, try to have the second line shorter than the first, resulting in an inverted-pyramid appearance.

WP Some word processing software will let you select an option that will center the text vertically on a page when it is printed.

It is easy to determine the line number on which you are keying text on a computer for some word processing programs, because the line number appears on the screen.

↓13

THE SECRETARY IN TODAY'S AUTOMATED OFFICE

Maintaining Traditional Skills While
Developing High-Tech Competence

Line 33 ——→ Prepared by

Phyllis G. Browne
Systems Analyst
The Western Office Group

December 9, 19--

↑13

REPORT 18
TABLE OF CONTENTS

Line: 6 inches (60 pica/70 elite)
Tab: center

LEADERS. Use leaders (rows of periods) to lead the eye across the page. Always leave 1 space *before* and *after* the row of periods. (Spaces may also be inserted between the periods, but all leaders must align vertically.)

WP Some word processors have a leader-tab feature that automatically inserts leaders when the user is tabbing from one point to the next.

Note: For roman numerals that take more than 1 space, use the margin release and backspace from the left margin.

↓13

CONTENTS

↓3

I.   THE TRADITIONAL SECRETARY .... 1 ↓2

   A.   Training 2
   B.   Hiring and Salary Levels 3
   C.   Career Advancement .... 3 ↓3

II. THE MODERN SECRETARY .... 4 ↓2

   A.   Training and Experience 4
   B.   Personality vs. Skills 5
   C.   Career Paths 6
   D.   Effect of Legislation 7
   E.   Feminism, Chauvinism, and Sexism .... 8 ↓3

III. CONTEMPORARY SECRETARIAL SKILLS .... 9 ↓2

   A.   Equipment Skills 10
   B.   Administration Skills 12
   C.   Technical Skills .... 14 ↓3

IV. LOOKING TO THE FUTURE 17

REPORT 58
BOUND REPORT:
APPENDIX (5)

TABLE 52
Spacing: single
Paper: plain, full sheet

Begin an appendix on a separate page with a 2-inch top margin.

start title on line 13

APPENDIX A 2

PARTS OF A BUSINESS LETTER 7

Standard Parts	~~Supplemental~~ Optional Parts	
		13
1. Letterhead	1. Attention line	19
2. Date line	2. Subject line	25
3. Inside address	3. Company signature	33
4. Salutation	4. Enclosure notation	40
5. Body	5. Copy notation	45
6. Complimentary closing	6. Postscript	53
7. Writer's identification		58
8. Reference initials		63

REPORT 59
BOUND REPORT:
TABLE OF CONTENTS

Line: 6 inches
(60 pica/70 elite)
Paper: plain, full sheet

Prepare a table of contents for your correspondence manual that is similar to the one shown below.

TABLE OF CONTENTS

I. Telephone Equipment Today 1
A. Key Systems 2
B. Private Branch Exchanges 2
C. Computerized Telephones 3
D. Voice/Data Networks 3
E. Other Equipment and Accessories 4
F. Voice Mail 5
I. Telephone Techniques 6
A. Answering Calls 7
B. Placing Calls 8
C. Communications Skills 9
I. Teleconferences 10
A. Audio Teleconferences 11
B. Video Teleconferences 12
C. Arranging a Teleconference 12

REPORT 60
BOUND REPORT:
TITLE PAGE

Paper: plain, full sheet

Prepare a title page for your correspondence manual that is similar to the one shown below.

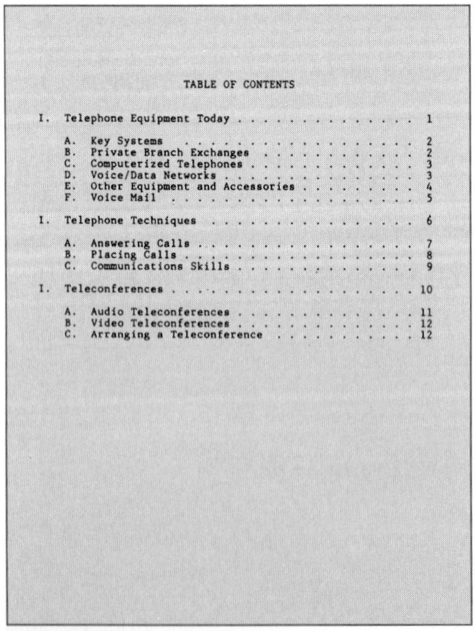

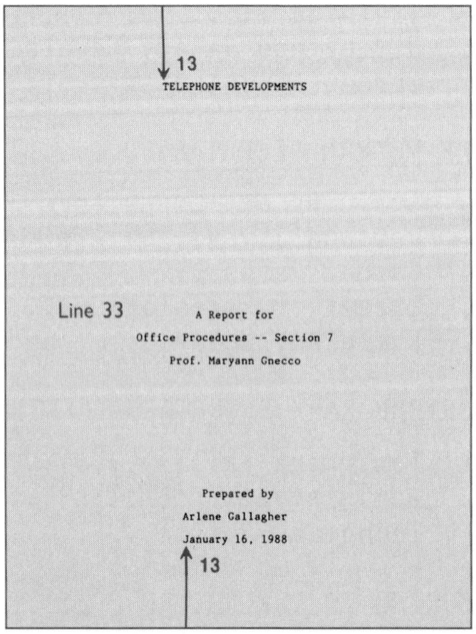

13
TELEPHONE DEVELOPMENTS

Line 33
A Report for
Office Procedures -- Section 7
Prof. Maryann Gnecco

Prepared by
Arlene Gallagher
January 16, 1988
13

REPORT 61
BOUND REPORT:
BIBLIOGRAPHY (6)

Line: 6 inches
(60 pica/70 elite)
Paper: plain, full sheet

Prepare a bibliography for your correspondence manual that is similar to the one shown below.

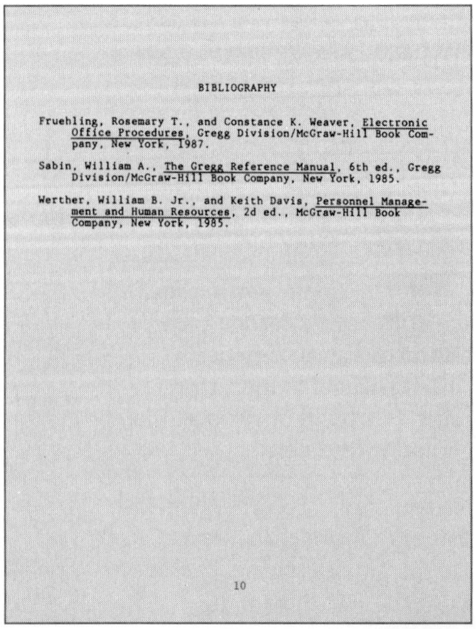

BIBLIOGRAPHY

Fruehling, Rosemary T., and Constance K. Weaver, Electronic Office Procedures, Gregg Division/McGraw-Hill Book Company, New York, 1987.

Sabin, William A., The Gregg Reference Manual, 6th ed., Gregg Division/McGraw-Hill Book Company, New York, 1985.

Werther, William B. Jr., and Keith Davis, Personnel Management and Human Resources, 2d ed., McGraw-Hill Book Company, New York, 1985.

10

LESSON 51

MEMORANDUMS

Line: 60 spaces
Tab: 5
Spacing: single
Drills: 2 times
Workguide: 93
Format Guide: 43–44
Tape: 20B

Goals: To increase speed and accuracy; to format memorandums on printed forms.

51-A. WARMUP

S 1 The girls with the keys may lay them down on the oak chair.
A 2 Tom quickly jeopardized his own life by giving the mixture.
N 3 The 10/23/89 invoice (#475) was for $132.86 plus $7.97 tax.

SKILLBUILDING

PRETEST. Take a 1-minute timing; compute your speed and count errors.

51-B. PRETEST: COMMON LETTER COMBINATIONS

4   At the conference last week, some person made a formal   12
5 motion that might be useful to us in the coming months. It   24
6 should enable us to easily comply with our building permit.   36
   | 1 | 2 | 3 | 4 | 5 | 6 | 7 | 8 | 9 | 10 | 11 | 12

PRACTICE.
   Speed Emphasis: If you made 2 or fewer errors on the Pretest, type each line twice.
   Accuracy Emphasis: If you made 3 or more errors, type each group of lines (as though it were a paragraph) twice.

51-C. PRACTICE: WORD BEGINNINGS

7 for forget formal format forces forums forked forest formed
8 con concur confer conned convoy consul convey convex condor
9 per perils period perish permit person peruse Persia pertly
10 com combat comedy coming commit common compel comply comets

51-D. PRACTICE: WORD ENDINGS

11 ing acting aiding boring buying ruling saving hiding dating
12 ble bubble dabble double enable feeble fumble tumble usable
13 ion action vision lesion nation bunion lotion motion legion
14 ful armful cupful earful eyeful joyful lawful useful woeful

POSTTEST. Repeat the Pretest and compare performance.

51-E. POSTTEST: COMMON LETTER COMBINATIONS

51-F. Tab: Every 11 spaces.

51-F. TECHNIQUE TYPING: TAB KEY

Alphabet						
15	Allen	Bates	Cohen	Drake	Evans	Fung
16	Gomez	Hogan	Innis	James	Kirby	Luke
17	Moore	North	Poole	Quinn	Reyes	Stan
18	Upton	Vogel	White	Xerox	Young	Zack

Number/Symbol						
19	$5.32	(451)	30.6%	18.3*	$6.84	#401
20	4,093	12:30	11'4"	5'10"	15/16	1.62
21	#3840	35-45	4:56*	3 & 4	5.42;	(4%)
22	11:50	(#47)	8.97%	$6-$7	23/24	#367

LESSON 135

FORMAL REPORT

Goals: To type 52 wam/5'/5e; to format the special pages of a formal report.

135-A. WARMUP

S 1 The woman owns half the lake and half the land by the town.
A 2 Valerie quickly mixed frozen strawberries with grape juice.
N 3 Items 2437, 2569, 2389, and 2450 were out of current stock.

SKILLBUILDING

135-B. PROGRESSIVE PRACTICE: NUMBERS

Turn to the Progressive Practice: Numbers routine at the back of the book. Take several 30-second timings, starting at the point where you left off the last time. Record your progress on Workguide page 289.

135-C. Spacing: double. Record your score.

135-C. SKILL MEASUREMENT: 5-MINUTE TIMED WRITING

4   Lots of hard work goes into planning a trip for a tour   12
5 group. Many people do not realize the amount of energy and   24
6 time that is required for this job. The person responsible   36
7 has to worry about both the itinerary and the travelers who   48
8 are going on the tour. Therefore, this person must be well   60
9 organized and very dependable. The person running the tour   72
10 takes credit when it is successful and also takes the blame   84
11 whenever it fails. The organizer's job is a difficult one.   96
12   Planning the itinerary is not so much a hard job as it   108
13 is a tedious one. Bus companies, airlines, hotels, and the   120
14 sight-seeing places must be called, and a time schedule has   132
15 to be arranged. All critical details should be confirmed a   144
16 few days before the trip is to begin. It is important that   156
17 each small detail be handled. This means that plans should   168
18 be made for rest stops, for meal times, and for relaxation. 180
19   The most troublesome aspect of planning tours pertains   192
20 to the individual vacationers. Each person is so different   204
21 in wants and needs. Individual preferences are bound to be   216
22 a problem for the organizer. One person wishes a room with   228
23 a view; another wants a seat by the window. Someone wishes   240
24 to stop at outlet stores; someone else hates outlet stores. 252
25 The job of tour leader is quite demanding.   260

| 1 | 2 | 3 | 4 | 5 | 6 | 7 | 8 | 9 | 10 | 11 | 12 |

51-G. FORMATTING A MEMORANDUM ON A PRINTED FORM

Although an interoffice memorandum can be typed on plain paper or letterhead stationery, it is often typed on a printed form with guide words, such as *To, From, Date,* and *Subject.* The forms may be either full or half sheets of paper, and the guide words may appear in different arrangements.

To format a memorandum on a printed form:

1. Set the left margin 2 or 3 spaces after the guide words; set the right margin to equal the left (by estimate).

2. Set a tab stop 2 or 3 spaces after the guide words in the second column.

3. Begin typing the insertions 2 or 3 spaces after the guide words, and align the insertions with the guide words at the bottom.

4. Separate the heading and the body with 2 blank lines.

5. Use reference initials and other notations.

To: George M. Dow	**From:** Patricia Hewson	6
General Manager	Media Relations	12
Subject: Accident at Site 5	**Date:** April 10, 19--	18

↓3

MEMO 5
ON PRINTED FORM

Paper: Workguide 93, top

WP

Because of the difficulty of aligning the heading data on a printer, printed forms are not used as frequently as plain paper for formatting memos on a word processor.

I have reviewed the technical reports from the chemical and 30
engineering departments and have also interviewed the operator 43
on duty the night of the accident. ~~Based on~~ *On the basis of* the information I 57
have on hand, I've *have* drafted the ~~enclosed~~ *attached* press release. 68

Would you please review this release and make any changes you 80
feel are necessary. Station KXAR-TV and the Morning Herald 92
have already called *to* asking for our side of the story. ~~Thus~~ So 104
I would like to issue this press release as soon as possible. 116

↓2

wpr 117
~~Enclosure~~ *Attachment* 119

To: *Patricia Hewson*	**From:** *George M. Dow*	6
Media Relations	*General Manager*	12
Subject: *Press Release*	**Date:** *April 11, 19--*	17

MEMO 6
ON PRINTED FORM

Paper: Workguide 93, bottom

You have done ~~a masterful~~ *an impressive* job on the press release, Pat. I have 30
no changes to suggest at all. As soon as you have our ~~attorney~~ *legal counsel* 44
review it, you may send it out. 50

Perhaps you should set up a press conference for me on Wednesday 86
afternoon--early enough to make the evening news. My office has 96
also recieved several calls from the News Media, and I've 96
refered all inquiries to your office. Please let me have a list 101
of likely questions by Tuesday afternoon. *and suggested responses* 114

pcb 115

134-E. FORMATTING A CORRESPONDENCE MANUAL (CONTINUED)

REPORT 57
BOUND REPORT (4)

Make your own decisions about page breaks, but keep in mind the space required for footnotes. Insert the correct page number in the heading.

Footnote 5. Compose a footnote using the same source given in footnote 2, but cite page 258.

Ellipses. Three periods separated by spaces, called an *ellipsis* (plural: *ellipses*), indicate an omission. If the omission is at the end of a sentence, four periods are used instead of three.

Footnote 6. Compose a footnote using the same source and page given in footnote 5.

Complimentary Closing. The closing is the signing-off phrase. Depending on the letter style, it will begin at the left margin or at the center. Only the first word is capitalized; the phrase is usually followed by a comma.

Writer's Identification. The writer's identification is typed under the space left for the handwritten signature. It should have the name of the writer, as well as any title if desired.

Reference Initials. Reference initials are the typist's initials. In some cases the dictator's initials are also included here.

B. OPTIONAL LETTER PARTS

In striving for more efficiency in handling correspondence, business writers have added a number of optional letter parts over the years.

Attention Line. The attention line is the second line of the inside address and is used when a letter is addressed to a company rather than an individual. With an attention line, keep the following in mind:

> When an attention line is used . . ., the letter is considered to be addressed to the organization rather than to the person named in the attention line. . . . Whenever possible, omit the attention line and address the letter directly to an individual. . . .[5]

Subject Line. The subject line appears between the salutation and the body of the letter. There is 1 blank line before and after it. It can be centered, or it can be blocked at the left margin. The term "Subject," "Re," or "In re" is used to introduce the subject line.

Company Signature. The company name is sometimes typed a double space below the complimentary closing to indicate the company's obligation or to stretch the length of the letter.

Enclosure Notation. The enclosure notation is a reminder to both the sender and the receiver of the letter that something is enclosed in the envelope.[6] There are a number of styles for including this notation.

Copy Notation. The copy notation lets the addressee know that copies were sent to the persons listed. There are several ways to type a copy notation.

Postscript. The postscript is used to highlight a particular thought or to express an afterthought. It is typed as a separate paragraph at the end of the letter.

Typing letters is a major task for an office typist. The guidelines discussed above are not intended as inflexible rules; they can—and should—be modified to fit specific occasions as good sense and good taste require.

(Continued on page 286.)

Line: 60 spaces
Tab: 5
Spacing: single
Drills: 2 times
Workguide: 95–97
Format Guide: 43–44
Tape: 21B

LESSON 52

MEMORANDUMS

Goals: To type 39 wam/3'/5e; to format memorandums with enumerations.

52-A. WARMUP

S 1 The eight men spent the day at work planting in the fields.
A 2 A few excited jackals squeezed by the open grove at midday.
N 3 My social security number (106-72-3854) was issued in 1967.

SKILLBUILDING

52-B. Change every singular noun to a plural noun. If you do so correctly, all lines will end evenly.

52-B. CONCENTRATION PRACTICE

4   If the man, woman, and child want to vacate the old
5 apartment, the manager must issue the permit to make the
6 transfer legal. The tenant must approve the plan before
7 the vacancy or listing can be printed in the newspaper.

Change every plural noun to a singular noun. If you do so correctly, all lines will end evenly.

8   The managers asked the secretaries to type the letters and
9 reports that the officers had dictated earlier. When the jobs
10 had been completed, the secretaries consulted your assistants.
11 Your assistants discovered the errors and had the jobs redone.

Change all first-person pronouns to the second person and vice versa; for example, change *I* to *you* and change *you* to *I* or *me*.

12   You must give me your recipe for success in your profession
13 if I intend to follow you. If I become a broker also, you
14 can help me by giving me some leads and other contacts; you
15 could also have me subcontract a few of your small accounts.

52-C. Spacing: double. Record your score.

52-C. SKILL MEASUREMENT: 3-MINUTE TIMED WRITING

16   A spelling mistake in a letter can be quite embarrass- 12
17 ing, and a typo in a legal document can be disastrous. But 24
18 no matter how careful you are, errors have a way of showing 36
19 up unexpectedly. 39
20   If you input your work on a computer, you can make use 51
21 of a spelling checker to locate some types of errors before 63
22 they show up in printed pages. Error-free output will jus- 75
23 tify the price. 78
24   The program has to analyze each word that is typed and 90
25 try to match it with a word stored in a dictionary on disk. 102
26 If no match can be found, it will flag the word as a possi- 114
27 ble misspelling. 117

| 1 | 2 | 3 | 4 | 5 | 6 | 7 | 8 | 9 | 10 | 11 | 12

FORMAL REPORT

Line: 60 spaces
Tab: 5, center
Spacing: single
Drills: 2 times
Format Guide: 131

Goals: To build speed and accuracy; to continue formatting a formal report.

134-A. WARMUP

S 1   He might make the early train if he can do his work by six.
A 2   Seizing the wax buffer, Joann quickly removed the big spot.
N 3   Invoice #6473 for $890.50 was mailed to 124 Fairbanks Road.

SKILLBUILDING

134-B. Tab: Every 12 spaces.

134-B. TECHNIQUE TYPING: TAB KEY

Alphabet

4	text	type	zone	modem	format
5	disk	jobs	word	video	search
6	copy	byte	menu	query	global

Numbers/Symbols

7	$8.60	$341	$75.50	5'11"	"Okay!"
8	21.3%	#D-8	19.75%	#3456	(5,340)
9	(341)	147#	"Hey!"	(R&D)	33 & 47

134-C. Take a 1-minute timing on the first paragraph to establish your base speed. Then take several 1-minute timings on the other paragraphs. As soon as you equal or exceed your base speed on one paragraph, advance to the next one.

134-C. SUSTAINED TYPING: ROUGH DRAFT

10   Many office workers look forward to a promotion on the   12
11   job. It should be realized that a number of items are used   24
12   by most managers when they consider a person for promotion.   36
13   Of course, seniority on the job is always a factor for   12
14   consideration. How ever, it shouldn't be the most critical.   24
15   The ability to perform the work must be carefully *analyzed* ~~considered~~.   36
16   Reviewing one's *previous* ~~prior~~ work record is another *factor* ~~thing~~   12
17   of great import*ance*. The ~~many~~ types of work and experience that   24
18   one has had are ~~very~~ important indicators of any *future* success.   36
19   Two final *factors* ~~points~~ which ~~can~~ *will* carry ~~much~~ *lots of* weight with   12
20   *most* ~~many~~ managers deals with the ~~success~~ *ratings* of the interviews and a   24
21   careful analysis of references given by *former* supervisors.   36

| 1 | 2 | 3 | 4 | 5 | 6 | 7 | 8 | 9 | 10 | 11 | 12 |

134-D. Compare this paragraph with the last paragraph of the timing on page 281. Type a list of the words that contain errors, correcting the errors as you type.

134-D. PRODUCTION PRACTICE: PROOFREADING

22   Working for a temperary agency is ideal for the worker
23   who wishes to have some free time during the summer. Taking
24   time off is as simple as one, two, three. It just requires
25   telling the agency when one is now available for work. One
26   can also find work thrugh a temporary agency that has more
27   flexable hours to meet individual needs.

52-D. FORMATTING MEMORANDUMS

MEMO 7
ON PRINTED FORM
Paper: Workguide 95

The abbreviation *RE* is sometimes used in place of the word *SUBJECT* in a memo or letter.

ENUMERATION. Treat each item as a separate paragraph with numbers at the left margin and turnover lines indented 4 spaces.

A copy notation on a memo is formatted the same way as on a business letter.

(TO:) Jileen Dagher, Shop Supervisor *(FROM:)* Evelyn Cunning- 9
ham, Human Resources Director *(DATE:)* October 19, 19— 18
(RE:) Performance Appraisal Form 23

Jileen, I've reviewed the draft appraisal form that your committee sub- 37
mitted on October 4, and I have these comments: 46

1. I suggest that you add a sentence under each category to help 60
explain what is meant. For example, under "Human Relations" you might 74
include this sentence: How effective was this employee in obtaining 88
cooperation, resolving conflict, and communicating with supervisors, 101
peers, and other personnel? 107

2. Add a summary evaluation, such as the following: "Indicate your 121
overall evaluation of this employee's performance, taking into considera- 135
tion the relative job importance of each of the categories above." 148

If your committee agrees with these two suggestions, I'm ready to 161
endorse your appraisal form and to seek the president's approval to place 176
the appraisal process into effect by January 1. Please let me know as soon 191
as your committee has acted. / *(Your initials)* / c: Legal Department 202

MEMO 8
ON PRINTED FORM
Paper: Workguide 97

(TO:) All Members of ASB Local 407 *(FROM:)* Evelyn Cunningham, 9
Human Resources Director *(DATE:)* October 19, 19— *(RE:)* An- 18
nual Performance Appraisal 23

As called for in our recent agreement, an annual performance appraisal 37
will be conducted for all covered employees. Basically, the agreement 51
requires each supervisor to compare each employee's job performance 65
with established job standards. 71

The purpose of the annual appraisal is to: 80

1. Document present job performance to provide management with 92
information needed to make decisions regarding salary, promotion, 106
transfer, and termination. 111

2. Aid in developing plans for improvement based on agreed-on goals, 125
strengths, and weaknesses. 130

3. Identify growth opportunities. 137

4. Provide feedback on the success of previous training and disclose 151
the need for additional training. 157

5. Provide the opportunity for formal feedback. 167

A joint labor-management committee is now developing an evaluation 180
form that will be submitted to management for approval. If you have any 195
questions or concerns about this new personnel policy, please call me at 210
Extension 1040. / *(Your initials)* 213

REPORT 56
BOUND REPORT (3)

Make your own decisions about page breaks, but keep in mind the space required for footnotes.

Technical reminders:
1. Italic (slanted) printing is underscored when typed.
2. Any short display is centered.
3. A footnote separation line is 2 inches long (20P/24E).
4. In a footnote, the title of a book is underscored, but the edition is not.
5. Quotations that take more than 3 typed lines are displayed single-spaced and indented 5 spaces from each margin.

Footnote abbreviations:
1. *Et al.* in a footnote means "and others" and is used when there are more than two authors.
2. *Op. cit.* means "in the book by this author named in a previous (but not the immediately preceding) footnote."
3. *Ibid.* means "same as the immediately preceding footnote"; it can be followed by a different page number.

All Latin footnote abbreviations have become so common that they are not underscored.

Short footnotes may be typed beside or below one another, whichever is better for the bottom margin on that page.

CORRESPONDENCE MANUAL   Page ?   5

Letterhead. The letterhead contains the company's name, address, and   19
phone number. It can range anywhere from 6 to 18 lines deep, with the   34
most common being 9 or 10 lines deep. If the letterhead is more than 12   48
lines deep, the date should be typed 3 lines below the bottom of the   62
letterhead.[2]   64

Date Line. The date line includes the month, day, and year that the   78
letter is typed. It is usually typed on line 15. The month should not be   93
abbreviated or written in figures. Separate the day and year with a   107
comma.   108

November 16, 1989   111

Inside Address. The inside address has the name of the addressee, the   126
street address, and the city, state, and ZIP Code. It is usually begun 5   141
lines below the date; it may be typed below the typewritten signature in   155
certain situations.[3] Lloyd gives the following advice about using a busi-   170
ness title: 172

    This title may be placed after the name, at the beginning of the   185
    next line, or on a line by itself. The line length of the inside address   200
    determines the position of the title. Keep these lines as nearly equal   214
    as possible.[4]   217

The following examples illustrate how the opening lines of the inside   231
address might be typed, with the title in various formats in order to keep   246
the lines as equal as possible.   252

Ms. Ernestine Gordon, President   258
Southwestern Insurance Company   264

Dr. Rosemarie Garrosino   269
Head, Pediatrics Division   274

Mr. Alan Rothberg   277
Chairman of the Board   281

Salutation. The salutation is typed a double space below the inside   295
address, with a colon following it unless open punctuation is used or the   310
letter is a social-business letter.   317
Body. The body contains the message. It is usually single-spaced, with   332
a blank line between paragraphs. The body is begun a double space   345
below the salutation.   349

---

[2]Alan C. Lloyd et al., *Gregg College Typing, Series Five,* Gregg Division,   364
McGraw-Hill Book Company, New York, 1985, p. 254.   374

[3]Sabin, op. cit., p. 273.   [4]Lloyd, op. cit.   (Continued on page 284.)   382

Line: 60 spaces
Tab: 5
Spacing: single
Drills: 2 times
Workguide: 99
Format Guide: 43–45
Tape: 22B

LESSON 53

PRINTED FORMS

Goals: To increase speed and accuracy; to format printed forms.

53-A. WARMUP

S 1 A man named Chris laid his six keys down on the blue chair.
A 2 Jack Fox didn't place my big quartz vase in the top drawer.
N 3 Read pages 495-527 before 8:30 a.m. Friday for English 106.

SKILLBUILDING

53-B. All of these words are among the 125 most frequently misspelled words in business correspondence.

53-B. PRODUCTION PRACTICE: SPELLING

4 audit member faculty position addition insurance activities
5 basis amount whether customer property questions industrial
6 other review subject division decision following facilities
7 while return section possible mortgage corporate experience
8 areas either control proposal approval education electrical

53-C. PROGRESSIVE PRACTICE: NUMBERS

Turn to the Progressive Practice: Numbers routine at the back of the book. Take several 30-second timings, starting at the point where you left off the last time. Record your progress on Workguide page 5.

53-D. Compare this memo with Memo 8 on page 107. Type a list of the words that contain errors, correcting the errors as you type.

53-D. PRODUCTION PRACTICE: PROOFREADING

9 As called for in our recent agreement, an annual job perfo-
10 rmance appraisal will be conducted for all covered employ-
11 ees. Basically, the agreement requires each supervisor to
12 compare each employees' performance with established job
13 standards.

14 The purpose of the annual appraisal is to:

15 1. Document present job performance to provide management
16   with information needed to make decisions regarding salary,
17   promotion, transfer, and termination.

18 2. Aid in developing plans for improving based on agreed-
19   upon goals, strengths, and weaknesses.

20 4. Provide feedback on the success of previous training and
21   disclose the need for additional training

22 5. Provide the opportunity for informal feedback.

23 A joint labor/management committee is developing an evalu-
24 ation form that will be submitted to management for ap-
25 praisal. If you have any questions or concerns about the
26 new personal policy, please call me at Extension 1040.

FORMAL REPORT

Line: 60 spaces
Tab: 5, center
Spacing: single
Drills: 2 times
Format Guide: 131

Goals: To type 52 wam/5'/5e; to continue formatting a formal report.

133-A. WARMUP

S 1 The eight men work down by the big lake for the rich widow.
A 2 I quickly gave a dozen boxes of city maps that were junked.
N 3 The lottery numbers of 9, 18, and 25 were worth $1,340,760.

SKILLBUILDING

133-B. PACED PRACTICE

Turn to the Paced Practice routine at the back of the book. Take several 2-minute timings, starting at the point where you left off the last time. Record your progress on Workguide page 290.

133-C. Spacing: double. Record your score.

133-C. SKILL MEASUREMENT: 5-MINUTE TIMED WRITING

4 Summer is the time of the year when many students look   12
5 for a good job. These students try to find a position that   24
6 pays good wages. They are also anxious to have a job which   36
7 might allow them to take some time off for rest and travel.   48
8 Of course, having a job that utilizes some skills that have   60
9 been learned in school is a real plus. A position that was   72
10 secured through a temporary agency can be quite attractive.   84
11   Many temporary agencies cannot find enough workers who   96
12 have the right skills for the jobs to be filled. A student   108
13 who has good typing skills along with knowledge of personal   120
14 computers and word processing is in a good position to fill   132
15 jobs for a temporary agency. The hourly wage paid for this   144
16 type of work can be quite high. In addition, such a worker   156
17 might be employed in a number of different firms during the   168
18 summer. This enables the student to make many contacts and   180
19 to learn how different firms complete various office tasks.   192
20   Working for a temporary agency is ideal for the worker   204
21 who wants to have some free time during the summer. Taking   216
22 time off is as simple as one, two, three! It just requires   228
23 telling the agency when one is not available for work. One   240
24 can also find work through a temporary agency that has more   252
25 flexible hours to meet individual needs.   260

| 1 | 2 | 3 | 4 | 5 | 6 | 7 | 8 | 9 | 10 | 11 | 12

53-E. PRINTED FORMS

Although printed forms vary in size and style, well-designed forms enable the typist to use the margins and tabs to input most of the data. (See example below.)

1. The left margin is set at the first column. Tabs are set for additional columns.
2. Number columns (Quantity, Cat. No., Unit Price, and Amount) align at the right and are centered visually within the vertical lines. (Since the numbers are not uniform in length, set a tab for the most common number of digits

and then either backspace or space forward for the other numbers.)

3. Word columns (Description) align at the left, 2 or 3 spaces after the vertical line. (Turnover lines are indented 3 spaces.)
4. The word *Total* begins at the start of the printed word *Description*.

Note: A purchase order is used by a company to order the goods or services it needs from another firm.

FORM 1
PURCHASE ORDER

Paper: Workguide 99

WP   For forms that are used frequently in the office, some word processors can be programmed to stop at the first blank space, pause while you key in the variable data, and then automatically move to the next blank, pause, and so on.

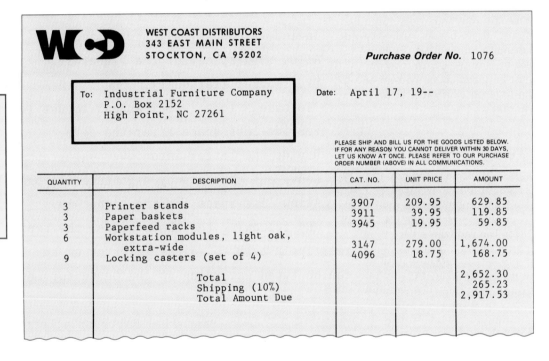

WCD   WEST COAST DISTRIBUTORS
343 EAST MAIN STREET
STOCKTON, CA 95202

Purchase Order No. 1076

To: Industrial Furniture Company
P.O. Box 2152
High Point, NC 27261

Date: April 17, 19--

PLEASE SHIP AND BILL US FOR THE GOODS LISTED BELOW. IF FOR ANY REASON YOU CANNOT DELIVER WITHIN 30 DAYS, LET US KNOW AT ONCE. PLEASE REFER TO OUR PURCHASE ORDER NUMBER (ABOVE) IN ALL COMMUNICATIONS.

QUANTITY	DESCRIPTION	CAT. NO.	UNIT PRICE	AMOUNT
3	Printer stands	3907	209.95	629.85
3	Paper baskets	3911	39.95	119.85
3	Paperfeed racks	3945	19.95	59.85
6	Workstation modules, light oak, extra-wide	3147	279.00	1,674.00
9	Locking casters (set of 4)	4096	18.75	168.75
	Total			2,652.30
	Shipping (10%)			265.23
	Total Amount Due			2,917.53

FORM 2
PURCHASE ORDER

Paper: Workguide 99

Purchase Order 1077, dated April 18, 19—, to Quality-First Computer Supplies, 1045 South Service Road, Plainview, NY 11803.

18 Data cartridges, 1/4 inch (Cat. No. 1980) @ 22.35 = 402.30

8 PC keyboard templates— MicroWord 3.2 (Cat. No. 8212) @ 12.95 = 103.60

9 Front-loading cartridges (Cat. No. 1840) @ 77.00 = 693.00

12 Space-saving copyholders (Cat. No. 6239) @ 34.95 = 419.40

Total = 1,618.30

Shipping/Handling = 243.00

Total Amount Due = 1,861.30

REPORT 55
BOUND REPORT (2)

CORRESPONDENCE MANUAL   Page 2   ↓3   5

An *expert* typist does not waste much time producing a letter.   18
B^y devising a method of expanding a short letter or ~~shortening~~ *telescoping*   31
a long letter, the typist can use the preceding placement   42
guide at all times ~~with no difficulty.~~ Some common methods   51
for achieving this objective are discussed below.   60

    To have a short letter appear better balanced: 70

SS
1. ~~Provide~~ *Allow* extra space after the date.   77
2. Divide the letter into more paragraphs.   86
3. ~~Include~~ *Insert* a company signature line.   93
4. Allow ~~more~~ *extra* space for the signature.   ← 5. Lower the reference   101
5.⁶ Use smaller stationery.   lines.   107
                                                                     112

    To have a long letter appear to use less space: 122

SS
1. ~~Provide~~ *Allow* less space after the date.   129
2. Divide the letter into fewer paragraphs.   138
3. ~~Leave out~~ *Omit* the company signature if possible.   146
4. Allow less space for the signature.   154
5. *Raise the reference lines.*   160
    By following the above hints, the typist should find it   171
relatively easy to adjust a letter of any length so that it   183
can be typed according to the Guide for Letter Placement.   195
                                                           ↓3

<u>Part II. Parts of a Letter</u>   200

    Business letters ~~correspondence~~ may have 14 or more dif- 208
ferent parts.[1] While some of these sections are ~~quite~~ stan-   219
dard, others are ~~considered~~ optional. (See Appendix A)   228

A. STANDARD LETTER PARTS   233

    There are several parts of a business letter that are   243
absolutely ~~mandatory~~ *essential* and without which the letter would ~~not~~ be 255
incomplete. A short description of each of these parts follows.   268

_____

    [1]William A. Sabin, <u>The Gregg Reference Manual</u>, 6th ed.,   279
Gregg Division, McGraw-Hill Book Company, New York, 1985,   291
p. 260.   292

(Continued on page 282.)

Sidebar notes

WP Most software allows you to type a header once, and it will automatically be printed at the top of each page.

If all enumerated items are 1-line items, single-space between the items.

Keep top and bottom margins in mind as you plan your page breaks. Page breaks will vary depending on whether you have pica or elite type. Each footnote must be typed at the bottom of the page on which it is cited in the text.

WP Some word processing software packages have a footnote feature that automatically places the divider line and leaves the correct bottom margin. Footnotes are automatically renumbered if you add or delete some.

Use appropriate spacing.

Footnotes may be typed as shown, with a raised figure, or with the number on the line with a period followed by two spaces. For example:
1. William A. Sabin....

Line: 60 spaces
Tab: 5
Spacing: single
Drills: 2 times
Format Guide: 45–46
Tape: 23B

LESSON 54

JOB-APPLICATION PAPERS

Goals: To type 39 wam/3'/5e; to format personal data sheets.

54-A. WARMUP

s 1 Both of the big firms in town also kept their workers busy.
A 2 Liz bought two very exquisite jackets from a downtown shop.
N 3 Pay Invoice No. 4036-B for $5,789.12 by 5:30 p.m. on May 2.

SKILLBUILDING

54-B. These words are among the 200 most frequently misspelled words in business correspondence.

54-B. PRODUCTION PRACTICE: SPELLING

4 using reason premium complete facility financial accounting
5 based recent receipt personal enclosed important successful
6 entry advise service eligible adequate equipment supervisor
7 means before absence security district receiving university
8 field annual support separate included completed authorized

54-C. Spacing: double. Record your score.

54-C. SKILL MEASUREMENT: 3-MINUTE TIMED WRITING

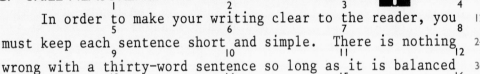

9   In order to make your writing clear to the reader, you   12
10 must keep each sentence short and simple. There is nothing   24
11 wrong with a thirty-word sentence so long as it is balanced   36
12 with some that are six, eight, or ten words long. However,   48
13 a short sentence that lacks other qualities of good writing   60
14 will have no use at all. Other good advice for a writer is   72
15 to emphasize common words and to use people as the subjects   84
16 of most of the sentences. This is how we talk, so the more   96
17 our writing sounds as though we were talking, the more eas-   108
18 ily our readers will understand what we write.   117

| 1 | 2 | 3 | 4 | 5 | 6 | 7 | 8 | 9 | 10 | 11 | 12 |

54-D. FORMATTING A PERSONAL DATA SHEET

At some point in your life, you will apply for a job. Generally, you will need a personal data sheet (or résumé), a letter of application, and a job-application form. You will prepare the personal data sheet in this lesson and the other two documents in Lesson 55. Since your job-application papers may create the first impression you make on the company, prepare them with care and accuracy.

A variety of styles is acceptable for formatting a personal data sheet. Choose a style that is attractive, and try to get all the needed information on one page.

Line: 60 spaces
Tab: 5, center
Spacing: single
Drills: 2 times
Format Guide: 129

Goals: To build speed and accuracy; to continue formatting a formal report.

132-A. WARMUP

S 1 Sue may go to work for the audit firm by the eighth of May.
A 2 Peggy would not analyze the jumbled tax forms very quickly.
N 3 His telephone number was changed from 691-8407 to 532-4876.

SKILLBUILDING

132-B. Type the paragraph twice, striving for fluency as symbols are typed.

132-B. SYMBOL TYPING

4 Order #514 was sent to Beek & Crane for the following: (1)
5 12 disks @ $3.40 each; (2) 3 rolls of continuous-feed paper
6 @ $12.50 each; and (3) 90 mailing labels @ $.05 each. This
7 invoice totaled $86.94, which also included a 5% sales tax.

PRETEST. Take a 1-minute timing; compute your speed and count errors.

132-C. PRETEST: DISCRIMINATION PRACTICE

8　　　Wisdom and genius are two important traits sought from　12
9 leaders and managers. Of course, the need for productivity　24
10 and loyalty is also very strong. Many businesses and firms　36
11 place quite a premium on finding leaders with these traits.　48
　　| 1 | 2 | 3 | 4 | 5 | 6 | 7 | 8 | 9 | 10 | 11 | 12

PRACTICE.
　Speed Emphasis: If you made no errors on the Pretest, type each line twice.
　Accuracy Emphasis: If you made 1 or more errors on the Pretest, type each group of lines (as though it were a paragraph) twice.

132-D. PRACTICE: LEFT HAND

12 rtr barter assert carton straw trace artist fort truck trip
13 asa basket asking ascent safer essay biased sand sadly safe
14 sds inside wisdom sadden dense desks beside kids desks dose
15 rer secure reason adhere purer after reflex redo alert doer

132-E. PRACTICE: RIGHT HAND

16 mnm manage solemn alumni named denim unmade main enemy mean
17 pop poorer oppose pompon roped pound option open point pool
18 olo locale oiling oblige along blown boldly loot loyal solo
19 iui united induce genius quite using medium suit quiet unit

POSTTEST. Repeat the Pretest and compare performance.

132-F. POSTTEST: DISCRIMINATION PRACTICE

132-G. Type each line twice. This drill gives practice in typing words that end in *able* or *ible*.

132-G. PRODUCTION PRACTICE: SPELLING

20 acceptable available favorable taxable profitable agreeable
21 negotiable advisable desirable movable deplorable debatable
22 incredible invisible divisible audible impossible illegible
23 accessible reducible plausible legible negligible indelible

FORM 3
PERSONAL DATA SHEET

Line: 6-inch
Tab: 15, center
Paper: plain

List all items in reverse chrono-
logical order (most recent first).

If work experience is your
strongest asset, list it first.

Include three references. (Be
sure to obtain permission before
using someone's name as a reference.)

TERRY M. MARTINA
↓2
145 Karluk Street
Anchorage, AK 99501
(907) 555-3942
↓3

Education   Federal Business College, Anchorage, Alaska
Degree: A.A. in Office Systems, May 1989
↓2
Courses in accounting, business communication,
computer software, machine transcription, office
procedures, office systems, records management,
typing, and word processing
↓2
Saint Vincent High School, Billings, Montana
Graduated: May 1987
↓3

Honors,   Tuition scholarship, Federal Business College
Awards,   Vice president, Office Careers Association
Activities   Member, Intramural Basketball Team
↓3

Part-Time   Flynn & Lynch, Anchorage, Alaska
Work Ex-   Position: Typist/File Clerk
perience   June 1987–Present
↓2
Better Burger, Billings, Montana
Position: Counter Clerk
May 1985–May 1987
↓3

References   Mrs. Susan M. Saifman, Instructor
Federal Business College, P.O. Box 1045,
Anchorage, AK 99506
Phone: (907) 555-7639
↓2
Mr. Robert N. Flynn, Attorney-at-Law
Flynn & Lynch, Route 4, Anchorage, AK 99509
Phone: (907) 555-3092
↓2
Ms. Elaine Harris, Principal
Saint Vincent High School, Billings, MT 59101
Phone: (406) 555-0992

FORM 4
PERSONAL DATA SHEET

Paper: plain

Prepare a personal data sheet for your own use in applying for a job.

131-C. FORMATTING A CORRESPONDENCE MANUAL

Use plain paper to format the correspondence manual. Before you begin, complete the Learning Guide on Workguide pages 333–334. Use the visual guide on Workguide page 336.

REPORT 54
BOUND REPORT (1)

TABLE 51

Line: 6 inches (60 pica/70 elite)
Tab: 5, center
Spacing: double
Paper: plain

The text of the correspondence manual is given in Lessons 131–135.

Note: To provide a wider left margin in a bound report: (1) use the visual guide on Workguide page 336, (2) move both margins and all tab stops 3 spaces to the right, or (3) move the paper guide 3 spaces to the left before inserting the paper.

Leave 3 blank lines (2 double spaces) before and after a table in the body of a report.

Footnote for a ruled table:
1. Type the footnote a double space below the final rule.
2. Use an asterisk to introduce the footnote.
3. Indent the first line 5 spaces, and type it to the width of the table.

CORRESPONDENCE MANUAL   4

Part I. Letter Placement   9

There is a general consensus on the need to have letters   21
arranged attractively on a sheet of paper or letterhead. This   33
means that the text will be centered between equal side mar-   45
gins. The bottom margin should be slightly bigger than the   57
side margins. In summary, the letter will appear "framed" on   69
the sheet of paper by its side, top, and bottom margins.   81

There is no one set formula to achieve this "framed look"   92
because of the different sizes of stationery, the lengths of   104
letters, and the depths of letterheads. In recent years there   117
has been a movement toward standardizing letter formatting.   129

Table 1 provides some basic information on the placement   140
of text in a typical letter.   146

Table 1   147

GUIDE FOR LETTER PLACEMENT   152

Letter Factor	Placement Guide	
		158
Position of date*	Line 15	163
Drop to address	5 lines	167
Length of line	6 inches	172
Length in spaces	60P, 70E	176

*On letterheads more than 2   182
inches deep, position the date 3 lines   190
below the bottom of the letterhead.   197

(Continued on page 280.)

LESSON 131

278

Line: 60 spaces
Tab: 5, center
Spacing: single
Drills: 2 times
Workguide: 101
Format Guide: 45—46
Tape: 23B

Goals: To increase speed and accuracy; to learn how to type on a printed line; to format a letter of application; to format a job-application form.

55-A. WARMUP

S 1 What in the world did the visitors do with their idle time?
A 2 Do not jeopardize an equal tax by having Mack vote swiftly.
N 3 The 193 men and 287 women voted 264 to 216 for the $50 tax.

55-B. PACED PRACTICE

Turn to the Paced Practice routine at the back of the book. Take several 2-minute timings, starting at the speed at which you left off the last time. Record your progress on Workguide page 6.

55-C. TYPING ON A PRINTED LINE

Note: If you are not sure of the position that a line of underscores will occupy or how far above it the letters will print, type the alphabet and underscore it; then note the *exact* relation of the letters to the underscore and of the underscore to the aligning scale on your machine.

When typing on a lined form, adjust the paper so that the line is in the position that a line of underscores would occupy. (See note in left margin.)

To adjust the paper slightly up or down, turn the platen with your right hand while your left hand presses the variable spacer in the left platen knob. To loosen the paper for adjustments, use the paper release.

Practice 1. Remove your paper from the machine. Using a pen and ruler, draw four straight lines (each about 3 to 4 inches long) on the sheet of paper.

Practice 2. Reinsert the paper, and type your name in the correct position on each line.

<u>Peggy Wojcek</u>	Too high
<u>Peggy Wojcek</u>	Too low
<u>Peggy Wojcek</u>	Just right

55-D. JOB-APPLICATION PAPERS

LETTER 18
JOB-APPLICATION LETTER IN MODIFIED-BLOCK STYLE
Paper: plain

Tell what job you are applying for and how you learned of the job.

Mention the highlights on your enclosed personal data sheet.

Close by requesting an interview.

February 15, 19— / Personnel Director / Fairbanks General Hospital / 107 McKinley Drive / Fairbanks, AK 99755 / Dear Sir or Madam: 12 / 23

    I would like to be considered an applicant for the position of records assistant that you advertised in the February 13 edition of the <u>Fairbanks Courier.</u>   37 / 52 / 54

    I will receive my A.A. degree in Office Systems from Federal Business College in May. As my enclosed personal data sheet shows, I have taken courses in records management, computer software, and word processing. These courses would be especially useful in your medical records department. In addition, I have had office experience as a typist/file clerk for a legal firm.   68 / 82 / 95 / 110 / 125 / 129

    I would enjoy working as a records assistant at Fairbanks General Hospital. If you wish to interview me for this position, please call me at (907) 555-3942.   142 / 157 / 160

    Sincerely, / Terry M. Martina / 145 Karluk Street / Anchorage, AK 99501 / Enclosure   172 / 174

Line: 60 spaces
Tab: 5, center
Spacing: single
Drills: 2 times
Workguide: 333–336
Format Guide: 129

FORMAL REPORT

Goals: To type 52 wam/5'/5e; to format a formal report.

131-A. WARMUP

S 1 Rickey works for us but may wish to work for the city firm.
A 2 I was quickly penalized five or six times by James Higgins.
N 3 Check 2104 for $683.25 gave us a new total balance of $927.

SKILLBUILDING

131-B. Spacing: double. Record your score.

131-B. SKILL MEASUREMENT: 5-MINUTE TIMED WRITING

4   A new job can be an exciting time. Whether it means a   12
5 new location or buying a new wardrobe, there is bound to be   24
6 quite a bit of excitement surrounding this new venture. It   36
7 is especially nice to meet new people and to learn some new   48
8 ways of doing things.   52
9   Of course, receiving the first paycheck from a new job   64
10 is also special. When reviewing the statement of earnings,   76
11 it can be frustrating to see the difference between the net   88
12 pay and the gross pay earned. The amount deducted in taxes   100
13 can be quite sizable.   104
14   The biggest tax deduction would be for the amount that   116
15 is withheld for federal income taxes. This amount is based   128
16 on the number of dependents that are claimed and the amount   140
17 of money that has been earned. The new tax law establishes   152
18 just a few tax rates.   156
19   The next large amount taken for taxes would be for the   168
20 social security tax. This tax was first started over fifty   180
21 years ago. There has been a steady increase in the amounts   192
22 withheld for it. There has been much discussion about this   204
23 program just recently.   208
24   The third tax that takes quite a bite from many checks   220
25 involves a state income tax. Just about every state in our   232
26 country has a state income tax. All these tax withholdings   244
27 added together help make your net pay quite a bit less than   256
28 your total gross pay.   260

| 1 | 2 | 3 | 4 | 5 | 6 | 7 | 8 | 9 | 10 | 11 | 12 |

FORM 5
JOB-APPLICATION FORM

Paper: Workguide 101

WP Printed forms, such as a job-application form, are most efficiently completed on a typewriter rather than a word processor. This is because it is difficult to adjust the printer to align the keyboarded copy with the guide words and printed lines.

It may be necessary to abbreviate some information on forms.

Remember: The line on the form should be in the position that a line of underscores would occupy.

Z+B ZIMMERMAN & BAUMGARDNER

Records Management Specialists

EMPLOYMENT APPLICATION

PERSONAL DATA

DATE February 15, 19--

NAME Terry M. Martina   SOCIAL SECURITY NO. 246-72-8480

PERMANENT ADDRESS 145 Karluk Street, Anchorage, AK 99501

TEMPORARY ADDRESS Same as above

TELEPHONE (907) 555-3942   MOST CONVENIENT TIMES TO CALL 1 p.m.-5 p.m.

TYPE OF WORK

TYPE OF JOB DESIRED Forms Secretary   DATE AVAILABLE FOR WORK May 19--

WHICH OF THE FOLLOWING BUSINESS MACHINES CAN YOU OPERATE WITH COMPETENCE?

x ELECTRONIC TYPEWRITER	x DEDICATED WORD PROCESSOR
x ELECTRONIC CALCULATOR	___ TELEX
x MACHINE TRANSCRIBER	___ MICROFILM MACHINE

WHICH OF THE FOLLOWING COMPUTER SOFTWARE PROGRAMS CAN YOU OPERATE WITH COMPETENCE?

x WORD PROCESSING	x SPREADSHEETS
x GRAPHICS	x DATA BASE
___ TELECOMMUNICATIONS	___ ACCOUNTING

EDUCATION (MOST RECENT FIRST)

INSTITUTION	CITY/STATE	DATE GRADUATED
Federal Business College	Anchorage, Alaska	May 1989
Saint Vincent High School	Billings, Montana	May 1987

WORK EXPERIENCE (MOST RECENT FIRST)

COMPANY	CITY/STATE	JOB TITLE	DATES (INCLUSIVE)
Flynn & Lynch	Anchorage, AK	Typist/File Clerk	June 1987-Present
Better Burger	Billings, MT	Counter Clerk	May 1985-May 1987

130-F. BUSINESS FORMS REVIEW

FORM 31
PURCHASE REQUISITION

Form: Workguide 329

Before completing 130-F, complete Learning Guide 17: Forms Typing on Workguide pages 327–328.

PURCHASE REQUISITION 807. On June 16, 19—, Allen Murphy from the Advertising Department on the 16th Floor orders these items, to be charged to Account 11-3567:

2 large-capacity, heavy-duty steel storage cabinets; 4 computer station organizers; 3 mobile file and storage pedestals; and 2 mobile steel service carts. The suggested source for these items is Billings Equipment Company, 1111 Main Street, Billings, MT 59105.

FORM 32
PURCHASE ORDER

Form: Workguide 329

PURCHASE ORDER 1896. On June 21, 19—, the Purchasing Department processes Purchase Requisition 807 and orders the following items from Billings Equipment Company:

2 large-capacity, heavy-duty steel storage cabinets (Catalog No. WHF-887W) @ $179.50 = $359.00; 4 computer station organizers (No. WEA-63) @ $109.95 = $439.80; 3 mobile file and storage pedestals (WFF-203) @ $77.50 = $232.50; and 2 mobile steel service carts (WES-3) @ $59.50 = $119.00; TOTAL = $1,150.30.

FORM 33
INVOICE

Form: Workguide 331

INVOICE 8614. On June 27, 19—, Billings Equipment Company invoices Boise Manufacturing, Inc., 1901 Main Street, Boise, ID 83702, for its Purchase Order 1896 for the following items:

2 large-capacity, heavy-duty steel storage cabinets @ $179.50 = $359.00; 4 computer station organizers @ $109.95 = $439.80; 3 mobile file and storage pedestals @ $77.50 = $232.50; and 2 mobile steel service carts @ $59.50 = $119.00; TOTAL = $1,150.30; LESS 10% TRADE DISCOUNT = $115.03; PLUS TAX AND SHIPPING = $118.75; TOTAL AMOUNT DUE = $1,154.02.

FORM 34
STATEMENT OF ACCOUNT

Form: Workguide 331

STATEMENT OF ACCOUNT. Billings Equipment Company prepares the monthly summary of its transactions with Boise Manufacturing, Inc., dated July 1:

6/1   Brought forward; balance of $4,560.40
6/6   Payment on account of $3,560.40 (credit); balance of $1,000.00
6/10   Invoice 8590 for $2,450.00 (charge); balance of $3,450.00
6/15   Payment on account of $1,000.00 (credit); balance of $2,450.00
6/27   Invoice 8614 for $1,154.02 (charge); balance of $3,604.02
6/27   Credit Memo 6781 for $432.50 (credit); balance of $3,171.52

Line: 60 spaces
Tab: 5, center
Spacing: single
Drills: 2 times
Workguide: 103–106
Format Guide: 47–48
Tape: 24A

LESSON **56**

SKILLBUILDING AND CORRESPONDENCE REVIEW

Goals: To type 40 wam/3′/5e; to review correspondence typing.

WP

To replace the word *kept* with the word *put* on a word processor, you would use the delete feature to remove the word *kept* and the insert feature to insert the word *put* in its place. The system would automatically move the rest of the line over to eliminate the extra space.

56-A.   WARMUP

S 1   The busy girls kept their eight wigs in a box on the shelf.
A 2   Vince knew that Maxine just passed her formal biology quiz.
N 3   They spoke to 478 people on July 26 between 9:15 and 10:30.

56-B.   PRODUCTION PRACTICE: ERROR CORRECTION

Spreading and squeezing are techniques used for making corrections that are shorter or longer than the original copy.
Spreading.   To make a correction fill an extra space, move the word an extra half space to the right, leaving a space and a half before and after it. The best way to do this is to use the half-space mechanism (if your machine has one) or to move the carrier by hand.
Squeezing.   If an extra letter must be inserted, move the word a half space to the left, leaving a half space before and after it.
Practice.   Type line 1 as it appears above. Then change the word *kept* to *put* and the word *wigs* to *gowns*. Do not retype the entire sentence.

SKILLBUILDING

56-C.   DIAGNOSTIC TYPING: ALPHABET

Turn to the Diagnostic Typing: Alphabet routine at the back of the book. Take the Pretest, and record your performance on Workguide page 5. Then practice the drill lines for those reaches on which you made errors.

56-D.   Spacing: double. Record your score.

56-D.   SKILL MEASUREMENT: 3-MINUTE TIMED WRITING

```
                    1                2                3                4
 4       Some students are quite shocked when they begin study-     12
                   5              6              7              8
 5   ing about word processing to discover that some jobs can be    24
                 9                10              11            12
 6   formatted quicker on a typewriter than on a word processor.    36
                13
 7   Is this really true?                                           40
                14              15              16            17
 8       Of course, it is.  For example, think about formatting     52
              18            19              20            21
 9   envelopes.  Their size makes it difficult to position these    64
            22              23              24            25
10   forms in printers for printing.  The same thing is true for    76
            26
11   all business forms.                                            80
            27          28              29            30
12       Likewise, short jobs that will never be revised should     92
          31            32            33            34
13   be typed on the typewriter; in other words, you should make   104
          35            36            37            38
14   good use of each machine by letting it do the types of jobs   116
          39            40
15   that it can do best.                                          120
     |   |   | 2  | 3  | 4  | 5  | 6  | 7  | 8  | 9  | 10 | 11 | 12
```

Line: 60 spaces
Tab: 5
Spacing: single
Drills: 2 times
Workguide: 327–331
Format Guide: 127

LESSON 130

SKILLBUILDING AND FORMS REVIEW

Goals: To improve speed and accuracy; to review business forms.

130-A.   WARMUP

S 1 Eight men wish to go by a lake if it is all right to do so.
A 2 We acquire jerky habits from having typed exercises lazily.
N 3 Albert sold more than 198 crates of #236 and #450 by May 7.

SKILLBUILDING

130-B. Take a 1-minute timing on the first paragraph to establish your base speed. Then take several 1-minute timings on the other paragraphs. As soon as you equal or exceed your base speed on one paragraph, advance to the next one.

130-B.   SUSTAINED TYPING: SYLLABIC INTENSITY

4   A teacher asked me the other day how our firm selected   12
5 new workers. It was soon clear that the main question con-   24
6 cerned the procedures used in selecting a top-notch worker.   36

7   The application form, data sheet, and letter of appli-   12
8 cation are reviewed first. The form can reveal a lot about   24
9 how a person can complete a job without a lot of direction.   36

10   The data sheet and letter are evaluated on their neat-   12
11 ness and formatting. Both are thoroughly analyzed for data   24
12 to be used when the applicant is invited for the interview.   36
   | 1 | 2 | 3 | 4 | 5 | 6 | 7 | 8 | 9 | 10 | 11 | 12

130-C.   TECHNIQUE TYPING: SHIFT/CAPS LOCK

13 Did the WANT AD section of the BOSTON NEWS help him at all?
14 ENTRANCE and EXIT signs were to be placed at various doors.
15 Their managers should read the article HOW TO MANAGE TODAY.
16 Was there a sign FOR RENT or FOR SALE in front of his home?
17 PROOFREAD ALL WORK signs may be necessary in their offices.
18 The title of their new monthly magazine is INFORMATION NOW.
19 He saw both the YIELD and CAUTION signs on the way to work.

130-D. These words are among the 250 most frequently misspelled words in business correspondence.

130-D.   PRODUCTION PRACTICE: SPELLING

20 through interest schedule commission appreciate immediately
21 account division decision industrial facilities established
22 courses personal security accounting electrical performance
23 current together prepared disability commitment association

130-E.   PROGRESSIVE PRACTICE: ALPHABET

Turn to the Progressive Practice: Alphabet routine at the back of the book. Take several 30-second timings, starting at the point where you left off the last time. Record your progress on Workguide page 289.

56-E. CORRESPONDENCE REVIEW

LETTER 19
MODIFIED-BLOCK STYLE

Paper: Workguide 103

Arrange enumerations with the numbers at the left margin and turnover lines indented 4 spaces.

November 18, 19— / Mr. Ibrahaim Abo-Motti / 145 King Street / North | 12
Pembroke, MA 02358 / Dear Mr. Abo-Motti: | 19

We want to extend our thanks to you for taking your first trip as a | 33
frequent flier on Worldwide Airlines. To show our appreciation, we are | 47
pleased to provide you with two special free gifts: | 58

1. One free upgrade to a first-class seat on any Worldwide flight you | 72
take this year. | 75

2. One free weekend (Friday and Saturday nights) at the Hartley Hotel | 89
in Boston. By copy of this letter, we are authorizing the reservation | 103
manager at the Hartley to send your room charges directly to us. | 116

You need only 20,000 miles to earn a free ticket on Worldwide. You | 130
are now well on your way to your first free ticket. Welcome aboard! | 143

Sincerely, / Marshall Dixon / Customer Relations / *(Your initials)* / c: | 153
Reservation Manager, Boston Hartley | 160

ENVELOPES 7 AND 8

Paper: Workguide 104

Prepare two standard large (No. 10) envelopes for Letter 19—one in upper- and lowercase letters with standard punctuation and one in all-capital letters with no punctuation.

LETTER 20
MODIFIED-BLOCK STYLE

Paper: Workguide 105

WP Some word processing centers measure output (productivity) in terms of the number of strokes or lines typed per day. Some software programs automatically compute the number of strokes, words, or lines produced.

November 18, 19-- / Mrs. Ann Byrd, Vice President / | 9
City National Bank / 204 North Hudson Avenue / | 17
Oklahoma City, OK 73102 / Dear Mrs. Byrd : | 25

On November 1, Worldwide Airlines added | 33
Charleston, West Virginia, and Providence, Rhode | 43
Island, to the list of cities we serve. | 51

There will be two daily flights from | 58
Charleston to Dallas / Fort Worth, with easy connections | 69
to over 100 other destinations, including Europe | 79
and the Pacific. Providence will have three | 88
nonstops daily to New York with convenient | 96
connections to over 100 Worldwide destinations. | 106

Since you are a frequent flier with Worldwide, | 115
we are sure that you would want to know of this | 125
additional service. Complete details are provided in | 136
the enclosed brochure. Welcome aboard! | 143

Sincerely, / Marshall Dixon / Customer Rela- | 151
tions / (Reference Initials) / Enclosure | 154

ENVELOPES 9 AND 10

Paper: Workguide 106

Prepare two standard small (No. 6¾) envelopes for Letter 20—one in upper- and lowercase letters with standard punctuation and one in all-capital letters with no punctuation.

129-D. FINANCIAL STATEMENT REVIEW

TABLE 50
BALANCE SHEET
(WITH LEADERS)

Spacing: single
Paper: plain, full sheet
Line: 70 spaces

Pivot from the right margin to find the point at which to set tabs for the money columns.

Spread-center the section headings.

Spread-center: leave 1 space between letters and 3 spaces between words.

Leave 2 blank lines above each section heading.

UNION STANDARD OFFICE EQUIPMENT, INC.   7

BALANCE SHEET   10

October 31, 19--   13

A S S E T S   15

Current Assets:		18
Cash	$ 7,504.25	21
Accounts Receivable	230.00	26
Merchandise Inventory	9,370.75	32
Office Supplies	960.00	36
Prepaid Insurance	780.40	41
Total Current Assets	$18,845.40	47
Fixed Assets:		49
Office Equipment	$ 3,230.00	55
Building	23,477.00	58
Land	9,785.00	60
Total Fixed Assets	36,492.00	66
Total Assets	$55,337.40	70

L I A B I L I T I E S   74

Current Liabilities:		78
Accounts Payable	$ 4,320.00	84
Notes Payable	500.00	87
State Income Taxes Payable	476.50	94
Federal Income Taxes Payable	1,653.10	101
Federal Unemploy. Taxes Payable	150.60	108
State Unemploy. Taxes Payable	540.00	115
FICA Taxes Payable	589.20	120
Total Current Liabilities	$ 8,229.40	127
Long-Term Liabilities:		132
Mortgage Payable	15,000.00	137
Total Liabilities	$23,229.40	142

O W N E R ' S   E Q U I T Y   147

Jason J. Lemke, Capital	32,108.00	154
Total Liabilities and Owner's Equity .	$55,337.40	163

SKILLBUILDING AND CORRESPONDENCE REVIEW

Line: 60 spaces
Tab: 5, center
Spacing: single
Drills: 2 times
Format Guide: 47–50
Tape: 24A

Goals: To build speed and accuracy; to review the formatting of personal-business letters and interoffice memorandums.

57-A. WARMUP

S 1 The name of the rich old man in their town is Henry Dudley.
A 2 Thomas F. Barrows of Phoenix, Arizona, jogged very quickly.
N 3 We purchased a new Model 45 for $1,760 on October 23, 1988.

SKILLBUILDING

57-B. TECHNIQUE TYPING: SHIFT/CAPS AND RETURN/ENTER KEYS

Take several 1-minute timings. Try not to slow down for the capital letters.

Shift Key

4　　Jim went to Iowa City, Iowa, in May to see Mr. Day. I　12
5　saw Jim at Big Joe's Deli on Oak Street on Monday. He said　24
6　the Blue Jays will play the Ink Blots on St. Patrick's Day.　36
7　If so, I will fly to El Paso on Key City Airlines with Jim.　48
　| 1 | 2 | 3 | 4 | 5 | 6 | 7 | 8 | 9 | 10 | 11 | 12

Type each sentence on a separate line. Do not slow down when you strike the return key.

Return Key

8　Who should go? Can you attend? Why not? Will Ann attend?
9　Someone should go. They need us. It won't take long. Ask
10　Ann to go. She may like it. Who knows? I can't go. I'll
11　be gone. If not, I'd go. Will you ask Ann? Thanks a lot.

57-C. PACED PRACTICE

Turn to the Paced Practice routine at the back of the book. Take several 2-minute timings, starting at the speed at which you left off the last time. Record your progress on Workguide page 6.

57-D. PRETEST: CLOSE REACHES

PRETEST. Take a 1-minute timing; compute your speed and count errors.

12　　Did anybody try to stymie the enemy when he loaded his　12
13　weapon? Sad to say, all fifty of them had no choice but to　24
14　attempt to avoid more bloodshed by not making a loud noise.　36
　| 1 | 2 | 3 | 4 | 5 | 6 | 7 | 8 | 9 | 10 | 11 | 12

57-E. PRACTICE: ADJACENT KEYS

PRACTICE.
　Speed Emphasis: If you made 2 or fewer errors on the Pretest, type each line twice.
　Accuracy Emphasis: If you made 3 or more errors, type each group of lines (as though it were a paragraph) twice.

15　tr traded tragic sentry trace tries stray extra metro retry
16　po pocket poorly teapot point poise pound spoke vapor tempo
17　sa salads sanded mimosa sadly safer usage essay visas psalm
18　oi boiled noises choice oiled doing coins avoid broil spoil

57-F. PRACTICE: CONSECUTIVE FINGERS

19　my myself myrtle myopia myths myrrh enemy foamy roomy slimy
20　ft drafts soften thrift after often fifty lifts craft graft
21　ny anyone canyon colony nylon nymph vinyl agony corny funny
22　lo loaded blouse pueblo loans locks along color hello cello

57-G. POSTTEST: CLOSE REACHES

POSTTEST. Repeat the Pretest and compare performance.

LESSON
129

SKILLBUILDING AND FINANCIAL STATEMENT REVIEW

Goals: To type 51 wam/5'/5/e; to review a financial statement.

129-A. WARMUP

S1 The fifteen new men cut more than half of all the new corn.
A2 My job was to pack a dozen equal boxes at night for Marvin.
N3 He paid $49.80 for an item that sold for $53.67 on July 21.

SKILLBUILDING

129-B. PROGRESSIVE PRACTICE: NUMBERS

Turn to the Progressive Practice: Numbers routine at the back of the book. Take several 30-second timings, starting at the point where you left off the last time. Record your progress on Workguide page 289.

129-C. Spacing: double. Record your score.

129-C. SKILL MEASUREMENT: 5-MINUTE TIMED WRITING

4   The topic of space management has become more and more   12
5 noticeable in the literature of the office today. Some ob- 24
6 jectives of space management are to provide sufficient room 36
7 and to maximize its use, to assure employees and the public 48
8 of comfort and convenience, to develop straight work flows, 60
9 to look at how people interact throughout the entire office 72
10 staff, and to provide alternatives for future layout needs. 84
11   Most often it has been found that large, open space is   96
12 better than small room spaces. Supervision and control are 108
13 more easily preserved, while communication between individ- 120
14 ual employees is more direct, and better light is possible. 132
15 An office requiring contact with the public, such as credit 144
16 or sales, must be placed so that the public can gain access 156
17 easily. Some business offices, however, must have privacy. 168
18   A unit which needs privacy, such as accounting, should   180
19 be away from easy access by the public. Often offices vary 192
20 in size according to the title of a staff member of a firm. 204
21 A top executive is given more space than other employees in 216
22 a firm. Departments that have a large volume of work which 228
23 is common to all of them are often situated near each other 240
24 to improve the flow of work. Space management is a must in 252
25 business today. 255

| 1 | 2 | 3 | 4 | 5 | 6 | 7 | 8 | 9 | 10 | 11 | 12 |

57-H. CORRESPONDENCE REVIEW

LETTER 21
PERSONAL-BUSINESS LETTER IN
MODIFIED-BLOCK STYLE

Paper: plain

November 19, 19--   3

Mr. Marshall Dixon, Manager   9
Customer Relations   12

Worldwide Airlines   16

2000 Cleveland Street   20

Dallas, TX 75215   23
Dear Mr. Dixon:
~~Gentlemen:~~   26

On August 15, 19--, I took Worldwide Flight 307 from Detroit[,Michigan,] to   41
Boston, (Mass). My ticket number was 437-0865, and my frequent   56
flier number ~~was~~ *is* 78228264.   61

~~Although~~ the flight was actually 632 miles, *but* I should have   71
recieved credit for 1,000 miles. *(Page 2 of)* Your sign-up brochure states   86
that all flights between 501 miles and 1,000 miles will   97
automatically receive credit for 1,000 miles. *Instead, I received*   110
credit for only 500 miles.   116
~~I am annoyed that this would happen.~~ Would you please correct   121
this error and give me credit for *#* an additional 500 miles on my   133
next account statement. *Thank you.*   140

Sincerely,   142

~~(Mr.)~~ Leonard Plachta   145
8800 Lucerne Avenue   149
Detroit, MI 48239   153

MEMO 9

Paper: plain

This memo, dated December 1, 19—, is from Marshall Dixon, Customer Relations, to Harriet
Small, Billing Department. The subject is Customer Billing Error.   28

Would you please verify that Mr. Plachta (letter en-   38
closed) is entitled to 1,000 miles for Flight [0]3[7], and if so,   51
credit him with an additional 500 miles on his next statement.   63

I frankly do not understand how such an error could   73
occur. I thought all mileage was calculated by the computer.   85
If so, the only opportunity for error would be if the opera-   97
tor entered the wrong flight number. ~~But that was obviously~~ *Is that what happened?*   109
~~not the case with Mr. Plachta.~~ Perhaps you can enlighten me.   116
After you check this out,   127
~~If an error was made,~~ please write *to* Mr. Plachta a~~letter~~ *nd explain*
the situation. *also*
~~of apology.~~ It would *also* be a nice gesture to give him a bonus   138
credit to help compensate for our error.   146

Closing lines?   149

128-G. BOXED TABLE REVIEW

TABLE 48
BOXED TABLE

Spacing: double
Paper: plain, full sheet

Special notes:
1. Extend all horizontal lines to the edges of the table.
2. Center the vertical lines within the 6 blank spaces between the columns.

REPORT OF SALES 3

Fourth Quarter, 19— 7

Rank	Name	Sales	Quota	
1	Klaus, Alberta	$150,225	$100,000	17
2	Mercer, Roger	110,374	100,000	22
3	Reed, Adele	105,189	97,000	27
4	Byrd, Ross	100,200	94,500	32
5	Lux, Jerry	96,876	90,000	37
6	Ketchum, Bernice	90,233	87,500	43
7	Cook, Joseph	89,761	85,000	48
TOTAL	. . . .	$742,858	$654,000	52

(Rank / Name / Sales / Quota header row = 11)

TABLE 49
BOXED TABLE WITH BRACED HEADING

Spacing: double
Paper: plain, full sheet

WP Some software programs have a draw feature that will allow you to insert the vertical lines.

Braced heading: a heading that is centered over two or more columns.

double-space

SELECTED FOREIGN EXCHANGE RATES 6

October 10, 19-- 9

Unit]	Units per American Dollar			
	this week	Last month	Last year	21
German mark	1.86	1.83	2.12	25
Swiss Franc	1.504	1.502	1.70	30
~~Japaneese Yen~~	~~151~~	~~1407~~	~~156~~	30
British pound	1.60	1.62	1.49	35
Canadian Dollar	1.33	1.33	1.39	40
French franc	6.18	6.09	6.887	45
~~Mexican peso~~	~~1394~~	~~132056~~	~~6.40~~	

(Units per American Dollar = 14)

LESSON 58

SKILLBUILDING AND REPORT REVIEW

Line: 60 spaces
Tab: 5, center
Spacing: single
Drills: 2 times
Format Guide: 49–50
Tape: 25A

Goals: To type 40 wam/3'/5e; to review report typing.

58-A. WARMUP

S 1 The maid will make up some snacks for the ten men at eight.
A 2 Jack's conquests near Oxbow proved not to faze Gil's enemy.
N 3 Use a 70-space elite line for Reports 19–23 on pages 48–56.

SKILLBUILDING

58-B. SUSTAINED TYPING: ROUGH DRAFT

58-B. Take a 1-minute timing on the first paragraph to establish your base speed. Then take several 1-minute timings on the remaining paragraphs. As soon as you equal or exceed your base speed on one paragraph, advance to the next one.

4   The early typing courses taught students to type using   12
5 only the two forefingers. Each student decided for himself   24
6 which finger to use for each key; there was no consistency.   36
7   As a joke, some~~one~~ body once bragged to the reigning ~~typing~~ speed   12
8 champion that he could type ~~with~~ using ⑧ fingers. The cham-   24
9 pion went home and taught himself to type that way. as well   36
10   It wasn't until ~~after~~ the second world # war that touch- typing   12
11 really caught on: the an Government had increased need for   24
12 trained typists, so they taut the military to type ~~by~~ touch.   36

  | | | 2 | 3 | 4 | 5 | 6 | 7 | 8 | 9 | 10 | 11 | 12

58-C. PROGRESSIVE PRACTICE: ALPHABET

Turn to the Progressive Practice: Alphabet routine at the back of the book. Take several 30-second timings, starting at the speed at which you left off the last time. Record your progress on Workguide page 5.

58-D. Spacing: double. Record your score.

58-D. SKILL MEASUREMENT: 3-MINUTE TIMED WRITING

13   By itself, the typewriter has brought about many major   12
14 changes in office routines, but at first it was not used in   24
15 an office. Mark Twain bought one of the first machines and   36
16 was the first one to turn in a typed manuscript for a book.   48
17   Court reporters were thought to be the main market for   60
18 typewriters. Next in order were lawyers and preachers. No   72
19 mention was ever made of the business use of the equipment.   84
20 Still, women seized the chance to enter an office by learn-   96
21 ing to type, and, as they say, the rest is history. Today,   108
22 typewriters and computers are the mainstay for office work.   120

  | | | 2 | 3 | 4 | 5 | 6 | 7 | 8 | 9 | 10 | 11 | 12

SKILLBUILDING AND BOXED TABLE REVIEW

Goals: To improve speed and accuracy; to review boxed tables.

128-A. WARMUP

S 1 Pamela may wish to pay for the signs for her downtown firm.
A 2 Jack typed four dozen requisitions for hollow moving boxes.
N 3 The 45 computers and 30 desks were ordered on May 26, 1987.

SKILLBUILDING

128-B. PACED PRACTICE

Turn to the Paced Practice routine at the back of the book. Take several 2-minute timings, starting at the point where you left off the last time. Record your progress on Workguide page 290.

128-C. Take several 1-minute timings. Slow down while typing the symbols, but keep your eyes on the copy.

128-C. SYMBOL TYPING

4   The new* contract called for an increase of $12.50 per   12
5 month for Miller & Smith employees. Mary and/or Mike indi-   24
6 cated that items #17 and #48 were "extras" in the contract.   36
7 The union steward (Heinz) liked it; Andrea did too. It was   48
8 approved on June 16 at 9:30 p.m. by a vote of three to one.   60
   | 1 | 2 | 3 | 4 | 5 | 6 | 7 | 8 | 9 | 10 | 11 | 12

128-D. Compare this copy with the material in Table 46 on page 270. Type a list of the errors, correcting the errors as you type.

128-D. PRODUCTION PRACTICE: PROOFREADING

9 Arizonia	2,718,425	1,774,399	749,587
10 California	23,667,656	19,917,069	10,586,223
11 Iowa	2,913,808	2,825,538	2,231,583
12 Michigan	9,262,087	8,881,826	6,137,766
13 New York	17,585,072	18,241,319	14,830,192
14 Wisonson	4,705,521	4,417,281	3,434,575

128-E. Make two copies. Copy 1: Type each sentence on a separate line. Copy 2: Type each sentence on a separate line, but tab-indent it 5 spaces.

128-E. TECHNIQUE TYPING: RETURN/ENTER AND TAB KEYS

15 Did you take the 3:40 train to Akron? No, I took the 4:50.
16 When is the first home football game? It is this Saturday.
17 I will help him type. It is great that you can assist him.

18 Where did you buy your boat? I bought it at Lynn's Marina.
19 When will the paper be completed? It should be done today.
20 Are you going to San Francisco? Yes, I plan to go in June.

128-F. PROGRESSIVE PRACTICE: NUMBERS

Turn to the Progressive Practice: Numbers routine at the back of the book. Take several 30-second timings, starting at the point where you left off the last time. Record your progress on Workguide page 289.

REPORT 19
TWO-PAGE UNBOUND REPORT
WITH FOOTNOTES

Visual guide: Workguide 59

Decide where to end your page. See the note on page 99 for page-ending decisions.

Each footnote must go on the same page on which it is cited in the text.

HOW TO READ A TELEPHONE BILL   6

By Elaine Daniels   9

Only two out of ten corporations even bother to check their tele-   22
phone bills.   Most pay them automatically, even though the average   35
corporate monthly bill is $94,000 and even though it's not impossible to   50
find that 25 percent of a bill has been overcharged.[1]   60

DECIPHERING THE BILL   64

Most managers find it difficult to pinpoint errors and decipher mul-   78
tipage telephone bills.   To clarify charges on the portion of the bill   92
dealing with basic services, experts suggest calling the local telephone   107
company and requesting an itemization of all costs associated with   120
monthly service.   123

"The first thing a prudent manager should do is identify the various   137
codes and services to make sure the company is getting all the services   151
for which it is being charged," states Carolyn Thering, president of Ther-   166
ing Communication Services.[2]   Frequently corporations find that they   180
are being billed for services that they thought had been disconnected.   194

Another communication consultant believes that the most frequent   207
errors are for services and equipment that at some point were discon-   220
nected; yet the charges remain on the monthly telephone bills.[3]   The   234
only way to get such charges deleted from the phone company's billing   248
computer is to make a request in writing.   256

NEED FOR EXPERTS   260

A consultant may be able to pinpoint charges that can be eliminated   273
from a company's bill. Because of the complexity of telephone codes,   287
tariffs, and billing procedures, it is difficult for many office managers to   303
decipher bills effectively.   308

Most experts say that it is cost-effective to pay a trained consultant to   323
come in at least once every two years to analyze telephone equipment,   337
usage, and billing. It is not unusual to find that the consultant will end up   353
saving the company three to four times his or her fee in yearly billings   367
for telephone usage.[4]   371

375

[1]J. A. Lindrup, <u>Cost-Effective Telecommunications Management</u>,   388
The Business Press, New York, 1987, p. 284.   396

[2]Carolyn Thering, "How to Read a Phone Bill," <u>Telecommunications</u>   409
<u>Quarterly</u>, December 1986, p. 386.   416

[3]Donald MacLeod and Dennis Lebsack, "Solving the Billing Maze,"   429
<u>Monthly Business Review</u>, May 1987, p. 113.   437

[4]Thering, op. cit., p. 215.   443

See the note on page 98 regarding the placement of footnotes on a partial page.

127-C. RULED TABLE REVIEW

TABLE 46
RULED TABLE

Spacing: double
Paper: plain, full sheet

Extend all horizontal lines to the edges of the table.

POPULATION BY SELECTED STATES

State	1980	1970	1950
Arizona	2,718,425	1,775,399	749,587
California	23,667,565	19,971,069	10,586,223
Iowa	2,913,808	2,825,368	2,231,853
Michigan	9,262,078	8,881,826	6,371,766
New York	17,558,072	18,241,391	14,830,192
Wisconsin	4,705,521	4,417,821	3,434,575
TOTAL	60,825,469	56,112,874	38,204,196

TABLE 47
RULED TABLE WITH FOOTNOTE

Spacing: double
Paper: plain, full sheet

Review formatting tables with footnotes on page 268.

Use periods across the width of a column to show that there is no entry.

PASSENGER CAR PRODUCTION BY MAKE *

Company	1987	1988
Crystal Motors Corporation	192,196	200,385
Detroit Motors Corporation	1,247,785	904,286
Hill Motor Company	1,775,257	1,547,680
Michigan Motors Corporation	4,344,737	3,975,291
National Corporation	. . . .	55,335
Point	74,785	98,207
Venus Ltd.	138,572	. . . .
TOTAL	7,773,332	6,781,184

* Only those cars made in the United States.

LESSON
59

Line: 60 spaces
Tab: 5, center
Spacing: single
Drills: 2 times
Format Guide: 49–51
Tape: 24B

SKILLBUILDING AND TABLE REVIEW

Goals: To build speed and accuracy; to review table typing.

59-A. WARMUP

S 1 Mr. Leo Burns is such a busy man he may not go to the game.
A 2 Felix might hit your jackpot even with the bad quiz answer.
N 3 Read pages 486-537 in Chapter 19 of your text for March 20.

SKILLBUILDING

59-B. DIAGNOSTIC TYPING: NUMBERS

Turn to the Diagnostic Typing: Numbers routine at the back of the book. Take the Pretest, and record your performance on Workguide page 5. Then practice the drill lines for those reaches on which you made errors.

PRETEST. Take a 1-minute timing; compute your speed and count errors.

59-C. PRETEST: ALTERNATE- AND ONE-HAND WORDS

4   I will defer the amendment that will attract a minimum   12
5 of a million visitors eastward to the island since it might   24
6 have created a problem. Did the auditors turn down my bid?   36
   | 1 | 2 | 3 | 4 | 5 | 6 | 7 | 8 | 9 | 10 | 11 | 12

PRACTICE.
   Speed Emphasis: If you made 2 or fewer errors on the Pretest, type each line twice.
   Accuracy Emphasis: If you made 3 or more errors, type each group of lines (as though it were a paragraph) twice.

59-D. PRACTICE: ALTERNATE HANDS

7 visible signs amendment visual height turndown suspend maps
8 element amend endowment signal handle ornament auditor half
9 figment usual authentic emblem island clemency dormant snap
10 problem chair shamrocks profit thrown blandish penalty form

59-E. PRACTICE: ONE HAND

11 trade poplin greater pumpkin eastward plumply barrage holly
12 exact kimono created minikin cassette opinion seaweed union
13 defer unhook reserve minimum attracts million scatter plump
14 serve uphill exceeds killjoy carefree homonym terrace onion

POSTTEST. Repeat the Pretest and compare performance.

59-G. Compare this footnote listing with that on page 119. Type a list of the words that contain errors, correcting the errors as you type.

59-F. POSTTEST: ALTERNATE- AND ONE-HAND WORDS

59-G. PRODUCTION PRACTICE: PROOFREADING

15   [1]J. A. Lindrup, <u>Cost-Effective Telecommunication</u>
16 Management, The Business Press, New York, 1987, p. 284.
17   [2]Carolyn Thering, "How to Read a Telephone Bill, <u>Telecom-</u>
18 <u>munication Quarterly</u>, December, 1986, p. 386.
19   [3]Donald Macleod and Denis Lebsack, "Solving the Billing
20 Billing Maize," <u>Monthly Business Review</u>, May 1978, p. 113.
21   [4]Thering, op. cit., page 215.

SKILLBUILDING AND RULED TABLE REVIEW

Line: 60 spaces
Tab: 5, center
Spacing: single
Drills: 2 times
Format Guide: 125

Goals: To type 51 wam/5'/5e; to review ruled tables.

127-A. WARMUP

S 1 Did Joe go to the show with them, or is he to go with Kurt?
A 2 Max had a zest for quiet living and placed work before joy.
N 3 Theresa received #357 on August 29 and #680 on December 14.

SKILLBUILDING

127-B. Spacing: double.
Record your score.

127-B. SKILL MEASUREMENT: 5-MINUTE TIMED WRITING

4   In order to be a good letter writer, one must follow a   12
5 set of guidelines that aids in writing letters. First, the   24
6 purpose must be clear. If the reader has to look more than   36
7 a few seconds for the message, the attention to the message   48
8 could be lost.   51
9   The message must be clear. The writer must know ahead   63
10 of time exactly what should be said so that the contents do   75
11 not puzzle the reader. Important facts should be presented   87
12 in a logical order. A well-developed outline aids in writ-   99
13 ing a letter.   102
14   To keep a reader's attention, the message must be kept   114
15 short. Sentences should be quite concise so they carry the   126
16 message in only the number of words required for the reader   138
17 to understand what is being stated. Poorly written letters   150
18 are confusing.   153
19   Simple language is often best. Avoid complicating the   165
20 simple idea with complex wording. The language of a letter   177
21 should be similar to the way a person ordinarily talks when   189
22 speaking face-to-face. Often a very formal business letter   201
23 may be stilted.   204
24   Letter-writing authorities often indicate that the you   216
25 attitude makes letters appealing to readers. No one is in-   228
26 terested in reading letters that revolve around an author's   240
27 interests. Put the readers first. Make them the center of   252
28 your messages.   255

| 1 | 2 | 3 | 4 | 5 | 6 | 7 | 8 | 9 | 10 | 11 | 12 |

59-H. TABLE REVIEW

TABLE 13

Spacing: single
Paper: full sheet

WORLDWIDE AIRLINES MONTHLY SUMMARY 7

Description	*Balance*	
		10
Previous balance	28,500	15
Credit miles added	5,000	19
Credit miles used for award	20,000	26
Current balance	13,500	30
Miles to next award	6,500	35

TABLE 14

Spacing: single
Paper: full sheet

WORLDWIDE FREQUENT-FLIER AWARDS 6

(Awards Issued Automatically) 12

Mileage	Airline Awards	Car-Rental Awards	
			20
10,000	1 first-class upgrade	1 large-car upgrade	29
20,000	1 domestic ticket	1 weekend day rental	37
30,000	1 international ticket	2 weekend day rentals	47
40,000	2 domestic tickets	2 weekday rentals	55
50,000	2 international tickets	3 weekday rentals	65

TABLE 15

Spacing: single
Paper: full sheet

WORLDWIDE AIRLINES MILEAGE STATEMENT 7

July 19— 9

Date	Flight Number	Itinerary	Credit Miles	
				11
				16
07/10/—	2806	Lansing, MI–Detroit, MI	500	24
07/10/—	143	Detroit, MI–Philadelphia, PA	1,000	33
07/14/—	235	Philadelphia, PA–Detroit, MI	1,000	41
07/14/—	2757	Detroit, MI–Lansing, MI	500	49
07/23/—	186	Detroit, MI–Boston, MA	1,000	57
07/24/—	456	Boston, MA–Detroit, MI	1,000	64

126-G. OPEN TABLE REVIEW

TABLE 44
OPEN TABLE

Spacing: double
Paper: plain, full sheet

Before completing 126-G, complete Learning Guide 16: Table Typing on Workguide page 325–326.

Center the table horizontally and vertically.

WEEKLY SALARY REPORT
Week Ending July 11, 19--

Employee	Hours Worked	Hourly Wage	Weekly Salary
Albert Campu	40	$ 9.50	$380.00
Liza Czich	38	7.50	285.00
Alex Lipka	36.5	8.75	319.38
Mary Rials	39.5	9.25	365.38
Janet Smith	40	9.00	360.00

FORMATTING TABLES WITH FOOTNOTES

To format footnotes in unruled and ruled tables, take the following steps:

Unruled Tables

1. Separate the footnote from the body of the table with a 1-inch underscore.
2. Single-space before typing the underscore, and double-space after typing it.
3. Type an asterisk or some other symbol at the beginning of a footnote to indicate its use in the table.
4. Type short footnotes beginning at the left margin; single-space between footnotes.
5. Indent the first line of long (two-line) footnotes 5 spaces; type turnover lines beginning at the left margin; double-space between footnotes. (**Note:** Do not mix styles in the same table—if one footnote is long, use the long format for all footnotes.)

Ruled Tables

1. Type the footnote a double space below the final rule.
2. Follow steps 3 through 5 for unruled tables.

Note: The symbol (such as an asterisk) used in the body of a table to indicate a footnote reference should be counted as part of the key line if it follows the longest entry in the column.

TABLE 45
OPEN TABLE

Spacing: double
Paper: plain, full sheet

Center the table horizontally and vertically.

COMMODITY PRICES OF THE WEEK*
September 1-7

Commodity	This Week	Last Week	Last Year
Aluminum	$ .83	$ .81	$ .54
Copper	.82	.83	.61
Cotton	.78	.75	.27
Gold	457.60	456.30	378.00
Wheat	2.69	2.62	2.46

*"Business Week Index," _Business Week_, September 7, 1987, p. 6.

Line: 60 spaces
Tab: 5
Spacing: single
Drills: 2 times
Workguide: 107–111
Format Guide: 51–52
Tape: 25B

LESSON
60

SKILLBUILDING AND FORMS REVIEW

Goals: To type 40 wam/3'/5e; to review forms typing.

60-A.   WARMUP

S 1 A bushel of corn was thrown to the turkeys by the neighbor.
A 2 Did Weldon give Liz your picturesque jukebox for Christmas?
3 3 Read pages 467-518 carefully for the weekend of July 29-30.

SKILLBUILDING

60-B.   PROGRESSIVE PRACTICE: ALPHABET

Turn to the Progressive Practice: Alphabet routine at the back of the book. Take several 30-second timings, starting at the speed at which you left off the last time. Record your progress on Workguide page 5.

60-C.   All of these words are among the 125 most misspelled words in business correspondence.

60-C.   PRODUCTION PRACTICE: SPELLING

4 their system through services received personnel appreciate
5 which during further interest material committee commission
6 there office general required schedule employees management
7 prior please present benefits business necessary procedures
8 first policy account provided contract available production

60-D.   Tab: Every 11 spaces.

60-D.   TECHNIQUE TYPING: TAB KEY

9   alas   away   aqua   area   aura   able
10 abut   aces   acid   acre   acts   arch
11 adds   aide   aged   awed   anew   apes
12 ache   ante   airy   ally   also   amid

60-E.   Spacing: double. Record your score.

60-E.   SKILL MEASUREMENT: 3-MINUTE TIMED WRITING

13   High-level spelling skills are the true mark of expert   12
14 typists. If your own skills are quite weak, begin today to   24
15 try to improve them. To begin with, learn how to spell all   36
16 the words in the above list. Next, start keeping a journal   48
17 of all words that you type that give you spelling problems.   60
18 After you have a page or two of such words, analyze them to   72
19 see if there is a pattern to your misspellings. Do most of   84
20 your words involve word beginnings or endings? Do many in-   96
21 volve similar-sounding words? Your journal can help you to   108
22 identify any problems to make your studying more efficient.   120
     | | | 2 | 3 | 4 | 5 | 6 | 7 | 8 | 9 | 10 | 11 | 12

LESSON
126

SKILLBUILDING AND OPEN TABLE REVIEW

Line: 60 spaces
Tab: 5, center
Spacing: single
Drills: 2 times
Workguide: 325–326
Format Guide: 125

Goals: To improve speed and accuracy; to review open tables; to learn to format a table with a footnote.

126-A. WARMUP

S 1 Sid can go to the lake with Bob if it is all right with Al.
A 2 Thomas A. Bignell quickly fixed the five jeopardized wires.
N 3 Please call 359-0678 for the 20 tickets on February 1 or 4.

SKILLBUILDING

126-B. Read through the entire copy before beginning to type.

126-B. PRODUCTION PRACTICE: ROUGH-DRAFT COPY

4   The way an office looks today is the result of quite a
5 few ~~minor~~ major changes over the past ~~thirty~~ twenty years. For example,
6 consider office ceilings. Many years ago, they were ornate,
7 but ceilings today ~~were~~ are functionally and designed to establish;
8 the character and atmosphere of interior spaces. Designing
9 ceilings today involves a number of ~~items~~ things such as texture,
10 height, fabrics coloring, lighting, and electrical systems.

PRETEST. Take a 1-minute timing; compute your speed and count errors.

126-C. PRETEST: VERTICAL REACHES

11   The senior lawyer was able to tackle the case in June.   12
12 She knew she would be making herself available to the court   24
13 for a third time in a month. She said she needed to revamp   36
14 her vacation plans to guard against whatever might go awry.   48
    | 1 | 2 | 3 | 4 | 5 | 6 | 7 | 8 | 9 | 10 | 11 | 12

PRACTICE.
 Speed Emphasis: If you made no errors on the Pretest, type each line twice.
 Accuracy Emphasis: If you made 1 or more errors on the Pretest, type each group of lines (as though it were a paragraph) twice.

126-D. PRACTICE: UP REACHES

15 aw awry away paws drawer awakes spawns brawny awards aweigh
16 se self seen sewn bosses paused senior seller seizes itself
17 ki kiln kilt kite skirts joking kinder bikini making unkind
18 rd hard lard cord hurdle overdo lizard inward boards upward

126-E. PRACTICE: DOWN REACHES

19 ac acid ache aces jacked facial actors tacked jackal places
20 kn knot knee knob knifes kneels knight knotty knocks knives
21 ab able blab ably tables fabric babies rabbit cabana cables
22 va vase vain vail evades revamp valley avails ravage canvas

POSTTEST. Repeat the Pretest and compare performance.

126-F. POSTTEST: VERTICAL REACHES

60-F. FORMS REVIEW

MEMO 10
Paper: Workguide 109

Send a memo dated December 2, 19— to the Personnel Department and Credit Union from Lisa Chiaverotti, Records Administrator, on the subject of Credit Verification.

I have recently applied for an automobile loan in the amount of $7,800 · 36
from City Imports in Fort Worth. As part of the loan process, I was · 50
required to complete the attached application for credit. I feel sure that · 65
City Imports will be contacting you to verify my employment and the · 79
amount in my credit-union account. · 86

You will note that I gave my salary level as of this coming January 1. · 100
Since that will be my salary during the period of the loan, I felt that it was · 116
appropriate to do so. Also, please note that although I had a credit-union · 131
loan for $500, that loan was repaid in full on November 1. · 143

I would appreciate your furnishing any information requested by City · 157
Imports. Please let me know if you have any questions. · 168

(Your initials) / Attachment · 170

FORM 6
APPLICATION FOR CREDIT

Paper: Workguide 111

APPLICATION FOR CREDIT

NAME _Lisa Chiaverotti_

ADDRESS _1801 North Lake Drive_

Fort Worth TX _76135_
Town or City · State · ZIP

HOW LONG AT ABOVE ADDRESS? _2½ years_

OWN OR RENT? _Own_

PREVIOUS ADDRESS _118 Harris Street, Apt. 3-B_

Fort Worth TX _76104_
Town or City · State · ZIP

CURRENT EMPLOYER _Worldwide Airlines_

EMPLOYER'S ADDRESS _2000 Cleveland Street_

Dallas TX _75215_
Town or City · State · ZIP

POSITION HELD _Records Administrator_

HOW LONG EMPLOYED? _6 years_

CURRENT SALARY _$27,600 a year_

SOCIAL SECURITY NUMBER _187-92-4036_

TELEPHONE _(817) 555-3180_

CHECKING ACCOUNT _City National Bank_
Name of Bank

SAVINGS ACCOUNT _Worldwide Credit Union_
Name of Bank

OTHER CREDIT OBLIGATIONS

Federal Mortgage Corp. _$68,000_
Creditor · Amount

City Card _$475_
Creditor · Amount

NAMES AND ADDRESSES OF TWO REFERENCES

Christopher Cardin, Manager, City National Bank
P.O. Box 1076, Dallas, TX 75221
Harriet Wolf, Publisher, Worldwide Airlines
2000 Cleveland St., Dallas, TX 75215

APPLICANT'S SIGNATURE _____

125-D. MEMORANDUM REVIEW

MEMO 22
Paper: plain

MEMO TO: Matthew Yeo, International Finnance Director   11
FROM: Lou Alonzo, Director of Sales   19
DATE: (Current Date)   24
SUBJECT: Current Forei*g*n Exchange Rate   32

As you are aware, the value of the *a*merican dollar has im-   43
proved over the past ~~twelve~~ *12* months. With the improvement of   55
the dollar, we ~~might~~ *should* see a steady increase*d* in our ~~overseas~~ *foreign*   66
market *y* *for transistors.*   71
I would like you to make an ~~comparison~~ *analysis* of last year's *European sales* ~~foreign~~   84
bud*get* with this year*'s* proposed budget to*o* determine what effect   97
the change in the doll*ar* will ~~make~~ *have* on our total i*n*c*o*me fo*r* the   110
year.   111
W*hen* you have made your analys*i*s, please let me know so that we   124
can make an*y* appointment with Ms. Katherine Lyons, our ~~sales~~   135
manager for international sales. *S*He will be very interested   147
in your projections.   151

(*Your initials*)   152
c: K. L*y*ons   154

MEMO 23
Paper: Workguide 323

(*TO:*) Harvey Morgan / Marketing Department / (*FROM:*) Larry Rogers /   9
Employee Relations / (*SUBJECT:*) Annual Fall Party / (*DATE: Current*)   20

In response to your recent memo regarding our annual fall party, I am   34
pleased to inform you that we will again be hosting this event for our   48
employees.   50
1. The fall party will be held at the Secor Hotel on October 25.   63
2. All employees and their immediate families are to be invited.   76
3. Invitations should be mailed by October 1.   85
4. A reception will be held at 6 p.m., followed by a dinner and dance at   100
7:30.   101
5. All directors and officers of the company are requested to be present.   116
As in the past, a raffle will be held after dinner. You will be pleased to   131
know that a deluxe four-door automobile will be the primary prize. Raf-   145
fle tickets will be distributed at the door, and all winners must be present   161
to receive their prizes.   166
If you have further questions at this time, please call me.   177
(*Your initials*)   178

PROGRESS TEST ON PART 3

Ask your instructor for the General Information Test on Part 3.

TEST 3-A
3-MINUTE TIMED WRITING

Line: 60 spaces
Tab: 5
Paper: Workguide 113

```
              1         2         3         4
    A limited partnership is a form of business enterprise    12
         5         6         7         8
in which all the risks of one or more of the owners will be   24
         9        10        11        12
restricted to the amount of assets each has invested in the   36
        13        14        15        16
firm.  This type of firm should have at least one owner who   48
        17        18        19        20
would assume the debts of the firm when called on to do so.   60
        21        22        23        24
Since limited partners will minimize their losses, they may   72
        25        26        27        28
not take part in running the new firm.  Because the expense   84
        29        30        31        32
of running some businesses is growing so quickly, this form   96
        33        34        35        36
of stock ownership has enjoyed much acceptance, most of all  108
        37        38        39        40
in high-risk industries such as in sports or entertainment.  120
|  1  |  2  |  3  |  4  |  5  |  6  |  7  |  8  |  9  | 10 | 11 | 12
```

**TEST 3-B
LETTER 22**
MODIFIED-BLOCK STYLE

Paper: Workguide 115

Use the current date.

Treat each item in the enumeration as a separate paragraph.

Please send the following letter to Mr. R. J. Caldwell, General Counsel / Consolidated Football League / 1603 Evans Street / Reston, VA 22091 / Dear Mr. Caldwell:

This letter will serve as official notification that ten investors have   41
completed their purchase of the Phoenix Phantoms from Mrs. L. J. Boggs.   56
The names, addresses, amount of investment, and affiliations of these ten   71
investors are given in the enclosed listing.   79

Mr. Thomas Keller will assume the role of general partner. The other   93
nine partners will be limited partners. Their rights will be restricted in   109
the following manner: 113

1. Their names will not appear in the name of the business.   125

2. They will be silent partners and will not be allowed to participate   139
in management.   142

3. They will not provide any services for the firm. This restriction   156
includes business as well as professional services.   166

The new management team will be in place on July 1. We look forward   180
to continuing the excellent working relationship established between   194
the former owner and the CFL.   200

Sincerely, / Patricia Muranka / Administrative Manager / *(Your initials)* / Enclosure   209
                                                                             212

Line: 60 spaces
Tab: 5
Spacing: single
Drills: 2 times
Workguide: 323
Format Guide: 123

LESSON 125

SKILLBUILDING AND MEMORANDUM REVIEW

Goals: To type 50 wam/5'/5e; to review memorandums.

125-A. WARMUP

S 1 He told us that some of the men did not find the right key.
A 2 The biweekly magazine for junior executives requested help.
N 3 During 1982 the attendance at all matches was over 543,670.

SKILLBUILDING

125-B. PROGRESSIVE PRACTICE: NUMBERS

Turn to the Progressive Practice: Numbers routine at the back of the book. Take several 30-second timings, starting at the point where you left off the last time. Record your progress on Workguide page 289.

125-C. Spacing: double. Record your score.

125-C. SKILL MEASUREMENT: 5-MINUTE TIMED WRITING

4 The way an office looks today is the result of quite a 12
5 few major changes over the past twenty years. For example, 24
6 consider office ceilings. Many years ago they were ornate, 36
7 but today ceilings are functional and designed to establish 48
8 the character and atmosphere of interior spaces. Designing 60
9 ceilings today involves a number of things such as texture, 72
10 height, fabric, coloring, lighting, and electrical systems. 84
11 Walls define space and territory. The movable wall is 96
12 popular now because it is flexible and allows changes in an 108
13 office design. Unfortunately, many a hard surface reflects 120
14 noise. Often hard surfaces are made of wood, glass, brick, 132
15 and plaster. These kinds of walls add to the character and 144
16 mood of an office. Many offices have a combination of wood 156
17 and brick, a combination which can add a feeling of warmth. 168
18 On the other hand, soft surfaces absorb noises, making 180
19 a serene, quiet work environment. Modern walls are made of 192
20 cork, fabric, carpet, and burlap. Walls define the charac- 204
21 ter of space by color and texture. Movable partitions have 216
22 preference over fixed wall structures in most cases. There 228
23 still are, however, a large number of offices which require 240
24 fixed walls such as those for doctors or lawyers. 250

| 1 | 2 | 3 | 4 | 5 | 6 | 7 | 8 | 9 | 10 | 11 | 12

SALE OF PHOENIX PHANTOMS
By Eileen Turner

On November 19, 1987, the Consolidated Football league (CFL) approved the sale of the Phoenix Phantoms for #23 million dollars to a group of ten investors known as Sports Invest, Inc.[1] This sale officially ended the 20-year ownership of the team by Mrs. L. #J. Boggs of Tempe, Arizona, and New York City.

OPERATIONAL MANAGEMENT

Louis Olivas was named managing partner of the new partnership and was given the voting trust, which gives him the power to represent the Phantoms in CFL matters. This action eliminates any real need for a single majority owner.

Still, as Olivas has himself pointed out, "The owners can always exercise their right to replace me if they wish."[23]

FORM OF NEW OWNERSHIP

The new owners are a group of 10 Arizona business people who have formed a Limited Partnership. They range in age from 33 to 65 and in ownership from 3% to 17%.[32]

_____

[1]Ron Turner, "Phantoms Have New Owner--Finally," The Arizona Herald, September 15, 1987, p. C-2.

[32]Andrew Shafley, "Does Phoenix have a Phantom Boss?" Sports Monthly, October, 1987, p. 114.

[23]Ibid.

SS

Please prepare Purchase Order 186, current date, to Software Plus, 2505 Main Street, Stratford, CT 06497.

Qty	Description	Stock No.	Price	Total
1	Ticketmaster software program version 3.2	807X	298.00	298.00
5	Time / Date utility	243T	39.95	199.75
2	Universal spelling checker	349S	89.95	179.90
	Total			677.65
	Shipping			78.50
	Total Amount Due			756.15

124-F.   SPECIAL STATIONERY

LETTER 70
BLOCK STYLE WITH STANDARD PUNCTUATION ON MONARCH STATIONERY

Paper: Workguide 317–318

Monarch stationery—7¼ by 10½ inches—accommodates up to 250 words on a 5-inch (50 pica/60 elite) line. The date goes on line 14; the address begins 5 lines below.

(*Current date*) / Ms. Alice L'Hullier / 256 Peachtree, NE / Atlanta, GA 14
30303 / Dear Ms. L'Hullier: 18

Thank you for agreeing to speak at our spring meeting on office sys- 32
tems. We have had numerous requests for such a meeting, and we know 46
that your research and practical experience are going to be welcomed 59
by our association. 63

Please send me a personal data sheet as soon as you are able to do so. 78
I want to prepare a series of announcements concerning your speech 91
and wish to include a brief synopsis of your work. If you have a recent 106
5" × 7" black-and-white glossy photograph of yourself, please send it 120
also. 121

I am enclosing a list of managers you might contact in order to be- 134
come better acquainted with office systems in northwestern Ohio. 147

As I indicated on the telephone, we will pay all expenses involved 160
with your trip and any additional costs you may incur in the preparation 175
of your speech. 178

Sincerely yours, / Paul Lyons / Systems Manager / (*Your initials*) / 186
Enclosure 188

LETTER 71
BLOCK STYLE WITH OPEN PUNCTUATION ON BARONIAL STATIONERY

Paper: Workguide 319–320

Baronial stationery—5½ by 8½ inches—accommodates up to 125 words on a 4-inch (40 pica/50 elite) line. Longer letters require a second page. The date goes on line 12. The address begins 4 lines below.

(*Current date*) / Mrs. Denise Bannon / 151 South Windsor Road / Clay- 13
mont, DE 19703 / Dear Mrs. Bannon 19

Mr. Arnold Hildy indicated that you will be responsible for making all 33
travel arrangements for the Light Wings Travel Club's trip to Las Vegas 47
this spring. 50

Enclosed is our latest brochure outlining various charter trips, accom- 64
modations, costs, and miscellaneous information that your group will 78
need. 79

Please call Ms. Debbie Lux at (302) 555-3800 when you are ready to 92
make your final plans and reservations. 100

Sincerely yours / Albert Hall / Sales Manager / (*Your initials*) / Enclo- 109
sure 110

LETTER 72
BLOCK STYLE WITH STANDARD PUNCTUATION ON BARONIAL STATIONERY

Paper: Workguide 321–322

(*Current date*) / Mrs. Louise Oxford / 101 Joyce Avenue / Chattanooga, 13
TN 37415 / Dear Mrs. Oxford: 18

Thank you for your recent letter concerning parking at our Meridian 32
Mall store. 34

We, too, are aware of the limited parking available to our customers. 48
We have been assured by the manager of the mall that everything is 62
being done to complete the new parking facility by the first of next 75
month. 77

In the meantime, we are providing valet parking for our customers. If 91
you will drive to the west entrance on your next visit, your car will be 105
parked while you shop and returned when you are ready to leave. 118

Sincerely yours, / Simon Firestone / (*Your initials*) 125

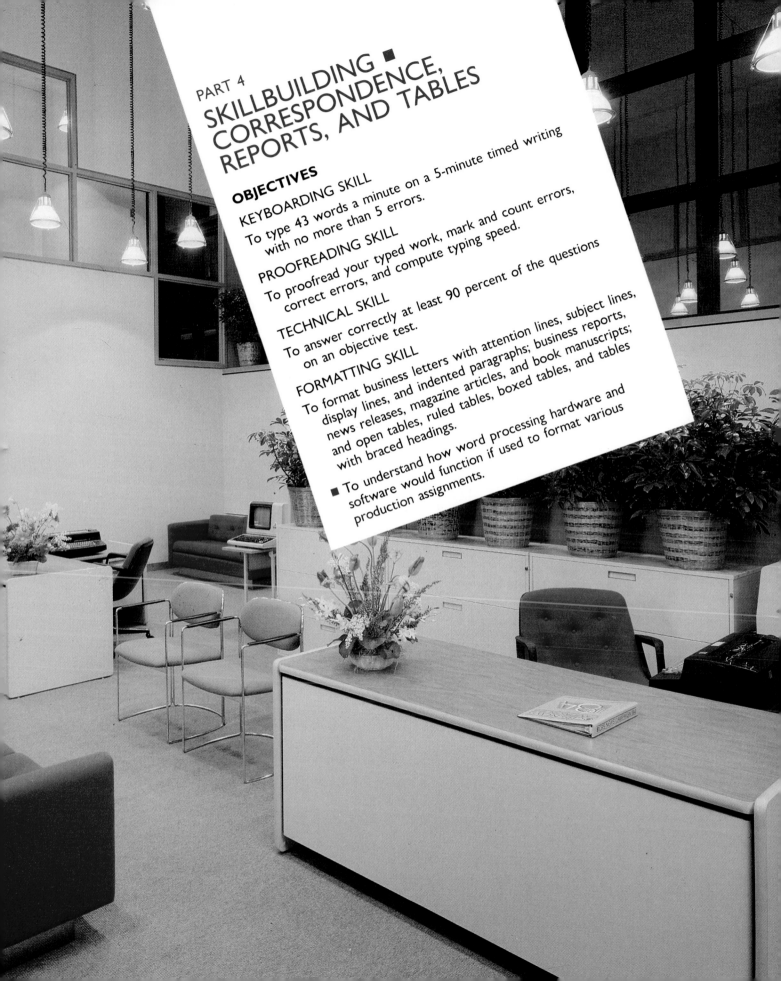

PART 4

SKILLBUILDING ■ CORRESPONDENCE, REPORTS, AND TABLES

OBJECTIVES

KEYBOARDING SKILL
To type 43 words a minute on a 5-minute timed writing with no more than 5 errors.

PROOFREADING SKILL
To proofread your typed work, mark and count errors, correct errors, and compute typing speed.

TECHNICAL SKILL
To answer correctly at least 90 percent of the questions on an objective test.

FORMATTING SKILL
To format business letters with attention lines, subject lines, display lines, and indented paragraphs; business reports; news releases, magazine articles, and book manuscripts; and open tables, ruled tables, boxed tables, and tables with braced headings.

■ To understand how word processing hardware and software would function if used to format various production assignments.

Line: 60 spaces
Tab: 5
Spacing: single
Drills: 2 times
Workguide: 317–322
Format Guide: 121

SKILLBUILDING AND SPECIAL STATIONERY

Goals: To improve speed and accuracy; to format letters on monarch and baronial stationery.

124-A.   WARMUP

S 1 Jan Mason took both of them for a ride in her new blue car.
A 2 Jack quietly gave some dog owners most of his prize boxers.
N 3 He will ship items #806, #734, and #651 on Flight 29 today.

SKILLBUILDING

PRETEST. Take a 1-minute timing; compute your speed and count errors.

124-B.   PRETEST: KEYBOARD REVIEW

4   Hall & Smith's catalog listed #489 (personal computer)   12
5 and #267 (disk) at a 15% discount. One-fourth (1/4) of all   24
6 of their items were on sale at 9:30 a.m. Ms. "Tillie" Yang   36
7 said the $7.50 tray sold well. However, the $9.65 did too.   48
   | 1 | 2 | 3 | 4 | 5 | 6 | 7 | 8 | 9 | 10 | 11 | 12

PRACTICE.

Speed Emphasis: If you made no errors on the Pretest, type each line twice.

Accuracy Emphasis: If you made 1 or more errors on the Pretest, type each group of lines (as though it were a paragraph) twice.

124-C.   PRACTICE: NUMBER AND SYMBOL KEYS

8   00 ;p0 000 0 pod, 00 pie, 00 par, 00 pale, 00 push, 00 past
9   11 aq1 111 1 ask, 11 add, 11 art, 11 quit, 11 zero, 11 zest
10 22 sw2 222 2 sew, 22 six, 22 was, 22 wise, 22 axes, 22 exam
11 33 de3 333 3 den, 33 dew, 33 end, 33 edge, 33 cede, 33 code
12 44 fr4 444 4 for, 44 far, 44 red, 44 rave, 44 very, 44 five
13 55 fr5 555 5 tar, 55 tag, 55 get, 55 gear, 55 boat, 55 verb
14 66 jy6 666 6 joy, 66 jog, 66 yet, 66 year, 66 nary, 66 navy
15 77 ju7 777 7 jug, 77 jib, 77 urn, 77 unto, 77 must, 77 mush
16 88 ki8 888 8 kit, 88 key, 88 icy, 88 inky, 88 kilt, 88 kite
17 99 lo9 999 9 lot, 99 log, 99 old, 99 oils, 99 loot, 99 oleo

18 % ft5% 18% 25% - ;--;- Smith-Brown's interest rate was 18%.
19 ." ;'"' ;"' "A" / ;//;/ "Ed" and/or "Bo" got it for 1/5 off.
20 $ fr4$ $18 $35 : ;:::;: Ken sold shares for $45 at 9:30 a.m.
21 _ ;p-_ ;-; _;_ () lo9(1p0) () Be on time (for once), Alan.
22 & ju7& j&j &j& ; ;;;;; Mo & Joe's sold it; but Al's didn't.
23 # de3# #82 #20 " ;'';' Jay's #67 and #33 were like Marie's.

POSTTEST. Repeat the Pretest and compare performance.

124-D.   POSTTEST: KEYBOARD REVIEW

124-E. Compare this paragraph with the first paragraph of the timing on page 261. Type a list of the words that contain errors, correcting the errors as you type.

124-E.   PRODUCTION PRACTICE: PROOFREADING

24   Being in charge of the budgit in a busines is often a
25 very exciting jib, objectives must be clear in order todo
26 an effictive job. These objectives are to paln activitiis,
27 to allocate specific rsecourses such as supplys, and to set
28 standards? Employees must be incolved at all levels in the
29 business to insure there acceptance of the budget. Studies
30 show that tehy want to be a part of budget dicision making.

LESSON

61

SKILLBUILDING AND WORD-DIVISION REVIEW

Line: 60 spaces
Tab: 5
Spacing: single
Drills: 2 times
Format Guide: 55

Goals: To improve speed and accuracy on alphabetic copy; to improve word-division skills.

S = Speed
A = Accuracy
N = Number

61-A. WARMUP

S 1 Nancy paid for the six pens that she got for the six girls.
A 2 Jack Bowman was very excited when my quilt got first prize.
N 3 Michael won the huge lottery with 8, 9, 17, 25, 39, and 40.

SKILLBUILDING

PRETEST. Take a 1-minute timing; compute your speed and count errors.

61-B. PRETEST: ALPHABETIC KEYBOARD REVIEW

4   As quickly as Liz raked the leaves, the wind blew them   12
5 back on the lawn. She fantasized about a giant vacuum that   24
6 just quietly plucks up extra junk and fills bags and boxes.   36
   | 1 | 2 | 3 | 4 | 5 | 6 | 7 | 8 | 9 | 10 | 11 | 12

PRACTICE.
1. Type lines 7 through 32 (A–Z) once.
2. Check the Pretest for those keys on which you made errors, and type the corresponding lines 2 more times.

61-C. PRACTICE: ALPHABET

7   A Amy Alex anew save cake alack badge afraid fearful Alaska
8   B Bea Bill bird abet base brake about aboard cobbler Brazil
9   C Cal Carl city acid crow click acute accrue lacking Ceylon
10 D Dot Dale dice edge daze drape adorn padded bedtime Denver

11 E Eve Emma be eve ease greed enrage excerpt eclipse England
12 F Fae Ford if fry fame hefty fluffy fearful fanfare Florida
13 G Guy Greg go gag gang rigid groggy lodging garbage Georgia
14 H Hal Hank oh hot hush bunch hither hatchet haughty Houston

15 I Ike Ivan ire lie into inset niacin lithium implied Ithaca
16 J Joe Jodi jam jab jury joker jacket perjury enjoyed Jasper
17 K Kim Kurt keg ark kilt knock kicked bracket package Kansas
18 L Lee Lois lay ale lack allot lively gallery fulfill London

19 M May Marty mine mimic hammer emblem member summary Montana
20 N Ned Nancy noun ninth banner animal notion enliven Norfolk
21 O Ola Oscar onto spoon potion noodle option opinion Oakland
22 P Pam Paula pulp primp appeal proper pauper peppery Prussia

23 Q Quent quip aqua quote equip quill conquer tranquil Quincy
24 R Ralph rest tray arrow razor rural rustler occurred Rwanda
25 S Sandy sues sash asset spots issue success scissors Sweden
26 T Trent tint that tempt start otter emotion attitude Toledo

(Continued on next page)

Make three copies: one c, one bc, and one file copy.

A blind copy (bc) notation is used if the addressee is not intended to know that one or more other persons are being sent a copy of the letter. The bc notation should be typed on the file copy at the left margin on the line below the reference initials (or on the line below the copy notation if one is used).

The bc notation is typed on the file copy after you remove the original and any copies that are not to show this information.

```
    Sincerely yours,


    Constance Buck
    President

    ek
    c:   George Ferns
    bc:  Dale Young
```

When preparing a letter with a blind copy on a computer, print one copy of the letter; then add the blind copy notation and print another copy.

123-D. SPECIAL LETTER FEATURES

(*Current date*) / Mr. Ashley Wells-Smith / Thames Tours / Queens Square BA1 / London / ENGLAND / Dear Ashley: 14 / 19

The Golden Wings Travel Club is again planning an excursion to European cities this fall. Would you be interested in helping me plan the tours of London? We will be in London the week of November 9–15.   33 / 48 / 60

As you know, the club consists of over 540 semiretired professionals who enjoy each other's company and traveling. Enclosed is a list of this year's members. As you can see, most of them are involved with processing information one way or another. A number of members are associated with health-related occupations. An asterisk after a member's name indicates that the member is planning to participate in this year's trip.   73 / 88 / 102 / 116 / 130 / 145

Would you please check with the Marble Arch Hotel to see if it has 30 single and 35 double rooms available from November 9 through the 14th. If it does, would you please reserve them for me whether or not you assist in planning the tours. I will send the hotel and you a list of the participants and their desired accommodations as soon as I hear from you.   159 / 172 / 186 / 202 / 216 / 217

The various city tours you arranged last year were very educational and interesting. Since many of this year's participants have never been to London, you may wish to provide them with a series of basic tourist tours. I am sure that a trip to Windsor Castle and Runnymede would be of interest to all. Could we include Hampton Court Palace if a trip to Windsor Castle should not materialize? Do you think that you can plan a boat trip down the Thames this year?   230 / 245 / 259 / 273 / 288 / 302 / 309

Can you provide a tour of some of the major business firms utilizing the latest technology for processing information? I am sure that many of the participants would be interested in visiting information processing centers and discussing with managers the latest in software, technology, and on-the-job requirements. We would also appreciate a tour of health-related institutions similar to the one last year.   323 / 338 / 352 / 367 / 381 / 391

The tour group will leave London on November 15 for Paris. I have contacted George Joyaux concerning the Paris tour.   405 / 415

Please let me know within a week whether you will be able to assist me with this year's tour. I *really* need your assistance if this tour is to be successful. If you have further questions, please call me collect at (302) 555-4471.   428 / 444 / 459 / 461

Sincerely yours, / GOLDEN WINGS TRAVEL CLUB / James Stopa / Treasurer / (*Your initials*) / Enclosure / c: J. Tong / bc: George Joyaux   471 / 481

```
27   U Ursula ugly pouch nurse uncut trust unique bureau Uruapan
28   V Violet vast cover serve valve avert lively voting Venezia
29   W Warren ward owner threw await swarm coward window Wyoming
30   X Xerxes axle oxide maxim excel vixen flaxen excite Xanthus

31   Y Yancy yak dye yelp yoga pray yummy trying skyway Yokosuka
32   Z Ziska zip zoo zero daze lazy ozone buzzer snazzy Zanzibar
```

POSTTEST. Repeat the Pretest and compare performance.

61-D. POSTTEST: ALPHABETIC KEYBOARD REVIEW

61-E. It is preferable not to divide a word at the end of a line. If it is necessary, though, follow these rules.

61-E. REVIEW OF WORD-DIVISION RULES

1. Do not divide words pronounced as one syllable *(brought, trimmed)*, contractions *(wouldn't, hasn't)*, or abbreviations *(NASA, f.o.b.)*.

2. Divide words only between syllables. Whenever you are unsure of where a syllable ends, consult a dictionary.

3. Leave at least three characters (the last will be a hyphen) on the upper line, and carry at least three characters (the last may be a punctuation mark) to the next line *(re- tain* and *broad- en;* but not *a- lert* or *seed- y).*

4. Divide compound words either at the hyphen *(self- contained)* or where the two words join to make a solid compound *(second- hand,* not *sec- ondhand,* and *winter- green,* not *win- tergreen).*

WP

Many word processors have an automatic hyphenation feature that will *(a)* automatically divide words too long to fit on one line or *(b)* highlight those words so that a hyphen can be inserted at the appropriate point.

61-F. Select the words in each line that can be divided, and type them with a hyphen to show where the division should be (example: *try- ing*).

61-F. PRODUCTION PRACTICE: WORD DIVISION

```
33   trying              rhyme           didn't
34   USAF                roadway         loudly
35   strayed             blamed          stepsister
36   wasn't              receive         extreme
37   scholarship         lonely,         caution
38   knowledge           crossing        self-evident
```

61-G. TECHNIQUE TYPING: MACHINE MANIPULATION

Backspace key

```
39   Margo Vashaw's shift starts at 4 p.m. and ends at midnight.
40   Gina Paull wrote two new books, Yuppies and Goals for 1990.
41   All of the girls and most of the boys were at the exhibits.
42   She asked if the computers are made only in gray and beige.
43   The order definitely listed three shirts and only two ties.
```

Tabulator key

Set two tab stops 25 and 50 spaces from the left margin. Then type each line, tabulating across from column to column.

```
44   daffodils           zinnias         carnations
45   marigolds           geraniums       begonias
46   roses               violets         daisies
47   hibiscus            delphiniums     phlox
48   sweet peas          iris            hollyhocks
```

61-H. PROGRESSIVE PRACTICE: ALPHABET

Turn to the Progressive Practice: Alphabet routine at the back of the book. Take several 30-second timings, starting at the point that you think is appropriate, that is, a speed at which you can type accurately. Record your progress on Workguide page 125.

Line: 60 spaces
Tab: 5
Spacing: single
Drills: 2 times
Workguide: 315–316
Format Guide: 121

LESSON 123

SKILLBUILDING AND SPECIAL LETTER FEATURES REVIEW

Goals: To type 50 wam/5'/5e; to review formatting special features in letters; to learn to format a blind copy (*bc*) notation.

123-A. WARMUP

s 1 Can he make the flight if he is to be on time for the show?
A 2 James Lennox, the banquet speaker, analyzed a few carvings.
N 3 She took Route 96 for 1,804 of the 3,257 miles on her trip.

> SKILLBUILDING

123-B. PROGRESSIVE PRACTICE: ALPHABET

Turn to the Progressive Practice: Alphabet routine at the back of the book. Take several 30-second timings, starting at the point where you left off the last time. Record your progress on Workguide page 289.

123-C. Spacing: double.
Record your score.

123-C. SKILL MEASUREMENT: 5-MINUTE TIMED WRITING

4   Being in charge of the budget in a business is often a   12
5   very exciting job. Objectives must be clear in order to do   24
6   an effective job. These objectives are to plan activities,   36
7   to allocate specific resources such as supplies, and to set   48
8   standards. Employees must be involved at all levels in the   60
9   business to ensure their acceptance of the budget. Studies   72
10 show that they want to be a part of budget decision making.   84
11 An operating budget is based on expected money that an   96
12 organization gets from the sale of goods and services. The   108
13 cash budget shows the cash flow, helping managers determine   120
14 how much cash to keep on hand to pay the bills. It is very   132
15 important. One reason cash budgets are so important may be   144
16 that they serve as business barometers. Significant change   156
17 in a cash budget may indicate a problem in bill collecting.   168
18 Another kind of budget in many businesses is the capi-   180
19 tal budget. The purpose of this budget is to outline long-   192
20 term expenses such as buying equipment. It is planned each   204
21 year and is often based on the various needs and the chang-   216
22 ing levels of productivity in each department. The balance   228
23 sheet forecasts the financial condition of the business and   240
24 lists its assets and liabilities for a given time.   250

| 1 | 2 | 3 | 4 | 5 | 6 | 7 | 8 | 9 | 10 | 11 | 12 |

SKILLBUILDING AND MEMORANDUM REVIEW

Line: 60 spaces
Tab: 5
Spacing: single
Drills: 2 times
Workguide: 139
Format Guide: 55

Goals: To improve speed and accuracy on numbers and symbols; to type 40 wam/3'/5e; to review the format for interoffice memorandums.

62-A. WARMUP

S 1 Len got them five boats so that they might make it on time.
A 2 Two excited queens looked very jumpy before he got a prize.
N 3 I counted 24 children in Room 306 at 8:57 a.m. on March 19.

SKILLBUILDING

PRETEST. Take a 1-minute timing; compute your speed and count errors.

62-B. PRETEST: NUMBER AND SYMBOL KEYBOARD REVIEW

4   The company paid $400 (25% of the total) for those #73 12
5 tiles. Gant & Nease and/or Dixon & Stahl <u>won't</u> sell 16,819 24
6 leftover "duds." A Dorfe-Moore share is $27 (58% more than 36
7 <u>one</u> year ago). The firm's owner/manager sold 39 #46 lamps. 48

| 1 | 1 | 2 | 3 | 4 | 5 | 6 | 7 | 8 | 9 | 10 | 11 | 12 |

PRACTICE.
1. Type lines 8 through 27 once.
2. Check the Pretest for those keys on which you made errors, and type the corresponding lines 2 more times.

62-C. PRACTICE: NUMBERS

8 0 ;p0 000 0 pins 00 pets 00 pals 00 parts 00 pails 00 plans
9 1 aq1 111 1 aunt 11 ants 11 apes 11 quips 11 zeros 11 zones
10 2 sw2 222 2 sets 22 sips 22 suns 22 suits 22 walls 22 watts
11 3 de3 333 3 dots 33 dams 33 eggs 33 elves 33 carts 33 colts

12 4 fr4 444 4 fads 44 figs 44 rims 44 roads 44 vases 44 volts
13 5 fr5 555 5 fins 55 fans 55 rats 55 rules 55 vines 55 vests
14 6 jy6 666 6 jabs 66 jugs 66 yaks 66 yards 66 masts 66 nests
15 7 ju7 777 7 jars 77 jets 77 ukes 77 units 77 males 77 notes

16 8 ki8 888 8 kegs 88 kits 88 imps 88 ideas 88 kilts 88 knots
17 9 lo9 999 9 lads 99 lids 99 oars 99 ovens 99 lumps 99 lists

62-D. PRACTICE: SYMBOLS

18 % f5% 28% 37% 49% 10% 65% 73% 91% 38% 47% 23% 119% and 150%
19 - ;p- all-new up-to-date life-support long-lived Cain-Smith
20 " ;'" "Tiny" "Buffy" "Cowboy" "Yes," he said, "I am going."
21 / ;/; we/they he/she yes/no and/or 1/8 5/12 37/92 and 46/89

22 $ f4$ $27 $89 $71 $70 $206 $382 $5,623 $6,912 and $2,582.39
23 _ ;-_ yes or <u>no</u>, he or <u>she</u>, <u>Micros and You</u>, <u>either</u> Al <u>or</u> Jo
24 () 19(;0) (fruit) (3%) (soldiers) (638) ($579) and (women)
25 ' ;'; I'm he's Jim's sisters' owner's won't isn't shouldn't

26 # d3# #45 #70 #46 #50 #54 #160 and 14# 74# 80# 51# and 475#
27 & j7& 39 & 34 & 581 & 104 & Harris & Parks, Garcia & Miller

POSTTEST. Repeat the Pretest and compare performance.

62-E. POSTTEST: NUMBER AND SYMBOL KEYBOARD REVIEW

122-E.   LETTER STYLE REVIEW

LETTER 66
PERSONAL-BUSINESS LETTER
Paper: plain

(*Current date*) / Mr. Robert Hatfield / 3320 North Arnoult Road / Metairie, LA 70002 / Dear Mr. Hatfield: 9 16 20

On behalf of the nominating committee that asked you to run for president of our condominium association, I wish to thank you for agreeing to do so. 28 37 46 49

I am sure that your running for this important office will induce others to accept such a responsibility in the future. If our condominium association is to succeed, we need a strong leader such as you. 58 67 76 86 90

The extension of Main Street is one of the major issues to be brought before the association next month. I believe that we need to thoroughly investigate the consequences of such a proposed extension. It has been stated that the extension would increase traffic threefold. 98 107 116 125 134 144 145

We appreciate your taking time from your important work to run for this office. 153 160

Sincerely, / Alice Meechum / 1201 Lake Avenue / Metairie, LA 70002 168 172

LETTER 67
SIMPLIFIED-STYLE LETTER

Paper: Workguide 313–314

(*Current date*) / Ms. Alicia Lopez / Employee Relations / Paramount Industries / 7210 Natalie Avenue, NE / Albuquerque, NM 87110 / APOLLO CORPORATE CREDIT CARD 9 17 24 29

Is your firm interested in both improving service to its employees who travel on business and simultaneously reducing costs? If so, you will be interested in our corporate credit card. 38 46 56 65 66

Three major advantages of the Apollo Corporate Card are as follows: 74 80
1. Check-cashing features. 85
2. Assured reservations. 90
3. Apollo Traveler's Checks. 96

The corporate card will provide you with a better opportunity to manage the money you spend on travel-related expenses. I urge you to complete the enclosed form and return it at once. We will then be able to make a detailed proposal as to how we can assist you and your employees who travel, while at the same time reducing your corporate travel costs. 104 113 123 132 141 150 159 167

JAMES J. JASON, MANAGER / (*Your initials*) / Enclosure 172 174

LETTER 68
PERSONAL-BUSINESS LETTER

Paper: plain

(*Current date*) / Wide-World Travel Agency / 330 South Main Street / Findlay, OH 45840 / Ladies and Gentlemen: 9 16 21

I will attend an international economics conference in Stockholm this fall. Do you have information on excursions to Europe that include the Scandinavian countries? 29 38 47 54

If you do, would you please send me the information. I am interested in the cities to be visited, accommodations, and costs of such tours. Many of my friends have found the tours of Lapland to be very interesting. Are tours of Lapland included with the tours of Norway, Sweden, and Finland? 62 72 80 90 100 108 112

The conference is to begin on October 15. I have made the necessary reservations for my stay in Stockholm from the 14th of October through the 19th. 121 130 139 142

Sincerely, / Frances Green / 150 South Grove Street / Bowling Green, OH 43402 150 156

62-F.   SKILL MEASUREMENT: 3-MINUTE TIMED WRITING

```
 28      One of the most exciting advances in the food business    12
 29  has been the development of take-out and home-delivery food    24
 30  service.  A whole new consumer demand has suddenly come for    36
 31  quick, convenient food service.  It came about because more    48
 32  and more husbands and wives are both working and need meals    60
 33  that they can pick up or have delivered quickly and easily.   72
 34      Our society also has a great many one-parent families,    84
 35  and these thrive doubly on the new food services.  Not only    96
 36  do they get more good meals but they can also enjoy them as   108
 37  a whole family together.  Business fulfills consumer needs.   120
```
```
  |  1  |  2  |  3  |  4  |  5  |  6  |  7  |  8  |  9  |  10  |  11  |  12
```

62-G.   INTEROFFICE MEMORANDUM REVIEW

↓13

MEMO 11*

Shown in pica
Line: 6 inches (60 pica/70 elite)
Tab: 10
Paper: plain, full sheet

*Memorandums 1–10 appear in Lessons 1–60.

MEMO 12

MEMO 11 COPY ON PRINTED FORM

Paper: Workguide 139

Retype Memo 11, this time using the memo form on Workguide page 139. When the left margin is set at the heading alignment point and the right margin is about the same as the left, the result is approximately a 6-inch line.

```
MEMO TO:  All Teachers, Phelps Middle School               9

FROM:     Gary A. Cramer, Jr., Principal                  17

DATE:     January 14, 19--                                22

SUBJECT:  In-Service Program for January 23, 19--         32
                                              ↓3

As provided for in the Master Agreement, no classes will be      44
scheduled on January 23, 19--.  However, all teachers will       56
report to the library at 9 a.m. for an in-service program that   68
will conclude at 3 p.m.  The Phelps PTA will serve lunch in      80
the lunchroom at 12 noon.                                        85

Mrs. Amy Weiss will conduct a workshop on the topic "The Young   98
Adolescent and Substance Abuse."  Particular attention will be  110
given to the teacher's role in the identification of involved   123
youngsters and subsequent responsibilities.  Mrs. Weiss is a    135
nationally known authority on this topic and is sponsored by    147
the State Health Department.                                    153

kle                                                             154
```

```
To:     All Teachers            From:  Gary A. Cramer, Jr.
        Phelps Middle School           Principal

Subject:  In-Service Program    Date:  January 14, 19--
          for January 23, 19--


As provided for in the Master Agreement, no classes will be
scheduled on January 23, 19--.  However, all teachers will
```

Line: 60 spaces
Tab: 5, center
Spacing: single
Drills: 2 times
Workguide: 313–314
Format Guide: 119

LESSON 122

SKILLBUILDING AND LETTER STYLE REVIEW

Goals: To improve speed and accuracy; to review personal-business and simplified-style letters.

122-A. WARMUP

S1 Sid asked her about some of the new fish items on the menu.
A2 The morning disc jockey won five bronze plaques for Maxine.
N3 He shipped 35 boxes each of items #890 and #467 on June 12.

SKILLBUILDING

PRETEST. Take a 1-minute timing; compute your speed and count errors.

122-B. PRETEST: KEYBOARD REVIEW

4   The skill of listening is just as important as are the   12
5   skills of speaking and writing. Quite often we hear an em-   24
6   ployer say that workers are not paying attention to what is   36
7   being said. Listening is expected of everybody and prized.   48
   | | 2 | 3 | 4 | 5 | 6 | 7 | 8 | 9 | 10 | 11 | 12

PRACTICE.
   Speed Emphasis: If you made no errors on the Pretest, type each line twice.
   Accuracy Emphasis: If you made 1 or more errors on the Pretest, type each group of lines (for example, lines 8–20), as though it were a paragraph, twice.

122-C. PRACTICE: ALPHABET KEYS

8   A Alan also last easy vain bacon canoe attest ballad author
9   B Beth baby able best bibb derby limbo budget burger bronze
10 C Chip coco cold care fact crazy civic carpet octave scopes
11 D Dave date adds drop dent adore diner redeem hidden worded
12 E Ella ease else eyed epic treat check esteem elated talked
13 F Faye fold fair cuff fort beefs draft friend grafts finder
14 G Glen good gold ages page vigor begun grates legion jargon
15 H Hope hash high huge such north laugh thrust though chided
16 I Iris into inch tile fill music pinch picnic impart deceit
17 J John junk just join jowl bijou banjo jabber junior hijack
18 K Kate cork kind seek hawk kitty knack kinder shrink awaken
19 L Lane look alas late lime elate skill locale collar bleach
20 M Mary mate maid main amen moody smile memory motion muffin

21 N Nate note neon wind fend longs mints noodle nation inland
22 O Opal oleo tool code fold opens order mascot report casino
23 P Paul pork pine spot tips props soupy dipped purple upbeat
24 Q Quip quiz quad quit quay quaff equal square piqued squirm
25 R Rose rage roar rare rate resin orbit arrear droves drench
26 S Sara suit sale easy skis sable ashes attest tassel assort
27 T Tony toot unto tile test stair trash fitted ratify stayed
28 U Ural undo unit used upon truth union assume scours adjust
29 V Vera vail veto vest wave value vivid evenly avowed lavish
30 W Wilt were avow crow gnaw swept waits awards winked wigwag
31 X Xeno exit jinx oxen axle sixty taxed coaxed exiled exceed
32 Y Yale yawl yard eyed stay dimly yeast choppy yearly yellow
33 Z Zeke zest zero zone cozy pizza tizzy dozing zapped sneeze

POSTTEST. Repeat the Pretest and compare performance.

122-D. POSTTEST: KEYBOARD REVIEW

SKILLBUILDING AND BUSINESS LETTER REVIEW

Line: 60 spaces
Tab: 5
Spacing: single
Drills: 2 times
Workguide: 141–146
Format Guide: 55

Goals: To improve speed and accuracy; to improve proofreading skills; to review the format for a business letter.

63-A. WARMUP

S 1 Chet said they might box if the size of that ring is right.
A 2 Five big Japanese fixed the axle and quickly zoomed onward.
N 3 I had 43 nickels, 58 dimes, and 67 quarters from the 1920s.

SKILLBUILDING

63-B. Take a 1-minute timing on the first paragraph to establish your base speed. Then take several 1-minute timings on the other paragraphs. As soon as you equal or exceed your base speed on one paragraph, advance to the next one.

63-B. SUSTAINED TYPING: SYLLABIC INTENSITY

4   People continue to rent autos for personal use and for   12
5 their work, and the car rental business just keeps growing.   24
6 When you rent a car, look carefully at the insurance costs.   36

7   It is likely that a good deal of insurance coverage is   12
8 a part of the standard rental cost. But you might be urged   24
9 to procure extra medical, property, and collision coverage.   36

10   Perhaps this is not necessary, as you may already have   12
11 the kind of protection you desire in your renter's or home-   24
12 owner's policy. And your own car policy may cover rentals.   36

| 1 | 2 | 3 | 4 | 5 | 6 | 7 | 8 | 9 | 10 | 11 | 12

63-C. Type a list of the words that contain errors, correcting the errors as you type.

63-C. PRODUCTION PRACTICE: PROOFREADING

13   Some manager have not given the proper amount of atte-

14 ntion to an office change that occured a few years ago.

15 The capital investments for an office worker exceeded those

16 for for a factory workers for the first time in history.

17 These costs can be directly traced to hte machines that are

18 used for the processing of infermation.

19   The question of cost justification must be faced by the

20 manager. Those who except a positive response to this

21 issue are then faced with the question of productivity: How

22 can our office workers become more productive in thier work?

23 More attention willbe given to this matter in the future.

63-D. Before typing Letter 23, study Workguide pages 141–142.

63-D. BUSINESS LETTER REVIEW

Using the visual guide for letter placement (Workguide page 143), type Letter 23 on the Workguide letterhead. Be sure to address the envelope on the reverse side of the letter-head.

121-C. LETTER STYLE REVIEW

LETTER 63
BLOCK STYLE, OPEN
PUNCTUATION
Paper: Workguide 307–308

(*Current date*) / The Dollar Bank / Attention: 9
Mr. Robert Scott / 5402 College Avenue / San   17
Diego, CA 92115 / Ladies and Gentlemen   24

I thought the last stockholders' meeting was   33
extremely well planned and successfully car-   42
ried out.   44

Your preliminary announcement of the   51
meeting and the proposed two-for-one stock   60
split and change of par value was very clear   69
and well documented. The use of the multicol-   78
ored graphs assisted in making the proxy state-   87
ment the best yet.   90

Your new directors are outstanding busi-   98
nesspeople in the community. You should be   107
commended for obtaining such a fine repre-   115
sentation from our major businesses.   122

It is also gratifying to know that the Dollar   132
Bank stock rose to $36.50 during the last quar-   141
ter of the year.   144

Again, congratulations to you and your asso-   153
ciates.   154

Sincerely yours / Alfred Black / President /   161
(*Your initials*) / PS: I am particularly happy to   168
learn that Mr. Ralph Bomeli, president, Bomeli   178
and Associates, was elected chairman of the   186
board.   188

LETTER 64
MODIFIED-BLOCK STYLE,
STANDARD PUNCTUATION
Paper: Workguide 309–310

(*Current date*) / Mr. Ernesto L. Gonzalez / 908   9
Elm Street / Manchester, NH 03101 / Dear Mr.   17
Gonzalez: / Subject: Partnership Agreement   25

Enclosed is a copy of the proposed partner-   34
ship agreement you and Mr. Hacker wish to   42
make.   43

The proposed agreement lists the following: 52
1. Partnership name, purpose, and place of   60
business.   62
2. Terms of agreement.   67
3. Amount each partner shall contribute to   76
be used by the partnership to establish its capi-   85
tal.   86
4. Proposed distribution of profits and   94
losses.   96
5. Salary each partner will draw in addition   105
to the distribution of profits and losses.   113

After you both have reviewed the instru-   121
ment, please call to make an appointment to   130
sign the agreement.   134

Sincerely yours, / Marjorie E. Conrad / Attor-   141
ney / (*Your initials*) / Enclosure / c: Mr.   146
Hacker   147

LETTER 65
MODIFIED-BLOCK STYLE WITH
INDENTED PARAGRAPHS,
OPEN PUNCTUATION
Paper: Workguide 311–312

(*Current date*) / Ms. Bernice A. Haddad / Sen-   9
ior Citizens Club / 480 Armour Road / Kansas   17
City, MO 64116 / Dear Ms. Haddad   22

Thank you for your invitation to speak be-   31
fore the senior citizens club next month.   39

I am very happy to accept your invitation   47
and will discuss the importance of making or   56
revising a last will and testament. As you know,   66
many senior citizens are under the impression   75
that once a will is made, it does not need to be   85
reviewed or revised.   89

Would you please duplicate the enclosed   97
questionnaire concerning a last will and testa-   106
ment and distribute it to your senior citizens.   116
Their answers will assist me in the preparation   126
of my talk. Please return the data as soon as   135
possible.   137

Sincerely yours / Albert D'Epiro / (*Your ini-*   143
tials) / Enclosure   145

Shown in pica
Line: 6 inches (60 pica/70 elite)
Tab: center
Paper: Workguide 145–146

*Letters 1–22 appear in Lessons
1–60.

Always respect a woman's preference in selecting *Miss, Mrs.,* or *Ms.* If her preference is unknown, use the title *Ms.*

2142 41st Street West, Topeka, KS 66609   (913) 555-7431

↓15

January 15, 19--   3
↓5

Mrs. Harriet Wong   7
Big Dollar Hardware, Inc.   12
1804 Elmwood Avenue   15
Manhattan, KS 66502   19
↓2

Dear Mrs. Wong: 22

All the questions that you posed in your recent letter were   34
excellent. The answers are illustrated by this letter and   46
the enclosed manual.   50

This letter is in the <u>modified-block</u> style, the style that is   63
most commonly used in business. Paragraphs may be blocked (as 75
in this letter) or indented 5 or more spaces.   84

Note that the date line and the closing lines start at the   96
center of the page. If this letter was being sent to a busi- 108
ness firm instead of a specific person in your firm, a company 121
salutation such as "Ladies and Gentlemen" would be appropriate. 134

Standard punctuation is used in this letter: a colon after   146
the salutation and a comma after the complimentary closing.   158
Also, the word <u>Enclosure</u> is typed below the reference initials 170
to serve as a reminder to both the sender and the recipient   182
that something is to be enclosed with the letter. The <u>c</u> no- 194
tation is a reminder that a copy of the letter is to be sent 207
to someone else.   210

                    Sincerely, ↓4   212

                    Karin A. Joyce, Director   217
                    Communications Department   222

eah   222
Enclosure   224
c: Vicki J. DeBlake   228
    Sales Department   232

Business letter in modified-block style.

LESSON
121

SKILLBUILDING AND LETTER STYLE REVIEW

Line: 60 spaces
Tab: 5, center
Spacing: single
Drills: 2 times
Workguide: 303–312
Format Guide: 119

Goals: To type 50 wam/5'/5e; to review block and modified-block letter styles.

121-A.   WARMUP

S 1 The man had to go to the hotel for a short meeting for her.
A 2 Did Alex Yentz win Jacqueline Kempt's five big door prizes?
N 3 A group of 105 left on the 6:34 plane at 7:38 from Gate 29.

SKILLBUILDING

121-B. Spacing: double. Record your score.

121-B.   SKILL MEASUREMENT: 5-MINUTE TIMED WRITING

4   Job analysis is one of a few ways to standardize work.   12
5   It is important not only to know what type of person should   24
6   be employed in the job but also to choose a worker in terms   36
7   of the education, experience, age, and other qualifications   48
8   necessary.   50
9   To break a job down into its parts, the following list   62
10 of items must be evaluated: job title, workplace, and sal-   74
11 ary range. Skill and quality of education, experience, and   86
12 training are judged. Another factor is if special training   98
13 is needed.   100
14   A job analyst notes what positions workers can advance   112
15 to when they wish to make a change of jobs. A job analysis   124
16 also lists the kinds of equipment a worker must operate, as   136
17 well as interpersonal skill, technical know-how, and physi-   148
18 cal skill.   150
19   The role an employee plays is also important. To whom   162
20 does a person send completed work? To whom does the worker   174
21 turn for supplies and information? These questions must be   186
22 determined for each position to clarify the lines of commu-   198
23 nication.   200
24   Many different methods of information gathering exist.   212
25 These include questionnaires, interviews, observations, and   224
26 logs and diaries. Each method has good and bad points con-   236
27 cerning accuracy and convenience. Firms should make a good   248
28 selection.   250

   | 1 | 2 | 3 | 4 | 5 | 6 | 7 | 8 | 9 | 10 | 11 | 12

Before completing 121-C, complete Learning Guide 15: Letter Typing on Workguide page 303.

Use the Visual Guide on Workguide page 305 for typing the letters in 121-C.

| Line: 60 spaces |
| Tab: 5 |
| Spacing: single |
| Drills: 2 times |
| Workguide: 147–150 |
| Format Guide: 57 |

SKILLBUILDING AND REPORT REVIEW

Goals: To improve speed and accuracy on alphabetic copy; to type 40 wam/5'/5e; to review correct formatting procedures for a report.

64-A. WARMUP

S 1 Both of the big men may be right as to which name is which.
A 2 Peggy Drexall would quiet the five zany back-room janitors.
N 3 Bus 53 stops at 110th Street and Arlo at 7:28 and 9:46 a.m.

SKILLBUILDING

64-B. PACED PRACTICE

Turn to the Paced Practice routine at the back of the book. Take several 2-minute timings, starting at the point that you think is appropriate. Record your progress on Workguide page 126.

64-C. Spacing: double. Record your score.

64-C. SKILL MEASUREMENT: 5-MINUTE TIMED WRITING

```
 4        Perhaps you have called at an office recently that had    12
 5   been familiar to you some years ago.  Do you recall how you    24
 6   reacted when you saw the changes that had taken place since    36
 7   your earlier visit?                                            40
 8        In response to similar questions, most people indicate    52
 9   that the modern furniture and new equipment stand out.  But    64
10   after observing the workers for a few hours, other types of    76
11   things are apparent.                                           80
12        While a sizable number of word processing machines can    92
13   be seen, there are also a lot of typewriters.  They seem to   104
14   be used for such jobs as the addressing of envelopes or the   116
15   filling in of forms.                                          120
16        In looking beyond the furniture or equipment, there is   132
17   excitement among the workers as they work together to reach   144
18   production goals.  Their managers have helped them initiate   156
19   suitable objectives.                                          160
20        The one thing that has most impressed me is the way in   172
21   which the workers are involved in the total operation.  The   184
22   morale of the people is high because they are involved with   196
23   the management team.                                          200
     |  1  |  2  |  3  |  4  |  5  |  6  |  7  |  8  |  9  |  10 |  11 |  12
```

PART 7

SKILLBUILDING ■ CORRESPONDENCE, TABLES, FINANCIAL STATEMENTS, FORMS, REPORTS ■ INTEGRATED OFFICE PROJECT: INSURANCE

OBJECTIVES

KEYBOARDING SKILL
To type 53 words a minute on a 5-minute timed writing with no more than 5 errors.

PROOFREADING SKILL
To proofread your typed work, mark errors and compute typing speed on timed writings, and correct errors on production work.

TECHNICAL SKILL
To answer correctly at least 90 percent of the questions on an objective test.

FORMATTING SKILL
To format memorandums, personal-business letters, and block-style and modified-block-style letters with attention lines, subject lines, and postscripts on regular, baronial, and monarch stationery.

To format open tables, ruled tables, a boxed table, a table with a braced heading, a financial statement, and forms.

To format a correspondence manual with footnotes, including an appendix, a table of contents, a title page, and a bibliography.

■ To apply high-level formatting skills while completing an integrated office project in insurance.

64-D. REPORT REVIEW

Each of the reports is to be typed on a full sheet of plain paper. Before typing the re-　ports, complete Workguide pages 147–148.

↓13

PERSONAL COMPUTER SOFTWARE	5
A Report to the Computer Committee	12
By Elizabeth A. Gray ↓3	16

What a computer can do depends on two things: what is　27

built into the machine and what software you have to make the　39

machine work. So, picking software is very, very important.　52

↓3

BASIC POLICY　54

↓2

There is one basic guideline for selecting software: it　66

must be compatible (usable) with your existing equipment.　77

↓3

TYPES OF SOFTWARE　81

The types of software from which you would get the　91

greatest benefit are word processing, spreadsheet, and data-　103

base programs.　106

Word Processing. The software used for word processing　117

makes it possible to revise letters, memorandums, and reports　130

by correcting or rearranging words, sentences, paragraphs or　142

even entire pages of text quickly.　149

Spreadsheet. Spreadsheets provide an easy and efficient　160

method for completing many kinds of statistical tasks. If you　173

expect to do inventory and payroll on your computer, a spread-　185

sheet makes the work easy and data easy to update.　196

Database. Many offices find that database packages are　207

great timesavers. Each database contains a vast amount of　219

information that may be extracted for computer tasks.　229

REPORT 21*
UNBOUND REPORT

Line: 6 inches (60 pica/70 elite)
Tab: 5, center
Spacing: double
Paper: plain, full sheet
Visual guide: Workguide 149

*Reports 1–20 appear in Lessons 1–60.

REPORT 22
BOUND REPORT

Line: 6 inches (60 pica/70 elite)
Tab: 5, center
Spacing: double
Paper: plain, full sheet
Visual guide: Workguide 150

Note: To provide a wider left margin in a bound report: (1) use the visual guide on Workguide page 150, (2) move both margins and all tab stops 3 spaces to the right, or (3) move the paper guide 3 spaces to the left before inserting the paper.

TEST 6-D
REPORT 53
TWO-PAGE UNBOUND REPORT
WITH FOOTNOTES

Spacing: double
Paper: Workguide 281

End page 1 at an appropriate
point.

EMPLOYEE PERFORMANCE APPRAISAL
By Carmello Rodriquez

Employee performance appraisal is extremely important in today's world of work. It is essential that all organizations have a method or plan in place for evaluating and analyzing the services provided by each employee, along with the work traits possessed by each individual. The purpose of this report is to discuss methods used in appraising employee performance and the frequency of such evaluations.

METHODS OF APPRAISING EMPLOYEE PERFORMANCE

There are many plans or methods for evaluating the performance of employees in a work situation. Three of the most commonly used methods are as follows:

1. Use of a rating scale.[1] The form includes factors that deal with the quantity and quality of work. A numeric value may be assigned to each factor, or a "Likert"-type scale may be used. This is a widely used method of evaluation, for it is easy to develop and administer.

2. Use of a narrative or essay evaluation.[2] This requires a written paragraph or more covering such topics as an employee's strengths, weaknesses, and potential. A problem with this type of evaluation is the difficulty of using it when comparing one employee with another.

3. Use of management by objectives or goal setting.[3] This method requires the employee and supervisor to agree on some short-range goals that will be met. This method is more results-oriented than traits-oriented.

FREQUENCY OF EMPLOYEE PERFORMANCE EVALUATIONS

In most firms or companies, the performance of workers is evaluated once a year, although more frequent reviews can be arranged in the event of promotional openings, poor performance, or outstanding performance. When a worker is in the first year of employment, there is often a probationary period; therefore, the evaluations might occur every three or six months.

An employee's anniversary date of employment is used most frequently for a performance evaluation. A pay increase or increment often depends on this performance evaluation.

---

[1]Thomas F. Housenick, *Performance Evaluation,* Best Publishing Company, Boston, 1987, p. 114.

[2]Charlotte A. Luna, *Employee Appraisal,* Bentley Book Company, Houston, 1988, p. 76.

[3]Ibid., p. 115.

Line: 60 spaces
Tab: 5
Spacing: single
Drills: 2 times
Workguide: 151–153
Format Guide: 57

SKILLBUILDING, TABLE AND FORM REVIEW

Goals: To improve speed and accuracy; to improve machine manipulation skills; to review formatting tables and forms.

65-A. WARMUP

S 1 Pam had to take the bus when she went to visit Laura Blake.
A 2 Everybody expects Jack's golf technique to help win prizes.
N 3 They may meet at 6:30 p.m. in Room 29, not 4:15 in Room 78.

SKILLBUILDING

65-B. TECHNIQUE TYPING: MACHINE MANIPULATION

Shift lock

4 Paul was told to use VACATION TRENDS for the revised title.
5 NO SMOKING signs are found in public and private buildings.
6 They now use COBOL as an important language in that course.
7 The magazine will be called either WP NEWS or INPUT/OUTPUT.
8 Cindy did not see the EMPLOYEES ONLY sign when she entered.

Margin release

Before typing lines 9–13, move the left margin 10 spaces to the right. Use the margin release to complete each line.

9 The regional managers asked Ronald to have a big fall sale.
10 As would be expected, planning the details took many hours.
11 After the prices were set, an advertising campaign started.
12 Several part-time salespersons were hired for the big sale.
13 Ronald got to work early that day to check all the details.

TABLE 16*
OPEN TABLE WITH BLOCKED COLUMN HEADINGS

Spacing: single
Paper: plain, full sheet

*Tables 1–15 appear in Lessons 1–60.

Review Notes
1. The key line consists of the longest item in each column plus 6 spaces between columns.
2. The column headings for this table are blocked at the left.
3. For additional review of tabulation, see page xiii in the Reference Section.

TABLE 17
TABLE 16 WITH CENTERED COLUMN HEADINGS

Spacing: single
Paper: plain, full sheet

65-C. TABLE REVIEW

Before typing Tables 16–18, complete Workguide pages 151–152 and study the information that accompanies each table, giving special attention to the placement of the headings.

Line			
1	ENROLLMENT REPORT FOR		4
2	IRA SEMINARS		7
3	↓3		
4			
5	Department	Date	No.	10
6			
7	Accounting	February 15	11	19
8	Maintenance	March 12	22	23
9	Personnel	February 28	7	26
10	Research	March 26	5	29
11	Sales	April 9	7	33
12	Shipping	April 23	13	38

Key Line: Maintenance 123456 February 15 123456 No.

(Current date)/Mr. Robert Hoxie, President/Acme   11
Tool and Dye/11 Grant Street/Bedford, VA 24523   20
Dear Mr. Hoxie: 24

    Congratulations on the formation of your   32
new company. Of course, a business must be   41
concerned with the benefits it can provide for   50
its employees. I would like to give you some   59
pertinent information about the services that   69
we could handle for you and your employees.   78
The enclosed brochures provide information   86
about each of the following: 92

    1. Life Insurance. We could provide your   101
employees with a group life insurance policy.   110
There would be a flat fee charged to you   118
as the employer, and your employees could   127
make individual contributions for additional   136
coverage.   138

    2. Medical Insurance. We have a medical   146
plan available for hospitalization and health   155
care. This plan is subscribed to by many   164
firms in Virginia and has many variations   172
depending on the family status of the different   180
workers.   182

    3. Stock/Savings Plan. We could arrange with   191
your individual employees to have a savings   200
plan that could provide for direct payroll   209
deposit. The plan allows for investment   217
in stocks, bonds, or mutual funds.   224

    Please contact me if you would be   231
interested in discussing any of these plans   239
in greater depth.   243

    Sincerely yours,/Martha Browning/   249
Industrial Account Agent/URS/Enclosures   257

TABLE 18
OPEN TABLE WITH CENTERED
COLUMN HEADINGS

Spacing: double
Paper: plain, full sheet

Review Notes
1. The underscore line is the full column width.
2. *TOTALS* is typed at the left margin.
3. The $ sign in the bottom line must align with the $ sign above it.

Beginning October 1, 19--   9

Month	Sales Quota	Actual Sales	Percent of Quota	
				11
				18
October	$224,760	$ 231,491	103.0	24
November	238,590	217,616	91.2	29
December	273,450	598,980	219.0	34
TOTALS	$736,800	$1,048,087	142.2	40

Key Line: November 123456 Sales Quota 123456 Actual Sales 123456 Percent of

65-D. FORM REVIEW

FORM 8*
PURCHASE ORDER

Workguide: 153

*Forms 1–7 appear in Lessons 1–60.

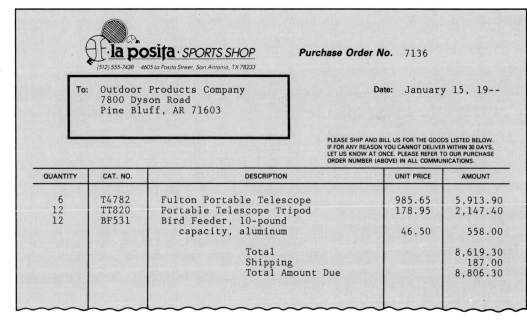

Ask your instructor for the General Information Test on Part 6.

TEST 6-A
5-MINUTE TIMED WRITING

Line: 60 spaces
Tab: 5
Paper: Workguide 275

```
          1                                              2
For many, many years the summer months have been known        12
     3                           4
as the lazy months.  It is at this time that a family might    24
     5                      6                    7
plan vacation trips because the children are not in school.    36
                       8                      9
Because of the nicer weather during the summer months, this    48
       10                       11                     12
is an especially good time to take advantage of the various    60
                      13                  14
water sports or to make travel plans for the entire family.    72
          15                              16
Water has always been an attraction.  A hot, humid day         84
   17                        18                      19
in July can be much more bearable with cool water.  Many of    96
                  20                       21
the water sports have become extremely popular.  Whether it   108
     22                        23                    24
means sailing on a sailboat, paddling a canoe, putting on a   120
                       25                      26
pair of water skis, or snorkeling in shallow waters, just a   132
          27                        28
little involvement with a water sport can be very relaxing.   144
       29                         30                      31
High on the list of summer activities for many is that        156
                  32                     33
chance to travel.  Whether visiting a nearby city or region   168
       34                         35                      36
or traveling to distant lands, this is a good time to visit   180
                       37                    38
and see places of interest and meet new people.  A trip can   192
                  39                     40
be planned to meet certain budget limitations.  It can also   204
     41                       42                      43
be arranged to use the various different methods of travel.   216
          44                              45
The lazy months of summer have a special appeal to all        228
     46                           47                      48
of us.  These months provide some time for relaxation and a   240
                  49                      50
time to slow the rapid pace of the rest of the year.          250
|  |  | 2 | 3 | 4 | 5 | 6 | 7 | 8 | 9 | 10 | 11 | 12
```

TEST 6-B
TABLE 43
RULED TABLE

Paper: Workguide 277

EMPIRE MANUFACTURING, INC.

Third-Quarter Sales Performance

Salesperson	Budgeted Sales	Actual Sales	Percent of Budget	
Kelly Benvenuto	$131,000	$127,987	97.7	29
Terence Cuddihy	104,000	100,776	96.9	35
Francisco Gonzalez	101,000	102,212	101.2	43
Ernestine Gordon	96,000	97,536	101.6	49
Wayne Johnson	84,000	88,788	105.7	55

(5, 11, 16, 22)

LESSON
66
BUSINESS LETTERS

Line: 60 spaces
Tab: 5
Spacing: single
Drills: 2 times
Workguide: 155–158
Format Guide: 59

Goals: To type 41 wam/5'/5e; to format business letters.

66-A. WARMUP

S 1 Dick and Mel did rush to the bus when it turned the corner.
A 2 J. Maddox took pictures of five quiet lions at the big zoo.
N 3 Please send me 35 cases of part number 907864 by August 12.

SKILLBUILDING

66-B. PROGRESSIVE PRACTICE: NUMBERS

Turn to the Progressive Practice: Numbers routine at the back of the book. Take several 30-second timings, starting at the point where you left off the last time. Record your progress on Workguide page 125.

66-C. Spacing: double. Record your score.

66-C. SKILL MEASUREMENT: 5-MINUTE TIMED WRITING

4   Each college senior faces a unique challenge: getting   12
5   prepared for his or her job search. On the day the diploma   24
6   is handed over, the candidate is expected to have the first   36
7   job lined up and waiting.   41
8   Before you knock on any business door, it is important   53
9   that you prepare a personal data sheet which tells what you   65
10 have done, what you can do, and especially what you hope to   77
11 do in your chosen career.   82
12   Your work record will be one of the factors in which a   94
13 company will be particularly interested. Your ability will   106
14 be important, but your willingness to work is even more so.   118
15 Emphasize the work record.   123
16   When you pause to think about a business's interest in   135
17 you, you'll realize what to tell about yourself. There may   147
18 be some interest in your polo playing, but your great drive   159
19 and fine health get more.   164
20   You are exceptionally lucky if you can match up goals,   176
21 college-learned skills, and job aspiration with the demands   188
22 of a fine entering job at a good salary in the career field   200
23 of your choice and desire.   205

    | 1 | 2 | 3 | 4 | 5 | 6 | 7 | 8 | 9 | 10 | 11 | 12

REPORT 52
TWO-PAGE BOUND REPORT
WITH ENDNOTES

Paper: plain

Plan for a 1-inch bottom margin
on the first page.

120-D. REPORT REVIEW

RECRUITING OFFICE EMPLOYEES

By Tara Kerr

Finding qualified, competent office employees has been more difficult than ever in the past few years. As the demand for office employees increases in the near future and as the supply dwindles, a good office manager or personnel director will have to maintain strong ties with some of the best suppliers of such employees. Two of these sources will be discussed in this report.

EDUCATIONAL INSTITUTIONS

Many secondary schools, private business schools, vocational schools, and community/junior colleges are able to provide entry- and middle-level office employees for business. Developing a strong linkage with such institutions through their work experience programs or through their career placement offices is essential.[1]

There has been a great deal written in recent months about the need for businesses to work closely with the educational institutions in their geographic area in order to ensure having a labor market that is competent. When working with postsecondary institutions, it might be beneficial to check their accreditation status; this can be indicative of their academic performance.[2]

EMPLOYMENT SERVICES

There are a number of different employment services that a business might contact when it is looking for an office worker. The largest public employment service is the U.S. Employment Service, which is supervised by the Department of Labor.[3] This service might be able to recommend office workers who are unemployed or underemployed. Private employment agencies are also used by many employers to find competent office workers. Usually, a fee is paid by the employer. Another source used frequently for seeking office workers is the temporary office help services. They "rent out" their workers for varying periods of time—a day, a week, a month, and so on.[4] These temporary workers can be very beneficial to many business firms.

NOTES

1. Arthur L. Jackson, "Hiring Office Workers," *Journal of Training and Development,* November 1987, p. 15.

2. Martha M. Diaz, *Accreditation Standards and Guidelines,* Educational Press, Atlanta, 1986, p. 134.

3. Jackson, p. 17.

4. Victoria S. Eng, "Temporaries Can Be Magic," *Office Automation Specialist,* January 1988, p. 37.

LETTER 24
MODIFIED-BLOCK STYLE

Shown in pica
Line: 6 inches (60 pica/70 elite)
Tab: center
Paper: Workguide 155–156

HI-TECK INDUSTRIES, INC.
3200 RIDGE ROAD
TOLEDO, OH 43614-2431
(419) 555-9265

(*Current date*)   4

An attention line is used to direct the letter to a particular
person or department. It is typed
on the second line of the inside
address.

ENVELOPES

Address No. 10 (large) envelopes for Letters 24 and 25. Use
the all-capital letters style recommended for electronic scanning as illustrated on page ix of
the Reference Section.

LETTER 25
MODIFIED-BLOCK STYLE

Paper: Workguide 157–158

Retype Letter 24. Address the
letter to Mr. Kearns, and omit
the attention line. Use the appropriate salutation.

Franklin Steel Products, Inc.   10
Attention: Mr. Conrad P. Kearns   16
2573 Green Valley Drive   21
Toledo, OH 43614-4941   25

Ladies and Gentlemen: 29

Because our company has doubled in size over the past year, we   42
are expanding our facilities. To this end, therefore, Hi-Teck   55
Industries purchased the Owens-Longyear Building at 3200 Ridge   66
Road three months ago.   72

Our consultant for redesigning the space and determining our   85
furnishing needs is Dr. Jason R. Roepke, of Northwest Business   97
Schools. He is preparing specifications, and in about two   109
weeks we will advertise to the trade our readiness to provide   121
specifications.   124

We invite your representative to tour our new building with   136
me. We feel that your firm will be in a better position to   148
bid wisely if you are familiar with our building. Please let   161
me hear from you.   164

                                        Sincerely yours,   167

                                        Vivian E. Goldsmith   171
                                        Facilities Coordinator   176

gls.0914   177
c: Dr. Jason R. Roepke   182

WP   A word processing
file reference number is
used in combination with
the reference initials. The
0914 indicates that this letter is stored on disk #9 as
document #14.

SKILLBUILDING AND REPORT REVIEW

Line: 60 spaces
Tab: 5, center
Spacing: single
Drills: 2 times
Format Guide: 113

Goals: To type 50 wam/5'/5e; to review formatting a two-page report with endnotes.

120-A. WARMUP

S 1 This audit can be done today if both girls handle it right.
A 2 Jeff amazed the audience by quickly giving six new reports.
N 3 Patricia had Seat 28A on Flight 467 at 5:30 on November 19.

SKILLBUILDING

120-B. PACED PRACTICE

Turn to the Paced Practice routine at the back of the book. Take several 2-minute timings, starting at the point where you left off the last time. Record your progress on Workguide page 125.

120-C. Spacing: double. Record your score.

120-C. SKILL MEASUREMENT: 5-MINUTE TIMED WRITING

```
4        Business is involved with a lot of different groups in    12
5    our society.  These groups include the workers of the firm;   24
6    the stockholders; the consumers or the public at large; all   36
7    the firms that compete with one another; the tax collectors   48
8    for all the city, state, and federal governments; and quite   60
9    a few others, from the health bureau to the welfare office.   72
10   It's hard to realize just how many persons and agencies are   84
11   influenced by every single business in every town and city.   96
12       Those who work for a firm are quite deeply involved in   108
13   its welfare for two reasons.  First, the efforts which they   120
14   exert will surely be a major factor in determining how much   132
15   success the business does or does not enjoy; and second, if   144
16   a firm does badly, not only the employees' incomes but also   156
17   their chances of advancement will be jeopardized.  Thus the   168
18   company has a right to employee loyalty; employees have the   180
19   right to expect a fair wage, good conditions, and a future.   192
20       Each business matters to the whole community.  It pro-   204
21   vides jobs for the citizens and revenue for the stores.  It   216
22   has an impact on market value of property and housing; this   228
23   means tax money for the town.  When a business does well, a   240
24   community will be a better place for its citizens.           250
     |  |  | 2 | 3 | 4 | 5 | 6 | 7 | 8 | 9 | 10 | 11 | 12
```

Line: 60 spaces
Tab: 5
Spacing: single
Drills: 2 times
Workguide: 159–162
Format Guide: 59

LESSON

67

BUSINESS LETTERS

Goals: To improve speed and accuracy; to format letters from handwritten and unarranged copy.

67-A. WARMUP

S 1 They paid for their tickets when they got to that ballpark.
A 2 Eve excitedly jumped when she found the big quartzite rock.
N 3 The 1:30 game drew a crowd of 78,569 on Sunday, October 24.

SKILLBUILDING

67-B. Make two copies. Copy 1: Type each sentence on a separate line. Copy 2: Type each sentence on a separate line, but tab-indent it 5 spaces.

67-B. TECHNIQUE TYPING: RETURN/ENTER AND TAB KEYS

4 Where is your new car? It is in the garage to be tuned up.
5 Are there big problems? No, there are a few routine items.
6 When will it be ready? I will pick it up Friday afternoon.

7 Do you need a ride tomorrow? Yes, that would be very nice.
8 I shall leave my house at 7:30. Will you be ready by 7:45?
9 Would you like a ride later? No, the bus schedule is fine.

10 The meeting will last all day. Will you join me for lunch?
11 Do you pick up the car today? It will be ready after work.
12 I will drop you off on my way home. You are a true friend.

67-C. Compare this paragraph with the second paragraph in Letter 24 on page 138. Type a list of the words that contain errors, correcting the errors as you type.

67-C. PRODUCTION PRACTICE: PROOFREADING

13 Our consultent for redisigning the space and determining
14 our furnishing need is Mr. Jason R. Reopke, of Northwest
15 business schools. He is preparing specifications, and in
16 about 2 weeks will advertize to the trade our readiness to
17 provide specification.

67-D. Take a 1-minute timing on the first paragraph to establish your base speed. Then take several 1-minute timings on the other paragraphs. As soon as you equal or exceed your base speed on one paragraph, advance to the next one.

67-D. SUSTAINED TYPING: SYLLABIC INTENSITY

18   As we have learned more and more about the benefits of   12
19 exercise, large numbers of people have gotten involved in a   24
20 broad range of sports. They want their workouts to be fun.   36

21   There are those who become puzzled after they discover   12
22 that they perform much better when they are practicing than   24
23 when competing. They can't keep their minds on their game.   36

24   Some of these discouraged athletes have sought counsel   12
25 from sports psychologists. They tell these special experts   24
26 that they handicap themselves because of these self-doubts.   36

27   Just as when working with professional athletes, there   12
28 is a basic challenge for the sports psychologist: What can   24
29 I do to rebuild confidence and refine concentration skills?   36

| 1 | 2 | 3 | 4 | 5 | 6 | 7 | 8 | 9 | 10 | 11 | 12

Each footnote must go on the same page on which it is cited in the text.

To maintain a 1-inch bottom margin after the footnotes are typed, plan the ending of the first page carefully.

Note: If the last page of a multipage report contains one or more footnotes, the divider line and footnotes should go at the bottom of the page rather than immediately below the last line of text.

The divider line is 2 inches long. Single-space before and double-space after the divider line.

Footnotes are single-spaced, with a double space between the footnotes.

119-G. REPORT REVIEW

ENTREPRENEURSHIP

By Thomas Clarke

Becoming an entrepreneur has had appeal for many people throughout history, and in a private enterprise system, individuals have the right to set up and operate their own businesses. For those who are willing to take the risk, being an entrepreneur is still a major incentive and/or goal.

In the past several years, there has been a tremendous growth in the number of new private businesses. The purpose of this report is to provide an insight into some of the statistics of entrepreneurship and the competencies needed for success as an entrepreneur.

ENTREPRENEURSHIP STATISTICS

There are over 600,000 small businesses created annually in the United States.[1] The number of small businesses has grown from 5.4 million in 1954 to more than 15 million in 1987.[2] When reviewing labor statistics, it will be found that a majority of the work force is employed by small businesses. It will also be noted that the number of women beginning their own businesses has been steadily growing. By 1990 the small-business sector will be responsible for more than 50 percent of the nation's gross national product.[3]

COMPETENCIES FOR SUCCESS

When an individual decides to open his or her own business, a number of factors should be reviewed. In order to succeed, the new entrepreneur must be able to have a complete knowledge of the business being formed, make short- and long-range plans, manage financial resources, manage human resources, organize and staff the new business, and solve problems and make decisions.[4]

Being a successful entrepreneur has many advantages and can be very exciting, but the critical skills needed for success should be understood and mastered.

---

[1]Robert E. Adams, "Growth of Small Businesses," *Small-Business Management,* October 1987, p. 114.

[2]Carolyn V. Nick, *American Private Enterprise,* Crane Publishing, Chicago, 1986, p. 85.

[3]Adams, p. 115.

[4]Susan R. Angelozzi, "Success as a Sole Proprietor," *American Business,* January 1988, p. 73.

67-E. BUSINESS LETTERS

Type Letters 26 and 27 on letterhead stationery. Follow the directions carefully.

LETTER 26
MODIFIED-BLOCK STYLE

Line: 6 inches (60 pica/70 elite)
Tab: center
Paper: Workguide 159–160

Use the current date and your own reference initials.

Mr. Dennis J. Simpson — 4
Purchasing Department — 8
Funtime Toys, Inc. — 12
1489 Bailey Avenue — 15
Jackson, MS 39203-1406 — 20

Dear Mr. Simpson: — 23

Your formal call for bids dated January 17, 19--, for bicycle — 35
wheels has been received. — 40
When our company began manufacturing three- and — 50
four-wheel all-terrain vehicles six months ago, we — 60
discontinued our production of bicycle wheels. Consequently, — 72
we will not be submitting a bid. — 79
Our long business relationship with you has been both — 90
pleasant and profitable. Perhaps we will resume that — 100
relationship at some point in the future. — 109

Sincerely yours, — 112

Henry P. Martin — 115
Director of Sales — 118

LETTER 27
MODIFIED-BLOCK STYLE

Line: 6 inches (60 pica/70 elite)
Tab: center
Paper: Workguide 161–162

Using the current date, please send the following letter to Mrs. Maria R. Giachino, — 5
Manager / Giachino Motorcycle Sales / 3984 34th Street / Meridian, MS 39305-4405 / — 21
Dear Mrs. Giachino: — 24

Your letter inquiring about Jackson three- and four-wheel all-terrain — 38
vehicles has been received. The addition of our products to your present — 54
line of motorcycles would be a wise decision. Most of our dealers have — 68
made similar arrangements. — 73

Our sales manager for your region, Sam Hodges, will contact you — 86
shortly to arrange a meeting with you. In the meantime, I hope you enjoy — 100
looking at the photos and reading the descriptions of our latest Jackson — 115
models in the enclosed brochures. — 122

We look forward to welcoming you to our growing list of dealers — 134
throughout the country. — 139

Sincerely, / Henry P. Martin / Director of Sales / *(Your initials)* / Enclo- — 152
sures / c: Sam Hodges — 156

SKILLBUILDING AND REPORT REVIEW

Line: 60 spaces
Tab: 5, center
Spacing: single
Drills: 2 times
Format Guide: 113

Goals: To build speed and accuracy; to review formatting a two-page report with footnotes.

119-A. WARMUP

S 1 Pam paid for the eight new signs that she got by the truck.
A 2 Paul said Buzz and Jack might quit five or six weeks early.
N 3 They drove 54 miles on Interstate 61 from 8:30 to 9:27 p.m.

SKILLBUILDING

119-B. Take a 1-minute timing on the first paragraph to establish your base speed. Then take successive 1-minute timings on the other paragraphs. As soon as you equal or exceed your base speed on one paragraph, advance to the next one.

119-B. SUSTAINED TYPING: NUMBERS

4 The employees of Bentley Financial Service were having 12
5 a blood drive for five of their coworkers. Tentative plans 24
6 were set to recruit 75 donors for May 19 starting at 8 a.m. 36

7 Each unit was assigned a goal for the number of donors 12
8 to recruit. Personnel had 14; Customer Service, 7; Records 24
9 Management, 8; Purchasing, 19; Accounting, 21; and Mail, 6. 36

10 As May 19 approached, there were 17 donors assigned to 12
11 give blood from 8 to 9 a.m.; 23 were assigned from 9 to 10; 24
12 and 24 were assigned for 10 to 11 a.m.--a sum of 64 donors. 36

| 1 | 2 | 3 | 4 | 5 | 6 | 7 | 8 | 9 | 10 | 11 | 12

PRETEST. Take a 1-minute timing; compute your speed and count errors.

119-C. PRETEST: ALTERNATE- AND ONE-HAND WORDS

13 Banks must not be carefree with their minimum reserves 12
14 or they might encounter a problem with the auditor. Such a 24
15 case might find a penalty being assessed. The opinion that 36
16 most eager bankers have is to exceed the required reserves. 48

| 1 | 2 | 3 | 4 | 5 | 6 | 7 | 8 | 9 | 10 | 11 | 12

PRACTICE.
   Speed Emphasis: If you made 2 or fewer errors on the Pretest, type each line twice.
   Accuracy Emphasis: If you made 3 or more errors on the Pretest, type each group of lines (as though it were a paragraph) twice.

119-D. PRACTICE: ALTERNATE HANDS

17 also amend maps island blame city problem panel formal down
18 snap rigid lens social visit with penalty right height half
19 chap burnt such enrich shape dish auditor spend eighty lamb
20 girl usual tick thrown laugh then suspend slept mantle kept

119-E. PRACTICE: ONE HAND

21 fad only craft pupil regret uphill drafted homonym carefree
22 bed join water nylon target pompon savages minimum exceeded
23 was hook great knoll teased kimono scatter pumpkin attracts
24 age milk eager union bazaar limply reserve opinion cassette

POSTTEST. Repeat the Pretest and compare performance.

119-F. POSTTEST: ALTERNATE- AND ONE-HAND WORDS

FORMAL LETTER

Line: 60 spaces
Tab: 5
Spacing: single
Drills: 2 times
Workguide: 163–164
Format Guide: 61

Goals: To type 41 wam/5′/5e; to format a letter with indented paragraphs and a formal letter.

68-A. WARMUP

S 1 She did not put the fish or lemons on that shaky top shelf.
A 2 Sixty big quail jumped over that back zoo wall before dawn.
N 3 I counted 29 or 30 cars in the lot at 4856 North 17 Avenue.

SKILLBUILDING

68-B. DIAGNOSTIC TYPING: ALPHABET

Turn to the Diagnostic Typing: Alphabet routine at the back of the book. Take the Pretest, and record your performance on Workguide page 125. Then practice the drill lines for those reaches on which you made errors.

68-C. Spacing: double. Record your score.

68-C. SKILL MEASUREMENT: 5-MINUTE TIMED WRITING

4 Most people are unaware of the great size of the paper   12
5 industry; they think that the industry is limited to things   24
6 that they note every day, like typing paper, newsprint, wax   36
7 paper, books, tissue paper, greeting cards, magazines, etc.   48
8 But the industry is a great deal bigger than that. It   60
9 includes an entire subindustry centered on nothing but what   72
10 is called packaging paper, which is the kind used for bags,   84
11 cartons, and boxes, found in thousands of sizes and shapes.   96
12 Packaging has become a whole industry in itself, as an   108
13 average shopping cart of supermarket goods will prove. The   120
14 six-packs, boxes within boxes, cans on cans taped together,   132
15 and so on, with colors and designs galore, in a single cart   144
16 will frequently provide twice as much package as content; a   156
17 perfect example is a dozen eggs--more box than eggs by far.   168
18 A little checking into the paper industry leads you to   180
19 the lumber industry, then to railroads and trucking, and so   192
20 on. Separate but related--that is the status of our indus-   204
21 tries.   205

| | 1 | 2 | 3 | 4 | 5 | 6 | 7 | 8 | 9 | 10 | 11 | 12 |

118-D. TABLE REVIEW

TABLE 40
OPEN TABLE

Spacing: single
Paper: plain

TABLE 41
RULED TABLE

Paper: plain

Retype Table 40 in ruled format.

EMPIRE MANUFACTURING, INC.

Expense Summaries for October

Individual	Department	Total
Estelle Citarelli	Accounting	$1,840.50
Kenneth Kardux	Purchasing	841.00
Lucille Lombardi	Marketing	3,642.75
John McAnelly	Production	3,342.50
William Velasquez	Research	640.80

TABLE 42
BOXED TABLE WITH BRACED
HEADING

Paper: plain

EMPIRE MANUFACTURING, INC.

Year-to-Date Sales of Lexington Products

Model	Quarter Sales Figures			Total for Year
	First Quarter	Second Quarter	Third Quarter	
115-300	$65,084	$57,850	$62,034	$184,968
115-304	48,312	47,312	49,319	144,943
118-102	23,482	24,500	26,358	74,340
118-210	34,549	36,412	33,880	104,841
119-560	29,587	29,484	30,125	89,196
120-210	18,587	21,348	19,957	59,892

118-E. FORMS REVIEW

FORM 29
INVOICE
Paper: Workguide 273

Invoice 1895 from Empire Manufacturing to Shelton Furniture, 113 Liston Avenue, Rocky Mount, NC 27801, for its Purchase Order 442: 12 ctns. of Arrow staples, 1/2″, T-50, @ $4.25 a carton = $51.00; 6 boxes of round-head bolts, 1 1/2″, @ $3.25 a box = $19.50; and 15 ctns. of nails unlimited, 2″, 6D, @ $8.00 a carton = $120.00. Invoice total = $190.50, plus 6% sales tax of $11.43. Total amount due = $201.93.

FORM 30
PURCHASE ORDER
Paper: Workguide 273

Purchase Order 145 to Maxwell Office Supplies, 18 South Brunswick Avenue, Lancaster, PA 17602: 10 reams of Prince copy paper, #1212, @ $14.00 a ream = $140; 2 boxes of Vinyltronic masters, #1684, @ $15.00 a box = $30; and 8 Techmatic ribbons, #841, @ $6.50 each = $52. Total amount of purchase order = $222.

68-D. LETTERS WITH INDENTED PARAGRAPHS

The following letter, addressed to a U.S. congresswoman, is in the modified-block style with indented paragraphs. However, the formal style illustrated at the bottom of the page is thought by many to be more appropriate when writing to public dignitaries.

LETTER 28
MODIFIED-BLOCK STYLE WITH
INDENTED PARAGRAPHS

Shown in pica
Line: 6 inches (60 pica/70 elite)
Tab: 5, center
Paper: plain, full sheet

The salutation *Dear Mrs. Garcia:* would also be appropriate.

Use the more formal complimentary closing, *Very truly yours,* because the letter is being sent to a public dignitary.

January 24, 19--   3

The Honorable Stella E. Garcia   9
House of Representatives   14
Washington, DC 20515   18

Dear Representative Garcia: 24

    On behalf of the Terre Haute Professional Women's Club, I   35
wish to thank you for your most informative and entertaining   47
presentation at our "Women in Politics" conference.   58

    The extensive preparation for your presentation was obvious.   69
The enthusiasm and interest of the audience were apparent   81
by the extensive question-and-answer session at the   93
conclusion of your remarks.   98

    We appreciate your taking the time from your important   109
work to speak to the members of our club and to help us become   122
better-informed citizens.   127

           Very truly yours,   130

           Susan M. Swafford   134
           1532 South 28 Street   138
           Terre Haute, IN 47803   142

(Your initials)   143

LETTER 29
FORMAL LETTER IN MODIFIED-
BLOCK STYLE WITH INDENTED
PARAGRAPHS

Retype Letter 28, but move the inside address to the bottom as illustrated to make the letter a "formal" or "official" letter. Return the carrier 5 times after the date to leave 4 blank lines before the salutation. Do not use reference initials.

~~~~~~

           Susan M. Swafford
           1532 South 28 Street
           Terre Haute, IN 47803   ↓5

The Honorable Stella E. Garcia
House of Representatives
Washington, DC 20515

~~~~~~

SKILLBUILDING; TABLE AND FORMS REVIEW

Line: 60 spaces
Tab: 5, center
Spacing: single
Drills: 2 times
Workguide: 273
Format Guide: 111

Goals: To type 50 wam/5'/5e; to review formatting tables and forms.

118-A. WARMUP

S 1 She will fight for the right to keep the profit for a gown.
A 2 Sixty equals only five dozen, but we promised Jackie eight.
N 3 Area codes 512, 806, 817, and 915 are all located in Texas.

SKILLBUILDING

118-B. PACED PRACTICE

Turn to the Paced Practice routine at the back of the book. Take several 2-minute timings, starting at the point where you left off the last time. Record your progress on Workguide page 125.

118-C. Spacing: double. Record your score.

118-C. SKILL MEASUREMENT: 5-MINUTE TIMED WRITING

4 Employee or fringe benefits have always been important   12
5 to office workers. Some of these benefits have been around 24
6 for a long time. For example, it is quite common to have a 36
7 company provide health-care benefits and insurance coverage 48
8 for its employees. Having benefits for sick-leave time and 60
9 vacation days is also quite normal. A new concern that has 72
10 been receiving lots of attention recently involves plans to 84
11 provide retirement benefits. Such plans might include tax- 96
12 sheltered annuities, profit sharing, or stock option plans. 108
13 A survey of leaders in personnel management would show 120
14 that many new benefits might be received by office workers. 132
15 For example, to meet the needs of the family with two work- 144
16 ing parents, or the family with just a single parent, there 156
17 are more and more firms that provide child-care facilities. 168
18 The concept of flexible working hours, whereby workers help 180
19 pick that time during the day when they will be on the job, 192
20 is another benefit which has assisted the space-age family. 204
21 There are many other benefits which can be received by 216
22 an office worker. It should be realized that companies are 228
23 paying a great deal of money in order to give their workers 240
24 a fringe-benefit package plan that is up to date. 250

| 1 | 2 | 3 | 4 | 5 | 6 | 7 | 8 | 9 | 10 | 11 | 12

Line: 60 spaces
Tab: 5
Spacing: single
Drills: 2 times
Workguide: 165
Format Guide: 61

LESSON
69

INTEROFFICE MEMORANDUMS

Goals: To improve speed and accuracy; to format interoffice memorandums.

69-A. WARMUP

S 1 Nancy may wish for a big bus when she sees all those girls.
A 2 Thieves quickly seized the extra banjo from two poor gents.
N 3 Models 74, 86, and 93 were out of stock for 15 to 20 weeks.

SKILLBUILDING

69-B. DIAGNOSTIC TYPING: NUMBERS

Turn to the Diagnostic Typing: Numbers routine at the back of the book. Take the Pretest, and record your performance on Workguide page 125. Then practice the drill lines for those reaches on which you made errors.

69-C. Clear all tabs. Then set four new tab stops every 12 spaces. Type each line, tabulating across from column to column.

69-C. TECHNIQUE TYPING: TAB KEY

4	await	berry	coins	dairy	eagle
5	fruit	gable	horse	igloo	jelly
6	knots	ledge	major	night	offer
7	phase	queen	roast	strap	toast
8	units	valve	waxed	yolks	zebra

PRETEST. Take a 1-minute timing; compute your speed and count errors.

69-D. PRETEST: VERTICAL REACHES

9   The third skier knelt on the knoll and secured a loose   12
10 ski as the race was about to begin. Each of the rival team 24
11 members awaited the starting signal way above the crowd. A 36
12 variety of trophies and awards would go to all the winners. 48
    | 1 | 2 | 3 | 4 | 5 | 6 | 7 | 8 | 9 | 10 | 11 | 12

PRACTICE.
   Speed Emphasis: If you made no more than 1 error on the Pretest, type each line twice.
   Accuracy Emphasis: If you made 2 or more errors on the Pretest, type each group of lines (for example, lines 13–16), as though it were a paragraph, twice.

69-E. PRACTICE: UP REACHES

13 aw away award crawl straw drawn sawed drawl await flaw lawn
14 se self sense raise these prose abuse users serve send seem
15 ki kind kites skill skier skims skips skits kilts king skid
16 rd lard third beard horde gourd board guard sword cord curd

69-F. PRACTICE: DOWN REACHES

17 ac ache track paced brace races facts crack acute back aces
18 kn knob knife kneel knows knack knelt known knoll knot knew
19 ab drab about label table above abide gable abbey able abet
20 va vain vague value valve evade naval rival avail vats vase

POSTTEST. Repeat the Pretest and compare performance.

69-G. POSTTEST: VERTICAL REACHES

117-H. CORRESPONDENCE REVIEW

MEMO 21
Paper: Workguide 271

Using the current date, type this memo from Valerie Walsh, Office Manager, to Charlotte Sabatini, Vice President for Administrative Services. The subject is Desktop Publishing.

As you know, I attended the North Jersey Business Show in Parsippany | 43
yesterday. I was particularly eager to get information about equipment | 55
that might help us in the production of our proposed newsletter. | 73

I visited with a number of exhibitors and saw some excellent demon- | 85
strations. One such demonstration was on the Vista 100—a piece of | 96
equipment that could be extremely useful to us as we consider the mer- | 108
its of publishing a newsletter for our clients. The equipment was exhib- | 120
ited by Raymond Miramontes of Office Automation in Clifton. | 139

Enclosed is a brochure on the Vista 100 as well as a copy of a letter I | 152
sent to Mr. Miramontes. Please let me have your reaction before I con- | 164
sider inviting him to demonstrate the equipment to our staff. | 175
(Closing lines?) | 180

LETTER 61
PERSONAL-BUSINESS LETTER IN
MODIFIED-BLOCK STYLE
Paper: plain

June 5, 19-- | 4

Ms. Gloria Koenig | 7
Customer Services | 11
Regency Resort | 14
1515 East Shore | 17
Lahaina, HI 96761 | 20

Dear Ms. Koenig: | 23

Thank you *very* so much for the assistance you gave ~~me and~~ my hus- | 34
band, *and me)* on our recent visit to your hotel in May. | 45

Due to the loss of our luggage on ~~our~~ *the* flight to Maui, we were | 57
quite upset at the prospect of not having our personal belong~~s~~ *ing* | 70
for any period of time. | 75

a few hours With your help, however, our luggage was retrieved from Hono- | 87
lulu within ~~the day~~ In addition, the upgraded room you as- | 100
signed to us made our entire 10-day visit ~~superb.~~ *fantastic.* To show | 112
our thanks for your time and effort, we ~~have sent~~ you a spe- | 125
cial package of Wisconsin cheeses. *are sending* | 132

We will be sure to recommend the Regency to our friends in | 143
Racine, *and* We ~~hope~~ *plan* to return to Maui ~~at some future time.~~ *again next year.* | 154

Sincerely, | 156

Nancy Anderson | 159
15 Hamilton Drive | 162
Racine, WI 53402 | 166

69-H. INTEROFFICE MEMORANDUMS

Memo 13 is displayed in the appropriate memorandum format. The same format is to be used for Memo 14, shown in unarranged form at the bottom of the page.

MEMO 13

Line: 6 inches (60 pica/70 elite)
Tab: 10
Paper: plain, full sheet

WP   Some word processors have a feature that automatically sets whatever top and bottom margins, side margins, and tabs are needed for recurring documents.

↓13

MEMO TO:	Dwight T. Wilson, Credit Manager	8
FROM:	Yvonne P. Johns	13
	Sales Manager, Zone 4	18
DATE:	January 25, 19--	23
SUBJECT:	Credit Terms (File 625-8) ↓3	30

I held a meeting yesterday with our sales representatives to   42
discuss the decline in sales in Zone 4. We found that the   54
basic problem lies in our credit terms, which are much more   66
stringent than those of our competitors.   74

As confirmed with your secretary this morning, I have set up a   86
meeting for 1:30 p.m. on Monday, February 2, in Conference   98
Room 1220 for all concerned with our credit rules and poli-   110
cies, as presently provided in File 625-8. I will appreciate   122
your coming to the meeting and your reviewing File 625-8 be-   134
fore the meeting. We shall be looking to you for alternatives   147
to our present policies.   152

daj   153

MEMO 14

Line: 6 inches (60 pica/70 elite)
Tab: 10
Paper: Workguide 165

Please send the following memo to Mr. R. N. Halsten, President. It is from James F.   7
Demings, Employee Services. Use the current date and an appropriate subject line.   20

This is a progress report on plans for the annual Hi-Teck Winter Ball,   35
to be held on February 11. As usual, the event will be held in the Regis-   49
Biltmore Hotel. Invitations have been sent to all home-office employees.   64
(Similar events have been scheduled for other employees at various sites   79
throughout the country.)   84

The menu has been planned, the orchestra has been selected, and the   97
Performance Awards recipients have been identified.   107

Let's hope that the weather will be more favorable than it was last   121
year, when we had a snowstorm on the night of the party!   132

SKILLBUILDING AND CORRESPONDENCE REVIEW

Line: 60 spaces
Tab: 5, center
Spacing: single
Drills: 2 times
Workguide: 271
Format Guide: 109

Goals: To build speed and accuracy; to review formatting an interoffice memo and a personal-business letter.

117-A. WARMUP

S 1 She may visit with the new owner down by the new city hall.
A 2 Jacqueline was glad her family took five or six big prizes.
N 3 Beverly got tickets 10, 29, 38, 47, and 56 for the concert.

SKILLBUILDING

117-B. NUMBER TYPING

4 Review pages 487–526 in Chapter 30 of the text by April 19.
5 Area codes 217, 309, 312, 618, and 815 are all in Illinois.
6 Invoices 2316, 2387, 2419, 2438, and 2507 were outstanding.
7 Checks were sent for $457.80, $389.92, $289.91, and $67.42.

117-C. PRETEST: CLOSE REACHES

PRETEST. Take a 1-minute timing; compute your speed and count errors.

8   Avoiding gloomy sales figures is a point of concern in   12
9 many firms. The same will be said for the need to trim any   24
10 losses in daily operations. Many firms look at sample ways   36
11 to obtain thrift and savings by trying to motivate workers.   48
   | 1 | 2 | 3 | 4 | 5 | 6 | 7 | 8 | 9 | 10 | 11 | 12

117-D. PRACTICE: ADJACENT KEYS

PRACTICE.
Speed Emphasis: If you made 2 or fewer errors on the Pretest, type each line twice.
Accuracy Emphasis: If you made 3 or more errors on the Pretest, type each group of lines (as though it were a paragraph) twice.

12 tr trim tree trait strap truce stripe pantry tremor truants
13 po post spot pours vapor poker powder oppose weapon pockets
14 sa sash same usage essay sadly safety dosage sample sailing
15 oi oily coin point voice doing choice boiled egoist loiters

117-E. PRACTICE: CONSECUTIVE FINGERS

16 my myth army foamy yummy myrrh stormy mystic gloomy mystery
17 ft left soft often after shift gifted crafts thrift uplifts
18 ny onyx deny nylon vinyl phony anyway skinny felony canyons
19 lo loss solo loser flood color locate floral ballot loaders

POSTTEST. Repeat the Pretest and compare performance.

117-F. POSTTEST: CLOSE REACHES

117-G. Compare this paragraph with the last paragraph of the timing on page 243. Type a list of the words that contain errors, correcting the errors as you type.

117-G. PRODUCTION PRACTICE: PROOFREADING

20   Students benfit greatly from the type of program. A
21 contact is made for futere employment, skills being learned
22 in school are applied on this job, exploring a job field can
23 start sooner, and money might be earnd earlier. A student
24 can utilze this program for carer advancement.

Line: 60
Tab: 5, center
Spacing: single
Drills: 2 times
Workguide: 167–170
Format Guide: 63

LESSON
70

BUSINESS LETTERS WITH VARIATIONS

Goals: To type 41 wam/5'/5e; to format business letters with 2-column tables.

70-A. WARMUP

S 1 Bob may fix the rotor on the motor when he visits us again.
A 2 Kyle mixed seven quarts of frozen grape juice with sherbet.
N 3 Order #459367 will likely be received within 18 or 20 days.

SKILLBUILDING

70-B. PACED PRACTICE

Turn to the Paced Practice routine at the back of the book. Take several 2-minute timings, starting at the point where you left off the last time. Record your progress on Workguide page 126.

70-C. Spacing: double.
Record your score.

70-C. SKILL MEASUREMENT: 5-MINUTE TIMED WRITING

```
 4        Seminars on the subject of time management continue to   12
 5   be in great demand throughout the nation.  The seminars are   24
 6   ordinarily held for staff supervisors and managers, but now   36
 7   and then the programs are open to anyone wishing to attend.   48
 8   The ideas promoted in the seminars are valid for everybody.   60
 9        The key ingredient in all plans for managing your time   72
10   is simply planning.  Those who plan their workday find that   84
11   they save time.  At the start of each office day, they list   96
12   the tasks that must be done, and next they set priorities--  108
13   that is, decide on the sequence in which to do those tasks.  120
14   Then they hold to their plan as exactly as the day permits.  132
15        Changes will have to be made, undoubtedly, as your day  144
16   advances, with new tasks unexpectedly rising and some older  156
17   carried-over tasks suddenly gaining new urgency and earning  168
18   higher priority--but any sensible person can adjust, right?  180
19   The main value of prioritizing the task sequence is that it  192
20   moves you from one task to the next without any big loss of  204
21   time.                                                        205
     |  1 |  2 |  3 |  4 |  5 |  6 |  7 |  8 |  9 | 10 | 11 | 12
```

LETTER 59
BLOCK STYLE,
OPEN PUNCTUATION

Paper: Workguide 267–268

116-C.   CORRESPONDENCE REVIEW

(*Current date*) / Mr. Andres Penabad / Office Automation Consultant /   14
Productivity Measurement Center / 15 Park Avenue / New York, NY   26
10016 / Dear Mr. Penabad   30

    When I was reading my copy of Management Techniques today, I was   43
interested in your article dealing with measuring productivity in the   57
office environment. I was especially interested in the following three   72
concepts: 73

    1.   Utilization of work measurement and work standards in the office.   87

    2.   Office operations that have been measured in the past and poten-   101
tial for new measurement standards.   108

    3.   Benefits of a work standards program.   116

    Please send me a copy of the brochure that you described in the   129
article. I might be able to use your consulting service for a productivity   144
program that we are undertaking here at Heritage.   154

    Sincerely yours / Valerie Walsh / Office Manager / (*Your initials*)   160

LETTER 60
BLOCK STYLE,
OPEN PUNCTUATION

Paper: Workguide 269–270

(Current date)/Mr. Raymond V. Miramontes / Office   10
Automation Equipment / 21 Lexington Avenue /   19
Clifton, NJ 07011 / Dear Mr. Miramontes   26

    It was good to talk with you at the   33
North Jersey Business Show in Parsippany   41
yesterday afternoon. The demonstration that   50
you provided on desktop publishing was very   59
interesting and informative.   65

    As I indicated, we are very eager to produce   74
a newsletter for our clients. It appears that   83
we could utilize the type of equipment you   92
demonstrated to meet our objective.   99

    As soon as I get my supervisor's approval,   107
I will call you to arrange a meeting in   115
our office so that you can give a demonstra-   124
tion to a number of our employees.   131

    Sincerely yours/Valerie Walsh/Office Manager/(Your initials)   140

70-D. BUSINESS LETTERS WITH VARIATIONS

Letters 30 and 31 are variations of the standard business letter. A subject line and a simple 2-column table are included, and the paragraphs are indented 5 spaces.

LETTER 30
MODIFIED-BLOCK STYLE WITH INDENTED PARAGRAPHS AND TABLE

Shown in pica
Line: 6 inches (60 pica/70 elite)
Tab: 5, center
Paper: Workguide 167–168

Before beginning to type, review the proofreaders' marks on page xiv in the Reference Section.

The subject line indicates what the letter is about. It is placed at the left margin a double space below the salutation. (The term *Re* or *In re* may be used in place of *Subject*.)

Center the table within the line of typing, with 6 spaces between columns.

LETTER 31
MODIFIED-BLOCK STYLE WITH INDENTED PARAGRAPHS AND TABLE

Paper: Workguide 169–170

Retype Letter 30, but address it to the first person listed in the table. Mr. Bierman's address is 2470 North 39 Street, Yakima, WA 98901. Miss Glover's name and company will replace his in the table. Remember to change the salutation.

WP
If Letter 30 had been typed on a word processor, you would have to retype only the changes. The remainder of the letter would be printed out automatically from the system's memory.

(Current date)   4

Ms. Sylvia A. Glover   8
Reade Paper Products, Inc.   13
1645 Leland Street   17
Greeley, CO 80631   20

Dear Ms. Glover: 23

Subject: Annual Convention Of APPA   31

Plans are underway for the annual convention of the the   41
American Paper Producers Association to be held in August in   54
Wausau, Wisconsin. As you have a special interest in futur-   66
istics, I am inviting you to participate on a panel at the   77
convention on a topic tentatively entitled "Paper Needs in   89
the 21st Century." The other panel members include: 100

Ralph E. Bierman   Clarkson Paper Co.   107
Elliott R. Treitz   DeRoche Paper Products, Inc.   116
Elizabeth A. Mahoski   National paper corporation   125

If you accept this invitation, I will set up a tele-conference   138
call for the five of us. Then, after you have selected a   149
chairperson, the panel will proceed with out further direc-   161
tion.   162

Please let me know if you will participate by calling me   173
collect at (218) 555-3690 within the next week.   182

Sincerely,   184

Benjamin L. Spahr   187
Program Chairperson   191

(Your initials)   192
c: Mr. Elisha A. Koenig   196
     Executive Vice President   201

LESSON 70   146

LESSON **116**

SKILLBUILDING AND CORRESPONDENCE REVIEW

Line: 60 spaces
Tab: 5
Spacing: single
Drills: 2 times
Workguide: 267–270
Format Guide: 109

Goals: To type 50 wam/5'/5e; to review correspondence typing.

116-A. WARMUP

S 1 If both girls handle the audit right, it can be done today.
A 2 Felix might hit your jackpot even with the bad quiz answer.
N 3 Our gross profit increased from $64,580 to $73,912 in 1989.

SKILLBUILDING

116-B. Spacing: double. Record your score.

116-B. SKILL MEASUREMENT: 5-MINUTE TIMED WRITING

4 In recent years there has been a strong growth in what 12
5 is called cooperative education. This type of program will 24
6 enable a student to combine work and school. The theory of 36
7 cooperative education first began at the college level. In 48
8 fact, some colleges started such a program more than eighty 60
9 years ago. There are some colleges where it is required to 72
10 enroll in such a program. More and more of the students in 84
11 colleges see the benefits that such a program will provide. 96

12 In the last three decades, high schools throughout the 108
13 country have also adopted work-experience programs for many 120
14 of their vocational areas. At first, many schools embraced 132
15 this concept because of funding that was available from the 144
16 government. To keep a solid cooperative education program, 156
17 it is essential to have a really good teacher, a supportive 168
18 group of business leaders, a strong group of school leaders 180
19 who back the program, and students who desire this program. 192

20 Students benefit greatly from this type of program. A 204
21 contact is made for future employment, skills being learned 216
22 in school are applied on the job, exploring a job field can 228
23 start sooner, and money might be earned earlier. A student 240
24 can utilize this program for career advancement. 250

| 1 | 2 | 3 | 4 | 5 | 6 | 7 | 8 | 9 | 10 | 11 | 12

LESSON
71

Line: 60 spaces
Tab: 5
Spacing: single
Drills: 2 times
Workguide: 149–150
Format Guide: 63

BUSINESS REPORTS

Goals: To improve speed and accuracy; to format business reports.

71-A. WARMUP

S 1 Kent and the eight big black dogs came down the dusty road.
A 2 Gramp quickly adjusted the tax bill size for Wendy Davison.
N 3 Al sold 40 tickets; Cyd, 28; Ed, 37; Rex, 19; and Sara, 56.

SKILLBUILDING

PRETEST. Take a 1-minute timing; compute your speed and count errors.

71-B. PRETEST: DISCRIMINATION PRACTICE

4   Lois said the rear of the long train was right next to   12
5 the column of poplar trees. A gunman had entered a red car 24
6 and stolen a case of grapefruit juice and ten cases of soda 36
7 pop. A policeman quickly arrested him; the train moved on. 48
   | | 2 | 3 | 4 | 5 | 6 | 7 | 8 | 9 | 10 | 11 | 12

PRACTICE.

Speed Emphasis: If you made no more than 1 error on the Pretest, type each line twice.

Accuracy Emphasis: If you made 2 or more errors on the Pretest, type each group of lines (as though it were a paragraph) twice.

71-C. PRACTICE: LEFT HAND

8   rtr art part trip sort trot start train skirt depart strobe
9   asa ash mass sand cash salt grass salad trash splash salmon
10 sds sad used suds said pods based drips curds stride guards
11 rer red rear fear rest pier tread lower press rental flower

71-D. PRACTICE: RIGHT HAND

12 mnm menu mine numb meant named melon column mention mansion
13 pop post poor coop point troop poise police popular operate
14 olo tool yolk loon spoil lodge color stroll lottery rolling
15 iui unit suit quit quiet unite juice sluice biscuit uniform

POSTTEST. Repeat the Pretest and compare performance.

71-E. POSTTEST: DISCRIMINATION PRACTICE

71-F. SUSTAINED TYPING: NUMBERS

71-F. Take a 1-minute timing on the first paragraph to establish your base speed. Then take several 1-minute timings on the other paragraphs. As soon as you equal or exceed your base speed on one paragraph, advance to the next one.

16   The 46 medical doctors and dentists told her that they   12
17 would volunteer to work at the 138th Street Clinic. All of 24
18 the building materials and construction labor were donated. 36

19   Each doctor and dentist devotes 8 to 20 hours per week   12
20 at the clinic. By the end of the seventh month, there were 24
21 between 735 and 1,496 outpatients being treated every week. 36

22   The 138th Street Clinic usually has 27 to 36 volunteer   12
23 nurses and 15 to 29 dental assistants who donate their time 24
24 to helping others. They work 10 to 14 hours each per week. 36
   | | 2 | 3 | 4 | 5 | 6 | 7 | 8 | 9 | 10 | 11 | 12

TABLE 38
RULED TABLE

Spacing: double
Paper: plain, full sheet

At the next executive board meeting of the National Conference of Realtors, Ms. Holden will report on the attendance at the last two annual conventions. Type the following ruled table for her use.

½ = TS = 2 blank lines

ATTENDANCE RECORD AT ANNUAL CONVENTIONS   8
NATIONAL CONFERENCE OF REALTORS   14

Comparison of Past Year With Previous Year   22

Region	Past Year	Previous Year	
East	350	338	30
Midwest	356	342	33
South	424	419	35
West	438	427	37
TOTAL	1,568	1,526	40

TABLE 39
BOXED TABLE

Spacing: double
Paper: plain, full sheet

Ms. Holden has received the information on membership statistics and wants to include it with the memo being sent to all executive board members. Type the following boxed table.

MEMBERSHIP STATISTICS   4
NATIONAL CONFERENCE OF REALTORS   10

Comparison of Past Year With Previous Year   19

Region	Past Year	Previous Year	Membership Change		
			Number	Percent	25/30
East	4,552	4,421	+131	+3.0	34
Midwest	3,762	3,854	-92	-2.4	39
South	3,876	3,662	+214	+5.8	44
West	4,430	4,215	+215	+5.1	48
TOTAL	16,620	16,152	+468	+2.9	53

71-G. BUSINESS REPORTS

Unless otherwise directed, type these business reports on a full sheet of plain paper.

REPORT 23
UNBOUND BUSINESS REPORT

Line: 6 inches (60 pica/70 elite)
Tab: 5, center
Spacing: double
Paper: plain, full sheet
Visual guide: Workguide 149

Displayed paragraphs are single-spaced and indented 5 spaces on each side.

REPORT 24
BOUND BUSINESS REPORT

Retype Report 23 as a bound business report.

Line: 6 inches (60 pica/70 elite)
Tab: 5, center
Spacing: double
Paper: plain, full sheet
Visual guide: Workguide 150

Note: To provide a wider left margin in a bound report: (1) use the visual guide on Workguide page 150, (2) move both margins and all tab stops 3 spaces to the right, or (3) move the paper guide 3 spaces to the left before inserting the paper.

↓13

WEEKLY SALE ITEMS   3
Effective March 1, 19 - - ↓3   8

As of March 1, 19--, all retail outlets of   17
Lone Star Associated Grocers will be required   26
to honor sale items advertised by the   33
warehouse distributor. This new sales and   42
advertising technique has been established to   51
better serve your needs and the needs of your   60
customers. The official policy is as follows: 69

All retail establishments of Lone   76
Star Associated Grocers will now   83
feature the same sale items each   89
week. These items will be determined   97
by the distribution manager at the   104
wholesale warehouse. Featured sale   111
items will be advertised in local   118
newspapers at warehouse expense. In   125
addition to featured warehouse   132
products, you may include five   138
in-store specials.   141

Sale items will be posted and mailed   149
in advance to ensure ample time for ordering   158
appropriate quantities. When we consolidate   167
sale items, customers will know that   174
those items advertised by the Lone Star   182
warehouse can be found at any Lone Star   190
food store. We plan to formally evaluate   199
this policy after a three-month trial period.   208

DEMOGRAPHICS AFFECTS *of* REAL ESTATE
By June Holden
(? Lines of 40 Spaces)

Demographics affect all phases of our society. Health care, entertainment activities, *labor market needs,* government legislation, educational pursuits, and leisure activities are all affected by changes in the demographics of our population. Of course, demographics also impact on the sale and purchase of residential real estate. ¶ In the next decade, individuals involved in the business of real estate should be aware of the following three facts: age shift in population, trade-up buyers, *and first-time buyers,*

Age Shift in Population

Most of All the demographic action for the next few years will be concentrated among the middle-agers--the graying, balding baby boomers and their immediate predecessors. The number of households in America occupied by *those* ~~the~~ under 30 years of age will ~~shrivel~~ *shrink* by 310,000 this year and by 400,000 in the next few years. That trend will accelerate even more *during* ~~in~~ the next ~~ten years.~~ *decade.*

FIRST-TIME BUYERS
(The number of) People who are buying their first home, the mainstay of the new-home market for the past decade, will take a sharp drop. Over 60 per cent of the baby boomers already own homes. They don't want a stripped-down starter unit anymore. They don't need one-bedroom condos, tiny town-houses, or government-housing bond programs as they used to.

Trade-Up Buyers *(ALL CAPS)*
Trade-up buyers will account for the big action in the real estate market in the next ~~ten years.~~ *decade.* Whether *they're* in their late thirties or forties, or early fifties, owners of existing homes will supply up to 75 per cent of the effective demand for new houses in the coming years--a change that everybody in residential real estate *should* ~~better~~ prepare for. ~~This is extremely important.~~

In dealing with these buyers, it will be necessary to think big.--Not just big in size. Think luxury, think amenities, think "life-style," and, above all, think quality. The trade-up buyers are tougher to sell to, because they are smarter than first-timers. They know more about construction quality. They want extra fireplaces, top-notch kitchens, elegant bathrooms, and two-car garages. They want homes with lots of living space and lots of conveniences.

SUMMARY
As a real estate agent, you should recognize the importance of preparing for the changing residential real estate market. Being aware of the age shift in population, first-time buyers, and trade-up buyers should help to make you a better real estate agent.

Line: 60 spaces
Tab: 5, center
Spacing: single
Drills: 2 times
Workguide: 171
Format Guide: 65

Goals: To type 42 wam/5'/5e; to format news releases.

72-A. WARMUP

S 1 Eight of them got to go with the girls to that rugby field.
A 2 Liza gave Max and Becky a quaint photo of a jar of flowers.
N 3 Our enrollments increased from 264 to 305 by the year 1987.

> SKILLBUILDING

72-B. PROGRESSIVE PRACTICE: ALPHABET

Turn to the Progressive Practice: Alphabet routine at the back of the book. Take several 30-second timings, starting at the point where you left off the last time. Record your progress on Workguide page 125.

72-C. Spacing: double. Record your score.

72-C. SKILL MEASUREMENT: 5-MINUTE TIMED WRITING

4   Someone in an office has to be responsible for keeping   12
5 an inventory of equipment and supplies. Without a doubt, a 24
6 computerized system is the way to go; a correct and current 36
7 listing is only minutes away.   42
8   A good inventory software program makes it possible to 54
9 print lists according to need. For example, there may be a 66
10 need for a list of all typewriters; or a list may be needed 78
11 for those bought six years ago.   84
12   There is a need for someone to identify those types of 96
13 data that should be entered for each supplies and equipment 108
14 category. Examples are serial numbers, vendors, brands, or 120
15 such things as size and color.   126
16   The system might well be judged by how well it fits in 138
17 with plans for reordering. A good system is one in which a 150
18 computer does much of the work by routinely printing a list 162
19 of those things to be ordered.   168
20   An automated ordering system will work only when there 180
21 is a real effort made to keep the files up to date. If the 192
22 inventory is not correct or current, there is no way that a 204
23 printout can be a proper list.   210

| 1 | 2 | 3 | 4 | 5 | 6 | 7 | 8 | 9 | 10 | 11 | 12

REVIEW OF OFFICER RESPONSIBILITIES   7

Pages 4 ~~to~~ *through* 7 of the bylaws were reviewed in detail, and as-   20
signments were made to officers as called for in that docu-   31
ment. There was only one minor change: Mr. Johnson rather   43
than Ms. Gancarz will assume responsibility for the exhibits   56
at the annual convention. All other responsibilities will   67
remain as ~~stated.~~   75
              indicated in that document.

EXECUTIVE BOARD MEETING ON APRIL 10 IN ST. LOUIS   84

   Ms. Holden will make all the necessary hotel arrangements   96
for the executive board meeting to be held in St. Louis on   108
April 10. Ms. Gancarz should ~~be prepared to~~ have a ~~proposed~~ 118
recommended
budget ready, with any ~~recommendations~~ for a dues increase.   130
Mrs. Lanzi should be prepared to distribute information on the   142
final program agenda for the June convention. The officers   154
will meet from 9 to 11 a.m. prior to the Executive Board   166
meeting.   *supporting data*   167

ANNUAL CONVENTION IN ST. LOUIS, JUNE 14-16   176

All contracts have been signed with the Redbird Hotel for   187
hosting ~~our~~ *the* annual convention June 14-16 in St. Louis. Ar- 199
rangements have been completed to have Dr. Susan Marki as ~~our~~ *the* 212
keynote speaker. A major part of the April 10 executive board   224
meeting will be devoted to discussing all the special func-   236
tions and activities for that convention. Ms. Holden will   248
work closely with all officers and Executive Board memembers   260
to be certain that all plans are being carried out.   270

Adjournment   272

The meeting was adjourned at 3:05 p.m.   280

                              Respectfully submitted,   285

                              Wayne Johnson,   287
                              Secretary   289

Distribution: Officers of National Conference of Realtors   301

Ms. Holden has submitted a magazine article for the *Realtors Bulletin*, which is to be prepared for membership distribution in April. Please retype the article on a 40-space line. After you have finished typing it, count the number of lines it contains, and type the number on the line below the byline. Double-space the article.

72-D. NEWS RELEASES

To format a news release:

1. Use a 6-inch line (60 pica/70 elite).
2. Double-space the body, and indent paragraphs 5 spaces.
3. On a printed form, align the identifying information with the guide words. On plain paper, begin the identifying information on line 7, aligned at the center tab.
4. Center the title of the news release in all-capital letters. Leave 2 blank lines above and below the title.
5. Type a date line: city, state, abbreviated date, and a dash before the first sentence.

REPORT 25
NEWS RELEASE

Shown in pica
Line: 6 inches (60 pica/70 elite)
Tab: 5, center
Spacing: double
Paper: Workguide 171

REPORT 26
NEWS RELEASE

Retype Report 25 on plain paper.
Line: 6 inches (60 pica/70 elite)
Tab: 5, center
Spacing: double
Paper: plain, full sheet

From the left margin, spread *NEWS RELEASE.* Leave 1 space between letters and 3 spaces between words. Begin *From Ellwood A. VanDyne* at center.

↓7

N E W S   R E L E A S E   From Ellwood A. VanDyne   11
Missouri Financial Corporation   17
2608 Parkmont Street   21
St. Louis, MO 63107   25
↓2
Release February 14, 19--   30
↓3

MFC HOLDS ~~ITS~~ ANNUAL MEETING   35
↓3

St. Louis, MO, Feb.12--The Missouri Financial Corporation   46

held its annual meeting of shareholders on February 11 in St.   58

Louis. Michael R. McGrath, chairman and chief executive of-   70

ficer, presided at the meeting attended by more than ~~100~~ 200   82

shareholders, directors, and employees. In his opening com-   94

ments, McGrath said, "Last year was indeed a busy year for the   106

Missouri Financial Corporation's employees and directors. We   119

added 11 community banks to our Company, our assets expanded   131

by 43% and our capital increased by 62%."   139

Shareholders were introduced to the new six directors   150

and to the presidents of The Missouri Financial Corporation's   163

new affiliates.   166

Joan D. Hudson, president and chief operations officer for MFC,   178

ended the meeting with a summary of the company's financial   190

performance over the past year.   197

Please retype these minutes. Then make a copy for each officer and one for our file.

If possible, the minutes should be typed on a word processor and stored in case any changes must be made when these minutes are read for approval at the April 10 meeting.

NATIONAL CONFERENCE OF REALTORS
Minutes of the Organizational Meeting
of New Officers
January 4, 19--

Attendance

The organizational meeting of the new officers of the National Conference of Realtors was held in the Conference Room of the headquarters building on Connecticut Ave. in Washington, DC, on Thursday, January 4. June Holden, the Executive Director, welcomed the four officers to headquarters and turned the meeting over to Joseph DiDomenico. Participants at the meeting were: Joseph DiDomenico, President; Linda Lanzi, Vice President; Wayne Johnson, Secretary; Valerie Gancarz, Treasurer; and June Holden, Executive Director.

ADOPTION OF AGENDA

President DiDomenico asked for adoption of the following agenda: Review of minutes; Review of Officer Responsibilities; Treasurer's Report; Executive Board Meeting on April 10 in St. Louis; the Annual Convention in St. Louis, on June 14–16; and Publications Schedule. This agenda was voted on and approved.

Review of Minutes

The minutes of the Executive Board meeting held at the conclusion of the annual conference last June 12–14 in Atlanta were reviewed. There was one correction that dealt with the scheduling of the fellowship banquet at the annual convention. At the meeting on June 14, it was decided to hold the fellowship banquet on the last day of the convention, not the next-to-last day as reported in the minutes. The correction was accepted.

TREASURER'S REPORT

Ms. Gancarz reported that the books had been audited by Pearson & Gersh of Washington, D.C., and found to be maintained appropriately. She distributed a written document by the auditors attesting to this fact. She reported that the current checkbook balance was $21,600. She gave all data supporting income and expenditures since last meeting. Review of all receipts and expenditures was completed and accepted.

A lengthy discussion took place regarding dues to be charged in the next membership year, beginning on July 1. After a great deal of much discussion, it was decided to table this question until the entire executive board meets on April 10 in St. Louis. A motion was made to this effect by Ms. Lanzi and was passed unanimously.

(Continued on next page.)

MAGAZINE ARTICLE

Line: 60 spaces
Tab: 5
Spacing: single
Drills: 2 times
Format Guide: 65

Goals: To improve speed and accuracy; to improve proofreading skills; to format a magazine article.

73-A.   WARMUP

S 1 Both of the men may take that bus when they go to the town.
A 2 Five excited girls and boys jumped when Jackie was quizzed.
N 3 Public Radio 64 raised that tower by 25 or 30 feet in 1987.

SKILLBUILDING

73-B.   PROGRESSIVE PRACTICE: NUMBERS

Turn to the Progressive Practice: Numbers routine at the back of the book. Take several 30-second timings, starting at the point where you left off the last time. Record your progress on Workguide page 125.

73-C.   Take a 1-minute timing on each line; compute your speed and count errors.

73-C.   ALPHABET REVIEW: INFREQUENT-LETTER PRACTICE

J 4 Jim got jam on Jack's jacket just as the old jaguar jumped.
5 Jovial Joe joked with Josh while they jogged in torn jeans.
K 6 Kay fell and kicked the black bike over when Kim backed up.
7 Kevin Packard knew that Rick and Kelly liked baked chicken.
  | 1 | 2 | 3 | 4 | 5 | 6 | 7 | 8 | 9 | 10 | 11 | 12

73-D.   DIAGNOSTIC TYPING: ALPHABET

Turn to the Diagnostic Typing: Alphabet routine at the back of the book. Take the Pretest and record your performance on Workguide page 125. Then practice the drill lines for those reaches on which you made errors.

73-E.   Compare these paragraphs with the second and third paragraphs in the news release on page 150. Type a list of the words that contain errors, correcting the errors as you type.

73-E.   PRODUCTION PRACTICE: PROOFREADING

8 In his opening comments, Mcgrath said, Last year was
9 indeed a busy year for the Missouri Financial Corporations
10 employees and directors. We added 12 community banks to our
11 company, our assets expended by 43 percent, and our capitol
12 increased by 62 per cent."
13 Share holders were introduced to the six new directors'
14 and to the presidents of the Missouri Financial Corpera-
15 tions new affiliates.

MEMO 20 — Paper: Plain

Our membership statistics have now been finalized for the past year. All executive board members are eager to have this information. Prepare the following memo that can be sent to each board member, along with the second table on page 242.

TO: Executive Board Members   7

FROM: June Holden, Executive Director   15

SUBJECT: Membership Statistics   21

DATE: January 8, 19--   27

I have just received the final numbers for our membership statistics the   35 / 42
past year. We had a total increase of   50
468 members in our four regions, which   58
represented a 2.9 percent gain. Our   65
records show a total of 16,620 members   73
compared with 16,152 from the previous   81
year.   82

Data for each region show an increase of   90
131 members in the East, 214 in the   97
South, and 215 in the West. The Midwest   105
showed a decrease of 92 members. Our   113
percentage changes ranged from +5.8   120
percent to -2.4 percent.   125

When our Executive Board   132
meeting in April in St. Louis, we will   140
discuss our membership goals for this   148
year and adopt objectives to be reached   156
for each region.   159

¶ Overall, I am pleased with these numbers;   166
however, I realize that we must be more   172
aggressive in our membership drive   178
this year.   184

LETTER 58 — BLOCK STYLE — Paper: Workguide 265–266

Type the following letter to the four officers listed in the directory on page 236 (DiDomenico, Lanzi, Johnson, and Gancarz). Include all four names and addresses on the one letter (two inside addresses blocked at the left; 2 inside addresses beginning at the center). Use the four first names as part of the salutation.

I thought that our organizational   6
meeting for the new officers went   12
smoothly on January 4. It was   19
good to have all of you on site;   25
my office staff was excited about   32
having the officers meet in our   38
office complex.   42
A check to cover the expenses   48
that you incurred for attending   54
the January 4 meeting has been   60
requested. You should receive   66
it within the next few days.   72
Enclosed is a copy of the   78
minutes of the meeting. Please   84
review them and contact me   90
if you have any questions. Of   96
course, we will formally adopt   102
these minutes when we have our   108
Executive Board meeting in   114
St. Louis on April 10.   119
I'm looking forward to seeing   125
you in St. Louis. In the   130
meantime, call me if you have   136
any questions or comments on   145
your assignments for that   147
April meeting.   150

73-F. MAGAZINE ARTICLE

In order to understand the reasons for the format, read the article carefully before typing.

REPORT 27
TWO-PAGE MAGAZINE
ARTICLE

Line: 40 spaces
Tab: 3, center
Spacing: double
Paper: plain, full sheet

Enumerations in a magazine article: (1) indent the first line 3 spaces, (2) begin turnover lines at the left margin, and (3) double-space.

↓13

TIPS FOR PUBLICATION   4
↓2

By Richard T. Parish   8
↓2

(42 lines of 40 spaces)   13
↓3

WHETHER OR NOT a magazine article gets   21
published is often determined by the appear-   30
ance of the typed manuscript. Many busy edi-   39
tors will not waste their time reading poorly   48
arranged or poorly typed manuscripts. They   57
receive many articles, far more than they can   66
read or publish. Therefore, it is in your best   75
interest to do a professional job when prepar-   85
ing your material for review.   90

There lies the secret of getting your maga-   99
zine article in print: Convince the editor that   109
the article was written by a professional for the   119
particular magazine that the editor manages.   127
↓3

FORMAT AND STYLE   130
↓2

In order to convince the editor, you must pre-   139
pare a quality manuscript. It must look profes-   149
sional. Here are a few suggestions: 156
1. Use quality typing paper.   162
2. Determine the average line length used   170

in the columns of the magazine. Use that line   180
length in your article, and do not exceed that   189
line length by more than 2 spaces on any one   198
line.   199
3. Indicate the total number of lines in your   208
article.   210
4. Double-space the article. Leave 2 blank   219
lines after each section of the article.   227
5. Type the author's name and the page   235
number on all pages.   239
6. Follow the style used for articles in the   248
magazine. This includes any distinctive fea-   257
tures, such as side headings.   263
↓3

THE END RESULT   266
↓2

If this seems like a lot of work, it is. But re-   276
member, the extra time and effort may be the   285
factors that determine whether or not your   293
magazine article is published.   299

(END)   300

```
                        Parish / 2

        1.  Use quality typing paper.
        2.  Determine the average line length
```

```
        may be the factors that determine
        whether or not your magazine article
        is published.
                    (END)
```

Continuation Pages of a Magazine Manuscript
1. Use the same line length as on page 1.
2. Type the heading (author's last name, a diagonal, and the page number) on line 7 at the right margin.
3. Triple-space before beginning to type the text.

LETTERS 56–57
BLOCK STYLE WITH OPEN PUNCTUATION

Paper: Workguide 255–258

I received requests from two members for our Pamphlet 86-510, *Adjustable-Rate Mortgages.* Please send the following letter to these two individuals, making appropriate changes in the inside address and salutation:

Mr. Jorge Gonzalez / Chula Vista Real Estate / 9
15 Vallecito Road / Chula Vista, CA 92012   16

Mrs. Roseanne Rinaldi / Land Development,   8
Inc. / 28 South Maple Street / Blacksburg, VA   16
24060   17

Dear   21

Your request for pamphlet 86-510, Ad-   28
justable-Rate Mortgages, has been re-   36
ceived and processed. You should ~~get~~ it   45
         receive
within the next few days.   50

Since the article dealing with ARM was   57
in our newsletter in November, we have   65
     numerous
had ~~many~~ requests from members like you   74
who wanted to have a copy of ~~this~~ pam-   81
          the
phlet.   83

If you have any questions about the   90
information included in the ~~pamphlet,~~   97
feel free to write directly to the au-   105
thor, whoÍse address appears on the   112
     of the   *requested*
inside front cover. She has ~~asked~~ that   122
we inform our membership of her will-   130
ingness to hear from readers.   135

Plans are moving along for our annual   143
conference, to be held June 14-16 at the   151
Redbird Hotel in St. Louis. Dr. Susan   159
Marki, author of the ARM pamphlet, will   167
be on the program; it would be a nice   175
~~chance~~ for you to meet her in person. I   184
hope you will plan to be with us.   190
opportunity   225

PS: We currently have a campaign   232
under way to recruit new members.   239
Encourage a professional acquaintance to   247
join our group.   250

FORMS 23–26
VOUCHER CHECKS

Paper: Workguide 259–261

The four officers of the association met in Washington, D.C., on January 4 to plan for the executive board meeting to be held in St. Louis on April 10 and to begin making preliminary plans for the national convention to be held June 14–16. Although we paid for their food and lodging while they were here, we still owe them for additional expenses that they incurred. Please total the amount due for each officer and prepare a voucher check for each one. Include the name and address on each check stub as well as a short explanation of what the check is for.

DiDomenico	Plane fare	$154.00
	Ground transportation	27.00
	Miscellaneous	6.50
Lanzi	Plane fare	$210.00
	Ground transportation	21.00
Johnson	Plane fare	$335.00
	Ground transportation	26.50
Gancarz	Plane fare	$347.00
	Ground transportation	28.00
	Miscellaneous	7.00

FORMS 27–28
PURCHASE ORDERS

Paper: Workguide 263

Type purchase orders for the following two orders that I have processed. Compute the total amount for each item by multiplying the number of units by the unit price, and then be sure to add all the amounts to figure the total amount of the purchase order. *Jan. 8*

PURCHASE ORDER 599. Order the following items from Gardner Office Supplies, 1430 Iowa Avenue, NW, Washington, DC 20015: 12 DCT ribbons @ $6.50 each (catalog number 5238-A); 4 cartons of *78.00* line printer paper, blue (No. 4173-B) @ $48 each; *192.00* and 20 double-sided disks (No. 6134-A) @ $2.40 *48.00* each.

PURCHASE ORDER 600. Order the following items from Devoe Computer Equipment, 157 South Pierpont Street, Vienna, VA 22180: 1 printer stand (No. 347) @ $95; 2 rolltop file containers (No. 741) @ $45; and 1 microstation table (No. 566) @ $175. *90.00*

Line: 60 spaces
Tab: 5
Spacing: single
Drills: 2 times
Workguide: 150
Format Guide: 67

LESSON
74

BOOK MANUSCRIPT

Goals: To type 42 wam/5'/5e; to format book manuscript pages.

74-A. WARMUP

S 1 Chan now works at the bake shop right next to the big park.
A 2 Vicky walked back for that amazingly exquisite prize jewel.
N 3 I need 10 mitts, 29 gloves, 38 bats, 47 balls, and 56 caps.

SKILLBUILDING

74-B. Take a 1-minute timing on each line; compute your speed and count errors.

74-B. ALPHABET REVIEW: INFREQUENT-LETTER PRACTICE

Q 4 She quickly questioned Quentin's request for equal quality.
5 Quincy quietly quoted the quip about the quartet's quarrel.
X 6 Maxine exhibited all except six boxes of extra onyx stones.
7 Max fixed those taxi exits for the six excited taxi owners.
   | 1 | 2 | 3 | 4 | 5 | 6 | 7 | 8 | 9 | 10 | 11 | 12

74-C. Spacing: double. Record your score.

74-C. SKILL MEASUREMENT: 5-MINUTE TIMED WRITING

8   There are some office workers who are quite naive with 12
9 respect to both diet and exercise habits. By the middle of 24
10 the morning, they are practically worn out; and the rest of 36
11 the day gets worse and worse. One reason is that doughnuts 48
12 and a giant cup of coffee are no substitute for a wholesome 60
13 breakfast. A sound breakfast along with a nutritious lunch 72
14 can supply the energy that is needed for a full day's work. 84
15   The common opinion that the evening meal should be the 96
16 big meal is just not supported by most food experts. Their 108
17 views are based on the idea that we need less energy during 120
18 the evening and when sleeping. Some folks are quite amazed 132
19 after becoming aware that some dietitians recommend as many 144
20 as six meals per day. Of course, the one catch is that the 156
21 meals must be modest; calorie totals are what really count. 168
22   Good eating habits and a regular exercise schedule are 180
23 just what the doctor ordered. The worker will have the pep 192
24 needed to perform an entire day's work; physical and mental 204
25 health are positively affected. 210
   | 1 | 2 | 3 | 4 | 5 | 6 | 7 | 8 | 9 | 10 | 11 | 12

INTEGRATED OFFICE PROJECT: NATIONAL CONFERENCE OF REALTORS

Situation: Today is Monday, January 8, 19—. You are working as an administrative assistant to Ms. June Holden, executive director of the National Conference of Realtors, located in Washington, D.C. Ms. Holden is responsible for handling all aspects of the work done by the organization. For example, she is responsible for keeping membership records current, for planning and organizing the annual convention, for preparing all publications and correspondence from headquarters, and for supervising the day-to-day activities of the office. She prefers the block letter style, with open punctuation and these closing lines:

Sincerely yours

June Holden
Executive Director

You are expected to make a copy of everything that you type. All typewritten copy should be in mailable form.

REPORT 48
DIRECTORY

Paper: plain
Spacing: single

Prepare a directory with the names and addresses of all members of the new executive board. This directory will replace pages 8 and 9 of last year's operations manual, so use those same page numbers with the side heading *Directory of Executive Board Members* on line 7 opposite the page number. Block-center the names and addresses. Type *Revised 1/19—* centered at the bottom of both pages.

<u>President</u>

Mr. Joseph DiDomenico
DiDomenico Realty Company
1572 Winston Street
Harrisburg, PA 17103
(717) 555-4807

<u>Vice President</u>

Mrs. ~~Loretta~~ Linda Lanzi
Windsor Realty
57 Winding Way ~~Blvd.~~
Windsor, CT ~~60950~~ 06095
(203) 555-6589

<u>Secretary</u>

Mr. Wayne Johnston
Breckenridge Real Estate
15 Lone Star ~~Road~~ Highway
Amarillo, TX 79102
(806) 555-2431

<u>Treasurer</u>

Ms. Valerie Gancarz
Lake Realty
R.D. 3, Box ~~81~~ 18
Brainerd, MN 56401
(218) 555-6834

<u>Regional Delegates:</u>
East, Midwest, South, West

Ms. ~~Christina~~ Tina Walsh
The Kramer Group
78 Oak Ridge ~~Street~~ Road
Albany, NY 12201
(518) 555-6004

Mrs. Hilda M. Lopez
Pashman Realty Company
3110 Lincoln Highway
Springfield, IL 62702
(217) 555-8844

Mr. ~~Hal~~ Harold Kessler
Bradgate Associates
17 Magnolia Drive
Shreveport, LA 71103
(318) 555-~~2550~~ 3345

Mr. James Yang
Yang Realtors
157 Vanderbilt Freeway
Spokane, WA 99204
(509) 555-1785

<u>Executive Director</u>

Ms. June Holden
National Conference of Realtors
127 Connecticut Avenue, Suite 110
Washington, DC 20015
(202) 555-1804

74-D. BOOK MANUSCRIPTS

(1) Book manuscripts are typed in standard "bound report" form. (2) Listings (other than numbered paragraphs) are single-spaced and indented 5 spaces. (3) The title of the book or chapter or the chapter number is identified in a condensed "running head" of two or three words typed in all capitals at the left margin on a line with the page number.

Note: For this job use the visual guide for bound reports on Workguide page 150.

REPORT 28
TWO-PAGE BOOK
MANUSCRIPT

Line: 6 inches (60 pica/70 elite)
Tab: 5
Spacing: double
Paper: plain
Visual guide: Workguide 150

CHAPTER 6   Page 125   3
                                          ↓3

You can do a great deal to help yourself   12
when you are interviewed for a job. The inter-   21
view is not a situation where the interviewer is   31
in total control and you are just a nervous and   40
helpless interviewee. If you try to remember   50
some dos and don'ts of interviewing, you will   59
increase your chances of being offered the   67
position you really want.   72
                         ↓3

Before the Interview   76

There are a number of things that you can   85
do in advance to prepare for the actual inter-   94
view. Some of these are as follows: 101

1. Practice your interviewing skills. Prepare   111
answers to questions that you think might be   120
asked. If feasible, have someone else ask the   129
questions as you hold a simulated interview.   138

2. Do some research on the company to   146
which you are applying. Some sources of infor-   155
mation are the library, civic organizations, and   165
the company itself.   169

3. Speak with your references. Let them   177
know the types of jobs for which you are ap-   186

plying so that they can make clear and relevant   196
recommendations.   199

4. Dress appropriately for the interview.   208
Use extreme care in the selection of your out-   217
fit. Your clothes should be comfortable, attrac-   227
tive, and appropriate for the business office.   236

5. Arrive a few minutes early for the inter-   245
view.   246
     ↓3

During the Interview   250

A good interview is like a pleasant conversa-   259
tion. It is a two-way process—an exchange of   268
information guided by polite questions. Be   277
prepared to ask a few questions yourself and to   287
answer a great many. A good answer is not   295
necessarily a brief one; the interviewer wants   305
you to give some long answers to indicate how   314
verbal you are, how poised you are, and   322
whether you have done your homework about   330
the company.   333
           ↓3

After the Interview   336

Within 24 hours you should have neatly   344
typed thank-you letters in the mail to those   353
people in the firm with whom you had signifi-   362
cant contact. These letters should be short but   372
personalized.   375

How long should you wait before inquiring   383
about the results of an interview? There is no   393
set answer to this. You might be wise to ask,   402
during the interview, when you might expect   411
to hear whether you got the job.   417

L. Retype this notice, correcting the errors as you type.

L. PRODUCTION PRACTICE: PROOFREADING

46 Our new mail service will begin on Monday, Febuary 17. It
47 is essential that all of are administrative support workers
48 have a through understanding of this new proceedure. To be
49 sure that everyone fully understands this new system, it is
50 necesary that you attend an orientation meeting on Monday,
51 Febuary 3, so that you will have all the particulars about
52 this new system. Call Debbie at 5147 if you can not attend.

M. Spacing: double. Record your score.

M. SKILL MEASUREMENT: 5-MINUTE TIMED WRITING

53   A major skill needed by all managers is the ability to   12

54 solve problems. The first step in that regard requires the   24

55 person to recognize the problem and to define it. Once the   36

56 problem is well defined, it is much easier to solve for all   48

57 concerned.   50

58   After the problem has been defined, it is essential to   62

59 get as much data as possible. Answers to questions of why,   74

60 when, how, who, what, and where can be extremely helpful in   86

61 allowing one to get the type of information needed to solve   98

62 a problem.   100

63   Once the relevant information has been collected, then   112

64 it is time to do a careful analysis to be sure that all the   124

65 data is understood. It is during this process that most of   136

66 the real learning about the problem takes place. This step   148

67 is critical.   150

68   Developing possible solutions to the problem is now in   162

69 order. Usually, there might be a number of ways in which a   174

70 problem might be solved. After careful thought, one choice   186

71 is made for the best way to solve the problem that has been   198

72 identified.   200

73   The final steps to be taken in solving a given problem   212

74 are to implement the chosen solution and then to be sure to   224

75 evaluate how well the solution is working. Managers should   236

76 be ready to go through the above steps when hoping to solve   248

77 a problem.   250

   | | | 2 | 3 | 4 | 5 | 6 | 7 | 8 | 9 | 10 | 11 | 12

BOOK MANUSCRIPT

Line: 60 spaces
Tab: 5
Spacing: single
Drills: 2 times
Format Guide: 67

Goals: To improve speed and accuracy; to format book manuscript pages with a table.

75-A. WARMUP

S 1 Heidi may lend the girl a pair of blue socks when she goes.
A 2 The girl squeezed pink tubes as May joined five wax pieces.
N 3 Exactly 463 of the 587 pens had been sold on May 19 and 20.

SKILLBUILDING

75-B. DIAGNOSTIC TYPING: NUMBERS

Turn to the Diagnostic Typing: Numbers routine at the back of the book. Take the Pretest, and record your performance on Workguide page 125. Then practice the drill lines for those reaches on which you made errors.

75-C. Take a 1-minute timing on each line; compute your speed and count errors.

75-C. ALPHABET REVIEW: INFREQUENT-LETTER PRACTICE

Y 4 Yes, they very nearly bought my yellow submarine yesterday.
5 You may see twenty lively young donkeys in many tiny yards.
Z 6 Liz and Buzz zoomed over and seized a sizable dozing zebra.
7 A dozen zany zealots zigzagged past a hazy frozen zoo zone.
| 1 | 2 | 3 | 4 | 5 | 6 | 7 | 8 | 9 | 10 | 11 | 12

75-D. PACED PRACTICE

Turn to the Paced Practice routine at the back of the book. Take several 2-minute timings, starting at the point where you left off the last time. Record your progress on Workguide page 125.

75-E. Make two copies. Copy 1: Type each sentence on a separate line. Copy 2: Type each sentence on a separate line, but tab-indent it 5 spaces.

75-E. TECHNIQUE TYPING: RETURN/ENTER AND TAB KEYS

8 Were those New York teams there? Yes, the Giants and Jets.
9 Did you see Los Angeles teams? I saw the Raiders and Rams.
10 And Chicago and Green Bay? Yes, the Bears and the Packers.
11 Any New England teams? Those Patriots represent them well.
12 What do you think of Minnesota? The Vikings are my choice.

13 Do they play basketball in Boston? The Celtics are superb.
14 Where do the Lakers play ball? They call Los Angeles home.
15 Did I see the Rockets and Supersonics? Yes, and the Bucks.
16 Which Southern teams do you enjoy? Atlanta is my favorite.
17 Does the Motor city have a team? The Pistons keep pumping.

18 Are there any Sox teams? I see both the Red and the White.
19 Where are the Pirates? They play home games in Pittsburgh.
20 They saw Indians in Cleveland? Yes, and Braves in Atlanta.
21 Which city backs those Brewers? Why, Milwaukee, of course.
22 What do you think of Minnesota? The Twins are my favorite.

G. ALPHABET REVIEW

16 Bored junior executives request help from weekly magazines.
17 Seizing the wax buffers, Joseph quickly removed a big spot.
18 The banquet speaker, James Boxell, analyzed a few carvings.

H. Tab: Every 12 spaces.

H. TECHNIQUE TYPING: TAB KEY

Alphabet

19 Susan	Patricia	Rosalie	Maria	Charlotte
20 Roberto	Thomas	Frank	Mark	Donald
21 Chicago	Boston	Atlanta	Miami	Las Vegas
22 Oregon	Iowa	Maine	Arizona	Alabama

Number/Symbol

23 2,221	7,892	6,453	8,056	9,314
24 4,567	8,732	9,013	1,197	5,018
25 $3.56	66.3%	(342)	#3127	5'10"
26 2 @ $5	1,034	$7.64	(PAL)	A & D

I. Type the paragraph, untangling the word transpositions.

I. CONCENTRATION PRACTICE

27   There been has a big increase in number the of workers
28 who employed are today by temporary agencies. This is fact
29 confirmed reviewing by the ads found in papers local and by
30 checking managers with of some local personnel departments.

J. This drill gives practice in typing words that end in *ar*, *er*, and *or*.

J. PRODUCTION PRACTICE: SPELLING

31 beggar calendar circular dollar regular similar spectacular
32 border employer prisoner writer voucher partner shareholder
33 debtor neighbor elevator doctor visitor auditor commentator

K. Take a 1-minute timing on the first paragraph to establish your base speed. Then take several 1-minute timings on the other paragraphs. As soon as you equal or exceed your base speed on one paragraph, advance to the next one.

K. SUSTAINED TYPING: NUMBERS

34 A committee was appointed in order to begin making the   12
35 plans for our annual meeting. It was made up of 12 members   24
36 from the Hills Region, 10 from Valley, and 8 from Stanhope.   36
37 The members in charge of exhibits are hoping to invite   12
38 34 exhibitors to utilize 50 booths in Convention Hall at 87   24
39 Midway. Last year we had 26 exhibitors at this conference.   36
40 The members in charge of the luncheon are hoping for a   12
41 total of 350 persons for lunch at $17.50 each. Last year a   24
42 ticket cost $16.40 for all those who attended the luncheon.   36
43 Attendance at last year's meeting was 1,230. The goal   12
44 for this year is to have 1,410 people. This will enable us   24
45 to project an increase of 180 people, a 14.63 percent rise.   36

| 1 | 2 | 3 | 4 | 5 | 6 | 7 | 8 | 9 | 10 | 11 | 12 |

75-F.   BOOK MANUSCRIPT WITH TABLE

As a table is to be inserted after the second paragraph of this manuscript, review the for-mat for an open table with blocked column headings at the bottom of page 135.

REPORT 29
TWO-PAGE BOOK
MANUSCRIPT WITH TABLE

Shown in pica
Line: 6 inches (60 pica/70 elite)
Tab: 5, center
Spacing: double
Paper: plain
Spacing for table: single

Leave 3 blank lines before and after a table in a book manuscript when it has a table number.

WP
   Many word pro-cessors allow you to put a code above and below a table so that it will not be divided between two pages.

SOFTWARE SALES TREND   Page 84   4
                                                          ↓3

As more and more typewriters are replaced by personal   15
computers, there is a greater need for software programs that   27
will adapt the computers for service as word processors for   39
business correspondence and reports.   46
   Accordingly, the sales of software programs are steadily   58
increasing also. The sales figures for one company, shown in   70
Table 4-C below, indicate the company's sales of its four main   83
types of software over a two-year period. In three of the   95
four categories, there were remarkable gains. The fourth type 107
(Database) lost ground slightly.   114
                                   ↓4

Table 4-C   115

SOFTWARE SALES COMPARISONS   121

Software	1987	1988	
Word Processing	728	952	128
Spreadsheets	372	492	131
Graphics	433	476	133
Data base	257	236	136

124

                                        ↓4

Word Processing. Sales of word processing packages rose   147
dramatically from 728 to 952, a 30.77 percent gain in a single 160
year.   161
   Spreadsheets. Business firms are becoming aware of how   172
easily financial data can be interpreted with a spreadsheet   184
program in a personal computer in lieu of the laborious use of 197
a calculator. Accordingly, sales are steadily rising.   208
   Graphics. Sales of graphics packages are also growing as   219
businesses discover the ease with which such packages can   231
translate data into many forms of charts and graphs.   241
   Database. Business has not yet warmed to database pro-   252
grams as wholeheartedly as to the other types. However, the   264
future of database programs is assured, and sales will mush-   276
room as manual filing systems are replaced by software that   288
makes the storage and retrieval of records simple and speedy.   301

UNIT **23**

Line: 60 spaces
Tab: 5, center
Spacing: single
Drills: 2 times
Workguide: 255–266
Format Guide: 103

INTEGRATED OFFICE PROJECT—ADMINISTRATIVE

GOALS FOR UNIT 23

1. To type 50 wam for 5 minutes with no more than 5 errors.
2. To format letters in block style.
3. To format voucher checks and purchase orders, performing simple mathematical calculations.
4. To format minutes of a meeting.
5. To format a magazine article.
6. To format a memo and tables.

A.   WARMUP

S 1   Kay goes to work for the audit firm by the eighth of April.
A 2   The very next question emphasized the growing lack of jobs.
N 3   Last night's attendance was 18,354; tonight we have 20,679.

SKILLBUILDING

PRETEST. Take a 1-minute timing; compute your speed and count errors.

B.   PRETEST: COMMON LETTER COMBINATIONS

4   We were careful to pick forty capable persons to serve   12
5   on the committee. Some complex questions concerning upkeep   24
6   of the condos were to be part of the discussions. A former   36
7   member made a motion to table the motion on building plans.   48
    | 1 | 2 | 3 | 4 | 5 | 6 | 7 | 8 | 9 | 10 | 11 | 12

PRACTICE.
   Speed Emphasis: If you made 2 or fewer errors on the Pretest, type each line twice.
   Accuracy Emphasis: If you made 3 or more errors on the Pretest, type each group of lines (as though it were a paragraph) twice.

C.   PRACTICE: WORD BEGINNINGS

8   for forty forth format former forget forest forearm forbear
9   con condo conic contra confer convey concur concern condemn
10 per peril perky period permit person peruse perform persist
11 com combo comic combat commit common combed compose complex

D.   PRACTICE: WORD ENDINGS

12 ing doing mixing living filing taping sending biking hiding
13 ble cable nimble fumble dabble bobble capable marble mumble
14 ion onion nation lotion motion option mention fusion legion
15 ful awful useful joyful earful lawful helpful sinful armful

POSTTEST. Repeat the Pretest and compare performance.

E.   POSTTEST: COMMON LETTER COMBINATIONS

F.   PACED PRACTICE

Turn to the Paced Practice routine at the back of the book. Take several 2-minute timings, starting at the point where you left off the last time. Record your progress on Workguide page 126.

LESSON 76

OPEN AND RULED TABLES

Line: 60 spaces
Tab: 5
Spacing: single
Drills: 2 times
Format Guide: 69

Goals: To type 43 wam/5'/5e; to format open and ruled tables.

76-A. WARMUP

S 1 That make of yacht may be the type that wins the big prize.
A 2 Jim quickly used up a single box of yellow razors to shave.
N 3 Our plane leaves from Gate 19 or 20 at either 7:53 or 8:46.

SKILLBUILDING

76-B. PACED PRACTICE

Turn to the Paced Practice routine at the back of the book. Take several 2-minute timings, starting at the point where you left off the last time. Record your progress on Workguide page 125.

76-C. Spacing: double. Record your score.

76-C. SKILL MEASUREMENT: 5-MINUTE TIMED WRITING

4   Wearing the proper clothes on the job will help you to   12
5   project a professional image; it is important, accordingly,   24
6   that you select and wear only quality clothing that will be   36
7   fresh and stylish for a long time.   43
8   It is also important that you dress and groom yourself   55
9   to match the level of your colleagues in an office: a case   67
10 of "keeping up with the Joneses." Do not dress much better   79
11 or less well than your coworkers.   86
12 Note also that the level of formality in dress depends   98
13 to some extent on the work done in your office. Executives   110
14 near the boardroom and their aides dress more formally than   122
15 artists in the advertising office.   129
16 Your first few days in the office will familiarize you   141
17 with the "code" of that office and give you some guidelines   153
18 you need for any modifications in your wardrobe that are to   165
19 be achieved to attain that "code."   172
20 Until you are cognizant of what is expected and have a   184
21 few salary checks in hand, it is wise to wear conservative,   196
22 classic business clothing and a minimum of accessories. It   208
23 is always safe to accent quality.   215

| 1 | 2 | 3 | 4 | 5 | 6 | 7 | 8 | 9 | 10 | 11 | 12 |

andthe evaluation has been completed, a new or improved salary   14

structure can be made so that every employee is equitibly   26

compensated. Tedesco and Mitchell (1974) further say that the   40

value of the job to the organizations is a major factor of   53

salary level. Other factors (Quible and Hyslop, 1984) that   62

should been sondered as going rates, the cost-of-living   73

index; leglisation, and collective bargining. Once all of the   86

factors have been considred; then salary ranges can be estab-   98

lished for the many job levels. The Following table is an   110

example of salary ranges for Buck Hardware Company.   120

Table 12   122

BIWEEKLY Salary Ranges   126

Job Level	Other Firms	Salary Ranges		
		Low	Medium	High
1	# 485	# 425	# 450	# 500	139
2	514	470	500	550	141
3	583	540	560	600	144
4	673	595	640	725	147
5	763	700	750	815	149

A regular schedule of (ranges salary) would show more job   160

levels; however, each job level should include those jobs   172

which have corresponding values to the organizations. For   183

example, Level 4 might include the secretary III and computer   196

II levels. The various jobs in each levels must be clerally   209

defined for all workers.   215

Please retype this page of the report I am writing for the home office. 77

76-D. OPEN AND RULED TABLES

Type Tables 19 and 20. Center each table on a full sheet of plain paper.

TABLE 19
OPEN TABLE WITH BLOCKED
COLUMN HEADINGS

Spacing: single
Paper: plain, full sheet

REGIONAL SALES COMPARISONS ↓2   5

January 19-- ↓3   8

Item	Region I	Region II	Region III	
110A	$21,707	$34,883	$ 32,664	19
120A	12,819	9,274	14,560	23
240B	5,114	6,932	24,646	27
270B	15,813	12,933	40,548	32
280B	10,001	11,295	2,746	36
330C	4,888	2,752	5,507	40
360C	3,917	3,921	6,775	43
TOTAL	$74,259	$81,990	$127,446	49

TABLE 20
RULED TABLE WITH CENTERED
COLUMN HEADINGS

Spacing: single
Paper: plain, full sheet

Notes
1. Horizontal placement is the same as in an open table.
2. The parts of the table are divided by horizontal rules.
3. A ruled line is preceded and followed by 1 blank line; therefore, single-space before typing it and double-space after typing it.
4. Column headings are not underscored separately.
5. All horizontal rules extend to the edges of the table.
6. Periods are typed across the width of a column to show that there is no entry.

↓23   SALES QUOTAS   2

↓2

Second Quarter, 19-- ↓1   6

Sales Manager	Region	Quota	
Burns, David S.	New England	$1,102,000	18
Chan, Chew Wah	Eastern	1,156,000	24
Getzen, Patti K.	Southern	1,114,000	31
Ludwig, Adele G.	North-Central	993,000	38
O'Brien, Sean F.	Plains	886,000	44
Oja, Gregory J.	Southwest	1,156,000	51
Upton, Gwen M.	Rocky Mountain	987,000	58
Woodbridge, Phillip J.	Western	1,134,000	65
TOTAL	.............(14)	$8,528,000	71

REPORT 46
MINUTES OF A MEETING

Paper: plain

Minutes of a meeting are a report of the business transacted at the meeting.

BUCK HARDWARE ~~OFFICE STAFF~~ MEETING   5
Aurora Storee   8
Minutes of the Meeting   12
May 5, 19--   14

The Buck Hawrdware staff of the Aurora store   23
held its monthly meeting on May 5, 19-- at   32
8:30 a.m. in the first-floor lounge. Franecs   41
Fowler presided.   44

ATTENDANCE

Put names in alphabetic order

Staff members present were Thomas Egegn, Vera   55
Case, Amy Jones, Clara Swihart, Clinton Jones,   64
Lyle Mason, and Gordon Thomas. *Add Susan Melnick*   74

MINUTES
APPROVED

The minutes of the April 3, 19--, meeting were   85
approved and read.   90

MANAGER'S
REPORT

Frances Fowler stated that she had met with the   101
vice president for sales, in the home office,   112
and was pleased to report ~~the~~ that the Aurora store   121
had topped its sales quota for the year. ~~to date~~.   131
She indicated that if sales continued at the   140
present pace, the Aurora sotre will again be   149
~~the~~ a pace maker store.   152

UNFINISHED
BUSINESS

Thomas Eggen reported that the computer system   164
would be in   168
operation by June 1. He indicated   177
that the store would save money through the   186
simplification of maintaining inventory con-   194
trol and sales. *with such a system.* He ~~indicated~~ stated that he would   203
soon be making a report to the home office.   213

NEW
BUSINESS

It was agreed that the annual summer sale would   223
be conducted the week of July 20. Vera Case,   234
as usual, will be instrumental in the promotion   244
of this sale.   246

ADJOURNMENT

The meeting was ajdourned at 10:00 a.m.   256

Respectfully submitted,   261

Clara Swihart, Secretary   266

Retype these minutes in final form for Clara. They are OK as far as I am concerned. 77

LESSON 77

RULED TABLES

Goals: To improve speed and accuracy; to format ruled tables.

77-A. WARMUP

S 1 Janet got the eight big maps and a box of pens at the park.
A 2 Pop was vexed when Liz jointly bought a famous rock quarry.
N 3 She typed 83 letters, 176 memos, 49 reports, and 205 notes.

SKILLBUILDING

77-B. PROGRESSIVE PRACTICE: NUMBERS

Turn to the Progressive Practice: Numbers routine at the back of the book. Take several 30-second timings, starting at the point where you left off the last time. Record your progress on Workguide page 125.

77-C. TECHNIQUE TYPING: TAB KEY

77-C. Clear all tabs. Then set four new tab stops every 12 spaces from the left margin. Type each line, tabulating across from column to column.

4 Dobson	Baraga	Alaska	17,321	42,689
5 Henley	Fenton	Hawaii	51,702	20,694
6 Jellis	Owosso	Kansas	38,569	37,700
7 Knight	Rumely	Nevada	48,518	43,861
8 Pelnar	Warren	Oregon	24,570	39,652

77-D. PRETEST: HORIZONTAL REACHES

PRETEST. Take a 1-minute timing; compute your speed and count errors.

9   Three peppy caddies and three happy adults watched her   12
10 wrap his wrist. A bough on the upper south side had fallen   24
11 on his arm. Gail opened up the gate so the farm boys could   36
12 take the young man to the hospital in the new pickup truck.   48
    | 1 | 2 | 3 | 4 | 5 | 6 | 7 | 8 | 9 | 10 | 11 | 12

77-E. PRACTICE: IN REACHES

PRACTICE.
   Speed Emphasis: If you made no more than 1 error on the Pretest, type each line twice.
   Accuracy Emphasis: If you made 2 or more errors on the Pretest, type each group of lines (as though it were a paragraph) twice.

13 wr wrap wren writ wrath wreck wring wrist write wrong wrote
14 ou ouch ours oust trout south tough proud sound bough dough
15 ad adds toad read trade radio bread adult tread caddy radar
16 py copy pyro pyre soapy happy poppy pylon pygmy peppy puppy

77-F. PRACTICE: OUT REACHES

17 yo your yoke yoga young youth yowls yodel yokel yours yolks
18 fa fame farm fact fault faith sofas fable fakes fades famed
19 up upon cups pups upend upper group upped upset rupee super
20 ga gate gaze gale gable gavel sugar gains gauge gaffe legal

77-G. POSTTEST: HORIZONTAL REACHES

POSTTEST. Repeat the Pretest and compare performance.

REPORT 44
MEETING AGENDA

Paper: plain

An agenda is a list of the items of business to be discussed at a meeting in the order in which they will be discussed. It is prepared (and sometimes distributed) prior to the meeting.

Retype on a full sheet for duplication. 77

BUCK HARDWARE STAFF MEETING   5

Aurora Stores   8

June 10, 19--   10

1. Approval of minutes of May 5 meeting.   18

2. Progress report on building ~~edition~~ addition and ~~expansion of~~ expanded   31
   parking lot: Norman Hedges.   35

3. Discussion ~~on~~ of attendance at the National Hardware Associ-   47
   ation's annual ~~session.~~ meeting   *Thomas*   52

4. Computer ~~installation~~ operations update: ~~T.~~ Eggan.   61

5. Home office visit: Jay Hoff.   67

        Frances Fowler   70
        Manager   72

REPORT 45
ITINERARY

Paper: plain

An itinerary is a schedule listing dates, times, and places.

MS FRANCES FOWLER   4

Itinerary for home office visit   — Center   10

June 10, 19--   12

8:15- 9:00	BREAKFAST .... Cafeteria	23
	Mr. Joseph Bird, president, host.	36
9:30-11:30 (30)	NEW PRODUCTS .... Room A	41
	Mr. Jay Hoff, Vice President for Sales,	49
	and staff will present new products to	57
	be sold through out let stores.	63
12:00- 1:30	LUNCH .... Cafeteria	74
2:00- 3:00	COMPUTER OPERATIONS UPDATE .... ~~Computer Center~~ Room A	85
	Mr. Paul Slocum, computer operations,	93
	will discuss new company-wide policies	100
	for computer confidentiality operations.	109
3:30- ~~4:30~~ 5:00	ACCOUNTING DEPARTMENT .... Room B	120
	Ms. Doris Vecker, department head, will re-	129
	view current accounting practices.	135

Retype on a full sheet of paper. I will review it when I return on Monday. 77

77-H. RULED TABLES

Type Tables 21–23. Center each table on a full sheet of paper.

TABLE 21
RULED TABLE

Spacing: single
Paper: plain, full sheet

Reminders
1. All horizontal lines extend to the edges of the table.
2. The $ sign must align at the top and bottom of a column.
3. Single-space before a ruled line, and double-space after it.
4. Use periods across the width of a column to show that there is no entry.

| CANDIDATES FOR PROMOTION | | | 5 |
| January 1, 19— | | | 8 |
Name	Title	Salary	11
Arndt, Daniel R.	Comptroller	$ 38,480	18
King, Jon J.	Senior Accountant	29,420	25
Lavine, Rhonda	Secretary	16,210	31
Rogers, Kristin	Chief Accountant	31,567	38
Weber, Kathy M.	Teller	14,890	43
TOTAL	. . . .	$130,567	49

TABLE 22
RULED TABLE

Spacing: single
Paper: plain, full sheet

Arrangement is by the size of the new salary.

| EMPLOYEE PROMOTIONS | | | 4 |
| Effective March 1, 19— | | | 8 |
Name	New Title	New Salary	13
Arndt, Daniel R.	Vice President	$ 48,000	21
Rogers, Kristin	Comptroller	34,500	27
King, Jon J.	Auditor	31,000	32
Lavine, Rhonda	Executive Secretary	19,700	40
Weber, Kathy M.	Secretary	16,500	46
TOTAL	. . . .	$149,700	52

TABLE 23
RULED TABLE

Spacing: single
Paper: plain, full sheet

Arrangement is by the percentage of increase.

Special Note: Unlike the $ sign, the % sign is used with every number if the word *Percent* does not appear in the column heading.

| SALARY INCREASES | | | | 3 |
| Effective March 1, 19-- | | | | 8 |
Name	Old Salary	New Salary	Increase	14
Arndt, Daniel R.	$ 38,480	$ 48,000	24.74%	21
Lavine, Rhonda	16,210	19,700	21.53%	28
Weber, Kathy M.	14,890	16,500	10.81%	34
Rogers, Kristin	31,567	34,500	9.29%	41
King, Jon J.	29,420	31,000	5.37%	47
AVERAGE	. . . .	. . . .	14.35%	52

Arndt, Daniel R. 123456 Old Salary 123456 New Salary 123456 Increase 62

Please type an invoice for the following items. Send to West End Nuts and Bolts, 1432 Broadway, Peoria, IL 61604. Refer to West End's Purchase Order 4682. 12 42-piece tool sets @ $21.50; 15 metric socket sets @ $4.50; 24 chisels @ $4.50; 50 plastic-handled screwdrivers @ $9.40; and one 6-drawer tool chest @ $114.99. Total the amount column, less 10% discount, plus 5% tax.

J.J.

FORM 21
CREDIT MEMORANDUM

Paper: Workguide 251

A *credit memorandum* shows the customer the changes in his or her account balance (for example, if merchandise was returned).

The customer's account is credited; that is, the amount has been deducted from the total owed.

Credit Memorandum

TO: Jonathon Black
     631 East End Street
     Edgewood, IL 64226

DATE:
CREDIT MEMO NO.: 3012
INVOICE NO.: 90599

YOUR ACCOUNT HAS BEEN CREDITED AS FOLLOWS:

Quantity	Cat. No.	Description	Price	Total
3 boxes	H-Z 6732	100-count 8" bolts (wrong size)	9.10	$27.30
		TOTAL		27.30
		LESS 10% TRADE DISCOUNT		3.73
		PLUS TAX AND SHIPPING	Tax O.K.	1.20
		TOTAL AMOUNT CREDITED		24.77

Check calculations and retype.

J.J.

FORM 22
STATEMENT OF ACCOUNT

Paper: Workguide 253

Prepare a statement of account for Black after you complete the credit memorandum. Subtract amount credited account. Complete balance column.

J.J.

Statement of Account
WITH: DATE:

Amount Enclosed
$

Please return this stub with your check.

DATE	REFERENCE	CHARGES	CREDITS	BALANCE
May 1	Brought forward			110.00
5	Invoice No. 93500	600.46		710.46
6	Invoice No. 93545	515.23		1,225.69
10	Payment on account		600.46	625.23
23	Invoice No. 9370	225.39		625.69
25	Payment on account		125.00	850.62
			25.85	851.08
June 3	Credit Memo 3012		—	726.08
				700.31

Pay the last amount in this column.

Line: 60 spaces
Tab: 5
Spacing: single
Drills: 2 times
Format Guide: 71

BOXED TABLES

Goals: To type 43 wam/5'/5e; to format boxed tables.

78-A.   WARMUP

S 1 Spring is a right time to rake the lawn and hose the drive.
A 2 Will Maggie quickly fix veal and pizza before they join us?
N 3 Game #24 of the 1987 season ended with a score of 60 to 53.

SKILLBUILDING

78-B.   PROGRESSIVE PRACTICE: ALPHABET

Turn to the Progressive Practice: Alphabet routine at the back of the book. Take several 30-second timings, starting at the point where you left off the last time. Record your progress on Workguide page 125.

78-C. Spacing: double. Record your score.

78-C.   SKILL MEASUREMENT: 5-MINUTE TIMED WRITING

```
                          1                          2
 4      There are professional organizations for every kind of    12
                     3                          4
 5  career field, including all the different career fields one    24
          5                          6                        7
 6  finds represented in the modern office.  For example, there    36
                  8                              9
 7  are associations for office managers, word processors, per-    48
              10                          11                  12
 8  sonnel directors, records managers, accountants, and dozens    60
                          13                          14
 9  of others.  The question is, why do all these groups exist?    72
                  15                          16
10      The basic answer is that birds of a feather will flock     84
          17                      18                      19
11  together--they always have and always will.  If you operate    96
                  20                          21
12  a computer and are proud of it, it is a pleasure to talk to   108
              22                          23                  24
13  other operators, to learn new things you can squeeze out of   120
                          25                      26
14  your computer, to explain your tricks of the trade, to find   132
                  27                          28
15  out about equipment changes, to discover new career fields.   144
          29                      30                          31
16  These are exciting aspects of the career of a professional.   156
                          32                          33
17      There is a social side too.  People interested in your    168
              34                          35                  36
18  kind of work are likely to be somewhat like you.  You enjoy   180
                          37                          38
19  them, make friendships, look forward to going with your new   192
                  39                          40
20  friends to the conventions and meetings in distant cities--   204
          41                      42                          43
21  a professional society puts zest in your job and life.        215
     |  |  |  2  |  3  |  4  |  5  |  6  |  7  |  8  |  9  |  10  |  11  |  12
```

Mr. Cheung asked me to review this rough-draft copy. It is OK. Since he is out of town, retype it for him. Mr. Cheung prefers the simplified letter style.

~~May~~ June 2, 19--   77   4

Mr. Bruce ~~B.~~ Manning, Manager   9
Joplin Distributors   13
2601 (N.) Meridian Avenue   18
Indianapolis, IN 46204   23

NEW COMPUTERIZED ~~PROGRAMS~~ SYSTEM   27

←On April 3O, 19--, Mr. Thomas Eggen joined us to ~~help us~~ assist   38
in putting all of our ~~store~~ operations on ~~mainframe.~~ a computerized system.   50

As you know, ~~Mr. Manning,~~ Bruce we have ~~grown~~ expanded considerably in ~~past~~ recent   62
years, by adding branch stores in Michigan. While we have utilized   75
computres for some operations, we feel it now would be expe-   87
dient to have ~~all of~~ our entire operations on a main frame to simp~~ily~~ lify   100
our inventory control and ~~distribution.~~ sales You will see some   110
changes within our store's opeartion within the next few month.   123

We are very pleased to have Mr. Eggen with us to ~~aid~~ help in ~~thei~~ this   136
reogranization. You may be hearing from ~~her~~ him with in the   147
month. He will explain the new procedures and how they will af-   160
fect our operations.   164

I am sure that you ~~know~~ are aware that we are the flag ship store ~~for~~ of   176
the Buck Hardware chain. If our new computerized system is suc-   190
cessful, I ~~am sure~~ believe that ~~top~~ management will want to install the   202
system in the other stores.   207

Please feel free to stop in our store the next time you are in   220
Aurora. We would like to have you see ~~the system and~~ what we   229
are able to do with this new computerzied system.   239

Robert Cheung, Controller   245

78-D. BOXED TABLES

In addition to the horizontal lines of a ruled table, a *boxed* table has vertical ruled lines to separate the columns. Type the table as you would a ruled table, including the horizontal ruled lines. After proofreading carefully, draw in the vertical lines: (1) Rest a black pen or pencil on the card holder of the type-writer, and turn the platen knob; or (2) remove the paper from the machine, and draw in the vertical lines with a black pen or pencil and a ruler. The lines divide the headings and columns but do not close in the sides of the table.

TABLE 24
BOXED TABLE

Spacing: single
Paper: plain, full sheet

Special Notes
1. Extend all horizontal lines to the edges of the table.
2. Center the vertical lines within the 6 blank spaces left between the columns.

Do not type the % sign in a column when the word *Percent* is used in the column heading.

L=25
margin-13-72
Tab, 30-40-53-65

COMPOSITION OF LAKESHORE WORK FORCE					7
Lower Harbor Branch Plant					12
February 1, 19--					15
Category	Male	Percent Male	Female	Percent Female	18 / 24
Factory	274	53	243	47	27
Office	21	25	62	75	30
Supervisory	22	55	18	45	34
Managerial	11	46	13	54	37

TABLE 25
BOXED TABLE

Spacing: single
Paper: plain, full sheet

You may abbreviate in tables when the entries would otherwise be too long.

HOUSE SALES				
Week of February 22, 19--				
Address	Type	Price	Agent	
2480 Ridge	3-bdrm. ranch	$ 94,500	Wilson	19
3600 Rice	lake cabin	38,900	Canale	25
1308 Birch	4-bdrm. bi-level	142,000	Prusi	33
18 Oak Lane	5-bdrm. 2-story	189,500	Gnauck	40
7803 Candace	4-bdrm. 2-story	93,600	Hart	48
809 Waldo	3-bdrm. ranch	87,200	Bjork	54
TOTAL	. . . .	$645,700	. . . .	61

(House Sales title line numbers: 2, 7, 11)

Please order the following items for me. List the department as Administration. Our account number is 10. Leave location blank. Purchase from Lowlar and Associates, 312 Summit Street, Normal, IL 61761

10 heavy-duty, 2-ply cotton American flags, size 3 x 5 ft

10 high-tensile-strength nylon American flags, size 4 x 6 ft

15 double-woven polyester American flags, size 5 x 8 ft

25 steel stacking chairs, chrome finish, 2-in-thick padded seat, 32 in overall height

J J

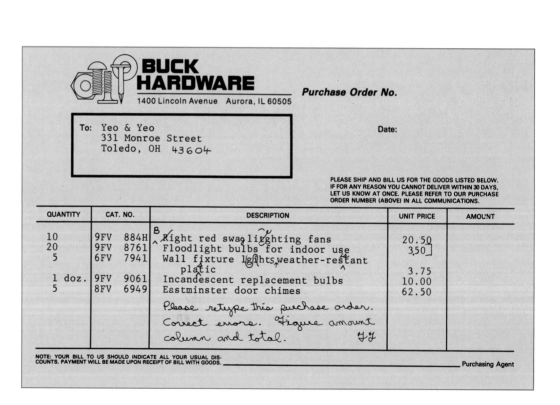

BUCK HARDWARE
1400 Lincoln Avenue   Aurora, IL 60505

Purchase Order No.

To: Yeo & Yeo
331 Monroe Street
Toledo, OH 43604

Date:

PLEASE SHIP AND BILL US FOR THE GOODS LISTED BELOW.
IF FOR ANY REASON YOU CANNOT DELIVER WITHIN 30 DAYS,
LET US KNOW AT ONCE. PLEASE REFER TO OUR PURCHASE
ORDER NUMBER (ABOVE) IN ALL COMMUNICATIONS.

QUANTITY	CAT. NO.	DESCRIPTION	UNIT PRICE	AMOUNT
10	9FV 884H	Bright red swag lighting fans	20.50	
20	9FV 8761	Floodlight bulbs for indoor use	3.50	
5	6FV 7941	Wall fixture lights, weather-restant plastic	3.75	
1 doz.	9FV 9061	Incandescent replacement bulbs	10.00	
5	8FV 6949	Eastminster door chimes	62.50	

Please retype this purchase order. Correct errors. Figure amount column and total. *J J*

NOTE: YOUR BILL TO US SHOULD INDICATE ALL YOUR USUAL DIS-
COUNTS. PAYMENT WILL BE MADE UPON RECEIPT OF BILL WITH GOODS.

_____ Purchasing Agent

BOXED TABLES WITH BRACED HEADINGS

Line: 60 spaces
Tab: 5
Spacing: single
Drills: 2 times
Format Guide: 71

Goals: To improve speed and accuracy; to format boxed tables with braced headings.

79-A. WARMUP

S 1 The keys to the big bus did not fit, so they may stay here.
A 2 Em will forget that Vicki quizzed six busy junior partners.
N 3 Merle was paid $609 on November 13 and $584 on November 27.

SKILLBUILDING

79-B. DIAGNOSTIC TYPING: ALPHABET

Turn to the Diagnostic Typing: Alphabet routine at the back of the book. Take the Pretest, and record your performance on Workguide page 125. Then practice the drill lines for those reaches on which you made errors.

79-C. PRODUCTION PRACTICE: PROOFREADING

79-C. Compare this copy with the material in lines 4–8 on page 159. Type a list of the errors, correcting the errors as you type.

4 Dobson	Barage	Alaska	17,221	42,689
5 Hanley	Fenton	Hawaii	51,502	20,694
6 Jellis	Owosso	Kanses	38,569	27,700
7 Knihgt	Rumely	Nevada	48,518	42,861
8 Palner	Warren	Oregon	42,570	39,652

79-D. SUSTAINED TYPING: NUMBERS

79-D. Take a 1-minute timing on the first paragraph to establish your base speed. Then take several 1-minute timings on the other paragraphs. As soon as you equal or exceed your base speed on one paragraph, advance to the next one.

9   Many young people soon see that their entry-level jobs 12
10 scarcely pay for necessities, and there is nothing left for 24
11 a savings program. Difficult as it may be, though, efforts 36
12 should be made to begin saving at the start of your career. 48

13   It is easy to understand that most of us don't realize 12
14 the effect of starting to save at a young age. The results 24
15 of saving $100 a month over 20 years are really surprising. 36
16 Money is not everything, but senior citizens need security. 48

17   The dollars saved will be working for the owner. When 12
18 that interest rate is 5.5 percent, the savings of $100 will 24
19 be worth over $43,000 at the end of that time. If this sum 36
20 impresses you, the next illustration will just astound you. 48

21   Let us suppose that those savings are earning interest 12
22 at a rate of 15 percent for a period of 30 years. The same 24
23 savings will be worth $700,000. A monthly increase to $200 36
24 results in almost a million and a half dollars in 30 years. 48

| 1 | 1 | 2 | 3 | 4 | 5 | 6 | 7 | 8 | 9 | 10 | 11 | 12

LETTER 54
BLOCK STYLE
Paper: Workguide 245–246

——————————————————June 2, 19——   4

Simmons ~~Supply~~ ^{Mower} Company   8
12500 Indiana Avenue   12
Chicago, IL 60604͞5   16

Gentlemen⊙   17

←—We are interest^{ed} in stock^{ing} a line of mowers for ~~resale~~ ^{sale} in   29
the Aur͜ora ~~store.~~ ^{area} Our ~~clients~~ ^{customers} have indicated an interest in   42
the Landrover mower.   46

We are particularly interested in ^a model^s that have 4-cy͜cle en-   58
gines with solid-start ignition and ~~have~~ a wheel ~~base~~ ^{size} from 7.0   70
x 1.͞5 to 8.0 x 2.0.   73

Our ~~clients~~ ^{customers} have ^{also} indicated aⁿ ~~desire~~ ^{interest} in mowers that have the   87
following features: 91
1. Presu͜rized lubrication, ~~with~~ ^{which} helps prevent head buildup.   103
2. Mech͜anical governors that help maintain blad^e speed in tall   116
    gr͜ass and weeds.   119
3. No-rust t͜anks that will not chip or corrode.   129
4. No-adjust carburetor^s that supply the exact fuel and air   141
    mixture for fast starting.   146
←—If you have models with ~~this~~ ^{these} features⊙ please send me a   157
catalog listing further specification^s.   165
Sincerely⊙   168
BU͞K͞C͞ HARDWARE   171

Franci͜es Fowler   174
Manager   175

    176

79-E. BOXED TABLES WITH BRACED HEADINGS

In addition to the regular column headings, it may be desirable at times to use an additional heading that relates to two or more columns. This is called a *braced heading,* and it should be typed so that it is centered over the columns to which it applies. For example, in Table 26 below, the heading *Male Members* applies to both the *Number* and the *Percent* columns.

To type a table with a braced heading:

1. Determine the vertical placement, and type the title. (Table 26 occupies 15 lines.)

2. Determine the horizontal placement, and set the left margin and the four tabs for the remaining columns.

3. Type the first horizontal rule; then go down 5 lines (thus leaving space for the braced heading) and type the column headings.

4. Roll the paper back 3 lines so that the braced heading *Male Members* will be a triple space above the column headings.

5. To center *Male Members* (12) over *Number* + 6 + *Percent* (19), indent *Male Members* 3 spaces from the start of *Number:* $19 - 12 = 7$; $7 \div 2 = 3\frac{1}{2} = 3$.

TABLE 26
BOXED TABLE WITH BRACED HEADING

Spacing: single
Paper: plain, full sheet

Note: Use of a braced heading *requires* that a table be typed in boxed style.

Note: The % sign is omitted after each number if the column heading makes it perfectly clear that the numbers in the column are percentages.

TABLE 27
BOXED TABLE WITH BRACED HEADING

Spacing: single
Paper: plain, full sheet

Note: When a table has a number, it is centered a double space above the title and typed in uppercase and lowercase letters.

CHIPPEWA ECONOMICS CLUB

Year	Male Members		Female Members	
	Number	Percent	Number	Percent
1965	102	88.7	13	11.3
1970	112	82.4	24	17.6
1975	122	68.5	56	31.5
1980	149	65.1	80	34.9
1985	133	55.4	107	44.6

Table 14
COMPOUND INTEREST
Accrued Annually

Year	Rate of 9%		
	Beginning Amount	Interest	Ending Amount
1	$50.00	$ 4.50	$54.50
2	54.50	4.91	59.41
3	59.41	5.35	64.76
4	64.76	5.83	70.59
5	70.59	6.35	76.94
TOTAL	....	$26.94	......

J. Spacing: double.
Record your score.

The content of this timing will give you some background about the company you will be working for in this in-basket exercise.

J. SKILL MEASUREMENT: 5-MINUTE TIMED WRITING

```
44      Buck Hardware is very pleased that you have accepted a        12
45  position as typist in our Aurora store.  You will find that       24
46  we are striving to provide the hardware needs of homeowners       36
47  for all of the area.  We are very glad that you are to work       48
48  here.                                                             49
49      You will be employed in the original store of the Buck        61
50  Hardware chain--a store well known for its service.  All of       73
51  its employees are genial and productive.  You will be happy       85
52  working with them as they eagerly assist new employees with       97
53  jobs.                                                             98
54      Our brands of hardware are sold through stores such as       110
55  the one in which you will be working.  We know our chain of      122
56  stores to be one of the best in the country.  You will rec-      134
57  ognize many of the brands because of our vigorous advertis-      146
58  ing.                                                             147
59      You are to work for the store manager.  The tasks that       159
60  you will be expected to complete include typing from rough-      171
61  draft copy, letters, memos, and business forms.  There will      183
62  be instances when you will be asked to make decisions about      195
63  work.                                                            196
64      Your office supervisor expects you to be able to carry       208
65  out your work with little or no explicit directions.  There      220
66  is an office manual for your use.  It is easy to read.  Use      232
67  it.  A good office manual can provide answers to many ques-      244
68  tions.                                                           245
```
| | 1 | 2 | 3 | 4 | 5 | 6 | 7 | 8 | 9 | 10 | 11 | 12 |

IN-BASKET EXERCISE: BUCK HARDWARE

Situation: Today is Wednesday, June 3, 19—. You are working as a typist for Ms. Frances Fowler, manager of the Buck Hardware store in Aurora, Illinois. Ms. Fowler is on a three-day vacation and has left the following jobs in your in-basket for you to complete during her absence.

Ms. Fowler prefers the block letter style with open punctuation and this closing:

Sincerely yours

BUCK HARDWARE

Frances Fowler
Manager

RULED AND BOXED TABLES

Line: 60 spaces
Tab: 5
Spacing: single
Drills: 2 times
Format Guide: 73

Goals: To type 43 wam/5'/5e; to format ruled and boxed tables.

80-A.   WARMUP

S 1 They may make some of their forms at that site by the dock.
A 2 Paula rejoiced at the amazing reviews of six quality books.
N 3 Please complete assignments 14 and 23 on pages 695 and 708.

SKILLBUILDING

80-B.   DIAGNOSTIC TYPING: NUMBERS

Turn to the Diagnostic Typing: Numbers routine at the back of the book. Take the Pretest, and record your performance on Workguide page 125. Then practice the drill lines for those reaches on which you made errors.

80-C.   SKILL MEASUREMENT: 5-MINUTE TIMED WRITING

80-C. Spacing: double. Record your score.

4   One day soon your boss will tell you that you may take   12
5   time off to attend your first professional convention. You   24
6   can help ensure that you have a very pleasant and rewarding   36
7   experience by heeding some advice from convention veterans.   48
8   First, have travel and hotel reservations confirmed in   60
9   writing well in advance of the convention. Early discounts   72
10 are particularly common for plane tickets. Also, the hotel   84
11 rooms will probably be available at lower convention rates.   96
12 Select your wardrobe for both work sessions and social   108
13 functions. Comfortable shoes are a must. And be sure that   120
14 you remember to bring your swimsuit and jogging gear if you   132
15 are one who wants to stick to that daily exercise schedule.   144
16 After registering at the convention headquarters, plan   156
17 to personalize your own schedule. There might be more than   168
18 one session planned for the same hour; and you will then be   180
19 forced to choose among the many speakers, panels, exhibits,   192
20 and other programs. Be sure to take good notes and collect   204
21 the handouts at sessions to share with workers at home.   215

| 1 | 2 | 3 | 4 | 5 | 6 | 7 | 8 | 9 | 10 | 11 | 12

F. Take a 1-minute timing on the first paragraph to establish your base speed. Then take several 1-minute timings on the other paragraphs. As soon as you equal or exceed your base speed on one paragraph, advance to the next one.

F. SUSTAINED TYPING: ROUGH DRAFT

16   The way that materials are arranged on a desk can cre-   12
17 ate an atmosphere where tasks are produced efficiently with   24
18 a minimum of confusion. Or it can create a situation where   36
19 little is completed.   40

20   Information processors must give consideration to when   12
21 and how each item on the desk is used: A plan must be made   24
22 for the placement of supplies and items which are used most   36
23 often in daily work.   40

24   Once the arrangement judgement is made, the information   12
25 processor should ensure that all materials and supplies are   24
26 placed in the same place each day. They will then be ready   36
27 when they are needed.   40

   | | | 2 | 3 | 4 | 5 | 6 | 7 | 8 | 9 | 10 | 11 | 12

G. Compare this passage with the first two paragraphs of the timing on page 225. Type a list of the words that contain errors, correcting the errors as you type.

G. PRODUCTION TECHNIQUE: PROOFREADING

28   Buck hardware is verry pleased thatyou have accepted a
29 position as typist in our Aurora store, You will find that
30 we are striving to provide the hawdware needs of homeowners
31 for all of the area. We are very glad that you our to work
32 hare.

33   You willbe employed in the original store of the Buck
34 Hardware chain--a store well known for its service, All of
35 it's employees are jenial and productive. You will be hapy
36 working with them as they eggerly assist new employees with
37 jobs?

H. Type each paragraph twice, or take two 1-minute timings on each paragraph.

H. SYMBOL TYPING

38   Barnes & Hall* quoted 80# @ $1.48 and 10# @ 56¢. They   12
39 will give a 12% discount. What a price! Can you match (on   24
40 account) this price? If so, call Bill and/or Liz tomorrow.   36

41   Shaffer's catalog* lists the sets @ $760.50 with a 10%   12
42 "cash discount." It is their end-of-the-year sale. Ask if   24
43 the price holds at #60 Meridan Place--their flagship store.   36

   | | | 2 | 3 | 4 | 5 | 6 | 7 | 8 | 9 | 10 | 11 | 12

I. PACED PRACTICE

Turn to the Paced Practice routine at the back of the book. Take several 2-minute timings, starting at the point where you left off the last time. Record your progress on Workguide page 125.

80-D. REVIEW OF RULED AND BOXED TABLES

TABLE 28
RULED TABLE

Spacing: single
Paper: plain, full sheet

QUALITY PERFORMANCE

January, 19--

Shift	Number Acceptable	Total Produced	%
A-Day	325	347	93.7
B-Day	315	362	87.0
C-Evening	3̶2̶3̶ 321	328	97.9
D-Evening	307	341	90.0
E-Late Night	342	408	8̶4̶.̶8̶ 83.8
F- Late Night	296	339	87.3
AVERAGE	318	354	9̶0̶.̶0̶

4
6
8
13
16
19
23
27
30
34
37

TABLE 29
BOXED TABLE WITH BRACED
HEADING

Spacing: double for the column
entries
Paper: plain, full sheet

ADVERTISING EXPENDITURES

Ficsal year 19--

]Month[	Media Type		Television TV	Totals
	Newspaper	Radio		
Jan.	$ 834	$ 721	$ 1,560	$ 3,115
Feb.	678	492	982	2,152
March	706	853	1,703	3,262
April	942	678	2,043	3,663
May	855	562 4̶6̶2̶	1,731	3 2,148
June	949	804	1,349	3,102
July	750	657	1,575	2,982
Aug.	1,782	1,046	2,782	5,610
Sept.	583	682	1,241	2,506
Oct.	797	734	1,402	2,933
Nov.	906	481	1,008	2,395
Dec.	1,782	1,673	3,781	7,236
Total	564 $11,5̶6̶2̶	$9,383	$21,157	$42,104

5
8
9
16
22
27
31
35
39
43
47
52
57
62
66
72
78

Line: 60 spaces
Tab: 5, center
Spacing: single
Drills: 2 times
Workguide: 245–253
Format Guide: 99

LESSONS
106–110

IN-BASKET EXERCISE:
BUCK HARDWARE

GOALS FOR UNIT 22

1. To type 49 wam for 5 minutes with no more than 5 errors.
2. To type letters with special features.
3. To type an agenda, an itinerary, and minutes of a meeting.
4. To type billing forms.
5. To type a report with a boxed table.
6. To follow directions.

A. WARMUP

S 1 Each of us must take the time to plan our part of the trip.
A 2 Jack Yeo's vague quip vexed and amazed his brother Wilfred.
N 3 On June 26 and July 10, I will use 54, 79, and 83 if I can.

SKILLBUILDING

PRETEST. Take a 1-minute timing; compute your speed and
count errors.

B. PRETEST: HORIZONTAL REACHES

4   Art enjoyed his royal blue race car. He bragged about   12
5   how he learned to push for those spurts of speed which made   24
6   him win races. The car had a lot of get-up-and-go. He had   36
7   daily meetings with his mechanics when a race date was set.   48
    | | | 2 | 3 | 4 | 5 | 6 | 7 | 8 | 9 | 10 | 11 | 12

PRACTICE.
    Speed Emphasis: If you made 2
or fewer errors on the Pretest,
type each line twice.
    Accuracy Emphasis: If you
made 3 or more errors on the
Pretest, type each group of lines
(as though it were a paragraph)
twice.

C. PRACTICE: IN REACHES

8   oy ahoy ploy toys loyal yodel royal enjoy decoy Lloyd annoy
9   ar fare arch mart march farms scars spear barns learn radar
10 pu pull push puts pulse spurt purge spuds pushy spurs pupil
11 lu luck blue lure lucid glued lumps value lulls bluff lunge

D. PRACTICE: OUT REACHES

12 ge gear gets ages getup raged geese lunge pages cagey forge
13 da dare date data dance adage dazed sedan daubs cedar daily
14 hi high hick hill hinge chief hires ethic hiked chili hitch
15 ra rate rare brag ranch brace ratio bravo rayon prawn races

POSTTEST. Repeat the Pretest
and compare performance.

E. POSTTEST: HORIZONTAL REACHES

PROGRESS TEST ON PART 4

TEST 4-A
5-MINUTE TIMED WRITING

Line: 60 spaces
Tab: 5
Spacing: double
Paper: Workguide 173

There is a great deal of concern today about the need,   12
indeed the urgency, to develop in youth the critical think-   24
ing that is so necessary for good judgment. Knowing how to   36
sort out the options, evaluate the best, and make the right   48
decisions based on reason--this is critical thinking. Note   60
that it demands a lot of knowledge about options, extensive   72
experience in sorting options, and the courage to take full   84
responsibility for the decision. It is a very heavy order.   96

To illustrate the point, suppose you were asked to buy   108
your firm or school a mainframe computer for a million dol-   120
lars. You would have to list the tasks the machine must do   132
and then go after all the available models that could serve   144
the tasks adequately. What options you would have to sort!   156
If you came up with a selection, it would be with the scary   168
realization that the machine would be known as your triumph   180
or a tragedy for the remainder of your professional career.   192

The two critical things about critical thinking are to   204
do it silently without criticizing the ideas of others.   215

| 1 | 2 | 3 | 4 | 5 | 6 | 7 | 8 | 9 | 10 | 11 | 12

TEST 4-B
LETTER 32
MODIFIED-BLOCK LETTER
WITH INDENTED PARAGRAPHS

Line: 6 inches (60 pica/70 elite)
Tab: 5, center
Paper: Workguide 175

(Current date) / Ms. Holly Miller / District Manager / MacPhee and   9
Green, Inc. / 901 Sherman Avenue / Denver, CO 80203 / Dear Holly: 20

Enclosed is a three-year analysis of our sales by district. I would like to   35
take this opportunity to congratulate you on the 28 percent increase in   50
sales over the past three years.   56

I am sure you will see that other districts had a larger increase in sales   71
than yours, but you must remember that your district was formed only   85
three years ago. If you were to compare previous sales analyses for dis-   100
tricts three years old, you would find that the sales increase in your   114
district topped all previous sales increases in a three-year period of time.   129

It is impossible for me to congratulate each employee in your district;   143
however, please extend my best wishes to all who have assisted in build-   158
ing our new district in the Rocky Mountain area.   167

Again, thank you for such a successful three years.   177

Sincerely yours, / Keith D. MacPhee / President / *(Your initials)* /   186
Enclosure   188

LETTER 52

Paper: Workguide 241–242

Send this letter to Ms. Jean Fernandez, President, Apex Appliances, 3116 Euclid Avenue, Cleveland, Ohio 44117. Send a copy to Harold Greco. AK

4
10
13
16
20
24

Welcome to the select group of Saturn Color tv dealers.

we
Your application has been approved, and I look forward to many

a *for.* *your firm and ours.*
years of successful business venture with both of us. We take

never
pride in the fact that we have seldom rec(s)inded a dealer ship

our
in the 35 years of manufacturing television sets. Our dealers

tell *working* *the*
will inform you that we are a family tied together to improve

quality and ser(v)ice of the television industry.

fine
We are aware of the reputation your company has for service

in *and therefore,*
and sales to the greater Cleveland area, it would be a plea-

sure to have you visit our offices at our expense as soon as

an
you have the opportunity to do so. Please let me know when

you can come to Woodmoore.

Again, congratulations to you, our newest dealer of the

nation's
country's best color television--the Saturn.

e
Sincerly yours,

35
48
63
75
88
100
111
124
139
151
163
168
179
188
191

LETTER 53

Paper: Workguide 243–244

Please send the same letter to Mr. Vance Lutz, General Manager, Avenue Stores, 331 Drexel Avenue, Chicago, Illinois 60653. Be sure to make the necessary change in the city.

194
198
199
202

TEST 4-C
TABLE 30
RULED TABLE

Tab: center
Spacing: single
Paper: Workguide 177

Center the table horizontally and vertically.

THREE-YEAR SALES ANALYSIS
(Current date)

Branch	Current Year	First Prior	Second Prior
Boston	$ 360,000	$ 275,000	$ 225,000
Chicago	425,000	375,000	350,000
Denver	275,000	230,000	200,000
Los Angeles	415,000	360,000	340,000
Pittsburgh	400,000	340,000	300,000
TOTAL	$1,875,000	$1,580,000	$1,415,000

TEST 4-D
REPORT 30
BOOK MANUSCRIPT PAGE 28
(BOUND REPORT)
Line: 6 inches (60 pica/70 elite)
Tab: 5
Spacing: double
Paper: Workguide 179

CORRESPONDENCE MANUAL   Page 28

Type the list single spaced with 1 blank line above and below the list as a whole.

REPORT HEADINGS

Reports often have several levels of headings to highlight the content of the text to follow and to help the reader focus on the central ideas. Too many headings, of course, clutter a report and may confuse the reader.

In preparing your text, be consistent in your style of positioning the headings to indicate their levels. there are at least three acceptable styles. They are as follows:

1. A centered heading is on a line by itself, with 2 blank lines above and 1 blank line below. It may be typed in all-capital letters or in capital and small letters that are underscored.

2. A side heading starts flush with the left margin, on a line by itself. It is typed in all-capital letters and preceded by 2 blank lines.

3. A paragraph heading begins a paragraph and is immediately followed by text on the same line. It is indented 5 spaces, with the first and principal words capitalized. It should be underscored and followed by a period (unless some other punctuation, such as a question mark, is required). The text then begins 2 spaces after the mark of punctuation.

3

INSTALLATION

    <u>Antenna</u>. Unless your television is connected by a cable

TV system or a centralized system, a good outdoor television

antenna is recommended for the best performance. If you are

located in an exceptionally good signal area that is free from

interference and ghost images, an indoor antenna may suffice.

    <u>Location</u>. Select the areas where sunlight and bright

indoor lighting will not fall directly on the screen and af-

fect the visibility.

    <u>Ventilation</u>. Proper ventilation keeps your TV running

cool. Air circulates through perforated screens or openings

in the back and bottom of the cabinet. <u>Do not block these</u>

<u>vents. If you do, you will shorten the life of your televi-</u>

<u>sion.</u>

POWER CONSIDERATIONS

<u>Viewing</u>. For maximum eye comfort, your set should be viewed from a distance of 3 to 6 feet or more.

<u>Power</u>. Your television receiver is designed to operate on 120V 60Hz ac. Insert the power plug into a 120 volt 60Hz outlet. DO NOT TRY TO OPERATE IT ON DC CURRENT.

<u>Power Cord</u>. Your power cord has been constructed according to the specifications required by Underwriter's Laboratories. It has one regular blade and fits only one way into a standard electrical outlet. If the blade will not enter either way, your outlet is probably old and nonstandard. A new outlet should be installed by a qualified electrician.

14
26
38
51
64
74
86
90
101
114
125
137
138
142
151
158
162
171
180
189
196
204
212
221
228
236
245
252
260
268

PART 5

SKILLBUILDING ■ CORRESPONDENCE, REPORTS, FORMS, AND TABLES

OBJECTIVES

KEYBOARDING SKILL

To type 47 words a minute on a 5-minute timed writing with no more than 5 errors.

PROOFREADING SKILL

To proofread your typed work, mark errors and compute typing speed on timed writings, and correct errors on production work.

TECHNICAL SKILL

To answer correctly at least 90 percent of the questions on an objective test.

FORMATTING SKILL

To format two-page letters and letters in block and simplified styles, for window envelopes, and on special stationery.

To format itineraries, minutes, a procedures manual, reports with author-year citations, and legal documents.

To format financial statements, tables, and forms.

■ To apply such word processing functions as formatting report headers and footers, completing an operator's log, using the mail-merge feature with a form letter, and formatting a newsletter using desktop publishing.

Retype and send with the memo to Rex Roy. AK

```
N E W S   R E L E A S E          From Anthony Koontz        9
                                 Vice President for Sales  13
                                 Saturn Appliances         17
                                 Woodmoor, MD 20901         20
END-OF-THE-WINTER SALE           Release February 18, 19--  25

                        SATURN COLOR TV                      29
```

WOODMORE, MD, February 18--No other manufacturer of tele-   41
vision can offer customers a 21-inch set for only $325. This 53
fabulous offer is being made during the annual End-of-the-Winter 65
sale of all Saturn Appliances.   71

The Saturn Color tv has been designed with the viewer in mind. 83
It has the brightest and clearest picture on the market today. 96
The remote control unit provides for the selection and hues of 109
color most appropriate for any viewer.   117

The 21-inch portable set can be placed on any currently   127
manufactured television stand. Its portable antenna provides 139
for its usage any where in the room or office. The specially 152
designed hand locks enables it to be carried from room to room. 164

Only saturn Appliances can provide such a superb set at such 177
a price and, especially, with a money-back guarantee if it does 189
not meet all viewer expectations.   196

The association of television dealers has selected the   207
Saturn Color 21-inch tv as the set of the year. This is the tenth 220
consecutive year that the 21-inch set has been rated in the   232
top-three sets of the year.   237

LESSON
81

Line: 60 spaces
Tab: 5
Spacing: single
Drills: 2 times
Workguide: 181–184
Format Guide: 75

LETTER STYLES

Goals: To improve speed and accuracy; to format letters in the block and simplified styles.

81-A. WARMUP

s 1 I wish both of us could also work with the men to make dye.
A 2 That judge quietly gave the six prizes back to those women.
N 3 Please call me at 555-6798 between 12:30 and 4:15 tomorrow.

SKILLBUILDING

PRETEST. Take a 1-minute timing; compute your speed and count errors.

81-B. PRETEST: COMMON LETTER COMBINATIONS

4   The insurance agents began to input the weekly renewal   12
5 data into the computer. They quickly decided which amounts   24
6 had to be increased by adding yearly totals to the formula.   36
   | | | 2 | 3 | 4 | 5 | 6 | 7 | 8 | 9 | 10 | 11 | 12

PRACTICE.
   Speed Emphasis: If you made no more than 1 error on the Pretest, type each line twice.
   Accuracy Emphasis: If you made 2 or more errors on the Pretest, type each group of lines (for example, lines 7–10), as though it were a paragraph, twice.

81-C. PRACTICE: WORD BEGINNINGS

7 re- react ready refer relax remit renew repel really reveal
8 in- incur index infer input inset inert inept inches insert
9 be- befit began being below beach beams bears beauty beside
10 de- deals debit debug decay deeds delay denim decent delude

81-D. PRACTICE: WORD ENDINGS

11 -ly apply daily early hilly lowly madly truly simply weekly
12 -ed acted added based cited dated hired sized opened showed
13 -nt agent count event front giant meant plant amount fluent
14 -al canal decal equal fatal ideal local usual actual visual

POSTTEST. Repeat the Pretest and compare performance.

81-E. POSTTEST: COMMON LETTER COMBINATIONS

81-F. PROGRESSIVE PRACTICE: ALPHABET

Turn to the Progressive Practice: Alphabet routine at the back of the book. Take several 30-second timings, starting at the point where you left off the last time. Record your progress on Workguide page 125.

81-G. These words are among the 200 most frequently misspelled words in business correspondence.

81-G. PRODUCTION PRACTICE: SPELLING

15 balance expense scheduled discussed opportunity development
16 because changes currently determine appropriate performance
17 members address procedure therefore maintenance corporation
18 medical courses permanent effective immediately appreciated
19 however council reference increased information association

MEMO 18

Paper: Workguide 237

Retype on printed form. Be sure to enclose news release. AK

TO:	Rex Ray, director of advertising	7
FROM:	Anthony Koontz, Vice President for Sales	17
DATE:	February 11, 19--	22
SUBJECT:	End-of-~~the Spring~~ Winter Sale ~~for~~ Saturn Color TV	31

Enclosed is a corrected copy of the End-of-Winter   41
Sale News release for our Saturn Color TV line. Distribute it   54
nation-wide.   56

I am particularly pleased that we are able to ~~sale~~ offer the 21-inch   69
portable for $225. As you know, it is our number one set, and   82
we should see a marked increase in the dollar volume of this   85
model at the end of the sale.   100

You are to be commended for the ~~great~~ excellent promotional materials   112
developed in your department.   118

MEMO 19

Paper: Workguide 237

Send this memo to Donna Palmer, Editor, Sales Department. Subject: Page 3 of Owner's Manual

AK   19

I have read page 3 of the Owner's   26
Manual and agree that we need more   33
information on installing the set.   40

You will see that I have added   46
material on viewing, power, and   52
power cord.   55

Please read the new copy. Perhaps   62
we should send a revised page to   68
the Engineering Department for its input.   76

If the Engineering Department suggests   84
changes, please let me know.   90

Note: It is unlikely that you will ever type letters in more than one or two styles while working for the same firm. Learning the different letter styles and technicalities in this unit will prepare you for typing letters in any office.

81-H.   LETTER STYLES

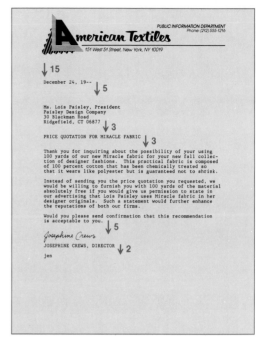

BLOCK STYLE.   All lines begin at the left margin.
OPEN PUNCTUATION.   No colon after salutation; no comma after complimentary closing.
SUBJECT LINE.   Comes after the salutation; double-space before and after.

SIMPLIFIED STYLE.   All lines begin at the left margin; no salutation or complimentary closing.
SUBJECT LINE.   Always included in a simplified-style letter; typed in all capitals without the word *Subject.*
WRITER'S IDENTIFICATION.   Typed in all capitals.

LETTER 33
BLOCK STYLE, OPEN PUNCTUATION

Paper: Workguide 181–182

June 24, 19— / Mr. William J. Kirtz / Mayflower Studios / 346 Claydon   14
Way / Sacramento, CA 95864 / Dear Mr. Kirtz / Subject: Photo Coverage   26
of Baker Speech   29

    Dr. Joseph Baker, the head of our research division, will be the key-   43
note speaker at the annual convention of the Industrial Chemists Asso-   57
ciation in Sacramento on Thursday, August 18, at Convention Hall at   70
10 a.m.   72

    Would you please take several photos of Dr. Baker delivering his   85
speech, talking with officers of the association, and sitting with the other   100
program participants on the dais. Then select the one best shot for pub-   115
licity purposes, and make 15 glossy prints. Deliver these prints to Helen   130
Sheldon in the pressroom on the second floor before 1 p.m. on Friday,   144
August 19.   146

    I would appreciate your sending us a written confirmation of your   159
acceptance of this assignment.   165

    Sincerely / Josephine Crews, Director / (*Your initials*)   172

LETTER 34
SIMPLIFIED STYLE

Paper: Workguide 183–184

Reformat Letter 33 in simplified style. Delete the salutation, the word *Subject,* and the complimentary closing.

Ms. Dorris Zollman, President   10

Zollman Enterprises, Inc.   15

8216 E. Vernon St.   19

Scottsdale, AZ 85257   23

Dear ~~Miss~~ *MS.* Zollman: 27

SUBJECT : SATURN COLOR TV SALES

We are happy to furnish you, a member of our board of direc-   37

tors, with the *following* sales information on our Saturn tv.   50

SATURN COLOR TV SALES   55

(1980-1990)   56

(In Millions of Dollars)   61

Projected

Region	1980	1985	1990
Eastern	$ 60,125	$ 57,700	$ 90,450
Central	48,780	54,175	59,320
Western	68,810	60,650	69,394
TOTAL	$ 187,715	$ 190,525	$ 220,164

As you know, our television is the most prestigious in the United States.   101

If we can be of further assistance to you; please let me know.   114

Sincerely Yours,   117

Anthony Koontz   120

Vice president for sales   125

126

single space table title

Center table

Read through this letter before retyping it

AK

LM24

Line: 60 spaces
Tab: 5, center
Spacing: single
Drills: 2 times
Workguide: 185–188
Format Guide: 75

SPECIAL LETTER PARTS

Goals: To type 44 wam/5'/5e; to format special letter parts.

82-A.   WARMUP

S 1 The chairman of a civic club also had to make an amendment.
A 2 Those folks who won big money prizes have vexed Jacqueline.
N 3 From 7:45 until 12:30, she copied 86 letters and 9 reports.

SKILLBUILDING

82-B.   PROGRESSIVE PRACTICE: NUMBERS

Turn to the Progressive Practice: Numbers routine at the back of the book. Take several 30-second timings, starting at the point where you left off the last time. Record your progress on Workguide page 125.

82-C.   Spacing: double. Record your score.

82-C.   SKILL MEASUREMENT: 5-MINUTE TIMED WRITING

4   The demand for writing instruments is growing in spite   12
5   of predictions that pens or pencils would be discarded when   24
6   complex equipment came into wide use. Pen and pencil sales   36
7   are strong, even in the high-tech office.   44
8   The huge increase in sales of writing tools shows that   56
9   word processing is done just as much by hand as by machine.   68
10 Such increases also point to a demand for specialized writ-   80
11 ing instruments in the electronic office.   88
12   Rolling ball pens, highlighter pens, and other instru-   100
13 ments designed for the electronic office are most in demand   112
14 today. These sales support the belief that automation will   124
15 assist the writing-instrument industry.   132
16   Highlighter pens and felt-tip markers are used to out-   144
17 line computer printouts. The new mechanical pencils with a   156
18 clutch have also gained a large share of the market. Sales   168
19 of fountain pens, however, have dropped.   176
20   More than half the work force is now made up of white-   188
21 collar workers. This means that today more and more people   200
22 need stylish writing tools. For some people, a pen is like   212
23 a badge of success--like a status symbol.   220

| 1 | 2 | 3 | 4 | 5 | 6 | 7 | 8 | 9 | 10 | 11 | 12 |

MEMO 17

Paper: Workguide 233

Memo to Art Wolfe, Sales Manager, Television Division.

Subject: Edridge Dealership

    Enclosed are the estimated sales for Saturn Color TV in Northwestern Ohio. Please have someone recheck the projected sales data. We do not want to mislead Edridge's.

    When this information is given to Edridge's, we must be sure that it's kept confidential by them.

c: B. J. Barnes. AK

| | 10 |
| 19 |
| 24 |
| 30 |
| 41 |
| 54 |
| 64 |
| 76 |
| 83 |
| 84 |
| 85 |
| 89 |

TABLE 37

Paper: plain, full sheet

8-6=2÷2=1

Type this table using a ruled format. Total the columns; send the table with the memo to Art Wolfe and B. J. Barnes

Projected Sales of Saturn Color TV Sets
By County in Northwestern Ohio
1990 – 1994

County	1990	1992	1994	
Defiance	880	910	915	29
Fulton	725	790	825	32
Lucas	1,780	1,900	2,400	36
Ottawa	645	725	780	39
Williams	450	600	650	42
Wood	800	950	975	45
Total	5,280	5875	6545	49

82-D. SPECIAL LETTER PARTS

An attention line may be typed immediately after the company name in both the inside address and the envelope address. An appropriate salutation is *Gentlemen:* or *Ladies and Gentlemen:*

Type a mailing notation on the line below the enclosure notation (if used) or on the line below the reference initials. A mailing notation comes before any copy notation:

   urs
Enclosure
By Federal Express
c: Legal Department

MODIFIED-BLOCK STYLE WITH INDENTED PARAGRAPHS

MILITARY-STYLE DATE. Type the day before the month instead of after, with no separating comma.

FOREIGN ADDRESS. Type the name of a foreign country in all capitals on a separate line.

```
                              15 March 19--


Mr. Abdul Majeed, Director
Worldwide Clipping Service
Industrial Building No. 2
P.O. Box 5082
Karachi 2
PAKISTAN

Dear Mr. Majeed:
```

LETTER 35
MODIFIED-BLOCK STYLE WITH INDENTED PARAGRAPHS

Tab: 5
Workguide: 185–186

March 14, 19— / Wayne State University / Attention: Finance Department / 4841 Cass Avenue / Detroit, MI 48202 / Ladies and Gentlemen: 14 / 26

    The annual meeting of the stockholders of American Textiles will be held next Friday, March 21, at 10 a.m. in Busch Auditorium. Inasmuch as our recent acquisition of North Carolina Mills will be a major item of discussion, this promises to be a lively meeting.   40 / 54 / 69 / 78

    Would you be interested in securing complimentary tickets to this meeting for your students majoring in finance? If so, simply let me know the number of tickets you would need, and I will have them available at the box office on Friday morning. The enclosed agenda shows the major items of business to be discussed.   92 / 106 / 121 / 135 / 142

    We look forward to having you and your students join us for this interesting and educational meeting.   155 / 162

    Sincerely, / Josephine Crews, Director / (*Your initials*) / Enclosure / Overnight Express   172 / 176

LETTER 36
MODIFIED-BLOCK STYLE WITH INDENTED PARAGRAPHS

Tab: 5
Workguide: 187–188

(*Same date as in Letter 35 but in military style*) / Professor Anne Rex / Commercial Studies Department / University of Aston / Gosta Green / Birmingham B4 7ET / ENGLAND / Dear Professor Rex: 8 / 20 / 29

    Same body as in Letter 35, but add this sentence at the beginning of the second paragraph: I know that the Aston Finance Club will be in Detroit on that day to participate in the Investment World Series at Wayne State University.   82 / 109

    Same closing lines, but change the mailing notation to Air Mail.   205

MODIFIED-BLOCK STYLE WITH
INDENTED PARAGRAPHS

Paper: Workguide 231–232

Note: When you are asked to sign a letter for someone else, write the person's name in your handwriting, and put your initials under the signature. Without your initials, the signature is forgery.

February 9, 19--   4

Edridge's, Inc.   7
Attention: Appliance Manager   13
321 Summit St.   16
Toledo, OH 43604   19

Gentlemen;   21

Thank you for your letter in which you inquired about your   33
firm's being the sold dealer in Northwestern Ohio for the Saturn   46
Color TV.   48

We are pleased to inform you that we would be most happy too   60
have your firm among our many fine dealers in ohio. As you   71
know; the Saturn has been selected by the association of   82
television dealers as the better televeision of the month. year.   92

The saturn color tv has a newly developed wide-angle   103
116-degree deflection picture tube which provides a bright and clear   116
picture. The single electro-static lens, the veritcal phosphor   129
strips; the power-saving narrow neck, and the precisely con-   141
trolled projection of the four colors beams are the result of the   154
unique design concepts of the saturn television system.   162

If you wish to become one of the selected dealers of the saturn   175
color tv, please complete the enclosed dealership contract. If   188
you have additional questions, about the contact or the saturn   201
Color TV; please write me.   206

Sincerely yours,   209

*I edited this rough-draft letter.
Send a copy to B. J. Barnes.
Sign my name.*   222

AK

Line: 60 spaces
Tab: 5, center
Spacing: single
Drills: 2 times
Workguide: 189–190
Format Guide: 77

Goals: To build speed and accuracy; to format a two-page letter.

83-A. WARMUP

S 1 Make my display for six of the eight pairs of giant rubies.
A 2 Virginia picked the jonquils and zinnias for my flower box.
N 3 Invoice 487 for $921.56 should be paid before September 30.

SKILLBUILDING

83-B. Take a 1-minute timing on the first paragraph to establish your base speed. Then take several 1-minute timings on the other paragraphs. As soon as you equal or exceed your base speed on one paragraph, advance to the next one.

83-B. SUSTAINED TYPING: ALTERNATE-HAND WORDS

4   The chairman of that civic club also had to make a new   12
5 amendment to change the shape of the map for downtown. The   24
6 rich visitor owns eight of the giant lots that are visible.   36

7   The problem with the audit is that the city will blame   12
8 our firm. Some may not wait for us to make a profit on the   24
9 deal. If that is the case, we shall refuse to participate.   36

10   I once lived in the downtown section of Baltimore. My   12
11 best neighbor there was a guy named Webster Lyon. The only   24
12 problem with him was that he tended to act like a busybody.   36

13   Phil and Edward had wasted a million pumpkins by scat-   12
14 tering the vegetables along the street in Sweetwater, Ohio.   24
15 Everyone was quite aggravated by the great waste of effort.   36

| 1 | 2 | 3 | 4 | 5 | 6 | 7 | 8 | 9 | 10 | 11 | 12

83-C. Compare this passage with the first two paragraphs of Letter 37 on page 175. Type a list of the words that contain errors, correcting the errors as you type.

83-C. PRODUCTION PRACTICE: PROOFREADING

16 American Textiles cordially invite the Channel 8 newsteam
17 to attend the opening of the Bank Street textile plant in
18 Dover on September 4 at 10 A.M. The opening of our new
19 plant is news worthy to the citizens of Dover for a variety
20 of reasons.

21 1. We will be employing 108 people from the Dover vicin-
22   ity, three-fourths of who will be members of the In-
23   ternational Ladies Garment Workers' Union.

83-D. TWO-PAGE LETTERS

Follow these guidelines when formatting a two-page business letter:

1. Type the first page on letterhead stationery and the second page on plain paper.
2. Use standard format for page 1.
3. Leave at least 1 inch for the bottom margin.

4. For the heading on page 2, type the addressee's name, the page number, and the date beginning on line 7, either blocked at the left margin or centered on one line, as illustrated on page 175.

K. Select the words that can be divided, and type them with a hyphen to show where the division should be (example: *prac-tice*).

K. PRODUCTION PRACTICE: WORD DIVISION

46	fought	already	distance
47	isn't	USN	gaiety
48	codify	overcast	bumpy
49	built	suppose	alone
50	epic	bunker	sister

L. Spacing: double. Record your score.

L. SKILL MEASUREMENT: 5-MINUTE TIMED WRITING

51	Welcome to Saturn Appliances. You may already know us	12
52	by our advertising or our logo. If you own a home, rent an	24
53	apartment or home, or still live with your parents, you may	36
54	recognize our name on the numerous household items we make.	48
55	Most of our appliances are sold through retail stores;	60
56	however, we do have some wholesale outlets. We believe our	72
57	appliances are better than any others in the field. All of	84
58	our television models have been top sellers in that market.	96
59	You will be working in an office that has a reputation	108
60	for excellence. In fact, all of our employees are proud of	120
61	their work. You will quickly understand this pride. It is	132
62	always found in a firm that is interested in its customers.	144
63	Your position in this unit is secretary in the offices	156
64	of the vice president for sales. The tasks to be completed	168
65	include typing rough-draft copy, letters, memos, and tables	180
66	to be used in marketing new products developed by the firm.	192
67	You will be expected to make many decisions as to work	204
68	priorities and formatting. Please pay special attention to	216
69	each of the directions you will be given. You will have an	228
70	opportunity to put your best skills to work in this office.	240

| 1 | 2 | 3 | 4 | 5 | 6 | 7 | 8 | 9 | 10 | 11 | 12 |

IN-BASKET EXERCISE: SATURN APPLIANCES

Situation: Today is Thursday, February 11, 19—. You are working as the secretary to Mr. Anthony Koontz, vice president for sales of Saturn Appliances, with headquarters in Woodmoor, Maryland. Mr. Koontz is attending a two-day meeting in New York City and has left the following jobs in your in-basket for you to complete during his absence.

Mr. Koontz prefers the modified-block letter style with blocked or indented paragraphs, standard punctuation, and this closing:

Sincerely yours,

Anthony Koontz
Vice President for Sales

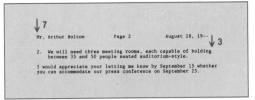

Either style of heading for continuation pages is acceptable for letters in modified-block style.

LETTER 37
TWO-PAGE LETTER IN MODIFIED-BLOCK STYLE

Line: 6 inches
Paper: Workguide 189–190

Indent the turnover lines of the enumeration 4 spaces.

Page-ending guidelines:
1. Do not divide the last word on a page.
2. Leave at least 2 lines of a paragraph at the bottom of the first page and carry forward at least 2 lines of the paragraph to the next page.
3. Page 2 should contain at least 2 lines of the body of the letter.

Use either style for the page-2 heading.

Type the table in ruled format. Leave 1 blank line before and after the table.

August 18, 19— / Ms. Margaretta J. Manninen / Director of Programming /   10
Spencer Broadcasting Company / 233 Spring Street / Dover, DE 19901 /   24
Dear Ms. Manninen: 26

American Textiles cordially invites the Channel 8 news team to attend   40
the opening of our Bank Street textile plant in Dover on September 4 at   55
10 a.m. The opening of our new plant is newsworthy to the citizens of   69
Dover for a variety of reasons: 75

1. We will be employing 180 people from the Dover vicinity, three-   88
fourths of whom will be members of the International Ladies' Garment   102
Workers' Union.   105

2. Located on 150 acres of parklike grounds, our Bank Street plant   119
contains the most advanced water system in the world. Water actually   133
leaves our plant cleaner than when we pumped it into our plant from   146
underground wells.   150

3. Our engineers have taken every step to ensure that this new facility   164
is completely compatible with the surrounding environment. It sur-   178
passes all government standards.   184

May I suggest that you use the two tickets in the enclosed envelope to   198
attend a private reception sponsored by the City Council on the evening   213
before the official opening of the plant. You will have an opportunity to   228
meet and interview the people who will actually be running this new   241
plant.   243

On September 4 the dedication schedule will be as follows: 254

Time	Event	Responsibility	
10:00 a.m.	Ribbon Cutting	Alan Brothers	259
11:00 a.m.	Plant Tour	Paul Feingold	266
12:15 p.m.	Lunch	Josephine Crews	273
2:15 p.m.	Golf Benefit	Josephine Crews	279
			286

We hope that you and your news team will be able to join us for this   300
happy event. Please call me if you need further information.   312
Sincerely, / Josephine Crews, Director / (*Your initials*) / Enclosure   322

F. TECHNIQUE TYPING: TAB KEY

16	admire	beacon	candle	desire	earful
17	detain	eludes	famous	grumpy	hearty
18	icicle	jalopy	kernel	ladder	method
19	nickel	ordeal	plunge	quince	runner
20	shrewd	thread	unused	vision	waving
21	duplex	yippee	zenith	agrees	barber
22	carrot	deacon	excess	folded	glance
23	hedges	incite	jester	kimono	lastly
24	memory	needle	oppose	pepped	rascal

G. DIAGNOSTIC TYPING: ALPHABET

Turn to the Diagnostic Typing: Alphabet routine at the back of the book. Take the Pretest, and record your performance on Workguide page 125. Then practice the drill lines for those reaches on which you made errors.

H. THINKING WHILE TYPING

25 A subcommittee chided a young sergeant for insubordination.
26 Their demographer worked for the Republicans and Democrats.
27 The English vaudevillian was unquestionably an entertainer.

28 The delicatessen served delightful petite cream delicacies.
29 A presumptuous professional aided in restoring the library.
30 The philanthropist from Massachusetts was a septuagenarian.

I. PRODUCTION PRACTICE: PROOFREADING

31   American business rans on printed forms. filling in a
32 form is a way of life in most offices. in fact; almost all
33 busnesss functions require a from at some point. Forms are
34 major time-savers, for they help to standardze office work;
35 Forms contain al the information which is constantly typed
36 right on them. They the typist fells in the variable data.
37 Repetitive typing is iliminated when you use printed forms.

J. TECHNIQUE TYPING: SHIFT AND RETURN/ENTER KEYS

38 John left for Ada, Ohio, in June to see Mr. James A. Smith.
39 Ann, Jill, John, Kermit, and Bill left for Utica, Michigan.
40 Bill was to go to Boston, Phoenix, Ely, Sitka, and Spokane.
41 She read Business Can Really Succeed Today in Tiffin, Ohio.

42 Tony can go. Jane won't be there. Do you know why? If he
43 can, fine. Anna likes to type. Jo left today. I can see.
44 Are they here? Can they? Will they? Why not? He may fly
45 home. What do you think? Should he? See me. He is here.

| Line: 60 spaces |
| Tab: 5, center |
| Spacing: single |
| Drills: 2 times |
| Workguide: 191–194 |
| Format Guide: 77 |

LESSON
84

SPECIAL STATIONERY

Goals: To type 44 wam/5′/5e; to format letters on special stationery.

84-A. WARMUP

S 1 The eighty fields of corn may produce many bushels for her.
A 2 My folks proved his expert eloquence was just a big hazard.
N 3 Our May 19—28 campaign sold 736 automobiles and 405 trucks.

SKILLBUILDING

84-B. All 26 capital letters are included in the passage. Keep your eyes on the copy, and try not to slow down for the capital letters.

84-B. TECHNIQUE TYPING: SHIFT KEY

4   Z. L. Ford from Eaton, Ohio, and Dr. B. I. Quincy from   12
5 Venice, Utah, attended the Miss America Pageant in Atlantic   24
6 City, New Jersey. They met Helen X. Wood from South Dakota   36
7 and Gay Y. Kane from Puerto Rico, who is Miss Congeniality.   48

| | | 2 | 3 | 4 | 5 | 6 | 7 | 8 | 9 | 10 | 11 | 12

84-C. Spacing: double. Record your score.

84-C. SKILL MEASUREMENT: 5-MINUTE TIMED WRITING

8   If anyone has been presented with a gift or has been a   12
9 guest in somebody's home, or on any number of other special   24
10 occasions, a thoughtful person will take the time to send a   36
11 thank-you letter. Your letter must express a sincere feel-   48
12 ing of gratitude; otherwise, it may have an insincere tone.   60
13   When couples have been guests, either the woman or the   72
14 man will usually write the thank-you notes for both people.   84
15 The note can be informal; a simple handwritten message will   96
16 often be sufficient. You should realize, however, that the   108
17 thank-you notes written in your office should most often be   120
18 typed either on regular letterhead or on smaller notepaper.   132
19   Regardless of the format of the note, the message that   144
20 you convey is that of a thoughtful person who takes time to   156
21 acknowledge an act of kindness which has been extended. If   168
22 you are a young person, the fact that you took the time and   180
23 made an effort to write a note will be greatly appreciated.   192
24 Always try to mention something unique or special about the   204
25 event so that the receiver will know the letter was written   216
26 just for him or her.   220

| | | 2 | 3 | 4 | 5 | 6 | 7 | 8 | 9 | 10 | 11 | 12

Line: 60 spaces
Tab: 5, center
Spacing: single
Drills: 2 times
Workguide: 231–242
Format Guide: 95

IN-BASKET EXERCISE: SATURN APPLIANCES

GOALS FOR UNIT 21

1. To type 48 wam for 5 minutes with no more than 5 errors.
2. To type correspondence, reports, and a news release.
3. To type ruled tables.
4. To follow directions.

A. WARMUP

S 1 Jack may give me the old tie to wear if he buys a new suit.
A 2 Why did Professor Black give you a quiz on the major taxes?
N 3 The 1989 sales were $178,240 compared with $65,330 in 1985.

SKILLBUILDING

PRETEST. Take a 1-minute timing; compute your speed and count errors.

B. PRETEST: DISCRIMINATION PRACTICE

4   Did the new clerk join your golf team? John indicated   12
5 to me that Beverly invited her prior to last Wednesday. He   24
6 believes she must give you a verbal commitment at once. We   36
7 should convince her to join because she is a gifted golfer.   48
   | 1 | 2 | 3 | 4 | 5 | 6 | 7 | 8 | 9 | 10 | 11 | 12

PRACTICE.
   Speed Emphasis: If you made 2 or fewer errors on the Pretest, type each line twice.
   Accuracy Emphasis: If you made 3 or more errors on the Pretest, type each group of lines (for example, lines 8–11), as though it were a paragraph, twice.

C. PRACTICE: LEFT HAND

vbv bevy verb bevel vibes breve viable braves verbal beaver
wew went week weans weigh weave wedges thawed weaker beware
ded dent need deals moved ceded heeded debate edging define
fgf guff gift flags foggy gaffe forget gifted guffaw fights

D. PRACTICE: RIGHT HAND

12 klk kale look kilts lakes knoll likely kettle kernel lacked
13 uyu buys your gummy dusty young unduly tryout uneasy jaunty
14 oio oils roil toils onion point oriole soiled ration joined
15 jhj jell heed eject wheat joked halved jalopy heckle jigsaw

POSTTEST. Repeat the Pretest and compare performance.

E. POSTTEST: DISCRIMINATION PRACTICE

DEEP LETTERHEAD. When the letterhead is deeper than 2 inches (12 lines), type the date 3 lines below the letterhead.

DISPLAY PARAGRAPHS. Indent 5 spaces from each margin. Double-space before and after.

COMPANY NAME IN CLOSING LINES. Type in all capitals a double space below the complimentary closing. Leave 3 blank lines between the company name and the writer's name.

LEFT-WEIGHTED STATIONERY. Move the margins and center tab ½ inch to the right of the widest item in the left column of the letterhead.

84-D. FORMATTING LETTERS ON SPECIAL STATIONERY

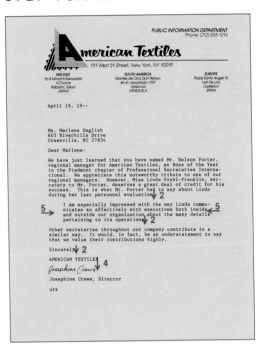

DEEP-LETTERHEAD STATIONERY. Letter shown in block style with standard punctuation.

LEFT-WEIGHTED STATIONERY. Letter shown in modified-block style with open punctuation.

LETTER 38
BLOCK STYLE ON DEEP-LETTERHEAD STATIONERY

Standard punctuation
Paper: Workguide 191–192

Treat this quotation as a display paragraph.

April 19, 19— / Mr. Raymond Mackenzie, Editor / Office Procedures Association / 1600 Wentworth Avenue South / Chicago, IL 60616 / Dear Mr. Mackenzie: 14 / 26 / 29

Thank you so much for your feature on our executive offices in your "Room at the Top" column in *Office Procedures* magazine. The article was well written and objective, and the photographs were superb. Your discussion of the wall coverings in the offices, however, was not completely accurate. You described them as follows: 43 / 57 / 71 / 85 / 95

The custom wall coverings appear to be made from a special type of designer fabric unusual for a wall covering. They are in subdued colors, perfectly matching the seating upholstery. 106 / 117 / 131

The wall coverings, which showed up so beautifully in your color photographs, are nothing more than our special-edition bed sheets fastened to the walls with heavy-duty staples. This practical decorating idea is one that any typical do-it-yourself decorator can accomplish in only a few hours. 144 / 158 / 174 / 188 / 190

Sincerely, / AMERICAN TEXTILES / Josephine Crews, Director / (*Your initials*) 202

LETTER 39
MODIFIED-BLOCK STYLE ON LEFT-WEIGHTED STATIONERY

Open punctuation
Paper: Workguide 193–194

Retype Letter 38 on left-weighted stationery in modified-block style with open punctuation. Use *Dear Raymond* as the salutation, and delete the company name in the closing lines.

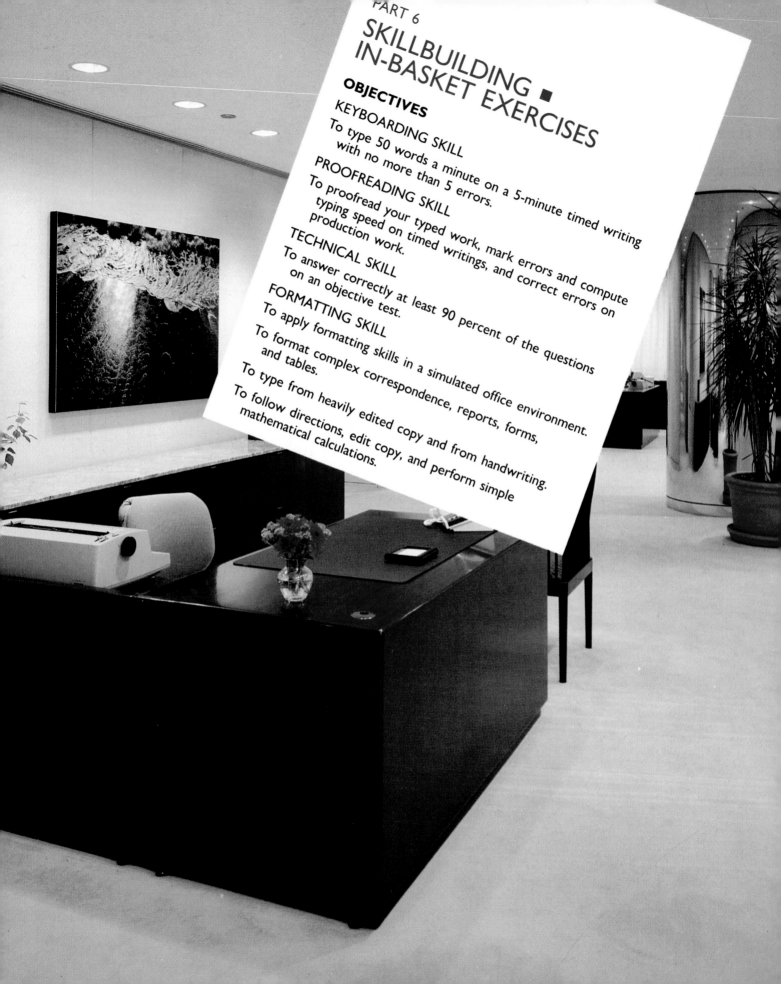

SKILLBUILDING ▪ IN-BASKET EXERCISES

OBJECTIVES

KEYBOARDING SKILL
To type 50 words a minute on a 5-minute timed writing with no more than 5 errors.

PROOFREADING SKILL
To proofread your typed work, mark errors and compute typing speed on timed writings, and correct errors on production work.

TECHNICAL SKILL
To answer correctly at least 90 percent of the questions on an objective test.

FORMATTING SKILL
To apply formatting skills in a simulated office environment.

To format complex correspondence, reports, forms, and tables.

To type from heavily edited copy and from handwriting.

To follow directions, edit copy, and perform simple mathematical calculations.

LETTERS WITH SPECIAL FEATURES

Line: 60 spaces
Tab: 5, center
Spacing: single
Drills: 2 times
Workguide: 195–198
Format Guide: 79

Goals: To improve speed and accuracy; to format letters with special features.

85-A. WARMUP

S 1 The busy men and women formed an endowment from the profit.
A 2 Jaffe quietly moved the dozen boxes by using a power truck.
N 3 Raymond Fox, 2573 East 189 Street, Apt. 61, Gary, IN 46408.

SKILLBUILDING

85-B. PACED PRACTICE

Turn to the Paced Practice routine at the back of the book. Take several 2-minute timings, starting where you left off last time. Record your progress on Workguide page 125.

85-C. This paragraph is made up of very short words, requiring the frequent use of the space bar. Type the paragraph twice. Do not pause before or after striking the space bar.

85-C. TECHNIQUE TYPING: SPACE BAR

4   If I may see you at one or two, I can get to my job by   12
5 six and not be too late. I will try to get a cab or jog to 24
6 the old inn so I can eat a hot dish of ham and eggs or have 36
7 some iced tea. Mr. Joe Cox and Ms. Pat Lee will see that I 48
8 get back to my home by ten. It should be a fun day for us. 60
   | | 2 | 3 | 4 | 5 | 6 | 7 | 8 | 9 | 10 | 11 | 12

85-D. Type this paragraph once, incorporating the indicated revisions. Then take several 1-minute timings, trying to increase your speed each time.

85-D. THINKING WHILE TYPING

Indent   By the time you have finished typing complete formatting all the jobs in these   12
10 5 lessons, you will have been exposed to the most common   24
11 features of business letters. Quite frankly, you may have   36
12 become an expert at formatting; that is a very good thing   48
13 because typing memos and letters is a frequent office task. 60
   | | 2 | 3 | 4 | 5 | 6 | 7 | 8 | 9 | 10 | 11 | 12

85-E. Either of the two formats for the inside address may be used with both block and modified-block letters.

85-E. LETTERS WITH SPECIAL FEATURES

If a letter is addressed to two people at different addresses, type each name and address either one under the other, with 1 blank line between, or side by side, with one address aligned at the left margin and the other at center. If a letter is addressed to two people at the same address, list each name on a separate line of the same inside address.

If a letter is to be signed by two people, type each name and title either one under the other, with 3 blank lines between, or side by side, with one name aligned at the left margin and the other aligned at center.

TEST 5-C
LETTER 49
BLOCK STYLE WITH OPEN
PUNCTUATION

Paper: Workguide 227

Supply an appropriate salutation,
the closing lines, and any necessary notations.

On February 23, 19—, Luis Enriques, controller, of Midstate Enterprises, sends a letter   4
to Classic Autos, Ltd., to the attention of Legal Affairs, 183 Bostock Lane, Nottingham   14
NG 10 4 EP, ENGLAND. The subject is Glenn Winchester. Mr. Enriques uses the com-   29
pany name, his name, and his title in the closing lines. Send a copy of the letter to the   30
Legal Department.   43

After searching through our files, I was able to locate the letter and   57
unpaid note to which you referred in your letter of January 25. Both are   72
dated June 9, 1983.   76

The letter shows that our company accepted a 30-day personal note   89
for $856.32 from Mr. Winchester for goods covered by Invoice 4336.   103
When the note was presented to the customer, he ignored it. We eventu-   117
ally turned the account over to our lawyers for collection. They also   131
were unsuccessful, and on June 30, 1984, we wrote off the obligation as   145
a loss on bad debts. Sincerely   152

PS: The statute of limitations has legally erased Mr. Winchester's debt   166
to our company.   169

TEST 5-D
REPORT 41
REPORT WITH AUTHOR/YEAR
CITATIONS

Spacing: double
Paper: Workguide 229

A REVIEW OF THE INFO II   5

By Keith R. Green   8

The Info II was released by Information Express on February 15, 1987,   22
exactly two years after the introduction of the original Info 16-bit ma-   36
chine (Mayhew, 1988, p. 42). This review summarizes the main features   51
and performance of the machine. A full review will be prepared later.   65

FEATURES   66

The Info II is powered by a 6802 processor and comes with 1 mega-   79
byte of RAM and two 800K drives. There is room for six expansion cards,   94
although Nubus notes that it will be some time before such cards are   108
available (1987, p. 85).   112

The standard monitor is a 12-inch monochrome monitor that displays   126
16 shades of gray at a resolution of 640 by 480 pixels. According to one   141
source, a 13-inch color monitor that offers 256 colors at the same resolu-   155
tion will be available by the third quarter (Adam and Lee, 1987, p. 6).   169

PERFORMANCE   172

Preliminary tests show that the Info II runs at twice the clock speed of   186
the Info I (Peters, 1988, pp. 43–44). When the machine is combined   200
with the faster disk drives, the result is, according to Vegas, "a system   215
that performs overall about four times faster than the original Info"   229
(1987, p. 183).   232

Note the use of the 9-digit ZIP Code in the letters in this lesson.

POSTSCRIPT NOTATION. Typed as the last item in the letter and preceded by 1 blank line. If the paragraphs of the letter are indented, indent the first line of the postscript too.

No. 10 window envelopes are often used in a word processing environment because of the difficulty of aligning envelopes correctly in a printer. A window envelope requires no typing, since the letter is folded so that the inside address is visible through the window.

Type the date on line 12, and triple-space before and after the inside address.

To fold a letter for a window envelope:

1. Place the letter *face down,* and fold the bottom third of the letter up toward the top.
2. Fold down the top third so that the address shows.
3. Insert the letter into the envelope so that the address shows through the window.

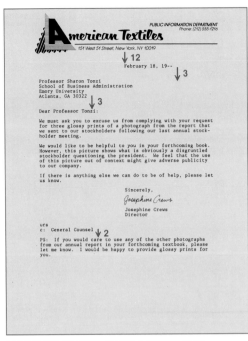

MODIFIED-BLOCK-STYLE LETTER FOR WINDOW ENVELOPE

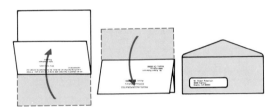

LETTER 40
BLOCK STYLE FOR WINDOW ENVELOPE

Paper: Workguide 195–196

After typing Letter 40, fold it for insertion into a window envelope.

Use either style shown on page 178 for the two writers in Letter 40 and for the two addresses in Letter 41.

February 18, 19— / Ms. June Underwood, Curator / Metropolitan Museum of Industry / P.O. Box 1892 / Houston, TX 77251-1892 / Dear Ms. Underwood:	13 / 26 / 28

February 18, 19— / Ms. June Underwood, Curator / Metropolitan Mu- 13
seum of Industry / P.O. Box 1892 / Houston, TX 77251-1892 / Dear Ms. 26
Underwood: 28

Thank you for your interest in the development of American Textiles. 42
We are sending you today under separate cover a copy of our company 55
history and a special booklet we published for our one hundredth anni- 69
versary celebration, which was held three years ago. 80

Because the topic of your forthcoming textbook is production meth- 93
ods, we are sure you will enjoy the enclosed photograph. 104

Please let us know if we can be of further assistance to you. If you 118
would like a personal tour of our newest plant or if you would like to 132
interview any of our technical people, we would be happy to make the 146
arrangements for you. 150

Sincerely, / Josephine Crews, Director / Public Information / William 163
D. Wallace, Director / Records Management / (*Your initials*) / Enclosure 174

PS: Inasmuch as we are sending you the original photograph of our 187
machinery, we would appreciate having it returned in the same protec- 200
tive envelope when you are finished with it. 210

LETTER 41
MODIFIED-BLOCK STYLE FOR REGULAR ENVELOPE

Paper: Workguide 197–198

Retype Letter 40, adding a second addressee: Professor James Tibbetts / School of Business / Eastern Montana College / Billings, MT 59101-0298. Use an appropriate salutation. Delete the postscript. Assume that the letter is written only by Josephine Crews but that a copy of the letter will be sent to William D. Wallace.

Ask your instructor for the General Information Test on Part 5.

PROGRESS TEST ON PART 5

TEST 5-A
5-MINUTE TIMED WRITING

Line: 60 spaces
Tab: 5
Paper: Workguide 223

No two business organizations are just alike. Most of   12
them, however, have similar traits and face problems common   24
to all. Financial management is one activity in which most   36
firms must engage. Each company must be financed, and each   48
must produce goods or services that can be exchanged with a   60
customer. The exchange can be for cash or credit. If cash   72
is exchanged, somebody has to plan how to handle and record   84
the receipt of the cash. If the exchange is based on cred-   96
it, the procedures for collecting the money at a later time   108
must be planned. Either way involves financial management.   120

The financial cycle is somewhat the same for each kind   132
of firm. You invest capital in something to sell; then you   144
sell it to recover your costs plus a profit. It may appear   156
to be quite an easy thing to do, but, of course, it is not.   168

All kinds of things might happen to disturb the smooth   180
running of the cycle. Prices or wages might go up or down.   192
New products may appear or new raw materials may be discov-   204
ered that may involve new ways of making a firm's products.   216
Managing a firm's funds is a complex task; and the need for   228
good financial management is great.   235

| 1 | 2 | 3 | 4 | 5 | 6 | 7 | 8 | 9 | 10 | 11 | 12 |

TEST 5-B
TABLE 36
INCOME STATEMENT WITH SPACED LEADERS

Line: 6 inches
Paper: Workguide 225

Leave 2 spaces between the number columns. Center the income statement horizontally and vertically.

NATURAL FLORAL DESIGN ← *(add 1 blank line)*   4
INCOME STATEMENT   7
For the Month Ended April 30, 19--   14

REVENUE FROM SALES		
Sales	$4,056.85	18 · 27
Less: Sales Returns	208.50	36
Net Sales	$3,848.35	45
EXPENSES		47
Raw Materials Expense	$1,256.90	56
Utilities Expense	195.25	65
Salaries Expense	1,150.00	74
Total Expenses	2,602.15	85
NET INCOME BEFORE TAXES	$1,246.20	94

LESSON

86

ITINERARIES

Line: 60 spaces
Tab: 5, center
Spacing: single
Drills: 2 times
Format Guide: 79

Goals: To type 45 wam/5'/5e; to use pivoting and leaders when formatting itineraries.

86-A. WARMUP

S 1 Eight of the idle visitors kept busy by forming a new game.
A 2 Sixty equals only five dozen, but we promised Jackie eight.
N 3 From June 8 to 9, I can be reached at 347-2056 after 1 p.m.

SKILLBUILDING

86-B. PROGRESSIVE PRACTICE: ALPHABET

Turn to the Progressive Practice: Alphabet routine at the back of the book. Take several 30-second timings, starting at the point where you left off the last time. Record your progress on Workguide page 125.

86-C. Spacing: double. Record your score.

86-C. SKILL MEASUREMENT: 5-MINUTE TIMED WRITING

4   To pivot a line means to make a line stop at a certain   12
5   point. In an announcement, for instance, if all your lines   24
6   end at the same point on the page, your typed job will have   36
7   quite a pleasing and professional appearance.   45
8   To pivot a line on electronic typewriters or computers   57
9   using word processing software, you simply enter the appro-   69
10 priate command, and the pivoting is done for you. However,   81
11 pivoting on most typewriters takes practice.   90
12   To pivot the copy on a standard typewriter, first move   102
13 your carrier one space beyond the point at which you want a   114
14 line to end. Then backspace once for every letter or space   126
15 in the line. Begin each line at this point.   135
16   Leaders are rows of periods that help to guide the eye   147
17 horizontally from one column to the next. You may use rows   159
18 of leaders for a table of contents or for any types of dis-   171
19 play jobs to make the displays more readable.   180
20   If the space between the columns is narrow, you should   192
21 use a solid row of leaders. When the space between columns   204
22 is wide, use spaced leaders that contain a space after each   216
23 period. Align all of the periods vertically.   225

| 1 | 2 | 3 | 4 | 5 | 6 | 7 | 8 | 9 | 10 | 11 | 12 |

100-D. FORMATTING A NEWSLETTER

Type the following one-page newsletter on the masthead form on Workguide page 221. Use a 35-space line for each column, with the following margins and center point for each column.

	Column 1			Column 2		
	Left	Right	Center	Left	Right	Center
Pica	5	40	22	45	80	62
Elite	10	45	27	55	90	72

REPORT 40
2-COLUMN NEWSLETTER

Paper: Workguide 221

Christine Olson, Editor   October 15, 19--

SPORTS CHAIN PURCHASED

MIDSTATE ENTERPRISES announced yesterday the signing of a letter of agreement to purchase Sports World Inc., a sports supply chain with ten stores in California, Arizona, and Texas. The chain is presently owned by two brothers from Utah.

In announcing the purchase, ME President R. J. Foyt said, "With the increase of leisure time, the earnings of most companies manufacturing sports equipment have far outdistanced the market in general. And Sports World has outdistanced the industry."

The purchase involves cash of $1.75 million plus the issuance of 45,000 shares of a new ME class of preferred stock to the owners of Sports World.

STRESS-MANAGEMENT CLASS

HAVE YOU felt tired, depressed, or irritable lately? If so, you are a prime candidate for the new stress-management class Dr. Camile Ariole will be offering. The course will meet from 4:30 until 6 p.m. each Wednesday for six weeks beginning November 3.

The course, designed for both management and the clerical staff, will teach workers how to minimize stress on the job, how to recognize it, and how to deal with it. Workers are asked to wear comfortable clothes and shoes to the class, which will meet in the cafeteria.

Phone Extension 4011 to register for the no-cost course.

COMPUTER DISCOUNT

BEGINNING IN January, employees who wish to purchase a computer for use at home will receive a 20 percent discount from the Computer Factory of St. Louis.

The discount, which applies to Computer Factory's entire line of hardware, was negotiated by Charles Sylvan, vice president for administration. It is available to any full-time employee of ME. Simply show your employee ID card when making the purchase. Software is not included.

CHOOSE YOUR OWN BENEFITS

CAFETERIA-STYLE benefits is the concept being studied by the Human Resources Department these days. The plan would give each employee a fixed dollar amount of benefits and then allow him or her to select particular benefits to "purchase" with that amount.

"The idea behind the new proposal," according to Diana Wong, personnel specialist, "is to enable each employee to get the maximum use out of his or her benefits without increasing the overall cost to the firm. For example, an employee whose spouse has full family medical coverage through his or her job may elect to forgo medical coverage altogether in order to add on dental insurance for the family."

Although the proposal is only in the planning stage, Wong would welcome employee reactions and suggestions. Call her at Extension 1040.

86-D. PRODUCTION PRACTICE: PIVOTING AND LEADERS

Read the information in 86-C. Then type the two practice exercises below, using a 40-space line. Leave 1 blank space before and after each row of leaders.

Practice 1: Solid Leaders

Marsha Rhodes .... Chairperson
Victor Gorge .... Vice Chairperson
Ronald J. Knutson .... Secretary
Liz Crudle .... Reporter

Practice 2: Spaced Leaders

Preface 1
Procedures 5
Findings 9
Recommendations 12

86-E. FORMATTING ITINERARIES

REPORT 31
ITINERARY

Line: 6 inches
Tab: 4, center

Itinerary: a proposed outline of a trip.

WP Some word processors have a leader-tab command that will automatically insert a row of periods from the point at which the tab key is depressed to the tab stop.

REPORT 32
ITINERARY

Line: 6 inches 15/90
Tab: 4, center

Retype Report 31. Use spaced leaders, and center the report vertically.

The periods must align vertically.

↓10	PORTLAND ITENERARY	4
	Arlene Gitsdorf	7
	March 12–15, 19-- ↓3	10

Thursday, March 12 ↓2   14

Detroit/Minneapolis .... North West 83   26
     Leave 5:10 p.m.; arrive 5:55 p.m.   32
     Seat 8D; nonstop ↓2   35

Minneapolis/Portland .... Northwest 2363   47
     Leave 6:30 p.m.; arrive 8:06 p.m.   54
     Seat 15C; nonstop; Dinner ↓3   59

Sunday, March 15   62

Portland/Minneapolis .... ~~United 1078~~ Northwest 360   74
     Leave 7:30 a.m.; arrive 12:26 p.m.   81
     seat 15H; one stop; breakfast   87

Detroit/Minneapolis .... Northwest 748   99
     Leave 1 p.m.; arrive 3:32 p.m.   105
     Seat 10D; nonstop; snack ↓4   110

Notes   111

1. Jack Weatherford, Assistant Western Regional Manager,   122
   will meet your flight on Thursday and return you to the   133
   airport on Sunday.   137

2. All seat assignments are aisle seats, and smoking is not   149
   allowed on any of the flights.   155

3. A single-room reservation, guaranteed for late arrival,   167
   has been made at the Airport Sheraton for March 12–14.   178

4. Important phone numbers: 184
   Jack Weatherford .... (503) 555-8029, Ext. 87   195
   Northwest Reservations .... (800) 555-1289   206
   ~~United Reservations~~ .... (800) 555-0536   217
   Airport Sheraton........(503)555-4031, Ext. 208   228

DESKTOP PUBLISHING

Line: 60 spaces
Tab: 5, center
Spacing: single
Drills: 2 times
Workguide: 221
Format Guide: 95

Goals: To type 47 wam/5'/5e; to format a one-page newsletter.

100-A. WARMUP

S 1 It was Kaye's turn to work in the town's big antique store.
A 2 Judy weaves quickly at a large beach for extra prize money.
N 3 The meeting ran from 12:45 until 3:50 in Room 678 on May 9.

SKILLBUILDING

100-B. PROGRESSIVE PRACTICE: NUMBERS

Turn to the Progressive Practice: Numbers routine at the back of the book. Take several 30-second timings, starting at the point where you left off the last time. Record your progress on Workguide page 125.

100-C. Spacing: double. Record your score.

100-C. SKILL MEASUREMENT: 5-MINUTE TIMED WRITING

4   Desktop publishing is a term that is now being used in   12
5   many offices to describe the process of printing brochures,   24
6   fliers, and company newsletters in-house rather than having   36
7   to send them out for printing. You can now use a computer,   48
8   software, and a high-quality printer to make quick work out   60
9   of your printing jobs. Here are two examples of such work.   72
10   Suppose your firm wanted to publish a small catalog of   84
11   its new products. You could first write the text on a word   96
12   processor and then copy your file into a desktop publishing   108
13   program. Then you might use a device known as a scanner to   120
14   copy a photograph of each product into your software files.   132
15   Using the special features of your software, you could then   144
16   move the pictures, called graphics, and the text around the   156
17   page until you had an attractive arrangement. You may need   168
18   to increase or reduce the size of the graphics to make them   180
19   fit on the page. Finally, you would print out the document   192
20   on a laser printer and reproduce as many copies as desired.   204
21   Or suppose you decided to start a newsletter. Desktop   216
22   publishing would permit you to compose and print columns of   228
23   text or photos with big headlines.   235

| 1 | 2 | 3 | 4 | 5 | 6 | 7 | 8 | 9 | 10 | 11 | 12 |

LESSON
87
MINUTES OF MEETINGS

Line: 60 spaces
Tab: 5, center
Spacing: single
Drills: 2 times
Format Guide: 81

Goals: To improve speed and accuracy; to format minutes of meetings.

87-A. WARMUP

S 1 The widow also kept six bushels of corn right in the field.
A 2 Seth and Virgil quickly flew from Phoenix, Arizona, by jet.
N 3 He moved to Apt. 5348-A at 9072 South Wright on October 16.

SKILLBUILDING

PRETEST. Take a 1-minute timing; compute your speed and count errors.

87-B. PRETEST: CLOSE REACHES

4   Old Uncle Evert lived northeast of the swamp, opposite   12
5 a dirty old shop. Last week we asked him to agree to allow   24
6 Aunt Gretel to purchase a jeweled sword for her next birth-   36
7 day. He fooled us all by getting her a new topaz necklace.   48
| | | 1 | | 2 | 3 | | 4 | 5 | 6 | | 7 | 8 | | 9 | | 10 | | 11 | | 12 |

PRACTICE.

Speed Emphasis: If you made no more than 1 error on the Pretest, type each line twice.

Accuracy Emphasis: If you made 2 or more errors on the Pretest, type each group of lines (as though it were a paragraph) twice.

87-C. PRACTICE: ADJACENT KEYS

8 as asked asset based basis class least visas ease fast mass
9 op opera roped topaz adopt scope troop shops open hope drop
10 we weary wedge weigh towed jewel fewer dwell wear weed week
11 rt birth dirty earth heart north alert worth dart port tort

87-D. PRACTICE: CONSECUTIVE FINGERS

12 sw swamp swift swoop sweet swear swank swirl swap sway swim
13 un uncle under undue unfit bunch begun funny unit aunt junk
14 gr grade grace angry agree group gross gripe grow gram grab
15 ol older olive solid extol spool fools stole bolt cold cool

POSTTEST. Repeat the Pretest and compare performance.

87-E. POSTTEST: CLOSE REACHES

87-F. DIAGNOSTIC TYPING: ALPHABET

Turn to the Diagnostic Typing: Alphabet routine at the back of the book. Take the Pretest, and record your performance on Workguide page 125. Then practice the drill lines for those reaches on which you made errors.

87-G. COMPOSING AT THE KEYBOARD

Say the answer in your mind; then type it.

Using the information in the 5-minute timing in 86-C on page 180, answer the following questions in complete sentences. Do not type the item numbers.

1. What does *pivoting* mean?
2. How do you pivot on a computer with word processing software?
3. What are the first two steps in pivoting on a standard typewriter?
4. What are *leaders*?
5. What are *spaced leaders*?

99-E. FORMATTING FORM LETTERS

LETTER 44
MASTER FORM LETTER

Paper: Workguide 215–216

Type the master form letter exactly as shown, with the variable information typed in all capitals and enclosed in parentheses.

WP
Automated equipment can merge the variables automatically to produce individual copies of a form letter.

Use a reference-initial format that identifies the file name under which the letter would be stored on a disk.

Compute the 10 percent balance for each account.

```
                              (CURRENT MONTH) 20, 19--                    5


(COMPANY)                                                                 7
Attention:  Accounts Payable                                            12
(STREET ADDRESS)                                                        15
(CITY), (STATE) (ZIP)                                                   20

Gentlemen:                                                              22

The (PREVIOUS MONTH) payment on your account has not been              33
received.  Our records show that the outstanding balance on            45
Account (ACCOUNT NO.) is now $(BALANCE).  That means that the          58
10 percent minimum payment which was due on (CURRENT MONTH) 15         70
was $(10% * BALANCE).                                                  74

Since your (NEXT MONTH) payment will be due shortly, won't you         87
take a few moments right now to write out a check for $(10% *          99
BALANCE) and send it to us in the enclosed postage-paid en-           111
velope.  You will be doing both yourself and us a big favor.          123

                         Sincerely,                                   125



                         Sharon J. Meyers                             128
                         Accounts Receivable                          132

(FILE NAME)                                                           134
Enclosure                                                             136
```

LETTERS 45–46
INDIVIDUAL FORM LETTERS

Paper: Workguide 217–220

Type the first two individual form letters (to Brown's Standard Service and Four Seasons Auto), inserting the appropriate information in the variable fields in standard format.

LETTERS 47–48

Paper: plain

If you are using automated equipment, type letters to Jerry's Transmission and R & D Auto Repair also.

Merge File = Accounts Receivable
Variable Fields = Company; Street Address; City; State; Zip;
Account No.; Balance

Brown's Standard Service; 433 South Salina Street; Syracuse;
NY; 13202; 3892461; 493.65

Four Seasons Auto; 125 River Road; Troy; NY; 12180; 1872396;
730.50

Jerry's Transmission; 83 Morgan Street; Stamford; CT; 06905;
0196823; 1,092.70

R & D Auto Repair; 321 Clearfield Avenue; Trenton; NJ;
08618; 5506413; 345.50

87-H. FORMATTING MINUTES OF A MEETING

RESONANCE COMMITTEE   4

Minutes of the Meeting ↓2   8

March 13, 19-- ↓3   11

REPORT 33
MINUTES OF A MEETING

Line: 6 inches
Tab: 15, center
Spacing: single
Paper: plain
Top margin: 2 inches

WP   Most word processing programs have a hanging-indent command for automatically returning at the end of each line and indenting to the first tab stop.

REPORT 34
MINUTES OF A MEETING

Retype these minutes in report format. Use single spacing. Type the side headings in all capitals, with a triple space before the heading and a double space after it.

Begin the closing lines at center.

ATTENDANCE   *The Resource Committee met on March 13, 19--,*   23

at the Airport Sheraton in Portland, Oregon,   32

in conjunction with the western regional meeting.   42

Put names in alphabetical order   *Members present were Michael Davis, D.S.*   50

Madsen, Cynthia Giovanni, and Edna Pintar.   59

Michael Davis, chairperson, called the   67

meeting to order at 2:30 p.m. ↓2   73

UNFINISHED BUSINESS   *The members of the committee reviewed the sales brochure*   85

on electronic copyboards. They agreed to purchase   97

an electronic copyboard for the conference   106

room. Cynthia Giovanni will secure quotations   115

from at least two suppliers.   124

NEW BUSINESS   *The committee reviewed a request from the*   136

Purchasing Department for two new electronic   145

typewriters. After much discussion about   153

the appropriate uses of electronic typewriters   162

versus microcomputers, the committee approved   170

the request.   174

A request from the Marketing Department for a   182

new photocopier was sent back to the department   191

for more justification.   197

ADJOURNMENT   *The meeting was adjourned at 4:45 p.m. The next*   210

meeting has been scheduled for May 4 in the   218

headquarters conference room. ↓2   225

Respectfully submitted, ↓4   229

D.S. Madsen, Secretary   234

Line: 60 spaces
Tab: 5, center
Spacing: single
Drills: 2 times
Workguide: 215–220
Format Guide: 93

MAIL MERGE

Goals: To improve speed and accuracy; to practice composition at the keyboard; to format form letters.

99-A. WARMUP

S 1 The idle field at the end of the right lane had a big rock.
A 2 Jacqueline was glad her family took five or six big prizes.
N 3 My Golden Wish credit card (No. 217-3846) expires in 05/89.

99-B. Compare this passage with the timed writing passage on page 204. Type a list of the words that contain errors, correcting the errors as you type.

99-B. PRODUCTION PRACTICE: PROOFREADING

4   Computers can not be used to access the performance of
5 office workers. With a special type of software, computers
6 can count the number of words of lines typed by the worker?
7 The data is then used to set output goals, price goods, re-
8 word the high achiever, and identify the need for training.
9   The computer reports a workers' output with no errors,
10 no matter what one's gender, age, race, physical condition,
11 or experience. Thus, this method of measurement allows all
12 all the workers to start out as equals. If the word output

99-C. COMPOSING AT THE KEYBOARD

99-C. Using correct memorandum format, compose a response to Memo 15 (page 205) from Frank Marsh to Luis Enriques.

Paragraph 1. Tell Luis that you think the draft of his report for the presentation to possible underwriters is superb. You believe it will do a tremendous selling job for the company.

Paragraph 2. Indicate that you do have one area of possible concern. You question whether he should even mention the recent losses by the automotive accessories divi-sion. Instead, you think that he should simply be prepared to explain the steps we've taken to solve the problem if questions arise.

Paragraph 3. Tell Luis that you've marked on the draft you've enclosed those topics which you think should be illustrated on visual aids. Close by wishing him good luck in his presentation.

SKILLBUILDING

99-D. Take a 1-minute timing on the first paragraph to establish your base speed. Then take several 1-minute timings on the other paragraphs. As soon as you equal or exceed your base speed on one paragraph, advance to the next one.

If you make the corrections indicated, your lines will end evenly.

99-D. SUSTAINED TYPING: ROUGH DRAFT

13   You are a word processing specialist in the offices of   12
14 the controller for Midstate Enterprises, which is comprised   24
15 of numerous companies that make a wide variety of products.   36

16   The controller is responsible for the firms' financial   12
17 matters, and he must ensure that the cash flow provides will   24
18 funds sufficient for day-to-day operations and emergencies.   36

19   The President depends up on the controller to reccommend   12
20 financial policy, arrange mergers with other companies, and   24
21 over see costs to ensure they do not exceed the cost budget.   36

22   An other 1 of the controllers' duties is too represent   12
23 the company before groups, persuading every one of them to   24
24 to recommend the your firm's stocks & bonds to their clients.   36

| 1 | 2 | 3 | 4 | 5 | 6 | 7 | 8 | 9 | 10 | 11 | 12

corporation   financial   all

PROCEDURES MANUAL

Line: 60 spaces
Tab: 5, center
Spacing: single
Drills: 2 times
Format Guide: 81

Goals: To type 45 wam/5'/5e; to format pages from a procedures manual.

88-A. WARMUP

S 1 The name of the new girl I work with in town is Ruth Blair.
A 2 Wes found my group's valuable quartz jackknife next to him.
N 3 Warehouse 8745 was 96 percent full from June 10 to June 23.

SKILLBUILDING

88-B. These words are among the 225 most frequently misspelled words in business correspondence.

88-B. PRODUCTION PRACTICE: SPELLING

4 lease project discuss initial together regarding assistance
5 issue already purpose limited prepared operating compliance
6 valve maximum library writing analysis operation sufficient
7 could request forward benefit probably recommend disability
8 until minimum current follows projects directors commitment

88-C. Spacing: double. Record your score

88-C. SKILL MEASUREMENT: 5-MINUTE TIMED WRITING

9   Now that your keyboarding skill is quite advanced, you   12
10 should begin next to develop your skill at composing at the   24
11 keyboard. If you can sit at your machine and type out your   36
12 memos and letters rather than having to first write them in   48
13 longhand, you will save much effort in your correspondence.   60
14   You may decide to begin by just typing out an informal   72
15 note to a friend or relative. The easiest way to begin the   84
16 note is to think in your mind what you want your first sen-   96
17 tence to say and then type the sentence. Continue this way   108
18 for the entire note--think a sentence, type a sentence. In   120
19 this way, you can concentrate on one aspect of composing at   132
20 a time. Do not be concerned about the format of your notes   144
21 initially; formatting details can be added at a later time.   156
22   If you begin to utilize your keyboarding skills to in-   168
23 put both personal and professional correspondence, you will   180
24 see that you save time. You will also increase your skills   192
25 because you will be spending more time at the keyboard. In   204
26 time, composing at the machine will become natural for you.   216
27 Then you can begin to add formatting details.   225

| 1 | 2 | 3 | 4 | 5 | 6 | 7 | 8 | 9 | 10 | 11 | 12

98-D. AUTOMATED TYPING TECHNICALITIES

An operator's log is sometimes used to record the output of word processing operators. For Memos 15 and 16 below and for the remaining jobs in this unit (Lessons 99 and 100), complete the operator's log shown on Workguide page 213. The directions are included on the form.

One problem of keyboarding on a computer is being able to quickly locate a document that has been stored on a disk for subsequent revision. Many operators use a reference-initial format that helps them de-termine where a job is stored on a disk. For example, the reference *cfw/L23* could mean that *Chris. F. Walters* typed *Letter 23* and the letter is stored on a disk under the file name *cfw/L23*. A reference notation would be typed on *all* documents. On reports and tables, the notation would be typed a double space below the last line of the job.

For Memos 15 and 16 below, use the new reference-initial format to specify where the jobs would be stored on a disk.

MEMO 15

Paper: plain

Use a reference-initial format that identifies the file name.

Send a memo to Frank Marsh, vice president, from Luis Enriques, controller, on August 31, 19—, on the subject of the presentation to underwriters. 20 27

I have just finished the enclosed draft of the report on our company's operations for presentation to a group of possible underwriters for our new bond issue. I hope that you will be able to provide some suggestions that I can use in preparing the final report. 42 56 71 80

I made a conscious effort to highlight our success in the manufacture and sale of filing equipment—especially our No-Search File. The report stresses the continuous growth of the outdoor sports equipment division. Reference is also made to the fact that we increased the dividend on our common stock twice within the past five years and that we have paid dividends continuously since 1910. 94 108 122 137 151 158

I ignored or just briefly touched on the losses sustained last quarter in the automotive accessories division, but I expect some sharp questioning on that topic. 173 187 191

I've just talked with Terry Winger in the Advertising Department about the preparation of charts to illustrate my presentation, but I haven't yet decided just what information I want to show. Maybe you have some ideas. 204 218 231 235

(Closing lines) 238

MEMO 16

Paper: plain

Use a reference-initial format that identifies the file name.

Retype Memo 15, making these revisions:

1. *Move* the third paragraph to make it the second paragraph.
2. *Delete* the last paragraph.
3. *Insert* this paragraph as the new last para-

graph: *I would appreciate your written comments on the enclosed draft as well as suggestions concerning the information I should show on charts and overhead transparencies.*

88-D. FORMATTING A PROCEDURES MANUAL

REPORT 35
PAGES 14 AND 15 OF A PROCEDURES MANUAL

Line: 6 inches
Tab: 4, 9
Spacing: single
Paper: plain
Top margin: 1 inch

Number pages consecutively, and pivot the page number from the right margin. Double-space between items.

```
                    ↓7
FORMATTING STYLE                              Page 14
                                                   ↓3
4.  Do not divide the last word on a page.  Leave at least
    two lines of a paragraph at the bottom of a page and carry
    at least two lines of a paragraph to the top of the fol-
    lowing page.
              ↓3
CAPITALIZATION
          ↓2
1.  Capitalize every proper noun and every adjective derived
```

FORMATTING STYLE   Page 14   5

4. Do not divide the last word on a page. Leave   17
   at least two lines of a paragraph at the bot-   26
   tom of a page, and carry at least two lines of 36
   a paragraph to the top of the following page.   45

CAPITALIZATION   48

1. Capitalize proper nouns and adjectives de-   57
   rived from proper nouns.   62
        the Bank of Detroit   65
        a Canadian citizen   69
2. Capitalize organizational terms such as *ad-*   78
   vertising department only when they are   86
   the actual names of units within your own   95
   organization and are modified by the word   103
   the.   104
        the Marketing Department   109
        our marketing department   114
3. Capitalize all official titles when they pre-   123
   cede personal names and are used in place   132
   of such personal titles as *Mr.* or *Ms.*   139
        President Joan Ross   143
        Joan Ross, president,   147
        our president, Joan Ross,   152
4. Capitalize directions only when they desig-   162
   nate definite regions or are part of a proper   171
   name.   172
        Tim lives in the East.   176
        Drive east to North Carolina.   182
5. Capitalize a noun followed by a number or   191
   letter except for the nouns *page, para-*   199
   graph, and *size.*   202
        Table 4, Policy C30, page 5   208
6. Capitalize the first word of each item dis-   217
   played in a list.   220

    Please provide this data: 225
    a. Name   227
    b. Phone number   230
7. Do not capitalize the first word of an indi-   240
   rect quotation, school courses that are not   249
   proper nouns, or seasons.   254
        He said that he will take word process-   261
        ing and English in the winter.   267

NUMBER EXPRESSION   271

1. Spell out numbers from 1 through 10, and   280
   use figures for numbers above 10.   286
        She rested three days.   291
        Please make 13 copies.   295
2. If several numbers both below and above   304
   10 are used in the same sentence, use fig-   312
   ures for all numbers.   316
        Buy 8 red and 16 blue binders.   322
3. Spell out a number at the beginning of a   331
   sentence.   333
        Thirty-two people attended.   339
4. Use figures for house and building numbers.   348
   Spell out the numbers 1 through 10 used as   357
   street names, and use figures for numbers   365
   above 10. Omit *st, d,* or *th* if a word such as 375
   East precedes the street number.   381
        8 Third Street, 10 14th Street   387
        187 East 14 Street   391
5. Do not use a decimal point with even   399
   amounts of money. Use the word *cents* for   407
   amounts under $1.   411
        $458   58 cents   413
6. Use figures to express time, whether with   422
   o'clock or with *a.m.* or *p.m.*   428
        10 o'clock, 8:30 p.m.   432
7. Express percentages in figures, and spell   441
   out *percent.*   444
        8 percent, 13.5 percent   448

Line: 60 spaces
Tab: 5
Spacing: single
Drills: 2 times
Workguide: 213
Format Guide: 93

LESSON
98

AUTOMATED TYPING TECHNICALITIES

Goals: To type 47 wam/5'/5e; to complete an operator's log; to move text in a document, delete text, and insert text.

98-A. WARMUP

S 1 The idle widow can visit both of the girls downtown in May.
A 2 The biweekly magazine for junior executives requested help.
N 3 Pages 245–306 of that 1987 yearbook contain the statistics.

SKILLBUILDING

98-B. These words are among the 250 most frequently misspelled words in business correspondence.

98-B. PRODUCTION PRACTICE: SPELLING

4 installation arrangements than approximately representative
5 requirements professional with international implementation
6 incorporated distribution well participation recommendation
7 organization construction area manufacturing correspondence

98-C. Spacing: double. Record your score.

98-C. SKILL MEASUREMENT: 5-MINUTE TIMED WRITING

8   Computers can now be used to assess the performance of   12
9 office workers. With a special type of software, computers   24
10 can count the number of words or lines typed by the worker.   36
11 The data is then used to set output goals, price goods, re-   48
12 ward the high achiever, and identify the need for training.   60
13   The computer reports a worker's output with no errors,   72
14 no matter what one's gender, age, race, physical condition,   84
15 or job experience. Thus this method of measurement permits   96
16 all the workers to start out as equals. If the work output   108
17 is outstanding, the record is clear, with no bias involved.   120
18   The amount of work one produces has been recognized as   132
19 a valid means of measuring one's performance; one new study   144
20 shows that millions of workers now have some parts of their   156
21 work measured by the computers on which they do their work.   168
22 Most of the jobs measured in this way entail doing the same   180
23 tasks over and over. Some jobs that are often measured are   192
24 data entry, word and order processing, or customer service.   204
25   A fair system of work measurement sets reachable goals   216
26 that account for all types of work, as well as for a short-   228
27 term difference in work functions.   235

| 1 | 2 | 3 | 4 | 5 | 6 | 7 | 8 | 9 | 10 | 11 | 12 |

REPORT WITH AUTHOR/ YEAR CITATIONS

Line: 60 spaces
Tab: 5, center
Spacing: single
Drills: 2 times
Format Guide: 83

Goals: To improve speed and accuracy; to format a report with author/year citations and a bibliography.

89-A. WARMUP

S 1 She also tore down both of the old docks when we went home.
A 2 As Elizabeth requested, Jack will pay for fixing my silver.
N 3 Version 3.76 of File 80 was released on September 24, 1988.

SKILLBUILDING

89-B. SUSTAINED TYPING: ROUGH DRAFT

89-B. Take a 1-minute timing on the first paragraph to establish your base speed. Then take several 1-minute timings on the other paragraphs. As soon as you equal or exceed your base speed on one paragraph, advance to the next one.

4   Whenever you use the words or ideas of other people in   12
5   a report, you have to provide the reader with the source of   24
6   the other people's work. There are various ways of format-   36
7   ting reference citations. Two methods are discussed below.   48
8   The use of footnotes is probably the most frequent means 12
9   of citing a reference. A number is typed raised at the ap-   24
10 propriate spot in the text, and the actual note is typed at   36
11 the bottom of that page, preceded by a 2-inch underscore.   48
12   Endnotes are used also to cite sources. A raised num-   12
13 ber is typed at an appropriate point in the text but   24
14 all of the notes are grouped together at the end of the re-   36
15 port on a seperate page. Thus end notes are easy to format. 48
16 You are all ready familiar with how to not format both foot- 12
17 notes and end notes. However there is still a 3d method   24
18 of sighting references that you have not tried. this new   36
19 method is the author/year method and it is the easiest.   48

| 1 | 2 | 3 | 4 | 5 | 6 | 7 | 8 | 9 | 10 | 11 | 12 |

89-C. COMPOSING AT THE KEYBOARD

89-C. Using the information in Report 36 on page 187, answer these questions in complete sentences. Do not type the item numbers.

1. How much of the author's name is typed within parentheses?
2. What punctuation is used between the author's name and the year?
3. What punctuation is used before and after the author's name and the year?
4. Where does the complete source note for each citation appear?
5. When is it appropriate to use only the year in a citation?

89-D. PRODUCTION PRACTICE: PROOFREADING

89-D. Compare this list of spelling words with the list in 88-B, page 184. Type a list of the words that are different or that are misspelled, correcting the errors as you type.

20 least project discuss initail together regarding assistence
21 issue already prupose limited prepared operation compliance
22 value maximum library writing analysis operating sufficient
23 could request forword benifit probably reccomend disability
24 until minimum currant follows projects directors comittment

97-G. FORMATTING REPORT HEADERS AND FOOTERS

A *header* is text that appears in the top margin of each page of a document. A *footer* appears in the bottom margin. Headers and footers are often used to show the name of a document or section of a document and the page number.

Begin typing a header on line 7 from the top and a footer on line 7 from the bottom. Begin the text a triple space after a header, and end a triple space before a footer.

If a document is to be printed on both sides of each sheet of paper, the page number is typically placed at the right margin for odd-numbered pages and at the left margin for even-numbered pages.

Type Report 39 as pages 4–7 of a report that will be photocopied on both sides. Type the headers and footers as shown at the right. Reverse the order of the items for odd-numbered pages; that is, type the page number and heading *EDITING COMMANDS* at the right on odd-numbered pages. *Note:* Report 39 represents four pages from a guide for using WordPerfect Version 4.2. The required steps differ for each word processing program.

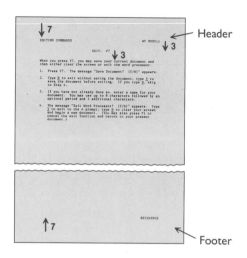

Header

Footer

REPORT 39
FOUR-PAGE REPORT WITH HEADERS AND FOOTERS

Spacing: single
Paper: plain

BLOCK: ALT-F4 — 3

Use the block function to define a portion of your text for use with other features. — 12, 20

To define a block: — 23

1. Position the cursor at the beginning of the block. — 32, 34

2. Press Alternate-F4. A blinking "Block" signal indicates that you are defining a block of text. — 43, 53, 54

3. Move the cursor to the end of the block. The block of text is highlighted. — 62, 69

The highlighted text has now been defined. You may now use any of the following features: Bold, Delete, Move, Print, Save, or Underline. — 78, 87, 96

BOLD: F6 — 98

Bold text prints darker than normal text. Bold appears brighter than the surrounding text on the screen of a monochrome monitor and in a different color on the screen of a color monitor. You may need to adjust the contrast and brightness on a monochrome monitor to see bold text. — 107, 115, 124, 134, 143, 152, 154

To define bold text: — 158

1. Press F6. Note that the Position number — 167

in the lower right corner of the screen is in bold. — 177, 178

2. Type your text. — 181

3. Press F6 to turn bold off. — 187

NOTE: If the text has already been entered, first define the block of text; then press F6. — 196, 206

CANCEL: F1 — 208

Pressing F1 will enable you to back out of a menu or message or to restore deleted text. (You must press F1 immediately after deleting the text. If you have made other changes, you cannot undelete text.) — 217, 226, 235, 242, 247

Pressing F1 will take you back to the previous screen. You can only restore the immediately preceding screen. Pressing F1 numerous times will have no effect. — 255, 264, 274, 279

CENTER TEXT: SHIFT-F6 — 283

Use the center function to center a line of text between the margins. — 293, 297

1. Position the cursor at the left margin. (If the cursor is not at the left margin, the text will be centered from the cursor position.) — 306, 317, 324

2. Press Shift-F6. — 328

3. Type the text. — 332

4. Press Return. — 335

You can center an existing line of text by moving the cursor to the beginning of the text and pressing Shift-F6. — 344, 353, 358

89-E. FORMATTING A REPORT WITH AUTHOR/YEAR CITATIONS

REPORT 36
TWO-PAGE REPORT WITH
AUTHOR/YEAR CITATIONS
Paper: plain

THE AUTHOR/YEAR METHOD OF CITATION 7

By Paula C. Holder 10

Except as noted below, all material in a report that comes from secondary sources must be documented in the form of reference citations. Such material might include specific facts and figures, opinions, direct quotations, and paraphrased material. 19 28 37 46 55 60

Two types of material do not need to be cited (Owens, 1988): (1) facts that are common knowledge to the readers of the report and (2) facts that can be verified easily. If in doubt about whether documentation is needed, provide the citation. 68 77 86 95 103 109

AUTHOR/YEAR FORMAT 113

In the author/year method of citation, the surname of the author and the year of publication are inserted at an appropriate point in the text. However, if only part of a source is being cited (for example, a particular statistic from a journal article), the page number on which the reference can be found is also included in the citation (Palmisano, 1985, p. 184). 121 131 140 150 160 170 179 186

According to Binnion (1983), if the name of the author occurs in the textual discussion, only the year of publication is cited in parentheses; otherwise, both name and year appear in parentheses, separated by a comma. 195 204 213 222 230

Although only the essential information is included in the text itself, the reader can refer to the bibliography for the title of the publication and other details. 238 248 258 263

ADVANTAGES 265

One of the reasons given for the growing popularity of this style of citation is that it gives the most important information about the source right in the body of the text so that the reader does not have to search for it. In addition, this style is not as distracting as footnotes might be (Marcy and Janis, 1986, pp. 203–204). 273 283 291 301 310 321 329 331

Another advantage often cited is that this style is easier for the typist to format. Thus, according to Robin, "fewer errors are likely to appear in a report that uses the author/year method of citation" (1981, p. 36). 339 349 359 368 375

Regardless of the method of citation used, the important point to remember is that references must be accurate and complete. Carelessness in citing references causes the researcher to lose credibility. 383 392 401 410 416

REPORT 37
BIBLIOGRAPHY
Paper: plain

BIBLIOGRAPHY 2

Binnion, Alice, *Formatting for the Computer Age,* Info Press, San Francisco, 1983. 11 19

Marcy, Alfred D., and R. J. Janis, "Ask the Experts," *Journal of Informational Sources,* Vol. XX, No. 3, October 1986, pp. 203–207. 28 36 44 45

Owens, Aaron, *The Student Researcher,* Scholastic Book Company, Portland, Oreg., 1988. 53 61 62

Palmisano, O. P., "He Reads the Fine Print," *Consumer Monthly,* February 1985, pp. 184–189. 71 78 80

Robin, Hilda, "Formatting Styles Used in Fortune 500 Companies," doctoral dissertation, Dickinson College, Springfield, N. Mex., 1981. 89 97 105 107

REPORT HEADERS AND FOOTERS

Line: 60 spaces
Tab: 5, center
Spacing: single
Drills: 2 times
Format Guide: 91

97-A. WARMUP

S 1 Helen put eighty of the giant ivory fish down on the shelf.
A 2 I quickly explained that many big jobs involve few hazards.
N 3 My lot at 4856 Oak Road is 107 feet wide and 329 feet long.

97-B. CONCENTRATION PRACTICE

When subsequent drafts of a document are to be distributed for review, hyphens are frequently used to show what material has been deleted, and all-capital letters are used to show what material has been added since the last draft.

Type one copy of the paragraph below as shown, using the backspace and hyphen keys to strike through the words that will be deleted and the shift lock to type in all capitals the words that will be added. Then type a second copy of the paragraph, making the changes indicated. Listen for the bell to end your lines.

4 Foreign, math, Greek, and VARIOUS graphic characters can be
5 displayed on your screen. To display such characters, hold
6 DOWN the control key and type V. You will see a box appear
7 at the bottom of the monitor. Then enter the DECIMAL VALUE
8 OF THE desired character. If the characters on your screen
9 do not match the PRINTED characters, you must then select a
10 new value to be sent to the printer from the setup program.

SKILLBUILDING

PRETEST. Take a 1-minute timing; compute your speed and count errors.

97-C. PRETEST: VERTICAL REACHES

11 　　　Just what does Dr. Carlson think is the basic cause of 12
12 Justin's scalp problem? A patch of hair at the back of his 24
13 neck can be treated with a new drug. I dread that it might 36
14 leave quite a bad scar, but Dr. Carlson thinks it will not. 48
　　| 1 | 2 | 3 | 4 | 5 | 6 | 7 | 8 | 9 | 10 | 11 | 12

PRACTICE.
　Speed Emphasis: If you made no more than 1 error on the Pretest, type each line twice.
　Accuracy Emphasis: If you made 2 or more errors on the Pretest, type each group of lines (as though it were a paragraph) twice.

97-D. PRACTICE: UP REACHES

15 at atlas atone attic batch gates sweat wheat atom bath what
16 dr draft drank dryer drain drama dread dream drag drew drug
17 ju judge juice jumpy junks juror julep jumbo judo jump just
18 es essay nests tests bless dress acres makes uses best rest

97-E. PRACTICE: DOWN REACHES

19 ca cable caddy cargo scare decay yucca pecan cage calm case
20 nk ankle blank crank blink think trunk brink bank junk sink
21 ba bacon badge basin tubal urban scuba basic baby back base
22 sc scale scalp scene scent scold scoop scope scan scar disc

POSTTEST. Repeat the Pretest and compare performance.

97-F. POSTTEST: VERTICAL REACHES

Line: 60 spaces
Tab: 5, center
Spacing: single
Drills: 2 times
Workguide: 199–202
Format Guide: 83

LESSON 90

LEGAL DOCUMENTS

Goals: To type 45 wam/5'/5e; to format legal documents.

90-A. WARMUP

S 1 Mable kept a big dog and a turkey on an island in the lake.
A 2 The ax point flew quickly over the beam and just grazed it.
N 3 Pages 489–507 showed 16 math problems and 23 word problems.

SKILLBUILDING

90-B. Take several 1-minute timings, trying to increase your speed each time. Technique tip: Do not slow down before or after striking the space bar.

90-B. TECHNIQUE TYPING: SPACE BAR

4   A man in a cab at the old pub can go up to the big bar 12
5 by the bay to ask the new boy for a box of cod if I ask him 24
6 to do so. He can fry a box of cod now, or he can put it on 36
7 ice for a day or two. We met an old man and his son at the 48
8 new inn; if they eat cod, it is up to you and me to fix it. 60
   | 1 | 2 | 3 | 4 | 5 | 6 | 7 | 8 | 9 | 10 | 11 | 12

90-C. Spacing: double. Record your score.

Study the information in 90-C before typing the documents in 90-D.

90-C. SKILL MEASUREMENT: 5-MINUTE TIMED WRITING

9   Even if you never work in a law office, you will quite 12
10 likely type legal documents occasionally. Examples of such 24
11 documents used in everyday affairs include contracts, bills 36
12 of sale, and powers of attorney. When possible, you should 48
13 use printed legal forms because they save time. When using 60
14 these forms, all you need to do is insert the needed infor- 72
15 mation. You should fill in every blank space with hyphens. 84
16   If a printed form is not available, you may use a spe- 96
17 cial type of paper, which has ruled lines running down both 108
18 left and right margins. All of the typing must be done be- 120
19 tween these vertical lines. There are standardized ways of 132
20 typing the forms: You should indent each of the paragraphs 144
21 ten spaces. You should type a cumulative page count at the 156
22 bottom of every page, you should spell out all figures, and 168
23 you should spread-center and type in all capitals the title 180
24 of every job. Spacing is usually double but may be single. 192
25   The final point to remember about legal typing is that 204
26 accuracy is of prime importance. In fact, most states will 216
27 not allow any erasures on names and amounts. 225
   | 1 | 2 | 3 | 4 | 5 | 6 | 7 | 8 | 9 | 10 | 11 | 12

96-D. FORMATTING LETTERS FOR WINDOW ENVELOPES

LETTER 42
BLOCK STYLE WITH OPEN PUNCTUATION

Paper: plain

Format Letter 42 for insertion into a window envelope. Fold the letter.

Type the letterhead data.

LETTER 43
MODIFIED-BLOCK STYLE WITH STANDARD PUNCTUATION

Paper: Workguide 211–212

Reformat Letter 42 on letterhead stationery for insertion into a regular No. 10 envelope. Omit the subject line.

↓⁴

MIDSTATE	1014 Locust Street	7
	St. Louis, MO 63101-2390	11
ENTERPRISES	Phone: (314) 555-0632	20

_____ ↓⁵

August 23, 19-- ↓³   35

Bondell, Vernon, and Otis   40
Attention: Leonard J. Craine   46
6012 Lehigh Avenue North   51
Chicago, IL 60646-4052 ↓³   55

Ladies and Gentlemen   59

Subject: New Bond Issue   64

At its last meeting, our board of directors authorized the   76
issuance of 9 percent 30-year bonds for $1,200,000 on May 1 of 88
next year. These bonds are for the financing of our new ro-   100
botics factory in Phoenix, as explained in the enclosed press   111
release.   114

As your company has secured the underwriting for the bonds we   126
offered in the past, we are asking that you pursue your usual   139
course of action in arranging interviews with possible under-   151
writers.   153

Although my own schedule is flexible throughout the next few   165
weeks, I wonder if Wednesday, June 8, would be a convenient   177
date for us to meet with the underwriters in the auditorium of 189
our headquarters building. If it is not, please suggest an   201
alternate date. I would like Ms. Janice Reynolds, our corpo-   214
rate attorney, to be present at this meeting.   223

We would also like to know if there are any new developments   235
in the bond market that might make it advisable to alter our   246
plans for this offering.   253

Sincerely yours   256

Luis Enriques, Controller   261

urs   262
Enclosure   264
c: Janice Reynolds   267

BLOCK-STYLE LETTER WITH OPEN PUNCTUATION—FORMATTED FOR WINDOW ENVELOPE

90-D. FORMATTING LEGAL DOCUMENTS

Study the illustrations below and the information contained in 90-C, page 188. Then type a bill of sale, once using legal paper and once using a preprinted legal form.

Note: For a two-page legal document, the cumulative page count (*Page 1 of 2, Page 2 of 2*) is centered 1 inch from the bottom. The second page has a 1½-inch top margin.

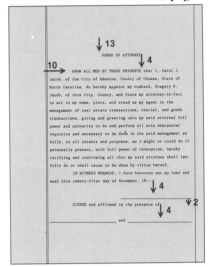

POWER OF ATTORNEY ON LEGAL PAPER

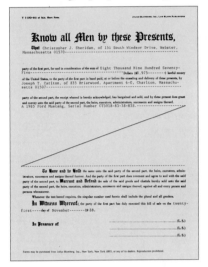

BILL OF SALE ON LEGAL FORM

REPORT 38
BILL OF SALE

Tab: 10 spaces
Top margin: 2 inches
Side margins: 2 spaces inside the vertical rules
Spacing: double
Paper: Workguide 199

Spread-center the title between the margins.

FORM 9
BILL OF SALE

Paper: Workguide 201–202

Using the information in Report 38, format a bill of sale using a preprinted form. Align the insertions with the preprinted words. Fill in any blank spaces within individual lines of the form with hyphens. Fill in any blank areas that occupy several blank lines with two horizontal underscores joined by a solid diagonal line drawn in black ink. This is called a *Z rule*.

BILL OF SALE ↓3   5

KNOW ALL MEN BY THESE PRESENTS that Polly A. Pitford, of 410 Mill Street, Hillsdale, Illinois 61257, party of the first part, for the sum of Two Thousand Two Hundred Fifty Dollars ($2,250), to me in hand paid, at or before the ensealing and delivery of these presents, by Alan R. Kullman, of 213 Northwest Avenue, Oakdale, Illinois 62268, party of the second part, does sell and grant and convey unto the said party of the second part, an IBM personal computer, Serial Number 7705863; a monochrome monitor, Serial Number 108632; and a Montrose business printer, Serial Number AE-1634.

TO HAVE AND TO HOLD the same unto the said party of the second part forever.   And the party of the first part does covenant and agree to defend the sale of the said goods against all and every person.

IN WITNESS WHEREOF, the party of the first part has duly executed this bill of sale on the seventh day of April, 19—. ↓4

_____ ↓2

SIGNED and affirmed in the presence of ↓4

_____ and _____

LESSON
96
WINDOW ENVELOPES

Line: 60 spaces
Tab: 5, center
Spacing: single
Drills: 2 times
Workguide: 211–212
Format Guide: 89

Goals: To type 47 wam/5'/5e; to format and fold letters for window envelopes.

96-A. WARMUP

S 1 If both of their fur chairs burn, throw them into the lake.
A 2 Jake Westman found exactly five quarters in the zipper bag.
N 3 On 12/30 I bought 45 shares of Amdex stock for $89.67 each.

SKILLBUILDING

96-B. PACED PRACTICE

Turn to the Paced Practice routine at the back of the book. Take several 2-minute timings, starting at the point where you left off the last time. Record your progress on Workguide page 125.

96-C. Spacing: double. Record your score.

96-C. SKILL MEASUREMENT: 5-MINUTE TIMED WRITING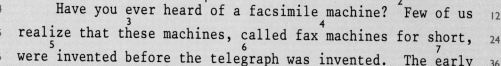

```
 4        Have you ever heard of a facsimile machine?  Few of us      12
 5   realize that these machines, called fax machines for short,      24
 6   were invented before the telegraph was invented.  The early      36
 7   units burned the image onto paper clamped onto a drum.           47
 8        The major element of a fax machine today is a scanner,      59
 9   which converts an image that is on a sheet of paper into an      71
10   audio signal.  The signal is then sent over a phone line to      83
11   the receiving location, where it is converted into text.         94
12        A technique much like that used in an office copier is     106
13   used to transfer these signals onto paper; the newest units     118
14   can transfer text at a rate of a thousand words per minute,     130
15   with graphs being transferred at about half that speed.         141
16        One of the nice features of fax machines today is that     153
17   a personal computer can be used to send or receive the data     165
18   by fax.  Thus, for instance, you can send a letter or photo     177
19   to your branch office for comment, revision, or filing.         188
20        The use of fax machines, along with modems, has opened     200
21   up a whole new world of communication for the modern office     212
22   worker.  No longer is he or she limited just to the mail or     224
23   to an overnight delivery service to transmit documents.         235
     |  |  | 2 | 3 | 4 | 5 | 6 | 7 | 8 | 9 | 10 | 11 | 12
```

WP   A modem is a device that enables data to be transmitted over telephone lines.

LESSON
91

ORDER FORMS

Line: 60 spaces
Tab: 5, center
Spacing: single
Drills: 2 times
Workguide: 203–205
Format Guide: 85

Goals: To improve speed and accuracy; to format order forms.

91-A. WARMUP

S 1 Did Jane blame the visitor from Guam for the world's chaos?
A 2 Jim Pitt quickly won over six men because of his good size.
N 3 Flight 569 departed at 12:07 and arrived in Dayton at 3:48.

91-B. With a pen and ruler, draw four rectangles about 1 by ½ inch. Then insert the paper into the machine, and visually center (both horizontally and vertically) the numbers at the right in the rectangles.

91-B. ALIGNMENT PRACTICE

536.48

29.49

76.21

3,073.48

SKILLBUILDING

91-C. PACED PRACTICE

Turn to the Paced Practice routine at the back of the book. Take several 2-minute tim- ings, starting where you left off last time. Record your progress on Workguide page 125.

91-D. Type each underlined word in all capitals instead. Type each word shown in all capitals with an underline instead.

Add one month to each month given.

Change *they*, *them*, and *their* to *we*, *us*, and *our*.

91-D. THINKING WHILE TYPING

4 WHEN you <u>are</u> taking a timed writing, do you <u>sometimes</u> START
5 to <u>daydream</u> instead of <u>concentrating</u> on what you are TRYING
6 to type? If you DO, you will see that MISTAKES <u>may</u> appear.

7 She received the January sales figures in March. However,
8 the April figures did not come in until August. We should
9 have asked for the October sales report in early November.

10 They hope you will give them their check before they leave. Should
11 you be leaving the office soon? They do not know, but at their
12 meetings with you, they said that they would work on their plans.

91-E. Disregarding format, compose the body of a letter to Mr. Roger Barnes. Provide an appropriate salutation and a complimentary closing. Compose the three paragraphs indicated.

91-E. COMPOSING AT THE KEYBOARD

Paragraph 1. Indicate that you have received his letter of August 14 and are pleased that he is enjoying his new copier.

Paragraph 2. Indicate that we do indeed provide an enlargement option for the Photron 215 that will enlarge copies up to 158 percent. This option, Part 38B, sells for $85 plus $4.50 shipping and can be easily installed by the user. If he wants to order this option, all he needs to do is give us a call at (832) 555-3895.

Paragraph 3. Thank him for writing, and ask him to please let us know when we can be of further service to him.

95-E. FORMATTING COMPLEX TABLES

Tables Turned Sideways. Paper turned sideways is 8½ inches long and contains 51 lines vertically (8½ × 6). It is 11 inches wide, so each line contains 132 elite spaces (11 × 12, with 66 as the center point) or 110 pica spaces (11 × 10, with 55 as the center point). Use these measurements for centering the table vertically and horizontally.

Two-Page Tables. If a table is typed on adjacent pages, divide it into two equal sections, making the division between columns. Divide the heading lines between the two pages.

Use a ½-inch right margin on the first page, and pivot the copy from the right margin. Use a ½-inch left margin for the second page. Pay special attention to vertical spacing to ensure that the two pages "line up."

After both pages are typed, trim the right margin of page 1 and the left margin of page 2, and tape the pages together on the *back* side. If necessary, use a straightedge and a black pen to connect the ruled lines.

TABLE 34
RULED TABLE TYPED SIDEWAYS

Spacing: single
Paper: full sheet

Center the table on one sheet of paper with the paper turned sideways.

Some word processing software and some printers permit sideways printing. If the printer accepts only 8½- by 11-inch paper and does not permit sideways printing, format the table as a two-page table and then tape the pages together.

TABLE 35
RULED TABLE TYPED ON ADJACENT PAGES

Spacing: single
Paper: 2 full sheets

Center the table on two sheets of paper. When you are finished, tape the two sheets together.

CASH-FLOW PROJECTIONS
130 East Boulevard

Category	Year 1	Year 2	Year 3	Year 4	Year 5	Year 6	Year 7	Year 8
Rents	64,800	67,522	70,358	73,313	76,392	79,600	82,943	86,427
Mgt. Fees	3,240	3,376	3,518	3,666	3,820	3,980	4,147	4,321
Administration	1,200	1,224	1,248	1,273	1,299	1,325	1,351	1,378
Utilities	5,900	6,254	6,629	7,027	7,449	7,896	8,369	8,871
Maintenance	9,000	9,270	9,548	9,835	10,130	10,433	10,746	11,069
Taxes	10,000	10,420	10,858	11,314	11,789	12,284	12,800	13,337
Insurance	1,300	1,339	1,379	1,421	1,463	1,507	1,552	1,599
Mortgage	32,344	32,344	32,344	32,344	32,344	32,344	32,344	32,344
Total	62,984	64,227	65,524	66,880	68,294	69,769	71,309	72,919
Cash Flow	1,816	3,295	4,834	6,433	8,098	9,831	11,634	13,508

(Page 1)   (Page 2)

91-F.   FORMATTING ORDER FORMS

Ordering goods is a two-step process in most companies. First, the department needing the goods prepares a *purchase requisition* and sends it to the purchasing department. Then the purchasing department prepares an official *purchase order* and sends it to the supplier.

To format these fill-in forms:

1. Align the fill-ins in the heading with the guide words.
2. Begin typing the body a double space below the ruled horizontal line. Set tabs as needed.
3. Visually center the information in the number columns.
4. Begin the description 2 spaces after the vertical rule.
5. Single-space each item; indent turnover lines 3 spaces.
6. Abbreviate as necessary; do not type the dollar sign.

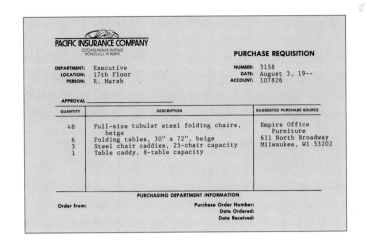

FORMS 10–11
PURCHASE REQUISITIONS

Paper: Workguide 203

FORMS 12–13
PURCHASE ORDERS

Paper: Workguide 205

PURCHASE REQUISITION 407. On November 1, 19—, J. Christopher from the Residential Department in Building C orders these items, to be charged to Account 482201:

1 heavy-duty 20-foot extension ladder; 4 full-view exterior doors with kickplate; 3 raised-panel exterior doors; and 3 double-glazed colonial doors. The suggested source for these items is Midwest Contracting Supplies, 2622 West Central, Wichita, KS 67203.

PURCHASE REQUISITION 415. On November 2, 19—, R. Lutz (Commercial Department, Building E) requisitions the following items, to be charged to Account 733404, which can be purchased at Universal Outlet, 1472 Florida Avenue, Hagerstown, MD 21740:

4 ctns. of light-oak trim kits for tub enclosure; 1 drop-in self-rimming thermoplastic sink (for 4-inch center faucet); 3 twin-panel tub enclosures with mirror panel, gold tone; and 2 doz. caulk and adhesive kits.

PURCHASE ORDER 4862. On November 6, 19—, the Purchasing Department processes Purchase Requisition 407 and orders the following items from Midwest Contracting Supplies:

1 heavy-duty 20-foot extension ladder (Catalog No. 634-8B) @ $88.99 = $88.99; 4 full-view exterior doors with kickplate (No. 251-6C) @ $219.99 = $879.96; 3 raised-panel exterior doors (No. 604-7B) @ $179.99 = $539.97; and 3 double-glazed colonial doors (No. 629-9H) @ $199.99 = $599.97; TOTAL = $2,108.89.

PURCHASE ORDER 4863. On November 6, 19—, the Purchasing Department processes Purchase Requisition 415 and orders the following items from Universal Outlet:

4 ctns. of light-oak trim kits for tub enclosure (Catalog No. 171) @ $12.80 = $51.20; 1 drop-in self-rimming thermoplastic sink (for 4-inch center faucet) (No. 876) @ $28.50 = $28.50; 3 twin-panel tub enclosures with mirror panel, gold tone (No. 355) @ $129.95 = $389.85; and 2 doz. caulk and adhesive kits (No. 201) @ $26.50 = $53.00; TOTAL = $522.55.

Line: 60 spaces
Tab: 5, center
Spacing: single
Drills: 2 times
Format Guide: 89

LESSON
95

COMPLEX TABLES

Goals: To increase speed and accuracy; to format a table typed sideways on a page; to format a two-page table.

95-A. WARMUP

S 1 The girls laid the eight keys down on the rock by the bush.
A 2 Five big jet planes zoomed quickly by the six steel towers.
N 3 Flight 106 may fly at 385 mph at an altitude of 9,742 feet.

95-B. Compare these lines from a balance sheet with those on page 197. Type a list of the words or figures that contain errors, correcting the errors as you type.

95-B. PRODUCTION PRACTICE: PROOFREADING

4 Prepaid Insurance .... ___454.00___
5   Total Currant Assets $19,693.75

6 Plant and Equipment
7   Land .... $ 8,045.00
8   Buildings 22,680.00
9   Office Equipment .... _2,875.50_
10   Total Plant and Equipment   34,005.50

11   Total Assets $53,699.25

SKILLBUILDING

95-C. PROGRESSIVE PRACTICE: ALPHABET

Turn to the Progressive Practice: Alphabet routine at the back of the book. Take several 30-second timings, starting at the point where you left off the last time. Record your progress on Workguide page 125.

95-D. Take a 1-minute timing on the first paragraph to establish your base speed. Then take several 1-minute timings on the other paragraphs. As soon as you equal or exceed your base speed on one paragraph, advance to the next one.

95-D. SUSTAINED TYPING: NUMBERS

12   When people talk about the national debt or the age of   12
13 the universe or the world population, they tend to speak in   24
14 millions, billions, and trillions. Can you think that big?   36

15   There were only 4 million Americans at the time of the   12
16 Constitutional Convention in 1787. It is 150 million kilo-   24
17 meters (nearly 93 million miles) from the earth to the sun.   36

18   The age of the earth is 4.65 billion years. The human   12
19 population is 5.1 billion people and will be 7.3 billion by   24
20 2001. To count to 1 billion would take 16,819,200 minutes.   36

21   To count to 1 trillion would take 32,000 years. World   12
22 military costs were $1.056 trillion in 1986. The U.S. bud-   24
23 get was $980,235,205 (or more than $0.98 trillion) in 1987.   36

   | 1 | 2 | 3 | 4 | 5 | 6 | 7 | 8 | 9 | 10 | 11 | 12

Line: 60 spaces
Tab: 5, center
Spacing: single
Drills: 2 times
Workguide: 207–209
Format Guide: 85

LESSON 92

BILLING FORMS

Goals: To type 46 wam/5'/5e; to format billing forms.

92-A. WARMUP

S 1 The shape of the ancient rifle was visible to Rob and Alan.
A 2 Brown jars would prevent the mixture from freezing quickly.
N 3 Jan had Seat 270 in Row 65, and Joe had Seat 138 in Row 94.

SKILLBUILDING

92-B. DIAGNOSTIC TYPING: ALPHABET

Turn to the Diagnostic Typing: Alphabet routine at the back of the book. Take the Pretest, and record your performance on Workguide page 125. Then practice the drill lines for those reaches on which you made errors.

92-C. SKILL MEASUREMENT: 5-MINUTE TIMED WRITING

92-C. Spacing: double. Record your score.

4   Many types of billing forms are used in business. The   12
5 forms that are prepared as a result of data that is already   24
6 in the computer are generally prepared on a computer. How-   36
7 ever, many forms are still typed on a typewriter.   46
8   For example, a purchase requisition is a form that may   58
9 be used to ask your purchasing department to order some new   70
10 merchandise for you. Since this is the first time the data   82
11 is being entered, a typewriter is frequently used.   92
12   Likewise, when the purchasing department gets a requi-   104
13 sition, it types out a new form, called the purchase order, 116
14 to be sent out to the vendor. Again, the data on this form 128
15 is used just once, so it is typed on a typewriter.   138
16   When the vendor receives the purchase order, depending   150
17 on its size, it will fill the order and prepare the invoice 162
18 using either a computer or a typewriter. Large firms often 174
19 use computers so that data can be accessed later.   184
20   At the end of the month, the vendor, who is the seller   196
21 of the goods, will prepare a statement of account to submit 208
22 to the buyer. If the invoice was prepared on the computer, 220
23 the statement then can be generated quite easily.   230

| 1 | 2 | 3 | 4 | 5 | 6 | 7 | 8 | 9 | 10 | 11 | 12

94-D. FORMATTING A BALANCE SHEET

TABLE 33
BALANCE SHEET
(WITH LEADERS)

Line: 60 spaces
Paper: full sheet

(12/77)

Center the table vertically.

Spread-center the section headings by leaving 1 space between letters and 3 spaces between words.

Leave 2 spaces between money columns.

Pivot from the right margin to find the point at which to set tabs for the money columns.

To keep your place when typing a financial statement, put a ruler or card under the line being typed and keep moving it as you go down the page.

WP

Many word processors have a calculator function that automatically provides totals and subtotals for the number columns—an especially useful feature for preparing financial statements.

WEST END SECRETARIAL SERVICE	6
BALANCE SHEET	8
November 30, 19--	12
A S S E T S	14
Current Assets:	17
Cash .... $ 9,543.50	27
Change Fund 35.00	36
Accounts Receivable 3,187.25	45
Merchandise Inventory 6,483.00	54
Prepaid Insurance 445.00	63
Total Current Assets $19,693.75	75
Plant and Equipment:	79
Land .... $ 8,450.00	88
Building 22,680.00	98
Office Equipment 2,875.50	107
Total Plant and Equipment 34,005.50	118
Total Assets $53,699.25	129
L I A B I L I T I E S	133
Current Liabilities:	137
Accounts Payable .... $ 5,548.50	147
Sales Taxes Payable 210.00	156
Federal Income Taxes Payable 360.00	165
FICA Taxes Payable 220.00	174
State Income Taxes Payable 145.00	183
Federal Unemploy. Taxes Payable ... 48.00	193
State Unemploy. Taxes Payable 176.00	202
Total Current Liabilities ...... $ 6,707.50	213
Long-Term Liabilities:	218
Mortgage Payable 14,000.00	230
Total Liabilities $20,707.50	241
O W N E R ' S E Q U I T Y	246
R. L. Wheatley, Capital 32,991.75	259
Total Liabilities and	263
Owner's Equity $53,699.25	274

92-D. FORMATTING BILLING FORMS

The buyer of goods prepares the purchase requisition and purchase order. The seller prepares the invoice and statement of account. An *invoice* (or bill) is an itemized list of the charges for providing the goods. A *statement of account* is a monthly summary of all transactions with the customer, showing each charge and credit and the cumulative balance.

FORMS 14–15
INVOICES

Paper: Workguide 207

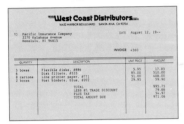

INVOICE 9076. On November 13, 19—, Midwest Contracting Supplies invoices Richard Moose, Builder, 1335 Dublin Road, Columbus, OH 43215, for its Purchase Order 4862 for the following items:

1 heavy-duty 20-foot extension ladder @ $88.99 = $88.99; 4 full-view exterior doors with kickplate @ $219.99 = $879.96; 3 raised-panel exterior doors @ $179.99 = $539.97; and 3 double-glazed colonial doors @ $199.99 = $599.97; TOTAL = $2,108.89; LESS 10% TRADE DISCOUNT = $210.89; PLUS TAX AND SHIPPING = $164.36; TOTAL AMOUNT DUE = $2,062.36.

INVOICE 6452. On November 28, 19—, Universal Outlet invoices Richard Moose, Builder, for its Purchase Order 4863 for the following items:

4 ctns. of light-oak trim kits for tub enclosure @ $12.80 = $51.20; 1 drop-in self-rimming thermoplastic sink @ $28.50 = $28.50; 3 twin-panel tub enclosures @ $129.95 = $389.85; and 2 doz. caulk and adhesive kits @ $26.50 = $53.00; TOTAL = $522.55; PLUS TAX = $28.30; TOTAL AMOUNT DUE = $550.85.

FORMS 16–17
STATEMENTS OF ACCOUNT

Paper: Workguide 209

STATEMENT OF ACCOUNT. Midwest Contracting Supplies prepares the monthly summary of its transactions with Richard Moose, Builder, dated December 1:

11/1	Brought forward; balance of $385.72
11/6	Invoice 9016 for $459.62 (charge); balance of $845.34
11/11	Payment on account of $385.72 (credit); balance of $459.62
11/13	Invoice 9076 for $2,062.36 (charge); balance of $2,521.98
11/22	Payment on account of $459.06 (credit); balance of $2,062.92
11/28	Invoice 9130 for $271.06 (charge); balance of $2,333.98

STATEMENT OF ACCOUNT. Universal Outlet prepares the monthly summary of its transactions with Richard Moose, Builder, dated December 1:

11/1	Brought forward; balance of $156.35
11/8	Payment on account of $156.35 (credit); balance of ---
11/13	Invoice 4560 for $485.76 (charge); balance of $485.76
11/21	Payment on account of $360.64 (credit); balance of $125.12
11/28	Credit Memo 2304 for $121.06 (credit); balance of $4.06
11/28	Invoice 6452 for $550.85 (charge); balance of $554.91

BALANCE SHEETS

Line: 60 spaces
Tab: 5, center
Spacing: single
Drills: 2 times
Format Guide: 87

Goals: To type 46 wam/5'/5e; to format a balance sheet.

94-A. WARMUP

S 1 The maid paid for the big bowl of fish with her own checks.
A 2 Six of the women quietly gave the prizes back to the judge.
N 3 On March 30, 15 of the 26 girls and 49 of the 78 boys left.

SKILLBUILDING

94-B. These words are among the 250 most frequently misspelled words in business correspondence.

94-B. PRODUCTION PRACTICE: SPELLING

4 officer location technical attention provisions cooperation
5 similar proposed indicated secretary previously implemented
6 quality expenses presently executive especially recommended
7 patient judgment extension requested assessment alternative

94-C. Spacing: double. Record your score.

94-C. SKILL MEASUREMENT: 5-MINUTE TIMED WRITING

8   Claims have been made that modern electronic equipment 12
9 will lessen the need for paper in the modern office. A lot 24
10 of office experts now predict that the office of the future 36
11 will be a paperless office. Just how likely is such a pre- 48
12 diction to come true? The fact of the matter is that sales 60
13 of paper have grown in the past two or three years. Compu- 72
14 ter and copy paper and business forms are leading the list. 84
15   One of the reasons given for the high sales is the in- 96
16 creased use of computers, causing a greater need for paper. 108
17 One other reason is the change in the national economy from 120
18 one that is based on making goods to one based on providing 132
19 services. These industries, such as insurance and banking, 144
20 generate much more paperwork. One more factor is that more 156
21 government rules and greater foreign operations now require 168
22 that more forms and other types of papers be typed and also 180
23 that more copies of each of these papers be made; in short, 192
24 office workers are now generating more papers than ever be- 204
25 fore, whether in the form of a computer printout, facsimile 216
26 copy, or photocopy. Thus, the view of the paperless office 228
27 is a myth. 230

  | 1 | 2 | 3 | 4 | 5 | 6 | 7 | 8 | 9 | 10 | 11 | 12

FINANCIAL STATEMENTS

Line: 60 spaces
Tab: 5, center
Spacing: single
Drills: 2 times
Format Guide: 87

Goals: To improve speed and accuracy; to format financial statements.

93-A. WARMUP

S 1 The name of their new theme park at Ruby Lake was The Keys.
A 2 Dave quickly froze the two mixtures in brown jugs and pots.
N 3 I bought a size 10 shoe for $47.85 plus $2.39 tax on May 6.

SKILLBUILDING

93-B. DIAGNOSTIC TYPING: NUMBERS

Turn to the Diagnostic Typing: Numbers routine at the back of the book. Take the Pretest, and record your performance on Workguide page 125. Then practice the drill lines for those reaches on which you made errors.

93-C. PRETEST: ALTERNATE- AND ONE-HAND WORDS

PRETEST. Take a 1-minute timing; compute your speed and count errors.

4   The usual visitors to the rocky island are either from   12
5 the city of Lakeland or Honolulu. They like to visit hilly   24
6 areas and taste the giant fruit. The eight signs that girl   36
7 made gave us an extra boost and some added revenue as well.   48
    | 1 | 2 | 3 | 4 | 5 | 6 | 7 | 8 | 9 | 10 | 11 | 12

93-D. PRACTICE: ALTERNATE-HAND WORDS

PRACTICE.
   Speed Emphasis: If you made no more than 1 error on the Pretest, type each line twice.
   Accuracy Emphasis: If you made 2 or more errors on the Pretest, type each group of lines (as though it were a paragraph) twice.

8 also angle field bushel ancient emblem panel sight fish big
9 both blame fight formal element handle proxy signs girl and
10 city chair giant island visitor profit right their laid cut
11 down eight laugh theory chaotic visual shape usual work she

93-E. PRACTICE: ONE-HAND WORDS

12 acts hilly award uphill average poplin refer jolly adds him
13 area jumpy based homily baggage you'll serve union beat ink
14 case onion brave limply greater kimono taste plump draw oil
15 gave pupil extra unhook wastage unholy wages imply star you

POSTTEST. Repeat the Pretest and compare performance.

93-F. POSTTEST: ALTERNATE- AND ONE-HAND WORDS

93-G. COMPOSING AT THE KEYBOARD

93-G. Using correct format, compose a memorandum to Ms. Sandra Weston from Donald Bovee on May 4 on the subject of the annual report. Incorporate the information indicated.

Paragraph 1. Tell Ms. Weston you understand her concern that the individual sections for the annual report are running late. Assure her that you're concerned as well.
Paragraph 2. Tell her that next week you plan to write each division head personally and request that the division report be submitted directly to you. You'll give the division heads a deadline date of May 31.
Paragraph 3. Thank Ms. Weston for her concern about this important project, and ask her to let you know if she runs into additional problems or if there is any other way in which you can help.

93-H. FORMATTING FINANCIAL STATEMENTS

TABLE 31
INCOME STATEMENT
WITH LEADERS

Line: 70 spaces
Spacing: single
Paper: full sheet

Pivot money columns from right margin
Leave 2 spaces between number columns
Center vertically

To type the double underscore, use the variable spacer to align the bottom underscore.

WEST END SECRETARIAL SERVICE   7

INCOME STATEMENT   ↓2   9

For the Month Ended November↓2 30, 19--   16
           ↓3

REVENUE FROM SALES		20
Sales.	$12,630.25	30
Less: Sales Returns and		35
Allowances	$190.50	41
Sales Discount.	45.75	236.25	50
Net Sales.	$12,394.00	58
COST OF GOODS SOLD.	7,245.00	67
GROSS PROFIT ON SALES	$5,149.00	76
OPERATING EXPENSES.		80
Advertising Expense.	$ 112.85	88
Delivery Expense	120.30	96
Insurance Expense.	40.60	103
Payroll Taxes Expense.	195.00	111
Salaries Expense	2,800.00	118
Supplies Expense	55.70	126
Utilities Expense.	243.35	134
Total Operating Expenses.	3,567.80	141
NET INCOME BEFORE TAXES	$ 1,581.20	149

TABLE 32
BOXED TABLE WITH BRACED
HEADINGS

Spacing: double
Paper: centered on full sheet

6 spaces between stub and number column
2 spaces between all number columns

WEST END SECRETARIAL SERVICE   7

COMPARISON OF ACTUAL AND PROJECTED OPERATIONS   15

For the Month Ended November 30, 19--   22

Category	Actual		Projected		
	Amount	% of Sales	Amount	% of Sales	33
Revenue From Sales	$12,394	100.0	$12,500	100.0	42
Cost of Goods Sold	7,245	58.5	7,250	58.0	49
Gross Profit on Sales	5,149	41.5	5,250	42.0	57
Operating Expenses	3,5678	28.8	3,500	28.0	64
Net Income Before Taxes	$ 1,581	12.8	$ 1,750	14.0	73

SKILLBUILDING ■

DIAGNOSTIC TYPING: ALPHABET

Line: 60 spaces
Spacing: single

The Diagnostic Typing: Alphabet program is designed to diagnose and then correct your keystroking errors. You may use this program at any time.

Directions

1. Type the Pretest/Posttest passage once, proofread it, and circle errors.
2. In the error chart on Workguide pages 5, 125, or 289, write the date, the number of errors you made on each key, and your total number of errors. For example, if you typed *rhe* for *the,* that would count as 1 error on the letter *t.*
3. For any letter on which you made 2 or more errors, select the corresponding drill lines and type them twice. If you made only 1 error, type the drill once.
4. If you made no errors on the Pretest/Posttest passage, turn to the practice on troublesome pairs on page SB-3 and type each line once. This section provides intensive practice on those pairs of keys which are most commonly confused.
5. Finally, retype the Pretest/Posttest, and compare your performance with your Pretest.

PRETEST/POSTTEST

Jacob and Zeke Koufax quietly enjoyed jazz music on my new jukebox. My six or seven pieces of exquisite equipment helped both create lovely music by Richard Wagner; I picked five very quaint waltzes from Gregg Ward's jazz recordings.

PRACTICE: INDIVIDUAL REACHES

```
aa Isaac badge carry dared eager faced gains habit dials AA
aa jaunt kayak label mamma Nancy oasis paint Qatar rapid AA
aa safer taken guard vague waves exact yacht Zaire Aaron AA


bb about ebbed ebony rugby fiber elbow amber unbar oboes BB
bb arbor cubic oxbow maybe abate abbot debit libel album BB
bb embed obeys urban tubes Sybil above lobby webby bribe BB


cc acted occur recap icing ulcer emcee uncle ocean force CC
cc scale itchy bucks excel Joyce acute yucca decal micro CC
cc mulch McCoy incur octet birch scrub latch couch cycle CC


dd admit daddy edict Magda ideal older index oddly order DD
dd outdo udder crowd Floyd adapt added Edith Idaho folds DD
dd under modem sword misdo fudge rowdy Lydia adept buddy DD


ee aegis beach cents dense eerie fence germs hence piece EE
ee jewel keyed leads media nerve poems penny reach seize EE
ee teach guest verse Wendy Xerox years zesty aerie begin EE
```

Almost everyone has experienced interviewing for a job during his or her life. For some persons, the interview is a traumatic time. But when a candidate adequately prepares for this interview, it doesn't need to be very frightening. A person should apply only for the jobs for which he or she is professionally prepared. Before an interview one should obtain detailed information about the company with which he or she is seeking employment.

One should learn the name of the person conducting the interview and use the name during the interview. It's also best to take a neat copy of your data sheet. It goes without saying that suitable business dress is always expected. The applicant will be judged on appearance, poise, and personability as well as competence. At the end of the interview, it is smart to stand, shake hands, and use the interviewer's name in the closing.

Are you an active listener? Listening is a skill that few people possess. It is one important way to bring about change in people. Listening is not a passive activity, and it is the most effective agent for personality development. Quality listening brings about change in people's attitudes toward themselves and others' values. People who have been listened to become more open to their experiences, less defensive, fairer, or less authoritative.

Listening builds deep positive relationships and tends to alter constructively the attitudes of the listener. Active listening on the job is extremely important whether an employee is in the top levels of management or works at the lower end of the hierarchy. Everyone should try to analyze his or her listening habits to see whether some improvement could be made. Smoother human interaction should certainly result and yield more job satisfaction.

```
ff after defer offer jiffy gulfs infer often dwarf cuffs FF
ff awful afoul refer affix edify Wolfe infra aloof scarf FF
ff bluff afoot defer daffy fifty sulfa softy surfs stuff FF

gg again edges egged soggy igloo Elgin angel ogled Marge GG
gg outgo auger pygmy agaze Edgar Egypt buggy light bulge GG
gg singe doggy organ fugle agree hedge began baggy Niger GG

hh ahead abhor chili Nehru ghost Elihu khaki Lhasa unhat HH
hh aloha phony myrrh shale Ethan while yahoo choir jehad HH
hh ghoul Khmer Delhi Ohara photo rhino shake think while HH

ii aired bides cider dices eight fifth vigil highs radii II
ii jiffy kinds lives mired niece oiled piped rigid siren II
ii tired build visit wider exist yield aimed binds cigar II

jj major eject fjord Ouija enjoy Cajun Fijis Benjy bijou JJ
jj banjo jabot jacks jaded jails Japan jaunt jazzy jeans JJ
jj jeeps jeers jelly jerks jibed jiffy jilts joint joker JJ

kk Akron locks vodka peeks mikes sulky links okras larks KK
kk skins Yukon hawks tykes makes socks seeks hiker sulks KK
kk tanks Tokyo jerky pesky nukes gawks maker ducks cheek KK

ll alarm blame clank idled elope flame glows Chloe Iliak LL
ll ankle Lloyd inlet olive plane burly sleet atlas Tulsa LL
ll yowls axles nylon alone blunt claim idler elite flute LL

mm among adman demit pigmy times calms comma unman omits MM
mm armor smell umber axmen lymph gizmo amass admit demon MM
mm dogma imply films mommy omits armed smear bumpy axman MM

nn ankle Abner envoy gnome Johns input knife kilns hymns NN
nn Donna onion apnea Arnes snore undid owned cynic angle NN
nn entry gnash inset knoll nanny onset barns sneer unfit NN

oo aorta bolts coats dolls peony fouls goofs hoped iotas OO
oo jolts kooky loins moral noise poled Roger soaks total OO
oo quote voter would Saxon yo-yo zones bombs colts doles OO

pp apple epoch flips alpha ample input droop puppy sharp PP
pp spunk soups expel typed April Epsom slips helps empty PP
pp unpin optic peppy corps spite upset types apply creep PP

qq Iraqi equal pique roque squad tuque aquae equip toque QQ
qq squab squat squak squaw quail qualm quart queen quell QQ
qq query quest quick quiet quilt quirk quota quote quoth QQ

rr array bring crave drive erode freak grain three irate RR
rr kraft inrun orate Barry tramp urges livre wrote lyric RR
rr Ezars armor broth crown drawl erect freer grade throw RR
```

Most of us have had occasion to write business letters from time to time whether to apply for a job, to comment on a product or service, or to place an order. Often it seems to be an easy task to sit and let our thoughts flow freely. In other cases we seem to struggle over the proper wording, trying to say it in just the right way. Writing is a skill that comes with practice and, most of all, with study. One can learn.

There are many writing principles that must be studied to ensure successful letters. Some of these principles are as follows: Use language in your letters that you would be comfortable using face-to-face. Words should be simple and direct. Words should be carefully chosen. Always be positive. Emphasize the bright side of a situation when possible. Be kind. Write the way you would like people to talk in person.

One of the most important areas for a business student to study is report writing. Many people who have worked in business organizations indicated that one of the areas they felt least prepared for was report writing. Most people in college do not know that they'll probably be asked to write reports on the job. Fortunately, most schools are aware of this deficit today and are trying to correct the situation. They are succeeding.

In recent years there has been quite a big increase in the range of report writing courses in the business curricula. Reports might be categorized as vertical, horizontal, and radial. Vertical reports go up and down in the organization and may include policy statements or status reports. Horizontal reports move from person to person or department to department and are informational. Radial reports may be publicized research.

```
ss ashen bombs specs binds bares leafs bangs sighs issue SS
ss necks mills teams turns solos stops stirs dress diets SS
ss usury Slavs stows abyss asked stabs cords mares beefs SS

tt attic debts pacts width Ethel often eight itchy alter TT
tt until motto optic earth stops petty couth newts extra TT
tt myths Aztec atone doubt facts veldt ether sight Italy TT

uu audio bumps cured dumps deuce fuels gulps huffy opium UU
uu junta kudos lulls mumps nudge outdo purer ruler super UU
uu tulip revue exult yucca azure auger burns curve duels UU

vv avows event ivory elves envoy overt larva mauve savvy VV
vv avant every rivet Elvis anvil coves curvy divvy avert VV
vv evict given valve ovens serve paves evade wives hover VV

ww awash bwana dwarf brews Gwenn schwa kiwis Elwin unwed WW
ww owner Irwin sweet twins byway awake dwell pewee tower WW
ww Erwin swims twirl awful dwelt Dewey owlet swamp twine WW

xx axiom exile fixed Bronx toxin Sioux Exxon pyxie axman XX
xx exert fixes Leonx oxbow beaux calyx maxim exact sixth XX
xx proxy taxes excel mixed boxer axing Texas sixty epoxy XX

yy maybe bylaw cynic dying eying unify gypsy hypos Benjy YY
yy Tokyo hilly rummy Ronny loyal pygmy diary Syria types YY
yy buyer vying Wyatt epoxy crazy kayak Byram cycle bawdy YY

zz Azure Czech adzes bezel dizzy Franz froze Liszt ritzy ZZ
zz abuzz tizzy hazed czars maize Ginza oozes blitz fuzzy ZZ
zz jazzy mazes mezzo sized woozy Hertz dizzy Hazel Gomez ZZ
```

PRACTICE: TROUBLESOME PAIRS

A/S Sal said he asked Sara Ash for a sample of the raisins.
B/V Beverly believes Bob behaved very bravely in Beaverton.
C/D Clyde and Dick decided they could decode an old decree.

E/W We wondered whether Andrew waited for Walter and Wendy.
F/G Griffin goofed in figuring their gifted golfer's score.
H/J Joseph joshed with Judith when John jogged to Johnetta.

I/O A novice violinist spoiled Orville Olin's piccolo solo.
K/L Kelly, unlike Blake, liked to walk as quickly as Karla.
M/N Many women managed to move among the mounds of masonry.

O/P A pollster polled a population in Phoenix by telephone.
Q/A Quincy acquired one quality quartz ring at the banquet.
R/T Three skaters traded their tartan trench coats to Bart.

U/Y Buy your supply of gifts during your busy July journey.
X/C The exemptions exceed the expert's wildest expectation.
Z/A Eliza gazed as four lazy zebra zigzagged near a gazebo.

82 wam   Do you enjoy the work you do most of the time? Do you look forward to going to work each day? Although some people talk about their work as being unpleasant, the majority of men and women usually find their work generally satisfying. If not, the problem could be that there is a poor fit between the job and the worker. Quality of life at work is a major concern of management, unions, and labor.

When jobs become dull and routinized, one becomes less productive because he or she does not feel challenged. The concept of job enrichment greatly enhances the types of experiences an employee deals with every day by upgrading the responsibilities of the job. Opportunity for growth is the key to job enrichment. An organization should select a few jobs that have the best potential for enrichment.

84 wam   More and more women are moving into the executive levels in business and industry. Many of the women who pursue careers in management today have moved into their positions after gaining experience as office support personnel. This background gives them a special appreciation for the myriad contributions made by such workers as typists, file clerks, word processors, and secretaries throughout the whole firm.

Other women have acquired their managerial roles after earning degrees and gaining experience through jobs in such fields as finance, marketing, accounting, and law. But the measure of success as a manager, no matter what the degrees or past experiences are, is how well one can identify goals and problems and then drive toward the realization of those goals and the resolution of those problems for the company.

DIAGNOSTIC TYPING: NUMBERS

Line: 60 spaces
Spacing: single

The Diagnostic Typing: Numbers program is designed to diagnose and then correct your keystroking errors. You may use this program at any time.

Directions

1. Type the Pretest/Posttest passage once, proofread it, and circle errors.
2. In the error chart on Workguide pages 5, 125, or 289, write the date, the number of errors you made on each key, and your total number of errors. For example, if you typed *24* for *25,* that would count as 1 error on the number *5.*

3. For any number on which you made 2 or more errors, select the corresponding drill lines and type them twice. If you made only 1 error, type the drill once.
4. Make one copy of the drills on page SB-5 that contain all the numbers. (If you made no errors on the Pretest/Posttest passage, type the drills that contain all the numbers, repeat, and then repeat again as you strive to reach new speed levels.)
5. Finally, retype the Pretest/Posttest, and compare your performance with your Pretest.

PRETEST/POSTTEST

My inventory records dated December 31, 1989, revealed
we had 458 pints, 2,069 quarts, and 4,774 gallons of paint.
We had 2,053 brushes, 568 scrapers, 12,063 wallpaper rolls,
897 knives, 5,692 mixers, 480 ladders, and 371 step stools.

PRACTICE: INDIVIDUAL REACHES

1 aq aq1 aq1qa 111 ants 101 aunts 131 apples 171 animals a1
They got 11 answers correct for the 11 questions in BE 121.
Those 11 adults loaded the 711 animals between 1 and 2 p.m.
All 111 agreed that 21 of those 31 are worthy of the honor.

2 sw sw2 sw2ws 222 sets 242 steps 226 salads 252 saddles s2
The 272 summer tourists saw the 22 soldiers and 32 sailors.
Your September 2 date was all right for 292 of 322 persons.
The 22 surgeons said 221 of those 225 operations went well.

3 de de3 de3ed 333 dots 303 drops 313 demons 393 dollars d3
Bus 333 departed at 3 p.m. with the 43 dentists and 5 boys.
She left 33 dolls and 73 decoys at 353 West Addison Street.
The 13 doctors helped some of the 33 druggists in Room 336.

4 fr fr4 fr4rf 444 fans 844 farms 444 fishes 644 fiddles f4
My 44 friends bought 84 farms and sold over 144 franchises.
She sold 44 fish and 440 beef dinners for $9.40 per dinner.
The '54 Ford had only 40,434 fairly smooth miles by July 4.

78 wam   The ergonomics experts emphasize the major role furniture plays in the well-being of office workers. Many years ago, we paid little attention to whether our chair and desk suited our utility and comfort needs. But now we know that various styles, sizes, shapes, and colors have quite an impact on our quality and quantity of work. An informed manager plans area surroundings.

The colors in the workplace may have important effects on one's moods. Studies show that the cool colors, such as blue and green, are quiet and relaxing. Cool colors should be used in offices that are located in warm areas, in south or west sections of the building. The warm colors, such as red, yellow, and orange, are cheerful and add zip to a job, which improves worker morale.

80 wam   Today we hear a great deal about the importance of human relations in management. Job-related human interaction is a comparatively new concern. This can be easily seen if we look at the history of leadership theories as they apply to management practice. When people first started to study leadership, it was expected that certain qualities, such as height, could predict effective leaders.

Next, exceptional leaders were analyzed to see whether they had similar qualities. However, that proposal was not any more successful than the earlier approaches. Now it is generally known that many elements combine to make a person an effective leader. Also, a specific leader's proficiency varies from one situation to another; everyone must develop a style that aids him or her on the job.

5 fr fr5 fr5rf 555 furs 655 foxes 555 flares 455 fingers f5
They now own 155 restaurants, 45 food stores, and 55 farms.
They ordered 45, 55, 65, and 75 yards of that new material.
Flight 855 flew over Farmington at 5:50 p.m. on December 5.

6 jy jy6 jy6yj 666 jets 266 jeeps 666 jewels 866 jaguars j6
Purchase orders numbered 6667 and 6668 were sent yesterday.
Those 66 jazz players played for 46 juveniles in Room 6966.
The 6 judges reviewed the 66 journals on November 16 or 26.

7 ju ju7 ju7uj 777 jays 377 jokes 777 joists 577 juniors j7
The 17 jets carried 977 jocular passengers above 77 cities.
Those 277 jumping beans went to 77 junior scouts on May 17.
The 7 jockeys rode 77 jumpy horses between March 17 and 27.

8 ki ki8 ki8ik 888 keys 488 kites 888 knives 788 kittens k8
My 8 kennels housed 83 dogs, 28 kids, and 88 other animals.
The 18 kind ladies tied 88 knots in the 880 pieces of rope.
The 8 men saw 88 kelp bass, 38 kingfish, and 98 king crabs.

9 lo lo9 lo9ol 999 lads 599 larks 999 ladies 699 leaders 19
All 999 leaves fell from the 9 large oaks at 389 Largemont.
The 99 linemen put 399 large rolls of tape on for 19 games.
Those 99 lawyers put 899 legal-size sheets in the 19 limos.

0 ;p ;p0 ;p0p; 100 pens 900 pages 200 pandas 800 pencils ;0
There were 1,000 people who lived in the 300 private homes.
The 10 party stores are open from 1:00 p.m. until 9:00 p.m.
They edited 500 pages in 1 book and 1,000 pages in 2 books.

All numbers   a1a s2s d3d f4f f5f j6j j7j k8k 191 ;0; Add 5 and 9 and 16.
Those 67 jumpsuits were shipped to 238 Birch on October 14.
Invoices numbered 294 and 307 are to be paid by November 5.
Flight 674 is scheduled to leave from Gate 18 at 11:35 a.m.

All numbers   a1a s2s d3d f4f f5f j6j j7j k8k 191 ;0; Add 6 and 8 and 29.
That 349-page script called for 18 actors and 20 actresses.
The check for $50 was sent to 705 Garfield Street, not 507.
The 14 researchers asked the 469 Californians 23 questions.

All numbers   a1a s2s d3d f4f f5f j6j j7j k8k 191 ;0; Add 3 and 4 and 70.
They built 1,200 houses on the 345-acre site by the canyon.
Her research showed that gold was at 397 in September 1986.
For $868 extra, they bought 27 new books and 62 used books.

All numbers   a1a s2s d3d f4f f5f j6j j7j k8k 191 ;0; Add 5 and 7 and 68.
A bank auditor arrived on May 26, 1988, and left on May 30.
The 4 owners open the stores from 9:30 a.m. until 6:00 p.m.
After 1,374 miles on the bus, she must then drive 125 more.

A major part of office activity is deciding what kinds of equipment will best meet company objectives. One should analyze every system, checking for easy and flexible usage. The next step is then defining the requirements of each job in terms of volume of work, space needed, and how each cost fits into the overall budget. Organize types of functions, above all.

     A complete itemized checklist of every task identifies various functions performed by each employee. This type of data can be obtained through questionnaires, interviews, or observation techniques. Some subjects covered are document creation, employee interaction, scheduling, typing, filing, and telephoning. Technology must then be selected to match job needs.

While technology has quite dramatically changed virtu- ally all office procedures in the last decade, attention to changing human interaction at the workplace owing to all of these changes has been largely neglected. Some people have a great deal of enthusiasm for working with different kinds of computers, while others view any computer as a threat, a fearsome complexity.

     It is expected that most people's jobs will in time be affected by computers. Therefore, it is imperative to ease employee qualms about learning to operate new equipment. A good idea is to nurture a positive attitude toward the com- puter by convincing employees of two things. First, office work is made easier. Second, they are much more apt to be- come more organized.

PROGRESSIVE PRACTICE: ALPHABET

This skillbuilding routine contains a series of 30-second timings that range from 16 wam to 100 wam. The first time you use these timings, select a passage that is 2 words a minute higher than your current speed. Take repeated timings on the passage until you can complete it within 30 seconds with no errors. When you have achieved your goal, record the date on the Progress Record on Workguide pages 5, 125, or 289. Then move on to the next passage and repeat the procedure.

16 wam   An author is the creator of a document.

18 wam   Access means to call up data out of storage.

20 wam   A byte represents one character to your computer.

22 wam   To store means to insert data in memory for later use.

24 wam   Soft copy is text that is displayed on your display screen.

26 wam   Memory is the part of a word processor that stores information.

28 wam   A menu is a list of choices to guide the operator through a function.

30 wam   A sheet feeder is a device that will insert sheets of paper into a printer.

32 wam   Boilerplate copy is a reusable passage that is stored until needed in a program.

34 wam   Downtime is the length of time that equipment is not usable because of a malfunction.

36 wam   To execute means to perform an action specified by an operator or by a computer program.

38 wam   Output is the result of a word processing operation. It is in either printed or magnetic form.

40 wam   Format refers to the physical features which affect the appearance and arrangement of a document.

68 wam   Enthusiasm is still another work trait that is eagerly
sought by most employers. Being enthusiastic means that an
employee has lots of positive energy. This is reflected in
actions toward the work as well as toward the employer. It
has been noted that enthusiasm can be catching. If workers
have enthusiasm, they can reach for gold.

It might pay to examine your level of enthusiasm for a
given job or project. Analyze whether you help to build up
people or whether you aid in giving coworkers a negative or
pessimistic attitude. There will always be quite a few job
opportunities for workers who are known to possess a wealth
of enthusiasm for the work they are given.

70 wam   Understanding is another work habit or trait that is a
requirement to be an excellent worker. In this society the
likelihood of working with people who have many differences
is quite probable. It is essential to have workers who can
understand and accept those differences that are evident in
the employees who are in the unit or the division.

On the job it is imperative that a worker realize that
employees will have different aptitudes and abilities. The
chances are also great that differences in race, ethnicity,
religion, work ethic, cultural background, and attitude can
be found. With so many possible differences, it is obvious
that a greater degree of understanding is needed.

72 wam   Reviewing the seven previous Paced Practice exercises,
it can be concluded that specific work habits or traits can
play a major role in determining the success of a worker at
a given job or task. Most managers would be quick to agree
on the importance of these traits. These habits would most
likely be on any performance appraisal forms you might see.

Of course, while these work habits are critical to the
success of an individual on the job, there is also the need
for specific competencies and abilities for a given job. A
new worker must size up the needed blend of these traits in
addition to those required competencies. As will be noted,
a worker needs many various skills to be a success at work.

42 wam A font is a set of type of one size or style which includes all letters, numbers, and punctuation marks.

44 wam Ergonomics is the science of adapting working conditions or equipment to meet most physical needs of workers.

46 wam Home position is the starting position of a document; it is typically the upper left corner of the display screen.

48 wam An electronic typewriter is a word processor which has only limited functions; it may or may not have a visual display.

50 wam An optical scanner is a device that can read text and enter it into a word processor without the need to rekeyboard the data.

52 wam Hardware refers to the physical equipment used, such as the central processing unit, display screen, keyboard, printer, or drive.

54 wam A peripheral device is any piece of equipment that will extend the capabilities of a system but that is not necessary for operation.

56 wam A split screen displays two or more different images at the same time; it can, for example, display two different pages of a legal document.

58 wam A daisy wheel is a printing element that is made of plastic or metal and is used on different printers. Each character is at the end of a spoke.

60 wam A cursor is a special character, often a blinking box or an underscore, which shows where the next typed character will appear on the display screen.

62 wam The hot zone is the area before the right margin, typically five to ten characters wide, where words may have to be divided or transferred to a new line.

64 wam Turnaround time is the length of time needed for a document to be keyboarded, edited, proofread, corrected if required, printed, and returned to the executive.

66 wam A local area network is a system that uses cable or another means to allow high-speed communication among various kinds of electronic equipment within a small area.

68 wam To search and replace means to direct the word processor to locate a character, word, or group of words wherever it occurs in the document and replace it with new text.

62 wam   Another trait or work habit essential for success on a
job is accuracy. Accurate workers are in much demand. The
worker who tallies numbers checks them very carefully to be
certain there are no errors. When reviewing documents, the
accurate worker has excellent proofreading skills to locate
all errors.

        Since accuracy is required on all jobs, it is critical
to possess this trait. An accurate worker is usually quite
thorough in all work that is undertaken or completed. If a
worker checks all work which is done and analyzes all steps
taken, it is likely that a high level of accuracy should be
attained.

64 wam   Efficiency is another work habit that is much admired.
This means that a worker is quick to complete an assignment
and to begin work on the next job. Efficient workers think
about saving steps and time when working. For example, one
should plan to make one trip to the copier versus going for
each individual job.

        Being efficient means having all the right tools to do
the right job. An efficient worker is able to zip along on
required jobs, concentrating on doing the job right. Being
efficient also means having all needed supplies for the job
within reach. This means that a worker can produce more in
a little less time.

66 wam   Cooperation is another desired work habit. This means
that an employee is thinking of all the team members when a
decision is made. A person who cooperates is willing to do
something for the benefit of the entire group. As a member
of a work unit or team, it is absolutely essential that you
take extra steps to cooperate.

        Cooperation may mean being a good sport if you have to
do something you would rather not do. It could also mean a
worker helps to correct a major error made by someone else.
If a worker has the interests of the organization at heart,
it should be a little easier to make a quick decision to be
cooperative in most endeavors.

70 wam   Indexing is the ability of a word processor to accumulate a list of words that appear in a document, including the page numbers, and then to print it out in alphabetic order.

72 wam   A control character is a special key that never prints; instead, it causes something to occur whenever the printer is activated; for instance, a special spacing or a tabulation.

74 wam   A facsimile is an exact copy of a document. It is also the process by which images, such as typed letters, signatures, and graphs, are scanned, transmitted, and then reprinted on paper.

76 wam   Compatibility refers to the ability of one machine to share information with another machine or to communicate with the other machine. It can be accomplished by using hardware or software.

78 wam   Indexing refers to determining the captions or titles under which a document would most likely be found. The term also encompasses cross-referencing each document under any other possible title.

80 wam   Wraparound is the ability of a word processor to automatically move words from one line to the next line and from one page to the next page as a result of insertions, deletions, or change of margin.

82 wam   The office is a place in which administrative functions are performed for an enterprise or organization; these administrative functions include consulting, recordkeeping, paperwork, or comparable jobs.

84 wam   List processing is the ability of a word processor to maintain lists of data that can be easily updated and sorted in alphabetic or numeric order. A list can also be added to a document stored in the system.

86 wam   A computer is an electronic device; it accepts data that is input and then processes the data and produces output. The computer performs its work by using one or more stored programs which give the instructions.

88 wam   The configuration is the components which make up your word processing system. Most systems include a keyboard that is used for entering data, a central processing unit, at least one disk drive, a screen, and a printer.

90 wam   A keypad meter is a device used to monitor usage of the office copier. It can be either a key or a coded card which, when inserted into your copier, unlocks the machine for use and keeps track of the number of copies made.

56 wam   Going to work has always been a major part of being an
adult. Of course, many adolescents also have jobs that can
keep them extremely busy. The work one does or the job one
holds is a critical factor in determining many other things
about the way a person is able to live.

Various work habits are as crucial to one's success as
the actual job skills and knowledge that one brings to that
job. If one is dependable, organized, accurate, efficient,
cooperative, enthusiastic, and understanding, one should be
quickly recognized by most supervisors.

58 wam   Being dependable is a desirable trait to have. When a
worker says that something will be done by a specific time,
it is quite assuring to a manager to know that a dependable
worker is assigned to it. Workers who are dependable learn
to utilize their time to achieve maximum results.

This trait can also be evident with workers who have a
good record for attendance. If a firm is to be productive,
it is essential to have workers on the job. Of course, the
dependable employee not only is on the job, but also is the
worker who can be counted on to be there on time.

60 wam   Organization is another trait that can be described as
necessary to exhibiting good work habits. To be organized,
a worker should have a sense of being able to plan the work
that is to be done and then to work that plan. It is quite
common to notice that competent workers are well organized.

If an office worker is organized, requests are handled
promptly, correspondence is answered quickly, and paperwork
does not accumulate on the desk. In addition, an organized
office worker returns all telephone calls without delay and
makes a list of things to be accomplished on a daily basis.

92 wam   An open office is a modern approach to office planning that combines modular furniture and an open layout. Workers are separated by panels, screens, or partitions instead of permanent walls; thus they have greater flexibility.

94 wam   To scroll means to show a large block of text by rolling it either horizontally or vertically past your display screen. As the text disappears from the top section of the monitor, new text appears at the bottom section of the monitor.

96 wam   Justification is a form of printing that inserts additional space between words or characters to force each line to the same length; it can be called right justification, since it forces all the lines to end at the same point at the right.

98 wam   A stop code is a command that makes a printer halt while it is printing to permit an operator to change the font or the paper in the printer. A stop code may be used when switching from elite to pica type or to a different color of ribbon.

100 wam   A computerized message system is a class of electronic mail that enables the operator to key in a message on a computer terminal and have it stored within the memory of the computer; the recipient can then have it displayed on his or her terminal.

50 wam   We all want to work in a pleasant environment where we
are surrounded with jovial people who never make a mistake.
The realities of the real world tell us, however, that this
likely will not happen; the use of corrective action may be
required.

    For the very reason that this trait is so difficult to
cultivate, all of us should strive to improve the manner in
which we accept constructive criticism. By recognizing the
positive intent of supervisors, each of us can accrue extra
benefits.

52 wam   The worker and the firm might be compared in some ways
with a child and the family unit. Just as a child at times
disagrees with a parent, the worker might question policies
of the company. In each case, there must be procedures for
conflict resolution.

    One option for a vexed child is to run away from home;
an employee may type a letter of resignation. A far better
option in both situations is the discussion of differences.
The child remains loyal to family, and the employee remains
loyal to the company.

54 wam   The person who aspires to a role in management must be
equal to the challenge. Those who have supervisory responsibilities must make fine judgments as decisions are formed
that affect the entire organization. The challenge of managing is difficult and lonely.

    While other labels are sometimes used to explain basic
functions of management, the concepts remain the same. The
four main functions are involved with planning, organizing,
actuating, and controlling of such components as personnel,
production, and sales of goods.

PROGRESSIVE PRACTICE: NUMBERS

Line: 60 spaces
Spacing: single

This skillbuilding routine contains a series of 30-second timings that range from 16 wam to 72 wam. The first time you use these timings, select a passage that is 4 to 6 words a minute *lower* than your current alphabetic speed. (The reason for selecting a lower speed goal is that sentences with numbers are more difficult to type.) Take repeated timings on the passage until you can complete it within 30 seconds with no errors. When you have achieved your goal, record the date on the Progress Record on Workguide pages 5, 125, or 289. Then move on to the next passage and repeat the procedure.

16 wam   There were now 21 children in Room 211.

18 wam   Fewer than 12 of the 121 boxes have arrived.

20 wam   Maybe 2 of the 21 applicants met all 12 criteria.

22 wam   There were 34 letters addressed to 434 West Cranbrook.

24 wam   Jan reported that there were 434 freshmen and 43 transfers.

26 wam   The principal assigned 3 of those 4 students to Room 343 at noon.

28 wam   Only 1 or 2 of the 34 latest invoices were more than 1 page in length.

30 wam   They met 11 of the 12 players who received awards from 3 of the 4 coaches.

32 wam   Those 5 vans carried 46 passengers on the first trip and 65 on the next 3 trips.

34 wam   We first saw 3 and then 4 beautiful eagles on Route 65 at 5 a.m. on Monday, June 12.

36 wam   The 6 companies produced 51 of the 62 records that received awards for 3 of 4 categories.

38 wam   The 12 trucks hauled the 87 cows and 65 horses to the farm, which was about 21 miles northeast.

40 wam   She moved from 87 Bayview Drive to 657 Cole Street and then 3 blocks south to 412 Gulbranson Avenue.

42 wam   My 7 or 8 buyers ordered 7 dozen in sizes 5 and 6 after the 14 to 32 percent discounts had been granted.

44 wam   There were 34 women and 121 men waiting in line at the gate for the 65 to 87 tickets to the Cape Cod concert.

42 wam   Newly employed workers are quite often judged by their
skills in informal verbal situations. A simple exchange of
greetings when being introduced to a customer is an example
that illustrates one situation.

A new employee might have a very good idea at a small-
group meeting. However, unless that idea can be verbalized
to the other members in a clear, concise manner, they won't
develop a proper appreciation.

44 wam   Many supervisors state that they want their workers to
use what they refer to as common sense. Common sense tells
a person to answer the phone, to open the mail, and to lock
the door at the end of the working day.

It is easy to see that this trait equates with the use
of good judgment. The prize employee will want to capitalize on each new experience that will help him or her to use
better judgments when making decisions.

46 wam   Every person should set as a goal the proper balancing
of the principal components in one's life. Few people will
disagree with the belief that the family is the most important of the four main ingredients in a human life.

Experts in the career education field are quick to say
that family must be joined with leisure time, vocation, and
citizenship in order to encompass one's full "career." The
right balance results in satisfaction and success.

48 wam   As we become an information society, there is an ever-
increasing awareness of office costs. Such costs are labor
intensive, and those who must justify them are increasingly
concerned about workers' use of time management principles.

Researchers in the time management area have developed
several techniques for examining office tasks and analyzing
routines. The realization that "time is money" is only the
beginning and must be followed with an educational program.

46 wam   Steve had listed 5 or 6 items on Purchase Order 241 when he saw that Purchase Requisition 87 contained 3 or 4 more.

48 wam   The item numbered 278 will sell for about 90 percent of the value of the 16 items that have a code number shown as 435.

50 wam   The manager stated that 98 of the 750 randomly selected new valves had about 264 defects, far in excess of the usual 31 norm.

52 wam   Half of the 625 volunteers received about 90 percent of the charity pledges. Approximately 83 of the 147 agencies will get funds.

54 wam   Merico hired 94 part-time workers to help the 378 full-time employees during that 62-day period when sales go up by 150 percent or more.

56 wam   Kaye only hit 1 for 6 in the first 29 games after an 8-game streak in which she batted 0 for 4. She then hit at a .573 average for 3 games.

58 wam   The mailman delivered 98 letters during the week to 734 Oak Street and also delivered 52 letters to 610 Pioneer Road as he returned on Route 58.

60 wam   Pat said that about 1 of 5 of the 379 swimmers had a chance of being among the top 20. The finest 6 of those 48 divers will receive about 16 awards.

62 wam   It rained from 3 to 6 inches, and 18 of the 21 farmers were fearful that 4 to 7 inches more would flood about 950 acres along 3 miles of the new Route 78.

64 wam   The 7 sacks weighed 48 pounds, more than the 30 pounds that I had thought. All 24 think the 92-pound bag is at least 6 or 9 or 15 pounds beyond what it weighs.

66 wam   They ordered 7 of those 8 options for 54 of the 63 vehicles last month. They now own over 120 dump trucks for use in 9 of the 15 regions in the new 20-county area.

68 wam   Andrew was 8 or 9 years old when they moved to 632 Glendale Street from the 1700 block of Horseshoe Lane about 45 miles directly southwest of Boca Raton, Florida 33434.

70 wam   Claire had read 575 pages in the 760-page book by March 30; David had read only 468 pages. Claire has read 29 of those optional books since October 9, and David has read 18.

72 wam   The school district has 985 elementary students, 507 middle school students, and 463 high school students; the total of 1,955 is 54, or 2.84 percent, over last year's grand total.

32 wam   Whichever career path is selected, the degree of pride shown in one's work has to be at a high level. Others will judge you by how well you do your work.

Your self-image is affected by what you believe others think of you as well as by what you think of yourself. The quality of your efforts impacts on both.

34 wam   If a matter is important to a supervisor or to a firm, it should be important to the worker. The responsible person can be depended on to put priorities in order.

The higher your job-satisfaction level, the greater is the likelihood that you will be pleased with all aspects of your life. Positive attitudes will bring rewards.

36 wam   Whenever people work together, attention must be given to the human relations factor. A quality organization will concern itself with interactional skills needed by workers.

Respect, courtesy, and patience are examples of just a few of the words that combine to bring about positive human relationships in the office as well as in other situations.

38 wam   The alarm didn't go off. The bus was late. The baby-sitter is sick. The car wouldn't start. And for some, the list of excuses goes on. Be thankful that this list is not like yours.

You will keep the tardy times to a minimum by planning and anticipating. And you will realize that those who jump the gun by quitting work early at the end of the day have a bad habit.

40 wam   Some people take forever to become acquainted with the office routines. Some must have every task explained along with a list of things to be done. Some go ahead and search for new things to do.

Initiative is a trait that managers look for in people who are promoted while on the job. A prized promotion with a nice pay raise can be the reward for demonstrating that a person has new ideas.

PACED PRACTICE

Line: 60 spaces
Spacing: single

The Paced Practice skillbuilding program builds speed and accuracy in short, easy steps, using individualized goals and immediate feedback. You may use this program at any time throughout the course.

This section contains a series of 2-minute timings for speeds ranging from 12 wam to 92 wam. The first time you use these timings, select a passage that is 2 wam higher than your current typing speed. Use this two-stage practice pattern to achieve each speed goal—first concentrate on speed, and then work on accuracy.

Have someone call out each ¼-minute interval as you type. Strive to be at the appropriate point in the passage marked by a small superior number as each ¼-minute interval is announced—typing neither too fast nor too slowly.

Speed Goal. Take successive timings on the same passage until you can complete it in 2 minutes without regard to errors.

When you have achieved your speed goal, record the date on the Progress Record on Workguide pages 6, 126, or 290. For example, if your speed goal was 58 wam, record the date beside *58s* (for *speed*). Then work on accuracy.

Accuracy Goal. To type accurately, you need to slow down—just a bit. Therefore, to reach your accuracy goal, drop back 2 wam to the previous passage. Take successive timings on this passage until you can complete it in 2 minutes with no more than 2 errors. When you have achieved your accuracy goal, record the date on the Progress Record.

For example, if you achieved your earlier speed goal of 58 wam, you should work on 56 wam for accuracy and record the date you achieved your goal beside *56a* (for *accuracy*). Then you would move up 4 wam (for example, to the 60-wam passage) and work for speed again.

12 wam

What is the meaning of work? Why do most people work?
The concept of work and careers is of interest to you.

14 wam

When doing something that is required, you think of it
as working.
When doing something that you want to do, you think of
it as fun.

16 wam

We often do not consider the amount of time and effort
spent doing a task.
If we did, we would realize that many people work hard
even while playing.

18 wam

For example, people sweat, strain, or even suffer dis-
comfort when playing a sport.
They do this for fun. If they were required to do it,
they might not be so willing.

20 wam
Spending time on a job is work. For most people, work is something they have to do to survive.

Today, work means more than staying alive. People expect different rewards from their jobs.

22 wam
Work can be interesting, and more and more workers are now saying that their work should be interesting.

Sure, there are many boring jobs, and every job always has some less exciting and more routine features.

24 wam
Today there are many different types of jobs which you may choose from which range from the routine to the exotic.

If you begin your planning early, you can work at different types of jobs and learn from the experience of each.

26 wam
Workers tend to identify with their careers, and their careers in a real sense give them a sense of importance and belonging.

People's jobs also help determine how they spend their spare time, who their friends are, and sometimes even where they live.

28 wam
Work can take place in school, in a factory or office, at home, or outside; it can be done for money or experience or even voluntarily.

It should be quite clear that work can be any activity that involves a type of responsibility. The same thing can be said about a job.

30 wam
A career relates to work that is done for pay. But it means more than a particular job; it is the pattern of work done throughout your lifetime.

A career suggests looking ahead, planning, and setting goals and reaching them. The well-planned career becomes a part of the individual's life.